Microsoft® Office

Access™ 2007

Comprehensive Concepts and Techniques

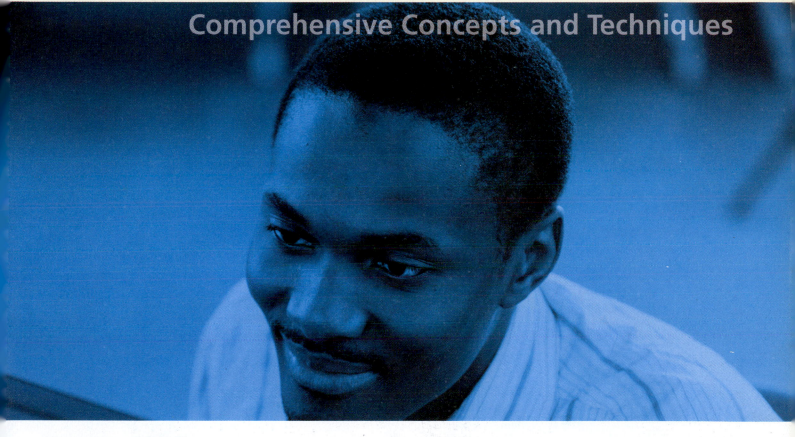

Gary B. Shelly

Thomas J. Cashman

Philip J. Pratt

Mary Z. Last

COURSE TECHNOLOGY
CENGAGE Learning™

Australia • Brazil • Japan • Korea • Mexico • Singapore • Spain • United Kingdom • United States

COURSE TECHNOLOGY
CENGAGE Learning™

Microsoft Office Access™ 2007
Comprehensive Concepts and Techniques
Gary B. Shelly, Thomas J. Cashman, Philip J. Pratt,
Mary Z. Last

Executive Editor: Alexandra Arnold

Senior Product Manager: Reed Curry

Associate Product Manager: Klenda Martinez

Editorial Assistant: Jon Farnham

Senior Marketing Manager: Joy Stark-Vancs

Marketing Coordinator: Julie Schuster

Print Buyer: Julio Esperas

Director of Production: Patty Stephan

Production Editor: Matthew Hutchinson

Developmental Editor: Amanda Brodkin

Proofreaders: John Bosco, Kim Kosmatka

Indexer: Rich Carlson

QA Manuscript Reviewers: John Freitas, Serge
   Palladino, Chris Scriver, Danielle Shaw, Marianne
   Snow, Teresa Storch

Art Director: Bruce Bond

Cover and Text Design: Joel Sadagursky

Cover Photo: Jon Chomitz

Compositor: GEX Publishing Services

Printer: Banta Menasha

For product information and technology assistance, contact us at
Cengage Learning Customer & Sales Support, 1-800-354-9706
For permission to use material from this text or product, submit all
requests online at **cengage.com/permissions**
Further permissions questions can be emailed to
permissionrequest@cengage.com

ISBN 13: 978-1-4188-4341-0

ISBN 10: 1-4188-4341-5

Course Technology
25 Thomson Place
Boston, Massachusetts 02210
USA

Cengage Learning is a leading provider of customized learning solutions with office
locations around the globe, including Singapore, the United Kingdom, Australia,
Mexico, Brazil, and Japan. Locate your local office at:
international.cengage.com/region

Cengage Learning products are represented in Canada by Nelson Education, Ltd.

For your lifelong learning solutions, visit **course.cengage.com**

Purchase any of our products at your local college store or at our preferred online store
www.ichapters.com

Printed in the United States of America
2 3 4 5 6 7 8 9 10 09 08

Microsoft® Office Access™ 2007

Comprehensive Concepts and Techniques

Contents

Microsoft Office Access 2007

CHAPTER NINE

Administering a Database System

WEB FEATURE

Sharing Access Data

Appendices

Preface

The Shelly Cashman Series® offers the finest textbooks in computer education. We are proud of the fact that our series of Microsoft Office 4.3, Microsoft Office 95, Microsoft Office 97, Microsoft Office 2000, Microsoft Office XP, and Microsoft Office 2003 textbooks have been the most widely used books in education. With each new edition of our Office books, we have made significant improvements based on the software and comments made by instructors and students.

Microsoft Office 2007 contains more changes in the user interface and feature set than all other previous versions combined. Recognizing that the new features and functionality of Microsoft Office 2007 would impact the way that students are taught skills, the Shelly Cashman Series development team carefully reviewed our pedagogy and analyzed its effectiveness in teaching today's Office student. An extensive customer survey produced results confirming what the series is best known for: its step-by-step, screen-by-screen instructions, its project-oriented approach, and the quality of its content.

We learned, though, that students entering computer courses today are different than students taking these classes just a few years ago. Students today read less, but need to retain more. They need not only to be able to perform skills, but to retain those skills and know how to apply them to different settings. Today's students need to be continually engaged and challenged to retain what they're learning.

As a result, we've renewed our commitment to focusing on the user and how they learn best. This commitment is reflected in every change we've made to our Office 2007 books.

Objectives of This Textbook

Microsoft Office Access 2007: Comprehensive Concepts and Techniques is intended for a ten- to fifteen-week period in a course that teaches Access 2007 as the primary component. No experience with a computer is assumed, and no mathematics beyond the high school freshman level is required. The objectives of this book are:

- To offer a comprehensive presentation of Microsoft Office Access 2007
- To expose students to practical examples of the computer as a useful tool
- To acquaint students with the proper procedures to create documents suitable for coursework, professional purposes, and personal use
- To help students discover the underlying functionality of Access 2007 so they can become more productive
- To develop an exercise-oriented approach that allows learning by doing

The Shelly Cashman Approach

Features of the Shelly Cashman Series Microsoft Office Access 2007 books include:

- **Project Orientation** Each chapter in the book presents a project with a practical problem and complete solution in an easy-to-understand approach.
- **Plan Ahead Boxes** The project orientation is enhanced by the inclusion of Plan Ahead boxes. These new features prepare students to create successful projects by encouraging them to think strategically about what they are trying to accomplish before they begin working.
- **Step-by-Step, Screen-by-Screen Instructions** Each of the tasks required to complete a project is clearly identified throughout the chapter. Now, the step-by-step instructions provide a context beyond point-and-click. Each step explains why students are performing a task, or the result of performing a certain action. Found on the screens accompanying each step, call-outs give students the information they need to know when they need to know it. Now, we've used color to distinguish the content in the call-outs. The Explanatory call-outs (in black) summarize

Q&A

What is a maximized window?

A maximized window fills the entire screen. When you maximize a window, the Maximize button changes to a Restore Down button.

Other Ways

1. Click Italic button on Mini toolbar
2. Right-click selected text, click Font on shortcut menu, click Font tab, click Italic in Font style list, click OK button
3. Click Font Dialog Box Launcher, click Font tab, click Italic in Font style list, click OK button
4. Press CTRL+I

BTW

Minimizing the Ribbon

If you want to minimize the Ribbon, right-click the Ribbon and then click Minimize the Ribbon on the shortcut menu, double-click the active tab, or press CTRL+F1. To restore a minimized Ribbon, right-click the Ribbon and then click Minimize the Ribbon on the shortcut menu, double-click any top-level tab, or press CTRL+F1. To use commands on a minimized Ribbon, click the top-level tab.

what is happening on the screen and the Navigational call-outs (in red) show students where to click.

- **Q&A** Found within many of the step-by-step sequences, Q&As raise the kinds of questions students may ask when working through a step sequence and provide answers about what they are doing, why they are doing it, and how that task might be approached differently.

- **Experimental Steps** These new steps, within our step-by-step instructions, encourage students to explore, experiment, and take advantage of the features of the Office 2007 new user interface. These steps are not necessary to complete the projects, but are designed to increase the confidence with the software and build problem-solving skills.

- **Thoroughly Tested Projects** Unparalleled quality is ensured because every screen in the book is produced by the author only after performing a step, and then each project must pass Course Technology's Quality Assurance program.

- **Other Ways Boxes and Quick Reference Summary** The Other Ways boxes displayed at the end of most of the step-by-step sequences specify the other ways to do the task completed in the steps. Thus, the steps and the Other Ways box make a comprehensive reference unit. A Quick Reference Summary at the end of the book contains all of the tasks presented in the chapters, and all ways identified of accomplishing the tasks.

- **BTW** These marginal annotations provide background information, tips, and answers to common questions that complement the topics covered, adding depth and perspective to the learning process.

- **Integration of the World Wide Web** The World Wide Web is integrated into the Access 2007 learning experience by (1) BTW annotations that send students to Web sites for up-to-date information and alternative approaches to tasks; (2) a Microsoft Business Certification Program Web page so students can prepare for the certification examinations; (3) a Quick Reference Summary Web page that summarizes the ways to complete tasks (mouse, Ribbon, shortcut menu, and keyboard); and (4) the Learn It Online section at the end of each chapter, which has chapter reinforcement exercises, learning games, and other types of student activities.

- **End-of-Chapter Student Activities** Extensive student activities at the end of each chapter provide the student with plenty of opportunities to reinforce the materials learned in the chapter through hands-on assignments. Several new types of activities have been added that challenge the student in new ways to expand their knowledge, and to apply their new skills to a project with personal relevance.

Organization of This Textbook

Microsoft Office Access 2007: Comprehensive Concepts and Techniques consists of nine chapters on Microsoft Office Access 2007, three special features, eight appendices, and a Quick Reference Summary.

End-of-Chapter Student Activities

A notable strength of the Shelly Cashman Series Microsoft Office Access 2007 books is the extensive student activities at the end of each chapter. Well-structured student activities can make the difference between students merely participating in a class and students retaining the information they learn. The activities in the Shelly Cashman Series Office books include the following.

CHAPTER SUMMARY A concluding paragraph, followed by a listing of the tasks completed within a chapter together with the pages on which the step-by-step, screen-by-screen explanations appear.

LEARN IT ONLINE Every chapter features a Learn It Online section that is comprised of six exercises. These exercises include True/False, Multiple Choice, Short Answer, Flash Cards, Practice Test, and Learning Games.

APPLY YOUR KNOWLEDGE This exercise usually requires students to open and manipulate a file from the Data Files that parallels the activities learned in the chapter. To obtain a copy of the Data Files for Students, follow the instructions on the inside back cover of this text.

EXTEND YOUR KNOWLEDGE This exercise allows students to extend and expand on the skills learned within the chapter.

MAKE IT RIGHT This exercise requires students to analyze a document, identify errors and issues, and correct those errors and issues using skills learned in the chapter.

IN THE LAB Three all new in-depth assignments per chapter require students to utilize the chapter concepts and techniques to solve problems on a computer.

CASES AND PLACES Five unique real-world case-study situations, including Make It Personal, an open-ended project that relates to student's personal lives, and one small-group activity.

Instructor Resources CD-ROM

The Shelly Cashman Series is dedicated to providing you with all of the tools you need to make your class a success. Information about all supplementary materials is available through your Course Technology representative or by calling one of the following telephone numbers: Colleges, Universities, and Continuing Ed departments, 1-800-648-7450; High Schools, 1-800-824-5179; and Career Colleges, Business, Government, Library and Resellers, 1-800-477-3692.

The Instructor Resources CD-ROM for this textbook include both teaching and testing aids. The contents of each item on the Instructor Resources CD-ROM (ISBN 1-4239-1226-8) are described on the following pages.

INSTRUCTOR'S MANUAL The Instructor's Manual consists of Microsoft Word files, which include chapter objectives, lecture notes, teaching tips, classroom activities, lab activities, quick quizzes, figures and boxed elements summarized in the chapters, and a glossary page. The new format of the Instructor's Manual will allow you to map through every chapter easily.

LECTURE SUCCESS SYSTEM The Lecture Success System consists of intermediate files that correspond to certain figures in the book, allowing you to step through the creation of a project in a chapter during a lecture without entering large amounts of data.

SYLLABUS Sample syllabi, which can be customized easily to a course, are included. The syllabi cover policies, class and lab assignments and exams, and procedural information.

FIGURE FILES Illustrations for every figure in the textbook are available in electronic form. Use this ancillary to present a slide show in lecture or to print transparencies for use in lecture with an overhead projector. If you have a personal computer and LCD device, this ancillary can be an effective tool for presenting lectures.

POWERPOINT PRESENTATIONS PowerPoint Presentations is a multimedia lecture presentation system that provides slides for each chapter. Presentations are based on chapter objectives. Use this presentation system to present well-organized lectures that are both interesting and knowledge based. PowerPoint Presentations provides consistent coverage at schools that use multiple lecturers.

SOLUTIONS TO EXERCISES Solutions are included for the end-of-chapter exercises, as well as the Chapter Reinforcement exercises. Rubrics and annotated solution files, as described below, are also included.

RUBRICS AND ANNOTATED SOLUTION FILES The grading rubrics provide a customizable framework for assigning point values to the laboratory exercises. Annotated solution files that correspond to the grading rubrics make it easy for you to compare students' results with the correct solutions whether you receive their homework as hard copy or via e-mail.

TEST BANK & TEST ENGINE In the ExamView test bank, you will find our standard question types (40 multiple-choice, 25 true/false, 20 completion) and new objective-based question types (5 modified multiple-choice, 5 modified true/false and 10 matching). Critical Thinking questions are also included (3 essays and 2 cases with 2 questions each) totaling the test bank to 112 questions for every chapter with page number references, and when appropriate, figure references. A version of the test bank you can print also is included. The test bank comes with a copy of the test engine, ExamView, the ultimate tool for your objective-based testing needs. ExamView is a state-of-the-art test builder that is easy to use. ExamView enables you to create paper-, LAN-, or Web-based tests from test banks designed specifically for your Course Technology textbook. Utilize the ultra-efficient QuickTest Wizard to create tests in less than five minutes by taking advantage of Course Technology's question banks, or customize your own exams from scratch.

LAB TESTS/TEST OUT The Lab Tests/Test Out exercises parallel the In the Lab assignments and are supplied for the purpose of testing students in the laboratory on the material covered in the chapter or testing students out of the course.

DATA FILES FOR STUDENTS All the files that are required by students to complete the exercises are included. You can distribute the files on the Instructor Resources CD-ROM to your students over a network, or you can have them follow the instructions on the inside back cover of this book to obtain a copy of the Data Files for Students.

ADDITIONAL ACTIVITIES FOR STUDENTS These additional activities consist of Chapter Reinforcement Exercises, which are true/false, multiple-choice, and short answer questions that help students gain confidence in the material learned.

Assessment & Training Solutions

SAM 2007

SAM 2007 helps bridge the gap between the classroom and the real world by allowing students to train and test on important computer skills in an active, hands-on environment.

SAM 2007's easy-to-use system includes powerful interactive exams, training or projects on critical applications such as Word, Excel, Access, PowerPoint, Outlook, Windows, the Internet, and much more. SAM simulates the application environment, allowing students to demonstrate their knowledge and think through the skills by performing real-world tasks.

Designed to be used with the Shelly Cashman series, SAM 2007 includes built-in page references so students can print helpful study guides that match the Shelly Cashman series textbooks used in class. Powerful administrative options allow instructors to schedule exams and assignments, secure tests, and run reports with almost limitless flexibility.

Student Edition Labs

Our Web-based interactive labs help students master hundreds of computer concepts, including input and output devices, file management and desktop applications, computer ethics, virus protection, and much more. Featuring up-to-the-minute content, eye-popping graphics, and rich animation, the highly interactive Student Edition Labs offer students an alternative way to learn through dynamic observation, step-by-step practice, and challenging review questions.

Online Content

Blackboard is the leading distance learning solution provider and class-management platform today. Course Technology has partnered with Blackboard to bring you premium online content. Instructors: Content for use with *Microsoft Office Access 2007: Comprehensive Concepts and Techniques* is available in a Blackboard Course Cartridge and may include topic reviews, case projects, review questions, test banks, practice tests, custom syllabi, and more.

   Course Technology also has solutions for several other learning management systems. Please visit course.com today to see what's available for this title.

CourseCasts Learning on the Go. Always Available...Always Relevant.

Want to keep up with the latest technology trends relevant to you? Visit our site to find a library of podcasts, CourseCasts, featuring a "CourseCast of the Week," and download them to your portable media player at http://coursecasts.course.com.

   Our fast-paced world is driven by technology. You know because you are an active participant — always on the go, always keeping up with technological trends, and always learning new ways to embrace technology to power your life.

   Ken Baldauf, a faculty member of the Florida State University (FSU) Computer Science Department, is responsible for teaching technology classes to thousands of FSU students each year. He knows what you know; he knows what you want to learn. He is also an expert in the latest technology and will sort through and aggregate the most pertinent news and information so you can spend your time e njoying technology, rather than trying to figure it out.

   Visit us at http://coursecasts.course.com to learn on the go!

CourseNotes

Course Technology's CourseNotes are six-panel quick reference cards that reinforce the most important and widely used features of a software application in a visual and user-friendly format. CourseNotes will serve as a great reference tool during and after the student completes the course. CourseNotes for Microsoft Office 2007, Word 2007, Excel 2007, Access 2007, PowerPoint 2007, Windows Vista, and more are available now!

About Our New Cover Look

Learning styles of students have changed, but the Shelly Cashman Series' dedication to their success has remained steadfast for over 30 years. We are committed to continually updating our approach and content to refl ect the way today's students learn and experi-

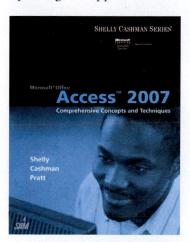

ence new technology. This focus on the user is refl ected in our bold new cover design, which features photographs of real students using the Shelly Cashman Series in their courses. Each book features a different user, refl ecting the many ages, experiences, and backgrounds of all of the students learning with our books. When you use the Shelly Cashman Series, you can be assured that you are learning computer skills using the most effective course-ware available. We would like to thank the administration and faculty at the participating schools for their help in making our vision a reality. Most of all, we'd like to thank the wonderful students from all over the world who learn from our texts and now appear on our covers.

To the Student . . . Getting the Most Out of Your Book

Welcome to *Microsoft Office Access 2007: Comprehensive Concepts and Techniques*. You can save yourself a lot of time and gain a better understanding of the Office 2007 programs if you spend a few minutes reviewing the figures and callouts in this section.

1 PROJECT ORIENTATION
Each chapter's project presents a practical problem and shows the solution in the first figure of the chapter. The project orientation lets you see firsthand how problems are solved from start to finish using application software and computers.

2 PROJECT PLANNING GUIDELINES AND PLAN AHEAD BOXES
Overall planning guidelines at the beginning of a chapter and Plan Ahead boxes throughout encourage you to think critically about how to accomplish the next goal before you actually begin working.

3 CONSISTENT STEP-BY-STEP, SCREEN-BY-SCREEN PRESENTATION
Chapter solutions are built using a step-by-step, screen-by-screen approach. This pedagogy allows you to build the solution on a computer as you read through the chapter. Generally, each step includes an explanation that indicates the result of the step.

4 MORE THAN JUST STEP-BY-STEP
BTW annotations in the margins of the book, Q&As in the steps, and substantive text in the paragraphs provide background information, tips, and answers to common questions that complement the topics covered, adding depth and perspective. When you finish with this book, you will be ready to use the Office programs to solve problems on your own. Experimental steps provide you with opportunities to step out on your own to try features of the programs, and pick up right where you left off in the chapter.

5 OTHER WAYS BOXES AND QUICK REFERENCE SUMMARY
Other Ways boxes that follow many of the step sequences and a Quick Reference Summary at the back of the book explain the other ways to complete the task presented, such as using the mouse, Ribbon, shortcut menu, and keyboard.

6 EMPHASIS ON GETTING HELP WHEN YOU NEED IT
The first project of each application and Appendix C show you how to use all the elements of Office Help. Being able to answer your own questions will increase your productivity and reduce your frustrations by minimizing the time it takes to learn how to complete a task.

7 REVIEW, REINFORCEMENT, AND EXTENSION
After you successfully step through a project in a chapter, a section titled Chapter Summary identifies the tasks with which you should be familiar. Terms you should know for test purposes are bold in the text. The SAM Training feature provides the opportunity for addional reinforcement on important skills covered in each chapter. The Learn It Online section at the end of each chapter offers reinforcement in the form of review questions, learning games, and practice tests. Also included are exercises that require you to extend your learning beyond the book.

8 LABORATORY EXERCISES
If you really want to learn how to use the programs, then you must design and implement solutions to problems on your own. Every chapter concludes with several carefully developed laboratory assignments that increase in complexity.

1 Creating and Using a Database

Objectives

You will have mastered the material in this chapter when you can:

- Describe databases and database management systems

- Design a database to satisfy a collection of requirements

- Start Access

- Describe the features of the Access window

- Create a database

- Create a table and add records

- Close a table

- Close a database and quit Access

- Open a database

- Print the contents of a table

- Create and print custom reports

- Create and use a split form

- Use the Access Help system

1 | Creating and Using a Database

What Is Microsoft Office Access 2007?

Microsoft Office Access 2007, usually referred to as simply Access, is a database management system. A database management system, such as Access, is a software tool that allows you to use a computer to create a database; add, change, and delete data in the database; sort the data in the database; retrieve data in the database; and create forms and reports using the data in the database. The term **database** describes a collection of data organized in a manner that allows access, retrieval, and use of that data. Some of the key features in Access are:

- **Data entry and update** Access provides easy mechanisms for adding, changing, and deleting data, including the capability of making mass changes in a single operation.

- **Queries (questions)** Access makes it possible to ask complex questions concerning the data in the database and then receive instant answers.

- **Forms** Access allows the user to produce attractive and useful forms for viewing and updating data.

- **Reports** Access includes report creation tools that make it easy to produce sophisticated reports for presenting data.

- **Web support** Access allows you to save objects, reports, and tables in HTML format so they can be viewed using a browser. You also can import and export documents in XML format as well as share data with others using SharePoint Services.

This latest version of Access has many new features to help you be more productive. Like the other Office applications, it features a new, improved interface utilizing the Ribbon. The new Navigation Pane makes navigating among the various objects in a database easier and more intuitive than in the past. The new version includes several professionally designed templates that you can use to quickly create a database. Sorting and filtering has been enhanced in this version. The new Layout view allows you to make changes to the design of forms and reports at the same time you are browsing the data. Datasheet view also has been enhanced to make creating tables more intuitive. Split form, a new form object, combines both a datasheet and a form as a single unit. Memo fields now support rich text, and there is a new Attachment data type. Using the Attachment data type, a field can contain an attached file, such as a document, image, or spreadsheet.

Project Planning Guidelines

The process of developing a database that communicates specific information requires careful analysis and planning. As a starting point, establish why the database is needed. Once the purpose is determined, analyze the intended users of the database and their unique needs. Then, gather information about the topic and decide what to include in the database. Finally, determine the database design and style that will be most successful at delivering the message. Details of these guidelines are provided in Appendix A. In addition, each project in this book provides practical applications of these planning considerations.

Project — Database Creation

JSP Recruiters is a recruiting firm that specializes in job placement for health care professionals. Because the recruiters at JSP have previous experience in the health care industry, the firm is able to provide quality candidates for employment in hospitals, clinics, medical laboratories, doctors' offices, and other health care facilities.

JSP Recruiters works with clients in need of health care professionals. It assigns each client to a specific recruiter. The recruiter works with the client to determine the necessary qualifications for each job candidate. The recruiter then contacts and does a preliminary review of the qualifications for each candidate before setting up a job interview between the client and the candidate. If the candidate is hired, the client pays a percentage of the new employee's annual salary to the recruiting firm, which then distributes a percentage of that client fee to the recruiter.

To ensure that operations run smoothly, JSP Recruiters organizes data on its clients and recruiters in a database, managed by Access. In this way, JSP keeps its data current and accurate while the firm's management can analyze the data for trends and produce a variety of useful reports.

In Access, a database consists of a collection of tables, each of which contains information on a specific subject. Figure 1–1 shows the database for JSP Recruiters. It consists of two tables. The Client table (Figure 1–1a) contains information about the clients to whom JSP provides services. The Recruiter table (Figure 1–1b) contains information about the recruiters to whom these clients are assigned.

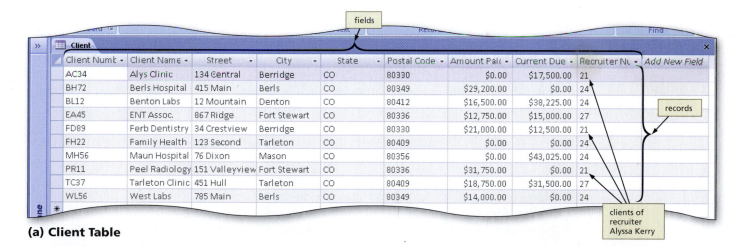

(a) Client Table

Client Number	Client Name	Street	City	State	Postal Code	Amount Paid	Current Due	Recruiter Number
AC34	Alys Clinic	134 Central	Berridge	CO	80330	$0.00	$17,500.00	21
BH72	Berls Hospital	415 Main	Berls	CO	80349	$29,200.00	$0.00	24
BL12	Benton Labs	12 Mountain	Denton	CO	80412	$16,500.00	$38,225.00	24
EA45	ENT Assoc.	867 Ridge	Fort Stewart	CO	80336	$12,750.00	$15,000.00	27
FD89	Ferb Dentistry	34 Crestview	Berridge	CO	80330	$21,000.00	$12,500.00	21
FH22	Family Health	123 Second	Tarleton	CO	80409	$0.00	$0.00	24
MH56	Maun Hospital	76 Dixon	Mason	CO	80356	$0.00	$43,025.00	24
PR11	Peel Radiology	151 Valleyview	Fort Stewart	CO	80336	$31,750.00	$0.00	21
TC37	Tarleton Clinic	451 Hull	Tarleton	CO	80409	$18,750.00	$31,500.00	27
WL56	West Labs	785 Main	Berls	CO	80349	$14,000.00	$0.00	24

(b) Recruiter Table

Recruiter Number	Last Name	First Name	Street	City	State	Postal Code	Rate	Commission
21	Kerry	Alyssa	261 Pointer	Tourin	CO	80416	0.10	$17,600.00
24	Reeves	Camden	3135 Brill	Denton	CO	80412	0.10	$19,900.00
27	Fernandez	Jaime	265 Maxwell	Charleston	CO	80380	0.09	$9,450.00
34	Lee	Jan	1827 Oak	Denton	CO	80413	0.08	$0.00

Figure 1–1

The rows in the tables are called **records**. A record contains information about a given person, product, or event. A row in the Client table, for example, contains information about a specific client.

The columns in the tables are called fields. A **field** contains a specific piece of information within a record. In the Client table, for example, the fourth field, City, contains the city where the client is located.

The first field in the Client table is the Client Number. JSP Recruiters assigns a number to each client. As is common to the way in which many organizations format client numbers, JSP Recruiters calls it a *number*, although it actually contains letters. The JSP client numbers consist of two uppercase letters followed by a two-digit number.

These numbers are unique; that is, no two clients are assigned the same number. Such a field can be used as a **unique identifier**. This simply means that a given client number will appear only in a single record in the table. Only one record exists, for example, in which the client number is BH72. A unique identifier also is called a **primary key**. Thus, the Client Number field is the primary key for the Client table.

The next seven fields in the Client table are Client Name, Street, City, State, Postal Code, Amount Paid, and Current Due. Note that the default width of the columns cuts off the names of some of the columns. The Amount Paid column contains the amount that the client has paid JSP Recruiters year to date (YTD) prior to the current period. The Current Due column contains the amount due to JSP for the current period. For example, client BL12 is Benton Labs. The address is 12 Mountain in Denton, Colorado. The postal code is 80412. The client has paid $16,500 for recruiting services so far this year. The amount due for the current period is $38,225.

JSP assigns each client a single recruiter. The last column in the Client table, Recruiter Number, gives the number of the client's recruiter.

The first field in the Recruiter table, Recruiter Number, is the number JSP Recruiters assigns to the recruiter. These numbers are unique, so Recruiter Number is the primary key of the Recruiter table.

The other fields in the Recruiter table are Last Name, First Name, Street, City, State, Postal Code, Rate, and Commission. The Rate field contains the percentage of the client fee that the recruiter earns, and the Commission field contains the total amount that JSP has paid the recruiter so far this year. For example, Recruiter 27 is Jaime Fernandez. His address is 265 Maxwell in Charleston, Colorado. The Postal Code is 80380. His commission rate is .09 (9%), and his commission is $9,450.

The recruiter number appears in both the Client table and the Recruiter table. It relates clients and recruiters. For example, in the Client table, you see that the recruiter number for client BL12 is 24. To find the name of this recruiter, look for the row in the Recruiter table that contains 24 in the Recruiter Number column. After you have found it, you know the client is assigned to Camden Reeves. To find all the clients assigned to Camden Reeves, you must look through the Client table for all the clients that contain 24 in the Recruiter Number column. His clients are BH72 (Berls Hospital), BL12 (Benton Labs), FH22 (Family Health), MH56 (Maun Hospital), and WL56 (West Labs).

The last recruiter in the Recruiter table, Jan Lee, has not been assigned any clients yet; therefore, her recruiter number, 34, does not appear on any row in the Client table.

Overview

As you read this chapter, you will learn how to create the database shown in Figure 1–1 on the previous page by performing these general tasks:

- Design the database.
- Create a new blank database.

- Create a table and add the records.
- Preview and print the contents of a table.
- Create a second table and add the records.
- Create four reports.
- Create a form.

**Plan
Ahead**

Database design guidelines.

Database design refers to the arrangement of data into tables and fields. In the example in this chapter the design is specified, but in many cases, you will have to determine the design based on what you want the system to accomplish.

When designing a database, the actions you take and the decisions you make will determine the tables and fields that will be included in the database. As you create a database, such as the project shown in Figure 1–1 on page AC 3, you should follow these general guidelines:

1. **Identify the tables.** Examine the requirements for the database in order to identify the main objects that are involved. There will be a table for each object you identified.

   In one database, for example, the main objects might be departments and employees. Thus, there would be two tables: one for departments and the other for employees. In another database, the main objects might be clients and recruiters. In this case, there would also be two tables: one for clients and the other for recruiters. In still another database, the main objects might be books, publishers, and authors. Here there would be three tables: one for books, a second for publishers, and a third for authors.

2. **Determine the primary keys.** Recall that the primary key is the unique identifier for records in the table. For each table, determine the unique identifier, if there is one. For a Department table, for example, the unique identifier might be the Department Code. For a Book table, the unique identifier might be the ISBN number.

3. **Determine the additional fields.** The primary key will be a field or combination of fields in a table. There typically will be many additional fields, each of which contains a type of data. Examine the project requirements to determine these additional fields. For example, in an Employee table, the additional fields might include such fields as Employee Name, Street Address, City, State, Postal Code, Date Hired, Salary, and so on.

4. **Determine relationships among the tables.** Examine the list of tables you have created to see which tables are related. When you determine two tables are related, include matching fields in the two tables. For example, in a database containing employees and departments, there is a relationship between the two tables because one department can have many employees assigned to it. Department Code could be the matching field in the two tables.

5. **Determine data types for the fields.** For each field, determine the type of data the field can contain. One field, for example, might contain only numbers. Another field might contain currency amounts, while a third field might contain only dates. Some fields contain text data, meaning any combination of letters, numbers and special characters (!, ;, ', &, and so on). For example, in an Employee table, the Date Hired field would contain dates, the Salary field would contain currency amounts, and the Hours Worked field would contain numbers. The other fields in the Employee table would contain text data, such as Employee Name and Department Code.

6. **Identify and remove any unwanted redundancy. Redundancy** is the storing of a piece of data in more than one place. Redundancy usually, but not always, causes problems, such as wasted space, difficulties with update, and possible data inconsistency. Examine each table you have created to see if it contains redundancy and, if so, determine whether the redundancy causes these problems. If it does, remove the redundancy by splitting the table into two tables. For example, you may have a single table of employees. In addition to typical employee data (name, address, earnings, and so on), the table might contain Department Number and Department Name. If so, the Department Name could repeat multiple times.

(continued)

Plan Ahead

> *(continued)*
>
> Every employee whose department number is 12, for example, would have the same department name. It would be better to split the table into two tables, one for Employees and one for Department. In the Department table, the Department Name is stored only once.
>
> 7. **Determine a location for the database. The database you have designed will be stored in a single file. You need to determine a location in which to store the file.**
>
> When necessary, more specific details concerning the above guidelines are presented at appropriate points in the chapter. The chapter also will identify the actions performed and decisions made regarding these guidelines during the creation of the database shown in Figure 1–1 on page AC 3.

BTW

Database Design
For more information on database design methods and for techniques for identifying and eliminating redundancy, visit the Access 2007 Database Design Web page (scsite.com/ac2007/dbdesign).

Designing a Database

This section illustrates the database design process by showing how you would design the database for JSP Recruiters from a set of requirements. In this section, you will use a commonly accepted shorthand to represent the tables and fields that make up the database as well as the primary keys for the tables. For each table, you give the name of the table followed by a set of parentheses. Within the parentheses is a list of the fields in the table separated by commas. You underline the primary key. For example,

Product (<u>Product Code</u>, Description, On Hand, Price)

represents a table called Product. The Product table contains four fields: Product Code, Description, On Hand, and Price. The Product Code field is the primary key.

Database Requirements

JSP Recruiters needs to maintain information on both clients and recruiters. It currently keeps this data in the two Word tables and two Excel workbooks shown in Figure 1–2. They use Word tables for address information and Excel workbooks for financial information.

Client Number	Client Name	Street	City	State	Postal Code
AC34	Alys Clinic	134 Central	Berridge	CO	80330
BH72	Berls Hospital	415 Main	Berls	CO	80349
BL12	Benton Labs	12 Mountain	Denton	CO	80412
EA45	ENT Assoc.	867 Ridge	Fort Stewart	CO	80336
FD89	Ferb Dentistry	34 Crestview	Berridge	CO	80330
FH22	Family Health	123 Second	Tarleton	CO	80409
MH56	Maun Hospital	76 Dixon	Mason	CO	80356
PR11	Peel Radiology	151 Valleyview	Fort Stewart	CO	80336
TC37	Tarleton Clinic	451 Hull	Tarleton	CO	80409
WL56	West Labs	785 Main	Berls	CO	80349

**(a)
Client Address
Information
(Word Table)**

Figure 1–2

(b) Client Financial Information (Excel Workbook)

	A	B	C	D
1	Client Number	Client Name	Amount Paid	Current Due
2	AC34	Alys Clinic	$0.00	$17,500.00
3	BH72	Berls Hospital	$29,200.00	$0.00
4	BL12	Benton Labs	$16,500.00	$38,225.00
5	EA45	ENT Assoc.	$12,750.00	$15,000.00
6	FD89	Ferb Dentistry	$21,000.00	$12,500.00
7	FH22	Family Health	$0.00	$0.00
8	MH56	Maun Hospital	$0.00	$43,025.00
9	PR11	Peel Radiology	$31,750.00	$0.00
10	TC37	Tarleton Clinic	$18,750.00	$31,500.00
11	WL56	West Labs	$14,000.00	$0.00

(c) Recruiter Address Information (Word Table)

Recruiter Number	Last Name	First Name	Street	City	State	Postal Code
21	Kerry	Alyssa	261 Pointer	Tourin	CO	80416
24	Reeves	Camden	3135 Brill	Denton	CO	80412
27	Fernandez	Jaime	265 Maxwell	Charleston	CO	80380
34	Lee	Jan	1827 Oak	Denton	CO	80413

(d) Recruiter Financial Information (Excel Workbook)

	A	B	C	D	E
1	Recruiter Number	Last Name	First Name	Rate	Commission
2	21	Kerry	Alyssa	0.10	$17,600.00
3	24	Reeves	Camden	0.10	$19,900.00
4	27	Fernandez	Jaime	0.09	$9,450.00
5	34	Lee	Jan	0.08	$0.00

Figure 1–2 (continued)

For clients, JSP needs to maintain address data. It currently keeps this address data in a Word table (Figure 1–2a). It also maintains financial data for each client. This includes the amount paid and the current due from the client. It keeps these amounts along with the client name and number in the Excel workbook shown in Figure 1–2b.

JSP keeps recruiter address data in a Word table as shown in Figure 1–2c. Just as with clients, it keeps financial data for recruiters, including their rate and commission, in a separate Excel workbook, as shown in Figure 1–2d.

Finally, it keeps track of which clients are assigned to which recruiters. Currently, for example, clients AC34 (Alys Clinic), FD89 (Ferb Dentistry), and PR11 (Peel Radiology) are assigned to recruiter 21 (Alyssa Kerry). Clients BH72 (Berls Hospital), BL12 (Benton Labs), FH22 (Family Health), MH56 (Maun Hospital), and WL56 (West Labs) are assigned to recruiter 24 (Camden Reeves). Clients EA45 (ENT Assoc.) and TC37 (Tarleton Clinic) are assigned to recruiter 27 (Jaime Fernandez). JSP has an additional recruiter, Jan Lee, whose number has been assigned as 34, but who has not yet been assigned any clients.

Naming Tables and Fields

In designing your database, you must name the tables and fields. Thus, before beginning the design process, you must understand the rules for table and field names, which are:

1. Names can be up to 64 characters in length.
2. Names can contain letters, digits, and spaces, as well as most of the punctuation symbols.
3. Names cannot contain periods (.), exclamation points (!), accent graves (`), or square brackets ([ ]).
4. The same name cannot be used for two different fields in the same table.

The approach to naming tables and fields used in this text is to begin the names with an uppercase letter and to use lowercase for the other letters. In multiple-word names, each word begins with an uppercase letter, and there is a space between words (for example, Client Number). You should know that there are other approaches. Some people omit the space (ClientNumber). Still others use an underscore in place of the space (Client_Number). Finally, some use an underscore in place of a space, but use the same case for all letters (CLIENT_NUMBER or client_number).

Identifying the Tables

Now that you know the rules for naming tables and fields, you are ready to begin the design process. The first step is to identify the main objects involved in the requirements. For the JSP Recruiters database, the main objects are clients and recruiters. This leads to two tables, which you must name. Reasonable names for these two tables are:

Client
Recruiter

Determining the Primary Keys

The next step is to identify the fields that will be the primary keys. Client numbers uniquely identify clients, and recruiter numbers uniquely identify recruiters. Thus, the primary key for the Client table is the client number, and the primary key for the Recruiter table is the recruiter number. Reasonable names for these fields would be Client Number and Recruiter Number, respectively. Adding these primary keys to the tables gives:

Client (<u>Client Number</u>)
Recruiter (<u>Recruiter Number</u>)

Determining Additional Fields

After identifying the primary keys, you need to determine and name the additional fields. In addition to the client number, the Client Address Information shown in Figure 1–2a on page AC 6 contains the client name, street, city, state, and postal code. These would be fields in the Client table. The Client Financial Information shown in Figure 1–2b also contains the client number and client name, which are already included in the Client table. The financial information also contains the amount paid and the current due. Adding the amount paid and current due fields to those already identified in the Client table and assigning reasonable names gives:

Client (<u>Client Number</u>, Client Name, Street, City, State, Postal Code,
Amount Paid, Current Due)

Similarly, examining the Recruiter Address Information in Figure 1–2c on page AC 7 adds the last name, first name, street, city, state, and postal code fields to the Recruiter table. In addition to the recruiter number, last name, and first name, the Recruiter Financial Information in Figure 1–2d would add the rate and commission. Adding these fields to the Recruiter table and assigning reasonable names gives:

Recruiter (<u>Recruiter Number</u>, Last Name, First Name, Street, City,

State, Postal Code, Rate, Commission)

Determining and Implementing Relationships Between the Tables

Plan Ahead

Determine relationships among the tables.
The most common type of relationship you will encounter between tables is the **one-to-many relationship**. This means that each row in the first table may be associated with *many* rows in the second table, but each row in the second table is associated with only *one* row in the first. The first table is called the "one" table and the second is called the "many" table. For example, there may be a relationship between departments and employees, in which each department can have many employees, but each employee is assigned to only one department. In this relationship, there would be two tables, Department and Employee. The Department table would be the "one" table in the relationship. The Employee table would be the "many" table.

To determine relationships among tables, you can follow these general guidelines:

1. Identify the "one" table.

2. Identify the "many" table.

3. Include the primary key from the "one" table as a field in the "many" table.

According to the requirements, each client has one recruiter, but each recruiter can have many clients. Thus, the Recruiter table is the "one" table, and the Client table is the "many" table. To implement this one-to-many relationship between recruiters and clients, add the Recruiter Number field (the primary key of the Recruiter table) to the Client table. This produces:

Client (<u>Client Number</u>, Client Name, Street, City, State, Postal Code, Amount Paid, Current Due, Recruiter Number)

Recruiter (<u>Recruiter Number</u>, Last Name, First Name, Street, City, State, Postal Code, Rate, Commission)

Determining Data Types for the Fields

Each field has a **data type**. This indicates the type of data that can be stored in the field. Three of the most commonly used data types are:

1. **Text** — The field can contain any characters. A maximum number of 255 characters is allowed in a field whose data type is Text.

2. **Number** — The field can contain only numbers. The numbers either can be positive or negative. Fields are assigned this type so they can be used in arithmetic operations. Fields that contain numbers but will not be used for arithmetic operations usually are assigned a data type of Text.

3. **Currency** — The field can contain only monetary data. The values will appear with currency symbols, such as dollar signs, commas, and decimal points, and with

BTW

Currency Symbols
To show the symbol for the Euro (€) instead of the dollar sign, change the Format property for the field whose data type is currency. To change the default symbols for currency, change the settings in the operating system using the Control Panel.

BTW

Field Size (Text Fields)
You can restrict the number of characters that can be entered in a text field by changing the field size. For example, if you change the field size for the Client Name field to 25, users will be unable to enter more than 25 characters in the field.

two digits following the decimal point. Like numeric fields, you can use currency fields in arithmetic operations. Access assigns a size to currency fields automatically.

Table 1–1 shows the other data types that are available.

Table 1–1 Additional Data Types	
Data Type	**Description**
Memo	Field can store a variable amount of text or combinations of text and numbers where the total number of characters may exceed 255.
Date/Time	Field can store dates and times.
AutoNumber	Field can store a unique sequential number that Access assigns to a record. Access will increment the number by 1 as each new record is added.
Yes/No	Field can store only one of two values. The choices are Yes/No, True/False, or On/Off.
OLE Object	Field can store an OLE object, which is an object linked to or embedded in the table.
Hyperlink	Field can store text that can be used as a hyperlink address.
Attachment	Field can contain an attached file. Images, spreadsheets, documents, charts, and so on can be attached to this field in a record in the database. You can view and edit the attached file.

In the Client table, because the Client Number, Client Name, Street, City, and State can all contain letters, their data types should be Text. The data type for Postal Code is Text instead of Number, because postal codes are not used in arithmetic operations. You do not add postal codes or find an average postal code, for example. The Amount Paid and Current Due fields both contain monetary data, so their data types should be Currency.

Similarly, in the Recruiter table, the data type for the Recruiter Number, Last Name, First Name, Street, City, State, and Postal Code fields all should be Text. The Commission field contains monetary amounts, so its data type should be Currency. The Rate field contains a number that is not a currency amount, so its data type should be Number.

Identifying and Removing Redundancy

Redundancy means storing the same fact in more than one place. It usually results from placing too many fields in a table — fields that really belong in separate tables — and often causes serious problems. If you had not realized there were two objects, clients and recruiters, for example, you might have placed all the data in a single Client table. Figure 1–3 shows a portion of this table with some sample data. Notice that the data for a given Recruiter (number, name, address, and so on) occurs on more than one record. The data for Camden Reeves is repeated in the figure.

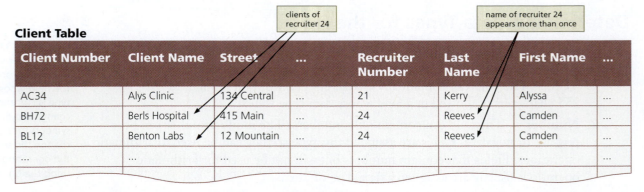

Client Table

Client Number	Client Name	Street	...	Recruiter Number	Last Name	First Name	...
AC34	Alys Clinic	134 Central	...	21	Kerry	Alyssa	...
BH72	Berls Hospital	415 Main	...	24	Reeves	Camden	...
BL12	Benton Labs	12 Mountain	...	24	Reeves	Camden	...
...	...	...	...	...	...	...	...

Figure 1–3

Storing this data on multiple records is an example of redundancy, which causes several problems, including:

1. Wasted storage space. The name of Recruiter 24 (Camden Reeves), for example, should be stored only once. Storing this fact several times is wasteful.

2. More difficult database updates. If, for example, Camden Reeves's name is spelled wrong and needs to be changed in the database, his name would need to be changed in several different places.

3. A possibility of inconsistent data. There is nothing to prohibit the recruiter's last name from being Reeves on client BH72's record and Reed on client BL12's record. The data would be inconsistent. In both cases, the recruiter number is 24, but the last names are different.

The solution to the problem is to place the redundant data in a separate table, one in which the data no longer will be redundant. If, for example, you place the data for recruiters in a separate table (Figure 1–4), the data for each recruiter will appear only once.

Client Table

Client Number	Client Name	Street	...	Recruiter Number
AC34	Alys Clinic	134 Central	...	21
BH72	Berls Hospital	415 Main	...	24 ← clients of recruiter 24
BL12	Benton Labs	12 Mountain	...	24 ←
...	...	...	...	...

Recruiter Table

Recruiter Number	Last Name	First Name	...
21	Kerry	Alyssa	...
24	Reeves ← name of recruiter 24 appears only once	Camden	...
...	...	...	...

Figure 1–4

Notice that you need to have the recruiter number in both tables. Without it, there would be no way to tell which recruiter is associated with which client. The remaining recruiter data, however, was removed from the Client table and placed in the Recruiter table. This new arrangement corrects the problems of redundancy in the following ways:

1. Because the data for each recruiter is stored only once, space is not wasted.

2. Changing the name of a recruiter is easy. You have only to change one row in the Recruiter table.

3. Because the data for a recruiter is stored only once, inconsistent data cannot occur. Designing to omit redundancy will help you to produce good and valid database designs.

You should always examine your design to see if it contains redundancy. If it does, you should decide whether you need to remove the redundancy by creating a separate table.

Postal Codes
Some organizations with many customers spread throughout the country will, in fact, have a separate table of postal codes, cities, and states. If you call such an organization to place an order, they typically will ask you for your postal code (or ZIP code), rather than asking for your city, state, and postal code. They then will indicate the city and state that correspond to that postal code and ask you if that is correct.

If you examine your design, you'll see that there is one area of redundancy (see the data in Figure 1–1 on page AC 3). Cities and states are both repeated. Every client whose postal code is 80330, for example, has Berridge as the city and CO as the state. To remove this redundancy, you would create a table whose primary key is Postal Code and that contains City and State as additional fields. City and State would be removed from the Client table. Having City, State, and Postal Code in a table is very common, however, and usually you would not take such action. There is no other redundancy in your tables.

Starting Access

If you are using a computer to step through the project in this chapter, and you want your screen to match the figures in this book, you should change your screen's resolution to 1024 × 768. For information about how to change a computer's resolution, read Appendix E.

Note: If you are using Windows XP, see Appendix F for alternate steps.

To Start Access

The following steps, which assume Windows Vista is running, start Access based on a typical installation. You may need to ask your instructor how to start Access for your computer.

- Click the Start button on the Windows Vista taskbar to display the Start menu.

- Click All Programs at the bottom of the left pane on the Start menu to display the All Programs list.

- Click Microsoft Office in the All Programs list to display the Microsoft Office list (Figure 1–5).

Figure 1–5

2

- Click Microsoft Office Access 2007 to start Access and display the Getting Started with Microsoft Office Access screen (Figure 1–6).

- If the Access window is not maximized, click the Maximize button next to the Close button on its title bar to maximize the window.

Q&A

What is a maximized window?

A maximized window fills the entire screen. When you maximize a window, the Maximize button changes to a Restore Down button.

Figure 1–6

Other Ways

1. Double-click Access icon on desktop, if one is present
2. Click Microsoft Office Access 2007 on Start menu

Creating a Database

In Access, all the tables, reports, forms, and queries that you create are stored in a single file called a database. Thus, before creating any of these objects, you first must create the database that will hold them. You can use either the Blank Database option or a template to create a new database. If you already know the tables and fields you want in your database, you would use the Blank Database option. If not, you can use a template. Templates can guide you by suggesting some commonly used databases. If you choose to create a database using a template, you would use the following steps.

To Create a Database Using a Template

1. If the template you wish to use is not already visible on the Getting Started with Microsoft Office Access page, double-click the links in the Template Categories pane to display the desired template.
2. Click the template you wish to use.
3. Enter a file name (or accept the suggested file name) and select a location for the database.
4. Click the Create button to create the database or the Download button to download the database and create the database, if necessary.

    When you create a database, the computer places it on a storage medium, such as a USB flash drive, CD, or hard disk. A saved database is referred to as a **file**. A **file name** is the name assigned to a file when it is saved.

BTW

Naming Files
File names can be a maximum of 260 characters including the file extension. The file extension for Access 2007 is .accdb. You can use either uppercase or lowercase letters in file names.

<table>
<tr><td>**Plan**
Ahead</td><td>**Determine where to create the database.**
When creating a database, you must decide which storage medium to use.

If you always work on the same computer and have no need to transport your database to a different location, then your computer's hard drive will suffice as a storage location. It is a good idea, however, to save a backup copy of your database on a separate medium in case the file becomes corrupted, or the computer's hard drive fails.

If you plan to work on your database in various locations or on multiple computers, then you can consider saving your projects on a portable medium, such as a USB flash drive or CD. The projects in this book are stored on a USB flash drive, which saves files quickly and reliably and can be reused. CDs are easily portable and serve as good backups for the final versions of projects because they generally can save files only one time.</td></tr>
</table>

To Create a Database

Because you already know the tables and fields you want in the JSP Recruiters database, you would use the Blank Database option rather than using a template. The following steps create a database, using the file name JSP Recruiters, on a USB flash drive.

Note: If you are using Windows XP, see Appendix F for alternate steps.

- With a USB flash drive connected to one of the computer's USB ports, click Blank Database to create a new blank database (Figure 1–7).

Figure 1–7

2

- Repeatedly press the DELETE key to delete the default name of Database1.

- Type JSP Recruiters in the File Name text box to replace the default file name of Database1 (your screen may show Database1.accdb). Do not press the ENTER key after typing the file name (Figure 1–8).

Q&A What characters can I use in a file name?

A file name can have a maximum of 260 characters, including spaces. The only invalid characters are the back-slash (\), slash (/), colon (:), asterisk (*), question mark (?), quotation mark ("), less than symbol (<), greater than symbol (>), and vertical bar (|).

3

- Click the 'Browse for a location to put your database' button to display the File New Database dialog box.

- If the Navigation Pane is not displayed in the Save As dialog box, click the Browse Folders button to expand the dialog box.

- If a Folders list is displayed below the Folders button, click the Folders button to remove the Folders list (Figure 1-9).

Q&A Do I have to save to a USB flash drive?

No. You can save to any device or folder. A **folder** is a specific location on a storage medium. You can save to the default folder or a different folder. You also can create your own folders, which is explained later in this book.

Figure 1–8

Figure 1–9

4

- If Computer is not displayed in the Favorite Links section, drag the top or bottom edge of the Save As dialog box until Computer is displayed.

- Click Computer in the Favorite Links section to display a list of available drives (Figure 1–10).

- If necessary, scroll until UDISK 2.0 (E:) appears in the list of available drives.

Q&A Why is my list of drives arranged and named differently?

The size of the Save As dialog box and your computer's configuration determine how the list is displayed and how the drives are named.

Figure 1–10

Q&A How do I save the file if I am not using a USB flash drive?

Use the same process, but select your desired save location in the Favorite Links section.

5

- Double-click UDISK 2.0 (E:) in the Computer list to select the USB flash drive, Drive E in this case, as the new save location (Figure 1–11).

Q&A What if my USB flash drive has a different name or letter?

It is very likely that your USB flash drive will have a different name and drive letter and be connected to a different port. Verify that the device in your Computer list is correct.

Figure 1–11

6

- Click the OK button to select the USB flash drive as the location for the database and to return to the Getting Started with Microsoft Office Access screen (Figure 1–12).

Figure 1–12

7

- Click the Create button to create the database on the USB flash drive with the file name, JSP Recruiters (Figure 1–13).

Q&A

How do I know that the JSP Recruiters database is created?

The name of the database appears in the title bar.

Figure 1–13

8

- If a Field List appears, click its Close button to remove the Field List from the screen (Figure 1–14).

Figure 1–14

Other Ways

1. Click Office Button, click Save, type file name, click Computer, select drive or folder, click Save button

2. Press CTRL+S or press SHIFT+F12, type file name, click Computer, select drive or folder, click Save button

The Access Window

The Access window consists of a variety of components to make your work more efficient and documents more professional. These include the Navigation Pane, Access work area, Ribbon, Mini toolbar and shortcut menus, Quick Access Toolbar, and Office Button. Some of these components are common to other Microsoft Office 2007 programs; others are unique to Access.

Navigation Pane and Access Work Area

You work on objects such as tables, forms, and reports in the **Access work area**. In the work area in Figure 1–14 on the previous page, a single table, Table1, is open in the work area. Figure 1–15 shows a work area with multiple objects open. **Object tabs** for the open objects appear at the top of the work area. You can select one of the open objects by clicking its tab. In the figure, the Client Form is the selected object. To the left of the work area is the Navigation Pane. The Navigation Pane contains a list of all the objects in the database. You use this pane to open an object. You also can customize the way objects are displayed in the Navigation Pane.

Figure 1–15

The Access work area in Figure 1–15 contains an insertion point, mouse pointer, scroll bar, and status bar. Other elements that may appear in the work area are discussed later in this and subsequent chapters.

Insertion Point The **insertion point** is a blinking vertical bar that indicates where text, graphics, and other items will be inserted. As you type, the insertion point moves to the right.

Mouse Pointer The **mouse pointer** becomes different shapes depending on the task you are performing in Access and the pointer's location on the screen. The mouse pointer in Figure 1–15 is the shape of an I-beam.

Scroll Bar   You use a **scroll bar** to display different portions of a database object in the Access window. At the right edge of the window is a **vertical scroll bar**. If an object is too wide to fit in the Access window, a **horizontal scroll bar** also appears at the bottom of the window. On a scroll bar, the position of the **scroll box** reflects the location of the portion of the database object that is displayed in the Access window. A **scroll arrow** is located at each end of a scroll bar. To scroll through, or display different portions of the object in the Access window, you can click a scroll arrow or drag the scroll box.

Status Bar   The **status bar**, located at the bottom of the Access window above the Windows Vista taskbar, presents information about the database object, the progress of current tasks, and the status of certain commands and keys; it also provides controls for viewing the object. As you type text or perform certain commands, various indicators may appear on the status bar.

The left edge of the status bar in Figure 1–15 shows that the form object is open in Form view. Toward the right edge are View buttons, which you can use to change the view that is currently displayed.

Ribbon

The **Ribbon**, located near the top of the Access window, is the control center in Access (Figure 1–16a). The Ribbon provides easy, central access to the tasks you perform while creating a database object. The Ribbon consists of tabs, groups, and commands. Each **tab** surrounds a collection of groups, and each group contains related commands.

When you start Access, the Ribbon displays four top-level tabs: Home, Create, External Data, and Database Tools. The **Home tab**, called the primary tab, contains the more frequently used commands. To display a different tab on the Ribbon, click the top-level tab. That is, to display the Create tab, click Create on the Ribbon. To return to the Home tab, click Home on the Ribbon. The tab currently displayed is called the **active tab**.

To allow more space in the Access work area, some users prefer to minimize the Ribbon, which hides the groups on the Ribbon and displays only the top-level tabs (Figure 1–16b). To use commands on a minimized Ribbon, click the top-level tab.

Each time you start Access, the Ribbon appears the same way it did the last time you used Access. The chapters in this book, however, begin with the Ribbon appearing as it did at the initial installation of the software. If you are stepping through this chapter on a computer and you want your Ribbon to match the figures in this book, read Appendix E.

BTW

Minimizing the Ribbon
If you want to minimize the Ribbon, right-click the Ribbon and then click Minimize the Ribbon on the shortcut menu, double-click the active tab, or press CTRL+F1. To restore a minimized Ribbon, right-click the Ribbon and then click Minimize the Ribbon on the shortcut menu, double-click any top-level tab, or press CTRL+F1. To use commands on a minimized Ribbon, click the top-level tab.

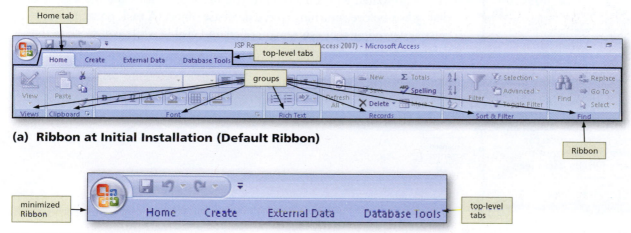

(a) Ribbon at Initial Installation (Default Ribbon)

(b) Minimized Ribbon

Figure 1–16

In addition to the top-level tabs, Access displays other tabs, called **contextual tabs**, when you perform certain tasks or work with objects such as datasheets. If you are working with a table in Datasheet view, for example, the Table Tools tab and its related subordinate Datasheet tab appear (Figure 1–17). When you are finished working with the table, the Table Tools and Datasheet tabs disappear from the Ribbon. Access determines when contextual tabs should appear and disappear based on tasks you perform. Some contextual tabs have more than one related subordinate tab.

Figure 1–17

Figure 1–18

Commands on the Ribbon include buttons, boxes (text boxes, check boxes, etc.), and galleries (Figure 1–18). A **gallery** is a set of choices, often graphical, arranged in a grid or in a list. You can scroll through choices on an in-Ribbon gallery by clicking the gallery's scroll arrows. Or, you can click a gallery's More button to view more gallery options on the screen at a time. Some buttons and boxes have arrows that, when clicked, also display a gallery; others always cause a gallery to be displayed when clicked. Many galleries support **live preview**, which is a feature that allows you to point to a gallery choice and see its effect in the database object — without actually selecting the choice.

Some commands on the Ribbon display an image to help you remember their function. When you point to a command on the Ribbon, all or part of the command glows in shades of yellow and orange, and an Enhanced ScreenTip appears on the screen. An **Enhanced ScreenTip** is an on-screen note that provides the name of the command, available keyboard shortcut(s), a description of the command, and sometimes instructions for how to obtain help about the command (Figure 1–19). Enhanced ScreenTips are more detailed than a typical ScreenTip, which usually only displays the name of the command.

The lower-right corner of some groups on the Ribbon has a small arrow, called a **Dialog Box Launcher**, which, when clicked, displays a dialog box or a task pane with additional options for the group (Figure 1–20). When presented with a dialog box, you make selections and must close the dialog box before returning to the database object. A **task pane**, by contrast, is a window that can remain open and visible while you work in the database object.

Figure 1–19

Figure 1–20

Mini Toolbar and Shortcut Menus

The **Mini toolbar**, which appears automatically based on tasks you perform, contains commands related to changing the appearance of text in a database object. All commands on the Mini toolbar also exist on the Ribbon. The purpose of the Mini toolbar is to minimize mouse movement. For example, if you want to use a command that currently is not displayed on the active tab, you can use the command on the Mini toolbar — instead of switching to a different tab to use the command.

When the Mini toolbar appears, it initially is transparent (Figure 1–21a). If you do not use the transparent Mini toolbar, it disappears from the screen. To use the Mini toolbar, move the mouse pointer into the toolbar, which causes the Mini toolbar to change from a transparent to bright appearance (Figure 1–21b).

A **shortcut menu**, which appears when you right-click an object, is a list of frequently used commands that relate to the right-clicked object. When you right-click a table, for example, a shortcut menu appears with commands related to the table (Figure 1–21c).

(a) Transparent Mini Toolbar

(b) Bright Mini Toolbar

(c) Shortcut Menu

Figure 1–21

Quick Access Toolbar

The **Quick Access Toolbar**, located by default above the Ribbon, provides easy access to frequently used commands (Figure 1–22a). The commands on the Quick Access Toolbar always are available, regardless of the task you are performing. Initially, the Quick Access Toolbar contains the Save, Undo, and Redo commands. If you click the Customize Quick Access Toolbar button, Access provides a list of commands you quickly can add to and remove from the Quick Access Toolbar (Figure 1–22b).

You also can add other commands to or delete commands from the Quick Access Toolbar so that it contains the commands you use most often. As you add commands to the Quick Access Toolbar, its commands may interfere with the title of the database object on the title bar. For this reason, Access provides an option of displaying the Quick Access Toolbar below the Ribbon (Figure 1–22c).

Figure 1–22

Each time you start Access, the Quick Access Toolbar appears the same way it did the last time you used Access. The chapters in this book, however, begin with the Quick Access Toolbar appearing as it did at the initial installation of the software. If you are stepping through this chapter on a computer, and you want your Quick Access Toolbar to match the figures in this book, you should reset your Quick Access Toolbar. For more information about how to reset the Quick Access Toolbar, read Appendix E.

Office Button

While the Ribbon is a control center for creating database objects, the **Office Button** is a central location for managing and sharing database objects. When you click the Office Button, located in the upper-left corner of the window, Access displays the Office Button menu (Figure 1–23). A **menu** contains a list of commands.

When you click the New, Open, and Print commands on the Office Button menu, Access displays a dialog box with additional options. The Save As, Print, Manage, and Publish commands have an arrow to their right. If you point to this arrow, Access displays a **submenu**, which is a list of additional commands associated with the selected command (Figure 1–24). For the Save As, Print, Manage, and Publish commands that do not display a dialog box when clicked, you can point either to the command or the arrow to display the submenu.

Figure 1–23

Figure 1–24

Key Tips

If you prefer using the keyboard instead of the mouse, you can press the ALT key on the keyboard to display a **Key Tip badge**, or keyboard code icon, for certain commands (Figure 1–25). To select a command using the keyboard, press its displayed code letter, or **Key Tip**. When you press a Key Tip, additional Key Tips related to the selected command may appear. For example, to select the New command on the Office Button menu, press the ALT key, then press the F key, then press the N key.

To remove the Key Tip badges from the screen, press the ALT key or the ESC key until all Key Tip badges disappear, or click the mouse anywhere in the Access window.

Figure 1–25

Creating a Table

When you first create your database, Access automatically creates a table for you. You can immediately begin defining the fields. If, for whatever reason, you do not have this table or inadvertently delete it, you can create the table by clicking Create on the Ribbon and then clicking the Table button on the Create tab. In either case, you are ready to define the fields.

BTW

Using Design View
The steps on pages AC 24 through AC 29 create the Client table using Datasheet view. To create the Client table using Design view, follow the steps in the PDF document located with the Data Files for Students on scsite.com. See the inside back cover of this book for instructions on accessing those files.

To Define the Fields in a Table

With the table already created, the next step is to define the fields in the table and to assign them data types. The fields in the Client table are Client Number, Client Name, Street, City, State, Postal Code, Amount Paid, Current Due, and Recruiter Number. The data type for the Amount Paid and Current Due fields is Currency. The data type for all other fields is Text. The following steps define the fields in the table.

1

● Right-click Add New Field to display a shortcut menu (Figure 1–26).

Q&A Why don't I delete the ID field first, before adding other fields?

You cannot delete the primary key in Datasheet view; you only can delete it in Design view. After adding the other fields, you will move to Design view, delete the ID field, and then make the Client Number the primary key.

Q&A Why does my shortcut menu look different?

You right-clicked within the column instead of right-clicking the column heading.

Figure 1–26

2

● Click Rename Column on the shortcut menu to display an insertion point.

● Type Client Number to assign a name to the new field.

● Press the DOWN ARROW key to complete the addition of the field (Figure 1–27).

Q&A Why doesn't the whole name appear?

The default column size is not large enough for Client Number to appear in its entirety. Later in this book, you will learn how to resize columns so that the entire name can appear.

Figure 1–27

3

- Right-click Add New Field to display a shortcut menu, click Rename Column on the shortcut menu to display an insertion point, type `Client Name` to assign a name to the new field, and then press the DOWN ARROW key to complete the addition of the field.

Q&A

Did I have to press the DOWN ARROW key? Couldn't I have just moved to the next field or pressed the ENTER key?

You could have pressed the TAB key or the ENTER key to move to the column heading for the next field. Pressing the DOWN ARROW key, however, completes the entry of the Client Number field and allows you to ensure that the column is assigned the correct data type.

- Using the same technique add the fields in the Client table up through and including the Amount Paid field.

- Click the Data Type box arrow to display the Data Type box menu (Figure 1–28).

Figure 1–28

4

- Click Currency to select Currency as the data type for the Amount Paid field (Figure 1–29).

Q&A

Why does Currency appear twice?

The second Currency is the format, which indicates how the data will be displayed. For the Currency data type, Access automatically sets the format to Currency, which is usually what you would want. You could change it to something else, if desired, by clicking the arrow and selecting the desired format.

Figure 1–29

5

- Click the right scroll arrow to shift the fields to the left and display the Add New Field column (Figure 1–30).

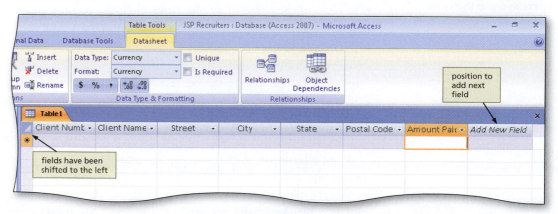

Figure 1–30

6

• Make the remaining entries from the Client table structure shown in Figure 1–31 to complete the structure. Be sure to select Currency as the data type for the Current Due field.

Figure 1–31

BTW

Creating a Table: Table Templates
Access includes table templates that assist you in creating some commonly used tables and fields. To use a template, click Create on the Ribbon and then click the Table Templates button on the Create tab. Click the desired template, make any adjustments you wish to the table that Access creates, and then save the table.

Making Changes to the Structure

When creating a table, check the entries carefully to ensure they are correct. If you discover a mistake while still typing the entry, you can correct the error by repeatedly pressing the BACKSPACE key until the incorrect characters are removed. Then, type the correct characters. If you do not discover a mistake until later, you can use the following techniques to make the necessary changes to the structure:

• To undo your most recent change, click the Undo button on the Quick Access Toolbar. If there is nothing that Access can undo, this button will be dim, and clicking it will have no effect.

• To delete a field, right-click the column heading for the field (the position containing the field name), and then click Delete Column on the shortcut menu.

• To change the name of a field, right-click the column heading for the field, click Rename Column on the shortcut menu, and then type the desired field name.

• To insert a field as the last field, right-click the Add New Field column heading, click Rename Column on the shortcut menu, type the desired field name, click the down arrow, and then ensure the correct data type is already selected.

• To insert a field between existing fields, right-click the column heading for the field that will follow the new field, and then click Insert Column on the shortcut menu. You then proceed just as you do when you insert a field as the last field.

As an alternative to these steps, you may want to start over. To do so, click the Close button for the window containing the table, and then click the No button in the Microsoft Office Access dialog box. Click Create on the Ribbon and then click the Table button to create a table. You then can repeat the process you used earlier to define the fields in the table.

To Save a Table

The Client table structure now is complete. The final step is to save and close the table within the database. At this time, you should give the table a name.

The following steps save the table, giving it the name, Client.

- Click the Save button on the Quick Access Toolbar to save the structure of the table (Figure 1–32).

Q&A

I have an extra row between the row containing the field names and the row that begins with the asterisk. What happened? Is this a problem? If so, how do I fix it?

You inadvertently added a record to the table by pressing some key after you pressed the DOWN ARROW key. Even pressing the Spacebar would add a record. You now have a record you do not want and it will cause problems when you attempt to assign a different primary key. To fix it, you need to delete the record, which you will do in Step 3.

Figure 1–32

- Type Client to change the name to be assigned to the table (Figure 1–33).

Figure 1–33

- Click the OK button to save the structure with the name, Client (Figure 1–34).

- If you have an additional record between the field names and the asterisk, click the record selector (the box at the beginning of the record), press the DELETE key, and then click the Yes button when Access asks you if you want to delete the record.

Figure 1–34

Other Ways

1. Click Office Button, click Save on the Office Button menu

2. Right-click tab for table, click Save on shortcut menu

3. Press CTRL+S

To Change the Primary Key

To change the primary key, you must first delete the ID field that Access created automatically. You then can designate the Client Number field as the primary key (see page AC 8). To delete the ID field, the table must appear in Design view rather than Datasheet view. You also can designate the Client Number field as the primary key within Design view. As you define or modify the fields, the **row selector**, the small box or bar that, when you click it, selects the entire row, indicates the field you currently are describing. The following steps move to Design view and then change the primary key.

- Click the Design View button on the status bar to move to Design view.

- Confirm that your data types match those shown in the figure. Make any necessary corrections to the data types (Figure 1-35).

Q&A

Did I have to save the table before moving to Design view?

Yes. If you had not saved it yourself, Access would have asked you to save it.

Figure 1–35

- Click the row selector for the ID field to select the field.

- Press the DELETE key to delete the field (Figure 1–36).

Q&A

What if I click the row selector for the wrong field before pressing the DELETE key?

Click the No button in the Microsoft Office Access dialog box. If you inadvertently clicked the Yes button, you have deleted the wrong field. You can fix this by clicking the Close button for the Client table, and then clicking the No button when asked if you want to save your changes.

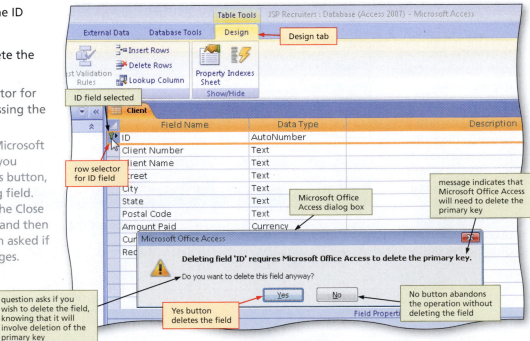

Figure 1–36

3

- Click the Yes button to complete the deletion of the field.

- With the Client Number field selected, click the Primary Key button to designate the Client Number field as the primary key.

- Click the Save button to save the changes (Figure 1–37).

Q&A

When I attempted to save the table I got an error message that indicates index or primary key cannot contain a null value. What did I do wrong and how do I fix it?

You inadvertently added a record to the table by pressing some key after you pressed the DOWN ARROW key. To fix it, click the OK button (you will need to do it twice) and then click the Primary Key button to remove the primary key. Click the Save button to save the table and then click the View button near the upper-left corner of the screen to return to datasheet view. Click the little box immediately to the left of the record you added and press the DELETE key. Click the Yes button when Access asks if it is OK to delete the record. Click the View button again and continue with these steps.

Figure 1–37

4

- Close the Client table by clicking the Close 'Client' button (Figure 1–38).

Q&A

What other changes can I make in Design view?

There are many. Two of the most common are changing the field size and adding a description. You can restrict the number of characters users can enter in a Text field by changing the field size. You also can enter a description for a field, which will appear on the Status bar when users are attempting to enter data in the field.

Figure 1–38

To Add Records to a Table

Creating a table by building the structure and saving the table is the first step in a two-step process. The second step is to add records to the table. To add records to a table, the table must be open. When making changes to tables, you work in Datasheet view. In **Datasheet view**, the table is represented as a collection of rows and columns called a **datasheet**.

You often add records in phases. You may, for example, not have enough time to add all the records in one session. The following steps open the Client table in Datasheet view and then add the first two records in the Client table (Figure 1–39).

Client Numb ▾	Client Name ▾	Street	▾	City	▾	State	▾	Postal Code ▾	Amount Paic ▾	Current Due ▾	Recruiter Nu ▾
AC34	Alys Clinic	134 Central		Berridge		CO		80330	$0.00	$17,500.00	21
BH72	Berls Hospital	415 Main		Berls		CO		80349	$29,200.00	$0.00	24

Figure 1–39

1
- Right-click the Client table in the Navigation Pane to display the shortcut menu (Figure 1–40).

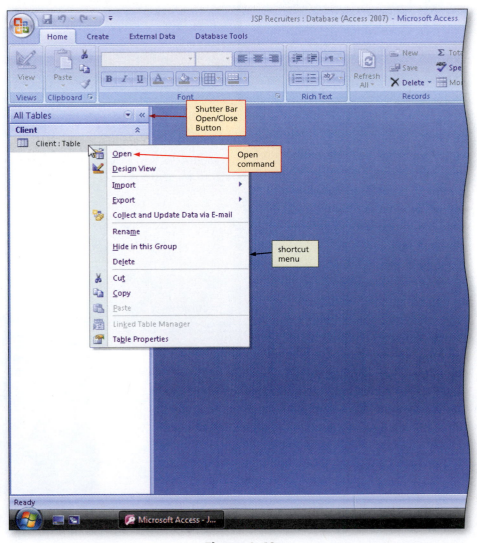

Figure 1–40

2

- Click Open on the shortcut menu to open the Client table in Datasheet view.

Q&A What if I want to return to Design view?

There are two ways to get to Design view. You could click Design View on the shortcut menu. Alternatively, you could click Open on the shortcut menu to open the table in Datasheet view and then click the Design View button on the Access status bar.

- Click the Shutter Bar Open/Close Button to hide the Navigation Pane (Figure 1–41).

Figure 1–41

3

- Click in the Client Number field and type AC34 to enter the first client number. Be sure you type the letters in uppercase so they are entered in the database correctly (Figure 1–42).

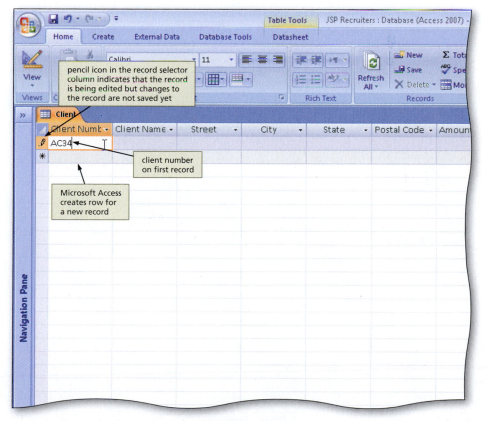

Figure 1–42

4

- Press the TAB key to complete the entry for the Client Number field.

- Enter the client name, street, city, state, and postal code by typing the following entries, pressing the TAB key after each one: `Alys Clinic` as the client name, `134 Central` as the street, `Berridge` as the city, `CO` as the state, and `80330` as the postal code.

- Type 0 to enter the amount paid (Figure 1–43).

 Q&A

Do I need to type a dollar sign?

You do not need to type dollar signs or commas. In addition, because the digits to the right of the decimal point are both zeros, you do not need to type either the decimal point or the zeros.

Figure 1–43

5

- Press the TAB key to complete the entry for the Amount Paid field.

- Type 17500 to enter the current due amount and then press the TAB key to move to the next field.

- Type 21 as the Recruiter number to complete data entry for the record (Figure 1–44).

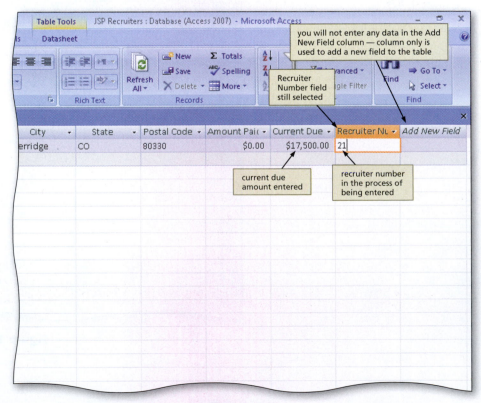

Figure 1–44

6

- Press the TAB key to complete the entry of the first record (Figure 1–45).

How and when do I save the record?

As soon as you have entered or modified a record and moved to another record, the original record is saved. This is different from other applications. The rows entered in an Excel worksheet, for example, are not saved until the entire worksheet is saved.

Figure 1–45

7

- Use the techniques shown in Steps 3 through 6 to enter the data for the second record in the Client table (Figure 1–46).

Figure 1–46

Undo and Redo

You also can undo multiple actions. To see a list of recent actions that you can undo, click the down arrow next to the Undo button on the Quick Access Toolbar. To redo the most recent action, click the Redo button on the Quick Access Toolbar. You also can redo multiple actions by clicking the down arrow next to the button.

Cut, Copy, and Paste

Just as in other Office applications, you can use buttons in the Clipboard group on the Home tab to cut, copy, and paste data. To cut data, select the data to be cut and click the Cut button. To copy data, select the data and click the Copy button. To paste data, select the desired location and click the Paste button.

AutoCorrect Options

Using the Office AutoCorrect feature, you can create entries that will replace abbreviations with spelled-out names and phrases automatically. For example, you can create the abbreviated entry *dbms* for *database management system*. Whenever you type dbms followed by a space or punctuation mark, Access automatically replaces dbms with database management system. To specify AutoCorrect rules and exceptions to the rules, click Access Options on the Office Button menu and then click Proofing in the Access Options dialog box.

Making Changes to the Data

Check your entries carefully to ensure they are correct. If you make a mistake and discover it before you press the TAB key, correct it by pressing the BACKSPACE key until the incorrect characters are removed and then typing the correct characters. If you do not discover a mistake until later, you can use the following techniques to make the necessary corrections to the data:

- To undo your most recent change, click the Undo button on the Quick Access Toolbar. If there is nothing that Access can undo, this button will be dim, and clicking it will have no effect.

- To add a record, click the New (blank) record button, shown in Figure 1–46 on the previous page, and then add the record. Do not worry about it being in the correct position in the table. Access will reposition the record based on the primary key, in this case, the Client Number.

- To delete a record, click the Record selector, shown in Figure 1–46, for the record to be deleted. Then press the DELETE key to delete the record, and click the Yes button when Access asks you to verify that you do indeed wish to delete the record.

- To change the contents of one or more fields in a record, the record must be on the screen. If it is not, use any appropriate technique, such as the UP ARROW and DOWN ARROW keys or the vertical scroll bar, to move to it. If the field you want to correct is not visible on the screen, use the horizontal scroll bar along the bottom of the screen to shift all the fields until the one you want appears. If the value in the field is currently highlighted, you can simply type the new value. If you would rather edit the existing value, you must have an insertion point in the field. You can place the insertion point by clicking in the field or by pressing F2. Once you have produced an insertion point, you can use the arrow keys, the DELETE key, and the BACKSPACE key in making the correction. You also can use the INSERT key to switch between Insert and Overtype mode. When you have made the change, press the TAB key to move to the next field.

If you cannot determine how to correct the data, you may find that you are "stuck" on the record. Access neither allows you to move to any other record until you have made the correction, nor allows you to close the table. If you encounter this situation, simply press the ESC key. Pressing the ESC key will remove from the screen the record you are trying to add. You then can move to any other record, close the table, or take any other action you desire.

AutoCorrect

Not visible in the Access window, the **AutoCorrect** feature of Access works behind the scenes, correcting common mistakes when you complete a text entry in a cell. AutoCorrect makes three types of corrections for you:

1. Corrects two initial capital letters by changing the second letter to lowercase.

2. Capitalizes the first letter in the names of days.

3. Replaces commonly misspelled words with their correct spelling. For example, it changes the misspelled word *recieve* to *receive* when you complete the entry. AutoCorrect will correct the spelling automatically of more than 400 commonly misspelled words.

To Close a Table

It is a good idea to close a table as soon as you have finished working with it. It keeps the screen from getting cluttered and prevents you from making accidental changes to the data in the table. The following steps close the Client table.

- Click the Close 'Client' button, shown in Figure 1–46 on page AC 33, to close the table (Figure 1–47).

Close button

clicking Shutter Bar Open/Close Button shows the Navigation Pane

Client table no longer appears

Figure 1–47

Other Ways

1. Right-click tab for table, click Close on shortcut menu

Quitting Access

If you save the object on which you are currently working and then quit Access, all Access windows close. If you have made changes to an object since the last time the object was saved, Access displays a dialog box asking if you want to save the changes you made before it closes that window. The dialog box contains three buttons with these resulting actions:

- Yes button — Saves the changes and then quits Access
- No button — Quits Access without saving changes
- Cancel button — Closes the dialog box and redisplays the database without saving the changes

If no changes have been made to any object since the last time the object was saved, Access will close all windows without displaying any dialog boxes.

To Quit Access

You saved your changes to the table and did not make any additional changes. You are ready to quit Access. The following step quits Access.

1 Click the Close button on the right side of the Access title bar, shown in Figure 1–47 on the previous page, to quit Access.

Starting Access and Opening a Database

Once you have created and later closed a database, you will need to open it in the future in order to use it. Opening a database requires that Access is running on your computer.

Note: If you are using Windows XP, see Appendix F for alternate steps.

To Start Access

The following steps, which assume Windows Vista is running, start Access.

1 Click the Start button on the Windows Vista taskbar to display the Start menu.

2 Click All Programs at the bottom of the left pane on the Start menu to display the All Programs list and then click Microsoft Office in the All Programs list to display the Microsoft Office list.

3 Click Microsoft Office Access 2007 on the Microsoft Office submenu to start Access and display the Getting Started with Microsoft Office Access window (Figure 1–48).

4 If the Access window is not maximized, click the Maximize button on its title bar to maximize the window.

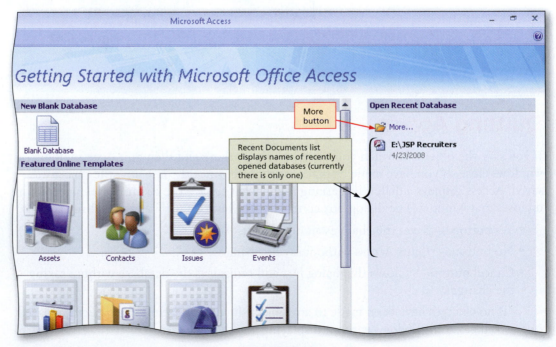

Figure 1–48

To Open a Database from Access

Note: If you are using Windows XP, see Appendix F for alternate steps.

Earlier in this chapter you created your database on a USB flash drive using the file name, JSP Recruiters. There are two ways to open the file containing your database. If the file you created appears in the Recent Documents list, you could click it to open the file. If not, you can use the More button to open the file. The following steps use the More button to open the JSP Recruiters database from the USB flash drive.

1

- With your USB flash drive connected to one of the computer's USB ports, click the More button, shown in Figure 1–48, to display the Open dialog box.

- If the Folders list is displayed below the Folders button, click the Folders button to remove the Folders list.

- If necessary, click Computer in the Favorite Links section.

- Double-click UDISK 2.0 (E:) to select the USB flash drive, Drive E in this case, as the new open location.

- Click JSP Recruiters to select the file name (Figure 1–49).

Q&A

How do I open the file if I am not using a USB flash drive?

Use the same process, but be certain to select your device in the Look in list. You might need to open multiple folders.

Figure 1–49

2

- Click the Open button to open the database (Figure 1–50).

Q&A

Why do I see the Access icon and name on the Windows Vista taskbar?

When you open an Access database, an Access program button is displayed on the taskbar. If the contents of a button cannot fit in the allotted button space, an ellipsis appears. If you point to a program button, its entire contents appear in a ScreenTip, which in this case would be the program name followed by the file name.

Figure 1–50

3

• If a Security Warning appears, as shown in Figure 1–50 on the previous page, click the Options button to display the Microsoft Office Security Options dialog box (Figure 1–51).

4

• Click the 'Enable this content' option button.

• Click the OK button to enable the content.

Q&A When would I want to disable the content?

You would want to disable the content if you suspected that your database might contain harmful content or damaging macros. Because you are the one who created the database and no one else has used it, you should have no such suspicions.

Figure 1–51

Other Ways

1. Click Office Button, double-click file name in Recent Documents list

2. Press CTRL+O, select file name, press ENTER

To Add Additional Records to a Table

You can add records to a table that already contains data using a process almost identical to that used to add records to an empty table. The only difference is that you place the insertion point after the last data record before you enter the additional data. To do so, use the **Navigation buttons**, which are buttons used to move within a table, found near the lower-left corner of the screen when a table is open. The purpose of each of the Navigation buttons is described in Table 1–2.

Table 1–2 Navigation Buttons in Datasheet View	
Button	**Purpose**
First record	Moves to the first record in the table
Previous record	Moves to the previous record
Next record	Moves to the next record
Last record	Moves to the last record in the table
New (blank) record	Moves to the end of the table to a position for entering a new record

The following steps add the remaining records (Figure 1–52) to the Client table.

Client Numb ▾	Client Name ▾	Street ▾	City ▾	State ▾	Postal Code ▾	Amount Paic ▾	Current Due ▾	Recruiter Nu ▾
BL12	Benton Labs	12 Mountain	Denton	CO	80412	$16,500.00	$38,225.00	24
EA45	ENT Assoc.	867 Ridge	Fort Stewart	CO	80336	$12,750.00	$15,000.00	27
FD89	Ferb Dentistry	34 Crestview	Berridge	CO	80330	$21,000.00	$12,500.00	21
FH22	Family Health	123 Second	Tarleton	CO	80409	$0.00	$0.00	24
MH56	Maun Hospital	76 Dixon	Mason	CO	80356	$0.00	$43,025.00	24
PR11	Peel Radiology	151 Valleyview	Fort Stewart	CO	80336	$31,750.00	$0.00	21
TC37	Tarleton Clinic	451 Hull	Tarleton	CO	80409	$18,750.00	$31,500.00	27
WL56	West Labs	785 Main	Berls	CO	80349	$14,000.00	$0.00	24

Figure 1–52

- If the Navigation Pane is hidden, click the Shutter Bar Open/Close Button, shown in Figure 1–47, to show the Navigation Pane (Figure 1–53).

Figure 1–53

- Right-click the Client table in the Navigation Pane to display a short-cut menu.

- Click Open on the shortcut menu to open the Client table in Datasheet view.

- Hide the Navigation Pane by clicking the Shutter Bar Open/Close button (Figure 1–54).

Figure 1–54

3

- Click the New (blank) record button to move to a position to enter a new record (Figure 1–55).

Q&A

Why click the New (blank) record button? Could you just click the Client Number on the first open record and then add the record?

You could click the Client Number on the first open record, provided that record appears on the screen. With only two records in the table, this is not a problem. Once a table contains more records than will fit on the screen, it is easier to click the New (blank) record button.

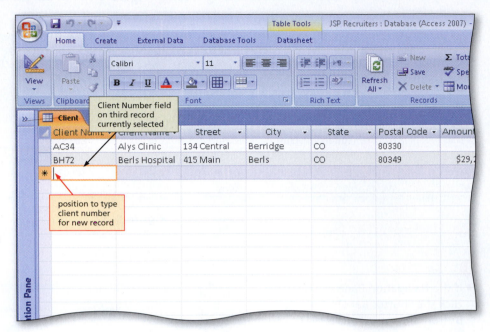

Figure 1–55

4

- Add the records shown in Figure 1–52 on the previous page, using the same techniques you used to add the first two records (Figure 1–56).

5

- Click the Close 'Client' button to close the table.

Figure 1–56

Other Ways

1. Click New button in Records group on Ribbon

2. Press CTRL+PLUS SIGN (+)

Previewing and Printing the Contents of a Table

When working with a database, you often will need to print a copy of the table contents. Figure 1–57 shows a printed copy of the contents of the Client table. (Yours may look slightly different, depending on your printer.) Because the Client table is wider substantially than the screen, it also will be wider than the normal printed page in portrait orientation. **Portrait orientation** means the printout is across the width of the page.

Client								
Client Number	Client Name	Street	City	State	Postal Code	Amount Paid	Current Due	Recruiter Numb
AC34	Alys Clinic	134 Central	Berridge	CO	80330	$0.00	$17,500.00	21
BH72	Berls Hospital	415 Main	Berls	CO	80349	$29,200.00	$0.00	24
BL12	Benton Labs	12 Mountain	Denton	CO	80412	$16,500.00	$38,225.00	24
EA45	ENT Assoc.	867 Ridge	Fort Stewart	CO	80336	$12,750.00	$15,000.00	27
FD89	Ferb Dentistry	34 Crestview	Berridge	CO	80330	$21,000.00	$12,500.00	21
FH22	Family Health	123 Second	Tarleton	CO	80409	$0.00	$0.00	24
MH56	Maun Hospital	76 Dixon	Mason	CO	80356	$0.00	$43,025.00	24
PR11	Peel Radiology	151 Valleyview	Fort Stewart	CO	80336	$31,750.00	$0.00	21
TC37	Tarleton Clinic	451 Hull	Tarleton	CO	80409	$18,750.00	$31,500.00	27
WL56	West Labs	785 Main	Berls	CO	80349	$14,000.00	$0.00	24

(4/23/2008)

Figure 1–57

Landscape orientation means the printout is across the length (height) of the page. Thus, to print the wide database table, use landscape orientation. If you are printing the contents of a table that fit on the screen, you will not need landscape orientation. A convenient way to change to landscape orientation is to preview what the printed copy will look like by using Print Preview. This allows you to determine whether landscape orientation is necessary and, if it is, to change the orientation easily to landscape. In addition, you also can use Print Preview to determine whether any adjustments are necessary to the page margins.

To Preview and Print the Contents of a Table

The following steps use Print Preview to preview and then print the Client table.

1

- If the Navigation Pane is hidden, show the Navigation Pane by clicking the Shutter Bar Open/ Close Button.

- Be sure the Client table is selected (Figure 1–58).

Q&A

Why do I have to be sure the Client table is selected? It is the only object in the database.

Figure 1–58

There is no issue when the database contains only one object. Ensuring that the correct object is selected is a good habit to form, however, to make sure that the object you print is the one you want.

2

- Click the Office Button to display the Office Button menu.

- Point to the Print command arrow to display the Print submenu (Figure 1–59).

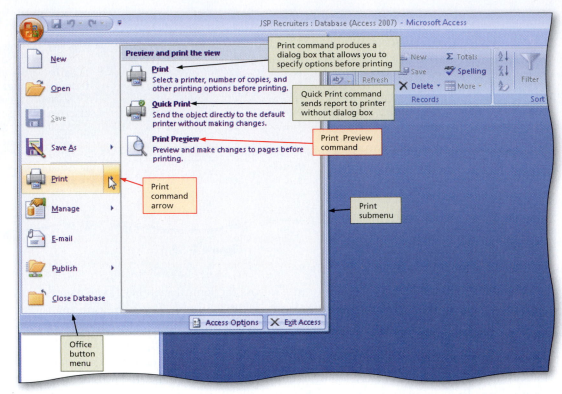

Figure 1–59

3

- Click Print Preview on the Print submenu to display a preview of the report (Figure 1–60).

Q&A

I can't read the report. Can I magnify a portion of the report?

Yes. Point the mouse pointer, whose shape will change to a magnifying glass, at the portion of the report that you wish to magnify, and then click. You can return the view of the report to the one shown in the figure by clicking a second time.

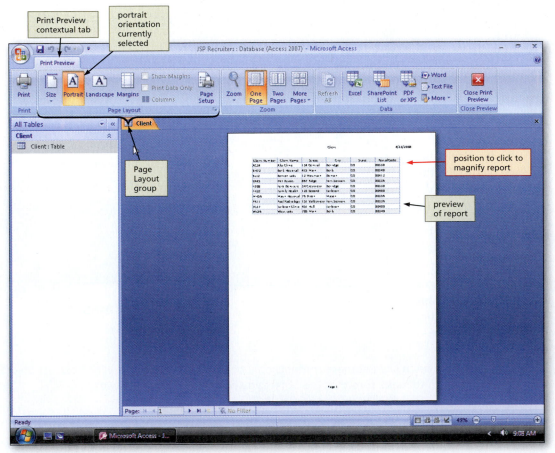

Figure 1–60

4

- Click the mouse pointer in the position shown in Figure 1–60 to magnify the upper-right section of the report (Figure 1–61).

Q&A

My report was already magnified in a different area. How can I see the area shown in the figure?

There are two ways. You can use the scroll bars to move to the desired portion of the report. You also can click the mouse pointer anywhere in the report to produce a screen like the one in Figure 1–60, and then click in the location shown in the figure.

Figure 1–61

5

- Click the Landscape button to change to landscape orientation (Figure 1–62).

6

- Click the Print button on the Print Preview tab to print the report.

- When the printer stops, retrieve the hard copy of the Client table.

- Click the Close Print Preview button to close the Print Preview window.

Q&A

How can I print multiple copies of my document other than clicking the Print button multiple times?

Click the Office Button, point to the arrow next to Print on the Office Button menu, click Print on the Print submenu, increase the number in the Number of Copies: box, and then click the OK button.

Q&A

How can I print a range of pages rather than printing the whole report?

Click the Office Button, point to the arrow next to Print on the Office Button menu, click Print on the Print submenu, click the Pages option button in the Print Range box, enter the desired page range, and then click the OK button.

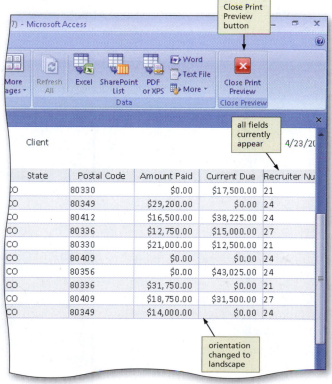

Figure 1–62

Other Ways
1. Press CTRL+P, press ENTER

BTW

Using Design View
The steps on pages
AC 44 through AC 48
create the Recruiter table
using Datasheet view. To
create the Recruiter table
using Design view, follow
the steps in the PDF
document located with
the Data Files for Students
on scsite.com. See the
inside back cover of this
book for instructions on
accessing those files.

Creating Additional Tables

The JSP Recruiters database contains two tables, the Client table and the Recruiter table. You need to create the Recruiter table and add records to it. Because you already used the default table that Access created when you created the database, you will need to first create the table. You can then add fields as you did with the Client table.

To Create an Additional Table

The fields to be added are Recruiter Number, Last Name, First Name, Street, City, State, Postal Code, Rate, and Commission. The data type for the Rate field is Number, and the data type for the Commission field is Currency. The data type for all other fields is Text. The following steps create the Recruiter table.

- Click Create on the Ribbon to display the Create tab (Figure 1–63).

Figure 1–63

- Click the Table button on the Create tab to create a new table (Figure 1–64).

Q&A

Could I save the table now so I can assign it the name I want, rather than Table1?

You certainly can. Be aware, however, that you will still need to save it again once you have added all your fields.

Figure 1–64

- Right-click Add New Field to display a shortcut menu.

- Click Rename Column on the short-cut menu to display an insertion point.

- Type `Recruiter Number` to assign a name to the new field.

- Press the DOWN ARROW key to complete the addition of the field.

- Using the same technique, add the Last Name, First Name, Street, City, State, Postal Code, and Rate fields.

- Click the Data Type box arrow to display the Data Type box menu (Figure 1–65).

Figure 1–65

- Click Number on the Data Type box menu to select the Number data type and assign the Number data type to the Rate field.

- Add the Commission field and assign it the Currency data type.

- Click the Save button to display the Save As dialog box (Figure 1–66).

Figure 1–66

⑤

- Type `Recruiter` to assign a name to the table.

- Click the OK button (Figure 1–67).

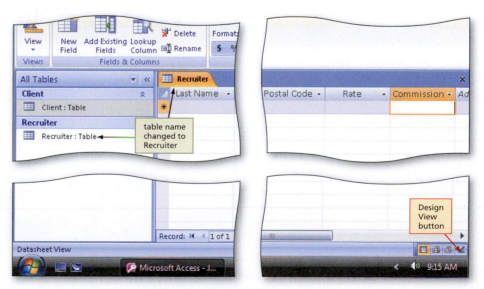

Figure 1–67

To Modify the Primary Key and Field Properties

Fields whose data type is Number often require you to change the field size. Table 1–3 shows the possible field sizes for Number fields.

Table 1–3 Field Sizes for Number Fields	
Field Size	**Description**
Byte	Integer value in the range of 0 to 255.
Integer	Integer value in the range of -32,768 to 32,767.
Long Integer	Integer value in the range of -2,147,483,648 to 2,147,483,647.
Single	Numeric values with decimal places to seven significant digits — requires four bytes of storage.
Double	Numeric values with decimal places to more accuracy than Single — requires eight bytes of storage.
Replication ID	Special identifier required for replication.
Decimal	Numeric values with decimal places to more accuracy than Single — requires 12 bytes of storage.

Because the values in the Rate field have decimal places, only Single, Double, or Decimal would be possible choices. The difference between these choices concerns the amount of accuracy. Double is more accurate than Single, for example, but requires more storage space. Because the rates are only two decimal places, Single is a perfectly acceptable choice.

In addition to changing the field size, you should also change the format to Fixed (a fixed number of decimal places) and the number of decimal places to 2.

The following steps move to Design view, delete the ID field, and make the Recruiter Number field the primary key. They then change the field size of the Rate field to Single, the format to Fixed, and the number of decimal places to 2.

1

- Click the Design View button on the status bar to move to Design view (Figure 1–68).

Figure 1–68

2

- Click the row selector for the ID field to select the field.

- Press the DELETE key to delete the field.

- Click the Yes button to complete the deletion of the field.

- With the Recruiter Number field selected, click the Primary Key button to designate the Recruiter Number field as the primary key.

- Click the row selector for the Rate field to select the field (Figure 1–69).

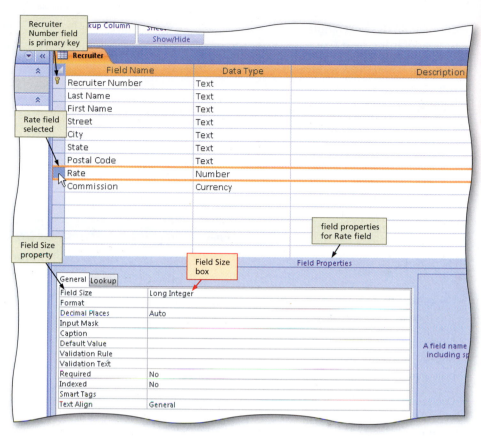

Figure 1–69

3

- Click the Field Size box to display the Field Size box arrow.

- Click the Field Size box arrow to display the Field Size box menu (Figure 1–70).

Q&A

What would happen if I left the field size set to Long Integer?

If the field size is Long Integer, no decimal places can be stored. Thus a value of .10 would be stored as 0. If you enter your rates and the values all appear as 0, chances are you did not change the field size.

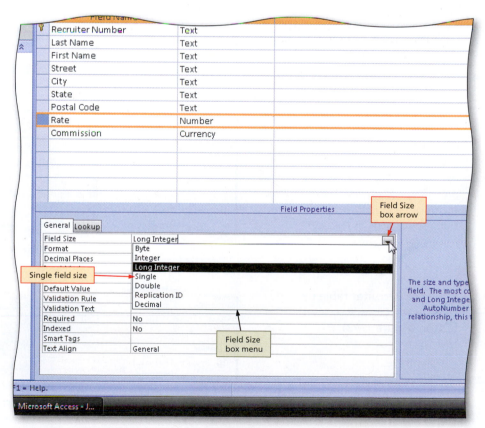

Figure 1–70

4

- Click Single to select single precision as the field size.

- Click the Format box to display the Format box arrow (Figure 1–71).

- Click the Format box arrow to open the Format box menu.

Figure 1–71

5

- Click Fixed to select fixed as the format.

- Click the Decimal Places box to display the Decimal Places box arrow.

- Click the Decimal Places box arrow to enter the number of decimal places.

- Click 2 to select 2 as the number of decimal places.

- Click the Save button to save your changes (Figure 1–72).

Q&A

What is the purpose of the error checking button?

You changed the number of decimal places. The error checking button gives you a quick way of making the same change everywhere Rate appears. So far, you have not added any data, nor have you created any forms or reports that use the Rate field, so no such changes are necessary.

Figure 1–72

6

- Close the Recruiter table by clicking the Close 'Recruiter' button (Figure 1–73).

Figure 1–73

To Add Records to an Additional Table

The following steps add the records shown in Figure 1–74 to the Recruiter table.

Recruiter Nu ▾	Last Name ▾	First Name ▾	Street ▾	City ▾	State ▾	Postal Code ▾	Rate ▾	Commission ▾
21	Kerry	Alyssa	261 Pointer	Tourin	CO	80416	0.10	$17,600.00
24	Reeves	Camden	3135 Brill	Denton	CO	80412	0.10	$19,900.00
27	Fernandez	Jaime	265 Maxwell	Charleston	CO	80380	0.09	$9,450.00
34	Lee	Jan	1827 Oak	Denton	CO	80413	0.08	$0.00

Figure 1–74

- Open the Recruiter table in Datasheet view and then hide the Navigation Pane.

- Enter the Recruiter data from Figure 1–74 (Figure 1–75).

 Experiment

- Click in the Rate field on any of the records. Be sure the Datasheet tab is selected. Click the Format box arrow and then click each of the formats in the Format box menu to see the effect on the values in the Rate field. When finished, click Fixed in the Format box menu.

Figure 1–75

- Click the Close 'Recruiter' button to close the table and remove the datasheet from the screen.

Creating a Report

JSP Recruiters needs the following reports. You will create the four reports shown in Figure 1–76 in this section.

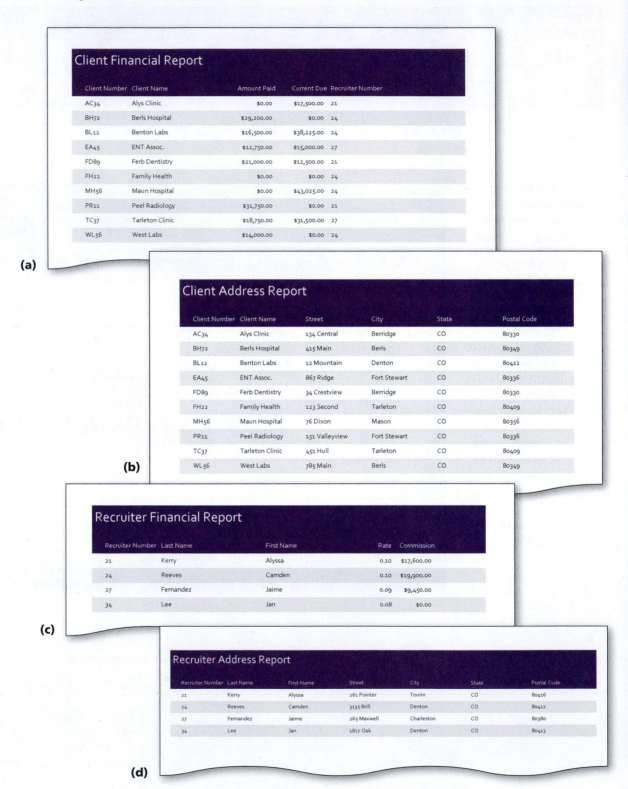

Figure 1–76

To Create a Report

You will first create the report shown in Figure 1–76a. The records in the report are sorted (ordered) by Client Number. To ensure that the records appear in this order, you will specify that the records are to be sorted on the Client Number field. The following steps create the report in Figure 1–76a.

- Be sure the Client table is selected in the Navigation Pane.

- Click Create on the Ribbon to display the Create tab.

- Click the Report Wizard button to display the Report Wizard dialog box (Figure 1–77).

Q&A   What would have happened if the Recruiter table were selected instead of the Client table?

The list of available fields would have contained fields from the Recruiter table rather than the Client table.

Q&A   If the list contained Recruiter table fields, how could I make it contain Client table fields?

Click the arrow in the Tables/Queries box and then click the Client table in the list that appears.

Figure 1–77

- Click the Add Field button to add the Client Number field.

- Click the Add Field button to add the Client Name field.

- Click the Amount Paid field, and then click the Add Field button to add the Amount Paid field.

- Click the Add Field button to add the Current Due field.

- Click the Add Field button to add the Recruiter Number field (Figure 1–78).

Figure 1–78

3

- Click the Next button to display the next Report Wizard screen (Figure 1–79).

Q&A What is grouping?

Grouping means creating separate collections of records sharing some common characteristic. For example, you might want to group clients in the same Postal code or that have the same recruiter.

Q&A What if I realize that I have selected the wrong fields?

You can click the Back button to return to the previous screen and then correct the list of fields. You also could click the Cancel button and start over.

Figure 1–79

4

- Because you will not specify any grouping, click the Next button in the Report Wizard dialog box to display the next Report Wizard screen.

- Click the box arrow in the text box labeled 1 to display a list of available fields for sorting (Figure 1–80).

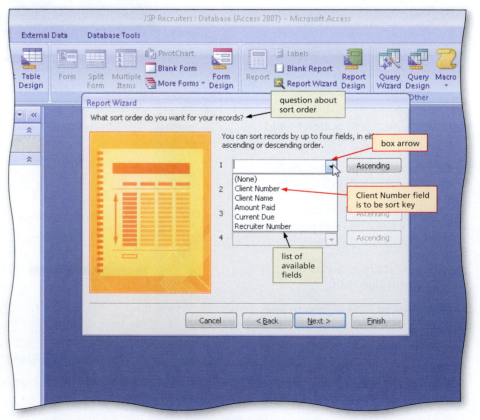

Figure 1–80

5

- Click the Client Number field to select the field as the sort key (Figure 1–81).

Q&A What if I want Descending order?

Click the Ascending button next to the sort key to change Ascending order to Descending. If you decide you want Ascending after all, click the button a second time.

Figure 1–81

6

- Click the Next button to display the next Report Wizard screen (Figure 1–82).

 Experiment

- Click different layouts and observe the effect on the sample report. When you have finished experimenting, click the Tabular option button for the layout and the Portrait option button for the orientation.

Figure 1–82

7

- Make sure that Tabular is selected as the Layout. (If it is not, click the Tabular option button to select Tabular layout.)

- Make sure Portrait is selected as the Orientation. (If it is not, click the Portrait option button to select Portrait orientation.)

- Click the Next button to display the next Report Wizard screen (Figure 1–83).

 Experiment

- Click different styles and observe the effect on the sample report. When you have finished experimenting, click the Module style.

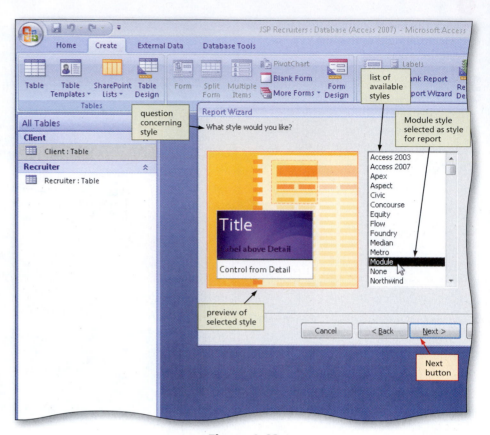

Figure 1–83

8

- Be sure the Module style is selected. (If it is not, click Module to select the Module style.)

- Click the Next button to display the next Report Wizard screen (Figure 1–84).

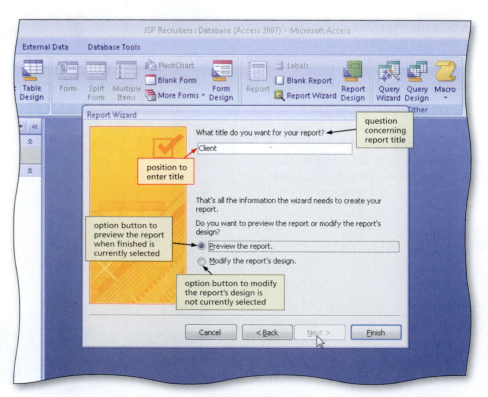

Figure 1–84

9

- Erase the current title, and then type `Client Financial Report` as the new title (Figure 1–85).

Q&A How do I erase the title?

You can highlight the existing title and then press the DELETE key. You can click at the end of the title and repeatedly press the BACKSPACE key. You can click at the beginning of the title and repeatedly press the DELETE key.

Q&A Could I just click after the word, Client, press the Spacebar, and then type Financial Report?

Yes. In general, you can edit the current title to produce the new title using the method with which you are most comfortable.

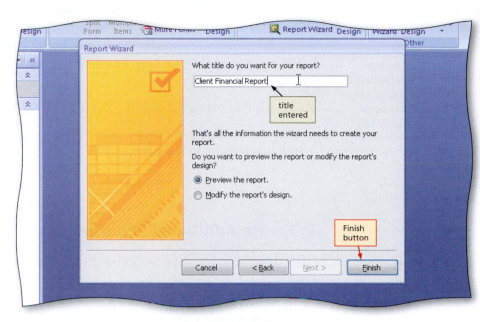

Figure 1–85

- Click the Finish button to produce the report (Figure 1–86).

10

- Click the Close 'Client Financial Report' button to remove the report from the screen.

Q&A Why didn't I have to save the report?

The Report Wizard saves the report automatically.

Figure 1–86

To Print a Report

Once you have created a report, you can print it at any time. The printed layout will reflect the layout you created. The data in the report will always reflect current data. The following step prints the Client Financial Report.

- With the Client Financial Report selected in the Navigation Pane, click the Office Button.

- Point to the arrow next to Print on the Office Button menu and then click Quick Print on the Print submenu to print the report.

To Create Additional Reports

The following steps produce the reports shown in Figure 1–76b, Figure 1–76c, and Figure 1–76d on page AC 50.

1 If necessary, click Create on the Ribbon to display the Create tab, and then click the Report Wizard button to display the Report Wizard dialog box.

2 Add the Client Number, Client Name, Street, City, State, and Postal Code fields by clicking each field and then clicking the Add Field button.

3 Click the Next button to move to the screen asking about grouping, and then click the Next button a second time to move to the screen asking about sort order.

4 Click the box arrow in the text box labeled 1, click the Client Number field to select the field as the sort key, and then click the Next button.

5 Make sure that Tabular is selected as the Layout and that Portrait is selected as the Orientation, and then click the Next button.

6 Make sure the Module style is selected, and then click the Next button.

7 Enter `Client Address Report` as the title and click the Finish button to produce the report.

8 Click the Close 'Client Address Report' button to close the Print Preview window.

9 Click the Recruiter table in the Navigation Pane, and then use the techniques shown in Steps 1 through 8 to produce the Recruiter Financial Report. The report is to contain the Recruiter Number, Last Name, First Name, Rate, and Commission fields. It is to be sorted by Recruiter Number. It is to have tabular layout, portrait orientation, and the Module Style. The title is to be Recruiter Financial Report.

10 With the Recruiter table selected in the Navigation Pane, use the techniques shown in Steps 1 through 8 to produce the Recruiter Address Report. The report is to contain the Recruiter Number, Last Name, First Name, Street, City, State, and Postal Code fields. It is to be sorted by Recruiter Number. It is to have tabular layout, landscape orientation, and the Module Style. The title is to be Recruiter Address Report.

11 Click the Close 'Recruiter Address Report' button to close the Print Preview window.

Using a Form to View Data

In Datasheet view, you can view many records at once. If there are many fields, however, only some of the fields in each record might be visible at a time. In **Form view**, where data is displayed in a form on the screen, you usually can see all the fields, but only for one record. To get the advantages from both, many database management systems allow you to easily switch between Datasheet view and Form view while maintaining position within the database. In Access 2007, you can view both a datasheet and a form simultaneously using a split form.

To Create a Split Form

A **split form** combines both a datasheet and a form, thus giving the advantages of both views. The following steps create a split form.

1
- Select the Client table in the Navigation Pane.

- If necessary, click Create on the Ribbon to display the Create tab (Figure 1–87).

Figure 1–87

2
- Click the Split Form button to create a split form. If a Field List appears, click its Close button to remove the Field List from the screen (Figure 1–88).

Q&A
Is the form automatically saved the way the report was created when I used the Report Wizard?

No. You must take specific action if you wish to save the form.

Figure 1–88

3

- Click the Save button to display the Save As dialog box (Figure 1–89).

Figure 1–89

4

- Type `Client Form` as the form name, and then click the OK button to save the form.

- If the form appears in Layout view, click the Form View button on the Access status bar to display the form in Form view (Figure 1–90).

Q&A

How can I recognize Layout view?

There are three ways. The left end of the Status bar will contain the words Layout View. There will be shading around the outside of the selected field in the form. The Layout View button will be selected in the right end of the Status bar.

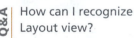

Figure 1–90

To Use a Split Form

After you have saved a form, you can use it at any time by right-clicking the form in the Navigation Pane and then clicking Open in the shortcut menu. If you plan to use the form to enter data, you must ensure you are viewing the form in Form view.

1
- Click the Next Record button four times to move to record 5 (Figure 1–91).

Q&A I inadvertently closed the form at the end of the previous steps. What should I do?

Right-click the form in the Navigation Pane and then click Open on the shortcut menu.

Q&A Do I have to take any special action for the form to be positioned on the same record as the datasheet?

No. The advantage to the split form is that changing the position on either the datasheet or the form automatically changes the position on the other.

Figure 1–91

2
- Click the Postal Code field on the second record in the datasheet to select the second record in both the datasheet and the form (Figure 1–92).

Experiment
- Click several fields in various records in the datasheet and observe the effect on the form.

3
- Click the Close 'Client Form' button to remove the form from the screen.

Figure 1–92

Changing Database Properties

Access helps you organize and identify your databases by using **database properties,** which are the details about a file. Database properties, also known as **metadata,** can include such information as the project author, title, or subject. **Keywords** are words or phrases that further describe the database. For example, a class name or database topic can describe the file's purpose or content.

Five different types of document properties exist, but the more common ones used in this book are standard and automatically updated properties. **Standard properties** are associated with all Microsoft Office documents and include author, title, and subject. **Automatically updated properties** include file system properties, such as the date you create or change a file, and statistics, such as the file size.

To Change Database Properties

The Database Properties dialog box contains areas where you can view and enter document properties. You can view and change information in this dialog box at any time while you are working on your database. It is a good idea to add your name and class name as database properties. The following steps use the Properties dialog box to change database properties.

- Click the Office Button to display the Office Button menu.

- Point to Manage on the Office Button menu to display the Manage submenu (Figure 1–93).

Q&A

What other types of actions besides changing properties can you take to prepare a database for distribution?

The Manage submenu provides commands to compact and repair a database as well as to back up a database.

Figure 1–93

- Click Database Properties on the Manage submenu to display the JSP Recruiters.accdb Properties dialog box (Figure 1–94).

Q&A

Why are some of the document properties in my Properties dialog box already filled in?

The person who installed Microsoft Office 2007 on your computer or network may have set or customized the properties.

Figure 1–94

❸

- If necessary, click the Summary tab.

- Click the Author text box and then type your name as the Author property. If a name already is displayed in the Author text box, delete it before typing your name.

- Click the Subject text box, if necessary delete any existing text, and then type your course and section as the Subject property.

- Click the Keywords text box, if necessary delete any existing text, and then type Healthcare, Recruiter as the Keywords property (Figure 1–95).

Q&A

What types of properties does Access collect automatically?

Access records such details as when the database was created, when it was last modified, total editing time, and the various objects contained in the database.

Figure 1–95

❹

- Click the OK button to save your changes and remove the JSP Recruiters.accdb Properties dialog box from the screen.

Access Help

At any time while using Access, you can find answers to questions and display information about various topics through **Access Help**. Used properly, this form of assistance can increase your productivity and reduce your frustrations by minimizing the time you spend learning how to use Access.

This section introduces you to Access Help. Additional information about using Access Help is available in Appendix C.

To Search for Access Help

Using Access Help, you can search for information based on phrases, such as create a form or change a data type, or key terms, such as copy, save, or format. Access Help responds with a list of search results displayed as links to a variety of resources. The following steps, which use Access Help to search for information about creating a form, assume you are connected to the Internet.

- Click the Microsoft Office Access Help button near the upper-right corner of the Access window to open the Access Help window.

- Type create a form in the 'Type words to search for' text box at the top of the Access Help window (Figure 1–96).

Figure 1–96

- Press the ENTER key to display the search results.

- Click the Maximize button on the Access Help window title bar to maximize the Help window unless it is already maximized (Figure 1–97).

Q&A

Where is the Access window with the JSP Recruiters database?

Access is open in the background, but the Access Help window sits on top of the Microsoft Access window. When the Access Help window is closed, the database will reappear.

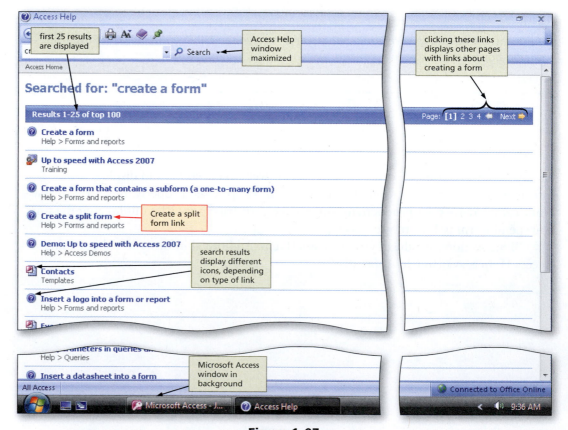

Figure 1–97

3

- Click the 'Create a split form' link to display information regarding creating a split form (Figure 1–98).

Q&A What is the purpose of the buttons at the top of the Access Help window?

Use the buttons in the upper-left corner of the Access Help window to navigate through the Help system, change the display, show the Access Help table of contents, and print the contents of the window.

4

- Click the Close button on the Access Help window title bar to close the Access Help window and make the database active.

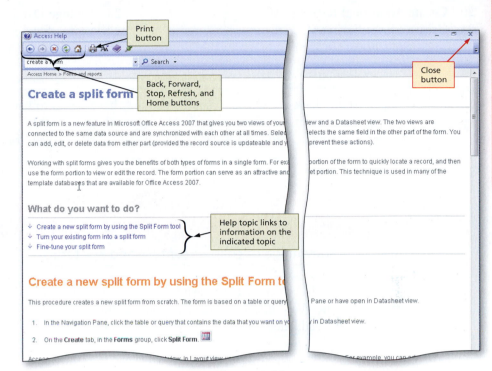

Figure 1–98

Other Ways

1. Press F1

To Quit Access

You saved all your changes and are ready to quit Access. The following step quits Access.

1 Click the Close button on the right side of the Access title bar to quit Access.

Chapter Summary

In this chapter you have learned to design a database, create an Access database, create tables and add records to them, print the contents of tables, create reports, and create forms. The items listed below include all the new Access skills you have learned in this chapter.

1. Start Access (AC 12)
2. Create a Database Using a Template (AC 13)
3. Create a Database (AC 14)
4. Define the Fields in a Table (AC 24)
5. Create a Table Using a Template (AC 26)
6. Save a Table (AC 27)
7. Change the Primary Key (AC 28)
8. Add Records to a Table (AC 30)
9. Close a Table (AC 35)
10. Quit Access (AC 36)
11. Start Access (AC 36)
12. Open a Database from Access (AC 37)
13. Add Additional Records to a Table (AC 38)
14. Preview and Print the Contents of a Table (AC 41)
15. Create an Additional Table (AC 44)
16. Modify the Primary Key and Field Properties (AC 46)
17. Add Records to an Additional Table (AC 49)
18. Create a Report (AC 51)
19. Print a Report (AC 56)

If you have a SAM user profile, you may have access to hands-on instruction, practice, and assessment. Log in to your SAM account (http://sam2007.course.com) to launch any assigned training activities or exams that relate to the skills covered in this chapter.

Learn It Online

Test your knowledge of chapter content and key terms.

Instructions: To complete the Learn It Online exercises, start your browser, click the Address bar, and then enter the Web address `scsite.com/ac2007/learn`. When the Access 2007 Learn It Online page is displayed, click the link for the exercise you want to complete and then read the instructions.

Chapter Reinforcement TF, MC, and SA
A series of true/false, multiple choice, and short answer questions that test your knowledge of the chapter content.

Flash Cards
An interactive learning environment where you identify chapter key terms associated with displayed definitions.

Practice Test
A series of multiple choice questions that test your knowledge of chapter content and key terms.

Who Wants To Be a Computer Genius?
An interactive game that challenges your knowledge of chapter content in the style of a television quiz show.

Wheel of Terms
An interactive game that challenges your knowledge of chapter key terms in the style of the television show *Wheel of Fortune*.

Crossword Puzzle Challenge
A crossword puzzle that challenges your knowledge of key terms presented in the chapter.

Apply Your Knowledge

Reinforce the skills and apply the concepts you learned in this chapter.

Changing Data, Creating a Form, and Creating a Report
Instructions: Start Access. Open the The Bike Delivers database. See the inside back cover of this book for instructions for downloading the Data Files for Students, or see your instructor for information on accessing the files required in this book.

The Bike Delivers uses motorbikes to provide courier services for local businesses. The Bike Delivers has a database that keeps track of its couriers and customers. The database has two tables. The Customer table (Figure 1–99a) contains data on the customers who use the services of The Bike Delivers. The Courier table (Figure 1–99b) contains data on the individuals employed by The Bike Delivers.

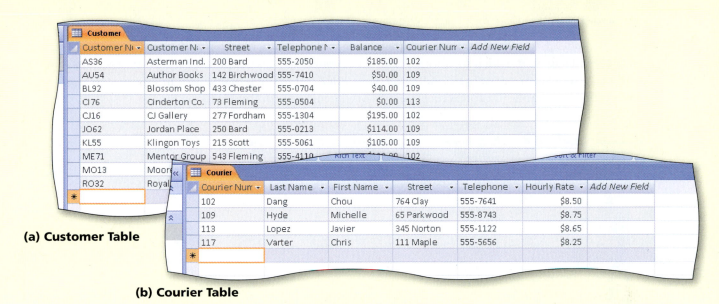

(a) Customer Table

(b) Courier Table

Figure 1–99

Perform the following tasks:

1. Open the Customer table and change the Courier Number for customer KL55 to 113.

2. Close the Customer table.

3. Create a split form for the Courier table. Use the name Courier for the form.

4. Open the form you created and change the street address for Michelle Hyde to 65 Park.

5. Close the Courier form.

6. Create the report shown in Figure 1–100 for the Customer table. The report uses the Module style.

7. Change the database properties, as specified by your instructor. Submit the revised database in the format specified by your instructor.

Figure 1–100

Extend Your Knowledge

Extend the skills you learned in this chapter and experiment with new skills. You may need to use Help to complete the assignment.

Changing Formats and Creating Grouped and Sorted Reports

Instructions: Start Access. Open the Camden Scott College database. See the inside back cover of this book for instructions for downloading the Data Files for Students, or see your instructor for information on accessing the files required in this book.

Continued >

Extend Your Knowledge *continued*

Camden Scott College is a small liberal arts college. The Human Resources Director has created an Access database in which to store information about candidates applying for faculty positions. You will make some changes to the Candidate table so that it looks like that shown in Figure 1–101 and create a report that both groups records and sorts them in ascending order.

Figure 1–101

Perform the following tasks:

1. Open the Candidate table in Datasheet view and change the column heading for the ID field to Candidate ID.

2. Save the change and open the table in Design view.

3. Select a format for the App Date field that will produce the look shown in Figure 1–101.

4. Change the data type for the Documentation field so that it will match that shown in Figure 1–101.

5. Save the changes.

6. Open the table in Datasheet view. The Human Resources department has received an application from Edward Klinger. Edward applied for the same position as Sarah Klinger on the same date as Sarah. Edward's phone number is 610-555-1111. He did submit all his documentation with his application. Add this record.

7. Add the Quick Print button to the Quick Access Toolbar.

8. Create a report for the Candidate table that lists the Department Code, App Date, Last Name, and First Name. Group the report by Department Code. Sort the report by App Date, Last Name, and then First Name. Choose your own report style and use Candidate by Department as the title of the report.

9. Remove the Quick Print button from the Quick Access Toolbar.

10. Change the database properties, as specified by your instructor. Submit the revised database in the format specified by your instructor.

Make It Right

Analyze a database and correct all errors and/or improve the design.

Correcting Errors in the Table Structure

Instructions: Start Access. Open the SciFi Scene database. See the inside back cover of this book for instructions for downloading the Data Files for Students, or see your instructor for information on accessing the files required in this book.

SciFi Scene is a database containing information on science fiction books. The Book table shown in Figure 1–102 contains a number of errors in the table structure. You are to correct these errors before any additional records can be added to the table. Book Code, not ID, is the primary key for the Book table. The column heading Titel is misspelled. The On Hand field represents the number of books on hand. The field will be used in arithmetic operations. Only whole numbers should be stored in the field. The Price field represents the price of the book. The current data type does not reflect this information.

Change the database properties, as specified by your instructor. Submit the revised database in the format specified by your instructor.

Figure 1–102

In the Lab

Design, create, modify, and/or use a database using the guidelines, concepts, and skills presented in this chapter. Labs are listed in order of increasing difficulty.

Lab 1: Creating the JMS TechWizards Database

Problem: JMS TechWizards is a local company that provides technical services to several small businesses in the area. The company currently keeps its records in two Excel workbooks. One Excel workbook (Figure 1–103a) contains information on the clients that JMS TechWizards serves. The other Excel workbook (Figure 1–103b) contains information on the technicians that JMS employs. JMS would like to store this data in a database and has asked for your help.

(a) Client Data (Excel Workbook)

(b) Technician Data (Excel Workbook)

Figure 1–103

Continued >

In the Lab *continued*

Instructions: Perform the following tasks:

1. Create a new database in which to store all the objects related to the technical services data. Call the database JMS TechWizards.

2. Create a table in which to store the data related to clients. Use the name Client for the table. The fields for the Client table are: Client Number, Client Name, Street, City, State, Postal Code, Telephone Number, Billed, Paid, and Technician Number. Client Number is the primary key. The Billed and Paid fields are currency data type.

3. Create a table in which to store the data related to technicians. Use the name Technician for the table. The fields for the Technician table are: Technician Number, Last Name, First Name, Street, City, State, Postal Code, Hourly Rate, and YTD Earnings. The primary key for the Technician table is Technician Number. Hourly rate and YTD Earnings are currency data type.

4. Add the data from the Client workbook in Figure 1–103a to the Client table.

5. Add the data from the Technician workbook in Figure 1–103b to the Technician table.

6. Create and save the reports shown in Figure 1–104a for the Client table and Figure 1–104b for the Technician table.

7. Change the database properties, as specified by your instructor. Submit the revised database in the format specified by your instructor.

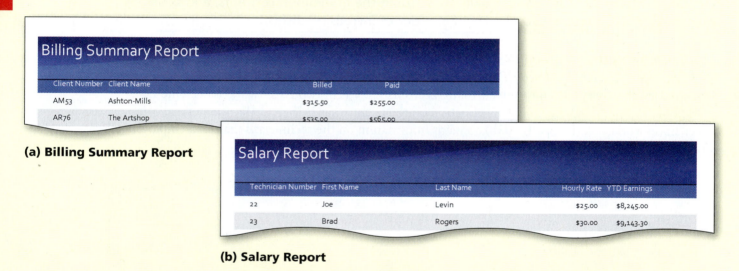

Billing Summary Report

Client Number	Client Name	Billed	Paid
AM53	Ashton-Mills	$315.50	$255.00
AR76	The Artshop	$535.00	$565.00

(a) Billing Summary Report

Salary Report

Technician Number	First Name	Last Name	Hourly Rate	YTD Earnings
22	Joe	Levin	$25.00	$8,245.00
23	Brad	Rogers	$30.00	$9,143.30

(b) Salary Report

Figure 1–104

In the Lab

Lab 2: Creating the Hockey Fan Zone Database

Problem: Your town has a minor league hockey team. The team store sells a variety of items with the team logo. The store purchases the items from suppliers that deal in specialty items for sports teams. Currently, the information about the items and suppliers is stored in the Excel workbook shown in Figure 1–105. You work part-time at the store, and your boss has asked you to create a database that will store the item and supplier information. You have already determined that you need two tables: an Item table and a Supplier table in which to store the information.

Instructions: Perform the following tasks:

1. Design a new database in which to store all the objects related to the items for sale. Call the database Hockey Fan Zone.

2. Use the information shown in Figure 1–105 to determine the primary keys and determine additional fields. Then, determine the relationships among tables and the data types. (See pages AC 10 and AC 11 for help in designing tables.)

3. Create the Item table using the information shown in Figure 1–105.

4. Create the Supplier table using the information shown in Figure 1–105.

5. Add the appropriate data to the Item table.

6. Add the appropriate data to the Supplier table.

7. Create a split form for the Item table. Use the name Item for the form.

8. Create the report shown in Figure 1–106 for the Item table.

9. Change the database properties, as specified by your instructor. Submit the database in the format specified by your instructor.

	Item Number	Description	On Hand	Cost	Selling Price	Supplier Code	Supplier Name	Telephone Number
2	3663	Ball Cap	30	$11.15	$18.95	LG	Logo Goods	517-555-3853
3	3683	Bumper Sticker	50	$0.95	$1.50	MN	Mary's Novelties	317-555-4747
4	4563	Earrings	10	$4.50	$7.00	LG	Logo Goods	517-555-3853
5	4593	Foam Finger	25	$2.95	$5.00	LG	Logo Goods	517-555-3853
6	5923	Jersey	12	$21.45	$24.75	AC	Ace Clothes	616-555-9228
7	6189	Koozies	35	$2.00	$4.00	MN	Mary's Novelties	317-555-4747
8	6343	Note Cube	7	$5.75	$8.00	MN	Mary's Novelties	317-555-4747
9	7810	Tee Shirt	32	$9.50	$14.95	AC	Ace Clothes	616-555-9228
10	7930	Visor	9	$11.95	$17.00	LG	Logo Goods	517-555-3853

Figure 1–105

Inventory Status Report

Item Number	Description	On Hand	Cost
3663	Ball Cap	30	$11.15
3683	Bumper Sticker	50	$0.95
4563	Earrings	10	$4.50
4593	Foam Finger	25	$2.95
5923	Jersey	12	$21.45
6189	Koozies	35	$2.00
6343	Note Cube	7	$5.75
7810	Tee Shirt	32	$9.50
7930	Visor	9	$11.95

Figure 1–106

In the Lab

Lab 3: Creating the Ada Beauty Supply Database

Problem: A distribution company supplies local beauty salons with items needed in the beauty industry. The distributor employs sales representatives who receive a base salary as well as a commission on sales. Currently, the distributor keeps data on customers and sales reps in two Word documents and two Excel workbooks.

Instructions: Using the data shown in Figure 1–107 on the next page, design the Ada Beauty Supply database. Use the database design guidelines in this chapter to help you in the design process.

Continued >

In the Lab *continued*

Customer Number	Customer Name	Street	Telephone
AM23	Amy's Salon	223 Johnson	555-2150
BB34	Bob the Barber	1939 Jackson	555-1939
BL15	Blondie's	3294 Devon	555-7510
CM09	Cut Mane	3140 Halsted	555-0604
CS12	Curl n Style	1632 Clark	555-0804
EG07	Elegante	1805 Boardway	555-1404
JS34	Just Cuts	2200 Lawrence	555-0313
LB20	Le Beauty	13 Devon	555-5161
NC25	Nancy's Place	1027 Wells	555-4210
RD03	Rose's Day Spa	787 Monroe	555-7657
TT21	Tan and Tone	1939 Congress	555-6554

(a) Customer Address Information (Word table)

	A	B	C	D	E
1	Customer Number	Customer Name	Balance	Amount Paid	Sales Rep Num
2	AM23	Amy's Salon	$195.00	$1,695.00	44
3	BB34	Bob the Barber	$150.00	$0.00	51
4	BL15	Blondie's	$555.00	$1,350.00	49
5	CM09	Cut Mane	$295.00	$1,080.00	51
6	CS12	Curl n Style	$145.00	$710.00	49
7	EG07	Elegante	$0.00	$1,700.00	44
8	JS34	Just Cuts	$360.00	$700.00	49
9	LB20	Le Beauty	$200.00	$1,250.00	51
10	NC25	Nancy's Place	$240.00	$550.00	44
11	RD03	Rose's Day Spa	$0.00	$975.00	51
12	TT21	Tan and Tone	$160.00	$725.00	44
13					
14					
15					
16					

(c) Customer Financial Information (Excel Workbook)

Sales Rep Number	Last Name	First Name	Street	City	State	Postal Code
44	Jones	Pat	43 Third	Lawncrest	WA	98084
49	Gupta	Pinn	678 Hillcrest	Manton	WA	98085
51	Ortiz	Gabe	982 Victoria	Lawncrest	WA	98084
55	Sinson	Terry	45 Elm	Manton	WA	98084

(b) Sales Rep Address Information (Word table)

	A	B	C	D	E	F
1	Sales Rep Number	Last Name	First Name	Salary	Comm Rate	Commission
2	44	Jones	Pat	$ 23,000.00	0.05	$613.50
3	49	Gupta	Pinn	$ 24,000.00	0.06	$616.60
4	51	Ortiz	Gabe	$ 22,500.00	0.05	$492.75
5	55	Sinson	Terry	$ 20,000.00	0.05	$0.00
6						

(d) Sales Rep Financial Information (Excel Workbook)

Figure 1–107

When you have completed the database design, create the database, create the tables, and add the data to the appropriate tables. Be sure to determine the correct data types.

Finally, prepare the Customer Status Report shown in Figure 1–108a and the Sales Rep Salary Report shown in Figure 1–108b. Change the database properties, as specified by your instructor. Submit the database in the format specified by your instructor.

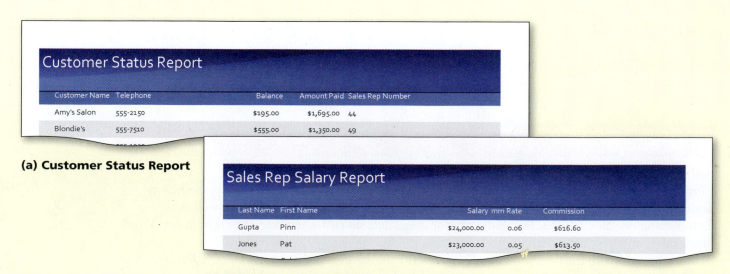

Customer Status Report

Customer Name	Telephone		Balance	Amount Paid	Sales Rep Number
Amy's Salon	555-2150		$195.00	$1,695.00	44
Blondie's	555-7510		$555.00	$1,350.00	49

(a) Customer Status Report

Sales Rep Salary Report

Last Name	First Name		Salary	mm Rate	Commission
Gupta	Pinn		$24,000.00	0.06	$616.60
Jones	Pat		$23,000.00	0.05	$613.50

(b) Sales Rep Salary Report

Figure 1–108

Cases and Places

Apply your creative thinking and problem solving skills to design and implement a solution.

• EASIER   •• MORE DIFFICULT

• 1: Design and Create an E-Commerce Database

Students often have very little money to furnish dorm rooms and apartments. You and two of your friends have decided to use the skills you learned in your e-commerce class to create a Web site specifically for college students to buy and sell used household furnishings.

Design and create a database to store the data that you need to manage this new business. Then create the necessary tables and enter the data from the Case 1-1 Second-Hand Goods document. See the inside back cover of this book for instructions for downloading the Data Files for Students, or see your instructor for information on accessing the files required in this book. Submit your assignment in the format specified by your instructor.

• 2: Design and Create a Rental Database

You are a part-time employee of BeachCondo Rentals. BeachCondo Rentals provides a rental service for condo owners who want to rent their units. The company rents units by the week. Currently, the company keeps information about its rentals in an Excel workbook.

Design and create a database to store the rental data. Then create the necessary tables and enter the data from the Case 1-2 BeachCondo Rentals workbook. See the inside back cover of this book for instructions for downloading the Data Files for Students, or see your instructor for information on accessing the files required in this book. Create an Available Rentals Report that lists the unit number, weekly rate, and owner number. Submit your assignment in the format specified by your instructor.

•• 3: Design and Create a Restaurant Database

Your school is sponsoring a conference that will draw participants from a wide geographical area. The conference director has asked for your help in preparing a database of restaurants that might be of interest to the participants. At a minimum, she needs to know the following: the type of restaurant (vegetarian, fast-food, fine dining, and so on), street address, telephone number, and opening and closing times and days. Because most of the participants will stay on campus, she also would like to know the approximate distance from campus. Additionally, she would like to know about any unique or special features the restaurants may have.

Design and create a database to meet the conference director's needs. Create the necessary tables, determine the necessary fields, enter some sample data, and prepare a sample report to show the director. Submit your assignment in the format specified by your instructor.

•• 4: Design and Create a Database to Help You Find a Job

Make It Personal

Conducting a job search requires careful preparation. In addition to preparing a resume and cover letter, you will need to research the companies for which you are interested in working and contact these companies to let them know of your interest and qualifications.

Microsoft Access includes a Contacts table template that can create a table that will help you keep track of your job contacts. Create a database to keep track of the companies that are of interest to you. Submit your assignment in the format specified by your instructor.

Continued >

Cases and Places *continued*

•• 5: Design a Database that Tracks Student Data

Working Together

Keeping track of students is an enormous task for school administrators. Microsoft Access can help school administrators manage student data. The Database Wizard includes a Students template that can create a database that will maintain many different types of data on students, such as allergies, medications, and emergency contact information.

Have each member of your team explore the features of the Database Wizard and determine individually which tables and fields should be included in a Students database. As a group, review your choices and decide on one common design. Prepare a short paper for your instructor that explains why your team chose the particular database design.

After agreeing on the database design, assign one member to create the database using the Database Wizard. Every other team member should contribute data and add the data to the database. Submit your assignment in the format specified by your instructor.

2 Querying a Database

Objectives

You will have mastered the material in this chapter when you can:

- Create queries using the Simple Query Wizard
- Print query results
- Create queries using Design view
- Include fields in the design grid
- Use text and numeric data in criteria
- Create and use parameter queries
- Save a query and use the saved query
- Use compound criteria in queries
- Sort data in queries
- Join tables in queries
- Create a report from a query
- Perform calculations in queries
- Calculate statistics in queries
- Create crosstab queries
- Customize the Navigation Pane

2 | Querying a Database

Introduction

A database management system such as Access offers many useful features, among them the capability of answering questions, the answers to which are found in the database. When you pose a question to Access, or any other database management system, the question is called a query. A **query** is simply a question presented in a way that Access can process.

Thus, to find the answer to a question, you first create a corresponding query using the techniques illustrated in this chapter. After you have created the query, you instruct Access to display the query results; that is, to perform the steps necessary to obtain the answer. Access then displays the answer in Datasheet view.

Project — Querying a Database

Organizations and individuals achieve several benefits from storing data in a database and using Access to manage the database. One of the most important benefits is the capability of easily finding the answers to questions such as those shown in Figure 2-1 and the following, which concern the data in the JSP Recruiters database:

1. What are the number, name, the amount paid, and the current due of client FD89?
2. Which clients' names begin with Be?
3. Which clients are located in Berridge?
4. Which clients have a current due of $0.00?
5. Which clients have an amount paid that is more than $20,000.00?
6. Which clients of recruiter 21 have an amount paid that is more than $20,000.00?
7. In what cities are all the clients located?
8. What is the total amount (amount paid + current due) for each client?
9. What is the client number and name of each client, and what is the number and name of the recruiter to whom each client is assigned?

In addition to these questions, JSP Recruiters needs to find information about clients located in a specific city, but they want to enter a different city each time they ask the question. A parameter query would enable this. The agency also has a special way it wants to summarize data. A crosstab query will present the data in the desired form.

Give me the number, name, amount paid, and current due for all clients whose name starts with Be.

Give me the number, name, amount paid, and current due for client FD89.

Give me the number, name, amount paid, current due, and recruiter number for all clients whose amount paid is more than $20,000 and whose recruiter number is 21.

Summarize the total amount paid by city and by recruiter.

List the client number, name, recruiter number, and amount paid for all clients. Sort the results by recruiter number and amount paid.

Give me the average amount paid by clients of each recruiter.

For each recruiter, list the number, last name, and first name. Also, list the client number and name for each of the recruiter's clients.

List the client number, client name, amount paid, current due, and the total amount (amount paid plus current due) for each client.

Figure 2–1

Overview

As you read this chapter, you will learn how to query a database by performing these general tasks:

- Create queries using the Simple Query Wizard and Design view
- Use criteria in queries
- Create and use parameter queries
- Sort data in queries
- Join tables in queries
- Perform calculations in queries
- Create crosstab queries

Plan Ahead

Query Design Guidelines

When posing a question to Access, you must design an appropriate query. In the process of designing a query, the decisions you make will determine the fields, tables, criteria, order, and special calculations included in the query. To design a query, you should follow these general guidelines:

1. **Identify the fields.** Examine the question or request to determine which fields from the tables in the database are involved. Examine the contents of these fields to make sure you understand how the data is stored.

2. **Identify restrictions.** Unless the question or request calls for all records, determine the restrictions, that is, the conditions records must satisfy in order to be included in the results.

3. **Determine whether special order is required.** Examine the question or request to determine whether the results must appear in some specific order.

4. **Determine whether more than one table is required.** If all the fields identified in Step 1 are in the same table, no special action is required. If this is not the case, identify all tables represented by those fields.

5. **Determine whether calculations are required.** Examine the question or request to determine whether, in addition to the fields determined in Step 1, calculations must be included. Results of mathematical operations typically are not stored in the database because they can be calculated easily when necessary. Such calculations include individual record calculations (for example, adding the values in two fields) or group calculations (for example, finding the total of the values in a particular field on all the records).

6. **If data is to be summarized, determine whether a crosstab query would be appropriate.** If data is to be grouped by two different types of information, you can use a crosstab query. You will need to identify the two types of information. One of the types will form the row headings and the other will form the column headings in the query results.

When necessary, more specific details concerning the above decisions and/or actions are presented at appropriate points in the chapter.

Starting Access

If you are using a computer to step through the project in this chapter and you want your screen to match the figures in this book, you should change your screen's resolution to 1024 × 768. For information about how to change a computer's resolution, read Appendix E.

To Start Access

The following steps, which assume Windows Vista is running, start Access.

Note: If you are using Windows XP, see Appendix F for alternate steps.

1 Click the Start button on the Windows Vista taskbar to display the Start menu.

2 Click All Programs at the bottom of the left Pane on the Start menu to display the All Programs list and then click Microsoft Office in the All Programs list to display the Microsoft Office list.

3 Click Microsoft Office Access 2007 on the Microsoft Office list to start Access and display the Getting Started with Microsoft Office Access window.

4 If the Access window is not maximized, click the Maximize button on its title bar to maximize the window.

To Open a Database

In Chapter 1, you created your database on a USB flash drive using the file name, JSP Recruiters. There are two ways to open the file containing your database. If the file you created appears in the Recent Documents list, you can click it to open the file. If not, you can use the More button to open the file. The following steps use the More button to open the JSP Recruiters database from the USB flash drive.

Note: If you are using Windows XP, see Appendix F for alternate steps.

1 With your USB flash drive connected to one of the computer's USB ports, click the More button to display the Open dialog box.

2 If the Folders list is displayed below the Folders button, click the Folders button to remove the Folders list.

3 If necessary, click Computer in the Favorite Links section and then double-click UDISK 2.0 (E:) to select the USB flash drive, Drive E in this case, as the new open location. (Your drive letter might be different.)

4 Click JSP Recruiters to select the file name.

5 Click the Open button to open the database.

6 If a Security Warning appears, click the Options button to display the Microsoft Office Security Options dialog box.

7 With the option button to enable this content selected, click the OK button to enable the content.

Creating Queries

Queries are simply questions, the answers to which are in the database. Access contains a powerful query feature. Through the use of this feature, you can find the answers to a wide variety of complex questions.

To Use the Simple Query Wizard to Create a Query

Once you have examined the question you wish to ask to determine the fields involved in the question, you can begin creating the query. If there are no restrictions involved in the query, nor any special order or calculations, you can use the Simple Query wizard. The following steps use the Simple Query wizard to create a query to display the number, name, and recruiter number of all clients.

1

- If the Navigation Pane is hidden, click the Shutter Bar Open/Close Button to show the Navigation Pane.

- Be sure the Client table is selected.

- Click Create on the Ribbon to display the Create tab.

- Click the Query Wizard button on the Create tab to display the New Query dialog box (Figure 2–2).

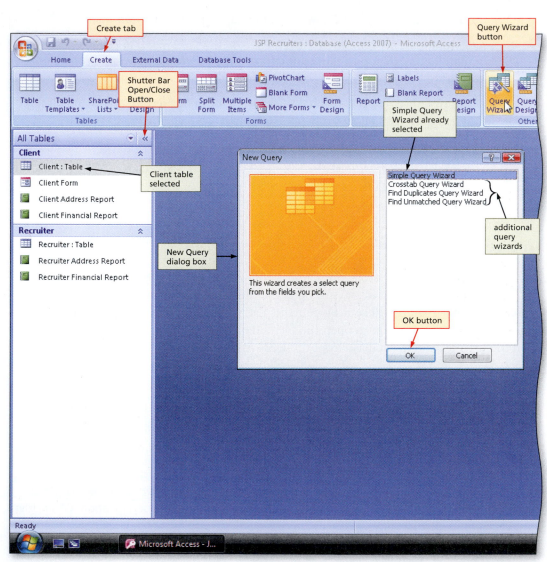

Figure 2–2

2

- Be sure Simple Query Wizard is selected, and then click the OK button to display the Simple Query Wizard dialog box (Figure 2–3).

Q&A

This looks like the screen I saw in the Report Wizard. Do I select fields in the same way?

Yes. In fact, you will see a similar screen in other wizards and you always select the fields just as you did in the Report Wizard.

Figure 2–3

3

- Click the Add Field button to add the Client Number field.

- Click the Add Field button a second time to add the Client Name field.

- Click the Recruiter Number field, and then click the Add Field button to add the Recruiter Number field.

- Click the Next button.

- Be sure the title of the query is Client Query.

- Click the Finish button to create the query (Figure 2–4).

Figure 2–4

• Click the Close button for the Client Query to remove the query results from the screen.

Q&A

If I want to use this query in the future, do I need to save the query?

Normally you would. The one exception is a query created by the wizard. The wizard automatically saves the query it creates.

Using Queries

After you have created and saved a query, you can use it in a variety of ways:

• To view the results of the query, open it by right-clicking the query in the Navigation Pane and clicking Open on the shortcut menu.

• To print the results with the query open, click the Office Button, point to Print on the Office Button menu, and then click Quick Print on the Print submenu.

• If you want to change the design of the query, right-click the query and then click Design View on the shortcut menu to open the query in Design view.

• To print the query without first opening it, be sure the query is selected in the Navigation Pane and then click the Office Button, point to Print on the Office Button menu, and then click Quick Print on the Print submenu.

You can switch between views of a query by using the View button (Figure 2–5). Clicking the arrow at the bottom of the button produces the View button menu as shown in the figure. You then click the desired view in the menu. The two views you will use in this chapter are Datasheet view (see the results) and Design view (change the design). You also can click the top part of the button, in which case, you will switch to the view identified by the icon on the button. In the figure, the button contains the icon for Design view, so clicking the button would change to Design view. For the most part, the icon on the button represents the view you want, so you can usually simply click the button.

Figure 2–5

To Use a Criterion in a Query

After you have determined the fields to be included in a query, you will determine whether there are any restrictions on the records that are to be included. For example, you might only want to include those clients whose recruiter number is 24. In such a case, you need to enter the 24 as a **criterion**, which is a condition that the records to be included must satisfy. To do so, you will open the query in Design view, enter the criterion below the appropriate field, and then view the results of the query. The following steps enter a criterion to include only the clients of recruiter 24 and then view the query results.

1
- Right-click Client Query to produce a shortcut menu (Figure 2–6).

Figure 2–6

2
- Click Design View on the shortcut menu to open the query in Design view (Figure 2–7). (Your field names may be enclosed in brackets.)

Figure 2–7

3

• Click the Criteria row in the Recruiter Number column of the grid, and then type 24 as the criterion (Figure 2–8).

Q&A The Recruiter Number field is a text field. Do I need to enclose the value for a text field in quotation marks?

You could, but it is not necessary, because Access inserts the quotation marks for you automatically.

Figure 2–8

4

• Click the View button to display the results in Datasheet view (Figure 2–9).

Q&A Could I click the View button arrow and then click Datasheet view?

Yes. If the icon representing the view you want appears on the View button, however, it is easier just to click the button.

Figure 2–9

5

• Close the Client Query window by clicking the Close 'Client Query' button.

• When asked if you want to save your changes, click the No button.

Q&A If I saved the query, what would happen the next time I ran the query?

You would see only clients of recruiter 24.

Other Ways

1. Click Run button on Ribbon

2. Click Datasheet View button on status bar

To Print the Results of a Query

To print the results of a query, use the same techniques you learned in Chapter 1 on pages AC 41 and AC 42 to print the data in the table. The following steps print the current query results.

1 With the Client Query selected in the Navigation Pane, click the Office Button.

2 Point to Print on the Office Button menu.

3 Click Quick Print on the Print submenu.

To Create a Query in Design View

Most of the time you will use Design view to create queries. Once you have created a new query in Design view, you can specify fields, criteria, sorting, calculations, and so on. The following steps create a new query in Design view.

1

• Hide the Navigation Pane.

• Click Create on the Ribbon to display the Create tab.

• Click the Query Design button to create a new query (Figure 2–10).

Q&A
Is it necessary to hide the Navigation Pane?

No. It gives you more room for the query, however, so it is usually a good practice to hide it.

Figure 2–10

2

- With the Client table selected, click the Add button in the Show Table dialog box to add the Client table to the query.

- Click the Close button in the Show Table dialog box to remove the dialog box from the screen.

Q&A

What if I inadvertently add the wrong table?

Right-click the table that you added in error and click Remove Table on the shortcut menu. You also can just close the query, indicate that you don't want to save it, and then start over.

- Drag the lower edge of the field box down far enough so all fields in the Client table appear (Figure 2–11).

Q&A

How do I drag the lower edge?

Point to the lower edge, press and hold the left mouse button, move the mouse pointer to the new position for the lower edge, and then release the left mouse button. While the mouse pointer points to the lower edge of the field list, its shape changes to a double-headed arrow.

Q&A

Is it essential that I resize the field box?

No. You can always scroll through the list of fields using the scroll bar. If you can resize the field box so all fields appear, it is usually more convenient.

Figure 2–11

To Add Fields to the Design Grid

Once you have a new query displayed in Design view, you are ready to create the query by making entries in the design grid in the lower Pane of the window. You add the fields you want included in the Field row in the grid. Only the fields that appear in the design grid will be included in the results of the query. The following step includes the client number, client name, amount paid, and current due for all clients by adding only those fields in the design grid.

1
- Double-click the Client Number field in the field list to add the Client Number field to the query.

Q&A What if I add the wrong field?

Click just above the field name in the design grid to select the column and then press the DELETE key to remove the field.

- Double-click the Client Name field in the field list to add the Client Name field to the query.

- Add the Amount Paid field to the query by double-clicking the Amount Paid field in the field list.

- Add the Current Due field to the query (Figure 2–12).

Q&A What if I want to include all fields? Do I have to add each field individually?

No. Instead of adding individual fields, you can double-click the asterisk (*) to add the asterisk to the design grid.

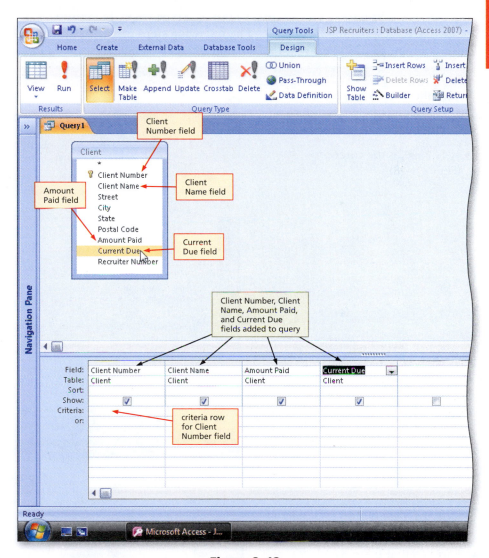

Figure 2–12

Entering Criteria

When you use queries, usually you are looking for those records that satisfy some criterion. In the simple query you created earlier, for example, you entered a criterion to restrict the records that were included to those on which the recruiter number was 24. In another query, you might want the name, amount paid, and current due amounts of the client whose number is FD89, for example, or of those clients whose names start with the letters, Be. You enter criteria in the Criteria row in the design grid below the field name to which the criterion applies. For example, to indicate that the client number must be FD89, you first must add the Client Number field to the design grid. You then would type FD89 in the Criteria row below the Client Number field.

To Use Text Data in a Criterion

To use **text data** (data in a field whose data type is Text) in criteria, simply type the text in the Criteria row below the corresponding field name. The following steps query the Client table and display the client number, client name, amount paid, and current due amount of client FD89.

- Click the Criteria row for the Client Number field to produce an insertion point.

- Type FD89 as the criterion (Figure 2–13).

Figure 2–13

2

- Click the View button to display the query results (Figure 2–14).

Q&A

I noticed that there is a View button on both the Home tab and the Design tab. Do they both have the same effect?

Yes. Use whichever one you find most convenient.

Figure 2–14

To Use a Wildcard

Microsoft Access supports wildcards. **Wildcards** are symbols that represent any character or combination of characters. One common wildcard, the **asterisk** (*), represents any collection of characters. Thus Be* represents the letters, Be, followed by any collection of characters. Another wildcard symbol is the **question mark** (?), which represents any individual character. Thus T?m represents the letter, T, followed by any single character followed by the letter, m, such as Tim or Tom.

The following steps use a wildcard to find the number, name, amount paid, and current due of those clients whose names begin with Be. Because you do not know how many characters will follow the Be, the asterisk is appropriate.

1
- Click the View button to return to Design view.

- If necessary, click the Criteria row below the Client Number field to produce an insertion point.

- Use the DELETE or BACKSPACE key as necessary to delete the current entry.

- Click the Criteria row below the Client Name field to produce an insertion point.

- Type Be* as the criterion (Figure 2–15).

Figure 2–15

2
- View the query results by clicking the View button (Figure 2–16).

 Experiment
- Vary the case of the letters in the criteria and view the results to determine whether case makes a difference when entering a wildcard.

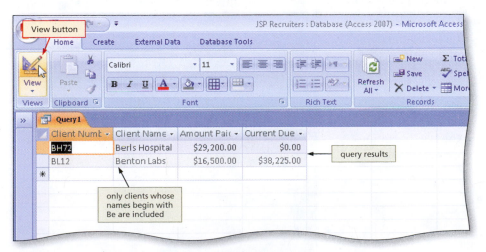

Figure 2–16

To Use Criteria for a Field Not Included in the Results

In some cases, you may have criteria for a particular field that should not appear in the results of the query. For example, you may want to see the client number, client name, amount paid, and current due for all clients located in Berridge. The criteria involve the City field, which is not one of the fields to be included in the results.

To enter a criterion for the City field, it must be included in the design grid. Normally, this also would mean it would appear in the results. To prevent this from happening, remove the check mark from its Show check box in the Show row of the grid. The following steps display the client number, client name, amount paid, and current due for clients located in Berridge.

- Click the View button to return to Design view.

- Erase the criterion in the Client Name field.

- Include the City field in the query.

- Type Berridge as the criterion for the City field (Figure 2–17).

Figure 2–17

- Click the Show check box for the City field to remove the check mark (Figure 2–18).

Q&A

Could I have removed the check mark before entering the criterion?

Yes. The order in which you performed the two operations does not matter.

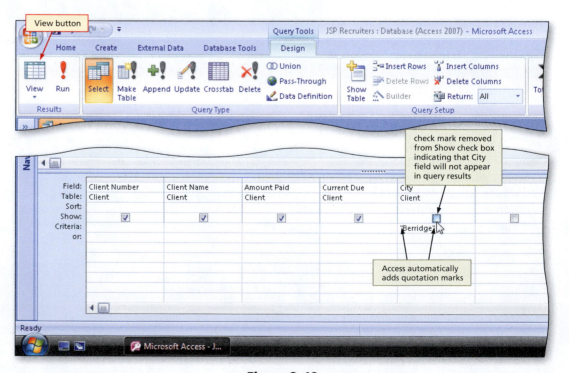

Figure 2–18

3
- View the query results (Figure 2–19).

🔍 **Experiment**

- Click the View button to return to Design view, enter a different city name, and view the results. Repeat this process with a variety of city names, including at least one city name that is not in the database.

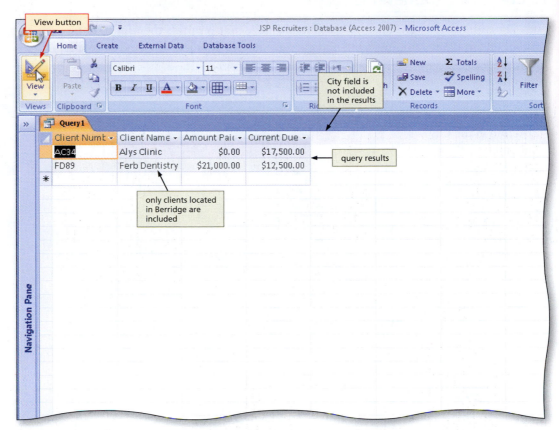

Figure 2–19

Creating a Parameter Query

If you wanted to find clients located in Fort Stewart rather than Berridge, you would either have to create a new query or modify the existing query by replacing Berridge with Fort Stewart as the criterion. Rather than giving a specific criterion when you first create the query, on occasion, you may want to be able to enter part of the criterion when you view the query results and then have the appropriate results appear. For example, to include all the clients located in Berridge, you could enter Berridge as a criterion in the City field. From that point on, every time you ran the query, only the clients in Berridge would appear.

A better way is to allow the user to enter the city at the time the user wants to view the results. Thus a user could view the query results, enter Berridge as the city and then see all the clients in Berridge. Later, the user could use the same query, but enter Fort Stewart as the city, and then see all the clients in Fort Stewart.

To enable this flexibility, you create a **parameter query**, which is a query that prompts for input whenever it is used. You enter a parameter, rather than a specific value, as the criterion. You create a parameter by enclosing a value in a criterion in square brackets. It is important that the value in the brackets does not match the name of any field. If you enter a field name in square brackets, Access assumes you want that particular field and does not prompt the user for input. For example, you could place [Enter City] as the criterion in the City field.

BTW

Removing a Table from a Query
If you add the wrong table to a query or have an extra table in the query, you can remove it by right-clicking the field list for the table and then clicking Remove Table on the shortcut menu.

To Create a Parameter Query

The following steps create a parameter query that prompts the user to enter a city, and then displays the client number, client name, amount paid, and current due for all clients located in that city.

1

- Return to Design view.

- Erase the current criterion in the City column, and then type [Enter City] as the new criterion (Figure 2–20).

Q&A

What is the purpose of the square brackets?

The square brackets indicate that the text entered is not text that the value in the column must match. Without the brackets, for example, Access would search for records on which the city is Enter City.

Q&A

What if I typed a field name in the square brackets?

Access would simply use the value in that field. In order to create a parameter query, it is essential that the text typed in the square brackets not be a field name.

Figure 2–20

2

- Click the View button to display the Enter Parameter Value dialog box (Figure 2–21).

Figure 2–21

3

- Type Fort Stewart as the parameter value in the Enter City text box and then click the OK button (Figure 2–22).

Experiment

- Try other characters between the square brackets. In each case, view the results. When finished, change the characters between the square brackets back to Enter City.

Figure 2–22

Each time you use this query, you will be asked to enter a city. Only clients in the city you enter will be included in the results.

To Save a Query

In many cases, you will want to repeatedly use the queries you construct. By saving the query, you eliminate the need to repeat all your entries. The following steps save the query you just have created and assign it the name Client-City Query.

1

- Click the Save button on the Quick Access Toolbar to open the Save As dialog box.

Q&A

Can I also save from Design view?

Yes. You can save the query when you view it in Design view just as you can save the query when you view the query results in Datasheet view.

- Type Client-City Query in the Query Name text box (Figure 2–23).

Figure 2–23

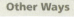

● Click the OK button to save the query (Figure 2–24).

● Click the Close 'Client-City Query' button to close the query and remove it from the screen.

Other Ways

1. Right-click tab for query, click Save on shortcut menu
2. Press CTRL+S

Figure 2–24

To Use a Saved Query

Once you have saved a query, you can use and manipulate it at any time in the future by opening it. When you right-click the query in the Navigation Pane, Access displays a shortcut menu containing commands that allow you to open and change the design of the query. You also can print the results by clicking the Office Button, pointing to Print on the Office button menu, and then clicking Quick Print on the Print submenu.

The query always uses the data that is currently in the table. Thus, if changes have been made to the data since the last time you ran the query, the results of the query may be different. The following steps use the query named Client-City Query.

1

● Show the Navigation Pane.

● Right-click the Client-City Query to produce a shortcut menu.

● Click Open on the shortcut menu to open the query and display the Enter Parameter Value dialog box (Figure 2–25).

Q&A

What would have happened if there were no parameters?

You would immediately see the results without needing to furnish any additional information.

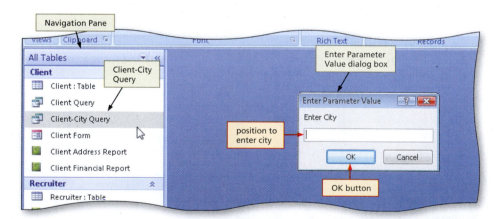

Figure 2–25

2

● Type `Fort Stewart` in the Enter City text box, and then click the OK button to display the results using Fort Stewart as the city as shown in Figure 2–24.

● Click the Close 'Client-City Query' button, shown in Figure 2–24, to close the query.

To Use a Number in a Criterion

To enter a number in a criterion, type the number without any dollar signs or commas. The following steps display all clients whose current due amount is $0.00.

1
- Hide the Navigation Pane.
- Click Create on the Ribbon to display the Create tab.
- Click the Query Design button to create a new query.
- With the Client table selected, click the Add button in the Show Table dialog box to add the Client table to the query.
- Click the Close button in the Show Table dialog box to remove the dialog box from the screen.
- Drag the lower edge of the field box down far enough so all fields in the Client table are displayed.
- Include the Client Number, Client Name, Amount Paid, and Current Due fields in the query.
- Type 0 as the criterion for the Current Due field (Figure 2–26).

Figure 2–26

Q&A
Do I need to enter a dollar sign and decimal point?

No. Access will interpret 0 as $0.00, because the data type for the Current Due field is currency.

2
- View the query results (Figure 2–27).

Q&A
Why did Access display the results as $0.00 when I only entered 0?

Access uses the format for the field to determine how to display the result. In this case the format indicated that Access should include the dollar sign and decimal point.

Figure 2–27

To Use a Comparison Operator in a Criterion

Unless you specify otherwise, Access assumes that the criteria you enter involve equality (exact matches). In the last query, for example, you were requesting those clients whose current due amount is equal to 0 (zero). If you want something other than an exact match, you must enter the appropriate **comparison operator**. The comparison operators are > (greater than), < (less than), >= (greater than or equal to), <= (less than or equal to), and NOT (not equal to).

The following steps use the > operator to find all clients whose amount paid is more than $20,000.00.

- Return to Design view.

- Erase the 0 in the Current Due column.

- Type **>20000** as the criterion for the Amount Paid field (Figure 2–28).

Figure 2–28

- View the query results (Figure 2–29).

🔍 Experiment

- Return to Design view. Try a different criterion involving a comparison operator in the Amount Paid field and view the results. When finished, return to Design view, enter the original criterion (>20000) in the Amount Paid field, and view the results.

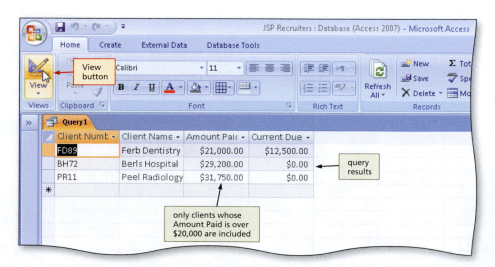

Figure 2–29

Using Compound Criteria

Often you will have more than one criterion that the data for which you are searching must satisfy. This type of criterion is called a **compound criterion**. Two types of compound criteria exist.

In an **AND criterion**, each individual criterion must be true in order for the compound criterion to be true. For example, an AND criterion would allow you to find those clients that have an amount paid greater than $20,000.00 and whose recruiter is recruiter 21.

Conversely, an **OR criterion** is true provided either individual criterion is true. An OR criterion would allow you to find those clients that have an amount paid greater than $20,000.00 or whose recruiter is recruiter 21. In this case, any client whose amount paid is greater than $20,000.00 would be included in the answer, regardless of whether the client's recruiter is recruiter 21. Likewise, any client whose recruiter is recruiter 21 would be included, regardless of whether the client had an amount paid greater than $20,000.00.

BTW

The BETWEEN Operator

The BETWEEN operator allows you to search for a range of values in one field. For example, to find all clients whose amount paid is between $10,000 and $20,000, you would enter Between 10000 and 20000 in the Criteria row for the Amount Paid field.

To Use a Compound Criterion Involving AND

To combine criteria with AND, place the criteria on the same line. The following steps use an AND criterion to find those clients whose amount paid is greater than $20,000.00 and whose recruiter is recruiter 21.

• Return to Design view.

• Include the Recruiter Number field in the query.

• Type 21 as the criterion for the Recruiter Number field (Figure 2–30).

Figure 2–30

• View the query results (Figure 2–31).

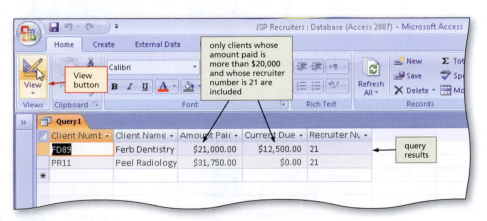

Figure 2–31

To Use a Compound Criterion Involving OR

To combine criteria with OR, the criteria must go on separate lines in the Criteria area of the grid. The following steps use an OR criterion to find those clients whose amount paid is greater than $20,000.00 or whose recruiter is recruiter 21 (or both).

- Return to Design view.

- If necessary, click the Criteria entry for the Recruiter Number field and then use the BACKSPACE key or the DELETE key to erase the entry ("21").

- Click the or: row (the row below the Criteria row) for the Recruiter Number field and then type 21 as the entry (Figure 2–32).

Figure 2–32

- View the query results (Figure 2–33).

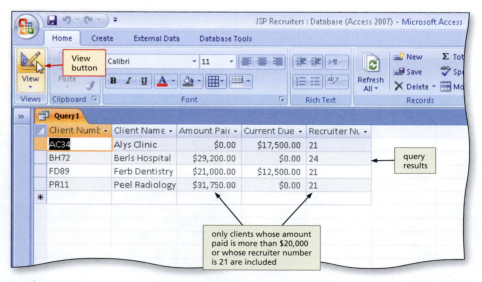

Figure 2–33

Sorting

In some queries, the order in which the records appear really does not matter. All you need to be concerned about are the records that appear in the results. It does not matter which one is first or which one is last.

In other queries, however, the order can be very important. You may want to see the cities in which clients are located and would like them arranged alphabetically. Perhaps you want to see the clients listed by recruiter number. Further, within all the clients of any given recruiter, you might want them to be listed by amount paid from largest amount to smallest.

To order the records in the answer to a query in a particular way, you **sort** the records. The field or fields on which the records are sorted is called the **sort key**. If you are sorting on more than one field (such as sorting by amount paid within recruiter number), the more important field (Recruiter Number) is called the **major key** (also called the **primary sort key**) and the less important field (Amount Paid) is called the **minor key** (also called the **secondary sort key**).

To sort in Microsoft Access, specify the sort order in the Sort row of the design grid below the field that is the sort key. If you specify more than one sort key, the sort key on the left will be the major sort key and the one on the right will be the minor key.

The following are guidelines related to sorting in queries.

BTW

OR Criteria in a Single Field
If you want to combine two criteria with OR in a single field, you can place the criteria on separate lines, or you can place the criteria on the same line with the word OR in between them. For example, to include those records in which the city is Berls or Mason, you could type Berls OR Mason in the Criteria row. You also can use the IN operator, which consists of the word IN followed by the criteria in parentheses. For example, you would type IN (Berls, Mason).

Determine whether special order is required.

1. **Determine whether sorting is required**. Examine the query or request to see if it contains words such as "order" or "sort" that would imply that the order of the query results is important. If so, you need to sort the query.

2. **Determine the sort key(s)**. If sorting is required, identify the field or fields on which the results are to be sorted. Look for words such as "ordered by" or "sort the results by," both of which would indicate that the specified field is a sort key.

3. **If using two sort keys, determine major and minor key**. If you are using two sort keys, determine which one is more important. That will be the major key. Look for words such as "sort by amount paid within recruiter number," which imply that the overall order is by recruiter number. Thus, the Recruiter Number field would be the major sort key and the Amount Paid field would be the minor sort key.

4. **Determine sort order**. Words such as "increasing," "ascending," or "low-to-high" imply Ascending order. Words such as "decreasing," "descending," or "high-to-low" imply Descending order. Sorting in alphabetical order implies Ascending order. If there are no words to imply a particular order, you would typically use Ascending.

5. **Determine restrictions**. Examine the query or request to see if there are any special restrictions. One common restriction is to exclude duplicates. Another common restriction is to list only a certain number of records, for example to list only the first five records.

Plan Ahead

To Clear the Design Grid

If the fields you want to include in the next query are different from those in the previous query, it is usually simpler to start with a clear grid, that is, one with no fields already in the design grid. You always can clear the entries in the design grid by closing the query and then starting over. A simpler approach to clearing the entries is to select all the entries and then press the DELETE key. The following steps return to Design view and clear the design grid.

- Return to Design view.

- Click just above the Client Number column heading in the grid to select the column.

I clicked above the column heading, but the column is not selected. What should I do?

You didn't point to the correct location. Be sure the mouse pointer turns to a down-pointing arrow and then click again.

- Hold the SHIFT key down and click just above the Recruiter Number column heading to select all the columns (Figure 2–34).

Figure 2–34

- Press the DELETE key to clear the design grid.

To Sort Data in a Query

If you have determined in the design process that a query is to be sorted, you must identify the sort key, that is, the field on which the results are to be sorted. In creating the query, you will need to specify the sort key to Access. The following steps sort the cities in the Client table by indicating that the City field is to be sorted. The steps specify Ascending sort order.

- Include the City field in the design grid.

- Click the Sort row below the City field, and then click the Sort row arrow to display a menu of possible sort orders (Figure 2–35).

Figure 2–35

2

- Click Ascending to select Ascending sort order (Figure 2–36).

Figure 2–36

3

- View the query results (Figure 2–37).

Experiment

- Return to Design view and change the sort order to Descending. View the results. Return to Design view and change the sort order back to Ascending. View the results.

 Q&A

Why do some cities appear more than once?

More than one client is located in those cities.

Figure 2–37

To Omit Duplicates

When you sort data, duplicates normally are included. In Figure 2–37 on the previous page, for example, Berridge appeared twice, as did Fort Stewart and Tarleton. These duplicates do not add any value, so you can eliminate them from the results. To eliminate duplicates, display the query's property sheet. A **property sheet** is a window containing the various properties of the object. To omit duplicates, you will use the property sheet to change the Unique Values property from No to Yes.

The following steps produce a sorted list of the cities in the Client table in which each city is listed only once.

 1

- Return to Design view.

- Click the second field in the design grid (the empty field following City).

- If necessary, click Design on the Ribbon to display the Design tab.

- Click the Property Sheet button on the Design tab to display the property sheet (Figure 2–38).

Q&A

My property sheet looks different. What should I do?

If your sheet looks different, you clicked the wrong place and will have to close the property sheet and repeat this step.

Figure 2–38

 2

- Click the Unique Values property box, and then click the arrow that appears to produce a menu of available choices for Unique Values (Figure 2–39).

Figure 2–39

3

- Click Yes and then close the Query Properties sheet by clicking its Close button.

- View the query results (Figure 2–40).

Figure 2–40

Other Ways

1. Right-click second field in design grid, click Properties on shortcut menu

To Sort on Multiple Keys

The following steps sort on multiple keys. Specifically, the data is to be sorted by amount paid (low to high) within recruiter number, which means that the Recruiter Number field is the major key and the Amount Paid field is the minor key.

1

- Return to Design view.

- Clear the design grid.

- Include the Client Number, Client Name, Recruiter Number, and Amount Paid fields in the query in this order.

- Select Ascending as the sort order for both the Recruiter Number field and the Amount Paid field (Figure 2–41).

Figure 2–41

2

• View the query results (Figure 2–42).

Experiment

• Return to Design view and try other sort combinations for the Recruiter Number and Amount Paid fields, such as Ascending for Recruiter Number and Descending for Amount Paid. In each case, view the results to see the effect of the changes. When finished, select Ascending as the sort order for both fields.

Q&A

What if the Amount Paid field is to the left of the Recruiter Number?

It is important to remember that the major sort key must appear to the left of the minor sort key in the design grid. If you attempted to sort by amount paid within recruiter number, but placed the Amount Paid field to the left of the Recruiter Number field, your results would be incorrect.

Figure 2–42

To Create a Top-Values Query

Rather than show all the results of a query, you may want to show only a specified number of records or a percentage of records. Creating a **top-values query** allows you to quantify the results. When you sort records, you can limit results to those records having the highest (descending sort) or lowest (ascending sort) values. To do so, first create a query that sorts the data in the desired order. Next, use the Return box on the Design tab to change the number of records to be included from All to the desired number or percentage. The following steps show the first five records that were included in the results of the previous query.

1

• Return to Design view.

• If necessary, click Design on the Ribbon to display the Design tab.

• Click the Return box arrow on the Design tab to display the Return box menu (Figure 2–43).

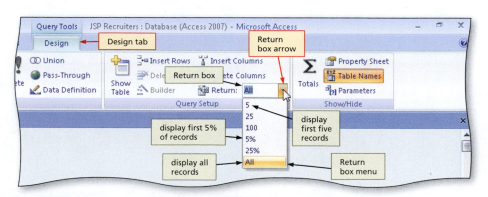

Figure 2–43

2

- Click 5 in the Return box menu to specify that the query results should contain the first five rows.

Q&A

Could I have typed the 5? What about other numbers that do not appear in the list?

Yes, you could have typed the 5. For numbers not appearing in the list, you must type the number.

- View the query results (Figure 2–44).

3

- Close the query by clicking the Close 'Query1' button.

- When asked if you want to save your changes, click the No button.

Q&A

Do I need to close the query before creating my next query?

Not necessarily. When you use a top-values query, however, it is important to change the value in the Return box back to All. If you do not change the Return value back to All, the previous value will remain in effect. Consequently, you may very well not get all the records you should in the next query. A good practice whenever you use a top-values query is to close the query as soon as you are done. That way, you will begin your next query from scratch, which guarantees that the value is set back to All.

Figure 2–44

Joining Tables

In designing a query, you need to determine whether more than one table is required. If the question being asked involves data from both the Client and Recruiter tables, for example, both tables are required for the query. Such a query may require listing the number and name of each client along with the number and name of the client's recruiter. The client's name is in the Client table, whereas the recruiter's name is in the Recruiter table. Thus, this query cannot be completed using a single table; both the Client and Recruiter tables are required. You need to **join** the tables; that is, to find records in the two tables that have identical values in matching fields (Figure 2–45). In this example, you need to find records in the Client table and the Recruiter table that have the same value in the Recruiter Number fields.

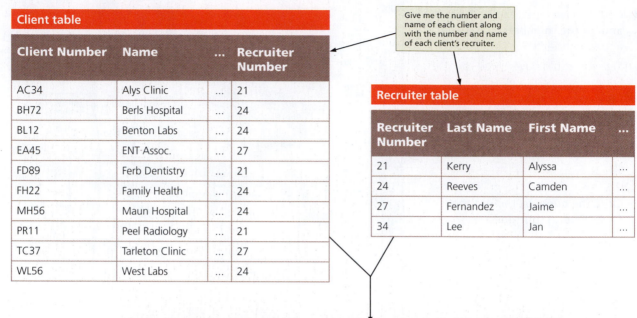

Figure 2–45

BTW

Join Types
The type of join that finds records from both tables that have identical values in matching fields is called an inner join. An inner join is the default join in Access. Outer joins are used to show all the records in one table as well as the common records; that is, the records that share the same value in the join field. In a left outer join, all rows from the table on the left are included. In a right outer join, all rows from the table on the right are included.

The following are guidelines related to joining tables.

Plan Ahead

Determine whether more than one table is required.

1. **Determine whether more than one table is required.** Examine the query or request to see if all the fields involved in the request are in one table. If the fields are in two (or more) tables, you need to join the tables.

2. **Determine the matching fields.** If joining is required, identify the matching fields in the two tables that have identical values. Look for the same column name in the two tables or for column names that are similar.

(continued)

(continued)

Plan Ahead

3. **Determine whether sorting is required.** Queries that join tables often are used as the basis for a report. If this is the case, it may be necessary to sort the results. For example, the Recruiter-Client Report is based on a query that joins the Recruiter and Client tables. The query is sorted by recruiter number and client number.

4. **Determine restrictions.** Examine the query or request to see if there are any special restrictions. For example, the query may only want clients whose current due amount is $0.00.

5. **Determine join properties.** Examine the query or request to see if you only want records from both tables that have identical values in matching fields. If you want to see records in one of the tables that do not have identical values, then you need to change the join properties. When two tables have fields with the same name, you also need to determine which table contains the field to be used in the query. For example, if you want to see all recruiters, even if they have no clients, then you should include the recruiter number from the Recruiter table in the design grid. If you want only records with identical values in matching fields, then it does not matter which matching field you select.

To Join Tables

If you have determined in the design process that you need to join tables, you will first bring field lists for both tables to the upper Pane of the Query window. Access will draw a line, called a **join line**, between matching fields in the two tables indicating that the tables are related. You then can select fields from either table. Access joins the tables automatically.

The first step is to create a new query and add the Recruiter table to the query. Then, add the Client table to the query. A join line will appear connecting the Recruiter Number fields in the two field lists. This join line indicates how the tables are related; that is, linked through these matching fields. (If you fail to give the matching fields the same name, Access will not insert the line. You can insert it manually, however, by clicking one of the two matching fields and dragging the mouse pointer to the other matching field.)

The following steps create a new query, add the Client table, and then select the appropriate fields.

1
- Click Create on the Ribbon to display the Create tab.

- Click the Query Design button to create a new query.

- Click the Recruiter table in the Show Table dialog box to select the table.

- Click the Add button to add a field list for the Recruiter table to the query (Figure 2–46).

Figure 2–46

2

- Click the Client table in the Show Table dialog box.

- Click the Add button to add a field list for the Client table.

- Close the Show Table dialog box by clicking the Close button.

- Expand the size of the field lists so all the fields in the Recruiter and Client tables appear (Figure 2–47).

Q&A I didn't get a join line. What should I do?

Ensure that the names of the matching fields are exactly the same, the data types are the same, and the matching field is the primary key in one of the two tables. If all of these are true and you still don't have a join line, you can produce one by pointing to one of the matching fields and dragging to the other matching field.

Figure 2–47

3

- In the design grid, include the Recruiter Number, Last Name, and First Name fields from the Recruiter table as well as the Client Number and Client Name fields from the Client table.

- Select Ascending as the sort order for both the Recruiter Number field and the Client Number field (Figure 2–48).

Figure 2–48

4

- View the query results (Figure 2–49).

Figure 2–49

To Save the Query

The following steps save the query.

1

- Click the Save button on the Quick Access Toolbar to display the Save As dialog box.

- Type `Recruiter-Client Query` as the query name (Figure 2–50).

2

- Click the OK button to save the query.

Figure 2–50

To Change Join Properties

Normally records that do not match do not appear in the results of a join query. A recruiter such as Jan Lee, for whom no clients currently exist, for example, would not appear. To cause such a record to be displayed, you need to change the **join properties**, which are the properties that indicate which records appear in a join, of the query, as in the following steps.

1

• Return to Design view.

• Right-click the join line to produce a shortcut menu (Figure 2–51).

Q&A

I don't see Join Properties on my shortcut menu. What should I do?

If Join Properties does not appear on your shortcut menu, you did not point to the appropriate portion of the join line. You will need to point to the correct portion and right-click again.

Figure 2–51

2

• Click Join Properties on the shortcut menu to display the Join Properties dialog box (Figure 2–52).

Q&A

How do the options in the Join Properties dialog box match the various types of joins described earlier?

Option button 1 gives an inner join, option button 2 gives a left join, and option button 3 gives a right join.

Figure 2–52

3

- Click option button 2 to include all records from the Recruiter table regardless of whether they match any clients.

- Click the OK button.

- View the query results by clicking the View button (Figure 2–53).

- Click the Save button on the Quick Access Toolbar.

 Experiment

- Return to Design view, change the Join properties, and select option button 3. View the results to see the effect of this option. When done, return to Design view, change the Join properties, and once again select option button 2.

Figure 2–53

4

- Close the Recruiter-Client Query by clicking the Close 'Recruiter-Client Query' button. Click No if asked to save the changes to the query.

To Create a Report Involving a Join

The following steps create the report shown in Figure 2–54. The records in the report are sorted (ordered) by Client Number within Recruiter Number. To ensure that the records appear in this order, the steps specify that the Recruiter Number and Client Number fields are sort keys.

Recruiter-Client Report

Recruiter Number	Last Name	First Name	Client Number	Client Name
21	Kerry	Alyssa	AC34	Alys Clinic
21	Kerry	Alyssa	FD89	Ferb Dentistry
21	Kerry	Alyssa	PR11	Peel Radiology
24	Reeves	Camden	BH72	Berls Hospital
24	Reeves	Camden	BL12	Benton Labs
24	Reeves	Camden	FH22	Family Health
24	Reeves	Camden	MH56	Maun Hospital
24	Reeves	Camden	WL56	West Labs
27	Fernandez	Jaime	EA45	ENT Assoc.
27	Fernandez	Jaime	TC37	Tarleton Clinic
34	Lee	Jan		

Figure 2–54

1

- Show the Navigation Pane and be sure the Recruiter-Client Query is selected in the Navigation Pane.

Q&A

I have two copies of Recruiter-Client Query. Does it matter which one I use?

No. There are two copies because the recruiter-Client Query involves two tables. It does not matter which one you select.

- Click Create on the Ribbon to display the Create tab.

- Click the Report Wizard button to display the Report Wizard dialog box (Figure 2–55).

Figure 2–55

2

- Click the Add All Fields button to add all the fields in the Recruiter-Client Query.

- Click the Next button to display the next Report Wizard screen (Figure 2–56).

Figure 2–56

- Because you will not specify any grouping, click the Next button in the Report Wizard dialog box to display the next Report Wizard screen.

- Because you already specified the sort order in the query, click the Next button again to display the next Report Wizard screen.

- Make sure that Tabular is selected as the Layout and Portrait is selected as the Orientation.

- Click the Next button to display the next Report Wizard screen.

- Be sure the Module style is selected.

- Click the Next button to display the next Report Wizard screen.

Figure 2–57

- Erase the current title, and then type Recruiter-Client Report as the new title.

- Click the Finish button to produce the report (Figure 2–57).

- Click the Close button for the Recruiter-Client Report to remove the report from the screen.

To Print a Report

Once you have created a report, you can print it at any time. The layout will reflect the layout you created. The data in the report will always reflect current data. The following step prints the Recruiter-Client Report.

1. With the Recruiter-Client Report selected in the Navigation Pane, click the Office Button, point to Print on the Office button menu, and then click Quick Print on the Print submenu to print the report.

To Restrict the Records in a Join

Sometimes you will want to join tables, but you will not want to include all possible records. For example, you would like to create a report showing only those clients whose Amount Paid is greater than $20,000, but you do not want the Amount Paid field to appear in the results. In such cases, you will relate the tables and include fields just as you did before. You also will include criteria. To include only those clients whose amount paid is more than $20,000.00, you will include >20000 as a criterion for the Amount Paid field.

The following steps modify the Recruiter-Client query to restrict the records that will be included in the join.

- Open the Recruiter-Client Query in Design view and hide the Navigation Pane.

- Add the Amount Paid field to the query.

- Type >20000 as the criterion for the Amount Paid field and then click the Show check box for the Amount Paid field to remove the check mark (Figure 2–58).

Figure 2–58

- View the query results (Figure 2–59).

- Close the query by clicking the Close 'Recruiter-Client Query' button.

- When asked if you want to save your changes, click the No button.

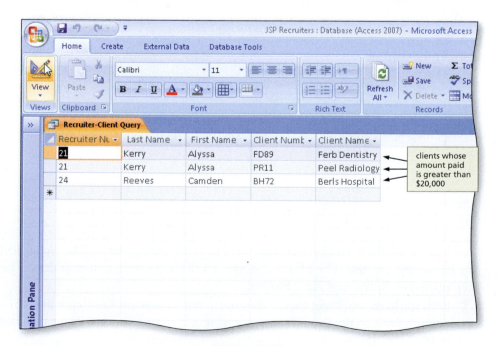

Figure 2–59

Calculations

If you have determined that a special calculation is required for a query, you then need to determine whether the calculation is an individual record calculation (for example, adding the values in two fields) or a group calculation (for example, finding the total of the values in a particular field on all the records).

JSP Recruiters may want to know the total amount (amount paid plus current due) from each client. This would seem to pose a problem because the Client table does not include a field for total amount. You can calculate it, however, because the total amount is equal to the amount paid plus the current due. A field that can be computed from other fields is called a **calculated field**. A calculated field is an individual record calculation.

JSP also may want to calculate the average amount paid for the clients of each recruiter. That is, they want the average for the clients of recruiter 21, the average for the clients of recruiter 24, and so on. This type of calculation is called a group calculation, because it involves groups of records. In this example, the clients of recruiter 21 would form one group, the clients of recruiter 24 would be a second, and the clients of recruiter 27 form a third group.

The following are guidelines related to calculations in queries.

Plan Ahead

Determine whether calculations are required.

1. **Determine whether calculations are required.** Examine the query or request to see if there are special calculations to be included. Look for words such as "total," "sum," "compute," or "calculate."

2. **Determine a name for the calculated field.** If calculations are required, decide on the name for the field. Assign a name that helps identify the contents of the field. For example, if you are adding the cost of a number of items, the name "Total Cost" would be appropriate. The name, also called an **alias**, becomes the column name when the query is run.

3. **Determine the format for the calculated field.** Determine how the calculated field should appear. If the calculation involves monetary amounts, you would use the currency format. If the calculated value contains decimals, determine how many decimal places to display.

To Use a Calculated Field in a Query

If you have determined that you need a calculated field in a query, you enter a name (alias) for the calculated field, a colon, and then the expression in one of the columns in the Field row. Any fields included in the expression must be enclosed in square brackets [ ]. For the total amount, for example, you will type Total Amount:[Amount Paid]+[Current Due] as the expression.

You can type the expression directly into the Field row. You will not be able to see the entire entry, however, because the Field row is not large enough. The preferred way is to select the column in the Field row and then use the Zoom command on its shortcut menu. When Access displays the Zoom dialog box, you can enter the expression.

You are not restricted to addition in calculations. You can use subtraction (-), multiplication (*), or division (/). You also can include parentheses in your calculations to indicate which calculations should be done first.

The steps on the next page use a calculated field to display the number, name, amount paid, current due, and the total amount for all clients.

1

- Create a query with a field list for the Client table.

- Add the Client Number, Client Name, Amount Paid, and Current Due fields to the query.

- Right-click the Field row in the first open column in the design grid to display a shortcut menu (Figure 2–60).

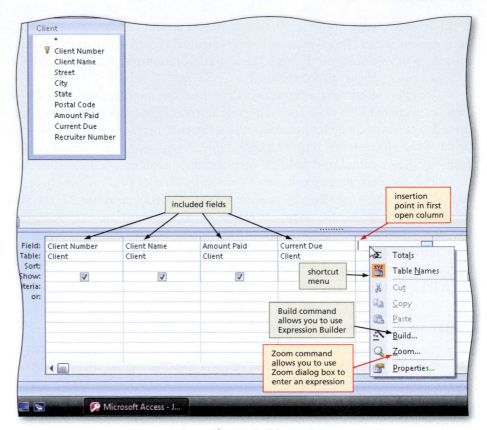

Figure 2–60

2

- Click Zoom on the shortcut menu to display the Zoom dialog box.

- Type `Total Amount:[Amount Paid]+[Current Due]` in the Zoom dialog box (Figure 2–61).

 Q&A

Do I always need to put square brackets around field names?

If the field name does not contain spaces, square brackets are technically not necessary, although it is still acceptable to use the brackets. It is a good practice, however, to get in the habit of using the brackets.

Figure 2–61

3

- Click the OK button to enter the expression (Figure 2–62).

Figure 2–62

4

- View the query results (Figure 2–63).

 Experiment

- Return to Design view and try other expressions. In at least one case, omit the Total Amount and the colon. In at least one case, intentionally misspell a field name. In each case, view the results to see the effect of your changes. When finished, re-enter the original expression.

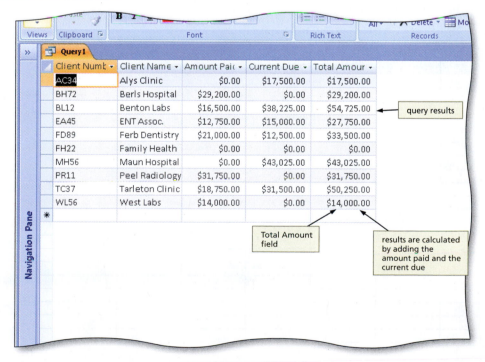

Figure 2–63

Instead of clicking Zoom on the shortcut menu, you can click Build. Access displays the Expression Builder dialog box that provides assistance in creating the expression. If you know the expression you will need, however, it is often easier to enter it using the Zoom command.

To Change a Caption

You can change the way items appear in the results of a query by changing their format. You also can change a query result's heading at the top of a column by changing the caption. Just as when you omitted duplicates, you will make this change by using a property sheet. In the property sheet, you can change the desired property, such as the format, the number of decimal places, or the caption. The following steps change the caption of the Amount Paid field to Paid and the caption of the Current Due field to Due.

- Return to Design view.

- Click Design on the Ribbon to display the Design tab.

- Click the Amount Paid field in the design grid, and then click the Property Sheet button on the Design tab.

- Click the Caption box, and then type Paid as the caption (Figure 2–64).

Q&A

My property sheet looks different. What should I do?

If your sheet looks different, you clicked the wrong place and will have to close the property sheet and repeat this step.

Figure 2–64

2

- Close the property sheet by clicking its Close button.

- Click the Current Due field in the design grid, and then click the Property Sheet button on the Design tab.

- Click the Caption box, and then type Due as the caption.

- Close the Property Sheet by clicking its Close button.

- View the query results (Figure 2–65).

3

- Click the Close 'Query1' button to close the query.

- When asked if you want to save your changes, click the No button.

Q&A

What would happen if I clicked the Yes button instead of the No button?

If you had saved the query, the changes you made to the properties would be saved in the database along with the query.

Figure 2–65

Other Ways

1. Right-click field in design grid, click Properties on shortcut menu

Calculating Statistics

For group calculations, Microsoft Access supports several built-in statistics: COUNT (count of the number of records), SUM (total), AVG (average), MAX (largest value), MIN (smallest value), STDEV (standard deviation), VAR (variance), FIRST (first value), and LAST (last value). These statistics are called aggregate functions. An **aggregate function** is a function that performs some mathematical function against a group of records. To use any of these aggregate functions in a query, you include it in the Total row in the design grid. The Total row routinely does not appear in the grid. To include it, click the Totals button on the Design tab.

To Calculate Statistics

The following steps create a new query for the Client table, include the Total row in the design grid, and then calculate the average amount paid for all clients.

- Create a new query with a field list for the Client table.

- If necessary, click Design on the Ribbon to display the Design tab.

- Add the Amount Paid field to the query.

- Click the Totals button on the Design tab to include the Total row in the design grid (Figure 2-66).

Figure 2–66

- Click the Total row in the Amount Paid column to display the Total box arrow.

- Click the Total box arrow to display the Total list (Figure 2–67).

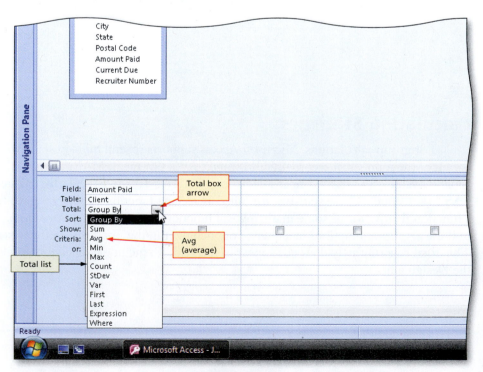

Figure 2–67

3

- Click Avg to indicate that Access is to calculate an average (Figure 2–68).

Figure 2–68

4

- View the query results (Figure 2–69).

 Experiment

- Return to Design view and try other aggregate functions. In each case, view the results to see the effect of your selection. When finished, select average once again.

Figure 2–69

To Use Criteria in Calculating Statistics

Sometimes calculating statistics for all the records in the table is appropriate. In other cases, however, you will need to calculate the statistics for only those records that satisfy certain criteria. To enter a criterion in a field, first you select Where as the entry in the Total row for the field, and then enter the criterion in the Criteria row. The following steps use this technique to calculate the average amount paid for clients of recruiter 21.

- Return to Design view.

- Include the Recruiter Number field in the design grid.

- Click the Total box arrow in the Recruiter Number column to produce a Total list (Figure 2–70).

Figure 2–70

- Click Where.

- Type 21 as the criterion for the Recruiter Number field (Figure 2–71).

Figure 2–71

- View the query results (Figure 2–72).

average amounts paid by clients of recruiter 21

Figure 2–72

To Use Grouping

Another way statistics often are used is in combination with grouping; that is, statistics are calculated for groups of records. You may, for example, need to calculate the average amount paid for the clients of each recruiter. You will want the average for the clients of recruiter 21, the average for clients of recruiter 24, and so on.

Grouping means creating groups of records that share some common characteristic. In grouping by Recruiter Number, for example, the clients of recruiter 21 would form one group, the clients of recruiter 24 would form a second, and the clients of recruiter 27 form a third group. The calculations then are made for each group. To indicate grouping in Access, select Group By as the entry in the Total row for the field to be used for grouping.

The following steps calculate the average amount paid for clients of each recruiter.

- Return to Design view and clear the design grid.

- Include the Recruiter Number field in the query.

- Include the Amount Paid field in the query.

- Select Avg as the calculation in the Total row for the Amount Paid field (Figure 2–73).

Q&A

Why didn't I need to change the entry in the Total Row for the Recruiter Number field?

Group By currently is the entry in the Total row for the Recruiter Number field, which is correct; thus, it was not changed.

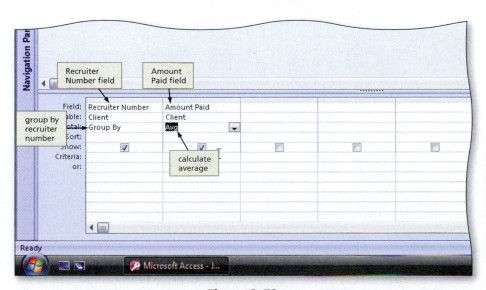

Recruiter Number field

Amount Paid field

group by recruiter number

calculate average

Figure 2–73

2

• View the query results (Figure 2–74).

3

• Close the query.

• Do not save your changes.

Figure 2–74

BTW

Certification
The Microsoft Certified Application Specialist (MCAS) program provides an opportunity for you to obtain a valuable industry credential — proof that you have the Access 2007 skills required by employers. For more information, see Appendix G or visit the Access 2007 Certification Web page (scsite.com/ac2007/cert).

Crosstab Queries

Crosstab queries are useful for summarizing data. A crosstab query calculates a statistic (for example, sum, average, or count) for data that is grouped by two different types of information. One of the types will appear down the side of the resulting datasheet, and the other will appear across the top.

For example, if you have determined that a query must summarize the sum of the amounts paid grouped by both city and recruiter number, you could have cities as the row headings, that is, down the side. You could have recruiter numbers as the column headings, that is, across the top. The entries within the data sheet represent the total of the amounts paid. Figure 2–75 shows a crosstab in which the total of amount paid is grouped by both city and recruiter number with cities down the left-hand side and recruiter numbers across the top. For example, the entry in the row labeled Fort Stewart and in the column labeled 21 represents the total of the amount paid by all clients of recruiter 21 who are located in Fort Stewart.

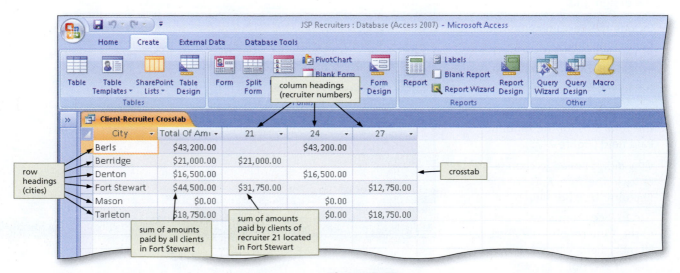

Figure 2–75

To Create a Crosstab Query

The following steps use the Crosstab Query wizard to create a crosstab query.

1

- Click Create on the Ribbon to display the Create tab.

- Click the Query Wizard button to display the New Query dialog box (Figure 2–76).

Figure 2–76

2

- Click Crosstab Query Wizard in the New Query dialog box.

- Click the OK button to display the Crosstab Query Wizard (Figure 2–77).

Figure 2–77

3

- With the Tables option button selected and the Client table selected, click the Next button to display the next Crosstab Query Wizard screen.

- Click the City field, and then click the Add Field button to select the City field for row headings (Figure 2–78).

Figure 2–78

4

- Click the Next button to display the next Crosstab Query Wizard screen.

- Click the Recruiter Number field to select the Recruiter Number field for column headings (Figure 2–79).

Figure 2–79

5

- Click the Next button to display the next Crosstab Query Wizard screen.

- Click the Amount Paid field to select the Amount Paid field for calculations.

🔍 **Experiment**

- Click other fields. For each field, examine the list of calculations that are available. When finished, click the Amount Paid field again.

- Click Sum to select Sum as the calculation to be performed (Figure 2–80).

Q&A
My list of functions is different. What did I do wrong?

Either you clicked the wrong field, or the Amount Paid field has the wrong data type. If you mistakenly assigned it the Text data type for example, you would not see Sum in the list of available calculations.

Figure 2–80

 6

- Click the Next button to display the next Crosstab Query Wizard screen.

- Type `Client-Recruiter Crosstab` as the name of the query (Figure 2–81).

 7

- Click the Finish button to produce the crosstab shown in Figure 2–75 on page AC 122.

- Close the query.

Q&A
If I want to view the crosstab at some future date, can I just open the query?

Yes.

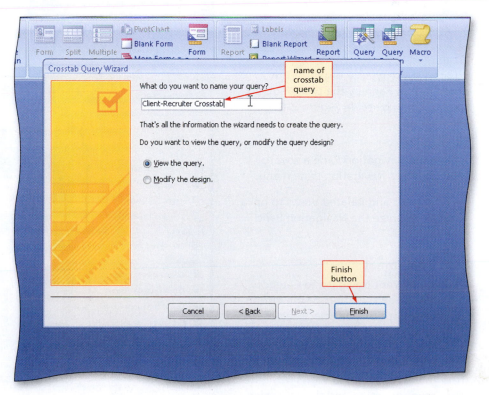

Figure 2–81

To Customize the Navigation Pane

Currently the entries in the Navigation Pane are organized by table. That is, the queries, forms, and reports associated with a particular table appear after the name of the table. In addition, all tables are included. You might want to change the way the information is organized. For example, you might wish to have all the queries appear together, all the forms appear together, and all the reports appear together, regardless of the table on which they are based. The following steps change the organization of the Navigation Pane.

- If necessary, click the Shutter Bar Open/Close Button to show the Navigation Pane.

- Click the Navigation Pane arrow to produce the Navigation Pane menu (Figure 2–82).

Q&A

If the Navigation Pane gets too cluttered, can I hide the objects in a group? For example, if the organization is by table, can I hide the objects (forms, queries, reports) for the table group and only show the table name?

Yes. Click the up arrow on the group bar. The objects under the table group will no longer appear and the up arrow will become a down arrow. To redisplay the objects, click the down arrow.

Figure 2–82

- Click Object Type to organize the Navigation Pane by the type of object rather than by table (Figure 2–83).

- Click the Navigation Pane arrow to produce the Navigation Pane menu.

- Click Tables and Related Views to once again organize the Navigation Pane by table.

Experiment

- Select different Navigate To Category options to see the effect of the option. With each option you select, select different Filter By Group options to see the effect of the filtering. When you have finished experimenting, select the Tables and Related Views Navigate To Category option and the All Tables Filter By Group option.

Figure 2–83

To Quit Access

You saved all your changes and are ready to quit Access. The following step quits Access.

 Click the Close button on the right side of the Access title bar to quit Access.

BTW

Quick Reference
For a table that lists how to complete the tasks covered in this book using the mouse, Ribbon, shortcut menu, and keyboard, see the Quick Reference Summary at the back of this book, or visit the Access 2007 Quick Reference Web page (scsite.com/ac2007/qr).

Chapter Summary

In this chapter you have learned to create queries, enter fields, enter criteria, use text and numeric data in queries, use wildcards, use compound criteria, create parameter queries, sort data in queries, join tables in queries, perform calculations in queries, create crosstab queries, and customize the Navigation Pane. The following list includes all the new Access skills you have learned in this chapter.

1. Use the Simple Query Wizard to Create a Query (AC 78)
2. Use a Criterion in a Query (AC 81)
3. Print the Results of a Query (AC 83)
4. Create a Query in Design View (AC 83)
5. Add Fields to the Design Grid (AC 85)
6. Use Text Data in a Criterion (AC 86)
7. Use a Wildcard (AC 87)
8. Use Criteria for a Field Not Included in the Results (AC 88)
9. Create a Parameter Query (AC 90)
10. Save a Query (AC 91)
11. Use a Saved Query (AC 92)
12. Use a Number in a Criterion (AC 93)
13. Use a Comparison Operator in a Criterion (AC 94)
14. Use a Compound Criterion Involving AND (AC 95)
15. Use a Compound Criterion Involving OR (AC 96)
16. Clear the Design Grid (AC 98)
17. Sort Data in a Query (AC 98)
18. Omit Duplicates (AC 100)
19. Sort on Multiple Keys (AC 101)
20. Create a Top-Values Query (AC 102)
21. Join Tables (AC 105)
22. Save the Query (AC 107)
23. Change Join Properties (AC 108)
24. Create a Report Involving a Join (AC 109)
25. Print a Report (AC 111)
26. Restrict the Records in a Join (AC 112)
27. Use a Calculated Field in a Query (AC 113)
28. Change a Caption (AC 116)
29. Calculate Statistics (AC 118)
30. Use Criteria in Calculating Statistics (AC 120)
31. Use Grouping (AC 121)
32. Create a Crosstab Query (AC 123)
33. Customize the Navigation Pane (AC 126)

 If you have a SAM user profile, you may have access to hands-on instruction, practice, and assessment. Log in to your SAM account (http://sam2007.course.com) to launch any assigned training activities or exams that relate to the skills covered in this chapter.

Learn It Online

Test your knowledge of chapter content and key terms.

Instructions: To complete the Learn It Online exercises, start your browser, click the Address bar, and then enter the Web address scsite.com/ac2007/learn. When the Access 2007 Learn It Online page is displayed, click the link for the exercise you want to complete and then read the instructions.

Chapter Reinforcement TF, MC, and SA
A series of true/false, multiple choice, and short answer questions that test your knowledge of the chapter content.

Flash Cards
An interactive learning environment where you identify chapter key terms associated with displayed definitions.

Practice Test
A series of multiple choice questions that test your knowledge of chapter content and key terms.

Who Wants To Be a Computer Genius?
An interactive game that challenges your knowledge of chapter content in the style of a television quiz show.

Wheel of Terms
An interactive game that challenges your knowledge of chapter key terms in the style of the television show *Wheel of Fortune*.

Crossword Puzzle Challenge
A crossword puzzle that challenges your knowledge of key terms presented in the chapter.

Apply Your Knowledge

Reinforce the skills and apply the concepts you learned in this chapter.

Using the Query Wizard, Creating a Parameter Query, Joining Tables, and Creating a Report
Instructions: Start Access. Open the The Bike Delivers database that you modified in Apply Your Knowledge in Chapter 1 on page AC 64. (If you did not complete this exercise, see your instructor for a copy of the modified database.)

Perform the following tasks:
1. Use the Simple Query Wizard to create a query for the Customer table. Include the Customer Name, Balance, and Courier Number in the query. Assign the name, Customer Query, to the query.
2. Create a query for the Customer table and add the Customer Number, Customer Name, Courier Number, and Balance fields to the design grid. Sort the records in descending order by Balance. Add a criterion for the Courier Number field that allows the user to enter a different courier each time the query is run. Save the query as Courier Parameter Query.
3. Create a query that joins the Courier and the Customer tables. Add the Courier Number, First Name, and Last Name fields from the Courier table and the Customer Number and Customer Name fields from the Customer table. Sort the records in ascending order by Courier Number and Customer Number. All couriers should appear in the result even if they currently have no customers. Save the query as Courier-Customer Query.
4. Create the report shown in Figure 2–84. The report uses the Courier-Customer Query.

Courier-Customer Report

Courier Number	Customer Number	First Name	Last Name	Customer Name
102	AS36	Chou	Dang	Asterman Ind.
102	CJ16	Chou	Dang	CJ Gallery
102	ME71	Chou	Dang	Mentor Group
109	AU54	Michelle	Hyde	Author Books
109	BL92	Mich...	Hyde	...m Shop

Figure 2–84

5. Submit the revised database in the format specified by your instructor.

Extend Your Knowledge

Extend the skills you learned in this chapter and experiment with new skills. You may need to use Help to complete the assignment.

Creating Crosstab Queries, Creating Queries Using Criteria

Instructions: Start Access. Open the Groom n Fluff database. See the inside back cover of this book for instructions for downloading the Data Files for Students, or see your instructor for information on accessing the files required in this book.

Groom n Fluff is a small pet grooming business. The owner has created an Access database in which to store information about the customers she serves and the pet groomers she employs. You will create the crosstab query shown in Figure 2–85. You also will query the database using specified criteria.

Figure 2–85

Continued >

Extend Your Knowledge *continued*

Perform the following tasks:

1. Create the crosstab query shown in Figure 2–85 on the previous page. The crosstab groups the average of customers' balances by city and groomer number.

2. Create a query to find all customers who do not live in Grant City. Include the Customer Number, Last Name, and Balance fields in the design grid. Save the query as Not Criteria Query.

3. Create a query to find all customers who do not have a telephone number. Include the Customer Number, Last Name, First Name, Street, and City fields in the query results. Save the query as Missing Values Query.

4. Create a query to find all customers whose balance is between $20.00 and $60.00. Include the Customer Number, Last Name, and Balance fields in the design grid. Save the query as Number Range Query.

5. Create a query to find all customers where the groomer number is 203 or 205 and the balance is greater than $40.00. Include the Customer Number, Last Name, First Name, Balance, and Groomer Number fields in the design grid. Save the query as Compound Criteria Query.

6. Change the database properties, as specified by your instructor. Submit the revised database in the format specified by your instructor.

Make It Right

Analyze a database and correct all errors and/or improve the design.

Correcting Errors in the Query Design

Instructions: Start Access. Open the Keep It Green database. See the inside back cover of this book for instructions for downloading the Data Files for Students, or see your instructor for information on accessing the files required in this book.

Keep It Green is a database maintained by a small landscaping business. The queries shown in Figure 2–86 contain a number of errors that need to be corrected before the queries run properly. The sort query shown in Figure 2–86a displays the query results in the proper order (First Name, Last Name, Street, City) but it is sorted incorrectly. The query results should be sorted by last name within city in ascending order. Also the caption for the Street field should be Address. Save the query with your changes.

When you try to run the join query for the Keep It Green database, the message shown in Figure 2–86b appears. The query joins the Worker table and the Customer table. It also calculates the total amount for each customer. The query should be sorted in alphabetical order by worker last name and customer last name. Correct the error that is causing the message shown in Figure 2–86b and sort the records properly. Save the query with your changes.

Change the database properties, as specified by your instructor. Submit the revised database in the format specified by your instructor.

STUDENT ASSIGNMENTS

(a) Incorrect Sort Query

(b) Incorrect Join Query

Figure 2–86

In the Lab

Design, create, modify, and/or use a database following the guidelines, concepts, and skills presented in this chapter. Labs are listed in order of increasing difficulty.

Lab 1: Querying the JMS TechWizards Database

Problem: The management of JMS TechWizards has determined a number of questions it wants the database management system to answer. You must obtain answers to the questions posed by management.

Instructions: Use the database created in the In the Lab 1 of Chapter 1 on page AC 67 for this assignment or see your instructor for information on accessing the files required for this book. Perform the following tasks:

1. Open the JMS TechWizards database and create a new query for the Client table that includes the Client Number, Client Name, and Technician Number fields in the design grid for all clients where the technician number is 23. Save the query as Lab 2-1 Step 1 Query.

2. Create a query that includes the Client Number, Client Name, and Paid fields for all clients located in Liberty Corner with a paid amount greater than $500.00. Save the query as Lab2-1 Step 2 Query.

3. Create a query that includes the Client Number, Client Name, Street, and City fields for all clients whose names begin with Gr. Save the query as Lab 2-1 Step 3 Query.

4. Create a query that lists all cities in descending order. Each city should appear only once. Save the query as Lab 2-1 Step 4 Query.

5. Create a query that allows the user to enter the city to search when the query is run. The query results should display the Client Number, Client Name, and Billed. Test the query by searching for those records where the client is located in Anderson. Save the query as Client-City Query.

Continued >

STUDENT ASSIGNMENTS

6. Include the Client Number, Client Name, and Billed fields in the design grid. Sort the records in descending order by the Billed field. Display only the top 25 percent of the records in the query result. Save the query as Lab 2-1 Step 6 Query.

7. Join the Technician and the Client table. Include the Technician Number, First Name, and Last Name fields from the Technician table. Include the Client Number, Client Name, and Billed from the Client table. Sort the records in ascending order by technician's last name and client name. All technicians should appear in the result even if they currently have no clients. Save the query as Technician-Client query.

8. Open the Technician-Client query in Design view and remove the Client table. Add the Hourly Rate field to the design grid following the Last Name field. Calculate the number of hours each technician has worked (YTD Earnings/Hourly Rate). Assign the alias Hours Worked to the calculated field. Change the caption for the Hourly Rate field to Rate. Display hours worked as an integer (0 decimal places). Use the Save As command to save the query as Lab 2-1 Step 8 Query.

9. Create a query to display the average billed amount for all clients. Save the query as Lab 2-1 Step 9 Query.

10. Create a query to count the number of clients for technician 23. Save the query as Lab 2-1 Step 10 Query.

11. Create a query to display the average billed amount for each technician. Save the query as Lab 2-1 Step 11 Query.

12. Create the crosstab shown in Figure 2–87. The crosstab groups total of clients' paid amounts by city and technician number. Save the crosstab as City-Technician Crosstab.

13. Submit the revised database in the format specified by your instructor.

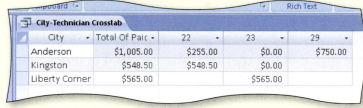

City	Total Of Paic	22	23	29
Anderson	$1,005.00	$255.00	$0.00	$750.00
Kingston	$548.50	$548.50	$0.00	
Liberty Corner	$565.00		$565.00	

Figure 2–87

In the Lab

Lab 2: Querying the Hockey Fan Zone Database

Problem: The management of the Hockey Fan Zone store has determined a number of questions it wants the database management system to answer. You must obtain answers to the questions posed by management.

Instructions: Use the database created in the In the Lab 2 of Chapter 1 on page AC 68 for this assignment, or see your instructor for information on accessing the files required for this book. Perform the following tasks:

1. Open the Hockey Fan Zone database and use the query wizard to create a query that includes the Item Number, Description, On Hand, and Cost fields for all records in the Item table. Name the query Lab 2-2 Step 1 Query.

2. Create a query that includes the Item Number, Description, Cost, and Supplier Code fields for all products where the Supplier Code is LG. Save the query as Lab 2-2 Step 2 Query.

3. Create a query that includes the Item Number and Description fields for all products where the description starts with the letter B. Save the query as Lab 2-2 Step 3 Query.

4. Create a query that includes the Item Number and Description field for all products with a cost less than $5.00. Save the query as Lab 2-2 Step 4 Query.

5. Create a query that includes the Item Number and Description field for all products with a selling price greater than $15.00. Save the query as Lab 2-2 Step 5 Query.

6. Create a query that includes all fields for all products with a selling price greater than $10.00 and where the number on hand is fewer than 10. Save the query as Lab 2-2 Step 6 Query.

7. Create a query that includes all fields for all products that have a selling price greater than $15.00 or a supplier code of AC. Save the query as Lab 2-2 Step 7 Query.

8. Join the Supplier table and the Item table. Include the Supplier Code and Supplier Name fields from the Supplier table and the Item Number, Description, On Hand, and Cost fields from the Item table. Sort the records in ascending order by Supplier Code and Item Number. Save the query as Supplier-Item Query. Note that the Report Wizard limits the size of the On Hand column header because it is a number field.

9. Create the report shown in Figure 2–88. The report uses the Supplier-Item query and the Module style.

Supplier-Item Report

Supplier Code	Item Number	Supplier Name	Description	Hand	Cost
AC	5923	Ace Clothes	Jersey	12	$21.45
AC	7810	Ace Clothes	Tee Shirt	32	$9.50
LG	3663	Logo Goods	Ball Cap	30	$11.15
LG	4563	Logo Goods	Earrings	10	$4.50
LG	4593	Logo Goods	Foam Finger	25	$2.95
LG	7930	Logo Goods	Visor	9	$11.95
MN	3683	Mary's Novelties	Bumper Sticker	50	$0.95
MN	6189	Mary's Novelties	Koozies	35	$2.00
MN	6343	Mary's Novelties	Note Cube	7	$5.75

Figure 2–88

10. Create a query that includes the Item Number, Description, On Hand, and Cost fields. Calculate the inventory value (on hand * cost) for all records in the table. Change the caption for the On Hand column to In Stock. Format inventory value as currency with two decimal places. Sort the records in descending order by inventory value. Save the query as Lab 2-2 Step 10 Query.

11. Create a query that calculates and displays the average cost of all items. Save the query as Lab 2-2 Step 11 Query.

12. Create a query that calculates and displays the average cost of items grouped by supplier code. Save the query as Lab 2-2 Step 12 Query.

13. Submit the revised database in the format specified by your instructor.

In the Lab

Lab 3: Querying the Ada Beauty Supply Database

Problem: The management of Ada Beauty Supply has determined a number of questions it wants the database management system to answer. You must obtain answers to the questions posed by management.

Instructions: Use the database created in the In the Lab 3 of Chapter 1 on page AC 69 for this assignment, or see your instructor for information on accessing the files required for this book. For Part 1 and Part 3, save each query using a format similar to the following: Lab 2-3 Part 1a Query, Lab 2-3 Part 3a Query, and so on. Submit the revised database in the format specified by your instructor.

Instructions Part 1: Create a new query for the Customer table and include the Customer Number, Customer Name, Balance, and Amount Paid fields in the design grid. Answer the following questions: (a) Which customers' names begin with C? (b) Which customers are located on Devon? (c) Which customers have a balance of $0.00? (d) Which customers have a balance greater than $200.00 and have an amount paid less than $800.00? (e) Which two customers have the highest balances? (f) For each customer, what is the total of the balance and amount paid amounts?

Instructions Part 2: Join the Sales Rep and the Customer table. Include the Sales Rep Number, First Name, and Last Name from the Sales Rep table and the Customer Number, Customer Name, and Amount Paid from the Customer table in the design grid. Sort the records in ascending order by Sales Rep Number and Customer Number. All sales reps should appear in the result even if they currently have no customers. Save the query as Sales Rep-Customer Query.

Instructions Part 3: Calculate the following statistics: (a) What is the average balance for customers assigned to sales rep 44? (b) What is the total balance for all customers? (c) What is the total amount paid for each sales rep?

Cases and Places

Apply your creative thinking and problem solving skills to design and implement a solution.

● EASIER   ●● MORE DIFFICULT

● 1: Querying the Second Hand Goods Database

Use the Second Hand Goods database you created in Cases and Places 1 in Chapter 1 on page AC 71 for this assignment, or see your instructor for information on accessing the files required for this book. Create queries for the following:

a. Find the number and description of all items that contain the word Table.

b. Find the item number, description, and condition of the item that has the earliest posting date.

c. Find the total price of each item available for sale. Show the item description and total price.

d. Find the seller of each item. Show the seller's first name and last name as well as the item description, price, quantity, and date posted. Sort the results by item description within seller last name.

e. Create a parameter query that will allow the user to enter an item description when the query is run. The user should see all fields in the query result.

f. Find all items posted between June 1, 2007 and June 4, 2007. The user should see all fields in the query result.

Submit the revised database in the format specified by your instructor.

● 2: Querying the BeachCondo Rentals Database

Use the BeachCondo Rentals database you created in Cases and Places 2 in Chapter 1 on page AC 71 for this assignment, or see your instructor for information on accessing the files required for this book. Create queries for the following:

a. Find all units that rent for less than $1,000 per week and have at least two bedrooms. The user should see all fields in the query result.

b. Find all units that are on the fourth floor. (Hint: The first digit of the Unit Number field indicates the floor.) Include the Unit Number and the Weekly Rate fields in the query result.

c. Find all units that have more than one bedroom and more than one bathroom and provide linens. Include the Unit Number, Bedrooms, and Weekly Rate fields in the query result.

d. Owner BE20 offers a 15 percent discount on the weekly rate if renters rent for more than one week. What is the discounted weekly rental rate for his units? Your result should include the unit number, bedrooms, bathrooms, sleeps, and discounted weekly rate in your result. Be sure the discounted rate appears as currency.

e. List the owner's first and last name as well as telephone number. Also include the unit number and the weekly rate. All owners should appear in the result even if they currently have no rental units.

f. Find the highest and lowest weekly rate.

Submit the revised database in the format specified by your instructor.

●● 3: Querying the Restaurant Database

Use the restaurant database you created in Cases and Places 3 in Chapter 1 on page AC 71 for this assignment, or see your instructor for information on accessing the files required for this book. Using the Plan Ahead guidelines presented in this chapter, determine at least five questions the conference director might want to ask the database. Using a word processing program, such as Microsoft Word, write the questions in your own words. Then, design the queries for Access. Run and save each query. Submit the Word document and the revised database in the format specified by your instructor.

Continued >

•• 4: Designing Queries to Help in Your Job Search

Make It Personal

Use the contacts database you created in Cases and Places 4 in Chapter 1 on page AC 71 for this assignment, or see your instructor for information on accessing the files required for this book. Consider your own personal job situation. What questions would you want to ask this database? Using a word processing program, such as Microsoft Word, write the questions in your own words. Can your database answer the questions that you listed? If it can, design the queries for Access. Run and save each query. In your Word document, identify which questions were posed to Access and which questions could not be answered. For questions that could not be answered, explain why your database cannot answer the question. Submit the Word document and the revised database in the format specified by your instructor.

•• 5: Creating Queries to Analyze Data

Working Together

Obtain a copy of the weather page of your local newspaper. As a team, choose 30 cities of interest. Create a database that contains one table and has five fields (City, State or Province, High Temp, Low Temp, Sky). Use the newspaper's abbreviations for Sky; for example, c for cloudy, r for rain and so on. Create queries that do the following:

a. Display the five cities with the highest high temperatures.

b. Calculate the difference between the high and low temperatures for each city.

c. Display the average high and low temperature for all cities.

d. List the states or provinces in your table. Each state or province should appear only once.

Write a one-page paper that explains what the team learned from querying the database and any conclusions you can draw about the data — for example, describe the Sky conditions for the cities with the least difference in high and low temperature. Submit the assignment in the format specified by your instructor.

3 | Maintaining a Database

Objectives

You will have mastered the material in this chapter when you can:

- Add, change, and delete records
- Search for records
- Filter records
- Update a table design
- Format a datasheet
- Use action queries to update records

- Specify validation rules, default values, and formats
- Create and use single-valued and multivalued Lookup fields
- Specify referential integrity
- Use a subdatasheet
- Sort records

3 | Maintaining a Database

Introduction

Once a database has been created and loaded with data, it must be maintained. **Maintaining the database** means modifying the data to keep it up-to-date, such as adding new records, changing the data for existing records, and deleting records. Updating can include mass updates or mass deletions; that is, updates to, or deletions of, many records at the same time.

Maintenance of a database can also involve the need to **restructure the database** periodically; that is, to change the database structure. Restructuring can include adding new fields — including both Lookup and multivalued fields — to a table, changing the characteristics of existing fields, and removing existing fields. It also includes the creation of validation rules and referential integrity. Validation rules ensure validity of the data in the database, while referential integrity ensures the validity of the relationships.

Maintaining a database also can include filtering records, a process that ensures that only the records that satisfy some criterion appear when viewing and updating the data in a table. Changing the appearance of a datasheet is a maintenance activity. Finally, backing up the database as well as compacting and repairing a database are database maintenance tasks as well.

Project — Maintaining a Database

JSP Recruiters faces the task of keeping its database up-to-date. As the agency takes on new clients and recruiters, it will need to add new records, make changes to existing records, and delete records. JSP managers have found they must change the structure of the database to categorize the clients by type. They will do this by adding a Client Type field to the Client table. They also want to track the specialties that are of interest to clients. They will do so by adding a Specialties Needed field to the Client table. Because clients may need more than one specialty, this field will be a multivalued field. Along with these changes, JSP staff want to change the appearance of a datasheet when displaying data.

JSP would like the ability to make mass updates, that is, to update or delete many records in a single operation. They want rules that make sure users can enter only valid data into the database, and they want to ensure that it is not possible for the database to contain a client who is not associated with a specific recruiter. Finally, they want to improve the efficiency of certain types of processing, specifically sorting and retrieving data.

Figure 3–1 summarizes some of the various types of activities involved in maintaining the JSP Recruiters database.

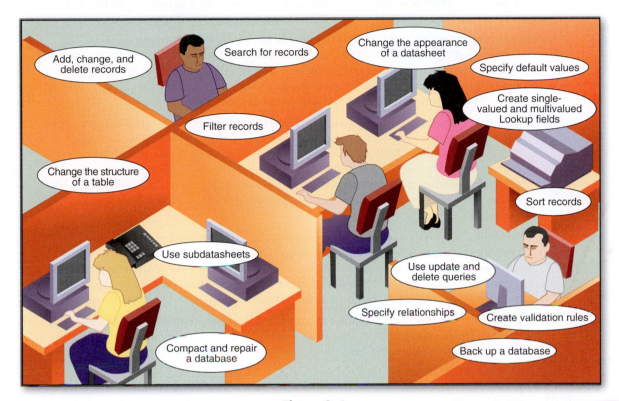

Figure 3–1

Overview

As you read through this chapter, you will learn how to maintain a database by performing these general tasks:

• Add, change, and delete records.

• Filter records so that only those records that satisfy some criterion appear in a datasheet or form.

• Change the structure of a table.

• Make mass changes to a table.

• Create validation rules to ensure that the database contains only valid data.

• Change the appearance of a datasheet.

• Enforce relationships by creating referential integrity.

• Order records.

• Perform special database operations such as backing up a database and compacting a database.

**Plan
Ahead**

Database Maintenance Guidelines

1. **Determine when it is necessary to add, change, or delete records in a database.** Decide when updates are necessary. Also determine whether the updates are to be made to individual records or whether mass updates would be more efficient. For example, if a state changes an area code, a mass update would be more efficient.

2. **Determine whether you should filter records.** For each situation where a user will be working with a table in the database, examine whether it might be desirable to have the records filtered, that is, have only those records that satisfy some criterion appear. For example, if a user only wants to make changes to clients in a particular city, it would be easier to view only those records rather than all the records in the table.

3. **Determine whether additional fields are necessary or whether existing fields should be deleted.** Have there been any changes to the initial requirements that would require the addition of a field (or fields) to one of the tables? If so, you will need to add the field to the appropriate table. Also, now that the database has been in operation for a period of time, determine whether all the fields actually are being used. If some fields are not in use, verify that they are, in fact, no longer needed. If so, you can delete the field from the table.

4. **Determine whether validation rules, default values, and formats are necessary.** Can you improve the accuracy of the data entry process by enforcing data validation? What values are allowed for a particular field? Are there some fields in which one particular value is used more than another? You can control the values that are entered in a field by modifying the table design to include default values, formats, and validation rules.

5. **Determine whether changes to the format of a datasheet are desirable.** Can you improve the appearance of the Datasheet view of your tables? Once you have decided on a particular appearance, it is a good idea to be consistent throughout all your tables except in special circumstances.

6. **Identify related tables in order to implement relationships between the tables.** Examine the database design you created earlier to identify related tables. For each pair of related tables, you will need to make decisions about the implementation of the relationship between the tables.

    When necessary, more specific details concerning the above decisions and/or actions are presented at appropriate points in the chapter. The chapter also will identify the use of these guidelines in database maintenance tasks such as those shown in Figure 3–1 on the previous page.

Starting Access

If you are using a computer to step through the project in this chapter and you want your screen to match the figures in this book, you should change your screen's resolution to 1024 × 768. For information about how to change a computer's resolution, read Appendix E.

To Start Access

The following steps, which assume Windows Vista is running, start Access.

1 Click the Start button on the Windows Vista taskbar to display the Start menu.

2 Click All Programs at the bottom of the left Pane on the Start menu to display the All Programs list and then click Microsoft Office in the All Programs list to display the Microsoft Office list.

3 Click Microsoft Office Access 2007 on the Microsoft Office list to start Access and display the Getting Started with Microsoft Office Access window.

4 If the Access window is not maximized, click the Maximize button on its title bar to maximize the window.

> **Note:** If you are using Windows XP, see Appendix F for alternate steps.

To Open a Database

In Chapter 1, you created your database on a USB flash drive using the file name, JSP Recruiters. There are two ways to open the file containing your database. If the file you created appears in the Recent Documents list, you can click it to open the file. If not, you can use the More button to open the file. The following steps use the More button to open the JSP Recruiters database from the USB flash drive.

1 With your USB flash drive connected to one of the computer's USB ports, click the More button to display the Open dialog box.

2 If the Folders list is displayed below the Folders button, click the Folders button to remove the Folders list.

3 If necessary, click Computer in the Favorite Links section and then double-click UDISK 2.0 (E:) to select the USB flash drive, as the new open location. (Your drive letter might be different.)

4 Click JSP Recruiters to select the file name.

5 Click the Open button to open the database.

6 If a Security Warning appears, click the Options button to display the Microsoft Office Security Options dialog box.

7 Click the Enable this content option button.

8 Click the OK button to enable the content.

> **Note:** If you are using Windows XP, see Appendix F for alternate steps.

Updating Records

Keeping the data in a database up-to-date requires updating records in three ways: adding new records, changing the data in existing records, and deleting existing records.

Adding Records

In Chapter 1, you added records to a database using Datasheet view; that is, as you added records, the records appeared on the screen in a datasheet. The data looked like a table. When you need to add additional records, you can use the same techniques.

In Chapter 1, you used a split form to view records. The split form contained both a form and a datasheet. You can use either portion to add records. You also can use a simple form, that is, a form that does not contain a datasheet. Whether you use a simple form or the form portion of a split form, you can use the form to update the table. To add new records, change existing records, or delete records, you use the same techniques you used in Datasheet view. The following steps create a simple form and then add a record to the Client table using the form.

To Create a Simple Form

Rather than using a split form, you may wish just to view the data in a form without also having a datasheet on the screen. If you already have created such a form, you can open it. If not, you can create a simple form to use. The following steps create a simple form.

1

- Show the Navigation Pane if it is currently hidden.

- If necessary, click the Client table in the Navigation Pane to select it.

- Click Create on the Ribbon to display the Create tab (Figure 3–2).

Figure 3–2

2

• Click the Form button
on the Create tab to
create a simple form
(Figure 3–3).

Q&A

How can I tell which
view of the form
is currently on the
screen?

Point to the button
that is highlighted in
the lower-right cor-
ner of the screen. The
ScreenTip indicates
the current view.
At the present time,
the form appears in
Layout view.

Q&A

Which view should I
use if I want to enter
records?

Form view.

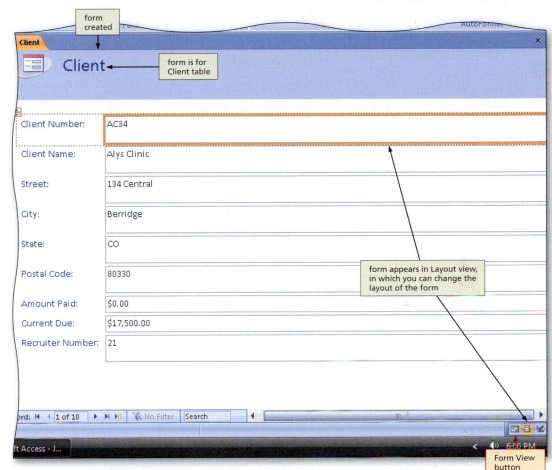

Figure 3–3

3

• Click the Form View button to
display the form in Form view
(Figure 3–4).

Q&A

Could I use the View button to
display the form in Form view?

Yes. Click the arrow at the
bottom of the button and then
click Form View.

 Experiment

• Click the various navigation
buttons (First record, Next
record, Previous record, and
Last record) to see each
button's effect. Click the
Current Record box, change
the record number, and press
the ENTER key to see how to
move to a specific record.

Figure 3–4

To Use a Form to Add Records

Once a form is open in Form view you can add records using the same techniques you used to add records in Datasheet view. The following steps use the form just created to add records.

- Click the New (blank) record button on the Navigation bar to enter a new record, and then type the data for the new record as shown in Figure 3–5. Press the TAB key after typing the data in each field, except after typing the data for the final field (Recruiter Number).

- Press the TAB key to complete the entry of the record.

- Click the Close 'Client' button to close the Client form.

- Click the No button when asked if you want to save your changes.

Q&A Why not save the form?

If you wish to use this form frequently in the future, you would probably save it. It is very easy to re-create the form whenever you need it, however.

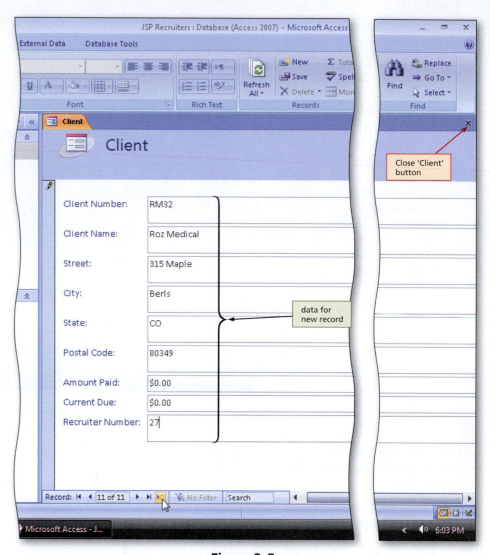

Figure 3–5

Other Ways

1. Click New button on Ribbon
2. Press CTRL+PLUS SIGN (+)

To Search for a Record

In the database environment, **searching** means looking for records that satisfy some criteria. Looking for the client whose number is MH56 is an example of searching. The queries in Chapter 2 also were examples of searching. Access had to locate those records that satisfied the criteria.

A need for searching also exists when using Form view or Datasheet view. To update client MH56, for example, first you need to find the client.

The following steps show how to search for the client whose number is MH56.

1

- Right-click Client Form in the Navigation Pane and click Open on the shortcut menu to open the form in Form view.

- Hide the Navigation Pane (Figure 3–6).

Q&A

Which command on the shortcut menu gives me Form view? I see both Layout view and Design view, but no option for Form view.

The Open command opens the form in Form view.

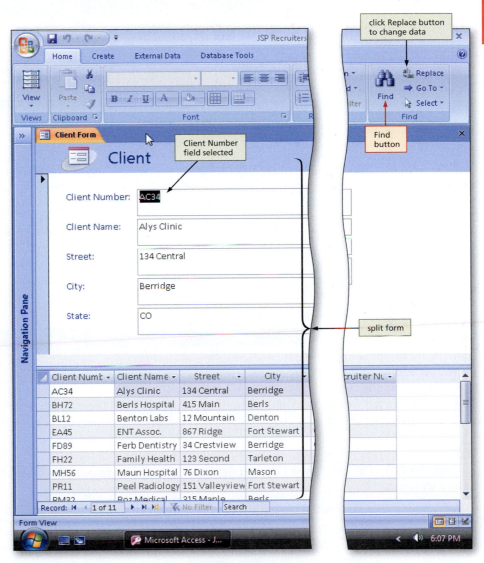

Figure 3–6

2

- Click the Find button on the Home tab to display the Find and Replace dialog box.

- Type MH56 in the Find What text box.

- Click the Find Next button in the Find and Replace dialog box to find client MH56 (Figure 3–7).

Q&A

Can I also find records in Datasheet view or in Form view?

Yes. You use the same process to find records whether you are viewing the data with split form, in Datasheet view, or in Form view.

Experiment

- Find records using other client numbers. Try to find a record using a client number that does not

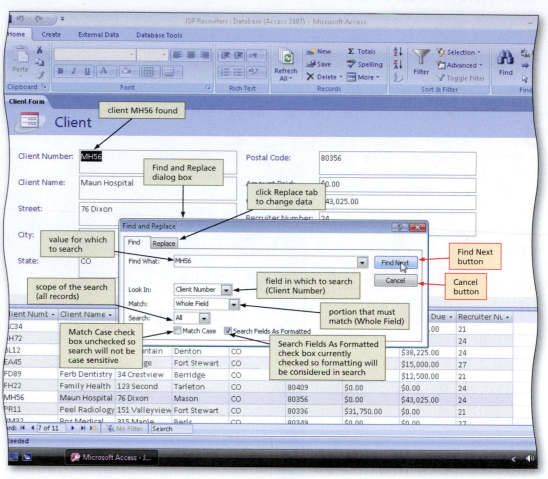

Figure 3–7

exist. Click in a different field and try to find records based on the value in that field. Try to use wildcards just as you did in queries. When done, once again locate client MH56.

3

- Click the Cancel button in the Find and Replace dialog box to remove the dialog box from the screen.

Q&A

Why does the button in the dialog box read Find Next rather than simply Find?

In some cases, after locating a record that satisfies a criterion, you might need to find the next record that satisfies the same criterion. For example, if you just found the first client whose recruiter number is 24, you then may want to find the second such client, then the third, and so on. To do so, click the Find Next button. You will not need to retype the value each time.

Q&A

Can I replace one value with another using this dialog box?

Yes. Either click the Replace button on the Ribbon or the Replace tab in the Find and Replace dialog box. You then can enter both the value to find and the replacement value.

Other Ways

1. Press CTRL+F

To Update the Contents of a Record

After locating the record to be changed, select the field to be changed by clicking the field. You also can press the TAB key repeatedly. Then make the appropriate changes. (Clicking the field automatically produces an insertion point. If you use the TAB key, you will need to press F2 to produce an insertion point.)

The following step uses Form view to change the name of client MH56 from Maun Hospital to Munn Hospital by deleting the letters au and then inserting the letters un after the letter M.

1

- Click in the Client Name field in the datasheet for client MH56 after the letter M to select the field.

- Press the DELETE key twice to delete the letters au.

- Type the letters un after the letter M.

- Press the TAB key to complete the change and move to the next field (Figure 3–8).

Q&A
Could I have changed the contents of the field in the form?

Yes. You first will need to ensure the record to be changed appears in the form. You can then change the value just as in the datasheet.

Q&A
Do I need to save my change?

No. Once you move to another record or close this table, the change to the name will become permanent.

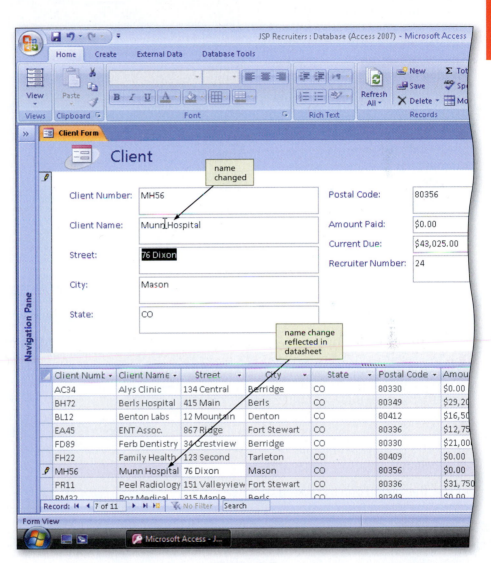

Figure 3–8

To Delete a Record

When records no longer are needed, **delete the records** (remove them) from the table. If client EA45 no longer is served by JSP Recruiters and its final payment is made, the record can be deleted. The following steps delete client EA45.

1

- With the Client Form open, click the record selector in the data-sheet (the small box that appears to the left of the first field) of the record on which the client number is EA45 (Figure 3–9).

Q&A

That technique works in the data-sheet portion. How do I select the record in the form portion?

With the desired record appearing in the form, click the record selector (the triangle in front of the record) to select the entire record.

Figure 3–9

2

- Press the DELETE key to delete the record (Figure 3–10).

3

- Click the Yes button to complete the deletion.

- Close the Client Form by clicking the Close 'Client Form' button.

Figure 3–10

Other Ways

1. Click Delete button on Ribbon

Filtering Records

You can use the Find button in either Datasheet view or Form view to locate a record quickly that satisfies some criterion (for example, the client number is MH56). All records appear, however, not just the record or records that satisfy the criterion. To have only the record or records that satisfy the criterion appear, use a **filter**. Four types of filters are available: Filter By Selection, Common Filters, Filter By Form, and Advanced Filter/Sort. You can use a filter in either Datasheet view or Form view.

**Plan
Ahead**

Determine whether you should filter records.

If you determine that it is desirable to have only those records that satisfy some criterion appear, you have two choices. You can create a query or create a filter. The following guidelines apply to this decision.

1. If you think that you frequently will want to display records that satisfy precisely this same criterion, you should consider creating a query whose results only contain the records that satisfy the criterion. To display those records in the future, simply open the query.

2. If you are viewing data in a datasheet or form and decide you want to restrict the records to be included, it is easier to create a filter than create a query. You can create and use the filter while you are viewing the data.

3. If you have created a filter that you would like to be able to use again in the future, you can save the filter as a query.

   If you have decided that it is appropriate to use a filter, you need to decide which type of filter to use.

1. If your criterion for filtering is that the value in a particular field matches or does not match a certain specific value, you can use Filter By Selection.

2. If your criterion only involves a single field but is more complex, for example, that the value in the field begins with a certain collection of letters, you can use a Common Filter.

3. If your criterion involves more than one field, use Filter By Form.

4. If your criterion involves more than a single And or Or, or if it involves sorting, you will probably find it simpler to use Advanced Filter/Sort.

To Use Filter By Selection

The simplest type of filter is called **Filter By Selection**. To use Filter By Selection, you give Access an example of the data you want by selecting the data within the table. You then choose the option you want on the Selection menu. If you have determined that you only want to display those clients located in Berridge, Filter By Selection is appropriate. The following steps use Filter By Selection in Datasheet view to display only the records for clients in Berridge.

- Open the Client Form and hide the Navigation Pane.

- Click the City field on the first record in the datasheet portion of the form to select Berridge as the city (Figure 3–11).

Could I have selected the City field on the fourth record, which is also Berridge?

Yes. It does not matter which record you select as long as the city is Berridge.

Figure 3–11

2

- Click the Selection button on the Home tab to display the Selection menu (Figure 3–12).

Figure 3–12

3

- Click Equals "Berridge" to select only those clients whose city is Berridge (Figure 3–13).

Q&A

Can I also filter in Datasheet view or in Form view?

Yes. Filtering works the same whether you are viewing the data with split form, in Datasheet view, or in Form view.

Experiment

- Try each of the other values in the Selection menu to see their effect. When done, once again select those clients whose city is Berridge.

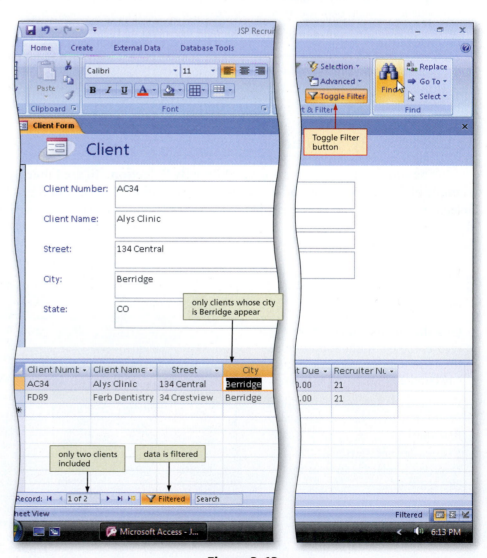

Figure 3–13

To Toggle a Filter

The following step toggles the filter to redisplay all records.

- Click the Toggle Filter button on the Home tab to toggle the filter and redisplay all records (Figure 3–14).

Q&A Does that action clear the filter?

No. The filter is still in place. If you click the Toggle Filter button a second time, you again will see only the filtered records.

Figure 3–14

TO CLEAR A FILTER

Once you have finished using a filter, you can clear the filter. After doing so, you no longer will be able to use the filter by pressing the Toggle Filter button. To clear a filter, you use the following steps.

1. Click the Advanced button on the Home tab.
2. Click Clear All Filters on the Advanced menu.

BTW

Using Wildcards in Filters
Both the question mark (?) and the asterisk (*) wildcards can be used in filters created using Advanced Filter/Sort.

To Use a Common Filter

You can filter individual fields by clicking the arrow to the right of the field name and using a Common Filter. If you have determined you want to include those clients whose city begins with Ber, Filter By Selection would not be appropriate. You would need to use a Common Filter. The following steps use a common filter to include only those clients whose city begins with Ber.

- Be sure the Home tab is selected.

- Click the City arrow to display the common filter menu.

- Point to the Text Filters command to display the custom text filters (Figure 3–15).

Q&A

I selected the City field and then clicked the Filter button on the Home tab. My screen looks the same. Is this right?

Yes. That is another legitimate way to display the common filter menu.

Figure 3–15

- Click Begins With to display the Custom Filter dialog box.

- Type Ber as the City begins with value (Figure 3–16).

Q&A

If I wanted certain cities included, could I use the check boxes?

Yes. Be sure the cities you want are the only ones checked. One way to do this is to click the Select All check box to remove all the check marks and then click the check boxes for the cities you want to include. Another way is to clear the check boxes for the cities you don't want. Use whichever technique you find more convenient.

Experiment

- Try other options in the Common Filter menu to see their effect. When done, once again select those clients whose city begins with Ber.

Figure 3–16

3

- Click the OK button to filter the records (Figure 3–17). (Your order may be different.)

Q&A

Can I use the same technique in Form view?

In Form view, you would need to click the field and then click the Filter button to display the Common Filter menu. The rest of the process would be the same.

4

- Click the Toggle Filter button on the Home tab to toggle the filter and redisplay all records.

	Street	City	State	Postal Code	Amount Paid	Current Due	Recruiter Nu
	134 Central	Berridge	CO	80330	$0.00	$17,500.00	21
al	415 Main	Berls	CO	80349	$29,200.00	$0.00	24
try	34 Crestview	Berridge	CO	80330	$21,000.00	$12,500.00	21
	785 Main	Berls	CO	80349	$14,000.00	$0.00	24
l	315 Maple	Berls	CO	80349	$0.00	$0.00	27

only clients whose city begins with Ber are included

Toggle Filter button

Figure 3–17

To Use Filter By Form

Filter By Selection is a quick and easy way to filter by the value in a single field. For more complex criteria, however, it is not appropriate. For example, if you determined you only wanted those clients whose postal code is 80330 and whose amount paid is 0, you could not use either the Filter by Selection or the Common Filter processes. Rather, you would use **Filter By Form**. The following steps use Filter By Form to restrict the records that appear.

1

- Click the Advanced button on the Home tab to display the Advanced menu (Figure 3–18).

Advanced button

Clear All Filters command

Filter By Form command

Clear All Filters

Filter By Form

Apply Filter/Sort

Advanced Filter/Sort...

Load from Query...

Save As Query

Delete Tab

Clear Grid

Close

Advanced menu

Postal Code:	80330
Amount Paid:	$0.00
Current Due:	$17,500.00

Figure 3–18

2

- Click Clear All Filters on the Advanced menu to clear the existing filter.

- Click the Advanced button on the Home tab to display the Advanced menu a second time.

- Click Filter By Form on the Advanced menu.

- Click the Postal Code field, click the arrow that appears, and then click 80330.

- Click the Amount Paid field, click the arrow that appears, and then click 0 (Figure 3–19).

Q&A

Is there any difference in the process if I am viewing a table in Datasheet view rather than in Form view or in a split form?

In Datasheet view, you will make your entries in a datasheet rather than a form. Otherwise, the process is the same.

- Click the Toggle Filter button on the Home tab to apply the filter (Figure 3–20).

Experiment

- Select Filter By Form again and enter different criteria. In each case, toggle the filter to see the effect of your selection. When done, once again select those clients whose postal code is 80330 and whose amount paid is 0.

Figure 3–19

Figure 3–20

To Use Advanced Filter/Sort

    In some cases, your criteria may be too complex even for Filter By Form. You might decide you want to include any client for which the postal code is 80330 and the amount paid is $0. You also may want to include any client whose amount paid is greater than $20,000, no matter where the client is located. Further, you might want to have the results sorted by name. To filter records using complex criteria, you need to use Advanced Filter/Sort as in the following steps.

- Click the Advanced button on the Home tab to display the Advanced menu, and then click Clear All Filters on the Advanced menu to clear the existing filter.

- Click the Advanced button on the Home tab to display the Advanced menu a second time.

- Click Advanced Filter/Sort on the Advanced menu.

- Include the Client Name field and select Ascending as the sort order.

- Include the Postal Code field and enter 80330 as the criterion.

- Scroll down so that the Amount Paid field is visible, include the Amount Paid field and enter 0 as the criterion in the Criteria row and >20000 as the criterion in the Or row (Figure 3–21).

Figure 3–21

2

- Click the Toggle Filter button on the Home tab to toggle the filter and view the results. Click the Client Form tab to view the Client table (Figure 3–22).

Experiment

- Select Advanced Filter/Sort again and enter different sorting options and criteria. In each case, toggle the filter to see the effect of your selection. When done, change back to the sorting options and criteria you entered in Step 1.

3

- Click Clear All Filters on the Advanced menu.

- Close the Client Form.

Figure 3–22

Filters and Queries

Filters and queries are related in three ways.

1. You can apply a filter to the results of a query just as you can apply a filter to a table.

2. When you have created a filter using either Filter By Form or Advanced Filter/Sort, you can save the filter settings as a query by using the Save As Query command on the Advanced menu.

3. You can restore filter settings that you previously saved in a query by using the Load From Query command on the Advanced menu.

Moving a Field in a Table Structure
If you add a field to a table and later realize the field is in the wrong location, you can move the field. To do so, click the row selector for the field and then drag the field to the new location.

Changing the Database Structure

When you initially create a database, you define its **structure**; that is, you assign names and types to all the fields. In many cases, the structure you first define will not continue to be appropriate as you use the database.

Perhaps a field currently in the table no longer is necessary. If no one ever uses a particular field, it is not needed in the table. Because it is occupying space and serving no useful purpose, you should remove it from the table. You also would need to delete the field from any forms, reports, or queries that include it.

More commonly, an organization will find that it needs to maintain additional information that was not anticipated at the time the database was first designed. The organization's own requirements may have changed. In addition, outside regulations that the organization must satisfy may change as well. In either case, the organization must add additional fields to an existing table.

To make any of these changes, you first must open the table in Design view.

TO DELETE A FIELD

If a field in one of your tables no longer is needed; for example, it serves no useful purpose or it may have been included by mistake, you should delete the field. To delete a field you would use the following steps.

1. Open the table in Design view.

2. Click the row selector for the field to be deleted.

3. Press the DELETE key.

4. When Access displays the dialog box requesting confirmation that you want to delete the field, click the Yes button.

To Add a New Field

You can add fields to a table in a database. JSP Recruiters has decided that it needs to categorize its clients. To do so requires an additional field, Client Type. The possible values for Client Type are MED (which indicates the client is a medical institution), DNT (which indicates the client is a dental organization), or LAB (which indicates the client is a lab). The following steps add the Client Type to the Client table immediately after the Postal Code field.

• Show the Navigation Pane, and then right-click the Client table to display a shortcut menu.

• Click Design View on the shortcut menu to open the Client table in Design view.

• Click the row selector for the Amount Paid field, and then press the INSERT key to insert a blank row above the Amount Paid row (Figure 3–23).

2

• Click the Field Name column for the new field. If necessary, erase any text that appears.

• Type Client Type as the field name and then press the TAB key.

Figure 3–23

Other Ways
1. Click Insert Rows button on Ribbon

To Create a Lookup Field

Because there are only three possible values for the Client Type field, you should make it easy for users to enter the appropriate value. A **Lookup field** allows the user to select from a list of values.

The following steps make the Client Type field a Lookup field.

● If necessary, click the Data Type column for the Client Type field, and then click the arrow to display the menu of available data types (Figure 3–24).

Figure 3–24

● Click Lookup Wizard, and then click the 'I will type in the values that I want.' option button to indicate that you will type in the values (Figure 3–25).

 When would I use the other option button?

You would use the other option button if the data to be entered in this field is found in another table or query.

Figure 3–25

3

- Click the Next button to display the next Lookup Wizard screen (Figure 3–26).

Figure 3–26

4

- Click the first row of the table (below Col1), and then type MED as the value in the first row.

- Press the DOWN ARROW key, and then type DNT as the value in the second row.

- Press the DOWN ARROW key, and then type LAB as the value in the third row (Figure 3–27).

Figure 3–27

5

- Click the Next button to display the next Lookup Wizard screen.

- Ensure Client Type is entered as the label for the lookup column and that the Allow Multiple Values check box is NOT checked (Figure 3–28).

6

- Click the Finish button to complete the definition of the Lookup Wizard field.

Q&A

Why does the data type for the Client Type field still show Text?

The data type is still Text because the values entered in the wizard were entered as text.

Figure 3–28

To Add a Multivalued Field

BTW

Multivalued Fields
If you plan to move your data to SQL Server at a later date, do not use multivalued fields. When you upsize a database containing multivalued fields to SQL Server, the field is converted to a memo field that contains the delimited set of values. This may mean that you need to do some redesign of your database.

Normally, fields contain only a single value. In Access 2007 it is possible to have **multivalued fields**, that is, fields that can contain more than one value. JSP Recruiters wants to use such a field to store the abbreviations of all the specialties their clients need (see Table 3–1 for the specialty abbreviations and descriptions). Unlike the Client Type, where each client only had one type, clients can require multiple specialty descriptions.

Table 3–1 Specialty Abbreviations and Descriptions	
Specialty Abbreviation	**Description**
CLS	Clinical Laboratory Specialist
CNA	Certified Nursing Assistant
CRNA	Certified Registered Nurse Anesthetist
DH	Dental Hygienist
Dnt	Dentist
EMT	Emergency Medical Technician
NP	Nurse Practitioner
OT	Occupational Therapist
PA	Physician Assistant
Phy	Physician
PT	Physical Therapist
RN	Registered Nurse
RT	Respiratory Therapist

One client might need CNA, PA, Phy, and RN employees (Certified Nursing Assistants, Physician Assistants, Physicians, and Registered Nurses). Another client might only need RTs (Respiratory Therapists).

To create a multivalued field, create a Lookup field being sure to check the Allow Multiple Values check box. The following steps create a multivalued field.

1 Click the row selector for the Amount Paid field, and then press the INSERT key to insert a blank row.

2 Click the Field Name column for the new field, type `Specialties Needed` as the field name.

3 Click the Data Type column for the Specialties Needed field, and then click Lookup Wizard in the menu of available data types to start the Lookup Wizard.

4 Click the 'I will type in the values that I want.' option button to indicate that you will type in the values.

5 Click the Next button to display the next Lookup Wizard screen.

6 Click the first row of the table (below Col1), and then type `CLS` as the value in the first row.

7 Enter the remaining values from the first column in Table 3–1. Before typing each value, press the DOWN ARROW key to move to a new row.

8 Click the Next button to display the next Lookup Wizard screen.

9 Ensure Specialties Needed is entered as the label for the lookup column.

10 Click the Allow Multiple Values check box to allow multiple values.

11 Click the Finish button to complete the definition of the Lookup Wizard field.

To Save the Changes and Close the Table

The following steps save the changes; that is, it saves the addition of the two new fields and closes the table.

1 Click the Save button on the Quick Access Toolbar to save the changes.

2 Click the Close 'Client' button.

TO MODIFY SINGLE OR MULTIVALUED LOOKUP FIELDS

You may find that you later want to change the list of choices in a Lookup field. If you find you need to modify a single or multivalued Lookup field you have created, you can use the following steps.

1. Open the table in Design view and select the field to be modified.
2. Click the Lookup Tab in the field properties.
3. Change the list in the Row Source property to change the desired list of values.

Mass Changes

In some cases, rather than making individual changes to records, you will want to make mass changes. That is, you will want to add, change, or delete many records in a single operation. You can do this with action queries. An **action query** adds, deletes, or changes data in a table. An **update query** allows you to make the same change to all records satisfying some criterion. If you omit the criterion, you will make the same changes to all records in the table. A **delete query** allows you to delete all the records satisfying some criterion. You can add the results of a query to an existing table by using an **append query**. You also can add the results to a new table by using a **make-table query**.

To Use an Update Query

The Client Type field is blank on every record. One approach to entering the information for the field would be to step through the entire table, assigning each record its appropriate value. If most of the clients have the same type, a simpler approach is available.

In the JSP Recruiters database, for example, most clients are type MED. Initially, you can set all the values to MED. To accomplish this quickly and easily, you can use an update query, which is a query that makes the same change to all the records satisfying a criterion. Later, you can change the type for dental organizations and labs.

The following steps use an update query to change the value in the Client Type field to MED for all the records. Because all records are to be updated, criteria are not required.

1
- Create a new query for the Client table and hide the Navigation Pane.

- Click the Update button on the Design tab, double-click the Client Type field to select the field, click the Update To row in the first column of the design grid, and then type MED as the new value (Figure 3–29).

Q&A Don't I have to enter a criterion?

If you only want the change to be made on some of the records, you would need to enter a criterion to identify those records. Without a criterion, the change will be made on all records, which is what you want in this update.

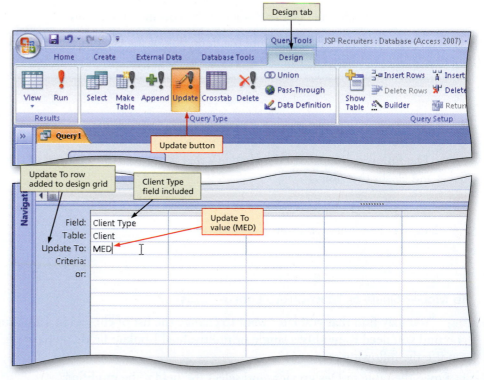

Figure 3–29

2

- Click the Run button on the Design tab to run the query and update the records (Figure 3–30).

Q&A

Why don't I click the View button to update the records?

The purpose of the View button is to simply view results. The Run button causes the updates specified by the query to take place.

Q&A

Why doesn't the dialog box appear on my screen when I click the Run button?

If the dialog box does not appear, it means that you did not choose the Enable this content option button when you first opened the database. Close the database, open it again, and enable the content in the Microsoft Office Security Options dialog box. Then, create and run the query again.

 Experiment

- Create an Update query to change the client type to DNT. Enter a criterion to restrict the records to be updated, and then run the query. Open the table to view your changes. When finished, create and run an Update query to change the client type to MED on all records.

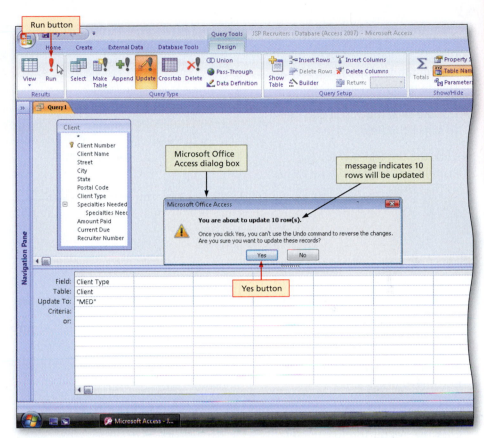

Figure 3–30

3

- Click the Yes button to make the changes.

Other Ways
1. Right-click any open area in upper Pane, point to Query Type on shortcut menu, click Update Query on Query Type submenu

To Use a Delete Query

In some cases, you may need to delete several records at a time. If, for example, all clients in a particular postal code are to be serviced by another firm, the clients with this postal code can be deleted from the JSP Recruiters database. Instead of deleting these clients individually, which could be very time-consuming in a large database, you can delete them in one operation by using a **delete query**, which is a query that will delete all the records satisfying the criteria entered in the query.

You can preview the data to be deleted in a delete query before actually performing the deletion. To do so, click the View button after you create the query, but before you run it. The records to be deleted then would appear in Datasheet view. To delete the records, click the View button again to change to Design view. Click the Run button, and then click the Yes button in the Microsoft Office Access dialog box when asked if you want to delete the records.

The following steps use a delete query to delete any client whose postal code is 80412 without first previewing the data to be deleted. (Only one such client currently exists in the database.)

- Clear the grid.

- Click the Delete button on the Design tab to make the query a Delete query (Figure 3–31).

- Double-click the Postal Code field to select the field.

- Click the Criteria row for the Postal Code field and type `80412` as the criterion.

Figure 3–31

- Run the query by clicking the Run button (Figure 3–32).

- Click the Yes button to complete the deletion.

- Close the Query window. Do not save the query.

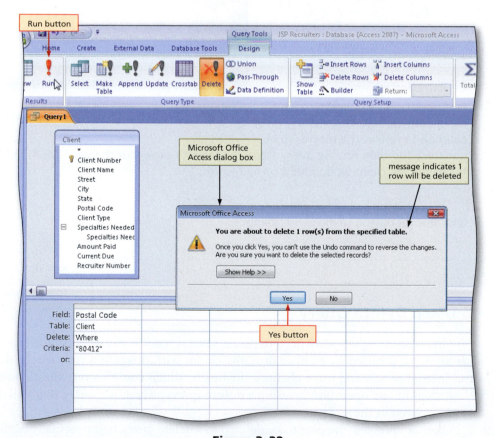

Figure 3–32

Other Ways

1. Right-click any open area in upper Pane, point to Query Type on shortcut menu, click Delete Query on Query Type submenu

To Use an Append Query

An append query adds a group of records from one table to the end of another table. For example, suppose that JSP Recruiters acquires some new clients and a database containing a table with those clients. To avoid entering all this information manually, you can append it to the Client table in the JSP Recruiters database using the append query. To create an append query, you would use the following steps.

1. Create a query for the table containing the records to append.
2. In Design view, indicate the fields to include, and then enter any necessary criteria.
3. View the query results to be sure you have specified the correct data, and then return to Design view.
4. Click the Append button on the Design tab.
5. When Access displays the Append dialog box, specify the name of the table to receive the new records and its location. Run the query by clicking the Run button on the Design tab.
6. When Access indicates the number of records to be appended, click the Yes button.

To Use a Make-Table Query

In some cases, you might want to add the records from an existing table to a new table, that is, a table that has not yet been created. If so, use a make-table query to add the records to a new table. Access will create this table as part of the process and add the records to it. To create a make-table query, you would use the following steps.

1. Create a query for the table containing the records to add.
2. In Design view, indicate the fields to include, and then enter any necessary criteria.
3. View the query results to be sure you have specified the correct data, and then return to Design view.
4. Click the Make Table button on the Design tab.
5. When Access displays the Make Table dialog box, specify the name of the table to receive the new records and its location. Run the query by clicking the Run button on the Design tab.
6. When Access indicates the number of records to be inserted, click the Yes button.

Validation Rules

You now have created, loaded, queried, and updated a database. Nothing you have done so far, however, makes sure that users enter only valid data. To ensure the entry of valid data, you create **validation rules**; that is, rules that a user must follow when entering the data. As you will see, Access will prevent users from entering data that does not follow the rules. The steps also specify **validation text**, which is the message that will appear if a user violates the validation rule.

Validation rules can indicate a **required field**, a field in which the user actually must enter data. For example, by making the Client Name field a required field, a user actually must enter a name (that is, the field cannot be blank). Validation rules can make sure a user's entry lies within a certain **range of values**; for example, that the values in the Amount Paid field are between $0.00 and $100,000.00. They can specify a **default value**; that is, a value that Access will display on the screen in a particular field before the user begins adding a record. To make data entry of client numbers more convenient, you also can have lowercase letters appear automatically as uppercase letters. Finally, validation rules can specify a collection of acceptable values; for example, that the only legitimate entries for the Client Type field are MED, DNT, and LAB.

BTW

Using Wildcards in Validation Rules
You can include wildcards in validation rules. For example, if you enter the expression, like C?, in the Validation Rule box for the State field, the only valid entries for the field will be CA, CO, and CT.

To Specify a Required Field

To specify that a field is to be required, change the value for the Required property from No to Yes. The following steps specify that the Client Name field is to be a required field.

1

- Show the Navigation Pane, and then open the Client table in Design view.

- Select the Client Name field by clicking its row selector.

- Click the Required property box in the Field Properties Pane, and then click the down arrow that appears.

- Click Yes in the list (Figure 3–33).

Q&A

What is the effect of this change?

Users cannot leave the Client Name field blank when entering or editing records.

Figure 3–33

To Specify a Range

The following step specifies that entries in the Amount Paid field must be between $0.00 and $100,000.00. To indicate this range, the criterion specifies that the amount paid value must be both >= 0 (greater than or equal to 0) and <= 100000 (less than or equal to 100000).

1

- Select the Amount Paid field by clicking its row selector, click the Validation Rule property box to produce an insertion point, and then type `>=0 and <=100000` as the rule.

- Click the Validation Text property box to produce an insertion point, and then type `Must be at least $0.00 and at most $100,000` as the text (Figure 3–34).

Q&A

What is the effect of this change?

Users now will be prohibited from entering an amount paid value that either is less than $0.00 or greater than $100,000.00 when they add records or change the value in the Amount Paid field.

Figure 3–34

To Specify a Default Value

To specify a default value, enter the value in the Default Value property box. The following step specifies MED as the default value for the Client Type field. This simply means that if users do not enter a client type, the type will be MED.

1

- Select the Client Type field. Click the Default Value property box to produce an insertion point, and then type =MED as the value (Figure 3–35).

Figure 3–35

To Specify a Collection of Allowable Values

The only allowable values for the Client Type field are MED, DNT, and LAB. An appropriate validation rule for this field prevents Access from accepting any entry other than these three possibilities. The following step specifies the legal values for the Client Type field.

1

- Make sure the Client Type field is selected.

- Click the Validation Rule property box to produce an insertion point and then type =MED Or =DNT Or =LAB as the validation rule.

- Click the Validation Text property box and then type Must be MED, DNT, or LAB as the validation text (Figure 3–36).

Q&A

What is the effect of this change?

Users now will be allowed to enter only MED, DNT, or LAB in the Client Type field when they add records or make changes to this field.

Figure 3–36

To Specify a Format

To affect the way data appears in a field, you can use a **format**. To use a format with a Text field, you enter a special symbol, called a **format symbol**, in the field's Format property box. The Format property uses different settings for different data types. The following step specifies a format for the Client Number field in the Client table and illustrates the way you enter a format. The format symbol used in the example is >, which causes Access to display lowercase letters automatically as uppercase letters. The format symbol < causes Access to display uppercase letters automatically as lowercase letters.

- Select the Client Number field.

- Click the Format property box and then type > (Figure 3–37).

Q&A

What is the effect of this change?

From this point on, any lowercase letters will appear automatically as uppercase when users add records or change the value in the Client Number field.

Q&A

Client numbers are supposed to be four characters long. Is there a way to ensure users don't type more than four characters?

Yes. The Field Size property dictates how many characters the users can type, so if you wanted to ensure that a maximum of four characters be allowed, you could change the field size from 255 to 4.

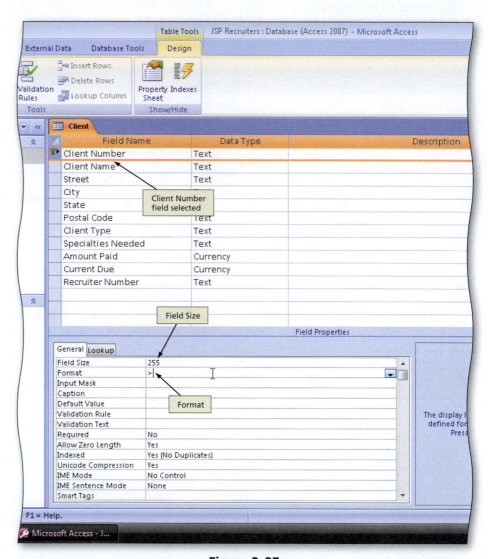

Figure 3–37

To Save the Validation Rules, Default Values, and Formats

The following steps save the validation rules, default values, and formats.

1
- Click the Save button on the Quick Access Toolbar to save the changes (Figure 3–38).

2
- Click the No button to save the changes without testing current data.

- Close the Client table.

Q&A

Should I always click the No button when saving validation rules?

If this were a database used to run a business or to solve some other critical need, you would click Yes. You would want to be sure that the data already in the database does not violate the rules.

Figure 3–38

Changing Data Types
It is possible to change the data type for a field that already contains data. Before you change a data type, however, you should consider what effect the change will have on other database objects, such as forms, queries, and reports. For example, you could convert a Text field to a Memo field if you find that you do not have enough space to store the data that you need. You also could convert a Number field to a Currency field or vice versa.

Updating a Table that Contains Validation Rules

When updating a table that contains validation rules, Access provides assistance in making sure the data entered is valid. It helps in making sure that data is formatted correctly. Access also will not accept invalid data. Entering a number that is out of the required range, for example, or entering a value that is not one of the possible choices, will produce an error message in the form of a dialog box. The database will not be updated until the error is corrected.

If the client number entered contains lowercase letters, such am49 (Figure 3–39), Access will display the data automatically as AM49 (Figure 3–40).

Figure 3–39

Figure 3–40

If the client type is not valid, such as xxx, Access will display the text message you specified (Figure 3–41) and not allow the data to enter the database.

Figure 3–41

If the amount paid value is not valid, such as 125000, which is too large, Access also displays the appropriate message (Figure 3–42) and refuses to accept the data.

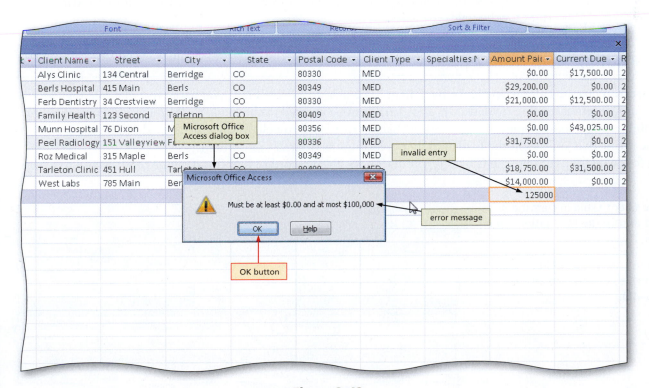

Figure 3–42

If a required field contains no data, Access indicates this by displaying an error message as soon as you attempt to leave the record (Figure 3–43). The field must contain a valid entry before Access will move to a different record.

Figure 3–43

When entering data into a field with a validation rule, you may find that Access displays the error message and you are unable to make the necessary correction. It may be that you cannot remember the validation rule you created or it was created incorrectly. In such a case, you neither can leave the field nor close the table because you have entered data into a field that violates the validation rule.

If this happens, first try again to type an acceptable entry. If this does not work, repeatedly press the BACKSPACE key to erase the contents of the field and then try to leave the field. If you are unsuccessful using this procedure, press the ESC key until the record is removed from the screen. The record will not be added to the database.

Should the need arise to take this drastic action, you probably have a faulty validation rule. Use the techniques of the previous sections to correct the existing validation rules for the field.

To Use a Lookup Field

Earlier, you changed all the entries in the Client Type field to MED. Thus, you have created a rule that will ensure that only legitimate values (MED, DNT, or LAB) can be entered in the field. You also made Client Type a Lookup field using a mass change. You can make changes to a Lookup field by clicking the field to be changed, clicking the arrow that appears in the field, and then selecting the desired value from the list.

The following steps change the Client Type value on the third record to DNT and on the ninth record to LAB.

- Open the Client table in Datasheet view and ensure the Navigation Pane is hidden.

- Click in the Client Type field on the third record to display the arrow (Figure 3–44).

Figure 3–44

2
- Click the down arrow to display the drop-down list of available choices for the Client Type field (Figure 3–45).

Could I type the value instead of selecting it from the list?

Yes. Once you have either deleted the previous value or selected the entire previous value, you can begin typing. You do not have to type the full entry. When you begin with the letter, D, for example, Access will automatically add the NT.

Figure 3–45

Experiment
- Select the Client Type field on the first record. Try to change the client type by typing various values. Try to type an invalid Client Type (like SPT). When finished, change the value on the record to MED.

3
- Click DNT to change the value.

- In a similar fashion, change MED on the ninth record to LAB (Figure 3–46).

Figure 3–46

To Use a Multivalued Lookup Field

Using a multivalued Lookup field is similar to using a regular Lookup field. The difference is that when you drop down the list, the entries all will be preceded by check boxes. You then can check all the entries that you want. The appropriate entries are shown in Figure 3–47. As indicated in the figure, the specialties needed for client AC34 are CNA, PA, Phy, and RN.

Client Number	Client Name	Specialties Needed
AC34	Alys Clinic	CNA, PA, Phy, RN
BH72	Berls Hospital	CLS, OT, PA, Phy, PT, RN
FD89	Ferb Dentistry	DH, Dnt
FH22	Family Health	NP, Phy, RN
MH56	Munn Hospital	CRNA, OT, Phy, PT, RN
PR11	Peel Radiology	RT
RM32	Roz Medical	CNA, NP, PA, Phy, RN
TC37	Tarleton Clinic	NP, PA, Phy, RN
WL56	West Labs	CLS

Figure 3–47

The following steps make the appropriate entries for the Specialties Needed field.

1

- Click the Specialties Needed field on the first record to display the arrow.

- Click the arrow to display the list of available specialties (Figure 3–48).

Q&A

All the specialties currently appear in the box. What if there were too many specialties to fit?

Access would automatically include a scroll bar that you could use to scroll through all the choices.

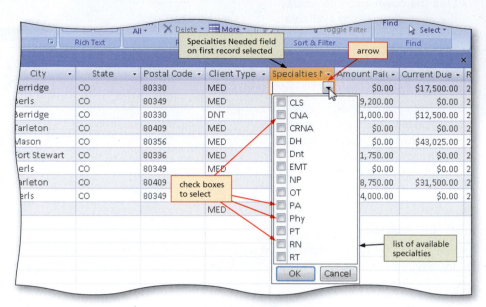

Figure 3–48

2

- Click the CNA, PA, Phy, and RN check boxes to select the specialties for the first client (Figure 3–49).

Figure 3–49

3

- Click the OK button to complete the selection.

- Using the same technique, enter the specialties given in Figure 3–47 on the previous page for the remaining clients (Figure 3–50).

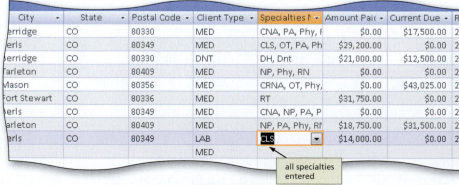

Figure 3–50

To Resize a Column in a Datasheet

The Access default column sizes do not always allow all the data in the field to appear. In some cases, the data may appear, but not the entire field name. You can correct this problem by **resizing** the column (changing its size) in the datasheet. In some instances, you may want to reduce the size of a column. The State field, for example, is short enough that it does not require all the space on the screen that is allotted to it. Changing a column width changes the **layout**, or design, of a table.

The following steps resize the columns in the Client table and save the changes to the layout.

1

- Point to the right boundary of the field selector for the Specialties Needed field (Figure 3–51) so that the mouse pointer becomes a doubled-ended arrow.

Figure 3–51

2

- Double-click the right boundary of the field selector for the Specialties Needed field to resize the field so that it best fits the data (Figure 3–52).

Figure 3–52

3

- Use the same technique to resize all the other fields to best fit the data. To resize the Amount Paid, Current Due, and Recruiter Number fields, you will need to scroll the fields by clicking the right scroll arrow shown in Figure 3–52 on the previous page (Figure 3–53).

4

- Save the changes to the layout by clicking the Save button on the Quick Access Toolbar.

- Close the Client table.

Q&A

What if I closed the table without saving the layout changes?

You would be asked if you want to save the changes.

Figure 3–53

ype	Specialties Needed	Amount Paid	Current Due	Recruiter Number	Add New Field
	CNA, PA, Phy, RN	$0.00	$17,500.00	21	
	CLS, OT, PA, Phy, PT, RN	$29,200.00	$0.00	24	
	DH, Dnt	$21,000.00	$12,500.00	21	
	NP, Phy, RN	$0.00	$0.00	24	
	CRNA, OT, Phy, PT, RN	$0.00	$43,025.00	24	
	RT	$31,750.00	$0.00	21	
	CNA, NP, PA, Phy, RN	$0.00	$0.00	27	
	NP, PA, Phy, RN	$18,750.00	$31,500.00	27	
	CLS	$14,000.00	$0.00	24	

Other Ways

1. Right-click field name, click Column Width

To Include Totals in a Datasheet

It is possible to include totals and other statistics at the bottom of a datasheet in a special row called the Total row. The following steps display the total of the commissions and the average of the rates for recruiters in the Total row.

1

- Open the Recruiter table in Datasheet view and hide the Navigation Pane.

- Click the Totals button on the Home tab to include the Total row in the datasheet (Figure 3–54).

Figure 3–54

2

• Click the Total row in the Commission column to display an arrow.

• Click the arrow to display a menu of available computations (Figure 3–55).

Q&A

Will I always get the same list?

No. You only will get the items that make sense for the type of data in the column. You cannot calculate the sum of text data, for example.

3

• Click Sum to calculate the sum of the commissions.

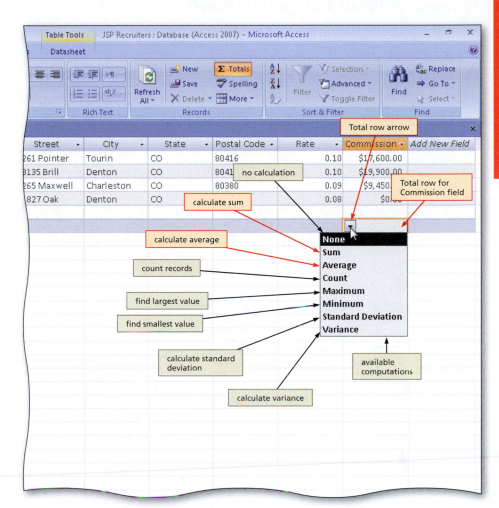

Figure 3–55

4

• Click the Total row in the Rate column to display an arrow.

• Click the arrow to display a menu of available computations.

• Click Average to calculate the average of the rates (Figure 3–56).

 Experiment

• Experiment with other statistics. When finished, once again select the sum of the commissions and the average of the rates.

Figure 3–56

To Remove Totals from a Datasheet

If you no longer want the totals to appear as part of the datasheet, you can remove the Total row. The following step removes the Total row.

- Click the Totals button on the Home tab to remove the Total row from the datasheet.

Changing the Appearance of a Datasheet

In addition to resizing columns and displaying totals, you can change the appearance of a datasheet in a variety of other ways. For example, you can change the appearance of grid-lines or change the text colors and font. Figure 3–57 shows the various buttons, found on the Home tab, that are available to change the Datasheet appearance.

Figure 3–57

The changes to the datasheet will be reflected not only on the screen, but also when you print or preview the datasheet.

Plan Ahead

Determine whether changes to the format of a datasheet are desirable.
You need to decide if changes to the format of a datasheet would improve its appearance and/or its usefulness. The following are the decisions you would make.

1. Would totals or other calculations be useful in the datasheet? If so, include the Total row and select the appropriate computations.

2. Would different gridlines make the datasheet more useful? If so, change to the desired gridlines.

3. Would alternating colors in the rows make them easier to read? If so, change the alternate fill color.

4. Would a different font and/or font color make the text stand out better? If so, change the font color and/or the font.

5. Is the font size appropriate? Can you see enough data at one time on the screen and yet have the data be readable? If not, change the font size to an appropriate value.

6. Is the column spacing appropriate? Are some columns wider than they need to be? Are there some columns where not all the data is visible? If so, change the column size.

As a general guideline, once you have decided on a particular look for a datasheet, all your datasheets should have the same look, unless there is a compelling reason for one of your datasheets to differ.

To Change Gridlines in a Datasheet

One of the changes you can make to a datasheet is which gridlines appear. You may feel that the appearance would be improved by having only horizontal gridlines. The following steps change the datasheet so that only horizontal gridlines are included.

- Open the Recruiter table in Datasheet view, if it is not already open.

- Click the box in the upper-left corner of the Datasheet selector to select the entire datasheet (Figure 3–58).

Figure 3–58

- Click the Gridlines button on the Home tab to display the Gridlines gallery (Figure 3–59).

Q&A

Does it matter whether I click the button or the arrow?

In this case, it does not matter. Either one will produce the same result.

- Click the Gridlines: Horizontal command in the Gridlines gallery to include only horizontal gridlines.

 Experiment

- Experiment with other gridline options. When finished, once again select horizontal gridlines.

Figure 3–59

To Change the Colors and Font in a Datasheet

You also may decide that you can improve the datasheet by changing the colors and the font. The following steps change the Alternate Fill color, a color that appears on every other row in the datasheet. They also change the font color, the font, and the font size.

- With the datasheet for the Recruiter table selected, click the Alternate Fill/Back Color button arrow to display the color palette (Figure 3–60).

Q&A

Does it matter whether I click the button or the arrow?

Yes. Clicking the arrow produces a color palette. Clicking the button applies the currently selected color. When in doubt, you should click the arrow.

Figure 3–60

- Click Aqua Blue (the second from the right color in the standard colors) to select aqua blue as the alternate color.

- Click the Font Color arrow, and then click Red (the second color in the bottom row) in the lower-left corner of standard colors to select Red as the font color.

- Click the Font box arrow, and then select Bodoni MT as the font. (If it is not available, select any font of your choice.)

- Click the Font Size box arrow, and select 10 as the font size (Figure 3–61).

Figure 3–61

Q&A

Does the order in which I make these selections make a difference?

No. You could have made these selections in any order.

Experiment

- Experiment with other colors, fonts, and font sizes. When finished, return to the options selected in this step.

Using the Datasheet Formatting Dialog Box

As an alternative to using the individual buttons, you can click the Datasheet Formatting Dialog Box Launcher, shown in Figure 3–61, to display the Datasheet Formatting dialog box (Figure 3–62). You can use the various options in the dialog box to make changes to the datasheet format. Once you are finished, click the OK button to apply your changes.

Figure 3–62

To Close the Datasheet Without Saving the Format Changes

The following steps show how to close the datasheet without saving the changes to the format. Because the changes are not saved, the next time you open the Recruiter table it will appear in the original format. If you had saved the changes, the changes would be reflected in its appearance.

1 Click the Close 'Recruiter' button to close the Recruiter table.

2 Click the No button in the Microsoft Office Access dialog box when asked if you want to save your changes.

Multivalued Field in Queries

You can use multivalued fields in queries just as you can use other fields. You have a choice concerning how the multiple values appear. You can choose to have them on a single row or on multiple rows.

To Query a Multivalued Field Showing Multiple Values on a Single Row

To include a multivalued field in the results of a query, place the field in the design grid just like any other field. The results will list all of the values for the multivalued field on a single row, just as in a datasheet. The following steps create a query to display the client number, client name, client type, and specialties needed for all clients.

- Create a query for the Client table and hide the Navigation Pane.

- Include the Client Number, Client Name, Client Type, and Specialties Needed fields (Figure 3–63).

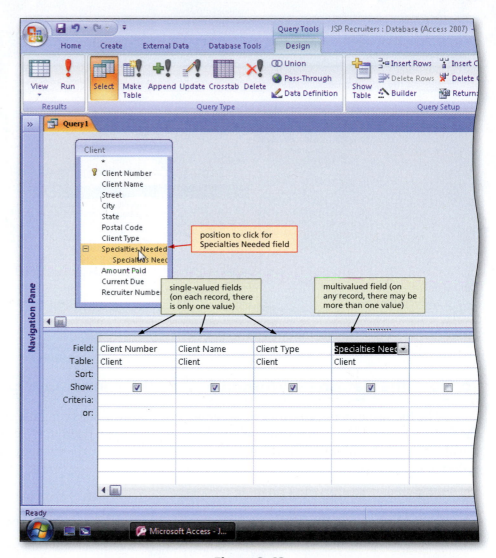

Figure 3–63

2

- View the results (Figure 3–64).

Q&A

Can I include criteria for the multi-valued field?

You can include criteria for the multivalued field when all the entries are displayed on a single row.

Experiment

- Return to Design view and enter various criteria in the Specialties Needed field. Run the queries. When finished, return to the options selected in this step.

Figure 3–64

To Query a Multivalued Field Showing Multiple Values on Multiple Rows

You may be interested in those clients requiring a particular specialty, for example, those clients needing an RN. Unfortunately, you cannot simply put the desired specialty in the Criteria row just as you would with other fields. Instead you need to change the query so that each specialty occurs on a different row by using the Value property. Once you have done so, you can enter criteria just as you would in any other query.

The following steps use the Value property to display each specialty on a separate row.

- Return to Design view and ensure the Client Number, Client Name, Client Type, and Specialties Needed fields are selected.

- Click the Specialties Needed field to produce an insertion point, and then type a period and the word `Value` after the word, Needed, to use the Value property (Figure 3–65).

Q&A I don't see the word, Specialties. Did I do something wrong?

No. There is not enough room to display the entire name. If you wanted to see it, you could point to the right boundary of the column selector and then either drag or double-click.

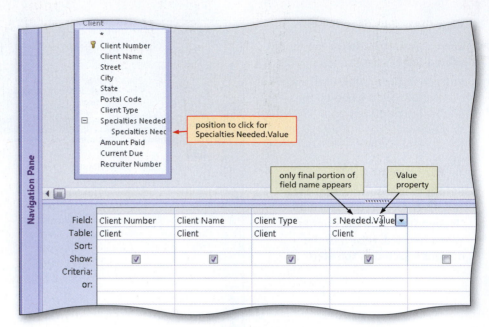

Figure 3–65

Q&A Do I need to type the word Value?

No. You also can double-click the second Specialties Needed entry in the field list.

- View the results (Figure 3–66).

Q&A Can I now include criteria for the multivalued field?

Yes. This is now just like any other query. There are no multiple values on any row.

- Close the query by clicking the Close 'Query1' button.

- When asked if you want to save the query, click the No button.

Figure 3–66

Referential Integrity

The property that ensures that the value in a foreign key must match that of another table's primary key is called **referential integrity**. A **foreign key** is a field in one table whose values are required to match the *primary key* of another table. In the Client table, the Recruiter Number field is a foreign key that must match the primary key of the Recruiter table; that is, the Recruiter number for any client must be a recruiter currently in the Recruiter table. A client whose Recruiter number is 92, for example, should not be stored because no such recruiter exists.

In Access, to specify referential integrity, you must define a relationship between the tables by using the Relationships command. Access then prohibits any updates to the database that would violate the referential integrity.

The type of relationship between two tables specified by the Relationships command is referred to as a **one-to-many relationship**. This means that *one* record in the first table is related to (matches) *many* records in the second table, but each record in the second table is related to only *one* record in the first. In the JSP Recruiters database, for example, a one-to-many relationship exists between the Recruiter table and the Client table. *One* recruiter is associated with *many* clients, but each client is associated with only a single recruiter. In general, the table containing the foreign key will be the *many* part of the relationship.

BTW

Relationships
You also can use the Relationships command to specify a one-to-one relationship. In a one-to-one relationship, one record in the first record is related to (matches) one record in the second table. In a one-to-one relationship, the matching fields are both primary keys. For example, if JSP Recruiters maintained a company car for each recruiter, the data concerning the cars might be kept in a Car table, in which the primary key is Recruiter Number—the same primary key as the Recruiter table. Thus, there would be a one-to-one relationship between recruiters and cars. Each recruiter is assigned one car and each car is assigned to one recruiter.

Plan Ahead

Identify related tables in order to implement relationships between the tables. When specifying referential integrity, you need to decide how to handle deletions. In the relationship between clients and recruiters, for example, deletion of a recruiter for whom clients exist, such as recruiter number 21, would violate referential integrity. Any clients for recruiter 21 no longer would relate to any recruiter in the database. You can handle this in two ways. For each relationship, you need to decide which of the approaches is appropriate.

1. The normal way to avoid this problem is to prohibit such a deletion.

2. The other option is to **cascade the delete.** This means that Access would allow the deletion but then delete all related records. For example, it would allow the deletion of the recruiter but then automatically delete any clients related to the deleted recruiter.

You also need to decide how to handle the update of the primary key. In the relationship between recruiters and clients, for example, changing the recruiter number for recruiter 21 to 12 in the Recruiter table would cause a problem. Clients are in the Client table on which the recruiter number is 21. These clients no longer would relate to any recruiter. You can handle this in two ways. For each relationship, you need to decide which of the approaches is appropriate.

1. The normal way of avoiding the problem is to prohibit this type of update.

2. The other option is to **cascade the update**. This means to allow the change, but make the corresponding change in the foreign key on all related records. In the relationship between clients and recruiters, for example, Access would allow the update but then automatically make the corresponding change for any client whose recruiter number was 21. It now will be 12.

To Specify Referential Integrity

The following steps use the Relationships command to specify referential integrity by specifying a relationship between the Recruiter and Client tables. The steps also ensure that update will cascade, but that delete will not.

1

- Click Database Tools on the Ribbon to display the Database Tools tab (Figure 3–67).

Figure 3–67

2

- Click the Relationships button on the Database Tools tab to open the Relationships window and display the Show Table dialog box (Figure 3–68).

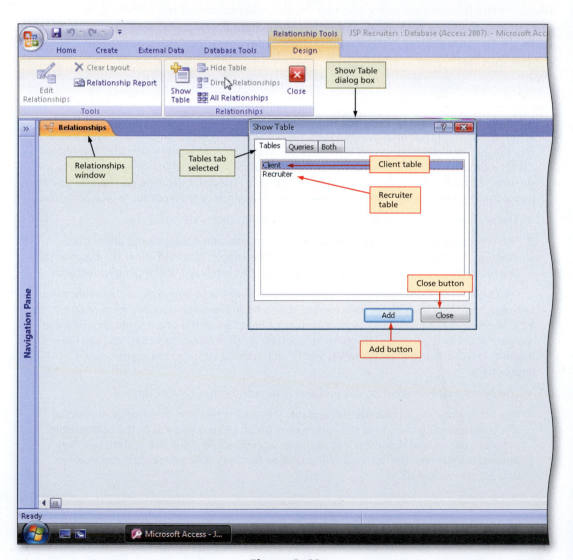

Figure 3–68

3

- Click the Recruiter table and then click the Add button to add the Recruiter table.

- Click the Client table and then click the Add button to add the Client table.

- Click the Close button in the Show Table dialog box to close the dialog box.

- Resize the field lists that appear so all fields are visible (Figure 3–69).

Q&A Do I need to resize the field lists?

No. You can use the scroll bars. Before completing the next step, however, you would need to make sure the Recruiter Number fields in both tables appear on the screen.

4

- Drag the Recruiter Number field in the Recruiter table field list to the Recruiter Number field in the Client table field list to open the Edit Relationships dialog box to create a relationship.

Q&A Do I actually move the field from the Recruiter table to the Client table?

No. The mouse pointer will change shape to indicate you are in the process of dragging, but the field does not move.

- Click the Enforce Referential Integrity check box.

Figure 3–69

5

- Click the Cascade Update Related Fields check box (Figure 3–70).

Q&A The Cascade check boxes were dim until I clicked the Enforce Referential Integrity check box. Is that correct?

Yes. Until you have chosen to enforce referential integrity, the cascade options have no meaning.

Q&A Can I change the join type like I can in queries?

Yes. Click the Join Type button in the Edit Relationships dialog box. Just as with queries, option button 1 creates an INNER join, option button 2 creates a LEFT join, and option button 3 creates a RIGHT join.

Figure 3–70

6

- Click the Create button to complete the creation of the relationship (Figure 3–71).

Q&A What is the symbol at the lower end of the join line?

It is the mathematical symbol for infinity. It is used here to denote the "many" end of the relationship.

Q&A Can I print a copy of the relationship?

Yes. Click the Relationship Report button on the Design tab to produce a report of the relationship. You can print the report. You also can save it as a report in the database for future use. If you do not want to save it, close the report after you have printed it and do not save the changes.

Figure 3–71

7

- Click the Save button on the Quick Access Toolbar to save the relationship you created.

- Close the Relationships window by clicking the Close 'Relationships' button.

Q&A Can I later modify the relationship if I want to change it in some way?

Yes. Click the Relationships button on the Database Tools tab. To add another table, click the Show Table button on the Design tab. To remove a table, click the Hide table button. To edit a relationship, select the relationship and click the Edit Relationships button.

Effect of Referential Integrity

Referential integrity now exists between the Recruiter and Client tables. Access now will reject any number in the Recruiter Number field in the Client table that does not match a Recruiter number in the Recruiter table. Attempting to change the recruiter number for a client to one that does not match any recruiter in the Recruiter table would result in the error message shown in Figure 3–72. Similarly, attempting to add a client whose recruiter number does not match would lead to the same error message.

Figure 3–72

Access also will reject the deletion of a recruiter for whom related clients exist. Attempting to delete recruiter 21 from the Recruiter table, for example, would result in the message shown in Figure 3–73.

Figure 3–73

Access would, however, allow the change of a recruiter number in the Recruiter table. Then it automatically makes the corresponding change to the recruiter number for all the recruiter's clients. For example, if you changed the recruiter number of recruiter 21 to 12, the same 12 would appear in the recruiter number field for clients.

To Use a Subdatasheet

Now that the Recruiter table is related to the Client table, it is possible to view the clients of a given recruiter when you are viewing the datasheet for the Recruiter table. The clients for the recruiter will appear below the recruiter in a **subdatasheet**. The availability of such a subdatasheet is indicated by a plus sign that appears in front of the rows in the Recruiter table. The following steps display the subdatasheet for recruiter 24.

- Open the Recruiter table and hide the Navigation Pane (Figure 3–74).

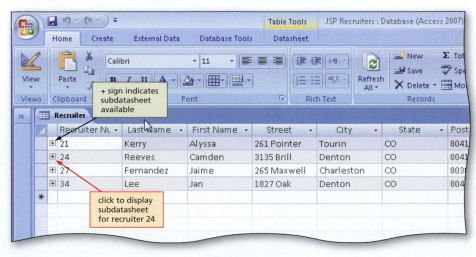

Figure 3–74

2

• Click the plus sign in front of the row for Recruiter 24 to display the subdatasheet (Figure 3–75).

Q&A

How do I hide the subdatasheet when I no longer want it to appear?

When you clicked the plus sign, it changed to a minus sign. Click the minus sign.

 Experiment

• Display subdatasheets for other recruiters. Display more than one subdatasheet at a time. Remove the subdatasheets from the screen.

Figure 3–75

3

• Close the Recruiter table.

TO FIND DUPLICATE RECORDS

One reason to include a primary key for a table is to eliminate duplicate records. A possibility still exists, however, that duplicate records can get into your database. Perhaps the same client was inadvertently added to the database with a new client number. You can detect this type of redundancy by searching to see if any client's names are duplicated. The **Find Duplicates Query Wizard** allows you to find duplicate records. The following steps illustrate how to use the Find Duplicates Query Wizard to find duplicate records.

1. Click Create on the Ribbon, and then click the Query Wizard button on the Create tab.
2. When Access displays the New Query dialog box, click the Find Duplicates Query Wizard and then click the OK button.
3. Identify the table and field or fields that might contain duplicate information.
4. Indicate any other fields you want displayed.
5. Finish the wizard to see any duplicate records.

TO FIND UNMATCHED RECORDS

Occasionally, you may want to find records in one table that have no matching records in another table. For example, you may want to determine which recruiters currently have no clients. The **Find Unmatched Query Wizard** allows you to find unmatched records. The following steps illustrate how to find unmatched records using the Find Unmatched Query Wizard.

1. Click Create on the Ribbon, and then click the Query Wizard button on the Create tab.
2. When Access displays the New Query dialog box, click the Find Unmatched Query Wizard and then click the OK button.
3. Identify the table that may contain unmatched records and then identify the related table.
4. Indicate the fields you want displayed.
5. Finish the wizard to see any duplicate records.

Ordering Records

Normally, Access sequences the records in the Client table by client number whenever listing them because the Client Number field is the primary key. You can change this order, if desired.

To Use the Ascending Button to Order Records

To change the order in which records appear, use the Ascending or Descending buttons. Either button reorders the records based on the field in which the insertion point is located.

The following steps order the records by city using the Ascending button.

- Open the Client table in Datasheet view and hide the Navigation Pane.

- Click the City field on the first record to select the field (Figure 3–76).

Q&A Did I have to click the field on the first record?

No. Any other record would have worked as well.

Figure 3–76

- Click the Ascending button on the Home tab to sort the records by City (Figure 3–77).

Q&A What if I wanted the cities to appear in reverse alphabetical order?

Click the Descending button.

Figure 3–77

🔍 **Experiment**

Sort the records by city in reverse order. When done, sort the records by city in the original order.

❸

- Close the table. When asked if you want to save your changes, click the No button.

Other Ways

1. Right-click field name, click Sort A to Z (for ascending) or Sort Z to A (for descending)

Special Database Operations

The special operations involved in maintaining a database are backup, recovery, compacting a database, and repairing a database.

Backup and Recovery

It is possible to damage or destroy a database. Users can enter data that is incorrect; programs that are updating the database can end abnormally during an update; a hardware problem can occur; and so on. After any such event has occurred, the database may contain invalid data. It even may be totally destroyed.

Obviously, you cannot allow a situation in which data has been damaged or destroyed to go uncorrected. You must somehow return the database to a correct state. This process is called recovery; that is, you **recover** the database.

The simplest approach to recovery involves periodically making a copy of the database (called a **backup copy** or a **save copy**). This is referred to as **backing up** the database. If a problem occurs, you correct the problem by copying this backup copy over the actual database, often referred to as the **live database**.

To backup the database that is currently open, you use the Back Up Database command on the Manage submenu on the Office Button menu. In the process, Access suggests a name that is a combination of the database name and the current date. For example, if you back up the JSP Recruiters database on April 20, 2008, Access will suggest the name JSP Recruiters_2008-04-20. You can change this name if you desire, although it is a good idea to use this name. By doing so, it will be easy to distinguish between all the backup copies you have made to determine which is the most recent. In addition, if you discover that a critical problem occurred on April 18, 2008, you may want to go back to the most recent backup before April 18. If, for example, the database was not backed up on April 17 but was backed up on April 16, you would use JSP Recruiters_2008-04-16.

The following steps back up a database to a file on a hard disk or high-capacity removable disk. You should check with your instructor before completing these steps.

To Back Up a Database

1. Open the database to be backed up.
2. Click the Office Button, and then point to Manage on the Office Button menu.
3. Click Back Up Database on the Manage submenu.
4. Select the desired location in the Save in box. If you do not want the name Access has suggested, enter the desired name in the File name text box.
5. Click the Save button.

Access creates a backup copy with the desired name in the desired location. Should you ever need to recover the database using this backup copy, you can simply copy it over the live version.

Compacting and Repairing a Database

As you add more data to a database, it naturally grows larger. When you delete an object (records, tables, forms, or queries), the space previously occupied by the object does not become available for additional objects. Instead, the additional objects are given new space, that is, space that was not already allocated. To remove this wasted space from the database, you must **compact** the database. The same option that compacts the database also repairs problems that may have occurred in the database.

To Compact and Repair a Database

1. Open the database to be compacted.
2. Click the Office Button, and then point to Manage on the Office Button menu.
3. Click Compact and Repair Database on the Manage submenu.

The database now is the compacted form of the original.

BTW

Certification
The Microsoft Certified Application Specialist (MCAS) program provides an opportunity for you to obtain a valuable industry credential — proof that you have the Access 2007 skills required by employers. For more information, see Appendix G or visit the Access 2007 Certification Web page (scsite.com/ac2007/cert).

BTW

Quick Reference
For a table that lists how to complete the tasks covered in this book using the mouse, Ribbon, shortcut menu, and keyboard, see the Quick Reference Summary at the back of this book, or visit the Access 2007 Quick Reference Web page (scsite.com/ac2007/qr).

BTW

Compacting Error Message on Opening Database
If you open your database and receive a compact error message, you may not be able to view all the objects in your database. You also may not see your tables in tabbed windows. To redisplay all the objects in your database, click the Navigation Pane arrow to display the Navigation Pane menu. Make sure that Tables and Related Views is selected. To make sure that objects appear in tabbed windows, click the Microsoft Office button, click the Access Options button, click Current Database, and make sure the Tabbed Documents option button is selected in the Application Options category.

Additional Operations

Additional special operations include opening another database, closing a database without exiting Access, and saving a database with another name. They also include deleting a table (or other object) as well as renaming an object. Finally, you can change properties of a table or other object, such as the object's description.

When you open another database, Access automatically will close the database that had been open. Before deleting or renaming an object, you should ensure that the object has no dependent objects, that is, other objects that depend on the object you wish to delete.

The following steps describe how you could perform these operations.

TO OPEN ANOTHER DATABASE

1. Click the Office Button.
2. Click Open on the Office Button menu.
3. Select the database to be opened.
4. Click the Open button.

TO CLOSE A DATABASE WITHOUT EXITING ACCESS

1. Click the Office Button.
2. Click Close Database on the Office Button menu.

TO SAVE A DATABASE WITH ANOTHER NAME

1. Click the Office Button.
2. Point to Save As on the Office Button menu.
3. Select the desired format.
4. Enter a name and select a location for the new version.
5. Click the Save button.

TO CHECK FOR DEPENDENT OBJECTS

1. Ensure that the object you wish to check is selected.
2. Click Database Tools on the Ribbon to display the Database Tools tab.
3. Click the Object Dependencies button on the Database Tools tab.
4. Click the 'Objects that depend on me' option button to display any objects that depend on the selected object.

TO DELETE A TABLE OR OTHER OBJECT

1. Right-click the object.
2. Click Delete on the shortcut menu.
3. Click the Yes button in the Microsoft Office Access dialog box.

TO RENAME AN OBJECT

1. Right-click the object.
2. Click Rename on the shortcut menu.
3. Type the new name and press the ENTER key.

TO CHANGE OBJECT PROPERTIES

1. Right-click the object.

2. Click Table Properties (if the object is a table) or Object Properties on the shortcut menu.

3. Change the desired property and click the OK button.

To Quit Access

You saved all your changes and are ready to quit Access. The following step quits Access.

1 Click the Close button on the right side of the Access title bar to quit Access.

Chapter Summary

In this chapter you have learned how to use a form to add records to a table; search for records; delete records; filter records; create and use Lookup fields; create and use multivalued fields; make mass changes; create validation rules; change the appearance of a datasheet; specify referential integrity; and use subdatasheets. The following list includes all the new Access skills you have learned in this chapter.

1. Create a Simple Form (AC 142)
2. Use a Form to Add Records (AC 144)
3. Search for a Record (AC 145)
4. Update the Contents of a Record (AC 147)
5. Delete a Record (AC 148)
6. Use Filter By Selection (AC 149)
7. Toggle a Filter (AC 151)
8. Clear a Filter (AC 151)
9. Use a Common Filter (AC 152)
10. Use Filter By Form (AC 153)
11. Use Advanced Filter/Sort (AC 155)
12. Delete a Field (AC 157)
13. Add a New Field (AC 157)
14. Create a Lookup Field (AC 158)
15. Add a Multivalued Field (AC 160)
16. Save the Changes and Close the Table (AC 161)
17. Modify Single or Multivalued Lookup Fields (AC 161)
18. Use an Update Query (AC 162)
19. Use a Delete Query (AC 163)
20. Use an Append Query (AC 165)
21. Use a Make-Table Query (AC 165)
22. Specify a Required Field (AC 166)
23. Specify a Range (AC 166)
24. Specify a Default Value (AC 167)
25. Specify a Collection of Allowable Values (AC 167)
26. Specify a Format (AC 168)
27. Save the Validation Rules, Default Values, and Formats (AC 169)
28. Use a Lookup Field (AC 172)
29. Use a Multivalued Lookup Field (AC 173)
30. Resize a Column in a Datasheet (AC 175)
31. Include Totals in a Datasheet (AC 176)
32. Remove Totals from a Datasheet (AC 178)
33. Change Gridlines in a Datasheet (AC 179)
34. Change the Colors and Font in a Datasheet (AC 180)
35. Close the Datasheet Without Saving the Format Changes (AC 181)
36. Query a Multivalued Field Showing Multiple Values on a Single Row (AC 182)
37. Query a Multivalued Field Showing Multiple Values on Multiple Rows (AC 183)
38. Specify Referential Integrity (AC 186)
39. Use a Subdatasheet (AC 190)
40. Find Duplicate Records (AC 191)
41. Find Unmatched Records (AC 191)
42. Use the Ascending Button to Order Records (AC 192)
43. Back up a Database (AC 193)
44. Compact and Repair a Database (AC 193)
45. Open Another Database (AC 194)
46. Close a Database Without Exiting Access (AC 194)
47. Save a Database with Another Name (AC 194)
48. Check for Dependent Objects (AC 194)
49. Delete a Table or Other Object (AC 194)
50. Rename an Object (AC 194)
51. Change Object Properties (AC 194)

 If you have a SAM user profile, you may have access to hands-on instruction, practice, and assessment. Log in to your SAM account (http://sam2007.course.com) to launch any assigned training activities or exams that relate to the skills covered in this chapter.

Learn It Online

Test your knowledge of chapter content and key terms.

Instructions: To complete the Learn It Online exercises, start your browser, click the Address bar, and then enter the Web address scsite.com/ac2007/learn. When the Access 2007 Learn It Online page is displayed, click the link for the exercise you want to complete and then read the instructions.

Chapter Reinforcement TF, MC, and SA
A series of true/false, multiple choice, and short answer questions that test your knowledge of the chapter content.

Flash Cards
An interactive learning environment where you identify chapter key terms associated with displayed definitions.

Practice Test
A series of multiple choice questions that test your knowledge of chapter content and key terms.

Who Wants To Be a Computer Genius?
An interactive game that challenges your knowledge of chapter content in the style of a television quiz show.

Wheel of Terms
An interactive game that challenges your knowledge of chapter key terms in the style of the television show *Wheel of Fortune*.

Crossword Puzzle Challenge
A crossword puzzle that challenges your knowledge of key terms presented in the chapter.

Apply Your Knowledge

Reinforce the skills and apply the concepts you learned in this chapter.

Specifying Validation Rules, Updating Records, Formatting a Datasheet, and Creating Relationships
Instructions: Start Access. Open The Bike Delivers database that you modified in Apply Your Knowledge in Chapter 2 on page AC 128. (If you did not complete this exercise, see your instructor for a copy of the modified database.)

Perform the following tasks:
1. Open the Customer table in Design view as shown in Figure 3–78.

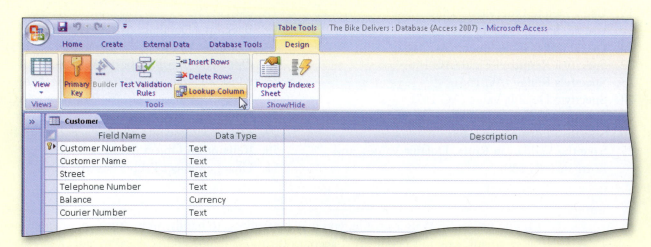

Figure 3–78

2. Format the Customer Number field so any lowercase letters appear in uppercase and make the Customer Name field a required field.

3. Specify that balance amounts must be between $0.0 and $1,000. Include validation text.

4. Save the changes to the Customer table.

5. Create a simple form for the Customer table and find the record for ME71 and change the customer name to Mentor Group Limited. Save the form as Customer Simple Form and close the form.

6. Open the Customer table in Datasheet view and use Filter By Selection to find the record for CI76. Delete the record. Remove the filter.

7. Resize all columns to best fit and remove the gridlines from the datasheet. Save the changes to the layout of the table. Close the Customer table.

8. Establish referential integrity between the Courier table (the one table) and the Customer table (the many table). Cascade the update but do not cascade the delete.

9. Submit the revised database in the format specified by your instructor.

Extend Your Knowledge

Extend the skills you learned in this chapter and experiment with new skills. You may need to use Help to complete the assignment.

Creating Action Queries, Changing Table Properties

Instructions: See the inside back cover of this book for instructions for downloading the Data Files for Students, or see your instructor for information on accessing the files required in this book.

Backyard is a retail business that specializes in products for the outdoors. The owner has created an Access database in which to store information about the products he sells. He recently acquired the inventory of a store that is going out of business. The inventory currently is stored in the Inventory database.

Perform the following tasks:

1. The owner needs to add the items stored in the Product table of the Inventory database to the Item table of the Backyard database. Create and run an append query to create the Item table for the Backyard database shown in Figure 3–79.

Item Code	Description	On Hand	Cost	Selling Price	Add New Field
BA35	Bat House	14	$43.50	$45.50	
BB01	Bird Bath	2	$54.00	$62.00	
BE19	Bee Sculpture	7	$39.80	$42.50	
BL06	Bug Mister	9	$14.35	$15.99	
BO22	Barn Owl Sculp	2	$37.50	$42.99	
BS10	Bunny Sprinkle	4	$41.95	$50.00	
BU24	Butterfly Stake	6	$36.10	$37.75	
FS11	Froggie Sprinkl	5	$41.95	$50.00	
GF12	Globe Feeder	12	$14.80	$16.25	
HF01	Hummingbird F	5	$11.35	$14.25	
LM05	Leaf Mister	3	$29.95	$35.95	
PM05	Purple Martin H	3	$67.10	$69.95	
SF03	Suet Feeder	7	$8.05	$9.95	
WF10	Window feede	10	$14.25	$15.95	

Figure 3–79

Continued >

STUDENT ASSIGNMENTS

Extend Your Knowledge *continued*

2. Open the Item table in the Backyard database and change the description for WF10 to Window Bird Feeder. Resize all columns to best fit the data.

3. Sort the datasheet in ascending order by Description.

4. Add a totals row to the datasheet and display the sum of the on hand items, and the average cost and average selling price.

5. Save the changes to the layout of the table. Close the table and rename it Product.

6. Update the table properties for the Product table to include the description, Updated to include items from Inventory database.

7. Using a query, delete all records in the Product table where the description starts with the letter S. Save the query as Delete Query.

8. Change the database properties, as specified by your instructor. Submit the revised database in the format specified by your instructor.

Make It Right

Analyze a database and correct all errors and/or improve the design.

Correcting Table Design Errors

Instructions: Start Access. Open the Care4Pets database. See the inside back cover of this book for instructions for downloading the Data Files for Students, or see your instructor for information on accessing the files required in this book.

Care4Pets provides a variety of services to pet owners. The owner of Care4Pets has decided that she could better manage her business if she added a multivalued field that lists the various types of pets her customers have. She created the field shown in Figure 3–80 but forgot to add Rabbit as one of the pet types. Modify the multivalued Lookup field to include Rabbit as a pet type.

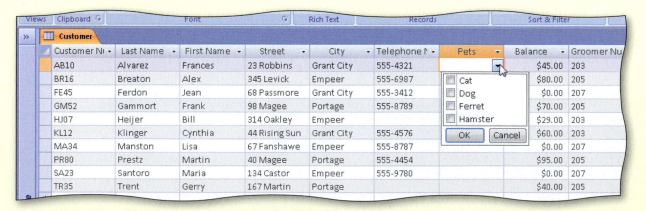

Figure 3–80

Finally, she wanted to add referential integrity between the Groomer table and the Customer table. The relationship shown in Figure 3–81 is not correct and must be fixed. She does not want to cascade the update or the delete. She also wants to create a report for the relationship. Use the name Relationships for Care4Pets for the report.

Figure 3–81

Submit the revised database in the format specified by your instructor.

In the Lab

Design, create, modify, and/or use a database following the guidelines, concepts, and skills presented in this chapter. Labs are listed in order of increasing difficulty.

Lab 1: Maintaining the JMS TechWizards Database

Problem: JMS TechWizards is expanding rapidly and needs to make some database changes to handle the expansion. The company needs to know more about its clients, such as the type of business, and it needs to ensure that data that is entered is valid. It also needs to update the records in the database.

Instructions: Use the database created in the In the Lab 1 of Chapter 1 on page AC 67 for this assignment or see your instructor for information on accessing the files required for this book.

Perform the following tasks:

1. Open the JMS TechWizards database and then open the Client table in Design view.

2. Add a Lookup field, Client Type, to the Client table. The field should appear after the Telephone Number field. The field will contain data on the type of client. The client types are MAN (Manufacturing), RET (Retail), and SER (Service). Save these changes to the structure.

3. Using a query, change all the entries in the Client Type column to RET. Save the query as Client Type Update Query.

4. Open the Client table and make the following changes. You can use the Find button, the Replace button, or Filter By Selection to locate the records to change:

   a. Change the client type for clients AM53 and SA56 to MAN.

   b. Change the client type for clients GR56, JE77, and ME17 to SER.

   c. Change the name of client SA56 to Sawyer Industries.

   d. Change the name of client ST21 to Steed's Department Store.

5. Resize all columns to best fit the data and remove the vertical gridlines. Save the changes to the layout of the table.

Continued >

In the Lab *continued*

6. Create the following validation rules for the Client table and save the changes.

   a. Specify the legal values MAN, RET, and SER for the Client Type field. Include validation text.

   b. Assign a default value of RET to the Client Type field.

   c. Ensure that any letters entered in the Client Number field appear as uppercase.

   d. Specify that the billed amount must be less than or equal to $1,500.00. Include validation text.

7. Open the Client table and use Filter By Form to find all records where the client is located in Anderson and has a client type of SER. Delete these records.

8. JMS has signed up a new retail store, Cray Meat Market (Client Number CR21) and needs to add the record to the Client table. The Meat Market is at 72 Main in Anderson, TX 78077. The phone number is 512-555-7766. Lee Torres is the technician assigned to the account. To date, they have not been billed for any services. Create a split form for the Client table and use this split form to add the record.

9. Specify referential integrity between the Technician table (the one table) and the Client table (the many table). Cascade the update but not the delete.

10. Compact the database and then back up the database.

11. Submit the revised database in the format specified by your instructor.

In the Lab

Lab 2: Maintaining the Hockey Fan Zone Database

Problem: The management of the Hockey Fan Zone store needs to change the database structure, add validation rules, and update records.

Instructions: Use the database created in the In the Lab 2 of Chapter 1 on page AC 68 for this assignment, or see your instructor for information on accessing the files required for this book.

Perform the following tasks:

1. Open the Hockey Fan Zone database and then open the Item table in Design view.

2. Add a Lookup field, Item Type to the Item table. The field should appear after the Description field. The field will contain data on the type of item for sale. The item types are CAP (caps and hats), CLO (clothing), and NOV (Novelties).

3. Make the following changes to the Item table:

   a. Change the field size for the On Hand field to Integer. The Format should be fixed and the decimal places should be 0.

   b. Make Description a required field.

   c. Specify the legal values CAP, CLO, and NOV for the Item Type field. Include validation text.

   d. Specify that number on hand must be between 0 and 75. Include validation text.

4. Save the changes to the table design. If a dialog box appears indicating that some data may be lost, click the Yes button.

5. Using a query, assign the value NOV to the Item Type field for all records. Save the query as Update Query.

6. Delete the split form for the Item table that you created in Chapter 1. The form does not include the Item Type field. Recreate the split form for the Item table.

7. Use the split form to change the item type for item numbers 3663 and 7930 to CAP. Change the item type for item numbers 5923 and 7810 to CLO.

8. Add the following items to the Item table.

3673	Blanket	NOV	5	$29.90	$34.00	AC
6078	Key Chain	NOV	20	$3.00	$5.00	MN
7550	Sweatshirt	CLO	8	$19.90	$22.95	LG

9. Create an advanced filter for the Item table. The filter should display the item number, item type, description, and number on hand for all items with less than 10 items on hand. Sort the filter by item type and description. Save the filter settings as a query and name the filter Reorder Filter.

10. Resize all columns in the Item table and the Supplier table to best fit.

11. Using a query, delete all records in the Item table where the description starts with the letter F. Save the query as Delete Query.

12. Specify referential integrity between the Supplier table (the one table) and the Item table (the many table). Cascade the update but not the delete.

13. Compact the database.

14. Submit the revised database in the format specified by your instructor.

In the Lab

Lab 3: Maintaining the Ada Beauty Supply Database

Problem: The management of Ada Beauty Supply has determined that some changes must be made to the database structure. A multivalued field must be added. Validation rules need to be added. Finally, some additions and deletions are required to the database.

Instructions: Use the Ada Beauty Supply database created in the In the Lab 3 of Chapter 1 on page AC 69 for this assignment, or see your instructor for information on accessing the files required for this book. Submit the revised database in the format specified by your instructor.

Instructions Part 1: Several changes must be made to the database structure. For example, management would like a multivalued field that lists the type of services each beauty salon offers. This knowledge can help the sales representatives better meet the needs of their customers. Table 3-2 lists the service abbreviations and descriptions that management would like in a Services Offered multivalued field.

Table 3–2 Service Abbreviations and Descriptions

Service Abbreviation	Description
FAC	Facial
HRS	Hair Styling
MNC	Manicure
PED	Pedicure
MST	Massage Therapy
TAN	Tanning

Management wants to ensure that an entry always appears in the Customer Name field and that any letters entered in the Customer Number field appear in uppercase. It also requires that the amount in the Balance field is never less than 0 or greater than $1,000. Make the changes to the database structure. Place the Services Offered field after the Telephone field.

Continued >

In the Lab *continued*

Instructions Part 2: The data for the Services Offered field shown in Figure 3–82 must be added to the database. The address for Elegante is incorrect. It should be 180 Broadway. Le Beauty has changed its name to Le Beauty Day Spa. Nancy's Place has gone out of business. A new salon, PamperMe Day Spa, just opened. The address for the spa is 2125 Lawrence and the phone number is 555-2401. The spa provides all services except hair styling and tanning.

Management wants to use PA10 as the customer number and Terry Sinson is the sales rep. The new spa has purchased $750 worth of supplies but has not paid for them. Format the datasheet to best fit the data.

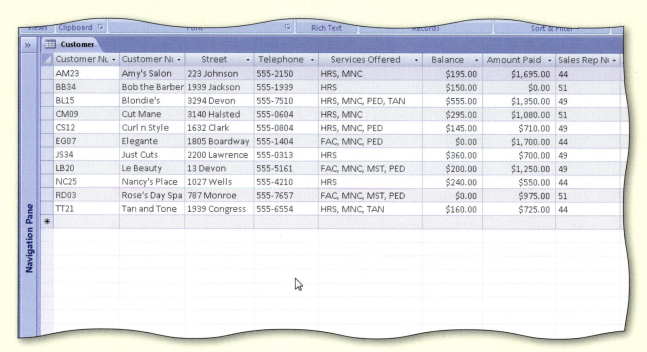

Customer Nu ▾	Customer Na ▾	Street ▾	Telephone ▾	Services Offered ▾	Balance ▾	Amount Paid ▾	Sales Rep Nι ▾
AM23	Amy's Salon	223 Johnson	555-2150	HRS, MNC	$195.00	$1,695.00	44
BB34	Bob the Barber	1939 Jackson	555-1939	HRS	$150.00	$0.00	51
BL15	Blondie's	3294 Devon	555-7510	HRS, MNC, PED, TAN	$555.00	$1,350.00	49
CM09	Cut Mane	3140 Halsted	555-0604	HRS, MNC	$295.00	$1,080.00	51
CS12	Curl n Style	1632 Clark	555-0804	HRS, MNC, PED	$145.00	$710.00	49
EG07	Elegante	1805 Boardway	555-1404	FAC, MNC, PED	$0.00	$1,700.00	44
JS34	Just Cuts	2200 Lawrence	555-0313	HRS	$360.00	$700.00	49
LB20	Le Beauty	13 Devon	555-5161	FAC, MNC, MST, PED	$200.00	$1,250.00	49
NC25	Nancy's Place	1027 Wells	555-4210	HRS	$240.00	$550.00	44
RD03	Rose's Day Spa	787 Monroe	555-7657	FAC, MNC, MST, PED	$0.00	$975.00	51
TT21	Tan and Tone	1939 Congress	555-6554	HRS, MNC, TAN	$160.00	$725.00	44

Figure 3–82

Instructions Part 3: Because the sales reps work on commission, management wants to make sure that customers are not assigned to a sales rep who is not in the database. It also wants the ability to change a sales rep number in the Sales Rep table and have the change applied to the Customer table. Create the appropriate relationship that would satisfy management's needs.

Cases and Places

Apply your creative thinking and problem solving skills to design and implement a solution.

• Easier   •• More Difficult

• 1: Maintaining the Second Hand Goods Database

Use the Second-Hand Goods database you created in Cases and Places 1 in Chapter 1 on page AC 71 for this assignment, or see your instructor for information on accessing the files required for this book. Perform each of the following tasks:

a. The Condition field should be a Lookup field. Only the current values in the database should be legal values.

b. A better description for the bookcases is 3-Shelf Bookcase.

c. The duvet has been sold.

d. The minimum price of any item is $2.00.

e. It would be easier to find items for sale if the default sort order for the item table were by description rather than by item number. Also, some of the descriptions are not displayed completely in Datasheet view.

f. Specify referential integrity. Cascade the update and the delete.

Submit the revised database in the format specified by your instructor.

• 2: Maintaining the BeachCondo Rentals database

Use the BeachCondo Rentals database you created in Cases and Places 2 in Chapter 1 on page AC 71 for this assignment, or see your instructor for information on accessing the files required for this book. Perform each of the following tasks:

a. Add the field, For Sale to the Condo Unit table, to indicate whether a condo unit is for sale. The field is a Yes/No field and should appear after the weekly rate.

b. All units owned by Alonso Bonita are for sale.

c. The Bedrooms, Bathrooms, and Sleeps fields always should contain data.

d. Most common condo units have one bedroom, one bathroom, and sleep two people. All condo units should have a minimum of one bedroom, one bathroom, and sleep two people.

e. No unit rents for less than $700 or more than $1,500.

f. Management has just received a new listing from Mark Graty. It is unit 300. The unit sleeps 10, has three bedrooms, has 2.5 bathrooms, and includes linens. The weekly rate is $1,400 and the owner is interested in selling the unit.

g. Specify referential integrity. Do not cascade the update or the delete.

Submit the revised database in the format specified by your instructor.

•• 3: Maintaining the Restaurant Database

Use the restaurant database you created in Cases and Places 3 in Chapter 1 on page AC 71 for this assignment, or see your instructor for information on accessing the files required for this book. Using the Plan Ahead guidelines presented in this chapter, determine what changes need to be made to your database. For example, a multivalued field could be useful to record opening days and times of a restaurant. Another multivalued field could record restaurant specialties. Create any necessary relationships. Examine the relationships to determine if the default join type is appropriate and whether you need to cascade the update and/or delete. Use a word processing program, such as

Continued >

Microsoft Word, to explain the changes you need to make to the database. Then, make the changes to the database. Submit the Word document and the revised database in the format specified by your instructor.

•• 4: Updating Your Contacts Database

Make It Personal

Use the contacts database you created in Cases and Places 4 in Chapter 1 on page AC 71 for this assignment, or see your instructor for information on accessing the files required for this book. Consider your own personal job situation. Has the focus of your job search changed? Are there specific jobs within the companies of interest that appeal to you? Have you contacted an individual within a company to express your interest? If so, consider creating another table with a one-to-one relationship between the individual contact and the company. Create a multivalued field to store those specific positions that would interest you. Review the fields in the contacts database. Are there any fields you need to add? Are there any fields you need to delete? Are there any tables that need to be deleted? Are there companies that need to be added to your database? Make any necessary changes to your database structure and update the database. Using a word processing program, such as Microsoft Word, explain what changes you made to your database and why you made the changes. Submit the Word document and the revised database in the format specified by your instructor.

•• 5: Understanding Action Queries, Query Wizards, and Table Design Changes

Working Together

With a make-table query, a user can create a new table from one or more tables in the database. The table can be stored in the same database or a new database. As a team, use the Access Help system to learn more about make-table queries. Then, choose either the Cases and Places 1 database or the Cases and Places 2 database and create a make-table query. For example, for the Hockey Fan Zone, the management could create a table named Supplier Call List that would include the item code, description, and cost of each item as well as the supplier name and telephone number. Write a one-page paper that (1) explains the purpose for which the new table is intended and (2) suggests at least two additional uses for make-table queries. Submit the paper and the database in the format specified by your instructor.

Open the Students database that you created in Chapter 1. As a team, review the data types for each of the fields that are in the database. Do any of these data types need to be changed? For example, is there a field that should store multiple values? Are there any fields that should contain validation rules? Change the data types and add validation rules as necessary. Examine the tables in your database. Delete any tables that you do not need. Determine the relationships among the remaining tables. Are there any one-to-one relationships or one-to-many relationships? Write a one-page paper that explains your reasons for changing (or not changing) the structure of the database. Submit the paper and the database in the format specified by your instructor.

Save the Ada Beauty Supply database as AdaTeam Beauty Supply. Research the purpose of the Find Unmatched Query Wizard and the Find Duplicates Query Wizard. Use the AdaTeam database and create queries using each of these wizards. Did the queries perform as expected? Open each query in Design view and modify it, for example, add another field to the query. What happened to the query results? Write a one-page paper that explains the purpose of each query wizard and describes the team's experiences with creating and modifying the queries. Submit the paper and database in the format specified by your instructor.

Integration Feature

Sharing Data Among Applications

Objectives

You will have mastered the material in this Integration Feature when you can:

- Import from or link to an Excel worksheet

- Import from or link to an Access database

- Import from or link to a text file

- Export data to Excel, Word, and text files

- Publish a report

- Export and import XML data

Integration Feature Introduction

It is not uncommon for people to use an application for some specific purpose, only to find later that another application may be better suited. For example, an organization initially might use Excel to maintain data on inventory only to discover later that the data would be better maintained in an Access database. This feature shows how to use data from other applications in Access. It also shows how to make Access data available to other applications.

Project — Sharing Data Among Applications

Camashaly specializes in sales of used computers and computer equipment. Employees have been using Microsoft Excel to automate a variety of tasks for several years. When determining to keep track of prices, item descriptions, serial numbers, and other data on the items for sale, the administrators originally decided to maintain the data as an Excel worksheet. Employees recently completed Microsoft Office training and now have decided they need to maintain the data in an Access database. They have two choices. They can **import** the data, which means to make a copy of the data as a table in the Access database. In this case, any changes made to the data in Access would not be reflected in the Excel worksheet. The other option is to **link** to the data in the worksheet. When data is linked, the data appears as a table in the Access database, but is, in fact, maintained in its original form in Excel. Any changes to the Excel data are thus automatically reflected when the linked table is viewed in Access. In this arrangement, Access would typically be used as a vehicle for viewing and querying the data, with actual updates being made in Excel.

Figure 1 illustrates the conversion process. The type of worksheet that can be converted is one in which the data is stored as a **list**, that is, a collection of rows and columns in which all the entries in a column represent the same type of data. In this type of list, the first row contains column headings rather than data. In the worksheet in Figure 1a, the first row contains the labels, which are entries indicating the type of data found in the column. The entry in the first column, for example, is Item Id, indicating that all the other values in the column are Item Ids. The entry in the second column is Description, indicating that all the other values in the column are descriptions. Other than the first row, which contains the labels, all the rows contain precisely the same type of data shown in the Access database in Figure 1b: an item Id in the first column, a description in the second column, the number of units on hand in the third column, and so on.

first row contains column headings that convert to field names in table

data

Item worksheet tab

Item table tab

field names

data

(a) Microsoft Excel Worksheet

(b) Microsoft Access Table

Figure 1

As the figures illustrate, the worksheet, shown in Figure 1a, is copied to an Access table, shown in Figure 1b. The columns in the worksheet become the fields. The column headings in the first row of the worksheet become the field names. The rows of the worksheet, other than the first row, which contains the labels, become the records in the table. In the process, each field will be assigned the data type that seems the most reasonable, given the data currently in the worksheet.

Organizations that currently use Access for their data needs often find that they need to export the data to other applications. JSP Recruiters has determined that it needs to make some of the data in its database available to other applications. Some users need the data in Excel; others want it placed in a Microsoft Word document. Still others want the ability to receive a report by e-mail.

You can **export** (copy) data from an Access database so that another application (for example, Excel) can use the data. Figure 2a on the next page shows the Recruiter-Client query exported to Excel and Figure 2b on the next page shows the same query exported to Word.

At times you may want to send a report to a user by e-mail. It would be prohibitive to send the whole database to the other user, just so the user could print or view the report. In addition, doing so would require the other user to have Microsoft Access installed. A better way is to publish the report as either a PDF or XPS (XML Paper Specification) file. A user with the appropriate software then can view and print the file. In Figure 2c, the report appears in the XML Paper Specification viewer. It looks just as it does in Access.

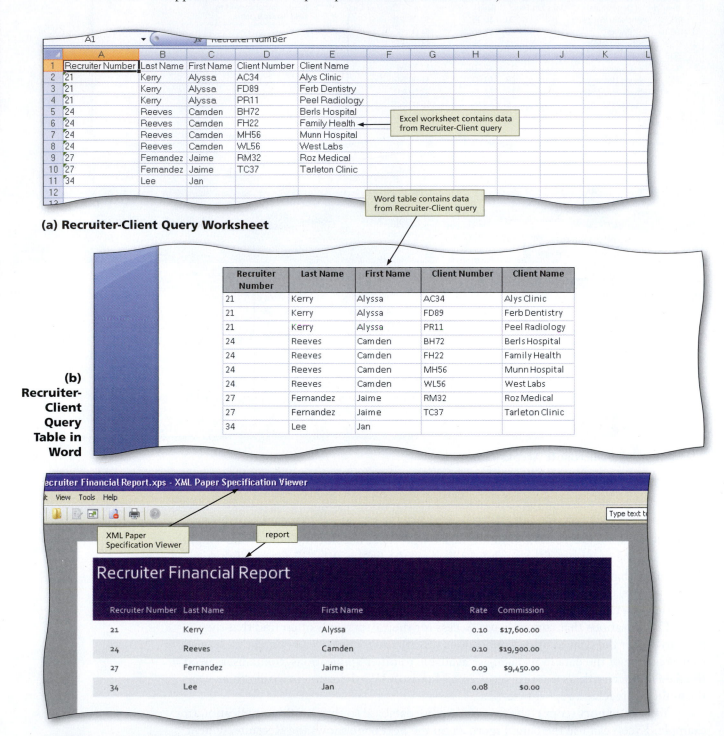

(a) Recruiter-Client Query Worksheet

(b) Recruiter-Client Query Table in Word

(c) XPS Version of Recruiter Financial Report

Figure 2

JSP Recruiters also would like to export the Client and Recruiter tables in such a way that they can be imported easily to a database used by a related organization, JSP Consulting, that handles various accounting functions for JSP Recruiters. The users have learned that the easiest way to do this is to use XML (Extensible Markup Language), which is a language that defines data records on a page, allowing for exchange of data between dissimilar applications. The XML format allows you to export and import both data and structure of multiple related tables in a single operation.

Overview

As you read through this feature, you will learn how to share data among applications by performing these general tasks:

- Import an Excel worksheet into an Access table
- Export a query to Excel
- Export a query to Word
- Publish a report as an XPS file
- Export multiple tables to an XML file
- Import multiple tables from an XML file

BTW

PDF and XPS Formats
Before you export to PDF and XPS formats, check to make sure you have the PDF or XPS button in the Export group on the External Data tab. If not, you must first install a free add-in program. To learn more about installing the add-in, type PDF in the Access Help window and follow the instructions. If you are using a computer in a school or work setting, check with your instructor or IT staff before installing any add-in program.

Plan Ahead

Guidelines for Sharing Data Among Applications

1. **Identify sources of external data for the database.** Does data already exist that you should incorporate into your database? Determine whether the data is in an Excel worksheet, another database, a text file, or some other application.

2. **Determine whether the data you have identified is in an appropriate format.** Is it a collection of rows and columns in which all the entries in a column represent the same type of data? Does the first row contain column headings rather than data? Is the data separated by tabs or by commas?

3. **Determine whether changes made to the data in the original data source should be reflected in the Access table.** If so, linking to the data source is the appropriate action. If not, importing the data would be appropriate.

4. **If the source of data is an Access database, determine whether, in addition to the tables, there are other objects to be imported.** If you import tables, you also can import queries, forms, and reports based on those tables. If, for example, the other database contained a report based on a table you are importing, you can import the report as well, thus saving you the effort of having to recreate the report.

5. **For data in your database that you want to make available to others, determine whether exporting the data is appropriate.** If you export the data, any changes that others make to the data will not be reflected in your database. If it is acceptable that these changes are not reflected, then exporting is appropriate. If not, the data will need to be linked. Linking must take place within the other application.

6. **If data is to be exported, determine the destination application.** The application that will receive the data determines the export process to be used. Common choices are Excel and Word. You also can export to text files in a variety of formats. For applications to which you cannot directly export data, you often can export an appropriately formatted text file that the other application can import. To make reports available to others, rather than exporting the report, you can publish the report, which is the process of making the report available to others on the Web. You can publish the report in either PDF or XPS format, so you would need to determine which is appropriate for the person who wants to be able to view the report.

When necessary, more specific details concerning the above decisions and/or actions are presented at appropriate positions within the feature. The feature also will identify the use of these guidelines in sharing data as shown in Figures 1 and 2.

Starting Access

If you are using a computer to step through the project in this chapter and you want your screen to match the figures in this book, you should change your screen's resolution to 1024×768. For information about how to change a computer's resolution, read Appendix E.

To Start Access

The following steps, which assume Windows is running, start Access.

Note: If you are using Windows XP, see Appendix F for alternate steps.

1 Click the Start button on the Windows taskbar to display the Start menu.

2 Click All Programs at the bottom of the left pane on the Start menu to display the All Programs list and then click Microsoft Office in the All Programs list to display the Microsoft Office list.

3 Click Microsoft Office Access 2007 on the Microsoft Office submenu to start Access and display the Getting Started with Microsoft Office Access window.

4 If the Access window is not maximized, click the Maximize button on its title bar to maximize the window.

To Create a New Database

Before importing data from another application to an Access database, you must ensure that a database exists. If there is no database, then you need to create one. The following steps create a database on a USB flash drive that will store the items for Camashaly.

Note: If you are using Windows XP, see Appendix F for alternate steps.

1 With a USB flash drive connected to one of the computer's USB ports, click Blank Database in the Getting Started with Microsoft Office Access screen to create a new blank database.

2 Type Camashaly in the File Name text box and then click the 'Browse for a location to put your database' button to display the File New Database dialog box.

3 Click Computer in the Favorite Links section to display a list of available drives and folders and then double-click UDISK 2.0 (E:) (your letter may be different) in the Computer list to select the USB flash drive as the new save location.

4 Click the OK button to select the USB flash drive as the location for the database and to return to the Getting Started with Microsoft Office Access screen.

5 Click the Create button to create the database on the USB flash drive with the file name, Camashaly.

Importing or Linking Data from Other Applications to Access

The process of importing or linking an Access database uses a wizard. Specifically, if the data is imported from an Excel worksheet, the process will use the **Import Spreadsheet Wizard**; if the data is linked to an Excel worksheet, the process will use the **Link Spreadsheet Wizard**. The wizard takes you through some basic steps, asking a few simple questions. After you have answered the questions, the wizard will import or link the data.

Identify sources of external data for the database: Excel worksheet.

You need to decide whether it is appropriate for data you currently keep in an Excel worksheet to be kept in a database instead. The following are some common reasons for using a database instead of a worksheet:

1. The worksheet contains a great deal of redundant data. As discussed in Chapter 1 on pages AC 10 and AC 12, databases can be designed to eliminate redundant data.

2. The data to be maintained consists of multiple interrelated items. For example, the JSP Recruiters database maintains data on two items, clients and recruiters, and these items are interrelated. A client has a single recruiter and each recruiter is responsible for several clients. The JSP Recruiters database is a very simple one. Databases easily can contain many separate, but interrelated, items.

3. You want to use the powerful query and report capabilities of Microsoft Access.

Plan Ahead

Determine whether the data you have identified is in an appropriate format: Excel worksheet.

Before importing or linking the Excel worksheet you have identified, you need to make sure it is in an appropriate format. The following are some of the actions you should take to ensure correct format:

1. Make sure the data is in the form of a list, a collection of rows and columns in which all the entries in a column represent the same type of data.

2. Make sure that there are no blank rows within the list. If there are, remove them prior to importing or linking.

3. Make sure there are no blank columns within the list. If there are, remove them prior to importing or linking.

4. Determine whether the first row contains column headings that will make appropriate field names in the resulting table. If not, you might consider adding such a row. In general, the process is simpler if the first row in the worksheet contains appropriate column headings.

Plan Ahead

To Import an Excel Worksheet

After Camashaly managers identified that a worksheet named Computer Items contains data that should be in a table in the database, they would import the data. You import a worksheet by using the Import Spreadsheet Wizard. In the process, you will indicate that the first row in the Computer Items worksheet contains the column headings. These column headings then will become the field names in the Access table. In addition, you will indicate the primary key for the table. As part of the process, you could, if appropriate, choose not to include all the fields from the worksheet in the resulting table.

The following steps import the Computer Items Excel worksheet.

Note: If you are using Windows XP, see Appendix F for alternate steps.

 1

- Click External Data on the Ribbon to display the External Data tab (Figure 3).

Figure 3

2

- Click the Excel button in the Import group on the External Data tab to display the Get External Data – Excel Spreadsheet dialog box.

- Click the Browse button in the Get External Data – Excel Spreadsheet dialog box.

- If necessary, click Computer in the Favorite Links section and then double-click UDISK 2.0 (E:) to select the USB flash drive.

- Click the Computer Items workbook, and then click the Open button to select the workbook (Figure 4).

Figure 4

3

- With the option button to import the data to a new table selected, click the OK button to display the Import Spreadsheet Wizard dialog box (Figure 5).

Q&A What happens if I select the option button to append records to an existing table?

Instead of the records being placed in a new table, they will be added to the existing table, provided the value in the primary key field does not duplicate that on an existing record.

Figure 5

4

- If necessary, click First Row Contains Column Headings to select it.

- Click the Next button (Figure 6).

Q&A When would I use the options on this screen?

You would use these options if you wanted to change properties for one or more fields. You can change the name, the data type, and whether the field is indexed. You also can indicate that some fields are not to be imported.

Figure 6

5

- Because the Field Options need not be specified, click the Next button (Figure 7).

Figure 7

6

- Click the 'Choose my own primary key.' option button (Figure 8).

Q&A

How do I decide which option button to select?

If one of the fields is an appropriate primary key, choose your own primary key from the list of fields. If you are sure you do not want a primary key, choose No primary key. Otherwise, let Access add the primary key.

Figure 8

7

- Because the Item Id field, which is the correct field, is already selected as the primary key, click the Next button.

- Be sure Item appears in the Import to Table text box.

- Click the Finish button to import the data (Figure 9).

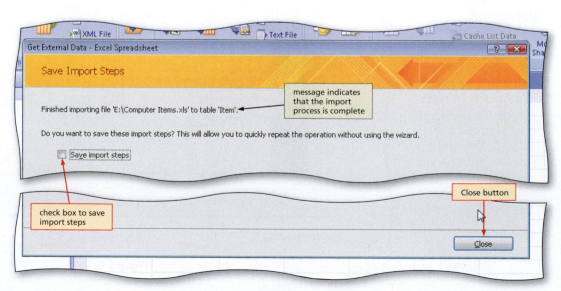

Figure 9

8
- Click the Save import steps check box to display the Save import steps options.

- If necessary, type `Import-Computer Items` in the Save as text box.

- Type `Import data from Computer Items workbook into Item table` in the Description text box (Figure 10).

Q&A

When would I create an Outlook task?

If the import operation is one you will repeat on a regular basis, you can create and schedule the import process just as you can schedule any other Outlook task.

Figure 10

9
- Click the Save Import button to save the import steps (Figure 11).

Figure 11

Other Ways

1. Right-click Table1 : Table in Navigation Pane, point to Import, click appropriate file format

Using the Access Table

After the Access version of the table has been created, you can use it as you would any other table. You can open the table in Datasheet view (Figure 1b on page AC 207). You can make changes to the data. You can create queries or reports that use the data in the table.

By clicking Design View on the table's shortcut menu, you can view the table's structure and make any necessary changes to the structure. The changes may include changing field sizes and types (for those that may not be correct), creating indexes, specifying the primary key, or adding additional fields. If you have imported multiple tables that are to be related, you will need to relate the tables. To accomplish any of these tasks, use the same steps you used in Chapter 3.

BTW

Linking versus Importing

When an external table or worksheet is imported, or converted, into an Access database, a copy of the data is placed as a table in the database. The original data still exists, just as it did before, but no further connection exists between it and the data in the database. Changes to the original data do not affect the data in the database. Likewise, changes in the database do not affect the original data.

It also is possible to link data stored in a variety of formats to Access databases by selecting the 'Link to the data source by creating a linked table' option button on the Get External Data - Excel Spreadsheet dialog box rather than the 'Import the source data into a new table in the current database' option button (Figure 4 on page AC 212). With linking, the connection is maintained.

When an Excel worksheet is linked, for example, the worksheet is not stored in the database. Instead Access simply establishes a connection to the worksheet so you can view the data in either Access or Excel. Any change made in the worksheet will be visible immediately in the table. For example, if you change an address in Excel and then view the table in Access, you would see the new address. If you add a new row in Excel and then view the table in Access, the row would appear as a new record. You cannot make changes to the table in Access. If you want to add, change, or delete data, you must make the changes in the worksheet because the data is stored in an Excel workbook.

To identify that a table is linked to other data, Access places an arrow in front of the table (Figure 12). In addition, the Excel icon in front of the name indicates that the data is linked to an Excel worksheet.

Figure 12

The Linked Table Manager

After you link tables between a worksheet and a database or between two databases, you can modify many of the linked table's features. For example, you can rename the linked table, set view properties, and set links between tables in queries. If you move, rename, or modify linked tables, you can use the **Linked Table Manager** to update the links. To do so, click Database Tools on the Ribbon to display the Database Tools tab. Then click the Linked Table Manager button on the Database Tools tab. The Linked Table Manager dialog box that appears includes instructions on how to update the links.

To Close a Database

The following steps show how to close the database.

1 Click the Office Button to display the Office Button menu.

2 Click Close Database on the Office Button menu.

Importing from or Linking to Data in Another Access Database

Just as you can import data from an Excel worksheet, you can import data from another Access database. Similarly, just as you can link to data in an Excel worksheet, you can link to data in another Access database.

<table>
<tr><td>

Identify sources of external data for the database: Access database.
You need to decide whether it is appropriate for you to import or link data in another Access database. The following are some common reasons for importing from or linking to another database:

1. You want to combine two databases into one. By importing, you can copy all objects (tables, queries, forms, reports, and so on) from one database to the other.

2. You want to create tables that are similar to tables in another database. When importing, you can choose to copy the table structure without the data. The table created in the process will have all the fields and field properties of the original, but will be empty.

3. You want to copy a collection of related objects from another database. In one operation you could, for example, copy a table along with all queries, forms, and reports that are based on that table.

4. You have several databases, but data in some tables is the same, for example, the Client table must be shared between some of the databases. By linking, any updates to the table in the source database are immediately available to anyone using any of the other databases.

</td><td>

Plan Ahead

</td></tr>
</table>

TO IMPORT DATA FROM ANOTHER ACCESS DATABASE

The following steps would import data from another Access database into the database that is currently open.

1. Click the Access button in the Import group on the External Data tab.
2. Select the database containing the data to be imported.
3. Be sure the 'Import tables, queries, forms, reports, macros, and modules into the current database' option button is selected and click the OK button.
4. In the Import Objects dialog box, select the tables, queries, forms, reports, macros, and/or modules you wish to import and then click the OK button.
5. Decide if you wish to save the import steps.

TO LINK TO DATA IN ANOTHER ACCESS DATABASE

The following steps would link tables in another Access database into the database that is currently open.

1. Click the Access button in the Import group on the External Data tab.
2. Select the database containing the tables to be linked.
3. Click the 'Link to the data source by creating a linked table' option button to link and then click the OK button.
4. In the Link tables dialog box, select the tables you wish to link and then click the OK button.

Text Files

Text files contain unformatted characters including both readable characters, such as numbers and letters, and some special characters, such as tabs, carriage returns, and line feeds. Typical extensions for text files that can be imported or linked into Access databases are txt, csv, asc, and tab.

To be able to use a text file for importing or linking, it must be organized into records (rows) and fields (columns). Records and fields can be organized in two ways: delimited files and fixed-width files.

In **delimited files**, each record is on a separate line and the fields are separated by a special character, called the **delimiter**. Common delimiters are tabs, semicolons, commas, and spaces. You also can choose any other value that does not appear within the field contents. The csv (comma separated values) file often used in Excel is an example of a delimited file.

In **fixed-width files**, the width of any field is the same on every record. For example, if the width of the first field on the first record is 12 characters, the width of the first field on every other record also must be 12 characters.

Plan Ahead

Identify sources of external data for the database: text file.
You need to decide whether it is appropriate for you to use external data stored in a text file. The following are some common reasons for using a text file for this purpose:

1. Data that you want to import is not available in a format that Access recognizes. You first would export the data from the original application to a text file and then import that text file into Access.

2. You manage data in Access but regularly receive data in text files from other users that needs to be incorporated into your database.

Plan Ahead

Determine whether the data you have identified is in an appropriate format: text file.
Before importing or linking the text file you have identified, you need to make sure it is in an appropriate format. The following are some of the actions you should take to ensure correct format:

1. Make sure the data in the text file consistently follows one of the available formats (delimited or fixed width). If the file is delimited, identify the delimiter and make sure the same one is used throughout. If the file is fixed-width, make sure each field on each record is the same width.

2. Make sure that there are no blank records within the file. If there are, remove them prior to importing or linking.

3. Make sure there are no blank fields within the list. If there are, remove them prior to importing or linking.

4. For each field, make sure the entries in each record represent the same type of data.

5. If it is a delimited file, determine whether the first row contains column headings that will make appropriate field names in the resulting table. If not, you should add such a row. In general, the process is simpler if the first row in a delimited file contains appropriate column headings.

6. Make sure there are no extra paragraph (carriage) returns at the end of the file. If there are, remove them prior to importing or linking.

TO IMPORT DATA FROM OR LINK DATA TO A TEXT FILE

To import data from or link data to a text file, you would use the following steps.

1. Click the Text File button in the Import group on the External Data tab.

2. Select the text file containing the data to be imported.

3. Be sure the 'Import the source into a new table in the current database' option button is selected if you wish to create a new table. Click the 'Append a copy of the records to the table' option button if you wish to add to an existing table, and then select the table. Click the 'Link to the data source by creating a linked table' option button if you wish to link the data. Once you have selected the correct option button, click the OK button.

4. Select the Delimited option button for a delimited file or the Fixed Width option button for a fixed-width file, and then click the Next button.

5a. For a delimited file, select the character that delimits the field values. If you know the file uses a text qualifier, which is a symbol used to enclose character values, select either the double quotation mark (") or the single quotation mark ('). If the first row contains field names, click the First Row contains Field Names check box. Once you have made your selections, click the Next button.

5b. For a fixed-width file, review the structure that Access recommends. If the recommended structure is not appropriate, follow the directions on the screen to add, remove, or adjust the lines. Once you have finished, click the Next button.

6. You can use the next screen if you need to change properties of one or more fields. When finished, click the Next button.

7. If you are importing, select the appropriate primary key, and then click the Next button. If you are linking, you will not have an opportunity to select a primary key.

8. Be sure the table name is correct, and then click the Finish button to import or link the data. Decide if you wish to save the import steps.

Using Saved Import Steps

You can use a set of saved import steps from within Access by clicking the Saved Imports button on the External Data tab. You then will see the Manage Data Tasks dialog box, as shown in Figure 13 on the next page. Select the set of saved import steps you want to repeat. (In this case only the import named Import-Computer Items exists.) Click the Run button to repeat the import steps you saved earlier. If you have created an Outlook task, you can schedule the import operation just as you schedule any other Outlook task.

Figure 13

Exporting Data from Access to Other Applications

Exporting is the process of copying database objects to another database, to a worksheet, or to some other format so another application (for example, Excel) can use the data. Businesses need the flexibility of using the same data in different applications. For example, numerical data in a table exported to Excel could be analyzed using Excel's powerful statistical functions. Data also could be exported as an RTF file for use in marketing brochures.

To Open a Database

Before exporting the JSP Recruiters data, you first must open the database. The following steps open the database.

Note: If you are using Windows XP, see Appendix F for alternate steps.

1 With your USB flash drive connected to one of the computer's USB ports, click the More button to display the Open dialog box.

2 If the Folders list is displayed below the Folders button, click the Folders button to remove the Folders list.

3 If necessary, click Computer in the Favorite Links section and then double-click UDISK 2.0 (E:) to select the USB flash drive as the new open location. (Your drive letter might be different.)

4 Click JSP Recruiters to select the file name.

5 Click the Open button to open the database.

6 If a Security Warning appears, click the Options button to display the Microsoft Office Security Options dialog box.

7 Click the 'Enable this content' option button and then click the OK button to enable the content.

To Export Data to Excel

Once JSP Recruiters has decided to make the Recruiter-Client Query available to Excel users, it needs to export the data. To export data to Excel, select the table or query to be exported, and then click the Excel button in the Export group on the External Data tab. The following steps export the Client-Recruiter Query to Excel and save the export steps.

1
- Click the Recruiter-Client Query in the Navigation Pane to select it.
- Click External Data on the Ribbon to display the External Data tab (Figure 14).

Figure 14

2

- Click the Excel button in the Export group on the External Data tab to display the Export – Excel Spreadsheet dialog box.

- Click the Browse button and select your USB flash drive as the file location.

- Be sure the file name is Recruiter-Client Query and then click the Save button (Figure 15).

Q&A Did I need to browse?

No. You could type the appropriate file location.

Q&A Could I change the name of the file?

You could change it. Simply replace the current file name with the one you want.

Q&A What if the file I want to export already exists?

Access will indicate that the file already exists and ask if you want to replace it. If you click the Yes button, the file you export will replace the old file. If you click the No button, you must either change the name of the export file or cancel the process.

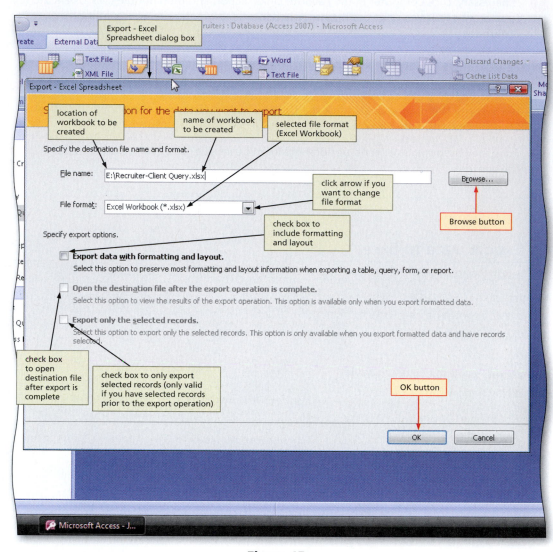

Figure 15

3
- Click the OK button to export the data (Figure 16).

4
- Click the Save export steps check box to display the Save export steps options.

- If necessary, type `Export-Recruiter-Client Query` in the Save as text box.

- Type `Export the Recruiter-Client Query without formatting` in the Description text box.

- Click the Save Export button to save the export steps.

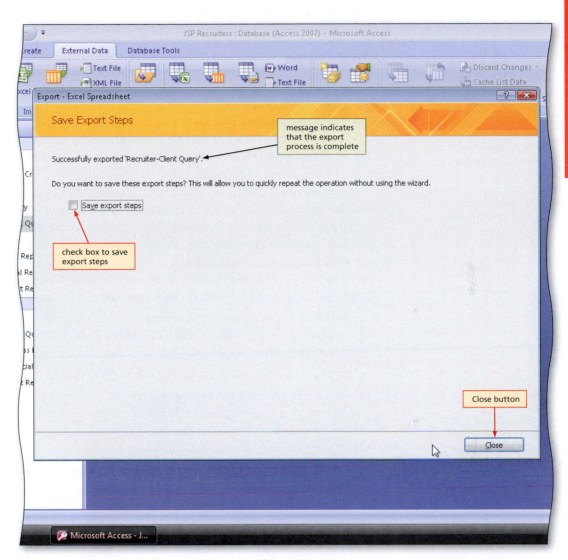

Figure 16

To Export Data to Word

Once JSP Recruiters has decided to also make the Recruiter-Client Query available to Word, it needs to export the data. There is a problem, however. It is not possible to export data to the standard Word format. It is possible, however to export the data as an RTF (rich text file), which Word can access. The following steps export the data to an RTF file. They do not save the export steps.

1 With the Recruiter-Client Query selected in the Navigation Pane and the External Data tab appearing on the screen, click the Word button in the Export group on the External Data tab to display the Export - RTF File dialog box.

2 Select your USB drive as the file location and make sure that Recruiter-Client Query is the file name.

3 If necessary, click the Save button and then click the OK button to export the data.

4 Because you will not save the export steps, click the Close button to close the Export - RTF File dialog box.

BTW

XPS Format
To view a file in XPS format, you need a viewer. You or the recipient of your file can download a free viewer from the Downloads section of Microsoft Office Online.

TO EXPORT DATA TO A TEXT FILE

When exporting data to a text file, you can choose to export the data with formatting and layout. This option preserves much of the formatting and layout in tables, queries, forms, and reports. For forms and reports, this is the only option.

If you do not need to preserve the formatting, you can choose either delimited or fixed-width as the format for the exported file. The most common option, especially if formatting is not an issue, is delimited. You can choose the delimiter and also whether to include field names on the first row. In many cases, delimiting with a comma and including the field names is a good choice.

To export data from a table or query to a comma-delimited file in which the first row contains the column headings, you would use the following steps.

1. With the object to be exported selected in the Navigation Pane and the External Data tab appearing on the Ribbon, click the Text File button in the Export group on the External Data tab to display the Export - Text File dialog box.

2. Select the name and location for the file to be created.

BTW

PDF Format
To view a PDF file, you must have a PDF reader installed on your computer. One such reader is the Acrobat Reader, available for free from Adobe Systems.

3. If you need to preserve formatting and layout, be sure the 'Export data with formatting and layout' check box is checked. If you do not need to preserve formatting and layout, make sure the check box is not checked. Once you have made your selection, click the OK button in the Export - Text File dialog box.

4. To create a delimited file, be sure the Delimited option button is selected. To create a fixed-width file, be sure the Fixed Width option button is selected. Once you have made your selection, click the Next button.

5a. If you are exporting to a delimited file, choose the delimiter that you want to separate your fields, such as a comma. Decide whether to include field names on the first row and, if so, click the Include Field Names on First Row check box. If you want to select a text qualifier, select it in the Text Qualifier list. When you have made your selections, click the Next button.

5b. If you are exporting to a fixed-width file, review the position of the vertical lines that separate your fields. If any lines are not positioned correctly, follow the directions on the screen to reposition them. When you have finished, click the Next button.

6. Click the Finish button to export the data.

7. Save the export steps if you wish, or simply click the Close button in the Export - Text File dialog box to close the dialog box without saving the export steps.

To Publish a Report

At JSP Recruiters, the staff would like to make the Recruiter Financial Report available through e-mail, which they can do by publishing the report as either a PDF or XPS file. The following steps publish the Recruiter Financial Report as an XPS file.

Note: If you are using Windows XP, see Appendix F for alternate steps.

- Click the Recruiter Financial Report in the Navigation Pane to select it.

- Click the 'PDF or XPS' button in the Export group on the External Data tab (see Figure 14 on page AC 221) to display the Publish as PDF or XPS dialog box.

- Select your USB drive as the file location. Make sure that Recruiter Financial Report is the file name and that XPS Document is the file type. If necessary, remove the check mark in the 'Open file after publishing' check box.

- Click the 'Standard (publishing online and printing)' option button to create a file that is appropriate for both publishing online and printing (Figure 17).

Q&A

How do I publish as PDF?

Change XPS Document to PDF in the Save as type box.

Figure 17

- Click the Publish button to publish the report as an XPS file.

- Because you will not save the export steps, click the Close button to close the Export - XPS dialog box.

Using Saved Export Steps

You can use a set of saved Export steps from within Access by clicking the Saved Exports button on the External Data tab. You then select the set of saved export steps you want to repeat and click the Run button in the Manage Data Tasks dialog box. If you have created an Outlook task, you can schedule the export operation just as you can schedule any other Outlook task.

BTW

Viewing or Printing the Report

To view or print the report stored in the XPS file, use the XML Paper Specification Viewer. If the XML Paper Specification Viewer is not installed on your system, you can obtain it from Microsoft. If you are unable to view or print XPS files, you alternatively can publish the report as a PDF. To do so, change the Save as type from XPS Document to PDF before clicking the Publish button.

XML

Just as Hypertext Markup Language (HTML) is the standard language for creating and displaying Web pages, **Extensible Markup Language (XML)** is the standard language for describing and delivering data on the Web. Another way of viewing the difference is that HTML handles the *appearance* of data within a Web page, whereas XML handles the *meaning* of data. XML is a data interchange standard that allows you to exchange data between dissimilar systems or applications. With XML, you can describe both the data and the structure **(schema)** of the data. You can export tables, queries, forms, or reports.

When exporting XML data, you can choose to export multiple related tables in a single operation to a single XML file. If you later import this XML data to another database, you will import all the tables in a single operation. Thus, the new database would contain each of the tables. All the fields would have the correct data types and sizes and the primary keys would be correct.

To Export XML Data

In exporting XML data, you indicate whether to just save the data or to save both the data and the schema (that is, the structure). If you have made changes to the appearance of the data, such as changing the font, and want these changes saved as well, you save what is known as the **presentation**. The data is saved in a file with the XML extension, the schema is saved in a file with the XSD extension, and the presentation is saved in a file with the XSL extension. The default choice, which usually is appropriate, is to save both the data and schema, but not the presentation. If multiple tables are related, such as the Client and Recruiter tables in the JSP Recruiters data, you can export both tables to a single file.

The following steps export both the Client and Recruiter tables to a single XML file called Client. The steps save the data and the schema, but do not save the presentation.

- Click the Client table in the Navigation Pane to select it.

- Click the More button in the Export group on the External Data tab to display the More button menu with additional export options (Figure 18).

Figure 18

- Click XML File on the More button menu to display the Export - XML File dialog box.

- Select your USB drive as the file location and make sure that Client is the file name (Figure 19).

Figure 19

3

- Click the OK button to display the Export XML dialog box (Figure 20).

Figure 20

4

- Click the More Options button to specify additional options (Figure 21).

Q&A

What is the purpose of the other tabs in this dialog box?

You can use the Schema tab to indicate whether you want primary key, index information, table properties, and field properties included (normally they are) and whether the schema information is to be stored in a separate file (normally it is). If you want to export the presentation, you can use the Presentation tab to indicate this fact and also specify options concerning how the Presentation will be exported.

Figure 21

5

- Click the expand indicator (the plus sign) to the left of [Lookup Data], and then click the Recruiter check box to select the Recruiter table (Figure 22).

6

- Click the OK button to export the data.

- Because you will not save the export steps, click the Close button to close the Export - XML File dialog box.

- Click the Close Database command on the Office Button menu.

Figure 22

To Create a New Database

Note: If you are using Windows XP, see Appendix F for alternate steps.

Before importing the data from the JSP Recruiters database, you need to create the new JSP Consulting database that will contain the data. The following steps create the JSP Consulting database on a USB flash drive.

1 With a USB flash drive connected to one of the computer's USB ports, click Blank Database in the Getting Started with Microsoft Office Access screen to create a new blank database.

2 Type JSP Consulting in the File Name text box and then click the 'Browse for a location to put your database' button to display the File New Database dialog box.

3 Click Computer in the Favorite Links section to display a list of available drives and folders and then click UDISK 2.0 (E:) (your letter may be different) in the Computer list to select the USB flash drive as the new save location.

4 Click the OK button to select the USB flash drive as the location for the database and to return to the Getting Started with Microsoft Office Access screen.

5 Click the Create button to create the database on the USB flash drive with the file name, JSP Consulting.

To Import XML Data

The following steps import both the Client and Recruiter tables stored in the XML file called Client. In addition to having the same data, the fields in both tables will have precisely the same data types and sizes as in the original database. Also, the same fields will have been designated primary keys.

Note: If you are using Windows XP, see Appendix F for alternate steps.

- With the JSP Consulting database open, click External Data on the Ribbon to display the External Data tab.

- Click the XML File button in the Import group on the External Data tab to display the Get External Data - XML File dialog box.

- Click the Browse button in the Get External Data - XML File dialog box to display the File Open dialog box.

- Click Computer and then double-click UDISK 2.0 (E:).

- Click the Client file to select it (Figure 23).

Q&A Should I click the xsd version?

No. If you do, you will import both tables, but none of the data. That is, the tables will be empty.

Figure 23

Access Integration Feature

2

● Click the Open button to return to the Get External Data - XML File dialog box (Figure 24).

Figure 24

3

● Click the OK button to display the Import XML dialog box (Figure 25).

4

● Be sure the Structure and Data option button is selected and then click the OK button to import the data.

● Because you will not save the import steps, click the Close button to close the Get External Data - XML File dialog box.

Figure 25

To Quit Access

You are ready to quit Access. The following step quits Access.

1 Click the Close button on the right side of the Access title bar to quit Access.

BTW

Certification
The Microsoft Certified Application Specialist (MCAS) program provides an opportunity for you to obtain a valuable industry credential — proof that you have the Access 2007 skills required by employers. For more information, see Appendix G or visit the Access 2007 Certification Web page (scsite.com/ac2007/cert).

Feature Summary

In this feature you have learned to import from and link to data in Excel worksheets, other Access databases, and text files; export data to Excel worksheets, Word documents, and text files; publish reports; and export and import XML data. The items listed below include all the new Access skills you have learned in this chapter.

1. Import an Excel Worksheet (AC 212)
2. Import Data from Another Access Database (AC 217)
3. Link to Data in Another Access Database (AC 217)
4. Import Data from or Link Data to a Text File (AC 219)
5. Export Data to Excel (AC 221)
6. Export Data to Word (AC 223)
7. Export Data to a Text File (AC 224)
8. Publish a Report (AC 225)
9. Export XML Data (AC 226)
10. Import XML Data (AC 228)

 If you have a SAM user profile, you may have access to hands-on instruction, practice, and assessment. Log in to your SAM account (http://sam2007.course.com) to launch any assigned training activities or exams that relate to the skills covered in this feature.

In the Lab

Design, create, modify, and/or use a database following the guidelines, concepts, and skills presented in this feature.

Lab 1: Importing Data to an Access Database

Problem: TAL Woodworks sells custom wood accessories for the home. TAL uses worksheets to keep track of inventory and customers. TAL realizes that customer data would be better handled if maintained in an Access database. The company wants to maintain the products inventory in Excel but also would like to be able to use the query and report features of Access.

Instructions: For this assignment, you will need two files: Customer.csv and Product.xlsx. See the inside back cover of this book for instructions for downloading the Data Files for Students, or see your instructor for information on accessing the files required in this book. Perform the following tasks:

1. Start Access and create a new database in which to store all the objects for TAL Woodworks. Call the database TAL Woodworks.

2. Import the Customer worksheet shown in Figure 26 into Access. The worksheet is saved as a .csv file.

	A	B	C	D	E	F	G	H	I	J	K
1	Customer Number	Name	Address	City	State	Balance					
2	AD23	Adson Gifts	407 Mallory	Tourin	CO	$ 205.00					
3	AR75	Arthur's Interiors	200 Mimberly	Denton	CO	$ 180.00					
4	BE28	Becker Design	224 Harbor Oak	Charleston	CO	$ 170.00					
5	CR66	Casa Grande	506 Mallory	Tourin	CO	$0.00					
6	DL60	Dee's Things	123 Village	Denton	CO	$ 235.00					
7	GR36	Grande Casa	1345 Fern	Charleston	CO	$ 204.00					
8	HA09	Hal's Gifts	568 Denmer	Berridge	CO	$ 245.00					
9	ME17	My House	879 Vinca	Berls	CO	$ 268.00					
10	RO44	Royal Interiors	677 Liatris	Berridge	CO	$0.00					
11	ST22	Steedman's	889 Lantana	Berls	CO	$ 123.00					
12											
13											
14											

Figure 26

3. Use Customer as the name of the table and Customer Number as the primary key.

4. Save the import steps. Be sure to enter a description for the saved steps.

5. Link the Product worksheet shown in Figure 27 to the database.

	A	B	C	D	E	F	G	H	I	J	K	L
1	Product Code	Description	On Hand	Cost	Selling Price							
2	101	Candy Dish	10	$4.00	$6.00							
3	103	Letter Opener	15	$2.00	$3.00							
4	104	Tray	5	$10.00	$15.00							
5	106	Salad Tongs	20	$3.00	$5.00							
6	110	Lazy Susan	8	$16.00	$20.00							
7	112	Spoon Set	21	$12.00	$14.00							
8	113	Salad Bowl	9	$18.00	$25.00							
9	115	Desk Organizer	8	$22.00	$30.00							
10	120	Book Ends	4	$27.00	$34.00							
11	121	Mobile	7	$34.00	$40.00							
12												
13												
14												

Figure 27

6. Rename the linked Product table as Inventory. Then, use the Linked Table Manager to update the link between the Excel worksheet and the Access table.

7. Import the Sales Rep table from the Ada Beauty Supply database that you modified in In the Lab 3 in Chapter 3 on page AC 201. (If you did not complete this exercise, see your instructor for a copy of the modified database.) Sales reps of Ada often sell gift items to salons.

8. Change the database properties, as specified by your instructor. Submit the database in the format specified by your instructor.

In the Lab

Lab 2: Exporting Data to Other Applications

Problem: JMS TechWizards wants to be able to export some of the data in its Access database to other applications. JMS wants to export the City-Technician Crosstab query for further processing in Excel. It also wants to use the Technician table in a Word document as well as e-mail the Salary Report to the company's accounting firm. The company has decided to branch out and offer consulting services. It wants to export the Client and Technician tables as a single XML file and then import it to a new database.

Instructions: Start Access. Open the JMS TechWizards database that you modified in In the Lab 1 in Chapter 3 on page AC 195. (If you did not complete this exercise, see your instructor for a copy of the modified database.) Perform the following tasks:

1. Export the City-Technician Crosstab query to Excel as shown in Figure 28. Save the export steps. Be sure to include a description.

Figure 28

2. Export the Technician table to a Word document. Do not save the export steps.

3. Publish the Salary Report as an XPS file.

4. Export both the Client and Technician tables in XML format. Be sure that both tables are exported to the same file. Do not save the export steps.

5. Create a new database called JMS TechConsultants.

6. Import the Client XML file containing both the Client and Technician tables to the JMS TechConsultants database.

7. Submit the Excel workbook, Word document, XPS file, and JMS TechConsultants database in the format specified by your instructor.

4 Creating Reports and Forms

Objectives

You will have mastered the material in this chapter when you can:

- Create reports and forms using wizards
- Group and sort in a report
- Add totals and subtotals to a report
- Resize columns
- Conditionally format controls
- Filter records in reports and forms
- Print reports and forms
- Add a field to a report or form
- Include gridlines
- Add a date
- Change the format of a control
- Move controls

4 | Creating Reports and Forms

Introduction

One of the advantages to maintaining data in a database is the ability to present the data in attractive reports and forms. Reports represent formatted printouts of data in a database. The data can come from one or more tables. Forms, on the other hand, are usually viewed on the screen, although they can be printed. They often are used to view specific data and also may be used to update data. Similar to reports, the data in the form can come from one or more tables. This chapter shows how to create reports and forms by creating two reports and a form. There are several ways to create both reports and forms. The most common is to use the Report or Form Wizard to create an initial report or form. If the layout created by the wizard is satisfactory, you are done. If not, you can use either Layout view or Design view to customize the report or form. In this chapter, you will use Layout view for this purpose. In later chapters, you will learn how to use Design view.

Project — Reports and Forms

JSP Recruiters has realized several benefits from using the database of clients and recruiters. JSP hopes to realize additional benefits using two custom reports that meet their specific needs. The first report is shown in Figure 4–1. The report features grouping. **Grouping** means creating separate collections of records sharing some common characteristic. In the report shown in Figure 4–1, for example, the records have been grouped by city. There are five separate groups: one each for Berls, Berridge, Fort Stewart, Mason, and Tarleton. The appropriate city appears before each group. The rows within the group include the client number, client name, amount paid, and current due. The total of the amount paid and current due amounts for the clients in the group (called a **subtotal**) appears after the group. At the end of the report is a grand total of the amount paid and current due amounts for all groups.

The second report, shown in Figure 4–2, includes subtotals of the amount paid and current due amounts after each group, and displays grand totals at the end. Like the report in Figure 4–1, the data is grouped, although this time it is grouped by recruiter number. This report, however, encompasses data from both the Recruiter table and the Client table. Not only does the recruiter number appear before each group, but the first name and last name of the recruiter appear as well. In addition, the column headings have been split over two lines.

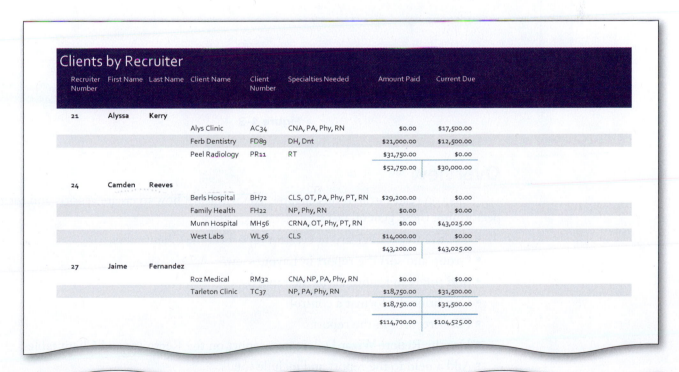

Figure 4–1

Figure 4–2

JSP also wants to improve the data entry process by using a custom form as shown in Figure 4–3. The form has a title and a date. It does not contain all the fields in the Client table, and the fields are in a different order. For this form, JSP likes the appearance of including the fields in a grid.

Figure 4–3

Overview

As you read through this chapter, you will learn how to create reports and forms by performing these general tasks:

- Use the Report Wizard to create a report on the Client table.
- Group and sort the report in Layout view.
- Add totals and subtotals to the report.
- Conditionally format a control.
- Filter records in the report.
- Use the Report Wizard to create a report on the Recruiter and Client tables.
- Add a field to the report and include totals.
- Use the Form Wizard to create a form on the Client table.
- Include gridlines and a date in the form.
- Add a field to the form.
- Filter and sort records in the form.

Report and Form Design Guidelines

1. **Determine whether the data should be presented in a report or a form.** Is it necessary to print the data, in which case a report would be the appropriate choice? Is it necessary to view the data on the screen, in which case a form would be the appropriate choice? Is the user going to update data? If so, a form is the appropriate choice.

2. **Determine the intended audience for the report or form.** Who will use the report or form? How will they use it? What data do they need? What level of detail do they need?

3. **Determine the tables that contain the data needed for the report or form.** Is all the data found in a single table or does it come from multiple related tables?

4. **Determine the fields that should appear on the report or form.** What data items are needed by the user of the report or form?

5. **Determine the organization of the report or form.** In what order should the fields appear? How should they be arranged? Should the records in a report be grouped in some way?

6. **Determine the format and style of the report or form.** What should be in the report or form heading? Do you want a title and date, for example? Do you want a logo? What should be in the body of the report and form? What should the style be? In other words, what visual characteristics should the various portions of the report or form have?

7. **Review the report or form after it has been in operation to determine whether any changes are warranted.** Is the order of the fields still appropriate? Are any additional fields required?

   When necessary, more specific details concerning the above decisions and/or actions are presented at appropriate points in the chapter. The chapter also will identify the actions performed and decisions made regarding these guidelines in the design of the reports and forms such as those shown in Figures 4–1, 4–2, and 4–3.

Starting Access

If you are using a computer to step through the project in this chapter and you want your screen to match the figures in this book, you should change your screen's resolution to 1024 × 768. For information about how to change a computer's resolution, read Appendix E.

To Start Access

The following steps, which assume Windows Vista is running, start Access.

Note: If you are using Windows XP, see Appendix F for alternate steps.

1 Click the Start button on the Windows Vista taskbar to display the Start menu.

2 Click All Programs at the bottom of the left pane on the Start menu to display the All Programs list and then click Microsoft Office on the All Programs list to display the Microsoft Office list.

3 Click Microsoft Office Access 2007 on the Microsoft Office list to start Access and display the Getting Started with Microsoft Office Access window.

4 If the Access window is not maximized, click the Maximize button on its title bar to maximize the window.

To Open a Database

Note: If you are using Windows XP, see Appendix F for alternate steps.

In Chapter 1, you created your database on a USB flash drive using the file name, JSP Recruiters. There are two ways to open the file containing your database. If the file you created appears in the Recent Documents list, you could click it to open the file. If not, you can use the More button to open the file. The following steps use the More button to open the JSP Recruiters database from the USB flash drive.

1 With your USB flash drive connected to one of the computer's USB ports, click the More button to display the Open dialog box.

2 If the Folders list is displayed below the Folders button, click the Folders button to remove the Folders list.

3 If necessary, click Computer in the Favorites Links section and then double-click UDISK 2.0 (E:) to select the USB flash drive, Drive E in this case, as the new open location.

4 Click JSP Recruiters to select the file name.

5 Click the Open button to open the database.

6 If a Security Warning appears, click the Options button to display the Microsoft Office Security Options dialog box.

7 With the option button to enable the content selected, click the OK button to enable the content.

Report Creation

Unless you want a report that simply lists all the fields and all the records in a table, the simplest way to create a report design is to use the Report Wizard. In some cases, the Report Wizard can produce exactly the desired report. Other times, however, you first must use the Report Wizard to produce a report that is as close as possible to the desired report. Then, use Layout view to modify the report and transform it into the correct report. In either case, once the report is created and saved, you can print it at any time. Access will use the current data in the database for the report, formatting and arranging it in exactly the way you specified when you created the report.

Plan Ahead

Determine the tables and fields that contain the data needed for the report.

1. **Examine the requirements for the report in general to determine the tables.** Do the requirements only relate to data in a single table, or does the data come from multiple tables? How are the tables related?

2. **Examine the specific requirements for the report to determine the fields necessary.** Look for all the data items that are specified for the report. Each should correspond to a field in a table or be able to be computed from a field in a table. This information gives you the list of fields.

3. **Determine the order of the fields.** Examine the requirements to determine the order in which the fields should appear. Be logical and consistent in your ordering. For example, in an address, the city should come before the state and the state should come before the postal code unless there is some compelling reason for another order.

TO CREATE A SIMPLE REPORT

A report that lists all the fields and all the records in a table without any special features is called a simple report. If you wanted to create a simple report, you would use the following steps.

1. Select the table for the report in the Navigation Pane.
2. Click the Create tab.
3. Click the Report button in the Reports group.

BTW

Creating Simple Reports
You also can base a simple report on a query. To modify a simple report, open the report in Layout view.

To Create a Report Using the Report Wizard

The following steps use the Report Wizard to create an initial version of the Clients by City report. After analyzing requirements, this version is to contain the City, Client Number, Client Name, Amount Paid, and Current Due fields. The fields all come from the Client table, so it is the only table required.

1

- Show the Navigation Pane if it is currently hidden.

- If necessary, click the Client table in the Navigation Pane to select it.

- Click Create on the Ribbon to display the Create tab.

- Click the Report Wizard button on the Create tab to start the Report Wizard (Figure 4–4).

Figure 4–4

2

- Click the City field and then click the Add Field button to add the City field to the list of selected fields (Figure 4–5).

Q&A

Why are there two Specialties Needed fields in the list?

They serve different purposes. If you were to select Specialties Needed, you would get all the specialties for a given client on one line. If you were to select Specialties Needed.Value, each specialty would be on a separate line. You are not selecting either one at this point.

Figure 4–5

3

● Using the same technique, add the Client Number, Client Name, Amount Paid, and Current Due fields (Figure 4–6).

Figure 4–6

4

● Click the Next button to display the next Report Wizard screen (Figure 4–7), which asks for grouping levels.

Figure 4–7

5

● Because you do not need to specify grouping levels, click the Next button to display the next Report Wizard screen, which asks for sort order (Figure 4–8).

Q&A

I thought the report involved grouping. Why do I not specify grouping at this point?

You could. You will specify it later, however, in a way that gives you more control over the grouping that is taking place.

Figure 4–8

6

● Because you do not need to specify a sort order, click the Next button to display the next Report Wizard screen, which asks for your report layout preference (Figure 4–9).

Q&A

Could I sort here?

You could. Again, in this report you will specify sorting later.

 Experiment

● Try different layouts to see the effect on the sample layout on the left. When finished, select the Tabular layout.

Figure 4–9

7

• With Tabular layout and Portrait orientation selected, click the Next button to display the next Report Wizard screen, which asks for a style.

• If necessary, click the Module style to select it (Figure 4–10).

 Experiment

• Try different styles to see the effect on the sample on the left. When finished, select the Module style.

Figure 4–10

8

• Click the Next button and then type Clients by City as the report title (Figure 4–11).

Figure 4–11

9

- Click the Finish button to produce the report (Figure 4–12).

10

- Click the Close 'Clients by City' button to close the report.

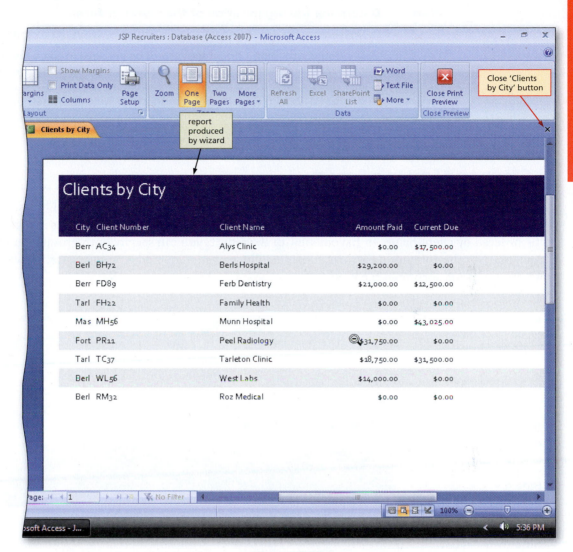

Figure 4–12

Using Layout View in a Report

When working with a report in Access, there are four different ways to view the report. They are Report view, Print Preview, Layout view, and Design view. Report view shows the report on the screen. Print Preview shows the report as it will appear when printed. Layout view is similar to Report view in that it shows the report on the screen, but it also allows you to make changes to the report. It is usually the easiest way to make such changes. Design view also allows you to make changes, but it does not show you the actual report. It is most useful when the changes you need to make are especially complex. In this chapter, you will use Layout view to modify the report.

Determine the organization of the report or form.

1. **Determine sort order.** Is there a special order in which the records should appear?

2. **Determine grouping.** Should the records be grouped in some fashion? If so, what should appear before the records in a group? If, for example, clients are grouped by city, the name of the city should probably appear before the group. What should appear after the group? For example, are there some fields for which subtotals should be calculated? If so, the subtotals would come after the group.

To Group and Sort in a Report

JSP has determined that the records in the report should be grouped by City. That is, all the clients of a given city should appear together immediately after the name of the city. Within the clients in a given city, the clients are to be ordered by client name. In Layout view of the report, you can specify both grouping and sorting by using the Group and Sort button on the Format tab. The following steps open the report in Layout view and then specify both grouping and sorting in the report.

- Right-click the Clients by City report in the Navigation Pane to produce a shortcut menu.

- Click Layout View on the shortcut menu to open the report in Layout view.

- Hide the Navigation Pane.

- If a field list appears, close the Field List by clicking its Close button.

- If necessary, click the Group & Sort button on the Format tab to produce the 'Add a group' and 'Add a sort' buttons (Figure 4–13).

Figure 4–13

2

- Click the 'Add a group' button to add a group (Figure 4–14).

Figure 4–14

3

- Click the City field in the field list to group records by city (Figure 4–15).

Q&A

Does the field on which I group have to be the first field?

No. If you select a field other than the first field, Access will move the field you select into the first position.

Q&A

I selected the wrong field for grouping. What should I do?

Click the arrow next to the control and select the correct field. If you decide you do not want to group after all, click the Delete button on the right-hand edge of the line containing the grouping field.

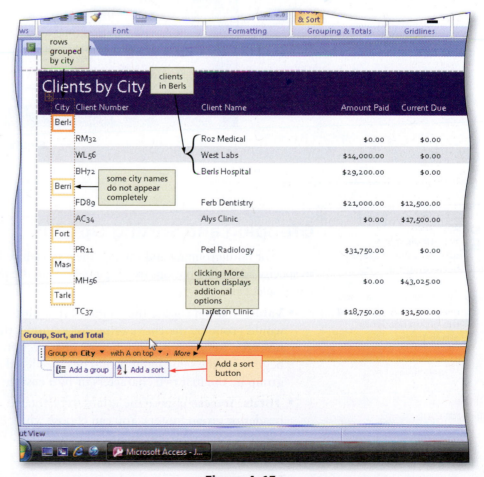

Figure 4–15

4

• Click the 'Add a sort' button to add a sort (Figure 4–16).

5

• Click the Client Name field in the field list to alphabetically sort by client name.

Q&A

I thought the report would be sorted by City, because I chose to group by City. What is the effect of choosing to sort by Client Name?

This sort takes place within groups. You are specifying that within the list of clients of the same city, the clients will be ordered by name.

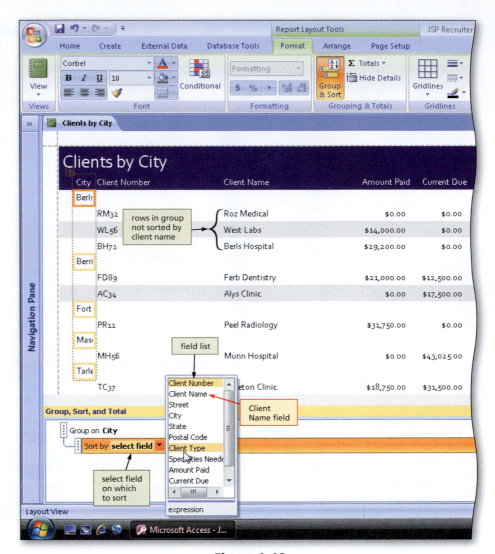

Figure 4–16

BTW

Grouping
You should allow sufficient white space between groups. If you feel the amount is insufficient, you can add more space by enlarging the group header or group footer.

Grouping and Sorting Options

For both grouping and sorting, there is a More button that you can click if you need to specify additional options (see Figure 4–15 on the previous page). The options you then could select are:

• **Value**. You can choose the length of the value on which to group. Typically you would group by the entire value, for example, the entire city name. You could choose, however, to only group on the first character, in which case all clients in cities that begin with the same letter would be considered a group. You also could choose to group by the first two characters or by a custom number of characters.

• **Totals**. You can choose the values to be totaled and where they are to appear (group header or group footer). You can choose whether there is to be a grand total, and also whether to show group totals as a percentage of the grand total.

• **Title**. You can customize the group title.

• **Header section**. You can choose to include or omit a header section for the group.

- **Footer section**. You can choose to include or omit a footer section for the group.
- **Keep together**. You can indicate whether Access is to attempt to keep portions of a group together on a page. The default is that it will not. You can specify that Access is to attempt to keep a whole group together on one page. If the group will not fit on the remainder of the page, Access will move the group header and the records in a group to the next page. Finally, you can choose to have Access keep the header and the first record together on one page. If the header would fit at the bottom of a page, but there would not be room for the first record, Access will move the header to the next page.

Understanding Report Sections

A report is divided into various sections to help clarify the presentation of data. In Design view, which you will use in later chapters, the sections are labeled on the screen. Even though they are not labeled in Layout view, it still is useful to understand the purpose of the various sections. A typical report consists of a Report Header section, Page Header section, Detail section, Page Footer section, and Report Footer section.

The contents of the **Report Header section** print once at the beginning of the report. In the Clients by City report, the title, Clients by City, is in the Report Header section. The contents of the **Report Footer section** print once at the end of the report. In the Clients by City report, the Report Footer section contains the grand totals of Amount Paid and Current Due. The contents of the **Page Header section** print once at the top of each page and typically contain the column headings. The contents of the **Page Footer section** print once at the bottom of each page and often contain a date and a page number. The contents of the **Detail section** print once for each record in the table, for example once for Roz Medical, once for West Labs, and so on. In this report, they contain the client number, client name, amount paid, and current due.

When the data in a report is grouped, there are two additional sections. The contents of the **Group Header section** are printed before the records in a particular group, and the contents of the **Group Footer section** are printed after the group. In the Clients by City report, the Group Header section contains the city name and the Group Footer section contains subtotals of Amount Paid and Current Due.

Understanding Controls

The various objects on a report are called **controls**. All the information on the report is contained in the controls. There is a control containing the title, Clients by City. There is a control containing each column heading (City, Client Number, Client Name, Amount Paid, and Current Due). There is a control in the Group Header section that displays the city and two controls in the Group Footer section. One displays the subtotal of Amount Paid and the other displays the subtotal of Current Due. In the Detail section, there are four controls, one containing the client number, one containing the client name, one containing the amount paid, and one containing the current due amount.

There are three types of controls: bound controls, unbound controls, and calculated controls. **Bound controls** are used to display data that comes from the database, such as the client number and name. **Unbound controls** are not associated with data from the database and are used to display such things as the report's title. Finally, **calculated controls** are used to display data that is calculated from other data, such as a total.

When working in Layout view, Access handles details concerning these controls for you automatically. When working in Design view, you will see and manipulate the controls.

To Add Totals and Subtotals

Along with determining to group data in this report, it also was determined that subtotals of Amount Paid and Current Due should be included. To add totals or other statistics, use the Totals button on the Format tab. You then select from a menu of aggregate functions, functions that perform some mathematical function against a group of records. The available aggregate functions are: Sum (total), Average, Count Records, Count Values, Max (largest value), Min (smallest value), Standard Deviation, and Variance. The following steps add totals of the Amount Paid and Current Due fields. Because the report is grouped, each group will have a subtotal, that is, a total for just the records in the group. At the end of the report, there will be a grand total, that is, a total for all records.

- Click the Amount Paid field on the first record to select the field.

Q&A Does it have to be the first record?

No. You could click the Amount Paid field on any record.

- Click the Totals button on the Format tab to display the list of available calculations (Figure 4–17).

Figure 4–17

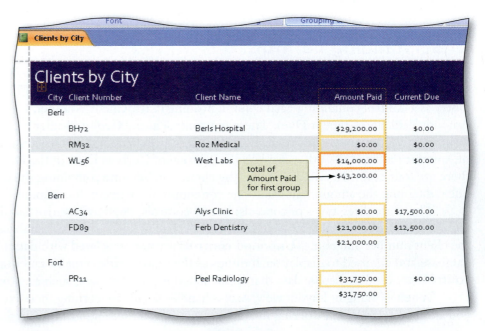

- Click Sum to calculate the sum of amount paid values (Figure 4–18).

Q&A Is Sum the same as Total?

Yes.

Figure 4–18

3

- Using the same technique as in Steps 1 and 2, add totals for the Current Due field (Figure 4–19).

Figure 4–19

To Resize Columns

In some cases, not all the data in the column appears because the column currently is too narrow. To resize a column, point to the boundary of the column so that the mouse pointer becomes a double-headed arrow. You can then drag the boundary of the column to resize the column. The following steps resize the columns.

1

- If necessary, close the Group, Sort, and Total pane by clicking the Group & Sort button on the Design tab.

- Click the City column heading.

- Point to the right boundary of the City column heading so that the pointer turns into a double-headed arrow.

- Drag the right boundary to the right so that the entire contents of the City column appear (Figure 4–20).

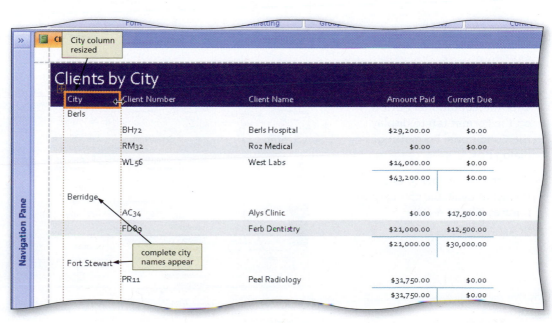

Figure 4–20

Determine the format and style of the report or form.

1. **Determine whether any special fonts and/or colors are warranted.** Would the look of the report or form be enhanced by changing a font, a color, or any other special effects?

2. **Determine whether conditional formatting is appropriate.** Are there any fields in which you would like to emphasize certain values by giving them a different appearance?

3. **Determine the appearance of the various components.** How should the various portions be formatted? Is one of the styles supplied by Access sufficient?

To Conditionally Format Controls

You can emphasize values in a column that satisfy some criterion by formatting them differently from other values. This emphasis is called **conditional formatting**. JSP management would like to emphasize values in the Current Due field that are greater than $0.00. The following steps conditionally format the Current Due field so that values in the field that are greater than $0.00 are in red.

1

- Click the Current Due field on the first record to select the field (Figure 4–21).

Q&A Does it have to be the first record?

No. You could click the field on any record.

Figure 4–21

2

- Click the Conditional button on the Format tab to display the Conditional Formatting dialog box.

- Click the box arrow to display the list of available comparison phrases (Figure 4–22).

Figure 4–22

3

• Click greater than to select the greater than operator.

• Type 0 as the greater than value.

• Click the Font/Fore Color button arrow for the format to be used when condition is true to display a color palette (Figure 4–23).

Figure 4–23

4

• Click the dark red color in the lower corner of the color palette to select the color (Figure 4–24).

Figure 4–24

5

- Click the OK button in the Conditional Formatting dialog box to change the formatting (Figure 4–25).

Q&A What if I have more than one condition?

Click the Add button to add additional conditions. You can include up to three conditions. For each condition, you specify the condition and the format to be used when the condition is true.

Q&A Can I change this conditional formatting at a later time?

Yes. Select the field for which you had applied conditional formatting on any record, click the Conditional button on the Format tab, make the necessary changes, and then click the OK button.

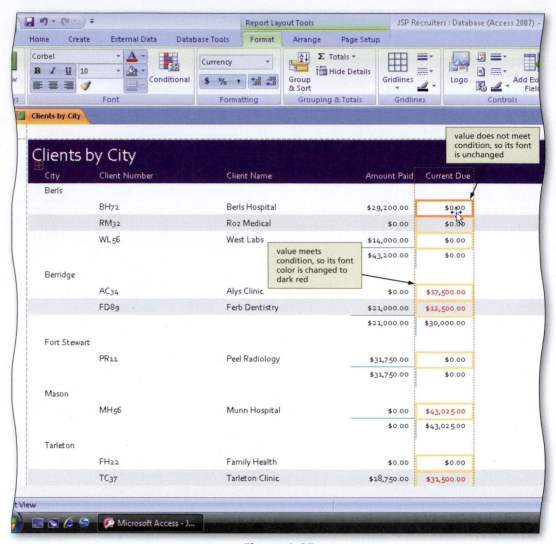

Figure 4–25

To Filter Records in a Report

You can filter records in a report just as you filter records in a datasheet. You can use the filter buttons on the Home tab in exactly the same fashion you do on a datasheet. If the filter involves only one field, right-clicking the field provides a simple way to filter. The following steps filter the records in the report to include only those records on which the amount paid is not $0.00.

1

- Right-click the Amount Paid field on the second record to display the shortcut menu (Figure 4–26).

Q&A Did I have to pick second record?

No. You could pick any record on which the Amount Paid is $0.00.

Figure 4–26

2

- Click Does Not Equal $0.00 on the shortcut menu to restrict the records to those on which the Amount Paid is not $0.00 (Figure 4–27).

Q&A When would you use Number Filters?

You would use Number Filters if you need filters that are not on the main shortcut menu or if you need the ability to enter specific values other than the ones shown on the shortcut menu. If those filters are insufficient for your needs, you can use Advanced Filter/Sort, which is accessible through the Advanced button on the Home tab.

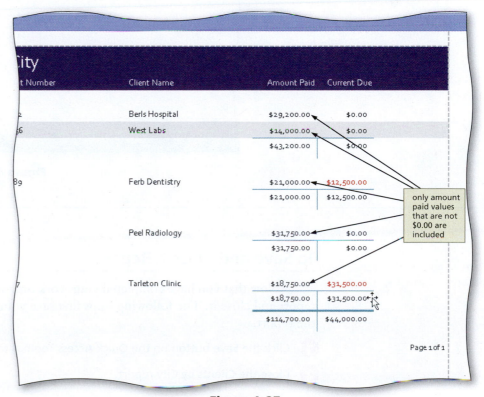

Figure 4–27

To Clear a Report Filter

When you no longer want the records to be filtered, you clear the filter. The following steps clear the filter on the Amount Paid field.

- Right-click the Amount Paid field on the first record to display the shortcut menu (Figure 4–28).

- Click Clear filter from Amount Paid on the shortcut menu to clear the filter and redisplay all records.

Experiment

- Try other filters on the shortcut menu for the Amount Paid field to see their effect. When done with each, clear the filter.

Figure 4–28

To Save and Close a Report

Now that you have completed your work on your report, you should save the report and close it. The following steps first save your work on the report and then close the report.

1. Click the Save button on the Quick Access Toolbar to save your work.

2. Close the Clients by City report.

The Arrange and Page Setup Tabs

When working on a report in Layout view, you can make additional layout changes by using the Arrange and/or Page Setup tabs. The Arrange tab is shown in Figure 4–29. Table 4–1 shows the buttons on the Arrange tab along with the Enhanced ScreenTips that describe their function.

Figure 4–29

Table 4–1 Arrange Tab	
Button	**Enhanced ScreenTip**
Tabular	Create a layout similar to a spreadsheet with labels across the top and data in columns below the labels.
Stacked	Create a layout similar to a paper form, with labels to the left of each field.
Remove	Remove the layout applied to the controls.
Control Margins	Specify the location of information displayed within the control.
Control Padding	Set the amount of spacing between controls and the gridlines of a layout.
Snap to Grid	Snap to grid.
Tab Order	Change the tab order of controls on the page.
Left	Align left.
Right	Align right.
Top	Align top.
Bottom	Align bottom.
Size to Fit	Size to fit.
Bring to Front	Bring the selected object in front of all other objects so that no part of it is hidden behind another object.
Send to Back	Send the selected object behind all other objects.
Property Sheet	Open this object's property sheet to set its properties.

The Page Setup tab is shown in Figure 4–30. Table 4–2 on the next page shows the buttons on the Page Setup tab along with the Enhanced ScreenTips that describe their function.

Figure 4–30

Table 4–2 Page Setup Tab	
Button	**Enhanced ScreenTip**
Size	Choose a paper size for the current section.
Portrait	Change to portrait orientation.
Landscape	Change to landscape orientation.
Margins	Select the margin sizes for the entire document or the current section.
Show Margins	Show margins.
Print Data Only	Print data only.
Columns	Columns.
Page Setup	Show the Page Setup dialog box.

To Print a Report

Once you have created a report, you can print it at any time. The printed layout will reflect the layout you created. The data in the report will always reflect current data. The following steps print the Clients by City report.

1 Show the Navigation Pane, ensure the Clients by City report is selected, and then click the Office Button to display the Microsoft Office menu.

2 Point to Print on the Office Button menu and then click Quick Print on the Print submenu to print the report.

Q&A How can I print a range of pages rather than printing the whole report?

Click the Office Button, point to Print on the Office Button menu, click Print on the Print submenu, click the Pages option button in the Print Range box, enter the desired page range, and then click the OK button.

Q&A What should I do if the report is too wide for the printed page?

You can adjust the margins or change the page orientation. You make both types of changes by opening the report in Layout view and then clicking the Page Setup tab. You can click the desired orientation button to change the orientation or click the Margins button to change to some preset margins. For custom margins, click the dialog box launcher in the lower-right corner of the Page Layout group.

To Create a Summary Report

You may determine that a report should be organized so that it only shows the overall group calculations, but not all the records. A report that includes the group calculations such as subtotals, but does not include the individual detail lines is called a **summary report**. If you wanted to create a summary report, you could use the following steps.

1. Create report including field on which you will group and fields you wish to summarize.

2. Group the report on the desired field.

3. Add the desired totals or other calculations.

4. Click the Hide Details button on the Format tab.

Multi-Table Reports

You may determine that the data required for a report comes from more than one table. You can use the Report Wizard to create a report on multiple tables just as you can use it to create reports on single tables.

To Create a Report that Involves Multiple Tables

The following steps use the Report Wizard to create a report that involves both the Recruiter and Client tables.

 1

- Show the Navigation Pane if it is currently hidden.

- Click the Recruiter table in the Navigation Pane to select it.

- Click Create on the Ribbon to display the Create tab.

- Click the Report Wizard button on the Create tab to start the Report Wizard (Figure 4–31).

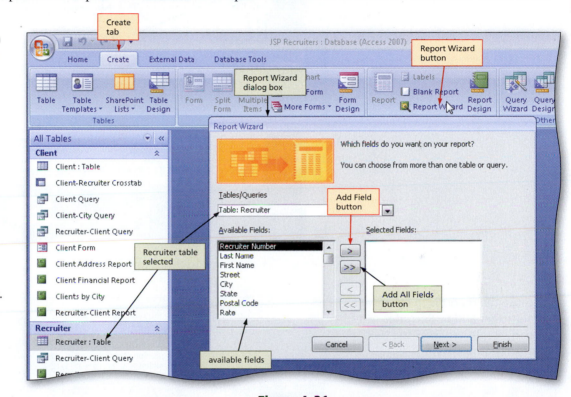

Figure 4–31

2

- Click the Add Field button to add the Recruiter Number field.

- Add the First Name field by clicking it and then clicking the Add Field button.

- Add the Last Name field in the same manner.

- Click the Tables/Queries arrow, and then click Table: Client in the Tables/Queries list box (Figure 4–32).

Figure 4–32

3

- Add the Client Number, Client Name, Amount Paid, and Current Due fields by clicking the field and then clicking the Add Field button.

- Click the Next button (Figure 4–33).

Figure 4–33

4

- Because the report is to be viewed by Recruiter and by Recruiter already is selected, click the Next button (Figure 4–34).

Figure 4–34

5

- Because no additional grouping levels are required, click the Next button.

- Click the box arrow in the text box labeled 1 and then click the Client Name field in the list to select Client Name for the sort order (Figure 4–35).

Q&A

When would I use the Summary Options button?

You would use the Summary Options button if you want to specify subtotals or other calculations within the wizard. You can also use it to produce a summary report by selecting Summary Only, which will omit all detail records from the report.

Figure 4–35

6

- Click the Next button, be sure the Stepped layout is selected, and then click the Landscape option button to select Landscape orientation (Figure 4–36).

Figure 4–36

7

• Click the Next button to display the next Report Wizard screen, which asks for a style (Figure 4–37).

Figure 4–37

8

• With the Module style selected, click the Next button and then type `Clients by Recruiter` as the report title (Figure 4–38).

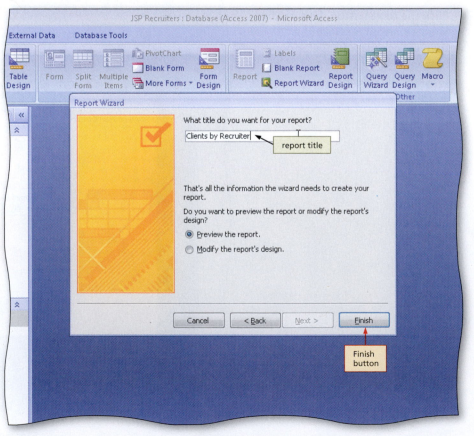

Figure 4–38

9

● Click the Finish button to produce the report (Figure 4–39).

Figure 4–39

10
● Click the magnifying glass mouse pointer somewhere within the report to view a complete page of the report (Figure 4–40).

 Experiment

● Zoom in on various positions within the report. When finished, view a complete page of the report.

Q&A
Why does Client Name appear before Client Number when we selected Client Number first in the Report Wizard?

When you specify sorting in the Report Wizard, Access places the field on which sorting is to occur first. This reversed the order of the Client Number and Client Name fields.

Q&A
Why are there pound signs (#) in the Current Due column?

The column is too small to hold the entire number. You can resize the column to display the entire number.

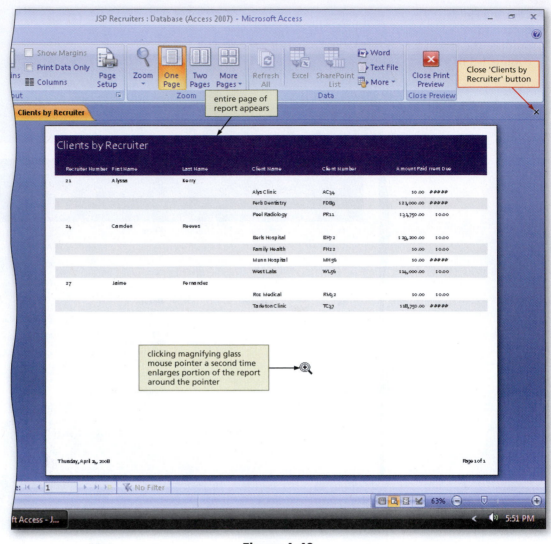

Figure 4–40

11
● Click the Close 'Clients by Recruiter' button to close the report and remove it from the screen.

To Resize Columns and Column Headings

The following steps resize the columns and the column headings in the Clients by Recruiter report.

1

- Open the Clients by Recruiter report in Layout view and then hide the Navigation Pane.

- Click the Recruiter Number column heading to select the column.

- Point to the lower boundary of the Recruiter Number column heading so that the mouse pointer changes to a double-headed arrow (Figure 4–41).

Could I point to the lower boundary of any other column as well?

Yes. It doesn't matter which one you point to. You will resize all of them at once.

Figure 4–41

2

- Increase the height of the column headings by dragging the lower portion of the column headings down to the approximate position shown in Figure 4–42 and then point to the right boundary of the Recruiter Number heading so that the mouse pointer changes to a double-headed arrow.

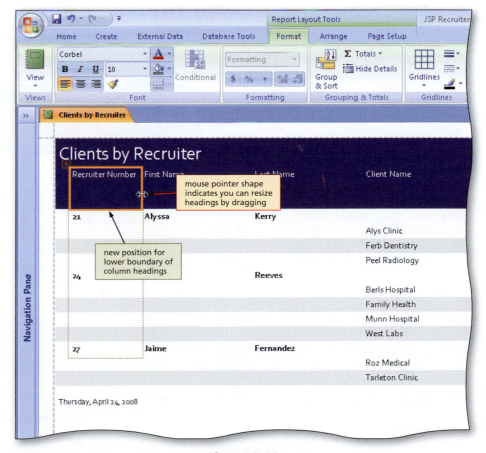

Figure 4–42

3
- Change the width of the Recruiter Number heading by dragging the pointer to the approximate position shown in Figure 4–43.

Q&A

Did I have to do anything special to extend the column heading over two lines?

If the column is too narrow for a two-word name to appear completely, Access will automatically split the name over two lines. If there is sufficient space for the two-word name, Access will not split the name. If you wish to split it you can do so by clicking the name to select it, clicking in front of the second word to produce an insertion point, holding the SHIFT key down and pressing the ENTER key.

Figure 4–43

4
- Using the same technique, change the width of the remaining columns to those shown in Figure 4–44.

Q&A

Do I have to be exact?

No. As long as your report looks close to the one in the figure it is fine.

Q&A

I'm not very good with dragging the mouse to make fine adjustments. Is there another way?

Yes. If you want to make a slight adjustment to the size of a control, you may find it easier to select the control, hold down the SHIFT key, and then use the appropriate arrow key to resize the control.

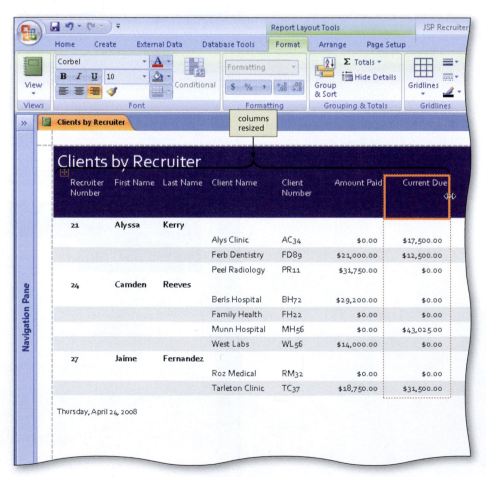

Figure 4–44

Review the report after it has been in operation to determine whether any changes are warranted.

Plan Ahead

1. **Determine whether the order of the fields is still the best order.** After a user has worked with a report or form for a period, he or she may feel that another order of the fields would work better than the original order.

2. **Determine whether any additional fields now are required.** Are there fields missing from the report that would be helpful?

To Add a Field

After reviewing the report, you may decide that the report should contain some additional field. You can use a field list to add the necessary field. The following steps use a field list to add the Specialties Needed field to the Clients by Recruiter report.

- If necessary, click the Add Existing Fields button on the Format tab to display a field list (Figure 4–45).

Q&A My field list does not look like the one in the figure. It does not have the two tables, and the link at the bottom has Show all tables. Yours has Show only fields in the current record source. What should I do?

Click the 'Show all tables' link. Your field list should then match the one in the figure.

Q&A What is the purpose of the Edit Table links in the field list?

If you click an Edit Table link, the table will appear in Datasheet view and you can make changes to it.

Figure 4–45

2

Q&A

- Point to the Specialties Needed field, press and hold the left mouse button, and then drag the mouse pointer until the line to the left of the mouse pointer is between the Client Number and Amount Paid fields (Figure 4–46).

What if I make a mistake?

You can delete the field by clicking the field and then pressing the DELETE key. You can move the field by dragging it to the correct position.

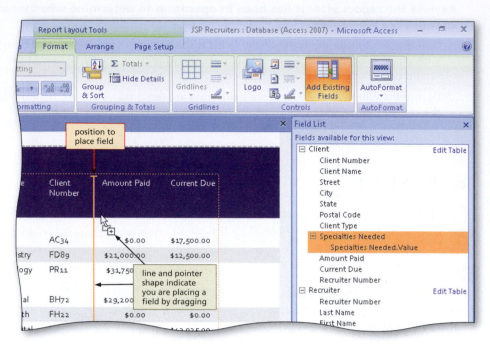

Figure 4–46

3

- Release the left mouse button to place the field (Figure 4–47).

Could I create a report in Layout view without using the Report Wizard just by dragging the fields into the positions I want?

Yes. You would click the Create tab, and then click Blank Report in the Reports group. You could then drag the fields from the field list.

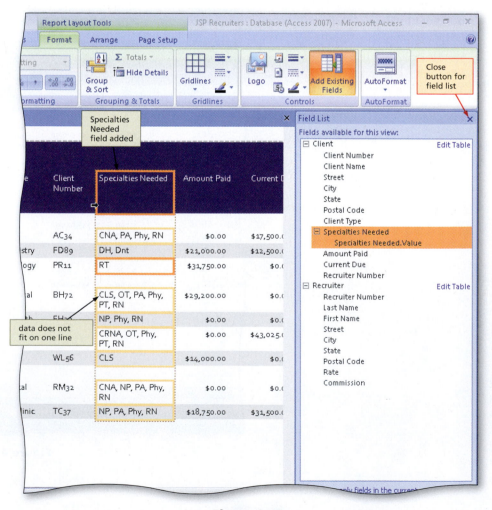

Figure 4–47

4

- Close the field list by clicking its Close button.

Could I also close the field list by clicking the Add Existing Field button a second time?

Yes. Use whichever method you find most convenient.

- Drag the right boundary of the Specialties Needed field to the approximate position shown in Figure 4–48.

Figure 4–48

Using the Value Property of a Multivalued Field

Rather than adding the Specialties Needed field, you could add the Value property of the Specialties Needed field. To do so, you would drag Specialties Needed.Value rather than Specialties Needed to the report. If you did so, each specialty would be on a separate line, as shown in Figure 4–49. If you compare the report in Figure 4–49 with the one shown in Figure 4–48, you will see that the four specialties needed by Alys Clinic, which appeared on one line in Figure 4–48, occupy four lines in the report shown in Figure 4–49.

BTW

Creating Reports in Layout View
You can create a report in Layout view without using the wizard. To do so, click Create on the Ribbon and then click the Blank Report button on the Create tab.

Figure 4–49

To Include Totals

The following steps add totals and subtotals for the Amount Paid and Current Due fields.

- Click the Amount Paid field on the first record to select the field.

- Click the Totals button on the Format tab to display the Totals menu (Figure 4–50).

Figure 4–50

2

- Click Sum in the Totals menu to calculate the sum of the amounts paid for the clients of each recruiter as well as the grand total.

- Click the Current Due field on the first record to select the field.

- Click the Totals button on the Format tab to display the Totals menu.

- Click Sum in the Totals menu to calculate the sum of the current due amounts for the clients of each recruiter as well as the grand total (Figure 4–51).

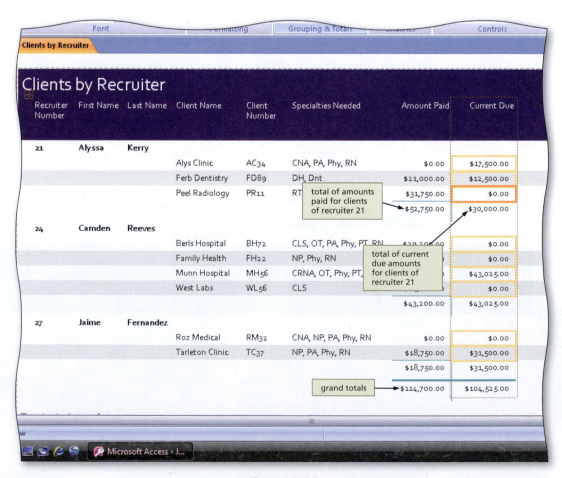

Figure 4–51

To Save and Close a Report

Now that you have completed your work on your report, you should save the report and close it. The following steps first save your work on the report and then close the report.

1 Click the Save button on the Quick Access Toolbar to save your work.

2 Close the Clients by Recruiter report.

To Print a Report

The following steps print the Clients by Recruiter report.

1 With the Clients by Recruiter report selected in the Navigation Pane, click the Office Button to display the Microsoft Office menu.

2 Point to the arrow next to print on the Office Button menu and then click Quick Print on the Print submenu to print the report.

Form Creation

As with reports, it is usually simplest to begin creating a form by using the wizard. Once you have used the Form Wizard to create a form, you can modify that form in either Layout view or Design view.

To Use the Form Wizard to Create a Form

The following steps use the Form Wizard to create an initial version of the Client Financial Form. This version contains the Client Number, Client Name, Client Type, Specialties Needed, Amount Paid, Current Due, and Recruiter Number fields.

1

- Be sure the Navigation Pane appears and the Client table is selected.

- Click Create on the Ribbon to display the Create tab.

- Click the More Forms button on the Create tab to display the More Forms menu (Figure 4–52).

Figure 4–52

• Click Form Wizard on the More Forms menu to start the Form Wizard.

• Add the Client Number, Client Name, Client Type, Specialties Needed, Amount Paid, Current Due, and Recruiter Number fields to the form (Figure 4–53).

Figure 4–53

• Click the Next button to display the next Form Wizard screen (Figure 4–54).

Figure 4–54

4
- Be sure the Columnar layout is selected, and then click the Next button to display the next Form Wizard screen (Figure 4–55).

Figure 4–55

5
- Be sure Module is selected, click the Next button, and then type `Client Financial Form` as the title for the form (Figure 4–56).

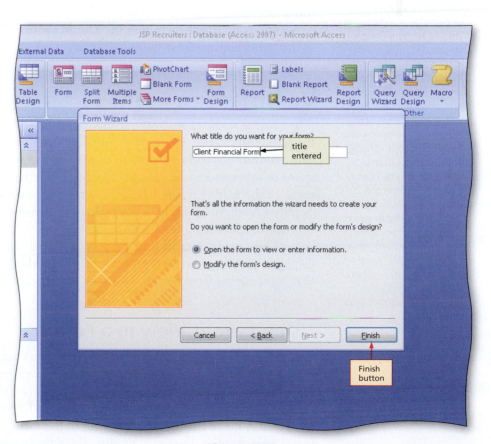

Figure 4–56

6
- Click the Finish button to complete and display the form (Figure 4–57).

7
- Click the Close 'Client Financial Form' button to close the form.

Figure 4–57

Form Design Considerations
Forms should be appealing visually and present data logically and clearly. Review your form to see if it presents the information effectively. Properly designed forms improve both the speed and accuracy of data entry. Forms that are cluttered or contain too many different effects (colors, fonts, frame styles, and so on) can be very hard on the eyes. Also, some colors are more difficult than others for individuals to see. Be consistent when creating forms. Once you decide on a general style for forms, stick with it throughout your database.

Understanding Form Sections

A form typically has only three sections. The **Form Header section** appears at the top of the form and usually contains the form title. It also may contain a logo and/or a date. The body of the form is in the **Detail section**. The **Form Footer section** appears at the bottom of the form and often is empty.

Understanding Controls

Just as with reports, the various items on a form are called controls. Forms include the same three types of controls: bound controls, unbound controls, and calculated controls. **Bound controls** are used to display data that comes from the database, such as the client number and name. Bound controls have attached labels that typically display the name of the field that supplies the data for the control. The **attached label** for the Client Number field, for example, is the portion of the screen immediately to the left of the field. It contains the words, Client Number.

Unbound controls are not associated with data from the database and are used to display such things as the form's title. Finally, **calculated controls** are used to display data that is calculated from other data in the database.

Using Layout View in a Form

When working with a form in Access, there are three different ways to view the report. They are Form view, Layout view, and Design view. Form view shows the form on the screen and allows you to use the form to update data. Layout view is similar to Form view in that it shows the form on the screen. In Layout view, you cannot update the data, but you can make changes to the layout of the form, which is usually the easiest way to make such changes. Design view also allows you to make changes, but it does not show you the actual form. It is most useful when the changes you need to make are especially complex. In this chapter, you will use Layout view to modify the form.

To Include Gridlines

You can make a variety of changes to the appearance of a form. One change is the inclusion of gridlines. The following steps modify the Client Financial Form to include horizontal and vertical gridlines.

- Open the Client Financial Form in Layout view and hide the Navigation Pane.

- If necessary, click Format on the Ribbon to display the Format tab.

- Ensure a field in the form is selected, then click the Gridlines button on the Format tab to display the Gridlines menu (Figure 4–58).

Figure 4–58

- Click Both on the Gridlines menu to specify both horizontal and vertical gridlines (Figure 4–59).

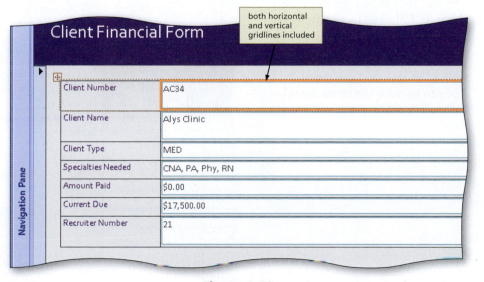

Figure 4–59

To Add a Date

You can add special items to reports and forms, such as a logo or title. You also can add the date and/or the time. In the case of reports, you can add a page number as well. To add any of these items, you use the appropriate button in the Controls group of the Format tab. The following steps use the Date and Time button to add a date to the Client Financial Form.

- Click in the Form header, outside the title (Client Financial Form) to select the Form header.

- Click the Date and Time button on the Format tab to display the Date and Time dialog box (Figure 4–60).

What is the relationship between the various check boxes and option buttons?

If the Include Date check box is checked, you must pick a date format from the three option buttons underneath the check box. If it is not checked, the option buttons will be dimmed. If the Include Time check box is checked, you must pick a time format from the three option buttons underneath the check box. If it is not checked, the option buttons will be dimmed.

Figure 4–60

2

- Click the option button for the second date format to select the format that shows the day of the month, followed by the abbreviation for the month, followed by the year.

- Click the Include Time check box to remove the check mark (Figure 4–61).

Figure 4–61

3

- Click the OK button in the Date and Time dialog box to add the date to the form (Figure 4–62).

Q&A

Why is the date so dark? I can hardly read it.

The letters are black, which does not work well with this color of the form heading. You need to change the color of the date to make it more visible.

Figure 4–62

To Change the Format of a Control

You can use the buttons in the Font group of the Format tab to change the format of a control. The following steps use the Font Color arrow in the Font group to change the color of the font in the control containing the date to white, so that it will be more visible.

1

- Click the Date control to select it.
- Be sure the Format tab appears.
- Click the Font Color arrow on the Format tab to display a color palette (Figure 4–63).

Figure 4–63

2

- Click the white color in the upper-left corner of the Standard Colors section to change the font color for the date to white (Figure 4–64).

Q&A Can I change the color of other controls the same way?

Yes. Select the control and then use the same steps to change the font color. You also can use other buttons on the Format tab to bold, italicize, underline, change the font, and so on.

Figure 4–64

To Move a Control

You can move a control by dragging the control. The following steps move the Date control to the lower edge of the form header.

1

- Point to the Date control so that the mouse pointer changes to a four-headed arrow and then drag the Date control to the lower boundary of the form heading (Figure 4–65).

Q&A I moved my pointer a little bit and it became a double-headed arrow. Can I still drag the pointer?

If you drag when the pointer is a double-headed arrow, you will resize the control. To move the control, it must be a four-headed arrow.

Q&A Could I drag other objects as well? For example, could I drag the title to the center of the form header?

Yes. Just be sure you are pointing at the object and the pointer is a four-headed arrow. You then can drag the object to the desired location.

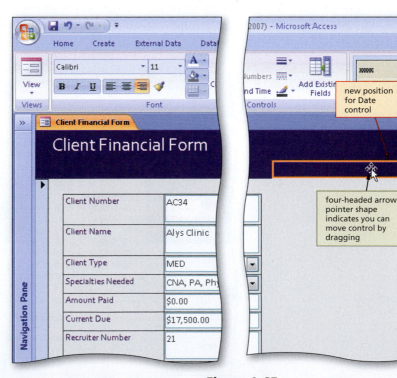

Figure 4–65

**Plan
Ahead**

Review the form after it has been in operation to determine whether any changes are warranted.

1. **Determine whether the order of the fields is still the best order.** After a user has worked with a form for a period, he or she may feel that another order of the fields would work better than the original order.

2. **Determine whether any additional fields now are required.** Are there fields missing from the form that would be helpful?

To Move Controls in a Control Layout

The controls for the fields are arranged in control layouts. A **control layout** is a guide that aligns the controls to give the form a uniform appearance. There are two types of control layouts. A **stacked layout** arranges the controls vertically with labels to the left of the control. A **tabular layout** arranges the controls horizontally with the labels across the top, typically in the Form header section. This form contains a stacked layout.

You can move a control within a control layout by dragging the control to the location you want. As you move it, a line will indicate the position where the control will be placed when you release the left mouse button. You can move more than one control in the same operation by selecting both controls prior to moving them.

The following steps move the Client Type and Specialties Needed fields so that they follow the Recruiter Number field.

- Click the control for the Client Type field to select it.

- Hold the SHIFT key down and click the control for the Specialties Needed field to select both fields (Figure 4–66).

Q&A

Why did I have to hold the SHIFT key down when I clicked the control for the Specialties Needed field?

If you did not hold the SHIFT key down, you would select only the Specialties Needed field. The Client Type field no longer would be selected.

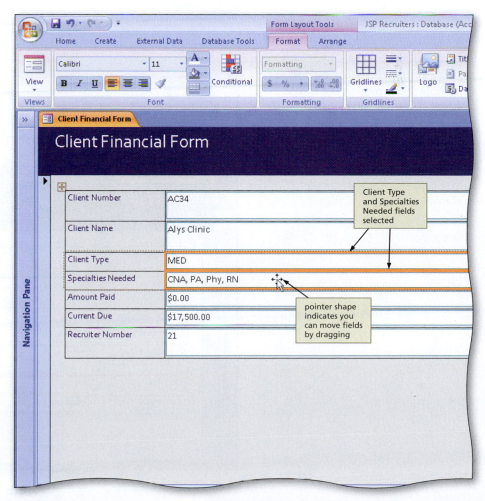

Figure 4–66

2

- Press the left mouse button and then drag the fields to the position shown in Figure 4–67.

Q&A

What is the purpose of the line by the mouse pointer?

It shows you where the fields will be positioned.

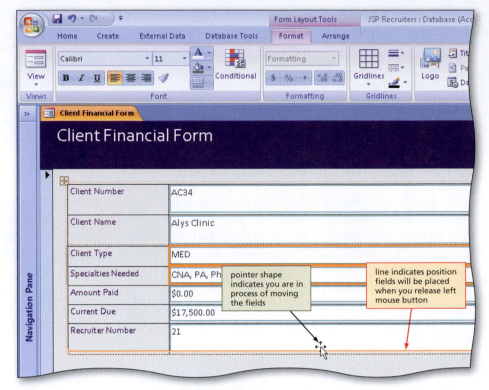

Figure 4–67

3

- Release the left mouse button to complete the movement of the fields (Figure 4–68).

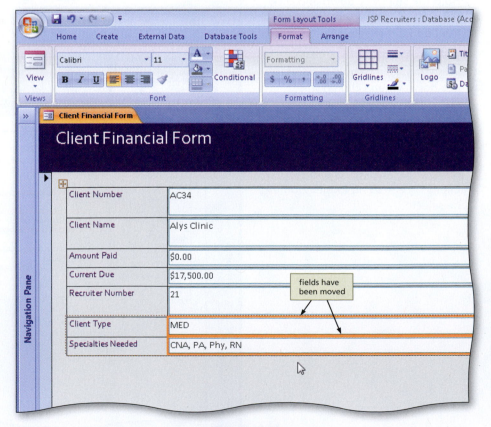

Figure 4–68

To Add a Field

Just as with a report, once you have created an initial form, you may decide that the form should contain an additional field. The following steps use a field list to add the City field to the Client Financial Form.

- Be sure the Format tab appears.

- Click the Add Existing Fields button to display a Field List (Figure 4–69).

Figure 4–69

- Point to the City field in the field list, press the left mouse button, and then drag the pointer to the position shown in Figure 4–70.

Q&A

Does it have to be exact?

The exact pointer position is not critical as long as the line is in the position shown in the figure.

Figure 4–70

3

- Release the left mouse button to place the field (Figure 4–71).

Q&A

What if I make a mistake?

Just as when you are modifying a report, you can delete the field by clicking the field and then pressing the DELETE key. You can move the field by dragging it to the correct position.

4

- Close the field list.

Figure 4–71

To Filter and Sort Using a Form

Just as in a datasheet, you can filter and sort using Advanced Filter/Sort, which is a command on the Advanced menu. The following steps use Advanced Filter/Sort to filter the records to those records whose city begins with the letters, Be. They also sort the records by client name.

1

- Click Home on the Ribbon to display the Home tab.

- Click the Advanced button on the Home tab to display the Advanced menu (Figure 4–72).

Figure 4–72

2

- Click Advanced Filter/Sort on the Advanced menu.

- Add the Client Name field and select Ascending sort order.

- Add the City field and type `like Be*` as the criterion for the city field (Figure 4–73).

Figure 4–73

3

- Click the Toggle Filter button on the Home tab to filter the records (Figure 4–74).

Q&A I can see only one record at a time in the form. How can I see which records are included?

You would have to scroll through the records. For example, you could repeatedly press the Next Record button.

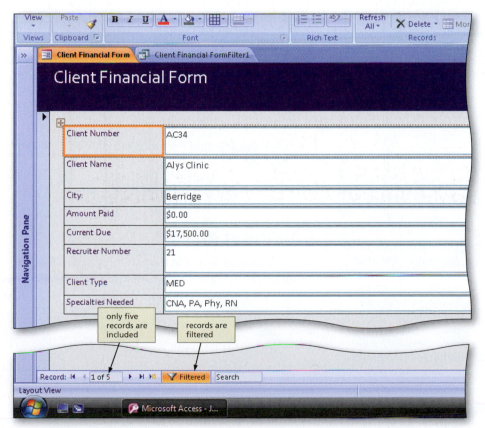

Figure 4–74

BTW

Creating and Removing Layouts
You can create and remove control layouts. To create a tabular layout, select the controls, click Arrange on the Ribbon and then click the Tabular button on the Arrange tab. To create a stacked layout, select the controls, click Arrange on the Ribbon and then click the Stacked button on the Arrange tab. To remove a tabular or stacked layout, select the fields with the layout you want to remove, click Arrange on the Ribbon and then click the Remove button on the Arrange tab.

To Clear a Form Filter

When you no longer want the records to be filtered, you clear the filter. The following steps clear the current filter for the Client Financial Form.

1 Click the Advanced button on the Home tab to display the Advanced menu.

2 Click Clear All Filters on the Advanced menu to clear the filter.

To Save and Close a Form

Now that you have completed your work on your form, you should save the form and close it. The following steps first save your work on the form and then close the form.

1 Click the Save button on the Quick Access Toolbar to save your work.

2 Close the Client Financial Form.

BTW

Creating Forms in Layout View
You can create a form in Layout view without using the wizard. To do so, click Create on the Ribbon and then click the Blank Form button on the Create tab.

To Print a Form

You can print all the records, a range of pages, or a selected record of a form by selecting the appropriate print range. In order to print the selected record, the form must be open. To print all records or a range of pages, the form simply can be highlighted in the Navigation Pane. The following steps open the Client Financial Form and then print the first record in the form, which is the selected record.

1 Open the Client Financial Form and then click the Office Button to display the Office Button menu.

2 Point to Print on the Office Button menu and then click Print on the Print submenu to display the Print dialog box.

3 Click the Selected Record(s) option button in the Page Range box, and then click the OK button.

BTW

Certification
The Microsoft Certified Application Specialist (MCAS) program provides an opportunity for you to obtain a valuable industry credential — proof that you have the Access 2007 skills required by employers. For more information, see Appendix G or visit the Access 2007 Certification Web page (scsite.com/ac2007/cert).

Changing an AutoFormat

An AutoFormat is a predefined style that can be applied to a report or form. You can apply or change an AutoFormat by using the AutoFormat group on the Format tab (see Figure 4–75). In viewing a form in Layout view, two AutoFormat selections appear on the screen. You can use the scroll arrows to see the previous two selections or the next two selections.

Figure 4–75

As an alternative, you can click the More button to display a gallery of all AutoFormat selections (Figure 4–76). In either case, once you select the desired AutoFormat, the characteristics of the AutoFormat will be applied to the form or report.

Figure 4–76

You also can use the AutoFormat Wizard to select an AutoFormat. Using the wizard, you can select whether the attributes in the form apply to the font, the color, and or the border. You also can create a new AutoFormat with the characteristics of the current form or report, update the selected AutoFormat with characteristics of the current form or report, or delete the selected AutoFormat.

BTW

Multiple Items Forms and Datasheet Forms
Access includes many different types of forms. A Multiple Items form is a form that shows multiple records in a datasheet with one record per row. To create a Multiple Items form, click the Multiple Items button on the Create tab. A Datasheet form displays a table in a datasheet. To create a Datasheet form, click the More Forms button arrow on the Create tab, and then click Datasheet.

BTW

Quick Reference
For a table that lists how to complete the tasks covered in this book using the mouse, Ribbon, shortcut menu, and keyboard, see the Quick Reference Summary at the back of this book, or visit the Access 2007 Quick Reference Web page (scsite.com/ac2007/qr).

To Apply an AutoFormat

If you wish to apply or change an AutoFormat, you would use the following steps.

1. Click the More button in the AutoFormat group on the Format tab.
2. Click the desired AutoFormat.

The Arrange Tab

Forms, like reports, have an Arrange tab that you can use to modify the form's layout. However, the Page Setup tab is not available for forms. The buttons on the Arrange tab and the functions of those buttons are just like the ones described in Table 4–1 on page AC 255, with one exception. When working with a form, there is an extra button, the Anchoring button. The function of this button is to tie a control to a section or another control so that it moves or resizes in conjunction with the movement or resizing of its parent.

To Quit Access

You saved all your changes and are ready to quit Access. The following step quits Access.

 Click the Close button on the right side of the Access title bar to quit Access.

Chapter Summary

In this chapter you have learned to use wizards to create reports and forms; modify the layout of reports and forms using Layout view; group and sort in a report, add totals to a report; conditionally format controls; filter records in reports and forms; resize and move controls; add fields to reports and forms; include gridlines; add a date; move controls in a control layout; and change an AutoFormat. The following list includes all the new Access skills you have learned in this chapter.

1. Create a Simple Report (AC 239)
2. Create a Report Using the Report Wizard (AC 239)
3. Group and Sort in a Report (AC 244)
4. Add Totals and Subtotals (AC 248)
5. Resize Columns (AC 249)
6. Conditionally Format Controls (AC 250)
7. Filter Records in a Report (AC 252)
8. Clear a Report Filter (AC 254)
9. Save and Close a Report (AC 254)
10. Print a Report (AC 256)
11. Create a Summary Report (AC 256)
12. Create a Report that Involves Multiple Tables (AC 257)
13. Resize Columns and Column Headings (AC 263)
14. Add a Field (AC 265)
15. Include Totals (AC 268)
16. Use the Form Wizard to Create a Form (AC 269)
17. Include Gridlines (AC 273)
18. Add a Date (AC 274)
19. Change the Format of a Control (AC 275)
20. Move a Control (AC 276)
21. Move Controls in a Control Layout (AC 277)
22. Add a Field (AC 279)
23. Filter and Sort Using a Form (AC 280)
24. Clear a Form Filter (AC 282)
25. Save and Close a Form (AC 282)
26. Print a Form (AC 282)
27. Apply an AutoFormat (AC 284)

 If you have a SAM user profile, you may have access to hands-on instruction, practice, and assessment. Log in to your SAM account (http://sam2007.course.com) to launch any assigned training activities or exams that relate to the skills covered in this chapter.

Learn It Online

Test your knowledge of chapter content and key terms.

Instructions: To complete the Learn It Online exercises, start your browser, click the Address bar, and then enter the Web address scsite.com/ac2007/learn. When the Access 2007 Learn It Online page is displayed, click the link for the exercise you want to complete and then read the instructions.

Chapter Reinforcement TF, MC, and SA

A series of true/false, multiple choice, and short answer questions that test your knowledge of the chapter content.

Flash Cards

An interactive learning environment where you identify chapter key terms associated with displayed definitions.

Practice Test

A series of multiple choice questions that test your knowledge of chapter content and key terms.

Who Wants To Be a Computer Genius?

An interactive game that challenges your knowledge of chapter content in the style of a television quiz show.

Wheel of Terms

An interactive game that challenges your knowledge of chapter key terms in the style of the television show *Wheel of Fortune*.

Crossword Puzzle Challenge

A crossword puzzle that challenges your knowledge of key terms presented in the chapter.

Apply Your Knowledge

Reinforce the skills and apply the concepts you learned in this chapter.

Creating a Report and a Form

Instructions: Start Access. If you are using the Microsoft Office Access 2007 Complete or the Microsoft Office Access 2007 Comprehensive text, open The Bike Delivers database that you used in Chapter 3. Otherwise, see the inside back cover of this book for instructions for downloading the Data Files for Students, or see your instructor for information on accessing the files required in this book.

Continued >

Apply Your Knowledge *continued*

Perform the following tasks:

1. Create the Customers by Courier report shown in Figure 4–77.

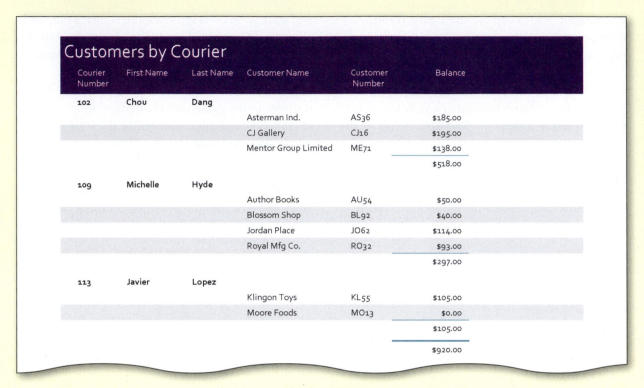

Figure 4–77

2. Create the Customer Update Form shown in Figure 4–78 for the Customer table. The form includes the current date and is similar in style to that shown in Figure 4–3 on page AC 236.

Figure 4–78

3. Submit the revised database in the format specified by your instructor.

Extend Your Knowledge

Extend the skills you learned in this chapter and experiment with new skills. You may need to use Help to complete the assignment.

Creating a Summary Report and a Justified Form

Instructions: See the inside back cover of this book for instructions for downloading the Data Files for Students, or see your instructor for information on accessing the files required in this book.

The Plant database contains data for a company that designs and maintains indoor landscapes. You will create the summary report shown in Figure 4–79. You also will create the form shown in Figure 4–80.

Figure 4–79

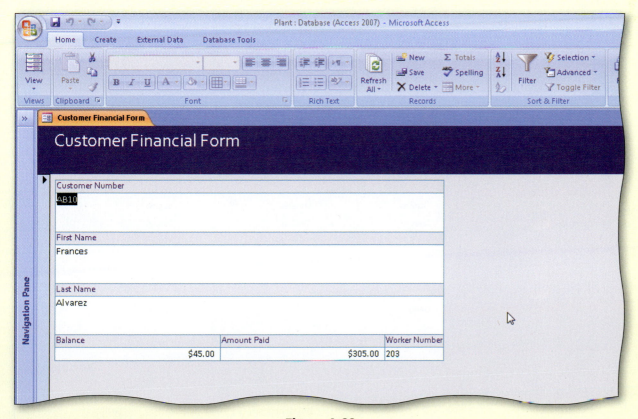

Figure 4–80

Continued >

Extend Your Knowledge *continued*

Perform the following tasks:

1. Create the summary report shown in Figure 4–79 on the previous page. Name the report Customers by City. The title of the report should be Customers by City Summary Report.

2. Create the Customer Financial Form shown in Figure 4–80 on the previous page. Please note that the form uses the Justified layout. Choose your own autoformat and apply it to the form. Save the form as Customer Financial Form AutoFormat.

3. Change the database properties, as specified by your instructor. Submit the revised database in the format specified by your instructor.

Make It Right

Analyze a database and correct all errors and/or improve the design.

Correcting Report Design and Form Design Errors

Instructions: Start Access. Open the Pet database. See the inside back cover of this book for instructions for downloading the Data Files for Students, or see your instructor for information on accessing the files required in this book.

The Pet database contains data for a company that provides a variety of services to pet owners. The owner of the company has created the report shown in Figure 4–81 using the Report Wizard but does not know how to adjust column sizes. She also does not know how to total the Balance field. She would like some way to differentiate customers with a zero balance.

Customers by City

City	Customer Number	First Name	Last Name	Balance
Em				
	BR16	Alex	Breaton	$80.00
	HJ07	Bill	Heijer	$29.00
	MA34	Lisa	Manston	$0.00
	SA23	Maria	Santoro	$0.00
Gra				
	AB10	Frances	Alvarez	$45.00
	FE45	Jean	Ferdon	$0.00
	KL12	Cynthia	Klinger	$60.00
Port				
	GM52	Frank	Gammort	$70.00
	PR80	Martin	Prestz	$95.00
	TR35	Gerry	Trent	$40.00

Figure 4–81

She also created the form shown in Figure 4–82 for the Customer table, but she forgot to add the Pets field. The field should appear before the Balance field.

Figure 4–82

Submit the revised database in the format specified by your instructor.

In the Lab

Design, create, modify, and/or use a database following the guidelines, concepts, and skills presented in this chapter. Labs are listed in order of increasing difficulty.

Lab 1: Presenting Data in the JMS TechWizards Database

Problem: The management of JMS TechWizards already has realized the benefits from the database of clients and technicians that you created. The management now would like to prepare reports and forms for the database.

Instructions: If you are using the Microsoft Office Access 2007 Complete or the Microsoft Office Access 2007 Comprehensive text, open JMS TechWizards database that you used in Chapter 3. Otherwise, see the inside back cover of this book for instructions for downloading the Data Files for Students, or see your instructor for information on accessing the files required in this book.

Continued >

In the Lab *continued*

Perform the following tasks:
1. Create the Clients by Type report shown in Figure 4–83 for the Client table. Group the report by Client Type and sort the records within Client Type by Client Name. Include totals for the Billed and Paid fields. If the amount in the Paid field is $0.00, it should appear in red.

Clients by Type

Client Type	Client Number	Client Name	Billed	Paid
MAN				
	AM53	Ashton-Mills	$315.50	$255.00
	SA56	Sawyer Industries	$372.25	$350.00
			$687.75	$605.00
RET				
	BE29	Bert's Supply	$229.50	$0.00
	CR21	Cray Meat Market	$0.00	$0.00
	DE76	D & E Grocery	$485.70	$400.00
	GU21	Grand Union	$228.00	$0.00
	ST21	Steed's Department Store	$0.00	$0.00
	AR76	The Artshop	$535.00	$565.00
			$1,478.20	$965.00
SER				
	GR56	Grant Cleaners	$215.00	$225.00
	ME17	Merry Café	$312.50	$323.50
			$527.50	$548.50
			$2,693.45	$2,118.50

Figure 4–83

2. Create the Clients by Technicians report shown in Figure 4–84. Be sure to adjust the column headings and include totals for the Billed and Paid fields.

Clients by Technician

Technician Number	First Name	Last Name	Client Name	Client Number	Client Type	Billed	Paid
22	Joe	Levin					
			Ashton-Mills	AM53	MAN	$315.50	$255.00
			Grant Cleaners	GR56	SER	$215.00	$225.00
			Merry Café	ME17	SER	$312.50	$323.50
						$843.00	$803.50
23	Brad	Rogers					
			Bert's Supply	BE29	RET	$229.50	$0.00
			Grand Union	GU21	RET	$228.00	$0.00
			Steed's Department Store	ST21	RET	$0.00	$0.00
			The Artshop	AR76	RET	$535.00	$565.00
						$992.50	$565.00
29	Maria	Rodriguez					
			D & E Grocery	DE76	RET	$485.70	$400.00
			Sawyer Industries	SA56	MAN	$372.25	$350.00
						$857.95	$750.00
32	Lee	Torres					
			Cray Meat Market	CR21	RET	$0.00	$0.00
						$0.00	$0.00
						$2,693.45	$2,118.50

Figure 4–84

3. Create the Client Financial Form shown in Figure 4–85.

Figure 4–85

4. Submit the revised database in the format specified by your instructor.

In the Lab

Lab 2: Presenting Data in the Hockey Fan Zone Database

Problem: The management of the Hockey Fan Zone store already has realized the benefits from the database of products and suppliers that you created. The management now would like to prepare reports and forms for the database.

Instructions: If you are using the Microsoft Office Access 2007 Complete or the Microsoft Office Access 2007 Comprehensive text, open the Hockey Fan Zone database that you used in Chapter 3. Otherwise, see the inside back cover of this book for instructions for downloading the Data Files for Students, or see your instructor for information on accessing the files required in this book.

Perform the following tasks:

1. Create the Items by Type report shown in Figure 4–86 for the Item table. The report is grouped by item type and sorted by description. Calculate the average cost and the average selling price for each item type and for all items.

Items by Type

Item Type	Item Number	Description	Cost	Selling Price
CAP				
	3663	Ball Cap	$11.15	$18.95
	7930	Visor	$11.95	$17.00
			$11.55	$17.98
CLO				
	5923	Jersey	$21.45	$24.75
	7550	Sweatshirt	$19.90	$22.95
	7810	Tee Shirt	$9.50	$14.95
			$16.95	$20.88
NOV				
	3673	Blanket	$29.90	$34.00
	3683	Bumper Sticker	$0.95	$1.50
	4563	Earrings	$4.50	$7.00
	6078	Key Chain	$3.00	$5.00
	6189	Koozies	$2.00	$4.00
	6343	Note Cube	$5.75	$8.00
			$7.68	$9.92
			$10.91	$14.37

Figure 4–86

2. Create the Items by Supplier report shown in Figure 4–87. If there are fewer than 10 items on hand, the value should appear in a red bold font.

Items by Supplier

Supplier Code	Supplier Name	Description	Item Number	On Hand	Cost
AC	Ace Clothes				
		Blanket	3673	5	$29.90
		Jersey	5923	12	$21.45
		Tee Shirt	7810	32	$9.50
LG	Logo Goods				
		Ball Cap	3663	30	$11.15
		Earrings	4563	10	$4.50
		Sweatshirt	7550	8	$19.90
		Visor	7930	9	$11.95
MN	Mary's Novelties				
		Bumper Sticker	3683	50	$0.95
		Key Chain	6078	20	$3.00
		Koozies	6189	35	$2.00
		Note Cube	6343	7	$5.75

Figure 4–87

3. Create the Item Update form shown in Figure 4–88. If there are fewer than 10 items on hand, the value should appear in a red bold font. Notice that the controls have been resized to a smaller width and that the figure shows the form with data for record 2 in the Item table.

Figure 4–88

4. Submit the revised database in the format specified by your instructor.

In the Lab

Lab 3: Maintaining the Ada Beauty Supply Database

Problem: The management of Ada Beauty Supply already has realized the benefits from the database you created. The management now would like to prepare reports and forms for the database.

Instructions: If you are using the Microsoft Office Access 2007 Complete or the Microsoft Office Access 2007 Comprehensive text, open the Ada Beauty Supply database that you used in Chapter 3. Otherwise, see the inside back cover of this book for instructions for downloading the Data Files for Students, or see your instructor for information on accessing the files required in this book. Submit the revised database in the format specified by your instructor.

Instructions Part 1: Create a report for Ada Beauty Supply. The report should be similar to the Clients by Recruiter report shown in Figure 4–2 on page AC 235 with the records grouped by Sales Rep Number. Include the Sales Rep Number, First Name, and Last Name from the Sales Rep table. Include the Customer Number, Customer Name, Services Offered, Balance, and Amount Paid fields from the Customer table. Provide subtotals and a grand total for the Balance and Amount Paid fields.

Instructions Part 2: Create a Customer Financial Form for Ada Beauty Supply that is similar to the Client Financial form shown in Figure 4–3 on page AC 236. The form should include Customer Number, Customer Name, Amount Paid, Balance, Sales Rep Number, and Services Offered.

Cases and Places

Apply your creative thinking and problem solving skills to design and implement a solution.

• EASIER   •• MORE DIFFICULT

• 1: Presenting Data in the Second-Hand Goods Database

If you are using the Microsoft Office Access 2007 Complete or the Microsoft Office Access 2007 Comprehensive text, open the Second-Hand Goods database that you used in Chapter 3. Otherwise, see the inside back cover of this book for instructions for downloading the Data Files for Students, or see your instructor for information on accessing the files required in this book. Use this database to create a report that groups items by seller. Include the seller code, first name, and last name from the Seller table. Include all fields except seller code from the Item table. Create a multiple items form and a datasheet form for the Item table. Submit the revised database in the format specified by your instructor.

• 2: Presenting Data in the BeachCondo Rentals database

If you are using the Microsoft Office Access 2007 Complete or the Microsoft Office Access 2007 Comprehensive text, open the BeachCondo Rentals database that you used in Chapter 3. Otherwise, see the inside back cover of this book for instructions for downloading the Data Files for Students, or see your instructor for information on accessing the files required in this book. The rental company needs a custom report that groups condo units by the number of bedrooms. Within each group, the records should be sorted in ascending order by weekly rate. The report should include all fields from the Condo Unit table except the For Sale field and the Owner Code field. The company also needs a form for the Condo Unit table that shows all fields except the For Sale field. Submit the revised database in the format specified by your instructor.

•• 3: Presenting Data in the Restaurant Database

If you are using the Microsoft Office Access 2007 Complete or the Microsoft Office Access 2007 Comprehensive text, open the restaurant database that you used in Chapter 3. Otherwise, see the inside back cover of this book for instructions for downloading the Data Files for Students, or see your instructor for information on accessing the files required in this book. Using the Plan Ahead guidelines presented in this chapter, determine what forms and reports you need to create. Create any necessary reports and forms. Include a logo on each report and form. You either can create your own logo or use Microsoft clip art. Write a short paper that explains why you chose to create the specific reports and forms. Submit the paper and the revised database in the format specified by your instructor.

•• 4: Presenting Data in Your Contacts Database

Make It Personal

If you are using the Microsoft Office Access 2007 Complete or the Microsoft Office Access 2007 Comprehensive text, open the contacts database that you used in Chapter 3. Otherwise, see the inside back cover of this book for instructions for downloading the Data Files for Students, or see your instructor for information on accessing the files required in this book. Consider your own personal job situation. What type of reports and forms would be useful to you? Do you need a report that lists all your contacts? Do you need a form to add each new contact that you make? Create any necessary reports and forms. Submit the revised database in the format specified by your instructor.

Continued >

Cases and Places *continued*

•• 5: Understanding Report and Form Formats and Styles

Working Together

The Report and Form Wizards offer several different styles and formats. Each member of the team should pick a different style and create the report shown in Figure 4–2 on page AC 235 and the form shown in Figure 4–3 on page AC 236 using the chosen styles. Compare the styles and as a team vote on which one you prefer. The project included general guidelines for designing reports and forms. Use the Internet to find more information about form design guidelines; for example, there are certain fonts that you should not use for a title and certain colors that are harder for individuals to see. Then, as a group, create a form that illustrates poor design features. Include a short write-up that explains what design principles were violated. Be sure to cite your references. Turn in each of the reports and forms that your team created using different styles. Also, turn in the poorly designed form and the write-up in the format specified by your instructor.

5 | Multi-Table Forms

Objectives

You will have mastered the material in this project when you can:

- Use Yes/No, Date, Memo, OLE Object, Attachment, and Hyperlink fields

- Use the Input Mask Wizard

- Update fields and enter data

- Change row and column size

- Create a form with a subform in Design view

- Modify a subform and form design

- Enhance the form title

- Change tab stops and tab order

- Use the form to view data and attachments

- Use Date, Memo, and Yes/No fields in a query

- View object dependencies

5 | Multi-Table Forms

Introduction

This chapter adds several additional fields to the JSP Recruiters database that require special data types. It then creates a form incorporating data from two tables. The two tables, Recruiter and Client, are related in a one-to-many relationship. That is, one recruiter is related to *many* clients, but each client is related to only *one* recruiter. The Recruiter table is called the "one" table in the relationship and the Client table is called the "many" table. The form will show one recruiter at a time, but also will include the many clients of that recruiter. This chapter also creates queries that use the added fields.

Project — Multi-Table Forms

JSP Recruiters uses its database to keep records about clients and recruiters. After several months, however, the administration has found that it needs to maintain additional data on its recruiters. JSP has a bonus program and it needs to add a field that indicates the recruiter's eligibility for the bonus program. JSP needs to store the start date of each recruiter in the database. JSP wants the database to contain a comment about each recruiter as well as the recruiter's picture. Additionally, recruiters now maintain files about potential contacts. Some of these files are maintained in Word and others in Excel. JSP would like a way to attach these files to the corresponding recruiter's record in the database. Finally, JSP wants to add the Phone Number field to the Recruiter table. Users should type only the digits in the telephone number and then have Access format the number appropriately. If the user enters 7195558364, for example, Access will format the number as (719) 555-8364.

After the proposed fields have been added to the database, JSP wants a form created that incorporates both the Client and Recruiter tables. The form includes some of the newly added fields along with some of the existing fields. The form also should include the client number, name, amount paid, and current due amount for the clients of each recruiter. JSP would like to see multiple clients on the screen at the same time (Figure 5–1). The database should provide the capability of scrolling through all the clients of a recruiter and of accessing any of the attachments concerning the recruiter's contact notes. Finally, JSP requires queries that use the Bonus, Start Date, and Comment fields.

Overview

As you read through this chapter, you will learn how to create reports and forms by performing these general tasks:

- Add the Bonus, Start Date, Comment, Picture, and Attachment fields to the Recruiter table and assign each field the appropriate data type.
- Add the Phone Number field to the Recruiter table and create an appropriate input mask.
- Create the Recruiter Master Form and add the fields from the Recruiter table at the appropriate positions.

Figure 5–1

- Add a subform containing the Client Number, Client Name, Amount Paid, and Current Due fields from the Client table.

- Enhance the form by assigning colors and various special effects.

- Create and run queries that involve the Bonus, Start Date, and Comment fields.

Report and Form Design Guidelines

1. **When new fields are needed, determine the purpose of those fields to see if they need special data types.** Does the field contain dates? Are the only values for the field Yes or No? Does the field contain an extended description of something? Does the field contain a picture? Is the purpose of the field to contain attachments of files created in other applications?

2. **When a form is required, determine whether the form requires data from more than one table.** Is all the data found in a single table or does it come from multiple related tables?

3. **If the form requires data from more than one table, determine the relationship between the tables.** Identify one-to-many relationships. For each relationship, identify the "one" table and the "many" table.

(continued)

Plan Ahead

**Plan
Ahead**

(continued)

4. **If the form requires data from more than one table, determine on which of the tables the form is to be based.** Which table contains data that is the main focus of the form? Is it a form about recruiters, for example, that happens to require some client data in order to be effective? Is it a form about clients that also includes some recruiter data as additional information?

5. **Determine the fields from each table that need to be on the form.** How exactly will the form be used? What fields are necessary to support this use? Are there any additional fields that, while not strictly necessary, would make the form more functional? For example, if a user is entering a recruiter number on a form based on clients, it may be helpful also to see the name of the recruiter with that number.

When necessary, more specific details concerning the above decisions and/or actions are presented at appropriate points within the chapter. The chapter also will identify the use of these guidelines in the design of forms such as the one shown in Figure 5–1 on the previous page.

Starting Access

If you are using a computer to step through the project in this chapter and you want your screen to match the figures in this book, you should change your screen's resolution to 1024 × 768. For information about how to change a computer's resolution, read Appendix E.

To Start Access

The following steps, which assume Windows Vista is running, start Access.

Note: If you are using Windows XP, see Appendix F for alternate steps.

1 Click the Start button on the Windows Vista taskbar to display the Start menu.

2 Click All Programs at the bottom of the left pane on the Start menu to display the All Programs list and then click Microsoft Office in the All Programs list to display the Microsoft Office list.

3 Click Microsoft Office Access 2007 on the Microsoft Office list to start Access and display the Getting Started with Microsoft Office Access window.

4 If the Access window is not maximized, click the Maximize button on its title bar to maximize the window.

To Open a Database

In Chapter 1, you created your database on a USB flash drive using the file name, JSP Recruiters. There are two ways to open the file containing your database. If the file you created appears in the Recent Documents list, you could click it to open the file. If not, you can use the More button to open the file. The following steps use the More button to open the JSP Recruiters database from the USB flash drive.

Note: If you are using Windows XP, see Appendix F for alternate steps.

1 With your USB flash drive connected to one of the computer's USB ports, click the More button to display the Open dialog box.

2 If the Folders list is displayed below the Folders button, click the Folders button to remove the Folders list.

3 If necessary, click Computer in the Favorite Links section and then double-click UDISK 2.0 (E:) to select the USB flash drive, Drive E in this case, as the new open location. (Your drive letter might be different.)

4 Click JSP Recruiters to select the file name.

5 Click the Open button to open the database.

6 If a Security Warning appears, click the Options button to display the Microsoft Office Security Options dialog box.

7 With the option button to enable the content selected, click the OK button to enable the content.

Determine the purpose of new fields to see if they need special data types.

Plan Ahead

1. **Determine whether an input mask is appropriate.** Should the data in the field be displayed in a special way; for example, with parentheses and a hyphen like a phone number or separated into three groups of digits like a Social Security number? Should Access assist the user in entering the data in the right format? For example, should Access automatically insert the parentheses and a hyphen when a user enters a phone number?

2. **Determine whether the Yes/No data type is appropriate.** Are the only possible field values Yes or No? Are the only possible values True or False? Are the only possible values On or Off? If any of these applies, the field is a good candidate for the Yes/No data type.

3. **Determine whether the Date data type is appropriate.** Does the field contain a date? If so, assigning it the Date data type accomplishes several things. First, Access will ensure that the only values entered in the field are legitimate dates. Second, you can perform date arithmetic. For example, you can subtract one date from another to find the number of days between the two dates. Finally, you can sort the field and the dates will sort correctly.

4. **Determine whether the Memo data type is appropriate.** Does the field contain text that is variable in length and that can potentially be very lengthy? If so, the Memo data type is appropriate. If you wish to use special text effects, such as bold and italics, you can assign the field the Memo data type and change the value of the field's Text Format property from Plain Text to Rich Text. You also can collect history on the changes to a memo field by changing the value of the field's Append Only property from No to Yes. If you do so, when you right-click the field and click Show Column History on the shortcut menu, you will see a record of all changes made to the field.

5. **Determine whether the OLE Object data type is appropriate.** Does the field contain objects created by other applications that support **OLE (Object Linking and Embedding)** as a server? Object Linking and Embedding is a feature of Microsoft Windows that creates a special relationship between Microsoft Access and the application that created the object. When you edit the object, Microsoft Access returns automatically to the application that created the object.

6. **Determine whether the Attachment data type is appropriate.** Will the field contain one or more attachments that were created in other application programs? If so, the Attachment data type is appropriate. It allows you to store multiple attachments on each record. You can view and manipulate these attachments in their original application.

7. **Determine whether the Hyperlink data type is appropriate.** Will the field contain links to other Office documents or to Web pages? If so, Hyperlink is appropriate.

Input Mask Characters
When you create an input mask, Access adds several characters. These characters control the literal values that appear when you enter data. For example, the first backslash in the input mask in Figure 5-8 on page AC 305 displays the opening parenthesis. The double quotes force Access to display the closing parenthesis and a space. The second backslash forces Access to display the hyphen that separates the first and second part of the phone number.

Adding Special Fields

Having analyzed the requirements for the new fields, JSP has determined some new fields to include in the Recruiter table. They need a Phone Number field and they want to assist the users in entering the correct format for a phone number, so it will use an input mask. An **input mask** specifies how data is to be entered and how it will appear. The Bonus field will be a Yes/No field, that is, its Data type will be Yes/No. The Start Date will be a Date field and the Comment field will be a Memo field. Because no special effects are required in the Comment field, the value of the Text Format property will remain Plain Text rather than Rich Text. Because JSP does not require a history of changes to the field, the value of the Append Only property will remain No. The Contact Notes field, which must be able to contain multiple attachments for each recruiter, will be an Attachment field. The only question is the Picture field. It could be either OLE Object or Attachment.

Certainly OLE Object is an appropriate data type for a picture. On the other hand, if an Attachment field contains a picture, the field will display the picture. For other types of attachments, such as Word documents and Excel spreadsheets, however, the Attachment field displays an icon representing the attachment. JSP Recruiters has decided to use OLE Object as the data type for two reasons. First, the form contains another field that must be an Attachment field, the Contact Notes field. In Datasheet view, an Attachment field appears as a paper clip rather than the field name. Thus, if the Picture field also were an Attachment field, the form would display two paper clips, leading to potential confusion. A second potential problem with using an Attachment field for pictures occurs when you have multiple attachments to a record. Only the first attachment routinely appears in the field on either a datasheet or form. Thus, if the picture were not the first attachment, it would not appear.

To Add Fields to a Table

You add the new fields to the Recruiter table by modifying the design of the table and inserting the fields at the appropriate position in the table structure. The following steps add the Bonus, Start Date, Comment, Picture, and Contact Notes fields to the Recruiter table.

1

- If necessary, show the Navigation Pane.

- Right-click the Recruiter table to display a shortcut menu (Figure 5–2).

Figure 5–2

2

- Click Design View on the shortcut menu to open the Recruiter table in Design view (Figure 5–3).

Figure 5–3

3

- Click the first open field to select the position for the first additional field.

- Type Bonus as the field name, press the TAB key, select Yes/No as the data type, and then press the TAB key twice to move to the next field.

- In a similar fashion, add a field with Start Date as the field name and Date/Time as the data type, a field with Comment as the field name and Memo as the data type, a field with Picture as the field name and OLE Object as the data type, and a field with Contact Notes as the field name and Attachment as the data type (Figure 5–4).

Q&A Why use Date as a data type for date fields rather than Text?

If you use Date, the computer will ensure that only legitimate dates are entered in the field. In addition, you can perform appropriate arithmetic with dates. You also can sort by date.

Figure 5–4

4

- Click the Save button on the Quick Access Toolbar to save your changes.

To Use the Input Mask Wizard

An **input mask** specifies how data is to be entered and how it will appear. You can enter an input mask directly or you can use the Input Mask Wizard. The wizard assists you in the creation of the input mask by allowing you to select from a list of the most frequently used input masks.

To use the Input Mask Wizard, select the Input Mask property and then select the Build button. The following steps add the Phone Number field and then specify how the telephone number is to appear by using the Input Mask Wizard.

- Click the row selector for the Rate field (shown in Figure 5–4 on the previous page), and then press the INSERT key to insert a blank row.

- Click the Field Name column for the new field.

- Type Phone Number as the field name and then press the TAB key.

- Click the Input Mask property box (Figure 5–5).

Q&A Do I need to change the data type?

No. Text is the appropriate data type for the Phone Number field.

Figure 5–5

- Click the Build button.

- If a dialog box appears asking you to save the table, click the Yes button. (If a dialog box displays a message that the Input Mask Wizard is not installed, check with your instructor before proceeding with the following steps.)

- Ensure that Phone Number is selected (Figure 5–6).

Experiment

- Click different input masks and enter data in the Try It text box to see the effect of the input mask. When done, click the Phone Number input mask.

Figure 5–6

3

- Click the Next button to move to the next screen, where you then are given the opportunity to change the input mask.

- Because you do not need to change the mask, click the Next button a second time (Figure 5–7).

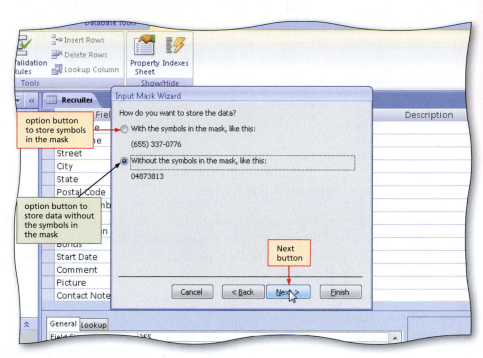

Figure 5–7

4

- Click the 'With the symbols in the mask, like this' option button, click the Next button, and then click the Finish button (Figure 5–8).

Q&A Why doesn't the data type change to Input Mask?

The data type of the Phone Number field is still Text. The only thing that changed is one of the field properties, the Input Mask property.

Q&A Could I have typed the value in the Input Mask property myself, rather than using the wizard?

Yes. Input masks can be complex, however, so it is usually easier and safer to use the wizard.

5

- Click the Save button on the Quick Access Toolbar to save your changes.

- Close the Recruiter table.

Figure 5–8

Updating the New Fields

After adding the new fields to the table, the next task is to enter data into the fields. The data type determines the manner in which this is accomplished. The following sections cover the methods for updating fields with an input mask, Yes/No fields, date fields, memo fields, OLE fields, and Attachment fields. They also show how you would enter data in Hyperlink fields.

To Enter Data Using an Input Mask

When you are entering data in a field that has an input mask, Access will insert the appropriate special characters in the proper positions. This means Access automatically will insert the parentheses around the area code, the space following the second parenthesis, and the hyphen in the Phone Number field. The following steps use the input mask to add the telephone numbers.

• Open the Recruiter table and hide the Navigation Pane.

• Click at the beginning of the Phone Number field on the first record to display an insertion point in the field (Figure 5–9).

Figure 5–9

• Type 7195558364 as the telephone number (Figure 5–10).

Q&A

Don't I need to type the parentheses, the space, and the hyphen?

No. Access will insert these automatically.

Figure 5–10

3

- Use the same technique to enter the remaining telephone numbers as shown in Figure 5–11.

Figure 5–11

To Enter Data in Yes/No Fields

Fields that are Yes/No fields contain check boxes. To set the value to Yes, place a check mark in the check box. To set a value to No, leave the check box blank. The following steps set the value of the Bonus field, a Yes/No field, to Yes for the first two records.

1

- Repeatedly click the right scroll arrow, shown in Figure 5–11, until the new fields appear.

- Click the check box in the Bonus field on the first record to place a check mark in the box (Figure 5–12).

Q&A

What is the meaning of the check mark?

A check mark indicates the value in the Bonus field is Yes. If there is no check mark, the value is No.

2

- Click the check box in the Bonus field on the second record to place a check mark in the box.

Figure 5–12

To Enter Data in Date Fields

To enter data in date fields, you simply can type the dates and include slashes (/). As an alternative, you can click the field, click the Calendar button that will appear next to the field, and then use the calendar to select the date. The following step adds the Start Dates for the recruiters without using the Calendar button.

 1

- Click the Start Date field on the first record, type 5/22/2004 as the date on the first record, and then press the DOWN ARROW key.

- Type 6/3/2004 as the start date on the second record, and then press the DOWN ARROW key.

- Type 10/3/2006 as the start date on the third record, and then press the DOWN ARROW key.

- Type 12/3/2007 as the start date on the fourth record (Figure 5–13).

Q&A How do I use the Calendar button?

Click the button to display a calendar. Scroll to the month and year you want and then click the desired day of the month.

Figure 5–13

Experiment

- Click the Calendar button and use it to assign a date. When finished, change the date to 12/3/2007.

To Enter Data in Memo Fields

To update a memo field, simply type the data in the field. With the current row and column spacing on the datasheet, only a small portion of the memo will appear. To correct this problem, you will change the spacing later to allow more room for the memo. The following steps enter each recruiter's comment.

 1

- If necessary, click the right scroll arrow so the Comment field appears.

- Click the Comment field on the first record, and then type Master's Degree in Healthcare Management; Treasurer of a national healthcare professional organization. as the entry (Figure 5–14).

Q&A Why don't I see the whole entry?

Currently, there is not room. You will address this problem shortly.

Figure 5–14

2

- Click the Comment field on the second record, and then type `Former hospital administrator; extensive human resources experience; frequent presenter at professional conferences.` as the entry.

- Click the Comment field on the third record, and then type `Former director of human resources at small hospital in Wyoming; Working on a Master's in Healthcare Management.` as the entry.

- Click the Comment field on the fourth record, and then type `Recently retired as a district school nurse; Hired to help expand recruiting services to K-12 school districts.` as the entry (Figure 5-15).

Figure 5–15

To Change the Row and Column Size

Only a small portion of the comments appears in the datasheet. To allow more of the information to appear, you can expand the size of the rows and the columns. You can change the size of a column by using the field selector. The **field selector** is the bar containing the field name. To change the size of a row, you use a record's **record selector**, which is the small box at the beginning of each record.

The following step resizes the column containing the Comment field and the rows of the table so a larger portion of the Comment field text will appear.

1

- Drag the line between the column headings for the Comment and Picture columns to the right to resize the Comment column to the approximate size shown in Figure 5–16.

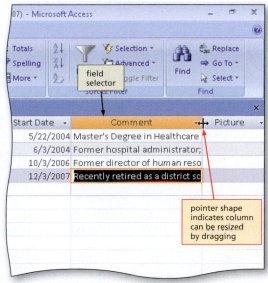

Figure 5–16

- Drag the lower edge of the record selector to approximately the position shown in Figure 5–17.

Q&A Can rows be different sizes?

No. All rows must be the same size.

Q&A Why does the value on the last record look different from the others?

It is the one that is currently selected.

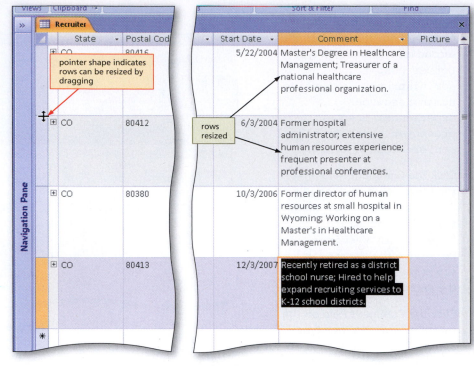

Other Ways

1. Right-click record selector, click Row Height to change row spacing
2. Right-click field selector, click Column Width to change column size

Figure 5–17

To Enter Data in OLE Fields

To insert data into an OLE field, you use the Insert Object command on the OLE field's shortcut menu. The Insert Object command presents a list of the various types of objects that can be inserted. Access then opens the corresponding application to create the object, for example, Microsoft Drawing. If the object already is created and stored in a file, as is the case in this project, you simply insert it directly from the file.

The following steps insert pictures into the Picture field. The steps assume that the pictures are located in a folder called AccessData on your USB drive. If your pictures are located elsewhere, you will need to make the appropriate changes.

- Ensure the Picture field appears on your screen, and then right-click the Picture field on the first record to produce a shortcut menu (Figure 5–18).

Figure 5–18

2

- Click Insert Object on the shortcut menu to display the Microsoft Office Access dialog box (Figure 5–19).

Figure 5–19

3

- Click the 'Create from File' option button, and then click the Browse button.

- Navigate to the AccessData folder on your USB drive in the Look in box. (If your pictures are located elsewhere, navigate to the folder where they are located instead of the AccessData folder.)

- Click Pict1 and then click the OK button to select the appropriate picture (Figure 5–20).

4

- Click the OK button.

- Insert the pictures into the second, third, and fourth records using the techniques illustrated in Steps 1 through 4. For the second record, select the picture named Pict2. For the third record, select the picture named Pict3. For the fourth record, select Pict4.

Figure 5–20

Bitmap Image

The entries in the Picture field all should be Bitmap images (BMP). They initially may be Pbrush, but, if so, they should change to Bitmap image after you close and reopen the table. If you see the word Package instead of Bitmap image or Pbrush, there is a problem either with the graphics filters that are installed or with the file associations for BMP files. In that case, you can use a slightly different technique to add the pictures. After right-clicking the Picture field, and clicking Insert Object, *do not* click the Create from File button. Instead, select the Paintbrush Picture object type from the list, select the Paste From command on the Edit menu of the Paintbrush window, select the desired BMP file, and then select the Exit command from the File menu to return to the datasheet. The entry in the Picture field then will be Bitmap image, as it should.

To Enter Data in Attachment Fields

To insert data into an Attachment field, you use the Manage Attachments command on the Attachment field's shortcut menu. The Manage Attachments command displays the Attachments dialog box which you can use to attach as many files as necessary to the field. The following steps attach two files to the first recruiter and one file to the fourth recruiter. The second and third recruiters currently have no attachments.

- Ensure the Contact Notes field, which has a paper clip in the field selector, appears on your screen, and then right-click the Contact Notes field on the first record to produce a shortcut menu (Figure 5–21).

Figure 5–21

- Click Manage Attachments on the shortcut menu to display the Attachments dialog box (Figure 5–22).

Figure 5–22

❸

- Click the Add button in the Attachments dialog box to add an attachment.

- Navigate to the AccessData folder on your USB drive in the Look in box. (If your files are located elsewhere, navigate to the folder where they are located instead of the AccessData folder.)

- Click Alyssa Kerry Clients, a Word file, and then click the Open button to attach the file.

- Click the Add button.

- Click the Alyssa Kerry Potential Clients, an Excel file, and then click the Open button to attach the file (Figure 5–23).

Figure 5–23

❹

- Click the OK button in the Attachments dialog box to close the Attachments dialog box.

- Using the same technique, attach the Jan Lee Potential Clients file to the fourth record (Figure 5–24). (The second and third records have no attachments.)

Figure 5–24

TO ENTER DATA IN HYPERLINK FIELDS

If you had a Hyperlink field, you would insert data by using the following steps.

1. Right-click the Hyperlink field in which you wish to enter data to display a shortcut menu.
2. Click Hyperlink on the shortcut menu to display the Hyperlink submenu.
3. Click Edit Hyperlink on the Hyperlink submenu to display the Insert Hyperlink dialog box.
4. Type the desired Web address in the Address text box.
5. Click the OK button.

To Save the Properties and Close the Table

The row and column spacing are table properties. When changing any table properties, the changes apply only as long as the table is active *unless they are saved*. Once you have saved them, they will apply every time you open the table.

To undo changes to the row height, right-click the row selector, click Row Height on the shortcut menu, and then click the Standard Height check box in the Row Height dialog box. To undo changes to the column width, right-click the field selector, click Column Width on the shortcut menu, and then click the Standard Width check box in the Column Width dialog box.

The following steps first save the properties and then close the table.

1 Click the Save button on the Quick Access Toolbar to save the changes to the table properties.

2 Close the table.

Viewing Pictures and Attachments in Datasheet View

Although the pictures do not appear on the screen, you can view them within the table. To view the picture of a particular recruiter, right-click the Picture field for the recruiter. Click Bitmap Image Object on the shortcut menu, and then click Open. The picture will appear. Once you have finished viewing the picture, close the window containing the picture by clicking its Close button.

You can view the attachments in the Contact Notes field by right-clicking the field and then clicking Manage Attachments on the shortcut menu. The attachments then appear in the Attachments dialog box. To view an attachment, click the attachment and then click the Open button in the dialog box. The attachment will appear in its original application. After you have finished viewing the attachment, close the original application and close the dialog box.

Multi-Table Form Techniques

With the additional fields in place, JSP Recruiters management is ready to incorporate data from both the Recruiter and Client tables in a single form. The form will display data concerning one recruiter. It also will display data concerning the many clients to which the recruiter is assigned. Formally, the relationship between recruiters and clients is called a **one-to-many relationship** (*one* recruiter services *many* clients). The Recruiter table is the "one" table in this relationship and the Client table is the "many" table.

To include the data for the many clients of a recruiter on the form, the client data will appear in a **subform**, which is a form that is contained within another form. The form in which the subform is contained is called the main form. Thus, the **main form** will contain recruiter data, and the subform will contain client data.

Determine on which of the tables the form is to be based.

Plan Ahead

1. **Determine the main table the form is intended to view and/or update.** What is the purpose of the form? Which table is it really intended to show? That would be the main table. Is there a table that could be omitted and still have the form make sense? That would NOT be the main table.

2. **Determine how the additional table should fit into the form.** If the additional table is the "many" part of the relationship, the data should probably be in a subform or datasheet. If the additional table is the "one" part of the relationship, the data probably should appear simply as fields on the form.

Determine the fields from each table to be included in the form.

Plan Ahead

1. **Determine the fields from the main table that should be included on the form.** What fields do users want on the form? Is there a particular order for the fields that would be most useful?

2. **Determine the fields from the additional table that should be included on the form.** What fields from the additional table would be helpful in updating or viewing the fields from the main table? Should users be able to change these fields via this form? (Often the answer will be no.)

To Create a Form in Design View

You can create a form in Design view, which gives you the most flexibility in laying out the form. You will be presented with a blank design on which you place objects. The following steps create a form in Design view.

1
- Show the Navigation Pane and be sure the Recruiter table is selected.

- Click Create on the Ribbon to display the Create tab (Figure 5–25).

Figure 5–25

- Click Form Design on the Create tab to create a new form in Design view.

- Hide the Navigation Pane.

- If a field list does not appear, click the Add Existing Fields button on the Design tab to display a field list (Figure 5–26). (Your list may show all fields in the Client table.)

- If the fields in the Recruiter table do not appear, click the expand indicator (+) in front of the Recruiter table to display the fields.

Figure 5–26

To Add a Control for a Field to the Form Design

To place a control for a field on a form, drag the field from the field list to the desired position. When you drag the field, you also drag the attached label for the field. The following steps place the Recruiter Number field on the form.

1

- Point to the Recruiter Number field in the field list for the Recruiter table, press the left mouse button, and then drag the field to the approximate position shown in Figure 5–27.

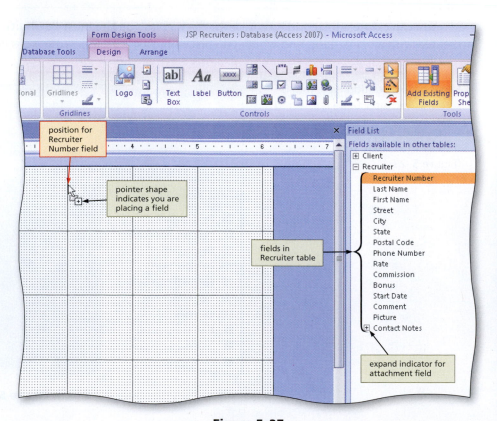

Figure 5–27

2

● Release the left mouse button to place a control for the field (Figure 5–28).

Figure 5–28

To Save the Form

Before continuing with the form creation, it is a good idea to save the form. The following steps save the form and assign it the name Recruiter Master Form.

1 Click the Save button on the Quick Access Toolbar.

2 Type `Recruiter Master Form` as the name of the form.

3 Click the OK button to save the form.

To Add Controls for Additional Fields

The following step places controls for the First Name, Last Name, Phone Number, Rate, Commission, Start Date, and Bonus fields on the form by dragging the fields from the field list.

- Drag the First Name, Last Name, Phone Number, Rate, Commission, Start Date, and Bonus fields to the approximate positions shown in Figure 5–29.

Q&A

Do I have to align them precisely?
You can, but you do not need to. In the next steps, you will instruct Access to align the fields properly.

Figure 5–29

To Align Controls

Often, you will want form controls to be aligned in some fashion. For example, the controls may be aligned so their right edges are even with each other. In another case, controls may be aligned so their top edges are even. While you can use the grid that appears in Design view to align controls, it is often easier to use alignment buttons. To ensure that a collection of controls is aligned properly with each other, select all of the affected controls, and then use the appropriate alignment button on the Arrange tab.

There are two ways to select multiple controls. One way is to use a ruler. If you click a position on the horizontal ruler, you will select all the controls for which a portion of the control is under that position on the ruler. Similarly, if you click a position on the vertical ruler, you will select all the controls for which a portion of the control is to the right of that position on the ruler.

The second way to select multiple controls is to select the first control by clicking it. Then, select all the other controls by holding down the SHIFT key while clicking the control.

The following steps select the First Name, Last Name, and Phone Number controls and then align them left.

1

- Click the First Name control (the white space, not the label) to select the control.

- Hold the SHIFT key down and click the Last Name control to select the Last Name control as well.

- Hold the SHIFT key down and click the Phone Number control to select the Phone Number control as well (Figure 5–30).

Q&A

I selected the wrong collection of fields. How can I start over?

Click anywhere outside the controls to deselect the controls, then begin the process again, making sure you do not hold the SHIFT key down when you select the first field.

Figure 5–30

2

- Click Arrange on the Ribbon to display the Arrange tab.

- Click the Left button on the Arrange tab to align the controls on the left.

- Release the SHIFT key.

- Using the same technique, align the Rate, Commission, and Start Date fields on the left.

- Click outside any of the selected controls to deselect the controls.

- Fine-tune your layout to match the one in Figure 5–31 by clicking and dragging controls individually.

Figure 5–31

To Move the Field List

Dragging from the field list onto the form is a problem if the field list covers the portion of the form where you wish to place the field. If that is the case, you can move the field list to a different location. The following step moves the field list in preparation for placing controls in the area it currently occupies.

- Move the field list to the approximate position shown in Figure 5–32 by dragging its title bar.

Q&A

My field list changed size when I moved it. How can I return it to its original size?

Point to the border of the field list so that the mouse pointer changes to a double-headed arrow. You then can drag to adjust the size.

Q&A

Can I make the field list smaller so I can see more of the screen?

Yes, you can adjust the size to whatever is most comfortable for you.

Figure 5–32

To Add Controls for the Remaining Fields

The following steps place controls for the Comment, Picture, and Contact Notes fields and also move their attached labels to the desired position.

- Drag the control for the Comment field from the field list to the approximate position shown in Figure 5–33.

Figure 5–33

• Move the label for the Comment field to the position shown in Figure 5–34 by dragging its move handle.

Q&A

I started to move the label and the control moved along with it. What did I do wrong?

You were not pointing at the handle to move the label independent of the control. Make sure you are pointing to the little box in the upper-left corner of the label.

Figure 5–34

❸

• Using the same technique, move the control for the Picture field to the approximate position shown in Figure 5–35 and move its label to the position shown in the figure.

Figure 5–35

4

- Click the control for the Picture field and drag the lower-right corner to the approximate position shown in Figure 5–36 to resize the control.

- Add a control for the Contact Notes field in the position shown in Figure 5–36 and move its attached label to the position shown in the figure.

5

- Close the field list by clicking its Close button.

Q&A Where will the field list be positioned the next time I display it?

Usually it will be in the position it was when you closed it. If that is the case and you want it in its typical position, move it there by dragging its title bar.

Figure 5–36

To Use a Shortcut Menu to Change the Fill/Back Color

You can use the Fill/Back Color button on the Design tab to change the background color of a form. In some cases, you also can use a shortcut menu. The following steps use a shortcut menu to change the background color of the form to gray.

1

- Right-click in the approximate position shown in Figure 5–37 to produce a shortcut menu.

Q&A Does it matter where I right-click?

You can right-click anywhere on the form as long as you are outside of all the controls.

Figure 5–37

2

- Point to the Fill/Back Color command arrow on the shortcut menu to display a color palette (Figure 5–38).

3

- Click the gray color shown in Figure 5–38 to change the fill/back color to gray.

Figure 5–38

To Add a Title

A form should have a descriptive title. The following step adds a title to the form.

1

- Click Design on the Ribbon to display the Design tab.

- Click the Title button on the Design tab (Figure 5–39).

Q&A Why is there a new section?

The form title belongs in the Form Header section. When you clicked the Title button, Access added the Form Header section automatically and placed the title in it.

Q&A Could I add a Form Header section without having to click the Title button?

Yes. Click the Form Header/Footer button on the Arrange tab.

Figure 5–39

To Place a Subform

To place a subform on a form, you use the Subform/Subreport tool on the Design tab. Provided you select the Control Wizards tool, a wizard will guide you through the process of adding the subform. The following steps use the Subform Wizard to place a subform.

- Be sure the Control Wizards tool is selected, click the Subform/Subreport button on the Design tab, and then move the mouse pointer to the approximate position shown in Figure 5–40.

Figure 5–40

- Click the position shown in Figure 5–40 and then ensure the 'Use existing Tables and Queries' option button is selected (Figure 5–41).

Figure 5–41

3

- Click the Next button.

- Click the Tables/Queries box arrow and then click Table: Client to select it as the table that contains the fields for the subform.

- Add the Client Number, Client Name, Amount Paid, and Current Due fields by clicking the field and then clicking the Add Field button (Figure 5–42).

Figure 5–42

4

- Click the Next button.

- Be sure the 'Choose from a list.' option button is selected (Figure 5–43).

Figure 5–43

5

- Click the Next button.

- Type **Clients of Recruiter** as the name of the subform (Figure 5–44).

Figure 5–44

6

- Click the Finish button to place the subform (Figure 5–45).

Figure 5–45

7

- Click the subform to select it.

- Move the subform to the approximate position shown in Figure 5–46 by dragging the subform and then resize it to the approximate size shown in the figure by dragging the appropriate sizing handles.

Figure 5–46

To Close and Save a Form

The following steps first save and then close the Recruiter Master Form.

1 Click the Save button on the Quick Access Toolbar to save the form.

2 Close the form by clicking the Close 'Recruiter Master Form' button.

To Modify a Subform

The next task is to resize the columns in the subform, which appears on the form in Datasheet view. The subform is a separate object in the database. The following steps open the subform and then resize the columns.

- Show the Navigation Pane.

- Right-click the Clients of Recruiter form to produce a shortcut menu.

- Click Open on the shortcut menu to open the form.

- Resize the columns to best fit the data by double-clicking the right boundaries of the field selectors (Figure 5–47).

Figure 5–47

- Save your changes and then close the subform.

- Open the Recruiter Master Form in Design view and then hide the Navigation Pane.

- Adjust the approximate size and position of the subform to the one shown in Figure 5–48.

Figure 5–48

3
- Click the View button to view the form in Form view (Figure 5–49).

Q&A
Could I have clicked the View button arrow and then clicked Form View?

Yes. You always can use the arrow. If the icon for the view you want appears on the face of the View button, however, you also can just click the button.

Q&A
Could I have clicked the Form View button in the lower-right corner of the screen to move to Form view?

Yes. Those buttons are always an option. Use whichever approach you find most convenient.

Figure 5–49

Size Mode

The portion of a picture that appears as well as the way it appears is determined by the **size mode**. The possible size modes are as follows:

1. **Clip** — Displays only the portion of the picture that will fit in the space allocated to it.

2. **Stretch** — Expands or shrinks the picture to fit the precise space allocated on the screen. For photographs, usually this is not a good choice, because fitting a photograph to the allocated space can distort the image, giving it a stretched appearance.

3. **Zoom** — Does the best job of fitting the picture to the allocated space without changing the look of the picture. The entire picture will appear and be proportioned correctly. Some white space may be visible around the picture, however.

Currently, the size mode should be Zoom, which is appropriate. If it were not and you wanted to change it, you would use the steps on the next page.

To Change the Size Mode

1. Click the control containing the picture, and then click the Property Sheet button on the Design tab to display the control's property sheet.
2. Click the Size Mode property, and then click the Size Mode property box arrow.
3. Click Zoom and then close the property sheet by clicking its Close button.

To Change Special Effects and Colors

Access allows you to change a variety of the characteristics of the labels in the form. You can change the border style and color, the background color, the font, and the font size. You also can give the label special effects, such as raised or sunken. The following steps change the font color and special effects of the labels.

- Click the View button arrow and then click Design View on the View button menu to return to Design view.

- Click the Recruiter Number label to select it.

- Select each of the remaining labels by holding down the SHIFT key while clicking the label. Be sure to include the label for the subform.

- Release the SHIFT key (Figure 5–50).

Q&A

Does the order in which I select the labels make a difference?

No. The only thing that is important is that they are all selected when you are done.

Figure 5–50

Multi-Table Form Techniques **AC** 331

2

- Click the Font Color arrow on the Design tab to display a color palette (Figure 5–51).

Figure 5–51

3

- Click the blue color in the second position from the right in the bottom row of Standard Colors to change the font color for the labels.

- Click the Property Sheet button on the Design tab to produce the property sheet for the selected labels.

- Change the Border Style to Solid and the Border Width to 3.

- Click the Special Effect property box to display the Special Effect property box arrow (Figure 5–52).

Q&A

The property sheet is too small to display the property box arrow. Can I change the size of the property sheet?

Yes. Point to the border of the property sheet so that the mouse pointer changes to a double-headed arrow. You then can drag to adjust the size.

Figure 5–52

4

- Click the Special Effect property box arrow and then select Etched as the special effect.

🔍 **Experiment**

- Try all the other special effects. In each case, view the form to see the special effect you selected and then return to Design view. When done, select Etched (Figure 5–53).

- Close the property sheet.

Figure 5–53

5

- Click the Recruiter Number control (the white space, not the label) to select it.

- Select each of the remaining controls by holding down the SHIFT key while clicking the control. Do not include the subform.

- Click the Property Sheet button on the Design tab to produce the property sheet for the selected controls.

- Select Sunken for the special effect (Figure 5–54).

Figure 5–54

6

- Close the property sheet by clicking its Close button.

- Click the View button to view the form in Form view (Figure 5–55).

Figure 5–55

To Enhance a Form Title

You can enhance the title in a variety of ways. These include moving it, resizing it, changing the font size, changing the alignment, and assigning it a special effect. The following steps enhance the form title.

1

- Click the View button arrow and then click Design View on the View button menu to return to Design view.

- Resize the Form Header section by dragging down the lower boundary of the section to the approximate position shown in Figure 5–56.

Figure 5–56

2

- Click the control containing the form title to select the control.
- Drag the control to the approximate position shown in Figure 5–57.
- Drag the lower-right sizing handle to resize the control to the approximate size shown in the figure.

Figure 5–57

3

- Click the Property Sheet button on the Design tab to display the control's property sheet.
- Click the Special Effect property box, click the Special Effect property box arrow, and then click Raised to change the Special Effect property value to Raised.
- In a similar fashion, change the Font Size property value to 20, the Text Align property value to Distribute, and the Font Weight property value to Semi-bold (Figure 5–58).

4

- Close the property sheet by clicking its Close button.

Figure 5–58

To Change a Tab Stop

If users repeatedly press the TAB key to move through the controls on the form, they should bypass the Bonus control, the Picture control, the Contact Notes control, and the subform. In order to force this to happen, the following steps change the value of the Tab Stop property for the control from Yes to No.

- Click the Bonus control to select it.

- Select the Picture control, the Contact Notes control, and the subform by holding down the SHIFT key while clicking each control (Figure 5–59).

- Click the Property Sheet button on the Design tab to display the property sheet. Make sure the All tab is selected, click the down scroll arrow until the Tab Stop property appears, click the Tab Stop property, click the Tab Stop property box arrow and then click No.

- Close the property sheet.

Q&A What is the effect of this change?

When anyone tabs through the controls, they will bypass the Bonus control, the Picture control, the Contact Notes control, and the subform.

Q&A I don't see the Tab Stop property. What did I do wrong?

You clicked the labels for the controls, not the controls.

- Click the Save button on the Quick Access Toolbar to save your changes.

Figure 5–59

- Click the View button to view the form in Form view. It looks like the one in Figure 5–1 on page AC 299.

- Close the form.

Changing the Tab Order

Users repeatedly can press the TAB key to move through the fields on a form. Access determines the order in which the fields are encountered in this process. If you prefer a different order, you can change the order by clicking the Tab Order button on the Arrange tab. You then can use the Tab Order dialog box (Figure 5–60) to change the order by dragging rows to their desired position as indicated in the dialog box.

Figure 5–60

TO ANCHOR CONTROLS

The Anchoring button on the Arrange tab allows you to tie (anchor) a control to a section or to another control so that it maintains the same distance between the control and the anchor position. To see the effect of anchoring, objects must appear in overlapping windows. To anchor controls you would use the following steps.

1. Select the control or controls that you want to anchor to the form.
2. Use the Anchor button arrow to display the different anchoring positions and select the desired position.
3. Change to overlapping windows. (Click the Office button, click the Access Options button, click Current Database in the left pane, click the Overlapping Windows option button, and then click the OK button. You will need to close and reopen the database for the change to take effect.)
4. To see the effect of anchoring, open your form and then resize the form by dragging the border of the form. The anchored objects should move appropriately.
5. Change back to tabbed documents. (Follow the instructions in Step 3, replacing the Overlapping Windows with Tabbed Documents.)

To Use the Form

To use a form to view data, right-click the form in the Navigation Pane, and then click Open on the shortcut menu that appears. You then can use the navigation buttons at the bottom of the screen to move among recruiters. You can use the navigation buttons in the subform to move among the clients of the recruiter currently shown on the screen. The following steps use the form to display desired data.

- Show the Navigation Pane if it is currently hidden.
- Right-click Recruiter Master Form and then click Open on the shortcut menu.
- Hide the Navigation Pane.
- Right-click the Contact Notes field to display a shortcut menu (Figure 5–61).

- Click the Manage Attachments command on the shortcut menu to display the Attachments dialog box (Figure 5–62).

Q&A How do I use this dialog box?

Select an attachment and click the Open button to view the attachment. Click the Add button to add a new attachment or the Remove button to remove the selected attachment. You can save the selected attachment as a file in whatever location you specify by clicking the Save button. You can save all attachments at once by clicking the Save All button.

Experiment

- Open each attachment to see how it looks in its original application. When finished, close the original application.

Figure 5–61

Figure 5–62

3
- Click the OK button to close the Attachments dialog box.
- Click the form's Next record button to display the data for recruiter 24 (Figure 5–63).

Figure 5–63

4
- Click the subform's Next record button twice to highlight the third client of recruiter 24 (Figure 5–64).

5
- Close the form.

Figure 5–64

Navigation in the Form

The previous steps illustrated the way you work with a main form and subform. Clicking the navigation buttons for the main form moves to a different recruiter. Clicking the navigation buttons for the subform moves to a different client of the recruiter who appears in the main form. The following are other actions you can take within the form.

1. To move from the last field in the main form to the first field in the subform, press the TAB key. To move back to the last field in the main form, press CTRL+SHIFT+TAB.

2. To move from the last field in the subform to the first field in the next record's main form, press CTRL+TAB.

3. To switch from the main form to the subform using the mouse, click anywhere in the subform. To switch back to the main form, click any control in the main form. Clicking the background of the main form will not cause the switch to occur.

To View Object Dependencies

In Access, you can view information on dependencies between database objects. Viewing a list of objects that use a specific object helps in the maintenance of a database and avoids errors when changes are made to the objects involved in the dependency. For example, many items depend on the Recruiter table. By clicking the Object Dependencies button, you can see what items depend on the object. You also can see the items on which the object depends. The following steps view the objects that depend on the Recruiter table.

1

- Display the Navigation Pane and click the Recruiter table.

- Click Database Tools on the Ribbon to display the Database Tools tab.

- Click the Object Dependencies button on the Database Tools tab to display the Object Dependencies Pane.

- Click the 'Objects that depend on me' option button to select it (Figure 5–65).

Figure 5–65

Experiment

- Click the 'Objects that I depend on' option button to see the objects on which the Recruiter table depends. Then try both options for other objects in the database. Try clicking the plus sign and the minus sign that appear in front of various objects.

2

- Close the Object Dependencies Pane by clicking its Close button.

BTW

Searching Memo Fields

When you search memo fields consider alternative spellings. For example, healthcare also can be written as health care.

Date, Memo, and Yes/No Fields in Queries

By specifying recruiter start dates using date fields, JSP Recruiters can run queries to find recruiters hired before or after a certain date. Other uses of the date field might include calculating an employee's length of service by subtracting the start date from the current date. Similarly, management can search for recruiters with specific qualifications by adding memos and Yes/No fields.

To use date fields in queries, you simply type the dates including the slashes. To search for records with a specific date, you must type the date. You also can use comparison operators. To find all the recruiters whose start date is prior to January 1, 2005, for example, you type <1/1/2005 as the criterion.

You also can use memo fields in queries. Typically, you will want to find all the records on which the memo field contains a specific word or phrase. To do so, you use wildcards. For example, to find all the recruiters who have the words, Healthcare Management, somewhere in the Comment field, you type *Healthcare Management* as the criterion.

To use Yes/No fields in queries, type the word Yes or the word No as the criterion. You can, if you wish, type True rather than Yes or False rather than No. The following steps create and run queries that use Date, Memo, and Yes/No fields.

BTW

Date Fields in Queries

To test for the current date in a query, type Date() in the Criteria row of the appropriate column. Typing <Date() in the Criteria row for Start Date, for example, finds those recruiters who started anytime before the date on which you run the query.

To Use Date, Memo, and Yes/No Fields in a Query

The following steps use Date, Memo, and Yes/No fields in queries.

1

- Create a query for the Recruiter table and include the Recruiter Number, Last Name, First Name, Start Date, Comment, and Bonus fields in the query (Figure 5–66).

Figure 5–66

2

- Click the Criteria row under the Comment field and then type `*Healthcare Management*` as the criterion.

- Click the Criteria row under the Start Date field, and then type `<1/1/2005` as the criterion (Figure 5–67).

Figure 5–67

3

- Click the View button to view the results (Figure 5–68).

Figure 5–68

4

- Click the View button to return to Design view (Figure 5–69).

Q&A

Why does the date have number signs (#) around it?

This is the date format in Access. You usually do not have to enter the number signs, because Access will insert them automatically.

Figure 5–69

5

- Erase the criterion in the Start Date field.

- Click the Criteria row under the Bonus field and then type `Yes` as the criterion (Figure 5–70).

Q&A

Do I have to type Yes?

You also could type True.

Figure 5–70

6

- Click the View button to view the results (Figure 5–71).

 Experiment

- Try other combinations of values in the Start Date field, the Comment field, and/or the Bonus field. In each case, view the results.

7

- Close the query without saving the results.

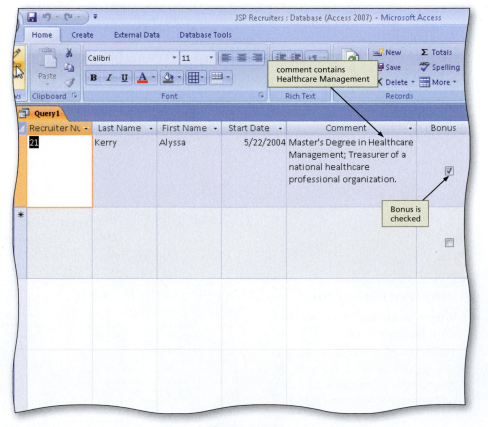

Figure 5–71

Datasheets in Forms

In forms created in Layout view, subforms are not available, but you can achieve similar functionality to subforms by including datasheets. Like subforms, the datasheets contain data for the "many" table in the relationship.

Creating a Simple Form with a Datasheet

If you create a form with the Form button for a table that is the "one" table in a one-to-many relationship, Access automatically includes the "many" table in a datasheet. If you create a form for the Recruiter table, for example, Access will include the Client table in a datasheet, as in Figure 5–72. The clients in the datasheet will be the clients of the recruiter currently on the screen, in this case Alyssa Kerry.

Figure 5–72

TO CREATE A SIMPLE FORM WITH A DATASHEET

To create a simple form with a datasheet, you would use the following steps.

1. Select the table that is the "one" part of a one-to-many relationship in the Navigation Pane.

2. Click Create on the Ribbon to display the Create tab.

3. Click the Form button on the Create tab to create the form.

Creating a Form with a Datasheet in Layout View

You can create a form with a datasheet in Layout view. To do so, you would first use the field list to add any fields from the "one" table as shown in Figure 5–73, in which fields from the Recruiter table have been added to the form.

Figure 5–73

Next you would use the field list to add a single field from the "many" table as shown in Figure 5–74, in which the Client Number field has been added. Access automatically will create a datasheet containing this field.

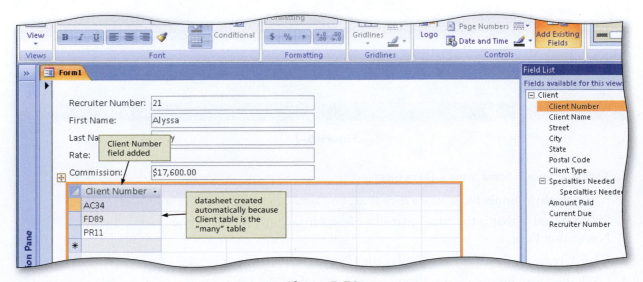

Figure 5–74

Finally, you would click the datasheet to select it and then use the field list to add the other fields from the "many" table that you wish to be included in the form, as shown in Figure 5–75.

Figure 5–75

To Create a Form with a Datasheet in Layout View

Specifically, to create a form with a datasheet in Layout view, you would use the following steps.

1. Click Create on the Ribbon to display the Create tab.
2. Click the Blank Form button on the Create tab to create a form in Layout view.
3. If a field list does not appear, click the Add Existing Fields button on the Format tab to display a field list.
4. Click Show All Tables to display the available tables.
5. Click the Expand indicator (the plus sign) for the "one" table to display the fields in the table and then drag the fields to the desired positions.
6. Click the Expand indicator for the "many" table and drag the first field for the datasheet onto the form to create the datasheet.
7. Click the datasheet to select it and then drag the remaining fields for the datasheet from the field list to the desired locations in the datasheet.

Creating a Multi-Table Form Based on the "Many" Table

All the forms discussed so far in this chapter were based on the "one" table, in this case, the Recruiter table. The records from the "one" table were included in a subform. You also can create a multi-table form based on the "many" table, in this case, the Client table. Such a form is shown in Figure 5–76.

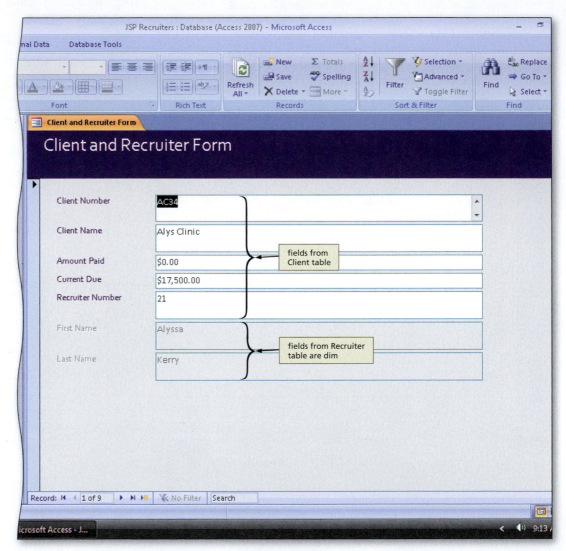

Figure 5–76

In this form, the Client Number, Client Name, Amount Paid, Current Due, and Recruiter Number fields are in the Client table. The First Name and Last Name fields are found in the Recruiter table and help to identify the recruiter whose number appears in the Recruiter Number field. To prevent the user from inadvertently changing the name of a recruiter, those fields have been disabled and appear dimmed. Disabling the fields from the "one" table in a form based on the "many" table is common practice.

To Create a Multi-Table Form Based on the "Many" Table

To create a multi-table form based on the "many" table, you would use the following steps.

1. Use the Form Wizard to create a form in which you first select fields from the "many" table and then select fields from the "one" table. Be sure the form is organized by the "many" table. Alternatively, you can create the form in Layout view by first placing the fields from the "many" table and then the fields from the "one" table.

2. In Layout view, select each of the fields from the "one" table, click the Property Sheet button on the Design tab to display the property sheet, and then change the value for the Enabled property from Yes to No. This will prevent users from inadvertently updating fields in the "one" table.

To Quit Access

You saved all your changes and are ready to quit Access. The following step quits Access.

1 Click the Close button on the right side of the Access title bar to quit Access.

Chapter Summary

In this chapter you have learned to use Yes/No, Date, Memo, OLE Object, and Attachment data types; create and use an input mask; create a form and add a subform; enhance the look of the controls on a form; use a form with a subform; create queries involving Yes/No, Date, and Memo fields; view object dependencies; and create forms containing datasheets in Layout view. The following list includes all the new Access skills you have learned in this chapter.

1. Add Fields to a Table (AC 302)
2. Use the Input Mask Wizard (AC 304)
3. Enter Data Using an Input Mask (AC 306)
4. Enter Data in Yes/No Fields (AC 307)
5. Enter Data in Date Fields (AC 308)
6. Enter Data in Memo Fields (AC 308)
7. Change the Row and Column Size (AC 309)
8. Enter Data in OLE Fields (AC 310)
9. Enter Data in Attachment Fields (AC 312)
10. Enter Data in Hyperlink Fields (AC 314)
11. Save the Properties and Close the Table (AC 314)
12. Create a Form in Design View (AC 315)
13. Add a Control for a Field to the Form Design (AC 316)
14. Add Controls for Additional Fields (AC 318)
15. Align Controls (AC 318)
16. Move the Field List (AC 320)
17. Add Control for the Remaining Fields (AC 320)
18. Use a Shortcut Menu to Change the Fill/Back Color (AC 322)
19. Add a Title (AC 323)
20. Place a Subform (AC 324)
21. Modify a Subform (AC 328)
22. Change the Size Mode (AC 330)
23. Change Special Effects and Colors (AC 330)
24. Enhance a Form Title (AC 333)
25. Change a Tab Stop (AC 335)
26. Use the Form (AC 337)
27. View Object Dependencies (AC 339)
28. Use Date, Memo, and Yes/No Fields in a Query (AC 340)
29. Create a Simple Form with a Datasheet (AC 343)
30. Create a Form with a Datasheet in Layout View (AC 345)
31. Create a Multi-Table Form Based on the "Many" Table (AC 347)

Learn It Online

Test your knowledge of chapter content and key terms.

Instructions: To complete the Learn It Online exercises, start your browser, click the Address bar, and then enter the Web address `scsite.com/ac2007/learn`. When the Access 2007 Learn It Online page is displayed, click the link for the exercise you want to complete and then read the instructions.

Chapter Reinforcement TF, MC, and SA
A series of true/false, multiple choice, and short answer questions that test your knowledge of the chapter content.

Flash Cards
An interactive learning environment where you identify chapter key terms associated with displayed definitions.

Practice Test
A series of multiple choice questions that test your knowledge of chapter content and key terms.

Who Wants To Be a Computer Genius?
An interactive game that challenges your knowledge of chapter content in the style of a television quiz show.

Wheel of Terms
An interactive game that challenges your knowledge of chapter key terms in the style of the television show *Wheel of Fortune*.

Crossword Puzzle Challenge
A crossword puzzle that challenges your knowledge of key terms presented in the chapter.

Apply Your Knowledge

Reinforce the skills and apply the concepts you learned in this chapter.

Adding Date and OLE Fields, Using an Input Mask Wizard, and Querying Date Fields
Instructions: Start Access. If you are using the Microsoft Office Access 2007 Complete or the Microsoft Office Access 2007 Comprehensive text, open The Bike Delivers database that you used in Chapter 4. Otherwise, see your instructor for information on accessing the files required in this book.

Perform the following tasks:

1. Add the Start Date and Picture fields to the Courier table structure, as shown in Figure 5–77.
   Create an input mask for the Start Date field. Use the Short Date input mask type.

Figure 5–77

2. Add the data shown in Figure 5–78 to the Courier table.

Data for Courier Table		
Courier Number	**Start Date**	**Picture**
102	03/01/2007	Pict2.bmp
109	01/15/2007	Pict4.bmp
113	10/12/2007	Pict3.bmp
117	01/11/2008	Pict1.bmp

Figure 5–78

Continued >

Apply Your Knowledge *continued*

3. Query the Courier table to find all couriers who started after January 1, 2008. Include the Courier Number, First Name, Last Name, and Hourly Rate in the query results. Save the query as Start Date Query.

4. Submit the revised database in the format specified by your instructor.

Extend Your Knowledge

Extend the skills you learned in this chapter and experiment with new skills. You may need to use Help to complete the assignment.

Adding Hyperlink Fields and Creating Multi-Table Forms

Instructions: Start Access. Open the Alyssa Ashton College database. See the inside back cover of this book for instructions on downloading the Data Files for Students, or contact your instructor for more information about accessing the required files.

The human resources director at Alyssa Ashton College maintains a database of faculty candidates. She would like a hyperlink field added to this database. You will add this field. You also will create the form shown in Figure 5–79.

Figure 5–79

Perform the following tasks:

1. Open the Candidate table in Design view and add a hyperlink field. Insert the field after the Documentation field. Use Web Page as the name of the field.

2. Open the Candidate table and add data for the hyperlink field to the first record. If the teachers at your school have individual Web pages, link to one of those pages. Otherwise, use your school home page as the URL.

3. Use the Form Wizard to create the multi-table form shown in Figure 5–79. The Candidate table appears as a subform in the form. The form uses the Module style. Change the title of the form to Department Candidate Form and increase the size of the subform.

4. Change the database properties, as specified by your instructor. Submit the revised database in the format specified by your instructor.

Make It Right

Analyze a database and correct all errors and/or improve the design.

Correcting Form Design Errors

Instructions: Start Access. Open the Landscape Exteriors database. See the inside back cover of this book for instructions on downloading the Data Files for Students, or contact your instructor for more information about accessing the required files.

The Landscape Exteriors database contains data for a company that provides landscaping services. The owner of the company has created the form shown in Figure 5–80 but she has encountered some problems with modifying the form.

Figure 5–80

Continued >

Make It Right *continued*

The form currently has the chiseled special effect for the Worker Number label. All labels should have a chiseled special effect. The Worker Number control has a sunken special effect. All other controls except the subform also should have the sunken special effect property. The subform is too big and needs to be resized. The First Name and Last Name labels should be aligned to the left. Finally, the form needs a title. The owner would like the title, Worker Master Form. The title should appear above the Worker Number control and should have a raised appearance with a font size of 20 and a font weight of bold.

Submit the revised database in the format specified by your instructor.

In the Lab

Design, create, modify, and/or use a database following the guidelines, concepts, and skills presented in this chapter. Labs are listed in order of increasing difficulty.

Lab 1: Creating Multi-Table Forms for the JMS TechWizards Database

Problem: JMS TechWizards needs to maintain additional data on each technician. The company needs to maintain the date each technician started as well as notes concerning the technician and a picture of the technician. The company wants a form that displays technician information and the clients for which they are responsible.

Instructions: If you are using the Microsoft Office Access 2007 Complete or the Microsoft Office Access 2007 Comprehensive text, open the JMS TechWizards database that you used in Chapter 4. Otherwise, see the inside back cover of this book for instructions on downloading the Data Files for Students, or contact your instructor for more information about accessing the required files.

Perform the following tasks:
1. Add the Start Date, Notes, and Picture fields to the end of the Technician table. The Text Format property for the Notes field should be rich text and users should be able to append data to the Notes field. Save the changes to the structure of the table.

2. Add the data shown in Figure 5–81 to the Technician table. Adjust the row and column spacing to best fit the data. Save the changes to the layout of the table.

Data for Technician Table			
Technician Number	**Start Date**	**Notes**	**Picture**
22	04/02/2007	Has MOS certification in Word, Excel, and Access.	Pict2.bmp
23	05/14/2007	Extensive network experience. Has a good rapport with clients.	Pict3.bmp
29	10/01/2007	Excellent diagnostic skills. Prefers to handle hardware problems.	Pict1.bmp
32	01/14/2008	Has MOS certification in Access.	Pict4.bmp

Figure 5–81

3. Create the form shown in Figure 5–82. Use Technician Master Form as the name of the form and Clients of Technician as the name of the subform. Change the tab order so users tab to the Notes field before the Start Date field. Users should not be able to tab through the Picture control. The title control has the following properties: raised special effect, a font size of 20, a font weight of semi-bold, and a text align of distribute. The remaining labels on the form have a chiseled special effect.

Figure 5–82

4. Query the Technician table to find all technicians who have MOS certification and started before January 1, 2008. Include the Technician Number, First Name, Last Name, and Notes fields in the query results. Save the query as MOS Query.

5. Submit the revised database in the format specified by your instructor.

In the Lab

Lab 2: Adding Fields and Creating Multi-Table Forms in the Hockey Fan Zone Database

Problem: The management of the Hockey Fan Zone store has found that they need to maintain additional data on suppliers. Management needs to know the last date an order was placed and whether the supplier accepts returns. Management also would like to attach Excel files to each supplier's record that contain historical cost data. The Hockey Fan Zone requires a form that displays information about the supplier as well as the items that are purchased from suppliers.

Instructions: If you are using the Microsoft Office Access 2007 Complete or the Microsoft Office Access 2007 Comprehensive text, open the Hockey Fan Zone database that you used in Chapter 4. Otherwise, see the inside back cover of this book for instructions on downloading the Data Files for Students, or contact your instructor for more information about accessing the required files.

Perform the following tasks:

1. Add the fields, Last Order Date, Returns, and Cost History to the end of the Supplier table structure. Last Order Date is a date field, Returns is a Yes/No field, and Cost History is an Attachments field. Create an input mask for the Last Order Date that uses the Short Date mask.

2. Add the data shown in Figure 5–83 to the Supplier table.

Data for Supplier Table			
Supplier Code	**Last Order Date**	**Returns**	**Cost History**
AC	02/25/2008	Yes	AC_History.xlsx
LG	03/21/2008	No	LG_History.xlsx
LG	03/04/2008	Yes	MN_History.xlsx

Figure 5–83

3. Create the form shown in Figure 5–84. Use Supplier Master Form as the name of the form and Items of Supplier as the name of the subform. The title control has the following properties: raised special effect, a font size of 20, a font weight of semi-bold, and a text align of distribute. The remaining labels on the form have a chiseled special effect.

Figure 5–84

4. Query the Supplier table to find all suppliers that accept returns. Include the Supplier Code and Name in the query results. Save the query as Returns Query.

5. Submit the revised database in the format specified by your instructor.

In the Lab

Lab 3: Maintaining the Ada Beauty Supply Database

Problem: The management of Ada Beauty Supply needs to maintain additional data on sales reps. Management needs to store the date the sales rep started, comments about each sales rep, and a picture of the sales rep. Management wants a form that displays sales rep information and the customers they represent.

Instructions: If you are using the Microsoft Office Access 2007 Complete or the Microsoft Office Access 2007 Comprehensive text, open the Ada Beauty Supply database that you used in Chapter 4. Otherwise, see the inside back cover of this book for instructions on downloading the Data Files for Students, or contact your instructor for more information about accessing the required files. Submit the revised database in the format specified by your instructor.

Continued >

In the Lab *continued*

Instructions Part 1: Add the Start Date, Notes, and Picture fields to the Sales Rep table and then add the data shown in Figure 5–85 to the Sales Rep table. Be sure the datasheet displays the entire comment.

Data for Sales Rep Table			
Sales Rep Number	**Start Date**	**Notes**	**Picture**
44	05/07/2007	Has an AA degree. Working on a BBA in Management.	Pict1.bmp
49	12/12/2006	Mentors new sales reps. Working on BBA in Marketing.	Pict2.bmp
51	02/15/2008	Former beautician. Cannot stand for long periods of time.	Pict3.bmp
55	03/06/2007	Excellent computer skills. Helps to train new employees.	Pict4.bmp

Figure 5–85

Instructions Part 2: Create the Sales Rep Master Form shown in Figure 5–86. The title control has a raised special effect with a font size of 20, a font weight of semi-bold, and a text align of distribute. The remaining labels on the form have no special effect. Users should not be able to tab to the Picture field.

Figure 5–86

Instructions Part 3: Find all sales reps that are former beauticians. Include the Sales Rep Number, First Name, and Last Name in the query result. Save the query as Beautician Query. Find all sales reps that started after February 1, 2008. Include the Sales Rep Number, First Name, Last Name, and Comm Rate in the query result. Save the query as Start Date Query.

Cases and Places

Apply your creative thinking and problem solving skills to design and implement a solution.

● EASIER ●● MORE DIFFICULT

● 1: Creating Multi-Table Forms for the Second-Hand Goods Database

If you are using the Microsoft Office Access 2007 Complete or the Microsoft Office Access 2007 Comprehensive text, open the Second-Hand Goods database that you used in Chapter 4. Otherwise, see the inside back cover of this book for instructions on downloading the Data Files for Students, or contact your instructor for more information about accessing the required files. Create a form for the Seller table that is similar in design to the form shown in Figure 5–87. Customize the form by adding your own special effects and changing the background color of the form. Include all fields. Create a form for the Item table that also includes the seller first name and the seller last name. Change the Enabled property for the seller first and last name so users cannot change the seller name data. Name the form Item Update Form. Submit the revised database in the format specified by your instructor.

Figure 5–87

Continued >

Cases and Places *continued*

• 2: Adding Fields and Creating Multi-Table Forms for the BeachCondo Rentals Database

If you are using the Microsoft Office Access 2007 Complete or the Microsoft Office Access 2007 Comprehensive text, open the BeachCondo Rentals database that you used in Chapter 4. Otherwise, see the inside back cover of this book for instructions on downloading the Data Files for Students, or contact your instructor for more information about accessing the required files. The rental company needs to store some notes concerning the owner's rental policies. Add a Notes field with a memo data type to the Owner table. Update the table with the data shown in Figure 5–88.

Data for Owner Table	
Owner Number	**Notes**
AB12	Will not rent to families with children under 18.
BE20	Will rent to families with children.
GR50	Allows dogs in unit.
HJ05	Will not rent during the month of April.
HJ05	Allows dogs in unit.

Figure 5–88

Create a form for the Owner table that is similar in design to the form shown in Figure 5–89. Customize the form by changing the special effects, the font color of the labels, and the background color of the form. Query the database to find all owners that allow dogs. Include the owner code, first name, last name, unit number, and weekly rate in the query results. Save the query as Pet Policy Query. Submit the revised database in the format specified by your instructor.

Figure 5–89

•• 3: Adding Fields to the Restaurant Database

If you are using the Microsoft Office Access 2007 Complete or the Microsoft Office Access 2007 Comprehensive text, open the restaurant database that you used in Chapter 4. Otherwise, see the inside back cover of this book for instructions on downloading the Data Files for Students, or contact your instructor for more information about accessing the required files. Using the Plan Ahead guidelines presented in this chapter, determine what additional fields you need to add to your database. For example, many restaurants maintain their own Web sites. You may want to include a hyperlink field for this data. You can use a memo field to store comments or notes about each restaurant. Add these fields to your database and update the fields with appropriate data. Review the different types of forms described in this chapter. Create at least two forms for your database that use these new fields. Use Layout view to create at least one form and then modify the form as necessary. Submit the revised database in the format specified by your instructor.

Continued >

Cases and Places *continued*

•• 4: Adding Fields to Your Contacts Database

Make It Personal

If you are using the Microsoft Office Access 2007 Complete or the Microsoft Office Access 2007 Comprehensive text, open the contacts database that you used in Chapter 4. Otherwise, see the inside back cover of this book for instructions on downloading the Data Files for Students, or contact your instructor for more information about accessing the required files. Consider your own personal job situation. What other fields would be useful to you? Do you need a hyperlink field with the URL of each of the companies in your contact database? Do you need an Attachment field in which to store correspondence that you have sent each company? Do you need to create new forms with the additional fields? Modify the database and create any necessary forms. Submit the revised database in the format specified by your instructor.

•• 5: Understanding Fields, Multi-Table Forms, and Object Dependencies

Working Together

Copy the JSP Recruiters database and rename the database to your team name. For example, if your team is the Fab Five, then name the database Fab Five. As a team, decide if there are any fields that could be added to the Client table. For example, it might be useful to have a hyperlink field that contains the URL for the client. Also, a field that contained additional notes about each client may be appropriate. Modify the Client table design to accommodate these new fields. Then, add data to the fields. You can use existing web pages for various medical institutions in your area. Create a multi-table form based on the Client table and include the recruiter's first and last name on the form. Users should not be able to update the recruiter name fields. Anchor the controls in the Client table and experiment with resizing the form. Determine the object dependencies for each table in the database. Write a short report that explains the importance of understanding object dependencies. Submit the report and the revised database in the format specified by your instructor.

6 Using Macros, Switchboards, PivotTables, and PivotCharts

Objectives

You will have mastered the material in this project when you can:

- Create and modify macros and macro groups

- Run macros

- Create a switchboard and switchboard pages

- Modify switchboard pages

- Use a switchboard

- Import data and create a query

- Create a PivotTable

- Change properties in a PivotTable

- Use a PivotTable

- Create a PivotChart and add a legend

- Change the chart type and organization of a PivotChart

- Remove drop zones in a PivotChart

- Assign axis titles and a chart title in a PivotChart

- Use a PivotChart

6 | Macros, Switchboards, PivotTables, and PivotCharts

Introduction

This chapter shows how to create and test macros and how to use these macros in the switchboard system that JSP Recruiters requires. With the switchboard system, users can access any form, table, or report simply by clicking the appropriate buttons on the switchboard. In this chapter, two additional tables are added to the database. A query incorporating these new tables then is used to create both a PivotTable and a PivotChart.

Project — Macros, Switchboards, PivotTables, and PivotCharts

Managers at JSP Recruiters have heard about switchboard systems that enable users to click a button or two to open any form or table, preview any report, or print any report. A **switchboard** like the one shown in Figure 6–1a is a form that includes buttons to perform a variety of actions. In this system, rather than having to use the Navigation Pane, the user simply clicks a button — View Form, View Table, View Report, Print Report, or Exit Application — to indicate the action to be taken. Other than Exit Application, clicking a button leads to another switchboard. For example, when a user clicks the View Form button, Access displays the View Form switchboard, as shown in Figure 6–1b. On this next-level form, the user clicks the button that identifies the form he or she wants to view. Similarly, when the user clicks the View Table button, Access displays a switchboard on which the user clicks a button to indicate the table he or she wants to view. Thus, viewing any form, table, or report, or printing any report requires clicking only two buttons. The administration at JSP would like such a switchboard system because they believe it will improve the user-friendliness of the system, thereby improving employee satisfaction and efficiency.

Before creating the switchboard, JSP will create **macros**, which are collections of actions designed to carry out specific tasks. To perform the actions in a macro, you run the macro. When a macro is run, Access will execute the various steps, called **actions**, in the macro. The switchboard system uses macros. Clicking certain buttons in the switchboard system will cause the appropriate macros to run.

Chapter 2 showed how to create a crosstab query, which is a query that calculates a statistic (for example, sum, average, or count) for data that is grouped by two different types of information. A PivotTable is similar. The PivotTable in Figure 6–1c, for example, displays the sum of hours spent and hours remaining grouped by seminar number and recruiter number. Unlike a crosstab, however, a PivotTable is dynamic, a feature that appeals to JSP. By clicking the plus or minus signs, JSP can expand and contract the level of detail that appears in the chart. Users can dynamically filter the data so that only certain seminars or recruiters are included. They even can use additional fields to filter the data. For example, they could specify that the data is only to reflect seminars offered to certain clients. Finally, they can change the organization. They might prefer to reverse

Figure 6–1

the roles of the rows and columns, having the rows represent recruiters and the columns represent seminars. Accomplishing this is a simple matter of dragging the fields to the desired positions.

JSP managers can represent the same data graphically by using a PivotChart like the one in Figure 6–1d on the previous page. In this particular chart, the colors of the sections of the bars represent the different seminars as indicated on the right of the chart. Across the bottom of the chart are the recruiters. The bars represent the hours spent or hours remaining for the recruiter. The total bar, ignoring colors, thus would represent the total hours spent or remaining by the recruiter. Unlike a regular chart, the PivotChart has the same dynamic capabilities as a PivotTable. You can change to a different chart type, you can reverse the roles of the rows and columns, and you can filter data with the same ease you can in a PivotChart.

PivotTables and PivotCharts are normally associated with Microsoft Excel. You always could export data from an Access database to Excel and then use Excel to create a PivotTable or PivotChart. Having PivotTable and PivotChart capabilities within Access, however, means that you do not have to go through that process.

Overview

As you read through this chapter, you will learn how to create macros, switchboards, PivotTables, and PivotCharts by performing these general tasks:

- Create a macro group contain ing the macros that will be used in the switchboard.
- Create a switchboard and add the switchboard pages.
- Add the items and actions to the switchboard pages.
- Create the tables, relationships, and query that will be used in creating a PivotTable and a PivotChart.
- Create and use a PivotTable.
- Create and use a PivotChart.

Plan Ahead

> ### Macro, Switchboard, PivotTable, and PivotChart Design Guidelines
>
> 1. **Determine when it would be beneficial to automate tasks in a macro.** Are there tasks involving multiple steps that would be more conveniently accomplished by running a macro than by carrying out all the individual steps? For example, to open a table in read-only mode and then display a message could be accomplished conveniently through a macro. Are there tasks that are to be performed when the user clicks buttons in a switchboard? These tasks can be placed in a macro, which can be run when the button is clicked.
>
> 2. **Determine whether it is appropriate to create a switchboard.** If you want to make it easy and convenient for users to perform a variety of tasks just by clicking buttons, consider creating a switchboard. You can associate the performance of the various tasks with the buttons in the switchboard.
>
> 3. **Determine the organization of the switchboard.** Determine the various tasks that need to be performed by clicking buttons. Decide the logical grouping of those buttons.
>
> 4. **Determine whether it is appropriate to present data as a PivotTable.** Do you need to calculate a statistic for data that is grouped by two different types of information? If so, you can consider either a crosstab query or a PivotTable. If you want the presentation to be interactive, that is, if you want to be able to easily change the organization of the data as well as to filter the data, then a PivotTable is appropriate.
>
> 5. **Determine the organization of the PivotTable.** Determine the fields for the rows, columns, data, and filters.
>
> *(continued)*

(continued)

Plan
Ahead

6. **Determine whether it is appropriate to present data as a PivotChart.** Do you want to summarize the same type of data as in a PivotTable, but graphically? Do you need the same ability to be able to change the organization of the presentation as well as to filter the data? If so, a PivotChart is appropriate.

7. **Determine the organization of the PivotChart.** Determine the fields for the x axis and the y axis. Decide which chart type would best display the data.

When necessary, more specific details concerning the above decisions and/or actions are presented at appropriate points in the chapter. The chapter also will identify the use of these guidelines in the design of switchboards, such as the one shown in Figures 6–1a and 6–1b on page AC 363, as well as PivotTables and PivotCharts, such as the ones shown in Figures 6–1c and 6–1d on page AC 363.

Starting Access

If you are using a computer to step through the project in this chapter and you want your screen to match the figures in this book, you should change your screen's resolution to 1024 × 768. For information about how to change a computer's resolution, read Appendix E.

To Start Access

The following steps, which assume Windows Vista is running, start Access.

Note: If you are using Windows XP, see Appendix F for alternate steps.

1 Click the Start button on the Windows Vista taskbar to display the Start menu.

2 Click All Programs at the bottom of the left pane on the Start menu to display the All Programs list and then click Microsoft Office in the All Programs list to display the Microsoft Office list.

3 Click Microsoft Office Access 2007 in the Microsoft Office list to start Access and display the Getting Started with Microsoft Office Access window.

4 If the Access window is not maximized, click the Maximize button on its title bar to maximize the window.

To Open a Database

In Chapter 1, you created your database on a USB flash drive using the file name, JSP Recruiters. There are two ways to open the file containing your database. If the file you created appears in the Recent Documents list, you could click it to open the file. If not, you can use the More button to open the file. The following steps use the More button to open the JSP Recruiters database from the USB flash drive.

Note: If you are using Windows XP, see Appendix F for alternate steps.

1 With your USB flash drive connected to one of the computer's USB ports, click the More button to display the Open dialog box.

2 If the Folders list is displayed below the Folders button, click the Folders button to remove the Folders list.

3 If necessary, click Computers in the Favorite Links section and then double-click UDISK 2.0 (E:) to select the USB flash drive, Drive E in this case, as the new open location. (Your drive letter might be different.)

4 Click JSP Recruiters to select the file name.

5 Click the Open button to open the database.

6 If a Security Warning appears, click the Options button to display the Microsoft Office Security Options dialog box.

7 With the option button to enable the content selected, click the OK button to enable the content.

Creating and Using Macros

Like other applications, Access allows you to create and use macros. Once you have created a macro, you can simply run the macro and Access will perform the various actions you specified. For example, the macro might open a table in Read-Only mode, a mode where changes to the table are prohibited, and then display a message indicating this fact.

A macro consists of a series of actions that Access performs when the macro is run; therefore, you will need to specify the actions when you create the macro. The actions are entered in a special window called a Macro Builder window. Once a macro is created, you can run it from the Navigation Pane by right-clicking the macro and then clicking Run on the shortcut menu. Macros also can be associated with items on switchboards. When you click the corresponding button on the switchboard, Access will run the macro. Whether a macro is run from the Navigation Pane or from a switchboard, the effect is the same: Access will execute the actions in the macro in the order in which they are entered.

In this chapter, you will learn how to create macros to open tables in read-only mode, open forms, preview reports, and print reports. As you enter actions, you will select them from a list box. The names of the actions are self-explanatory. The action to open a form, for example, is OpenForm. Thus, it is not necessary to memorize the specific actions that are available.

To Begin Creating a Macro

The following steps begin creating a macro, the purpose of which is to open the Client table in Read Only mode and then display a message to this effect. You will later add the appropriate actions to the macro.

- If necessary, hide the Navigation Pane.

- Click Create on the Ribbon to display the Create tab.

- Click the Macro button arrow to display the Macro button menu (Figure 6–2).

Figure 6–2

2

- Click Macro on the Macro menu to create a new macro (Figure 6–3).

Q&A Could I just click the Macro button instead of clicking the arrow?

In this case you could. Because the icon on the face of the button is the one for macro, clicking the button would produce the same results as clicking the arrow and then clicking Macro.

Figure 6–3

The Macro Builder Window

The first column in the Macro Builder window, also called the Macro window, is the Action column (see Figure 6–3). You enter the actions you want the macro to perform in this column. To enter an action, click the arrow in the Action column and then select the action from the list that appears. Many actions require additional information, called the **arguments** of the action. If you select such an action, the arguments will appear in the lower portion of the Macro Builder window and you can make any necessary changes to them. The second column contains the values you have assigned to these arguments. You can use the third column to enter a comment concerning the action if you wish.

The actions, the arguments, and the values for the arguments are shown in Table 6–1.

Table 6–1 Specifications for First Macro		
Action	**Argument to Change**	**New Value for Argument**
OpenTable	Table Name	Client
	View	Datasheet
	Data Mode	Read Only
MsgBox	Message	Table is open as read-only
	Beep	Yes
	Type	Information
	Title	JSP Recruiters

The macro begins by opening the Client table in read-only mode. That is, users can view the data, but cannot change it. The macro then displays a message indicating that the table is open in this mode. When the users click the OK button, the message will disappear.

To Add Actions to a Macro

To continue creating this macro, enter the actions. For each action, enter the action and comment in the appropriate text boxes, and then make the necessary changes to any arguments. The following steps add the actions to the macro that will open the Client table in Read Only mode and then display a message to this effect. They then save the macro.

- Click the box arrow in the first row of the Action column to display a menu of available actions (Figure 6–4).

Q&A

How can I tell the purpose of the various actions?

Select an action. A brief description of the action will appear in the lower-right corner of the screen. If you want detailed information on the selected action, press F1.

Experiment

- Select an action and then press F1 to view a detailed description. Close the Access Help window, press the box arrow and repeat the process for other actions. When finished, press the box arrow a final time.

Figure 6–4

- Scroll down until OpenTable appears and then click OpenTable to select it as the action (Figure 6–5).

Figure 6–5

3

- Click the Table Name argument to display an arrow.

- Click the arrow to display a list of available tables and then click Client to select the Client table.

- Click the Data Mode argument to display an arrow.

- Click the arrow to display a list of available choices for the Data Mode argument (Figure 6–6).

- Click Read Only to select Read Only as the value for the Data Mode argument.

Q&A

How can I tell the meaning of the various options?

A description appears in the lower-right corner of the screen. If that is not sufficient, press F1 for detailed information.

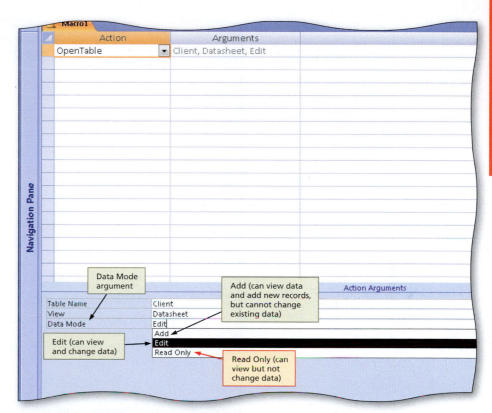

Figure 6–6

4

- Click the second row in the Action column and then click the arrow that appears to display a menu of available actions.

- Scroll down until MsgBox appears and then click MsgBox to select it as the action (Figure 6–7).

Figure 6–7

5

- Click the Message argument and type `Table is open as read-only` as the message.

- Click the Type argument, click the arrow that appears, and then select Information as the value for the Type argument.

Q&A

How can I tell the meaning of the various possibilities?

When you click the argument, Access displays a general description to the right of the argument. If you want further information at that point, press F1.

- Click the Title argument and type `JSP Recruiters` as the title (Figure 6–8).

Figure 6–8

 6

- Click the Save button on the Quick Access Toolbar and type `Open Client Table Read Only` as the name of the macro (Figure 6–9).

 7

- Click the OK button to save the macro.

- Close the macro.

Figure 6–9

Single-Stepping a Macro

You may have problems with a macro. The macro may abort. It may open the wrong table or produce a wrong message. If you have problems with a macro, you can **single-step the macro**, that is, proceed through a macro a step at a time in Design view. To do so, you would open the macro in Design view and then click the Single Step button on the Design tab (Figure 6–10).

Figure 6–10

You next would click the Run button on the Design tab. Access would display the Macro Single Step dialog box (Figure 6–11). The dialog box shows the action to be executed and the values of the various arguments. You can click the Step button to proceed to the next step. If you want to terminate the process, you can click the Stop All Macros button.

Figure 6–11

To Run a Macro

When you instruct Access to run a macro, Access will execute the steps in the macro. The following steps run the macro that was just created.

1 Show the Navigation Pane and scroll down, if necessary, so that the Open Client Table Read Only macro appears. It should be in a section of the Navigation Pane called Unrelated Objects, because it is not directly related to any of the tables in the database.

2 Right-click the Open Client Table Read Only macro and then click Run on the shortcut menu to run the macro (Figure 6–12).

3 Click the OK button in the JSP Recruiters dialog box and then close the Client table.

Figure 6–12

To Modify a Macro

You can modify a macro in the same way you first created it. You can change actions and/or arguments. You can insert a new action between two existing actions by clicking the position for the action and pressing the INSERT key to insert a new blank row. The following steps modify the macro you just created, adding a new step to customize the Navigation Pane so that only the tables in the database appear.

- Right-click the Open Client Table Read Only macro to display a shortcut menu.

- Click Design View on the shortcut menu to open the macro in Design view.

- Click the row selector on the row containing the MsgBox action to select the row, and then press the INSERT key to insert a new row.

- Click the new row.

- Click the Action column arrow on the new row, scroll down, and select NavigateTo as the action (Figure 6–13).

Figure 6–13

- Click the Category argument, click the arrow, and then click Object Type as the value for the Category argument.

- Click the Group argument, click the arrow, and then click Tables as the value for the Group argument (Figure 6–14).

- Save and then close the macro.

Q&A

Is it necessary to save and close the macro before running it?

No. You can run it in Design view by clicking the Run button on the Design tab.

Figure 6–14

To Run the Modified Macro

The following steps run the macro that you just modified.

1   Right-click the Open Client Table Read Only macro and then click Run on the shortcut menu to run the macro (Figure 6–15).

2   Click the OK button in the JSP Recruiters dialog box and then close the Client table.

Figure 6–15

To Reverse the Macro Action

The modified macro changed what is displayed in the Navigation Pane. The following steps return the Navigation Pane to its original state.

1   Click the Navigation Pane arrow to produce the Navigation Pane menu.

2   Click Tables and Related Views to once again organize the Navigation Pane by table (Figure 6–16).

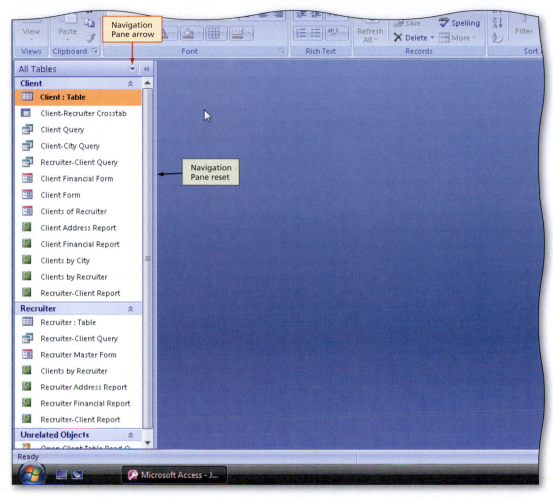

Figure 6–16

Errors in Macros

Macros can contain errors. For example, if you type the name of the table in the Table Name argument of the OpenTable action instead of selecting it from the list, you may type it incorrectly. Access then will not be able to execute the desired action. In that case, a Microsoft Office Access dialog box will appear, indicating the error and solution, as shown in Figure 6–17.

Figure 6–17

If such a dialog box appears, click the OK button. The Action Failed dialog box then appears (Figure 6–18). The dialog box indicates the macro that was being run, the action that Access was attempting to execute, and the arguments for the action. This information tells you which action needs to be corrected. To make the correction, click the Stop All Macros button, and then modify the design of the macro.

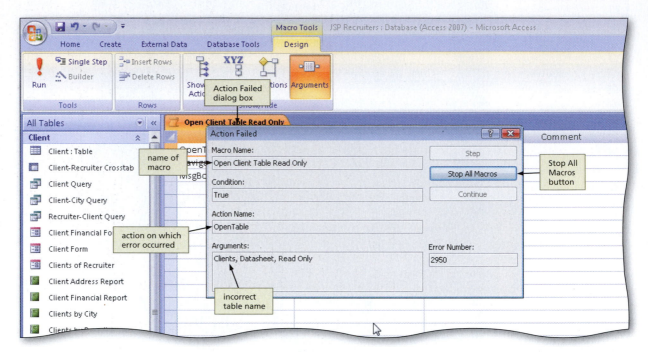

Figure 6–18

Additional Macros

The additional macros to be created are shown in Table 6–2. You will create these macros in the steps starting on page AC 377. The first column gives the name of the macro, and the second column indicates the actions for the macro. The third column contains the values of those arguments that may need to be changed. (Values for any arguments not listed can be left as they are.)

Table 6–2 Specifications for Additional Macros		
Macro Name	**Action**	**Argument(s) and Value(s)**
Open Client Table	OpenTable	Table Name: Client Data Mode: Read Only
	MsgBox	Message: Table is open as read-only Type: Information Title: JSP Recruiters
Open Recruiter Table	OpenTable	Table Name: Recruiter Data Mode: Read Only
	MsgBox	Message: Table is open as read-only Type: Information Title: JSP Recruiters
Open Client Form	OpenForm	Form Name: Client Form View: Form
Open Recruiter Master Form	OpenForm	Form Name: Recruiter Master Form View: Form

Table 6–2 Specifications for Additional Macros (*continued*)

Macro Name	Action	Argument(s) and Value(s)
Preview Client Address Report	OpenReport	Report Name: Client Address Report View: Report
Preview Client Financial Report	OpenReport	Report Name: Client Financial Report View: Report
Preview Clients by City Report	OpenReport	Report Name: Clients by City View: Report
Preview Clients by Recruiter Report	OpenReport	Report Name: Clients by Recruiter View: Report
Print Client Address Report	OpenReport	Report Name: Client Address Report View: Print
Print Client Financial Report	OpenReport	Report Name: Client Financial Report View: Print
Print Clients by City Report	OpenReport	Report Name: Clients by City View: Print
Print Clients by Recruiter Report	OpenReport	Report Name: Clients by Recruiter View: Print

To Create a Macro Group

If you have several macros, you can create a separate file for each one. Alternatively, you can create a single file, called a **macro group**, and place the macros in the single macro group.

To place multiple macros in a macro group, you add the macro names column to the macro and then assign a name to each macro. The following steps create the additional macros shown in Table 6–2 in a macro group called SB Macros, for Switchboard Macros.

1
- Click Create on the Ribbon to display the Create tab.
- Click the Macro button arrow to display the Macro menu.
- Click Macro on the Macro menu to create a new macro.
- Hide the Navigation Pane.
- Click the Macro Names button on the Design tab to display the Macro Name column (Figure 6–19).

Figure 6–19

2

- Type the name of the first macro in Table 6–2 on page AC 376 in the Macro Name column on the first row.

- In the Action column on the first row, select the first action in the first macro in Table 6–2 and then make the indicated changes to the arguments in the Actions Arguments pane at the bottom of the screen.

- In the Action column on the second row, select the second action in the first macro in Table 6–2 and then make the indicated changes to the arguments (Figure 6–20).

Q&A

This macro is very similar to the Open Client Table Read Only macro. Is there any way I can modify that macro and create the macro group?

You could, but it probably takes longer to modify the macro than to create a new one. You would need to open the Open Client Table Read Only macro in Design view, add the Action Name column, delete the Navigate To action and then use the Save As command on the Office menu rather than the Save button.

Figure 6–20

To Save the Macro Group

The following steps save the macro group.

1

- Click the Save button on the Quick Access Toolbar to display the Save As dialog box.

- Type SB Macros as the macro name (Figure 6–21).

2

- Click the OK button to save the macro group.

Figure 6–21

To Add the Remaining Macros to the Macro Group

You add the remaining macros to the macro group just as you added the first macro. The following steps add the remaining macros.

- Enter the remaining macro names, actions, and arguments shown in Table 6–2 on pages AC 372 and AC 373 (Figure 6–22).

Q&A

What is the meaning of the symbols that appear in front of the Print macros?

The symbol indicates that the indicated action will not be allowed if the database is not trusted. Because running certain macros can cause potential security risks, Access is alerting you to the threat.

- Click the Save button on the Quick Access Toolbar to save the macro group with the additional macros.

- Close the macro group.

Figure 6–22

Opening Databases Containing Macros

When a database contains macros, there is a chance a computer virus can attach to a macro. By default, Access disables macros when it opens a database and displays a Security Warning. If the database comes from a trusted source and you are sure that it does not contain any macro viruses, click the Options button and then enable the content in the Microsoft Office Security Options dialog box. You can make adjustments to Access security settings by clicking the Access Options button on the Office Button menu and then clicking Trust Center.

Creating and Using a Switchboard

A switchboard (see Figures 6–1a and 6–1b on page AC 363) is a special type of form. It contains buttons you can click to perform a variety of actions. Buttons on the main switchboard can lead to other more specialized switchboards. Clicking the View Form button, for example, causes Access to display the View Form switchboard. Switchboard buttons also can be used to open forms or tables. Clicking the Client Form button on the View Form switchboard opens the Client Form. Still other buttons cause reports to appear in a preview window or print reports.

Plan Ahead

Determine the organization of the switchboard.

1. **Determine all the tasks to be accomplished by clicking buttons in the switchboard.** Which tables need to be opened? Which forms? Which queries? Which reports?

2. **Determine any special requirements for the way the tasks are to be performed.** When you open a table, should a user be able to edit data or should the table be open read-only? Should a report be printed or simply viewed on the screen?

3. **Determine how to group the various tasks.** Should the tasks be grouped by function? If so, you could consider an organization such as View Table, View Form, and so on. Within the View Table category, you could list all the tables to be opened. Should the tasks be grouped by table? If so, you could consider an organization in which you are initially presented with a list of tables. When you select a specific table, you would have all the actions that could affect that table, for example, all queries, forms, and reports that are based on that table.

To Create a Switchboard

JSP Recruiters has determined that they want buttons on the switchboard to view the Client and Recruiter tables in a fashion that does not allow the data to be changed; to view the Client Form and the Recruiter Master Form; to view several reports; and to print the same collection of reports. The overall organization will be by task. Thus, the initial switchboard will contain buttons such as View Form, View Table, View Report, and Print Report.

To create a switchboard, you use the Switchboard Manager button on the Database Tools tab. If you have not previously created a switchboard, you will be asked if you wish to create one. The following steps create a switchboard for the JSP Recruiters database.

- Hide the Navigation Pane if it is not already hidden.

Q&A Do I have to hide the Navigation Pane in order to create a switchboard?

No. Hiding it just makes the screen less cluttered. Hiding it is a matter of personal preference.

- Click Database Tools on the Ribbon to display the Database Tools tab.

- Click the Switchboard Manager button on the Database Tools tab (Figure 6–23).

Q&A Is the message an error?

No. The message is simply an indication that you have not yet created a switchboard. If you click the Yes button, Access will create one for you.

Figure 6–23

2

- Click the Yes button to create a new switchboard (Figure 6–24).

Figure 6–24

Creating Switchboard Pages

The next step in creating the switchboard system is to create the individual switchboards within the system. These individual switchboards are called the **switchboard pages**. The switchboard pages to be created are listed in the first column of Table 6–3. You do not have to create the Main Switchboard page because Access has created it automatically (Figure 6–24). To create each of the other pages, use the New button in the Switchboard Manager dialog box, and then enter the name of the page.

Table 6–3 Specifications for Switchboard Pages and Items			
Switchboard Page	**Switchboard Item**	**Command**	**Additional Information**
Main Switchboard	View Form	Go to Switchboard	Switchboard: View Form
	View Table	Go to Switchboard	Switchboard: View Table
	View Report	Go to Switchboard	Switchboard: View Report
	Print Report	Go to Switchboard	Switchboard: Print Report
	Exit Application	Exit Application	None
View Form	Client Form	Run Macro	Macro: Open Client Form
	Recruiter Master Form	Run Macro	Macro: Open Recruiter Master Form
	Return to Main Switchboard	Go to Switchboard	Switchboard: Main Switchboard
View Table	Client Table	Run Macro	Macro: Open Client Table
	Recruiter Table	Run Macro	Macro: Open Recruiter Table
	Return to Main Switchboard	Go to Switchboard	Switchboard: Main Switchboard

Table 6–3 Specifications for Switchboard Pages and Items (*continued*)

Switchboard Page	Switchboard Item	Command	Additional Information
View Report	Client Address Report	Run Macro	Macro: Preview Client Address Report
	Client Financial Report	Run Macro	Macro: Preview Client Financial Report
	Clients by City Report	Run Macro	Macro: Preview Clients by City Report
	Clients by Recruiter Report	Run Macro	Macro: Preview Clients by Recruiter Report
	Return to Main Switchboard	Go to Switchboard	Switchboard: Main Switchboard
Print Report	Client Address Report	Run Macro	Macro: Print Client Address Report
	Client Financial Report	Run Macro	Macro: Print Client Financial Report
	Clients by City Report	Run Macro	Macro: Print Clients by City Report
	Clients by Recruiter Report	Run Macro	Macro: Print Clients by Recruiter Report
	Return to Main Switchboard	Go to Switchboard	Switchboard: Main Switchboard

To Create Switchboard Pages

The following steps create the switchboard pages.

1
- Click the New button in the Switchboard Manager dialog box.

- Type `View Form` as the name of the new switchboard page (Figure 6–25).

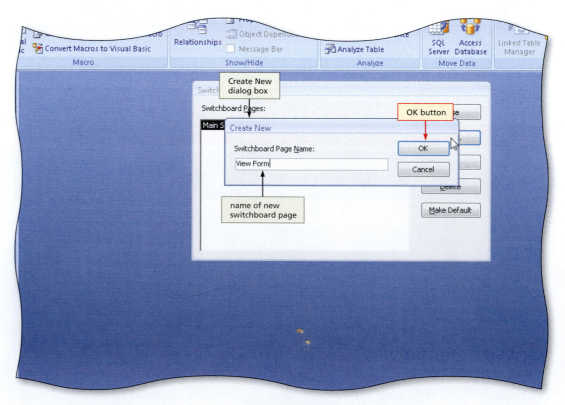

Figure 6–25

2

- Click the OK button to create the View Form switchboard page.

- Use the same technique to create the View Table, View Report, and Print Report switchboard pages (Figure 6–26).

Q&A

Why does Print Report appear at the top of the list?

In the Switchboard Manager dialog box, the pages are listed alphabetically. The switchboard will display the pages in the order in which you entered them. You can change the order of a page when you edit it.

Figure 6–26

To Modify the Main Switchboard Page

The switchboard pages now exist. Currently, there are no actions associated with the pages. You can modify a switchboard page by using the following procedure. Select the page in the Switchboard Manager dialog box, click the Edit button, and then add new items to the page, move existing items to a different position in the list of items, or delete items. For each item, you can indicate the command to be executed when the item is selected.

The following steps modify the Main Switchboard page.

1

- With the Main Switchboard (Default) page selected, click the Edit button to edit the Main switchboard (Figure 6–27).

Figure 6–27

2

- Click the New button, type `View Form` as the text, and then click the Switchboard box arrow to display a menu of available switchboards (Figure 6–28).

Q&A

What am I accomplishing here?

There will be a button on the main switchboard labeled View Form. When you click the View Form button on the main switchboard, Access will take the action you indicate, namely it will go to a switchboard page. Whichever page you select for the Switchboard argument is the one to which it will go.

Figure 6–28

3

- Click View Form and then click the OK button to add the item to the switchboard.

- Using the technique illustrated in Steps 2 and 3, add the View Table, View Report, and Print Report items to the Main Switchboard page. In each case, the command is Go to Switchboard. The names of the switchboards are the same as the name of the items. For example, the switchboard for the View Table item is called View Table.

- Click the New button, type `Exit Application` as the text, and click the Command box arrow to display a menu of available commands (Figure 6–29).

Figure 6–29

4

- Click Exit Application and then click the OK button to add the item to the switchboard.

- Click the Close button in the Edit Switchboard Page dialog box to indicate you have finished editing the Main Switchboard page.

Q&A

What is the purpose of the Exit Application button?

The Exit Application button closes the switchboard, closes the database, and returns you to the Getting Starting with Microsoft Office Access screen.

To Modify the Other Switchboard Pages

You modify the other switchboard pages from Table 6–3 on page AC 381 in exactly the same manner you modified the Main Switchboard page. The following steps modify the other switchboard pages.

1

• Click the View Form switchboard page (Figure 6–30).

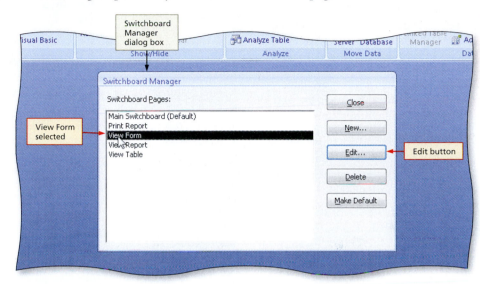

Figure 6–30

2

• Click the Edit button, click the New button to add a new item, type `Client Form` as the text, click the Command box arrow, and then click Run Macro.

• Click the Macro box arrow to display a menu of available macros (Figure 6–31).

Q&A Why do most of the macro names begin with SB Macros and then a period?

This is the notation used when macros are contained in a macro group. The name of the macro group and a period precede the name of the macro.

Q&A Why don't I click the New button? How do I add items to the View Form switchboard page?

You are actually editing the page, so you first click the Edit button. You then will be able to add items to the page.

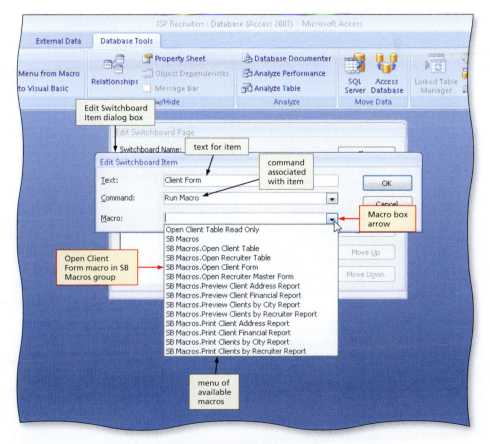

Figure 6–31

3

• Click Open Client Form, and then click the OK button.

• Click the New button, type `Recruiter Master Form` as the text, click the Command box arrow, and then click Run Macro.

• Click the Macro box arrow, click Open Recruiter Master Form, and then click the OK button.

• Click the New button, type `Return to Main Switchboard` as the text, and click the Switchboard box arrow (Figure 6–32).

Q&A

What is the purpose of the Return to Main Switchboard button?

The Return to Main Switchboard button returns you to the main switchboard page. Because the switchboard is really a series of menus, you always should include a button to return to the main menu, that is, the main switchboard.

Figure 6–32

4

• Click Main Switchboard in the list of available switchboards, and then click the OK button.

• Click the Close button in the Edit Switchboard Page dialog box to indicate you have finished editing the View Form switchboard.

• Use the techniques illustrated in Steps 1 through 3 to add the items indicated in Table 6–3 on page AC 381 to the other switchboards (Figure 6–33).

5

• Click the Close button in the Switchboard Manager dialog box.

Figure 6–33

To Open a Switchboard

The switchboard is complete and ready for use. Access has created a form called Switchboard that you will run to use the switchboard. It also has created a table called Switchboard Items. Do not modify this table. Switchboard Manager uses this table to keep track of the various switchboard pages and items.

To use the switchboard, select the switchboard in the Navigation Pane, and then click Open on the shortcut menu. The Main Switchboard then will appear. To take any action, click the appropriate buttons. When you have finished, click the Exit Application button. The switchboard will be removed from the screen, and the database will be closed. The following steps open a switchboard system for use.

1

- Show the Navigation Pane, scroll down so that the Switchboard form appears, and then right-click Switchboard (Figure 6–34).

What is the difference between Switchboard and Switchboard Items?

Switchboard is the form. Switchboard Items is a table containing information about the way the switchboard functions. You should not change the Switchboard Items table in any way; otherwise, your switchboard may not function.

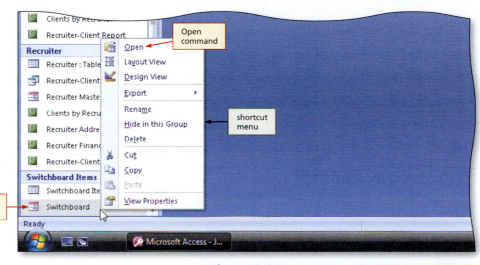

Figure 6–34

2

- Click Open on the shortcut menu to open the switchboard (Figure 6–35).

 Experiment

- Try the various buttons on the switchboard to see their effect.

Figure 6–35

BTW

Displaying a Switchboard
It is possible to have the switchboard appear automatically when the database is open. To do so, click Access Options on the Office Button menu and then click Current Database in the Access Options dialog box. Click the down arrow for the Display Form: list box and then select Switchboard. Click the OK button. When you next open the database, the Switchboard will appear.

Using the Switchboard

Click the View Form button to display the View Form switchboard page. Click the View Table button to display the View Table switchboard page. Click the View Report button to display the View Report switchboard page. Click the Print Report button to display the Print Report switchboard page. On each of the other switchboard pages, click the button for the form, table, or report you wish to view, or the report you wish to print. To return from one of the other switchboard pages to the Main Switchboard, click the Return to Main Switchboard button. To leave the switchboard system, click the Exit Application button.

If you discover a problem with the switchboard, click the Switchboard Manager button on the Database Tools tab. You can modify the switchboard system using the same techniques you used to create it.

To Close the Switchboard and Close the Database

To close the switchboard and the database, click the Exit Application button. To close the switchboard without closing the database, close the switchboard form by clicking the Close 'Switchboard' button. The following step closes the switchboard and closes the database.

1 Click the Exit Application button to remove the switchboard from the screen and close the database.

BTW

AutoNumber Field as Primary Key
When you create a table in Datasheet view, Access automatically creates an ID field with the AutoNumber data type as the primary key field. As you add records to the table, Access increments the ID field so that each record will have a unique value in the field. You can rename the ID field. You also can delete the ID field and choose another field as the primary key.

Additional Tables

Because the recruiters at JSP have experience in health-care administration, they are frequently asked to present seminars on various health-care related topics. JSP would like to incorporate this data in the JSP Recruiters database.

Before examining PivotTables and PivotCharts, you need to create the two additional tables. The first table, Seminar, is shown in Figures 6–36a and 6–36b. This table contains the specific seminars that the recruiters at JSP Recruiters offer to their clients. Each seminar has a number and a description. The table also includes the total hours for which the seminar usually is offered and the increments, that is, the standard time blocks in which the seminar usually is offered. The first row, for example, indicates that seminar S01 is called Assessing Patient Satisfaction. It typically is offered in two-hour increments for a total of eight hours.

(a)
Structure of Seminar Table

Field Name	Data Type	Primary Key?
Seminar Number	Text	Yes
Seminar Description	Text	
Hours	Number	
Increments	Number	

Figure 6–36

Seminar Number	Seminar Description	Hours	Increments
S01	Assessing Patient Satisfaction	8	2
S02	HIPAA Fundamentals	4	2
·S03	Medical Powers of Attorney	12	4
S04	OSHA Fundamentals	4	2
S05	Using Basic Medical Terminology	16	4
S06	Working in Teams	16	4
S07	Coping with Crisis Situations	8	2
S08	Personal Hygiene in the Medical Environment	2	1

(b)
Seminar Table

Figure 6–36 (continued)

The second table, Seminar Offerings, is shown in Figures 6–37a and 6–37b. Figure 6–37a, the structure, indicates that the table contains a client number, a seminar number, the total number of hours for which the seminar is scheduled, and the number of hours already spent in the seminar.

Field Name	Data Type	Primary Key?
Client Number	Text	Yes
Seminar Number	Text	Yes
Total Hours	Number	
Hours Spent	Number	

(a)
Structure
of Seminar
Offerings Table

Client Number	Seminar Number	Total Hours	Hours Spent
BH72	S02	4	0
BH72	S03	12	6
FH22	S04	4	2
FH22	S07	8	4
MH56	S06	16	8
MH56	S07	8	4
PR11	S05	16	4
TC37	S01	8	2
TC37	S07	8	4
TC37	S08	2	0

(b)
Seminar
Offerings Table

Figure 6–37

Figure 6–37b gives the data. For example, the first record shows that client number BH72 currently has scheduled seminar S02 (HIPAA Fundamentals). The seminar is scheduled for 4 hours and they have not yet spent any hours in class.

If you examine the data in Figure 6–37b, you see that the Client Number field cannot be the primary key. The first two records, for example, both have a client number of BH72. The Seminar Number field also cannot be the primary key. The fourth and sixth records, for example, both have seminar number S07. Rather, the primary key is the combination of both Client Number and Seminar Number.

Copy the Structure of a Table

If you want to create a table that has a structure similar to an existing table, you can copy the structure of the table only. To do so, select the existing table in the Navigation Pane and click Copy on the Home tab, then click Paste on the Home tab. When the Paste Table As dialog box appears, type the new table name and click the Structure Only option button. Then, click the OK button. To modify the new table, open it in Design view.

To Open the Database

Because clicking the Exit Application button closed the JSP Recruiters database, you need to open it again. The following steps use the More button to open the JSP Recruiters database from the USB flash drive.

1 With your USB flash drive connected to one of the computer's USB ports, click the More button to display the Open dialog box.

2 If the Folders list is displayed below the Folders button, click the Folders button to remove the Folders list.

3 If necessary, click Computers in the Favorite Links section and then double-click UDISK 2.0 (E:) to select the USB flash drive, Drive E in this case, as the new open location. (Your drive letter might be different.)

4 Click JSP Recruiters to select the file name.

5 Click the Open button to open the database.

6 If a Security Warning appears, click the Options button to display the Microsoft Office Security Options dialog box.

7 With the option button to enable the content selected, click the OK button to enable the content.

To Create the New Tables

You can create new tables in either Datasheet view or Design view. In Design view, you define the structure of the tables. The steps to create the new tables are similar to the steps you used previously to add fields to an existing table and to define primary keys. The only difference is the way you specify a primary key consisting of more than one field. First, you select both fields that make up the primary key by clicking the row selector for the first field, and then hold down the SHIFT key while clicking the row selector for the second field. Once the fields are selected, you can use the Primary Key button to indicate that the primary key consists of both fields.

The following steps create the tables in Design view.

1

• Hide the Navigation Pane.

• Click Create on the Ribbon to display the Create tab (Figure 6–38).

Figure 6–38

② Click the Table Design button to create a table in Design view.

● Enter the information for the fields in the Seminar table as indicated in Figure 6–36a on page AC 388, selecting Seminar Number as the primary key.

● Save the table using the name `Seminar` and close the table.

● Click the Table Design button on the Create tab to create a table in Design view.

● Enter the information for the fields in the Seminar Offerings table as indicated in Figure 6–37a on page AC 389.

Figure 6–39

● Click the row selector for the Client Number field.

● Hold down the SHIFT key and then click the row selector for the Seminar Number field so both fields are selected.

● Click the Primary Key button on the Design tab to select the combination of the two fields as the primary key (Figure 6–39).

③

● Save the table using the name `Seminar Offerings` and close the table.

To Import the Data

Now that the tables have been created, you need to add data to them. You either could enter the data, or if the data is already in electronic form, you could import the data. The data for the Seminar and Seminar Offerings tables are on your Data Disk as text files. The following steps import the data.

1 With the JSP Recruiters database open, click the External Data tab on the Ribbon and then click the Text File button in the Import group on the External Data tab to display the Get External Data - Text File dialog box.

2 Click the Browse button and select the location of the files to be imported (for example, the folder called AccessData on drive E:). Select the Seminar text file and click the Open button.

3 Select the 'Append a copy of records to the table' option button and the Seminar table and then click the OK button. Be sure the Delimited option button is selected and click the Next button. Click First Row Contains Field Names check box, click the Next button, and then click the Finish button.

4 Click the Close button to close the Get External Data – Text Box dialog box without saving the import steps.

5 Use the technique shown in Steps 1 through 4 to import the Seminar Offerings text file into the Seminar Offerings table.

BTW

Modify Composite Primary Keys
If you find that you have selected an incorrect field as part of a composite primary key, open the table in Design view, click any field that participates in the primary key, and click the Primary Key button on the Ribbon to remove the primary key. If the fields are adjacent to each other, click the row selector for the first field, hold down the SHIFT key and click the row selector for the second field. Then click the Primary Key button. If the fields are not adjacent to each other, use the CTRL key to select both fields.

To Relate Several Tables

Now that the tables have been created they need to be related to the existing tables. The Client and Seminar Offerings tables are related through the Client Number fields in both. The Seminar and Seminar Offerings tables are related through the Seminar Number fields in both. The following steps illustrate the process of relating the tables.

1 Close any open datasheet on the screen by clicking its Close button. Click Database Tools on the Ribbon to display the Database Tools tab and then click the Relationships button on the Database Tools tab.

2 Click the Show Table button.

3 Click the Seminar Offerings table, click the Add button, click the Seminar table, click the Add button again, and then click the Close button.

4 Point to the Client Number field in the Client table, press the left mouse button, drag to the Client Number in the Seminar Offerings table, and then release the left mouse button. Click the Enforce Referential Integrity check box in the Edit Relationships dialog box and then click the Create button.

5 Drag the Seminar Number field from the Seminar table to the Seminar Offerings table. Click Enforce Referential Integrity check box and then click the Create button to create the relationship (Figure 6–40).

6 Click the Close button in the Relationships group and then click the Yes button to save the changes.

Figure 6–40

PivotTables and PivotCharts

There are two alternatives to viewing data in Datasheet view or Form view. **PivotTable view** presents data as a **PivotTable**, that is, an interactive table that summarizes or analyzes data. PivotChart view presents data as a **PivotChart**, that is, a graphical representation of the data. PivotTables and PivotCharts allow you to view data in multiple dimensions, thus making it valuable for management decision-making. For example, PivotTables and PivotCharts can be used to analyze past data and predict future patterns and trends, a technique known as data mining.

In a PivotTable, you can show different levels of detail easily as well as change the organization or layout of the table by dragging items. You also can filter data by checking or unchecking values in drop-down lists. In a PivotChart, just as in a PivotTable, you can show different levels of detail or change the layout by dragging items. You also can filter data by checking or unchecking values in drop-down lists. You can change the type of chart that appears as well as customize the chart by adding axis titles, a chart title, and a legend. In this section, you will create a PivotTable and a PivotChart. Both the PivotTable and the PivotChart can be based on a table or a query. Both the PivotTable and PivotChart that you create in the following sections are based on a query.

BTW

PivotTable Form
You also can create a PivotTable form. To create a PivotTable form, select the table or query for the PivotTable form in the Navigation Pane, click Create on the Ribbon, click the More Forms button on the Create tab, and then click PivotTable. Click the Field List button on the Design tab to display the PivotTable field list. You then can use the steps shown in Figures 6–47 through 6–50 to create the PivotTable. When finished, save the form. When you open the form, you can use the PivotTable just as in Figures 6–51 through 6–57 on pages AC 400 through AC 402.

To Create the Query

Because the PivotTable and PivotChart you will create will be based on a query, you first must create the query. The following steps create the necessary query.

- Click Create on the Ribbon and then click the Query Design button on the Create tab to create a query.

- Click the Recruiter table and then click the Add button to add the Recruiter table to the query.

- Click the Client table and then click the Add button to add the Client table to the query.

- Click the Seminar Offerings table and then click the Add button to add the Seminar Offerings table to the query.

- Click the Close button for the Show Table dialog box.

- Resize the Recruiter and Client field lists so as many fields as possible appear (Figure 6–41).

Figure 6–41

2

- Double-click the Recruiter Number field from the Recruiter table and the Client Number field from the Client table.

- Double-click the Seminar Number and Hours Spent fields from the Seminar Offerings table.

- Right-click the Field row in the first open column to produce a shortcut menu (Figure 6–42).

Figure 6–42

3

- Click Zoom on the shortcut menu to display the Zoom dialog box, type `Hours Remaining:[Total Hours]-[Hours Spent]` in the Zoom dialog box to enter the expression for the field (Figure 6–43).

Figure 6–43

4

- Click the OK button and then click the View button on the Design tab to ensure your results are correct.

- Click the Save button on the Quick Access Toolbar and type `Recruiters and Seminar Offerings` as the name of the query (Figure 6–44).

5

- Click the OK button to save the query.

- Close the query.

Figure 6–44

PivotTables

Figure 6–45 shows a sample PivotTable. The rows in the table represent the seminars. The columns represent the recruiter numbers. Each column is subdivided into the total of the hours spent and the total of the hours remaining for seminars for those clients assigned to the recruiter. The last column shows the grand total for the items in each row. The last row shows the grand total for items in each column.

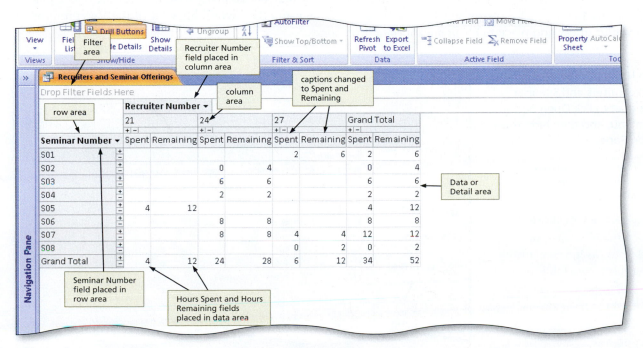

Figure 6–45

BTW

Certification
The Microsoft Certified Application Specialist (MCAS) program provides an opportunity for you to obtain a valuable industry credential—proof that you have the Access 2007 skills required by employers. For more information, see Appendix G or visit the Access 2007 Certification Web page (scsite.com/ac2007/cert).

To create the PivotTable, you place fields in predefined areas of the table called **drop zones**. In the PivotTable in Figure 6–45 on the previous page, the Seminar Number field has been placed in the row zone (also called row area), for example. The drop zones are listed and described in Table 6–4.

Table 6–4 PivotTable Drop Zones	
Zone	**Purpose**
Row	Data from fields in this area will appear as rows in the table.
Column	Data from fields in this area will appear as columns in the table.
Filter	Data from fields in this area will not appear in the table but can be used to restrict the data that appears.
Detail	Data from fields in this area will appear in the detail portion (the body) of the table.
Data	Summary data (for example, a sum) from fields in this area will appear in the detail portion (the body) of the table. Individual values will not appear.

Plan Ahead

Determine the organization of the PivotTable.

1. **Determine the field or fields that will be used for the rows and columns.** What do you want the rows in the grid to represent? What do you want the columns to represent? You can easily reverse the roles later if you wish.

2. **Determine the field or fields that will be summarized in the grid.** Precisely what calculations is the PivotTable intended to present?

3. **Determine the field or fields that will be used to filter the data.** Are there any fields in addition to the ones already identified that will be used to filter the data?

To Create a PivotTable

Applying the steps in the Plan Ahead, JSP Recruiters has determined that the rows will represent the Seminar Number field, the columns will represent the Recruiter Number field, the Hours Spent and Hours Remaining fields will be summarized in the grid. They also have determined that they may occasionally wish to filter the data using the Client Number field. The following steps create the PivotTable using the PivotTable view of the Recruiters and Seminar Offerings query and place fields in appropriate drop zones.

- Show the Navigation Pane, right-click the Recruiters and Seminar Offerings query, click Open on the shortcut menu, and then hide the Navigation Pane.

- Click the View button arrow to display the View button menu (Figure 6–46).

Q&A

Can I just click the View button?

No. Clicking the View button would move to Design view of the query. You want PivotTable view.

Figure 6–46

2

- Click PivotTable View to switch to PivotTable view of the query.

- If the PivotTable Field List does not appear, click the Field List button on the PivotTable tab to display the field list.

- Click Seminar Number in the field list, and then ensure Row Area appears next to the Add to button (Figure 6–47).

Figure 6–47

3

- Click the Add to button to add the Seminar Number field to the Row area.

- Click the Add to box arrow to display the list of available areas (Figure 6–48).

 Are the areas the same as drop zones?

Yes.

Figure 6–48

4

- Click Column Area, click the Recruiter Number field in the field list, and then click the Add to button to add the Recruiter Number field to the Column area.

- Click the arrow to display the list of available areas, click Data Area, click Hours Spent, and then click the Add to button to add the Hours Spent field to the Data area.

- Use the same technique to add the Hours Remaining field to the Data area.

- Close the PivotTable Field List by clicking its Close button (Figure 6–49).

Figure 6–49

Other Ways

1. Click PivotTable View on status bar

To Change Properties in a PivotTable

You can use the property sheet for the objects in a PivotTable to change characteristics of the objects. The following steps use the appropriate property sheet to change the caption for Sum of Hours Spent to Spent and for Sum of Hours Remaining to Remaining in order to reduce the size of the columns in the PivotTable.

1

- Click the Sum of Hours Spent box to select it, and then click the Property Sheet button on the Design tab to display a property sheet.

- Click the Captions tab in the property sheet (Figure 6–50).

2

- Delete the current entry in the Caption property box, type Spent as the new value for the Caption property, and then close the property sheet.

- Use the same technique to change the caption for the Sum of Hours Remaining box to Remaining.

Figure 6–50

To Save the PivotTable Changes

The following step saves the PivotTable changes.

1 Click the Save button on the Quick Access Toolbar.

BTW

Quick Reference
For a table that lists how to complete the tasks covered in this book using the mouse, Ribbon, shortcut menu, and keyboard, see the Quick Reference Summary at the back of this book, or visit the Access 2007 Quick Reference Web page (scsite.com/ac2007/qr).

To Use a PivotTable

To view data using a PivotTable as well as to take advantage of the formatting and filtering that a PivotTable provides, you must open it. If the PivotTable is associated with a query, this would involve opening the query and then switching to PivotTable view. You then can click appropriate plus (+) or minus (−) signs to hide or show data. You also can click appropriate arrows and then check or uncheck the various items that appear to restrict the data that appears. You can drag items from one location to another to change the layout of the PivotTable. The following steps use the PivotTable view of the Recruiters and Seminar Offerings query.

1

- Click the View button arrow, and then click PivotTable View.

Q&A

What if I had closed the query? How would I get back in?

Right-click the query in the Navigation Pane and click Open on the shortcut menu.

- Click the plus sign (+) under recruiter number 21 to remove the details for recruiter number 21 (Figure 6–51).

Figure 6–51

2

- Click the minus sign (−) under recruiter number 21 to again display data for recruiter number 21.

- Click the Recruiter Number arrow to display a list of available recruiter numbers (Figure 6–52).

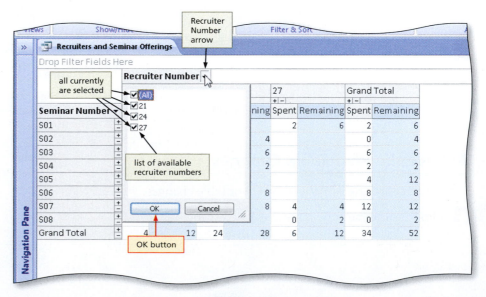

Figure 6–52

3

- Click the Check box for recruiter number 21 to remove the check mark, and then click the OK button to remove the data for recruiter number 21 (Figure 6–53).

🔍 **Experiment**

- Click the Recruiter Number arrow and then try different combinations of check marks to see the effect of your choice.

Figure 6–53

4

- Click the Recruiter Number arrow, click the All check box to display all recruiter numbers, and then click the OK button (Figure 6–54).

Figure 6–54

5

- Click the Field List button to display the PivotTable Field List. Click Client Number, click the arrow to display a list of available areas, click Filter Area, and then click the Add to button to add the Client Number field to the Filter area.

- Click the Client Number arrow (Figure 6–55).

Q&A

Why do I only see these clients and not the others?

These are the only clients who currently have seminars.

Figure 6–55

6
- Click the check boxes in front of clients BH72 and FH22 to remove the check marks, and then click the OK button so that the data for these clients will not be reflected in the PivotTable (Figure 6–56).

 Experiment
- Click the Client Number arrow and then try different combinations of check marks to see the effect of your choice.

Figure 6–56

7
- Click the Client Number arrow, click the All check box, and then click the OK button to display data for all clients.

- Drag the Recruiter Number field from the Column area to the Row area, and then drag Seminar Number field from the Row area to the Column area to reverse the organization (Figure 6–57).

 Q&A I think I dragged to the wrong area. How can I fix it?

You should be able to drag to the correct area. If you would rather start over, close the query without saving it, open the query, and then move to PivotTable view. You then can try again.

Figure 6–57

8
- Close the Recruiters and Seminar Offerings query without saving your changes.

Q&A What if I save my changes?

The next time you open the query and move to PivotTable view, you will see the new organization. The roles of the rows and columns would be interchanged.

PivotCharts

If you have not already created a PivotTable for a query or table, you can create a PivotChart for the query or table from scratch by placing fields in appropriate drop zones just as you did when you created a PivotTable. The drop zones are shown in Figure 6–58. Their purpose is described in Table 6–5.

Figure 6–58

Table 6–5 PivotChart Drop Zones		
Zone	**Purpose**	**Example**
Series	Data from fields in this area will appear as data series, which are represented by colored data markers such as bars. Related markers constitute a series and are assigned a specific color. The names and colors appear in the chart legend.	In the JSP Recruiters PivotChart, the Series area contains the Seminar Number field. The seminar numbers and related colors appear in a legend.
Category	Data from fields in this area will appear as categories, that is, related groups of data. Category labels appear across the x-axis (horizontal) of the chart provided the graph type selected has such an axis.	In the JSP Recruiters PivotChart, the Category area contains the Recruiter Number fields. The recruiter numbers are listed across the x-axis.
Filter	Data from fields in this area will not appear in the chart but can be used to restrict the data that appears.	JSP currently does not use this feature in this PivotChart. If they decide they only want seminars offered to certain clients, they would place the Client Number field in this area.
Data	Data from fields in this area will be summarized within the chart.	In the JSP Recruiters PivotChart, the Data area contains the Hours Spent and Hours Remaining fields. The sum of the values in these fields is represented by the bars in the chart.

<table>
<tr><td>

Plan Ahead

</td><td>

Determine the organization of the PivotChart.

1. **Determine the field or fields that will be used for the series.** What field or fields will be represented as data series, that is, as colored data markers like bars? Do you want these represented with a legend?

2. **Determine the field or fields that will be used for the categories.** What field or fields will be represented as categories, that is, as related groups of data? Labels for these fields will appear across the x-axis in those chart types that have an x-axis.

3. **Determine the field or fields that will be used for the data.** Which fields contain the data to be summarized in the chart?

4. **Determine the field or fields that will be used to filter the data.** Are there any fields in addition to the ones already identified that will be used to filter the data?

5. **Determine the type of chart.** What type of chart best represents the data? The most common types of charts are pie charts, line charts and bar charts. A pie chart shows percentages as slices of pies. A line chart uses lines to connect dots that show ordered observations. A bar chart uses bars to show frequencies or values for different categories.

</td></tr>
</table>

To Create a PivotChart and Add a Legend

If you are using the PivotChart view of a table or query and already have modified the PivotTable view, much of this work already is done. The same information is used wherever possible. You can, of course, modify any aspect of this information. You can remove fields from drop zones by clicking the field name and then pressing the DELETE key. You can add fields to drop zones just as you did with the PivotTable. You also can make other changes, including adding a legend, changing the chart type, changing captions, and adding titles.

JSP Recruiters has applied the steps in the Plan Ahead and determined that seminar numbers will be used for the series, the recruiters will be used for the categories, the Spent and Remaining fields will furnish the data, and the chart type will be 3D Stacked Column.

The following steps create the PivotChart using PivotChart view of the Recruiters and Seminar Offerings query and then add a legend.

• Show the Navigation Pane if it is currently hidden.

• Open the Recruiters and Seminar Offerings query.

• Hide the Navigation Pane.

• Click the View button arrow, and then click PivotChart View.

• If the Chart Field List appears, close the field list by clicking its Close button (Figure 6–59).

Figure 6–59

Q&A

Where did the data come from?

Because you already have created a PivotTable, Access has represented the data in your PivotTable in the PivotChart. You now can make a variety of changes to this PivotChart.

2

• Click the Legend button on the Design tab to display a legend (Figure 6–60).

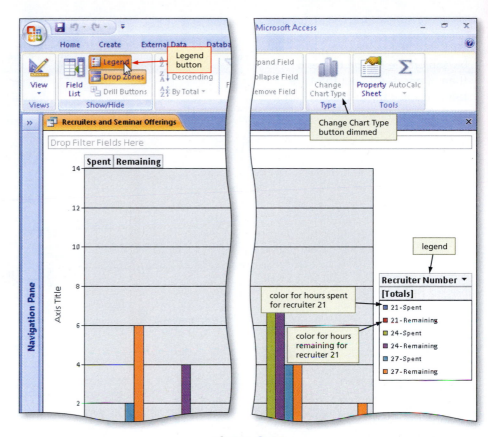

Figure 6–60

Other Ways

1. Click PivotChart View on status bar

To Change the Chart Type

Several types of charts are available. You might find a pie chart more useful than a bar chart, for example. To change the chart type, use the Chart Type button, and then select the desired chart type. The following steps change the chart type to 3D Stacked Column.

1

• If the Change Chart Type button is dimmed, click the Chartspace (that is, the white space in the chart) (Figure 6–61).

Does it matter where in the white space I click?

No.

Figure 6–61

2

- Click the Change Chart Type button on the Design tab, and then, if necessary, click the Type tab to display the available chart types (Figure 6–62).

Figure 6–62

3

- Click the 3D Stacked Column type to change the chart type, and then close the Properties window by clicking its Close button (Figure 6–63).

Experiment

- Click the Change Chart Type button and try other chart types to see how they present the data in the PivotChart. When done, select the 3D Stacked Column chart type.

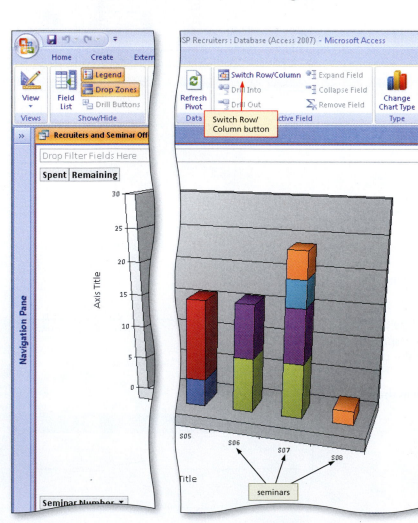

Figure 6–63

To Change PivotChart Orientation

The chart in Figure 6–63 has the seminar numbers along the horizontal axis and recruiter numbers in the legend. The heights of the bars represent the total number of hours for each seminar. Within a bar, the colors represent the recruiter and whether the amount represents hours remaining or hours spent (see legend). To change the chart orientation, you can click the By Row/By Column button. The following step changes the orientation so the recruiter numbers appear along the horizontal axis and the seminars appear in the legend.

1
- Click the Switch Row/Column button on the Design tab to change the organization (Figure 6–64).

Figure 6–64

To Assign Axis Titles

You can assign titles to an axis by clicking the Axis Title box for the axis you want to change, clicking the Property Sheet button on the Design tab, and then changing the Caption property to the title you want to assign. The following steps change the two axis titles to Hours and Recruiter.

- Click the axis title to the left of the chart, and then click the Property Sheet button on the Design tab.

- Click the Format tab in the Properties window, and then click the Caption box.

- Use the BACKSPACE or DELETE key to delete the old caption.

- Type Hours as the new caption (Figure 6–65).

- Close the property sheet to complete the change of the axis title.

- Use the same technique to change the other axis title to Recruiter.

Figure 6–65

Other Ways

1. Right-click Axis Title box, click Properties on shortcut menu

To Remove Drop Zones

You can remove the drop zones from the PivotChart to give the chart a cleaner look. To do so, use the Drop Zones button on the Design tab. If you later need to use the drop zones to perform some task, you can return them to the screen by using the Drop Zones button on the Design tab a second time. The following step removes the drop zones.

1

- Click the Drop Zones button on the Design tab to remove the drop zones (Figure 6–66).

Q&A

Why remove the drop zones? What if I want to use them later?

The PivotChart has a cleaner look without the drop zones. You can always bring them back whenever you need them by clicking the Drop Zones button again.

Figure 6–66

To Add a Chart Title

You can add a title to a PivotChart by clicking the Add Title button in the property sheet for the chart. You then can change the Caption property for the newly added title to assign the title of your choice. The following steps add a title to the PivotChart and then change the title's Caption property to Hours by Recruiter and Seminar.

1

- Click anywhere in the Chartspace (the white space) of the PivotChart, click Property Sheet button on the Design tab, and then, if necessary, click the General tab.

- Click the Add Title button (Figure 6–67).

Q&A

The title that was added is simply Chart Workspace Title. What if I want a more descriptive title?

In the next step, you will change the title to the one you want.

Figure 6–67

2

- Close the property sheet, click the newly added title, and then click the Property Sheet button on the Design tab.

 Q&A

Why did I have to change to a different property sheet?

The property sheet in Step 1 was the property sheet for the chart workspace. To change the title, you need to work with the property sheet for the title.

- Click the Format tab.

- Click the Caption box, and then use the BACKSPACE or DELETE key to erase the old caption.

- Type Hours by Recruiter and Seminar as the new caption and press the ENTER key to change the caption (Figure 6–68).

Figure 6–68

3

- Close the property sheet by clicking its Close button (Figure 6–69).

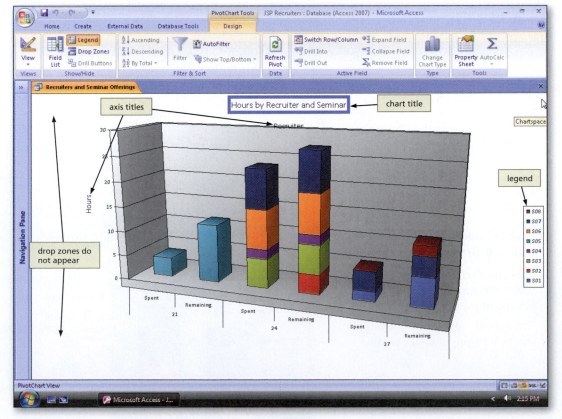

Figure 6–69

To Save the PivotChart Changes

The following step saves the PivotChart changes.

1 Click the Save button on the Quick Access Toolbar.

To Use a PivotChart

To use a PivotChart, you first must open the table or query with which it is associated and then switch to PivotChart view. You then can check or uncheck the various items that appear to restrict the data that appears. In order to do so, the drop zones must appear. If they do not, use the Drop Zones button on the Design tab to display them. You then can click the arrows. You also can drag fields to the drop zones.

You can make the same types of changes you made when you first created the PivotChart. You can change the chart type. You can change the orientation by clicking the By Row/By Column button. You can add or remove a legend. You can change titles. The following steps use the PivotChart view of the Recruiters and Seminar Offerings query.

1

- Be sure the Recruiters and Seminar Offerings query is open in PivotChart view.

- Click the Drop Zones button on the Design tab to display the drop zones (Figure 6–70).

Figure 6–70

2

- Click the Recruiter Number arrow to display the list of available recruiters (Figure 6–71).

Figure 6–71

3

- Click the check box for recruiter number 24 to remove the check mark, and then click the OK button (Figure 6–72).

Experiment

- Click the Recruiter Number arrow and then try different combinations of check marks to see the effect of your choice.

4

- Close the PivotChart without saving your changes.

Q&A

What would happen if I saved the changes?

The next time you view the PivotChart, the changes would be reflected. In particular, data for recruiter 24 would not be reflected in the PivotChart.

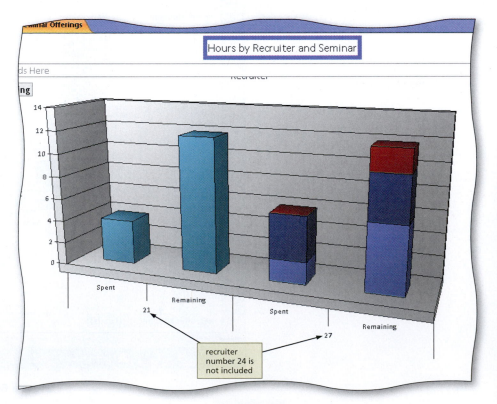

Figure 6–72

To Quit Access

You saved all your changes and are ready to quit Access. The following step quits Access.

 1 Click the Close button on the right side of the Access title bar to quit Access.

Chapter Summary

In this chapter you have learned to create and use macros; use the Switchboard Manager to create a switchboard, the switchboard pages, and the switchboard items, as well as to assign actions to the buttons on the switchboard pages; use a switchboard; create a table with a multiple-field primary key; create, customize, and use a PivotTable; and create, customize, and use a PivotChart. The following list includes all the new Access skills you have learned in this chapter.

1. Begin Creating a Macro (AC 366)
2. Add Actions to a Macro (AC 368)
3. Run a Macro (AC 372)
4. Modify a Macro (AC 373)
5. Run the Modified Macro (AC 374)
6. Reverse the Macro Action (AC 374)
7. Create a Macro Group (AC 377)
8. Save the Macro Group (AC 378)
9. Add the Remaining Macros to the Macro Group (AC 379)
10. Create a Switchboard (AC 380)
11. Create Switchboard Pages (AC 382)
12. Modify the Main Switchboard Page (AC 383)
13. Modify the Other Switchboard Pages (AC 385)
14. Open a Switchboard (AC 387)
15. Close the Switchboard and Close the Database (AC 388)
16. Create the New Tables (AC 390)
17. Import the Data (AC 391)
18. Relate Several Tables (AC 392)
19. Create the Query (AC 393)
20. Create a PivotTable (AC 396)
21. Change Properties in a PivotTable (AC 398)
22. Save the PivotTable Changes (AC 399)
23. Use a PivotTable (AC 400)
24. Create a PivotChart and Add a Legend (AC 404)
25. Change the Chart Type (AC 405)
26. Change PivotChart Orientation (AC 407)
27. Assign Axis Titles (AC 408)
28. Remove Drop Zones (AC 409)
29. Add a Chart Title (AC 409)
30. Save the PivotChart Changes (AC 411)
31. Use a PivotChart (AC 411)

 If you have a SAM user profile, you may have access to hands-on instruction, practice, and assessment. Log in to your SAM account (http://sam2007.course.com) to launch any assigned training activities or exams that relate to the skills covered in this chapter.

Learn It Online

Test your knowledge of chapter content and key terms.

Instructions: To complete the Learn It Online exercises, start your browser, click the Address bar, and then enter the Web address scsite.com/ac2007/learn. When the Access 2007 Learn It Online page is displayed, click the link for the exercise you want to complete and then read the instructions.

Chapter Reinforcement TF, MC, and SA

A series of true/false, multiple choice, and short answer questions that test your knowledge of the chapter content.

Flash Cards

An interactive learning environment where you identify chapter key terms associated with displayed definitions.

Practice Test

A series of multiple choice questions that test your knowledge of chapter content and key terms.

Who Wants To Be a Computer Genius?

An interactive game that challenges your knowledge of chapter content in the style of a television quiz show.

Wheel of Terms

An interactive game that challenges your knowledge of chapter key terms in the style of the television show *Wheel of Fortune*.

Crossword Puzzle Challenge

A crossword puzzle that challenges your knowledge of key terms presented in the chapter.

Apply Your Knowledge

Reinforce the skills and apply the concepts you learned in this chapter.

Adding Tables and Creating PivotTables and PivotCharts

Instructions: Start Access. If you are using the Microsoft Office Access 2007 Complete or the Microsoft Office Access 2007 Comprehensive text, open The Bike Delivers database that you used in Chapter 5. Otherwise, see your instructor for information on accessing the files required in this book. Perform the following tasks:

1. Create two tables in which to store data about the courier services performed for clients. The Services Offered table has the structure shown in Figure 6–73a and the Weekly Services table has the structure shown in Figure 6–73b. The Bike Delivers charges a set fee based on the type of service the client requests. At the end of each week, the company bills the clients.

(a) Structure of Services Offered Table

Field Name	Data Type	Primary Key?
Service Code	Text	Yes
Service Description	Text	
Fee	Currency	

Figure 6–73

Field Name	Data Type	Primary Key?
Customer Number	Text	Yes
Service Date	Date/Time (change Format Property to Short Date)	Yes
Service Time	Date/Time (change Format Property to Medium Time)	Yes
Service Code	Text	

(b) Structure of Weekly Services Table

Figure 6–73 (continued)

2. Import the Services Offered.txt file to the Services Offered table and the Weekly Services.txt file to the Weekly Services table.

3. Create a query that includes the Courier, Customer, Services Offered, and Weekly Services tables. Add the Courier Number from the Courier table, the Customer Number and Service Code from the Weekly Services table, and the Service Fee from the Services Offered table to the design grid. Save the query as Couriers and Services.

4. Create the PivotTable shown in Figure 6–74a and the PivotChart shown in Figure 6–74b.

(a) PivotTable

(b) PivotChart

Figure 6–74

5. Submit the revised database in the format specified by your instructor.

Extend Your Knowledge

Extend the skills you learned in this chapter and experiment with new skills. You may need to use Help to complete the assignment.

Modifying Macros and Switchboards

Instructions: Start Access. Open the Regional Books database. See the inside back cover of this book for instructions on downloading the Data Files for Students, or contact your instructor for more information about accessing the required files.

Regional Books, a local bookstore, has created macros and a switchboard. Because the company uses a dark red and gray color scheme on all their publicity materials, they would like the switchboard to reflect those colors. They also would like the name of the store to show on the main switchboard page. You will modify the switchboard page as shown in Figure 6–75. You also will modify a macro.

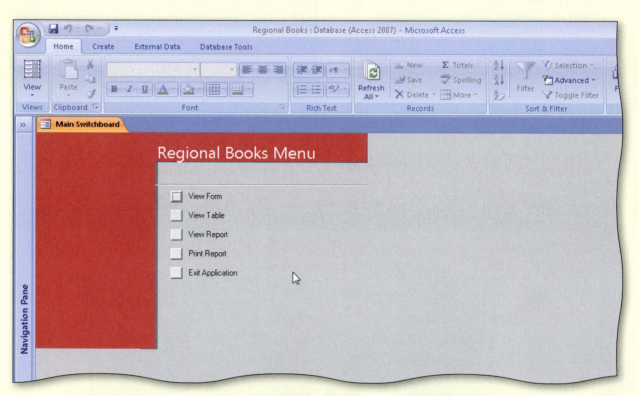

Figure 6–75

Perform the following tasks:

1. Open the switchboard in Design view and change the background color of the form to correspond to the colors shown in Figure 6–75. Change the title to Regional Books Menu.

2. Open the Open Publisher Table macro in Design view and change the Data Mode for the table so that it is read-only. A message box with an appropriate message should appear when the table is opened.

3. Change the database properties, as specified by your instructor. Submit the revised database in the format specified by your instructor.

Make It Right

Analyze a database and correct all errors and/or improve the design.

Correcting Form Design Errors

Instructions: Start Access. Open the College Dog Walkers database. See the inside back cover of this book for instructions on downloading the Data Files for Students, or contact your instructor for more information about accessing the required files.

The College Dog Walkers database contains data for an organization that provides dog walking services. The owner of the company has created the switchboard shown in Figure 6–76a but he forgot to add the Exit Application button to the main switchboard page. He also forgot to include a button on the View Form page shown in Figure 6–76b to let the user return to the main switchboard page.

(a) Main Switchboard

(b) View Form Switchboard Page

Figure 6–76

Correct these errors, and change the database properties as specified by your instructor. Submit the revised database in the format specified by your instructor.

In the Lab

Design, create, modify, and/or use a database following the guidelines, concepts, and skills presented in this chapter. Labs are listed in order of increasing difficulty.

Lab 1: Creating Macros, a Switchboard, and a PivotTable for the JMS TechWizards Database

Problem: JMS TechWizards would like an easy way to access the various tables, forms, and reports by simply clicking a button or two. This would make the database much easier to maintain and update. The company also needs to keep track of open service requests, that is, uncompleted requests for service.

Instructions: For this assignment you will use the JMS TechWizards database and the data files, Workorders.txt and Category.txt. If you are using the Microsoft Office Access 2007 Complete or the Microsoft Office Access 2007 Comprehensive text, open JMS TechWizards database that you used in Chapter 5. Otherwise, see the inside back cover of this book for instructions on downloading the Data Files for Students, or contact your instructor for more information about accessing the required files. The Workorders.txt and Category.txt files are text files that are included with the Data Files for Students.

Perform the following tasks:

1. Create a macro group that will include macros that will perform the following tasks: (a) open the Client table in read-only mode, (b) open the Technician table in read-only mode (c) open the Client form, (d) open the Technician Master Form, (e) preview the Billing Summary Report, (f) preview the Clients by Technician report, (g) preview the Clients by Type report, (h) print the Billing Summary Report, (i) print the Clients by Technician report, and (j) print the Clients by Type report. Name the macro group JMS Macros.

2. Create a switchboard for the JMS TechWizards database. Use the same design for your switchboard pages as the one illustrated in this chapter. For example, the View Table switchboard page should have three choices: Client Table, Technician Table, and Return to Main Switchboard. Include all the tables, forms, and reports for which you created macros in step 1.

3. Run the switchboard and correct any errors.

4. Create two tables in which to store the open request information. Use Category and Work Orders as the table names. The structure of the Category table is shown in Figure 6–77a and the structure of the Work Orders table is shown in Figure 6–77b. Because the structure of the Work Orders table is similar to the Seminar Offerings table in the JSP Recruiters database, copy the Seminar Offerings table and paste only the structure to the JMS TechWizards database. Import the Category.txt file to the Category table and the Workorders.txt file to the Work Orders table.

(a) Structure of Category Table

Field Name	Data Type	Primary Key?
Category Code	Text	Yes
Category Description	Text	

(b) Structure of Work Orders Table

Field Name	Data Type	Primary Key?
Client Number	Text	Yes
Category Code	Text	Yes
Total Hours (est)	Number	
Hours Spent	Number	

Figure 6–77

5. Add the Category and the Work Orders tables to the Relationships window. Establish a one-to-many relationship between the Category table and the Work Orders table. Establish a one-to-many relationship between the Client table and the Work Orders table.

6. Create a query that joins the Technician table, Client table, and Work Orders table. Include the technician number from the Technician table, the Client Number from the Client table, the category number from the Work Orders table, and hours spent from the Work Orders table in the design grid. Add a calculated field that calculates the hours remaining (Total Hours(est) - Hours Spent). Use Hours Remaining as the name of the calculated field. Run the query and save the query as Technicians and Work Orders.

7. Open the Technicians and Work Orders query and switch to PivotTable view. Create the PivotTable shown in Figure 6–78. Change the captions for the Hours Spent and Hour Remaining fields to Spent and Remaining, respectively.

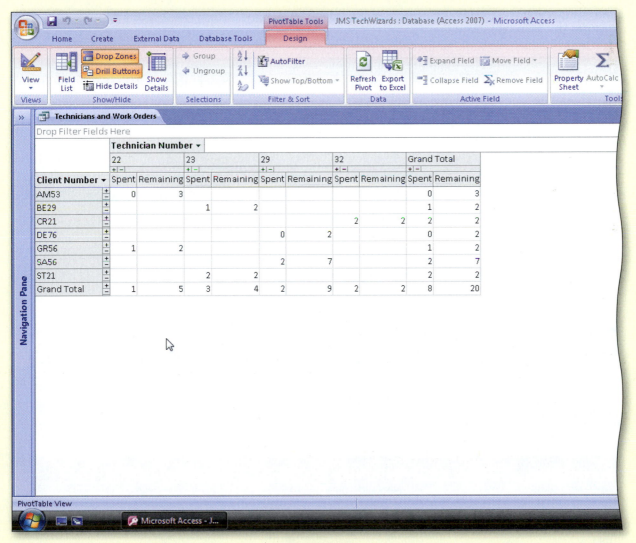

Client Number	Technician Number 22		23		29		32		Grand Total	
	Spent	Remaining	Spent	Remaining	Spent	Remaining	Spent	Remaining	Spent	Remaining
AM53	0	3							0	3
BE29			1	2					1	2
CR21							2	2	2	2
DE76					0	2			0	2
GR56	1	2							1	2
SA56					2	7			2	7
ST21			2	2					2	2
Grand Total	1	5	3	4	2	9	2	2	8	20

Figure 6–78

8. Submit the revised database in the format specified by your instructor.

In the Lab

Lab 2: Creating Macros and a Switchboard for the Hockey Fan Zone Database

Problem: The management of the Hockey Fan Zone store would like an easy way to access the store's various tables, forms, and reports, by simply clicking a button or two. This would make the database much easier to maintain and update. Management also needs to track items that are being reordered from suppliers. Management must know when an item was ordered and how many were ordered. Hockey Fan Zone may place an order with a supplier one day and then find it needs to order more of the same item before the original order is filled.

Instructions: If you are using the Microsoft Office Access 2007 Complete or the Microsoft Office Access 2007 Comprehensive text, open the Hockey Fan Zone database that you used in Chapter 5. Otherwise, see the inside back cover of this book for instructions on downloading the Data Files for Students, or contact your instructor for more information about accessing the required files. Perform the following tasks:

1. Create a macro group that includes macros to perform the following tasks: (a) open the Item table in read-only mode, (b) open the Supplier table in read-only mode, (c) open the Item Update Form, (d) open the Supplier Master Form, (e) preview the Inventory Status Report, (f) preview the Items by Supplier report, (g) preview the Items by Type report, (h) print the Inventory Status Report, (i) print the Items by Supplier report, and (j) print the Items by Type report. Name the macro group HFZ Macros.

2. Create a switchboard for the Hockey Fan Zone database. Use the same design for your switchboard pages as the one illustrated in this chapter. For example, the View Form switchboard page should have three choices: Item Update Form, Supplier Master Form, and Return to Main Switchboard. Include all the tables, forms, and reports for which you created macros in step 1.

3. Run the switchboard and correct any errors.

4. Create a table in which to store the item reorder information using the structure shown in Figure 6–79a. Use Reorder as the name of the table. Add the data shown in Figure 6–79b to the Reorder table.

(a) Structure of Reorder Table

Field Name	Data Type	Primary Key?
Item Number	Text	Yes
Date Ordered	Date/Time (Create an Input Mask and use Short Date)	Yes
Number Ordered	Number	

(b) Data for Reorder Table

Item Number	Date Ordered	Number Ordered
3673	4/15/2008	2
5923	4/21/2008	1
6343	4/1/2008	5
6343	4/4/2008	6
7550	4/3/2008	2
7550	4/5/2008	2
7930	4/11/2008	3
7930	4/14/2008	3

Figure 6–79

5. Add the Reorder table to the Relationships window and establish a one-to-many relationship between the Item table and the Reorder table.

6. Create a query that joins the Reorder table, Item table, and Supplier table. Include the item number from the Reorder table, the supplier code and number on hand from the Item table, and the number ordered from the Reorder table in the design grid. Run the query and save the query as Supplier and Number of Items.

7. Submit the revised database in the format specified by your instructor.

In the Lab

Lab 3: Creating Macros, a Switchboard, a PivotTable, and a PivotChart for the Ada Beauty Supply Database

Problem: Ada Beauty Supply wants an easy way to access the various tables, forms, and reports by simply clicking a button or two. The company also needs to track active accounts for the current week and wants the ability to easily change the way data is summarized and presented.

Instructions: If you are using the Microsoft Office Access 2007 Complete or the Microsoft Office Access 2007 Comprehensive text, open the Ada Beauty Supply database that you used in Chapter 5. Otherwise, see the inside back cover of this book for instructions on downloading the Data Files for Students, or contact your instructor for more information about accessing the required files. Submit the revised database in the format specified by your instructor.

Instructions Part 1:   Create a macro group that includes macros to open the Customer and Sales Rep tables, to open the Customer Financial Form and the Sales Rep Master, and to view and print the Customer Status Report and the Customers by Sales Rep report. Create a switchboard that uses these macros.

Instructions Part 2:   The management of Ada Beauty Supply want to maintain data on a weekly basis on the open orders for its customers. These are orders that have not yet been delivered. To track this information requires a new table, an Open Orders table. Create this table using the structure shown in Figure 6–80. Import the Open Orders.txt file into the Open Orders table. Then, update the relationship between the Customer table and the Open Orders table.

Field Name	Data Type	Primary Key?
Order Number	Text	Yes
Amount	Currency	
Customer Number	Text	

Figure 6–80

Continued >

In the Lab *continued*

Instructions Part 3:   The management wants to actively track the expected commissions on open orders by sales rep and customer. Create a query that includes the Sales Rep, Open Orders, and Customer tables. Include the sales rep number, customer number, and commission in the design grid. Add a calculated field that calculates the expected commission on the open orders amount, and then create the PivotTable shown in Figure 6–81.

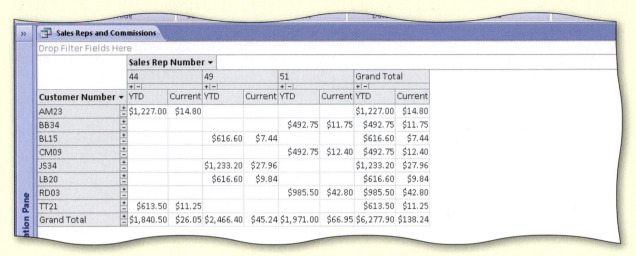

Customer Number ▾	YTD	Current	YTD	Current	YTD	Current	YTD	Current
	44		**49**		**51**		**Grand Total**	
AM23	$1,227.00	$14.80					$1,227.00	$14.80
BB34					$492.75	$11.75	$492.75	$11.75
BL15			$616.60	$7.44			$616.60	$7.44
CM09					$492.75	$12.40	$492.75	$12.40
JS34			$1,233.20	$27.96			$1,233.20	$27.96
LB20			$616.60	$9.84			$616.60	$9.84
RD03					$985.50	$42.80	$985.50	$42.80
TT21	$613.50	$11.25					$613.50	$11.25
Grand Total	$1,840.50	$26.05	$2,466.40	$45.24	$1,971.00	$66.95	$6,277.90	$138.24

Figure 6–81

Cases and Places

Apply your creative thinking and problem solving skills to design and implement a solution.

• EASIER   •• MORE DIFFICULT

• 1: Creating Macros and a Switchboard for the Second Hand Goods Database

If you are using the Microsoft Office Access 2007 Complete or the Microsoft Office Access 2007 Comprehensive text, open the Second Hand Goods database that you used in Chapter 5. Otherwise, see the inside back cover of this book for instructions on downloading the Data Files for Students, or contact your instructor for more information about accessing the required files. Create a macro group named SHG Macros. The macro group should include macros to open the two tables (Item and Seller), open the two forms (Item Update Form and Seller Master Form), and preview and print the Items by Seller report. For the two open-table macros, select Edit as the Data Mode and do not display a message box. Create the switchboard shown in Figure 6–82a that uses the macros in the macro group. The Forms and Tables switchboard pages are similar in design to the View Form and View Table pages in the chapter. The Reports page is shown in Figure 6–82b. Submit the revised database in the format specified by your instructor.

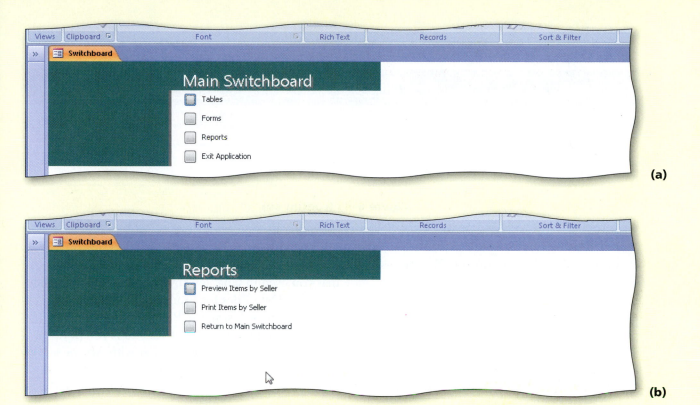

(a)

(b)

Figure 6–82

• 2: Adding Tables, Creating Macros, and a Switchboard for the BeachCondo Rentals Database

If you are using the Microsoft Office Access 2007 Complete or the Microsoft Office Access 2007 Comprehensive text, open the BeachCondo Rentals database that you used in Chapter 5. Otherwise, see the inside back cover of this book for instructions on downloading the Data Files for Students, or contact your instructor for more information about accessing the required files. Create a macro group named BCR Macro Group. The macro group should include macros to open the two tables (Condo Unit and Owner), open the two forms (Condo Unit Form and Owner Master Form) and preview and print the two reports (Available Rentals Report and Condos by Bedroom). Create a switchboard that uses the macros in the macro group. The switchboard should be similar in design to the one created in this chapter. The rental company must keep track of the units that are rented and the individuals who rent the units. Units are rented a week at a time and rentals start on Saturday. The structure of the tables that should contain this data, the Current Rentals and Renter tables, is shown in Figure 6–83a and Figure 6-83b. The data for the two tables is in separate worksheets in the data file, Rentals.xlsx. Create the Current Rentals table in Table Design view. Create the Renter table in Datasheet view. The data type for Renter Number is Text and it is the primary key for the Renter table. Then, import the data from the workbook. Finally, create the necessary relationships. There is a one-to-many relationship between the Renter and the Current Rentals table and a one-to-many relationship between the Condo Unit table and the Current Rentals table. Submit the revised database in the format specified by your instructor.

Field Name	Data Type	Primary Key?
Unit Number	Text	Yes
Start Date	Date/Time	Yes
Length	Number	
Renter Number	Text	

(a)
Structure of Current Rentals Table

Figure 6–83

Continued >

Cases and Places continued

Field Name	Data Type	Primary Key?
Renter Number	Text	Yes
First Name	Text	
Last Name	Text	
Telephone Number	Text	

(b) Structure of Renter Table

Figure 6–83 (continued)

••3: Creating Macros and a Switchboard for the Restaurant Database

If you are using the Microsoft Office Access 2007 Complete or the Microsoft Office Access 2007 Comprehensive text, open the restaurant database that you used in Chapter 5. Otherwise, see the inside back cover of this book for instructions on downloading the Data Files for Students, or contact your instructor for more information about accessing the required files. Using the Plan Ahead guidelines presented in this chapter, determine what macros you need to add to your database and if you need a switchboard. Because your database will be used by others who may not be familiar with Access, a switchboard probably would be beneficial. Determine what pages and what actions your switchboard should perform. Create the necessary macros and the switchboard. Submit the revised database in the format specified by your instructor.

••4: Enhancing Your Contacts Database

Make It Personal

If you are using the Microsoft Office Access 2007 Complete or the Microsoft Office Access 2007 Comprehensive text, open the contacts database that you used in Chapter 5. Otherwise, see the inside back cover of this book for instructions on downloading the Data Files for Students, or contact your instructor for more information about accessing the required files. Review the way in which you have used the Contacts database. Are there certain forms, reports, or queries that you open regularly? If so, consider creating a macro to automate these tasks. Review the companies in your database. Have you contacted different individuals at the same company? Are you interested in more than one position at the same company? If the answer is yes, consider creating additional tables similar to the Seminar Offerings table in this chapter. Modify the database and create any necessary forms. Submit the revised database in the format specified by your instructor.

••5: Understanding PivotTables and PivotCharts

Working Together

As a team, research the differences between a crosstab query and a PivotTable. Copy the JMS TechWizards database and rename the database to your team name. For example, if your team is TeamTogether, then name the database TeamTogether TechWizards. Modify the City-Technician crosstab query. What type of modifications are possible to a crosstab query? How difficult is it to make the changes? Create a PivotTable and a PivotChart from the same data. Create a PivotTable form. Discuss when a crosstab is appropriate and when a PivotTable is appropriate and use Microsoft Word to write a short paper that explains the differences. Why would you use a PivotTable form? Submit the Word document and the revised database in the format specified by your instructor.

SQL Feature
Using SQL

Objectives

You will have mastered the material in this project when you can:

- Change the font or font size for SQL queries

- Include fields and criteria in SQL queries

- Use computed fields and built-in functions in SQL queries

- Sort the results in SQL queries

- Use multiple functions in the same command

- Group the results in SQL queries

- Join tables in SQL queries

- Use subqueries

- Compare SQL queries with Access-generated SQL

- Use INSERT, UPDATE, and DELETE queries to update a database

SQL Feature Introduction

The language called **SQL (Structured Query Language)** is a very important language for querying and updating databases. It is the closest thing to a universal database language, because the vast majority of database management systems, including Access, use it in some fashion. Although some users will be able to do all their queries through the query features of Access instead of SQL, those in charge of administering and maintaining the database system certainly should be familiar with this important language. Access also can be used as an interface to other database management systems, such as SQL Server. To use or interface with SQL Server requires knowledge of SQL.

Project — Using SQL

JSP Recruiters administration realizes that there is a database language for queries that seems to be universal. The language, which is called SQL and is supported by virtually every DBMS, is an extremely powerful tool for querying a database. The administration wants staff at JSP to learn to use this language to broaden their capabilities in accessing JSP Recruiters data. In the process, they would like to create a wide variety of SQL queries. Similar to creating queries in Design view, SQL provides users a way of querying relational databases. In SQL, however, instead of making entries in the design grid, the user must type commands to obtain the desired results, as shown in Figure 1a. You then can click the View button to view the results just as when you are creating queries in Design view. The results for the query in Figure 1a are shown in Figure 1b.

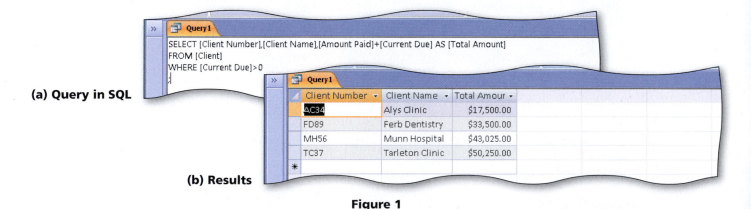

(a) Query in SQL

(b) Results

Figure 1

Overview

As you read through this feature, you will learn how to create SQL queries by performing these general tasks:

- Create queries involving criteria.
- Sort the results of a query.
- Group records in a query and perform group calculations.
- Join tables in queries.
- Create a query that involves a subquery.
- Update data using the INSERT, UPDATE, and DELETE commands.

**Plan
Ahead**

SQL Query Guidelines

1. **Select the fields for the query.** Examine the requirements for the query you are constructing to determine which fields are to be included.

2. **Determine which table or tables contain these fields.** For each field, determine the table in which it is located.

3. **Determine criteria.** Determine any criteria data you must satisfy to be included in the results. If there are more than two tables in the query, determine the criteria to be used to ensure the data matches correctly.

4. **Determine sort order.** Is the data to be sorted in some way? If so, by what field or fields is it to be sorted?

5. **Determine grouping.** Is the data to be grouped in some way? If so, by what field is it to be grouped? Are there any calculations to be made for the group?

6. **Determine any update operations to be performed.** Determine if rows need to be inserted, changed, or deleted. Determine the tables involved.

When necessary, more specific details concerning the above decisions and/or actions are presented at appropriate points in the feature. The feature also will identify the use of these guidelines in creating SQL queries such as the one shown in Figure 1.

Starting Access

If you are using a computer to step through the project in this feature and you want your screen to match the figures in this book, you should change your screen's resolution to 1024 × 768. For information about how to change a computer's resolution, read Appendix E.

To Start Access

The following steps, which assume Windows Vista is running, start Access.

Note: If you are using Windows XP, see Appendix F for alternate steps.

1 Click the Start button on the Windows Vista taskbar to display the Start menu.

2 Click All Programs at the bottom of the left pane on the Start menu to display the All Programs list and then click Microsoft Office in the All Programs list to display the Microsoft Office list.

3 Click Microsoft Office Access 2007 in the Microsoft Office list to start Access and display the Getting Started with Microsoft Office Access window.

4 If the Access window is not maximized, click the Maximize button on its title bar to maximize the window.

To Open a Database

In Chapter 1, you created your database on a USB flash drive using the file name, JSP Recruiters. There are two ways to open the file containing your database. If the file you created appears in the Recent Documents list, you could click it to open the file. If not, you can use the More button to open the file. The following steps use the More button to open the JSP Recruiters database from the USB flash drive.

Note: If you are using Windows XP, see Appendix F for alternate steps.

1 With your USB flash drive connected to one of the computer's USB ports, click the More button to display the Open dialog box.

2 If the Folders list is displayed below the Folders button, click the Folders button to remove the Folders list.

3 If necessary, click Computer in the Favorite Links section and then double-click UDISK 2.0 (E:) to select the USB flash drive, Drive E in this case, as the new open location. (Your drive letter might be different.)

4 Click JSP Recruiters to select the file name.

5 Click the Open button to open the database.

6 If a Security Warning appears, click the Options button to display the Microsoft Office Security Options dialog box.

7 With the option button to enable the content selected, click the OK button to enable the content.

SQL Background

Datasheet Font Size
You also can use the Access Options button to change the default font and font size for datasheets. To do so, click Datasheet in the Access Options dialog box and make the desired changes in the default font area.

SQL was developed under the name SEQUEL at the IBM San Jose research facilities as the data manipulation language for IBM's prototype relational model DBMS, System R, in the mid-1970s. In 1980, it was renamed SQL to avoid confusion with an unrelated hardware product called SEQUEL. It is used as the data manipulation language for IBM's current production offerings in the relational DBMS arena — SQL/DS and DB2. Most relational DBMSs, including Microsoft Access and Microsoft SQL Server, use a version of SQL as a data manipulation language.

Some people pronounce SQL by pronouncing the three letters, that is, "ess-que-ell." It is very common, however to pronounce it as the name under which it was developed originally, that is, "sequel." This text assumes you are pronouncing it as the word, sequel. That is why you will see the article, a, used before SQL. If it were pronounced ess-que-ell, you would use the article, an, before SQL. For example, this text will refer to "a SQL query" rather than "an SQL query."

To Change the Font Size

You can change the font and/or the font size for SQL queries using the Access Options button on the Office menu and then Object Designers in the list of options. There usually is not a compelling reason to change the font, unless there is a strong preference for some other font. It often is worthwhile to change the font size, however. With the default size of 8, the queries can be hard to read. Increasing the font size to 10 can make a big difference. The following steps change the font size for SQL queries to 10.

1

• Click the Office Button to display the Office Button menu, and then click Access Options to display the Access Options dialog box.

• Click Object Designers to display the Object Designers options.

• In the Query design area, Click the Size box arrow, and then click 10 in the list that appears to change the size to 10 (Figure 2).

2

• Click the OK button to close the Access Options dialog box.

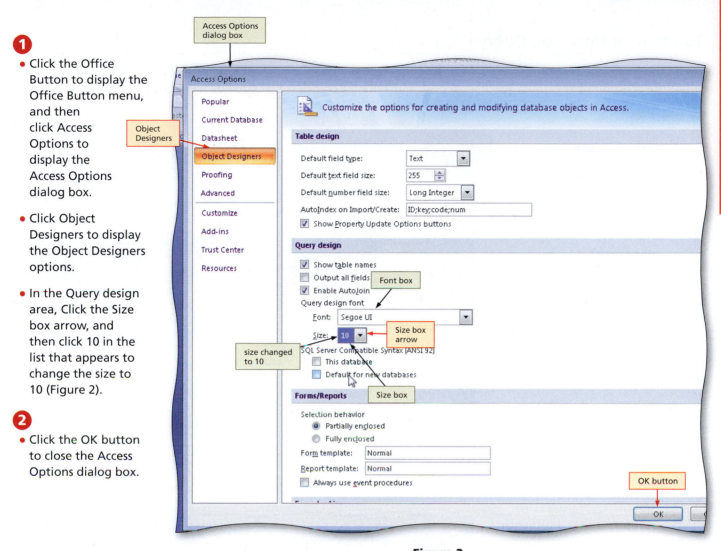

Figure 2

SQL Queries

When you query a database using SQL, you type commands in a blank window rather than filling in the design grid. When the command is complete, you can view your results just as you do with queries you create using the design grid.

To Create a New SQL Query

You begin the creation of a new **SQL query**, which is a query expressed using the SQL language, just as you begin the creation of any other query in Access. The only difference is that you will use SQL view instead of Design view. The following steps create a new SQL query.

1

• Hide the Navigation Pane.

• Click Create on the Ribbon to display the Create tab.

• Click the Query Design button on the Create tab to create a query.

• Close the Show Table dialog box without adding any tables.

• Click the View button arrow to display the View menu (Figure 3).

Q&A Why did the icon on the View button change to SQL and why are there only two items on the menu instead of the usual five?

Without any tables selected, you cannot view any results, nor can you view a PivotTable or PivotChart. You only can use the normal Design view or SQL view.

Figure 3

2

• Click SQL View to view the query in SQL view (Figure 4).

Q&A What happened to the design grid?

In SQL view, you specify the query by typing a SQL command rather than making entries in the design grid.

Figure 4

SQL Commands

The basic form of SQL expressions is quite simple: SELECT-FROM-WHERE. The command begins with a **SELECT clause**, which consists of the word, SELECT, followed by a list of those fields you want to include. The fields will appear in the results in the order in which they are listed in the expression. Next there is a **FROM clause**, which consists of the word, FROM, followed by a list of the table or tables involved in the query. Finally, there is an optional **WHERE clause**, which consists of the word, WHERE, followed by any criteria that the data you want to retrieve must satisfy. The command ends with a semicolon (;), which in this text will appear on a separate line.

SQL has no special format rules for placement of terms, capitalization, and so on. In this text, you place the word FROM on a new line, then place the word WHERE, when it is used, on the next line. This makes the commands easier to read. This text also shows words that are part of the SQL language in uppercase and others in a combination of uppercase and lowercase. Because it is a common convention, and necessary in some versions of SQL, place a semicolon (;) at the end of each command.

Unlike some other versions of SQL, Microsoft Access allows spaces within field names and table names. There is a restriction, however, to the way such names are used in SQL queries. When a name containing a space appears in SQL, it must be enclosed in square brackets. For example, Client Number must appear as [Client Number] because the name includes a space. On the other hand, City does not need to be enclosed in square brackets because its name does not include a space. For consistency, all names in this text are enclosed in square brackets. Thus, the City field would appear as [City] even though the brackets technically are not required by SQL.

To Include Only Certain Fields

To include only certain fields, list them after the word SELECT. If you want to list all rows in the table, you do not need to include the word WHERE. The following steps list the number, name, amount paid, and current due amount of all clients.

1

- Type `SELECT [Client Number],[Client Name],[Amount Paid],[Current Due]` as the first line of the command, and then press the ENTER key.

- Type `FROM [Client]` as the second line, press the ENTER key and then type a semicolon (;) on the third line.

- Click the View button to view the results (Figure 5).

Q&A
My screen displays a dialog box that asks me to enter a parameter value. What did I do wrong?

You typed a field name incorrectly. Click Cancel to close the dialog box and then correct your SQL statement.

(a) Query

(b) Results

Figure 5

To Prepare to Enter a New SQL Query

To enter a new SQL query, you could close the window, click the No button when asked if you want to save your changes, and then begin the process from scratch. A quicker alternative is to use the View menu and then select SQL View. You then will be returned to SQL view with the current command appearing. At that point, you could erase the current command and then enter a new one. (If the next command is similar to the previous one, it may be simpler to modify the current command instead of erasing it and starting over.) The following steps show how to prepare to enter a new SQL query.

1

• Click the View button arrow to display the View button menu (Figure 6).

2

• Click SQL View to return to SQL view.

Q&A Could I just click the View button or do I have to click the arrow?

Because the icon on the button is not the icon for SQL view, you must click the arrow.

Q&A Can I save the query if I want to use it again?

You certainly can. Click the Save button on the Quick Access Toolbar and assign a name in the Save As dialog box.

Figure 6

To Include All Fields

To include all fields, you could use the same approach as in the previous steps, that is, list each field in the Client table after the word SELECT. There is a shortcut, however. Instead of listing all the field names after SELECT, you can use the asterisk (*) symbol. This indicates that you want all fields listed in the order in which you described them to the system during data definition. The following steps list all fields and all records in the Client table.

1

- Delete the current command, type `SELECT *` as the first line of the command, and then press the ENTER key.

- Type `FROM [Client]` as the second line, press the ENTER key, and type a semicolon on the third line.

- Click the View button to view the results (Figure 7).

Q&A

Can I use copy and paste commands when I enter SQL commands?

Yes, you can use copy and paste as well as other editing techniques, such as replacing text.

(a) Query

(b) Results

Figure 7

Determine criteria.

Plan Ahead

1. **Determine the fields involved in the criteria.** For any criterion, determine the fields that are included in the criterion. Determine the data types for these fields. If the criterion uses a value that corresponds to a Text field, be sure to enclose the value in single quotation marks.

2. **Determine comparison operators.** When fields are being compared to other fields or to specific values, determine the appropriate comparison operator (equals, less than, greater than, and so on). If a wildcard is involved, then the query will use the LIKE operator.

3. **Determine join criteria.** If tables are being joined, determine the fields that must match.

4. **Determine compound criteria.** If more than one criterion is involved, determine whether all individual criteria are to be true, in which case you will use the AND operator, or whether only one individual criterion needs to be true, in which case you will use the OR operator.

To Use a Criterion Involving a Numeric Field

To restrict the records to be displayed, include the word WHERE followed by a criterion as part of the command. If the field involved is a numeric field, you simply type the value. The following steps list the client number and name of all clients whose current due amount is 0.

- Click the View button arrow, click SQL View to return to SQL view, and then delete the current command.

- Type SELECT [Client Number],[Client Name] as the first line of the command.

- Type FROM [Client] as the second line.

- Type WHERE [Current Due]=0 as the third line and then type a semicolon on the fourth line.

- Click the View button to view the results (Figure 8).

 Experiment

- Try the other comparison operators. In each case, view the results to see the effect of your choice.

Q&A

On my screen, the clients are listed in a different order. Did I do something wrong?

No. The order in which records appear in a query result is random unless you specifically order the records. You will see how to order records later in this feature.

(a) Query

(b) Results

Figure 8

Simple Criteria

The criterion following the word WHERE in the preceding query is called a simple criterion. A **simple criterion** has the form: field name, comparison operator, then either another field name or a value. The possible comparison operators are shown in Table 1. Note that there are two different versions for "not equal to" (<> and !=). You must use the one that is right for your particular implementation of SQL. If you use the wrong one, your system will let you know instantly. Simply use the other.

Table 1 Comparison Operators

Comparison Operator	Meaning
=	Equal to
<	Less than
>	Greater than
<=	Less than or equal to
>=	Greater than or equal to
<> or !=	Not equal to

To Use a Criterion Involving a Text Field

If the criterion involves a text field, the value must be enclosed in single quotation marks. The following example lists all clients located in Berls, that is, all clients for whom the value in the City field is Berls.

- Return to SQL view, delete the previous query, and type SELECT [Client Number],[Client Name] as the first line of the command.

- Type FROM [Client] as the second line.

- Type WHERE [City]='Berls' as the third line and type a semicolon on the fourth line.

- Click the View button to view the results (Figure 9).

(a) Query

(b) Results

Figure 9

BTW

BETWEEN Operator
The BETWEEN operator allows you to search for a range of values in one field. For example, to find all clients whose amount paid amount is between $20,000 and $30,000, the WHERE clause would be WHERE Amount Paid BETWEEN 20000 AND 30000.

Compound Criteria

The criteria you have seen so far are called simple criteria. The next examples require compound criteria. **Compound criteria** are formed by connecting two or more simple criteria using AND, OR, and NOT. When simple criteria are connected by the word AND, all the simple criteria must be true in order for the compound criterion to be true. When simple criteria are connected by the word OR, the compound criterion will be true whenever any of the simple criteria are true. Preceding a criterion by NOT reverses the truth or falsity of the original criterion. That is, if the original criterion is true, the new criterion will be false; if the original criterion is false, the new one will be true.

To Use a Compound Criterion

The following steps use a compound criterion to display the names of those clients located in Tarleton and for whom the current due amount is 0.

• Return to SQL view, delete the previous query, and type SELECT [Client Number],[Client Name] as the first line of the command.

• Type FROM [Client] as the second line.

• Type WHERE [City]='Tarleton' as the third line.

• Type AND [Current Due]=0 as the fourth line and type a semicolon on the fifth line.

• Click the View button to view the results (Figure 10).

Q&A

How do I form compound criteria that involve OR?

You use the same method to form compound criteria involving OR. Simply use the word OR instead of the word AND. In that case, the results would contain those records that satisfied either criterion or both.

(a) Query

(b) Results

Figure 10

To Use NOT in a Criterion

To use the word NOT in a criterion, precede the criterion with the word NOT. The following steps list the numbers and names of the clients not located in Tarleton.

 1

- Return to SQL view and delete the previous query.

- Type `SELECT [Client Number],[Client Name]` as the first line of the command.

- Type `FROM [Client]` as the second line.

- Type `WHERE NOT [City]= 'Tarleton'` as the third line and type a semicolon on the fourth line.

- View the results (Figure 11).

(a) Query

(b) Results

Figure 11

To Use a Computed Field

Just as with queries created in Design view, you can include fields in queries that are not in the database, but that can be computed from fields that are. Such a field is called a **computed** or **calculated field**. Such computations can involve addition (+), subtraction (−), multiplication (*), or division (/). The query in the following step computes the total amount, which is equal to the amount paid amount plus the current due amount.

To indicate the contents of the new field (the computed field), you must name the field by following the computation with the word AS and then the name you wish to assign the field. The name, also called an alias, becomes the column name when the query is run. The following step assigns the name Total Amount to the computed field. The step also lists the Client Number and Name for all clients for which the current due amount is greater than 0.

- Return to SQL view and delete the previous query.

- Type `SELECT [Client Number], [Client Name],[Amount Paid] +[Current Due] AS [Total Amount]` as the first line of the command.

- Type `FROM [Client]` as the second line.

- Type `WHERE [Current Due]>0` as the third line and type a semicolon on the fourth line.

- View the results (Figure 12).

(a) Query

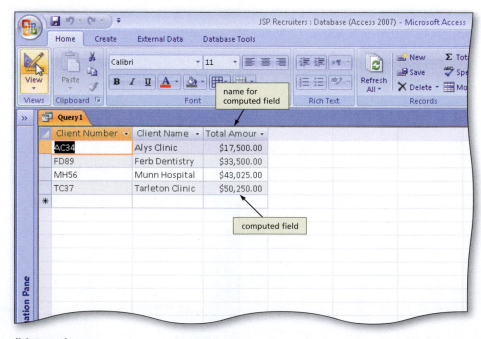

(b) Results

Figure 12

Sorting

The field on which data is to be sorted is called a **sort key**, or simply a **key**. If the data is to be sorted on two fields, the more important key is called the **major sort key** (also referred to as the **primary sort key**) and the less important key is called the **minor sort key** (also referred to as the **secondary sort key**). By following a sort key with the word DESC with no comma in between, you can specify descending sort order. If you do not specify DESC, the data will be sorted in ascending order.

To sort the output, you include an **ORDER BY clause**, which consists of the words ORDER BY followed by the sort key. If there are two sort keys, the major sort key is listed first. In queries that you construct in Design view, the more major sort key must be to the left of the minor sort key in the list of fields to be included. In SQL, there is no such restriction. The fields to be included in the query are in the SELECT clause and the fields to be used for sorting are in the ORDER BY clause. The two clauses are totally independent.

BTW

Union, Pass-Through, and Data Definition Queries
There are three queries that cannot be created in Design view. When you click the button for any of these three queries in Design view, the SQL view window opens. The Union query combines fields from more than one table into one query result set. The Pass-through query enables you to send SQL commands directly to ODBC (Open Database Connectivity) databases using the ODBC database's SQL syntax. The Data Definition query allows you to create or alter database tables or create indexes in Access directly.

Plan Ahead

Determine sort order.

1. **Determine whether data is to be sorted.** Examine the requirements for the query looking for words like "sorted by," "ordered by," "arranged by," and so on.

2. **Determine sort keys.** Look for the fields that follow "sorted by," "ordered by," or any other words that signify sorting. If the requirements for the query included "ordered by client name," then Client Name is a sort key.

3. **If there is more than one sort key, determine which one will be the major sort key and which will be the minor sort key.** Look for words that indicate which field is more important. For example, if the requirements indicate that the results are to be "ordered by amount paid within recruiter number," then Recruiter Number is the more important sort key.

To Sort the Results

The following step lists the client number, name, amount paid amount, current due amount, and recruiter number for all clients. The data is to be sorted by amount paid within recruiter number. That is, within the clients having the same recruiter number, the data is to be sorted further by amount paid amount. This means that the Recruiter Number field is the major (primary) sort key and the Amount Paid field is the minor (secondary) sort key.

1

- Return to SQL view and delete the previous query.

- Type `SELECT [Client Number], [Client Name],[Amount Paid],[Current Due], [Recruiter Number]` as the first line of the command.

- Type `FROM [Client]` as the second line.

- Type `ORDER BY [Recruiter Number],[Amount Paid]` as the third line and type a semicolon on the fourth line.

- View the results (Figure 13).

 Experiment

- Try reversing the order of the sort keys to see the effect. Also try to specify descending order for one or both of the sort keys. In each case, view the results to see the effect of your choice.

(a) Query

(b) Results

Figure 13

To Use a Built-In Function

SQL has **built-in** functions (also called **aggregate** functions) to calculate the number of entries, the sum or average of all the entries in a given column, and the largest or smallest of the entries in a given column. In SQL, these functions are called COUNT, SUM, AVG, MAX, and MIN, respectively.

The following step counts the number of clients assigned to recruiter number 21 by using the COUNT function with an asterisk (*).

1

- Return to SQL view and delete the previous query.

- Type SELECT COUNT(*) as the first line of the command.

- Type FROM [Client] as the second line.

- Type WHERE [Recruiter Number]='21' as the third line and type a semicolon on the fourth line.

(a) Query

- View the results (Figure 14).

Why does Expr1000 appear in the column heading of the results?

Because the column is a computed column, it does not have a name. Access assigns a generic expression name. You can add a name for the column by including the AS clause in the query; it is good practice to do so.

(b) Results

Figure 14

To Use Multiple Functions in the Same Command

The only differences between COUNT and SUM, other than the obvious fact that they are computing different statistics, are that first, in the case of SUM, you must specify the field for which you want a total, instead of an asterisk (*) and second, the field must be numeric. You could not calculate a sum of names or addresses, for example. The following step uses both the COUNT and SUM functions to count the number of clients and calculate the SUM (total) of their Amount Paid amounts.

- Return to SQL view and delete the previous query.

- Type SELECT COUNT(*), SUM([Amount Paid]) as the first line of the command.

- Type FROM [Client] as the second line and type a semicolon on the third line.

- View the results (Figure 15).

(a) Query

Experiment

- Try using the other functions in place of SUM. In each case, view the results to see the effect of your choice.

(b) Results

Figure 15

The use of AVG, MAX, and MIN is similar to SUM. The only difference is that a different statistic is calculated.

Grouping

Grouping means creating groups of records that share some common characteristic. In grouping clients by recruiter number, for example, the clients of recruiter 21 would form one group, the clients of recruiter 24 would be a second, and the clients of recruiter 27 would form a third.

Plan Ahead

Determine grouping.

1. **Determine whether data is to be grouped in some fashion.** Examine the requirements for the query to see if they contain individual rows or information about groups of rows.

2. **Determine the field or fields on which grouping is to take place.** By which field is the data to be grouped? Look to see if the requirements indicate a field along with several group calculations.

3. **Determine which fields or calculations are appropriate to display.** When rows are grouped, one line of output is produced for each group. The only things that may appear are statistics calculated for the group or fields whose values are the same for all rows in a group. For example, it would make sense to display the recruiter number, because all the clients in the group have the same recruiter number. It would not make sense to display the client number, because the client number will vary from one row in a group to another. (SQL could not determine which client number to display for the group.)

To Use Grouping

The following step calculates the totals of the Amount Paid fields, called Total Paid, and the Current Due fields, called Total Due, for the clients of each recruiter. To calculate the totals, the command will include the SUM([Amount Paid]) and SUM([Current Due]). To get totals for the clients of each recruiter the command also will include a **GROUP BY clause**, which consists of the words, GROUP BY, followed by the field used for grouping, in this case, Recruiter Number.

Including GROUP BY Recruiter Number will cause the clients for each recruiter to be grouped together; that is, all clients with the same recruiter number will form a group. Any statistics, such as totals, appearing after the word SELECT will be calculated for each of these groups. It is important to note that using GROUP BY does not imply that the information will be sorted.

The step also renames the total amount paid as Total Paid and the total current due as Total Due by including appropriate AS clauses.

1

- Return to SQL view and delete the previous query.

- Type `SELECT [Recruiter Number],SUM([Amount Paid]) AS [Total Paid],SUM([Current Due]) AS [Total Due]` as the first line of the command.

- Type `FROM [Client]` as the second line.

- Type `GROUP BY [Recruiter Number]` as the third line.

- Type `ORDER BY [Recruiter Number]` as the fourth line and type a semicolon on the fifth line.

- View the results (Figure 16).

(a) Query

(b) Results

Figure 16

Grouping Requirements

When rows are grouped, one line of output is produced for each group. The only things that may appear are statistics calculated for the group or fields whose values are the same for all rows in a group. For example, it would make sense to display the recruiter number, because all the clients in the group have the same recruiter number. It would not make sense to display the client number, because the client number will vary from one row in a group to another. (SQL could not determine which client number to display for the group.)

To Restrict the Groups that Appear

In some cases you only want to display certain groups. For example, you may want to display only those recruiters for whom the sum of the Current Due amounts are greater than $3,000. This restriction does not apply to individual rows, but instead to groups. Because WHERE applies only to rows, it is not appropriate to accomplish the kind of restriction you have here. Fortunately, there is a clause that is to groups what WHERE is to rows. The clause is the **HAVING clause**, which consists of the word, HAVING, followed by a criterion. It is used in the following step, which restricts the groups to be included to those on which the sum of the current due is greater than $40,000.00.

- Return to SQL view and delete the previous query.

- Click the beginning of the fourth line (ORDER BY [Recruiter Number]) and press the ENTER key to insert a new blank line.

- Click the beginning of the new blank line, and then type `HAVING SUM([Current Due])>40000` as the new fourth line.

- View the results (Figure 17).

(a) Query

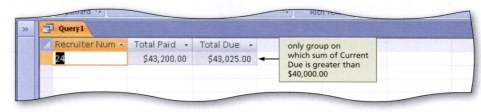

(b) Results

Figure 17

Inner Join
A join that compares the tables in the FROM clause and lists only those rows that satisfy the condition in the WHERE clause is called an inner join. SQL has an INNER JOIN clause. You could replace the FROM and WHERE clauses in the query shown in Figure 18a with FROM Client INNER JOIN Recruiter ON [Client].[Recruiter Number]=[Recruiter].[Recruiter Number] to get the same results as shown in Figure 18b.

Joining Tables

Many queries require data from more than one table. Just as with creating queries in Design view, it is necessary to be able to **join** tables, that is, to find rows in two tables that have identical values in matching fields. In SQL, this is accomplished through appropriate criteria following the word WHERE.

If you wish to list the client number, name, recruiter number, first name of the recruiter, and last name of the recruiter for all clients, you need data from both the Client and Recruiter tables. The Recruiter Number field is in both tables, the Client Number field is only in the Client table, and the First Name and Last Name fields are only in the Recruiter table. You need to access both tables in your SQL query, as follows:

1. In the SELECT clause, you indicate all fields you wish to appear.

2. In the FROM clause, you list all tables involved in the query.

3. In the WHERE clause, you give the criterion that will restrict the data to be retrieved to only those rows included in both of the two tables, that is, to the rows that have common values in matching fields.

Qualifying Fields

There is a problem in indicating the matching fields. The matching fields are both called Recruiter Number. There is a field in the Client table called Recruiter Number, as well as a field in the Recruiter table called Recruiter Number. In this case, if you only enter Recruiter Number, it will not be clear which table you mean. It is necessary to **qualify** Recruiter Number, that is, to specify to which field in which table you are referring. You do this by preceding the name of the field with the name of the table, followed by a period. The Recruiter Number field in the Client table, for example is [Client].[Recruiter Number].

Whenever there is potential ambiguity, you must qualify the fields involved. It is permissible to qualify other fields as well, even if there is no confusion. For example, instead of [Client Name], you could have typed [Client].[Client Name] to indicate the Client Name field in the Client table. Some people prefer to qualify all fields, and this is not a bad approach. In this text, you only will qualify fields when it is necessary to do so.

To Join Tables

The following step lists the client number, name, recruiter number, first name of the recruiter, and last name of the recruiter for all clients.

1

- Return to SQL view and delete the previous query.

- Type `SELECT [Client Number], [Client Name], [Client]. [Recruiter Number], [First Name], [Last Name]` as the first line of the command.

- Type `FROM [Client], [Recruiter]` as the second line.

- Type `WHERE [Client].[Recruiter Number]=[Recruiter]. [Recruiter Number]` as the third line and type a semicolon on the fourth line.

Q&A
What is the purpose of the WHERE clause?

The WHERE clause specifies that only rows on which the recruiter numbers match are to be included. Specifically, the recruiter number in the Client table ([Client].[Recruiter Number]) must be equal to the recruiter number in the Recruiter table ([Recruiter].[Recruiter Number]).

- View the results (Figure 18).

(a) Query

(b) Results

Figure 18

To Restrict the Records in a Join

You can restrict the records to be included in a join by creating a compound criterion. The criterion will include the criterion necessary to join the tables along with a criterion to restrict the records. The criteria will be connected with AND.

The following step lists the client number, client name, recruiter number, first name of the recruiter, and last name of the recruiter for all clients for which the current due amount is greater than 0.

- Return to SQL view and delete the previous query.

- Click immediately prior to the semicolon on the last line.

- Type AND [Current Due] > 0 and press the ENTER key.

- View the results (Figure 19).

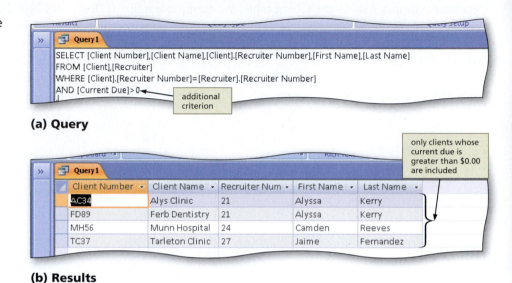

(a) Query

(b) Results

Figure 19

Aliases

When tables appear in the FROM clause, you can give each table an **alias**, or an alternative name, that you can use in the rest of the statement. You create an alias by typing the name of the table, pressing the Spacebar, and then typing the name of the alias. No commas or periods are necessary to separate the two names.

You can use an alias for two basic reasons. The first reason is for simplicity. Figure 20 shows the same query as in Figure 18 on the previous page, but with the Client table assigned the letter, C, as an alias and the Recruiter table assigned the letter, R. Whenever you need to qualify a field name, you can use the alias. Thus, you only need to type R.[Recruiter Number] rather than [Recruiter].[Recruiter Number].

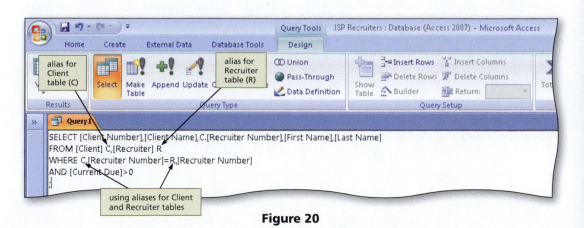

Figure 20

To Join a Table to Itself

The other use of aliases is in joining a table to itself. Joining a table to itself can be useful when you want to compare values in a column to other values in the same column. If you wanted to find the client numbers and names for all clients who are located in the same city and if you had two Client tables in your database, you would simply join the tables looking for rows where the cities were the same. Even though there is only one Client table, however, you actually can treat the Client table as two tables in the query by creating an alias. You would change the FROM clause to:

```
FROM CLIENT F, CLIENT S
```

SQL treats this clause as a query of two tables: one that has the alias F, and another that has the alias S. The fact that both tables are really the single Client table is not a problem. The following step assigns two aliases (F and S) to the Client table and lists the client number and client name of both clients as well as the city in which both are located.

1

- Return to SQL view and delete the previous query.

- Type `SELECT F.[Client Number],F.[Client Name], S.[Client Number],S.[Client Name],F.[City]` as the first line of the command.

- Type `FROM [Client] F, [Client] S` as the second line.

- Type `WHERE F.[City]=S.[City]` as the third line.

- Type `AND F.[Client Number]<S.[Client Number]` as the fourth line and type a semicolon on the fifth line.

- View the results (Figure 21).

Q&A

Why is the criterion F.[Client Number] < S.[Client Number] included in the query?

If you did not include this criterion, the query would contain four times as many results. On the first row in the results, for example, the first client number is AC34 and the second is FD89. Without this criterion there would be a row on which both the first and second client numbers are AC34, a row on which both are FD89, and a row on which the first is FD89 and the second is AC34. This criteria only selects the one row on which the first client number (AC34) is less than the second (FD89).

(a) Query

(b) Results

Figure 21

Subqueries

It is possible to place one query inside another. The inner query is called a **subquery** and it is evaluated first. Then the outer query can use the results of the subquery to find its results.

To Use a Subquery

The following step uses the query shown in Figure 22 as a subquery. This query selects recruiter numbers from those records in the Client table on which the city is Berls. In other words, it selects recruiter numbers for those recruiters who have at least one client located in Berls.

Figure 22

After the subquery is evaluated, the outer query will select the recruiter number, first name, and last name for those recruiters whose recruiter number is in the list produced by the subquery.

- Return to SQL view and delete the previous query.

- Type `SELECT [Recruiter Number],[First Name],[Last Name]` as the first line of the command.

- Type `FROM [Recruiter]` as the second line.

- Type `WHERE [Recruiter Number] IN` as the third line.

- Type `(SELECT [Recruiter Number]` as the fourth line.

- Type `FROM [Client]` as the fifth line.

- Type `WHERE [City]='Berls')` as the sixth line and type a semicolon on the seventh line.

- View the results (Figure 23).

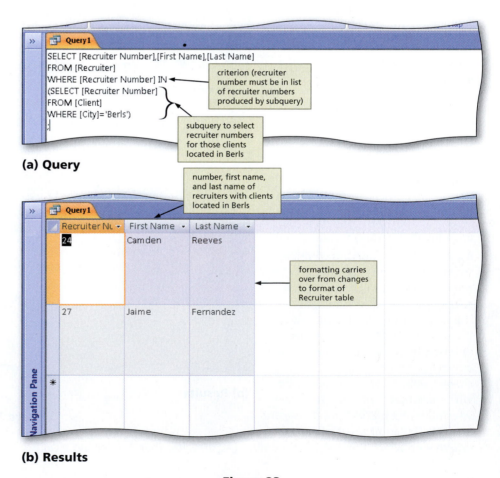

(a) Query

(b) Results

Figure 23

Using an IN Clause

The query in Figure 23 uses an IN clause with a subquery. You also can use an IN clause with a list as an alternative to an OR criterion when the OR criterion involves a single field. For example, to find clients whose city is Berls, Mason, or Tarleton, the criterion using IN would be City IN ('Berls', 'Mason', 'Tarleton'). The corresponding OR criterion would be City='Berls' OR City='Mason' OR City='Tarleton'. The choice of which one to use is a matter of personal preference.

You also can use this type of IN clause when creating queries in Design view. To use the criterion in the previous paragraph for example, include the City field in the design grid and enter the criterion in the Criteria row.

Comparison with Access-Generated SQL

When you create a query in Design view, Access automatically creates a corresponding SQL query that is similar to the queries you have created in this feature. The Access query shown in Figure 24, for example, was created in Design view and includes the Client Number and Client Name. The City field has a criterion (Berls), but the City field will not appear in the results.

BTW

Outer Joins
Sometimes you need to list all the rows from one of the tables in a join, regardless of whether they match any rows in the other table. For example, you can perform a join of the Client and Seminar Offerings table but display all clients — even the ones without seminar offerings. This type of join is called an outer join. In a left outer join, all rows from the table on the left (the table listed first in the query) will be included regardless of whether they match rows from the tables on the right (the table listed second in the query). Rows from the right will be included only if they match. In a right outer join, all rows from the table on the right will be included regardless of whether they match rows from the table on the left. The SQL clause for a left outer join is LEFT JOIN and the SQL clause for a right outer join is RIGHT JOIN.

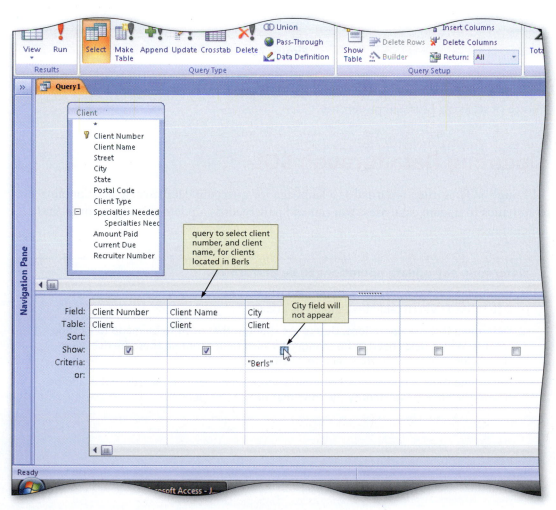

Figure 24

The SQL query that Access generates in correspondence to the Design view query is shown in Figure 25. The query is very similar to the queries you have entered, but there are three slight differences. First, the fields are qualified (Client.[Client Number] and Client.[Client Name]), even though they do not need to be. (Only one table is involved in the query, so no qualification is necessary.) Second, the City field is not enclosed in square brackets. The field legitimately is not enclosed in square brackets because there are no spaces or other special characters in the field name. Finally, there are extra parentheses in the criteria.

Figure 25

Both the style used by Access and the style you have been using are legitimate. The choice of style is a personal preference.

Updating Data through SQL

Although SQL is often regarded as a language for querying databases, it also contains commands to update databases. You can add new records, update existing records, and delete records.

Plan Ahead

> **Determine any update operations to be performed.**
>
> 1. **Determine INSERT operations.** Determine whether new records need to be added. Determine to which table they should be added.
>
> 2. **Determine UPDATE operations.** Determine changes that need to be made to existing records. Which fields need to be changed? Which tables contain these fields? What criteria identify the rows that need to be changed?
>
> 3. **Determine DELETE operations.** Determine which tables contain records that are to be deleted. What criteria identify the rows that need to be deleted?

To Use an INSERT Command

You can add records to a table by using the SQL INSERT command. The command consists of INSERT INTO followed by the name of the table into which the record is to be inserted. Next is the word VALUE followed by the values for the fields in the record. Values for Text fields must be enclosed within quotes. The following steps add a record that JSP Recruiters wants to add to the Seminar Offerings table. The record is for client PR11 and seminar S01 and indicates that the course will be offered for a total of 8 hours, of which 0 hours already have been spent.

 1

- If necessary, return to SQL view and delete the existing query.

- Type INSERT INTO [Seminar Offerings] as the first line of the command.

- Type VALUES as the second line.

- Type ('PR11','S01',8,0) as the third line and type a semicolon on the fourth line (Figure 26).

 2

- Run the query by clicking the Run button.

- When Access displays a message indicating the number of records to be inserted, click the Yes button to insert the records.

Q&A I clicked the View button and didn't get the message. Do I need to click the Run button?

Yes. You are making a change to the database so you must click the Run button or the change will not be made.

Q&A How can I see if the record was actually inserted?

Use a SELECT query to view the records in the Seminar Offerings table.

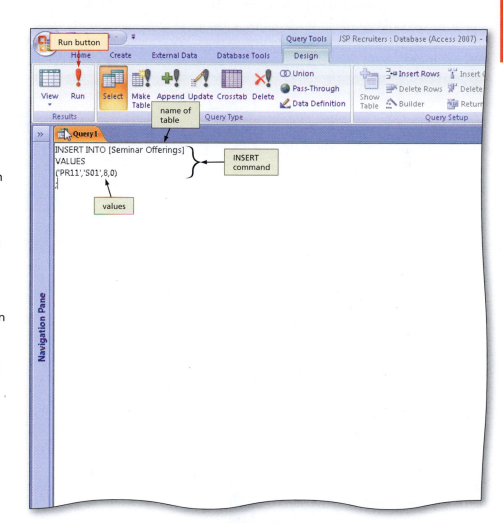

Figure 26

To Use an UPDATE Command

You can update records in SQL by using the UPDATE command. The command consists of UPDATE followed by the name of the table in which records are to be updated. Next, the command contains one or more SET clauses, which consist of the word SET followed by a field to be updated, an equal sign, and the new value. The SET clause indicates the change to be made. Finally, the query includes a WHERE clause. When you execute the command all records in the indicated table that satisfy the criterion will be updated. The following steps use the SQL UPDATE command to perform an update requested by JSP Recruiters. Specifically, they change the Hours Spent to 2 on all records in the Seminar Offerings table on which the client number is PR11 and the seminar number is S01. Because the combination of the Client Number and Seminar Number fields is the primary key, only one record will be updated.

1

- Delete the existing query.

- Type UPDATE [Seminar Offerings] as the first line of the command.

- Type SET [Hours Spent]=2 as the second line.

- Type WHERE [Client Number]= 'PR11' as the third line.

- Type AND [Seminar Number]= 'S01' as the fourth line and type a semicolon on the fifth line (Figure 27).

Q&A Do I need to change a field to a specific value like 2?

You could use an expression. For example, to add $100 to the Current Due amount, the SET clause would be SET [Current Due]=[Current Due]+100.

2

- Run the query by clicking the Run button.

- When Access displays a message indicating the number of records to be updated, click the Yes button to update the records.

Q&A How can I see if the update actually occurred?

Use a SELECT query to view the records in the Seminar Offerings table.

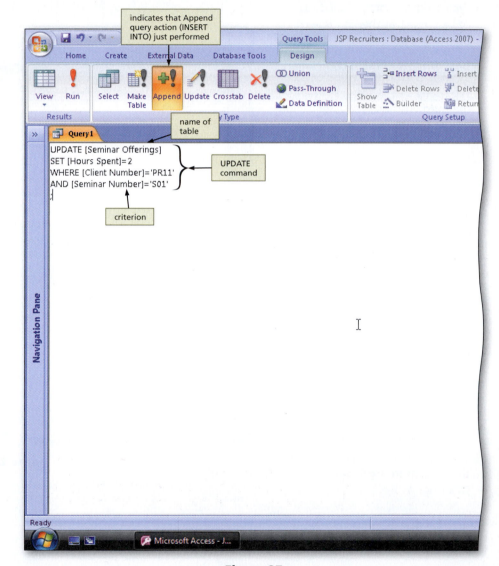

Figure 27

To Use a DELETE Command

You can delete records in SQL by using the DELETE command. The command consists of DELETE FROM followed by the name of the table from which records are to be deleted. Finally, there is a WHERE clause. When you execute the command, all records in the indicated table that satisfy the criterion will be deleted. The following steps use the SQL DELETE command to delete all records in the Seminar Offerings table on which the client number is PR11 and the seminar number is S01, as JSP Recruiters has requested. Because the combination of the Client Number and Seminar Number fields is the primary key, only one record will be deleted.

- Delete the existing query.

- Type DELETE FROM [Seminar Offerings] as the first line of the command.

- Type WHERE [Client Number]= 'PR11' as the second line.

- Type AND [Seminar Number]= 'S01' as the third line and type a semicolon on the fourth line (Figure 28).

- Run the query by clicking the Run button.

- When Access displays a message indicating the number of records to be deleted, click the Yes button to delete the records.

Q&A
How can I see if the deletion actually occurred?

Use a SELECT query to view the records in the Seminar Offerings table.

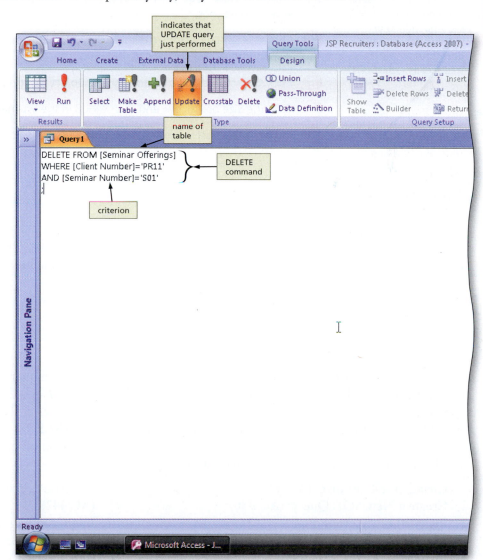

Figure 28

BTW

Certification
The Microsoft Certified Application Specialist (MCAS) program provides an opportunity for you to obtain a valuable industry credential — proof that you have the Access 2007 skills required by employers. For more information, see Appendix G or visit the Access 2007 Certification Web page (scsite.com/ac2007/cert).

BTW

Quick Reference
For a table that lists how to complete the tasks covered in this book using the mouse, Ribbon, shortcut menu, and keyboard, see the Quick Reference Summary at the back of this book, or visit the Access 2007 Quick Reference Web page (scsite.com/ac2007/qr).

Closing the Query and Restoring the Font Size

The following steps close the query and restore the font size to its default setting.

To Close a Query and Restore the Font Size

1 Click the Close 'Query1' button and then click the No button when asked if you want to save the changes.

2 Click the Office Button to display the Office Button menu, and then click Access Options to display the Access Options dialog box.

3 Click Object Designers to display the Object Designers options.

4 Click the Size box arrow, and then click 8 in the list that appears to change the size back to 8.

5 Click the OK button or the Close button for the Access Options dialog box.

To Quit Access

You are ready to quit Access. The following step quits Access.

1 Click the Close button on the right side of the Access title bar to quit Access.

Feature Summary

In this feature you have learned to create SQL queries; include fields in a query; use criteria involving both numeric and text fields as well as use compound criteria; use computed fields, rename the computation; sort the results of a query; use the built-in functions; group records in a query and also restrict the groups that appear in the results; join tables; restrict the records in a join; use subqueries; and use the INSERT, UPDATE, and DELETE commands to update data. Finally, you looked at the SQL query that is generated automatically by Access. The following list includes all the new Access skills you have learned in this feature.

1. Change the Font Size (AC 428)
2. Create a New SQL Query (AC 430)
3. Include Only Certain Fields (AC 431)
4. Prepare to Enter a New SQL Query (AC 432)
5. Include All Fields (AC 432)
6. Use a Criterion Involving a Numeric Field (AC 434)
7. Use a Criterion Involving a Text Field (AC 435)
8. Use a Compound Criterion (AC 436)
9. Use NOT in a Criterion (AC 437)
10. Use a Computed Field (AC 438)
11. Sort the Results (AC 440)
12. Use a Built-In Function (AC 441)
13. Use Multiple Functions in the Same Command (AC 442)
14. Use Grouping (AC 443)
15. Restrict the Groups that Appear (AC 444)
16. Join Tables (AC 445)
17. Restrict the Records in a Join (AC 446)
18. Join a Table to Itself (AC 447)
19. Use a Subquery (AC 448)
20. Use an INSERT Command (AC 451)
21. Use an UPDATE Command (AC 452)
22. Use a DELETE Command (AC 453)
23. Close a Query and Restore the Font Size (AC 454)

In the Lab

Design, create, modify, and/or use a database following the guidelines, concepts, and skills presented in this feature.

Lab 1: Querying the JMS TechWizards Database Using SQL

Problem: The management of JMS TechWizards would like to learn more about SQL and has determined a number of questions it wants SQL to answer. You must obtain the answers to the questions posed by management. Rather than save each query separately, you will copy the SQL query statement to Microsoft Office Word.

Instructions: Start Access. If you are using the Microsoft Office Access 2007 Complete or the Microsoft Office Access 2007 Comprehensive text, open the JMS TechWizards database that you used in Chapter 6. Otherwise, see the inside back cover of this book for instructions on downloading the Data Files for Students, or contact your instructor for more information about accessing the required files.

Perform the following tasks:

1. Open Microsoft Office Word, create a new document, and then type your name at the top. With both Access and Word open on the desktop, create the queries in SQL in Steps 2 through 11 below. For each query, run the query, print the query results (if instructed to do so by your instructor), and copy the SQL command to the Word document. To copy the SQL command, highlight the command and right-click. Click Copy on the shortcut menu. Switch to Word, click the location in the document where the command should appear, right-click, and click Paste on the shortcut menu. Save the document using the file name specified by your instructor.

2. Find all records in the Client table where the billed amount is less than $300.00. Display the client number, name, and technician number in the result.

3. Find all records in the Client table where the billed amount is greater than $350.00 and the city is Anderson. Display all fields in the query result.

4. Find all records in the Client table where the postal code is not 78077. Display the client number, name, and city in the query result.

5. Display the client number, name, technician number, first name, and last name for all clients. Sort the results in ascending order by technician number and client number.

6. Display and print the average billed amount grouped by technician number. Name the average balance as Average Billed.

7. Find the client numbers and names for every pair of clients who are located in the same city.

8. Use a subquery to find all technicians whose clients are located in Kingston. Display the recruiter number, first name, and last name.

9. Add the following record to the Work Orders table.

GR56	4	4	0

10. Update the Hours Spent field to 2 for those records where the Client Number is GR56 and the Category Number is 4.

11. Delete all records where the Client Number is GR56 and the Category Number is 4.

12. Change the document properties for the Word document and save the document using the file name specified by your instructor.

13. Submit in the format specified by your instructor.

In the Lab

Lab 2: Querying the Hockey Fan Zone Database Using SQL

Problem: The management of Hockey Fan Zone would like to learn more about SQL and has determined a number of questions it wants SQL to answer. You must obtain the answers to the questions posed by management.

Instructions: Start Access. If you are using the Microsoft Office Access 2007 Complete or the Microsoft Office Access 2007 Comprehensive text, open the JMS TechWizards database that you used in Chapter 6. Otherwise, see the inside back cover of this book for instructions on downloading the Data Files for Students, or contact your instructor for more information about accessing the required files.

Perform the following tasks:

1. Open Microsoft Office Word, create a new document, and then type your name at the top. With both Access and Word open on the desktop, create the queries in SQL in Steps 2 through 9 below. For each query, run the query, print the query results (if instructed to do so by your instructor), and copy the SQL command to the Word document. To copy the SQL command, highlight the command and right-click. Click Copy on the shortcut menu. Switch to Word, click the location in the document where the command should appear, right-click, and click Paste on the shortcut menu. Save the document using the file name specified by your instructor.

2. Find all records in the Item table where the difference between the cost of the item and the selling price of the item is greater than $4.00. Display the item number, description, cost, and selling price in the query result.

3. Display the item number, description, and total cost (cost * on hand) for all items. Name the computed field Total Cost.

4. Find all items where the description begins with the letter B. Include the item number and description in the query result.

5. Display the supplier name, item number, description, and cost for all items where the number on hand is less than 10. Sort the results in ascending order by supplier name and description.

6. Find the average cost by supplier.

7. Restrict records retrieved in step 6 to only those suppliers where the average cost is less than $20.00.

8. Find the total number of reordered items for each item in the Reorder table. Name the computed field Total Ordered.

9. Use the IN operator to find all items that are clothing or cap type. Display the item number, description, cost, and supplier code in the result. Sort the results by supplier code and item number.

10. Change the document properties for the Word document and save the document using the file name specified by your instructor.

11. Submit in the format specified by your instructor.

7 | Advanced Report Techniques

Objectives

You will have mastered the material in this project when you can:

- Change a caption
- Create queries for reports
- Create reports in Design view
- Add fields and text boxes to a report
- Format controls
- Group and ungroup controls

- Update multiple controls
- Add and modify a subreport
- Modify section properties
- Add a title, page number, and date
- Add totals and subtotals
- Create and print mailing labels

7 | Advanced Report Techniques

Introduction

In this chapter, you will create two reports in Design view. Both reports feature grouping and sorting. The first report contains a subreport, which is a report that is contained in another report. The subreport contains data from a query that is related to data in the main report. The second report uses aggregate functions to calculate subtotals and grand totals. It also uses a function to calculate a value where the calculation will vary from record to record depending on whether a given criterion is true. Finally, the steps in the chapter produce mailing labels.

Project — Advanced Report Techniques

The management at JSP Recruiters wants a master list of recruiters. This list should be available as an Access report. For each recruiter, the report is to include full details for all the clients assigned to the recruiter. In addition, for each of these clients for whom seminars currently are scheduled, the report should list the specific seminars being offered to the client. The actual report is shown in Figure 7–1a. The report is organized by recruiter. For each recruiter, the report lists the number, first name, and last name. Following the recruiter number and name, the report lists data for each client served by that recruiter. The client data includes the number, name, address, city, state, postal code, client type, specialties needed, amount paid, current due, and total amount. It also includes any seminars currently being offered to the client. For each seminar, it lists the number, description, total hours the seminar requires, hours already spent, and hours remaining.

Many organizations offer discounts as a way of rewarding current clients and attracting new clients. The management at JSP is considering offering a discount on the Current Due amount to its current clients. The exact amount of the discount depends on how much the client already has paid. If the amount paid is more than $20,000, the discount will be 4 percent of the current due amount. If the amount paid is $20,000 or less, then the discount will be 2 percent of the current due amount. To assist in determining the discount, JSP needs a report like the one shown in Figure 7–1b. The report groups clients by recruiter. It includes subtotals and grand totals of both the Amount Paid and Current Due fields. Finally, it shows the discount amount, which is calculated by multiplying the current due amount by .04 (4 percent) for those clients for whom the amount paid is more than $20,000 and by .02 (2 percent) for all others.

The management also wants to be able to produce mailing labels for their clients. These labels must align correctly with the particular labels they have purchased and must be sorted by postal code (Figure 7–1c).

(a) Recruiter Master List - Page 3

(b) Discount Report

(c) Mailing Labels

Figure 7–1

Overview

As you read through this chapter, you will learn how to create the reports and labels by performing these general tasks:

- Change a caption and create queries for a report.
- Create a report, specify grouping and sorting, and add fields and text boxes to the report.
- Add a subreport to the report.
- Create a second report, specify grouping and sorting, and add fields and text boxes to the report.
- Add totals and subtotals to the report, and add a text box that uses a function.
- Create mailing labels.

Plan Ahead

Report Design Guidelines

1. **Determine the intended audience and purpose of the report.** Who will use the report? How will they use it? What data do they need? What level of detail do they need?

2. **Determine the source of data for the report.** Is all the data found in a single table or does it come from multiple related tables? Is the data found in a query? Do you need to create multiple reports for a query where the criterion for a field changes? If so, use a parameter query and enter the criterion when you run the report. If the data comes from multiple related tables, you may wish to create a query and use the query as a source of data.

3. **Determine the fields that belong on the report.** What data items are needed by the user of the report?

4. **Determine the organization of the report.** In what order should the fields appear? How should they be arranged? Should the records in the report be grouped in some way? Should the report contain any subreports?

5. **Determine any calculations required for the report.** Should the report contain totals or subtotals? Are there any special calculations? For example, the Recruiter Master List contains a Total Amount field that is calculated by adding the contents of the Amount Paid field and the Current Due field. The Discount Report contains a Discount field, which is calculated by multiplying the amount in the Current Due field by 4 percent if the amount in the Amount Paid field is greater than $20,000 and by 2 percent otherwise.

6. **Determine the format and style of the report.** What information should be in the report heading? Do you want a title and date, for example? Do you want a logo? What should be in the body of the report? What should the style be? In other words, what visual characteristics should the various portions of the report have? Does the organization have specific style requirements for reports?

7. **For mailing labels, determine the contents, order, and type of label.** What fields should appear on the label and how should they be arranged? Is there a certain order (for example, by postal code) in which the labels should be printed? Who is the manufacturer and what is the style number for the labels? What are the dimensions for each label and how many labels print across a page?

When necessary, more specific details concerning the above decisions and/or actions are presented at appropriate positions within the chapter. The chapter also will identify the use of these guidelines in the design of the reports and labels such as the ones shown in Figure 7–1 on the previous page.

Starting Access

If you are using a computer to step through the project in this chapter and you want your screen to match the figures in this book, you should change your screen's resolution to 1024×768. For information about how to change a computer's resolution, read Appendix E.

To Start Access

The following steps, which assume Windows Vista is running, start Access.

Note: If you are using Windows XP, refer to Appendix F for alternate steps.

1 Click the Start button on the Windows Vista taskbar to display the Start menu.

2 Click All Programs at the bottom of the left pane on the Start menu to display the All Programs list, and then click Microsoft Office on the All Programs list to display the Microsoft Office list.

3 Click Microsoft Office Access 2007 on the Microsoft Office list to start Access and display the Getting Started with Microsoft Office Access window.

4 If the Access window is not maximized, click the Maximize button on its title bar to maximize the window.

To Open a Database

In Chapter 1, you created your database on a USB flash drive using the file name, JSP Recruiters. There are two ways to open the file containing your database. If the file you created appears in the Recent Documents list, you could click it to open the file. If not, you can use the More button to open the file. The following steps use the More button to open the JSP Recruiters database from the USB flash drive.

Note: If you are using Windows XP, refer to Appendix F for alternate steps.

1 With your USB flash drive connected to one of the computer's USB ports, click the More button to display the Open dialog box.

2 If the Folders list is displayed below the Folders button, click the Folders button to remove the Folders list.

3 If necessary, click Computers in the Favorite Links section and then double-click UDISK 2.0 (E:) to select the USB flash drive, Drive E in this case as the new open location. (Your drive letter might be different.)

4 Click JSP Recruiters to select the file name.

5 Click the Open button to open the database.

6 If a Security Warning appears, click the Options button to display the Microsoft Office Security Options dialog box.

7 With the option button to enable the content selected, click the OK button to enable the content.

Creating Reports in Design View

You do not have to use the wizard when you create a report. You simply can create the report in Design view. In the previous reports you created, you used the wizard to create an initial report, and then used Layout view to modify the design the wizard created. You also can use Design view to modify a report created by the wizard. If you do not use the wizard before moving to Design view, the design will be empty. It then is up to you to place all the fields in the desired locations. It also is up to you to specify any sorting or grouping that is required.

Whether you use the wizard or simply use Design view, you must decide the table or query on which the report is to be based. If the report is to be based on a query, you first must create the query, unless, of course, it already exists.

To Change a Caption

Normally, the field name will appear as the label for a field on a form or report and as the column name in Datasheet view. If you would rather have a different name appear, you can change the field's caption to the desired name. Because JSP wants to shorten Specialties Needed to Spec Needed on reports and forms, the following steps change the caption of the Specialties Needed field to Spec Needed.

- Open the Client table in Design view.

- Click the row selector for the Specialties Needed field to select the field.

- Click the Caption property box and then type `Spec Needed` as the new caption (Figure 7–2).

- Click the Save button on the Quick Access Toolbar to save the change.

- Close the Client table.

Q&A

Will the column heading for the field change when the table is displayed in Datasheet view?

Yes. When the table appears in Datasheet view and when any query results appear in Datasheet view, the column heading will show the changed caption.

Figure 7–2

To Create a Query for the Report

The analysis of JSP requirements for the reports shows that it would be convenient to use two queries for the report. These queries do not yet exist. The first query relates recruiters and clients and the second query relates seminars and seminar offerings. The following steps create the Recruiters and Clients query.

1 Hide the Navigation Pane, click Create on the Ribbon to display the Create tab, and then click the Query Design button on the Create tab to create a new query.

2 Click the Recruiter table, click the Add button, click the Client table, click the Add button, and then click the Close button to close the Show Table dialog box.

③ Double-click the Recruiter Number, First Name, and Last Name fields from the Recruiter table. Double-click the Client Number, Client Name, Street, City, State, Postal Code, Client Type, Specialties Needed, Amount Paid, and Current Due fields from the Client table to add the fields to the design grid.

④ View the query results and scroll through the fields to make sure you have included all the necessary fields. If you have omitted a field, return to Design view and add it.

⑤ Click the Save button on the Quick Access Toolbar to save the query, type `Recruiters and Clients` as the name of the query, and then click the OK button.

⑥ Close the query.

To Create an Additional Query for the Report

JSP Recruiters needs to include the number of hours that remain in a seminar offering in the Recruiter Master List shown in Figure 7–1a on page AC 459. The following steps create the Seminar Offerings and Seminars query that includes a calculated field for hours remaining.

①
- Click Create on the Ribbon to display the Create tab and then click the Query Design button on the Create tab to create a new query.

- Click the Seminar table, click the Add button, click the Seminar Offerings table, click the Add button, and then click the Close button to close the Show Table dialog box.

- Double-click the Client Number and Seminar Number fields from the Seminar Offerings table. Double-click the Seminar Description field from the Seminar table. Double-click the Total Hours and Hours Spent fields from the Seminar Offerings table to add the fields to the design grid.

Figure 7–3

- Click the first open column in the design grid to select it.

- Click the Builder button on the Design tab to display the Expression Builder dialog box (Figure 7–3).

2

- Double-click Tables to display a list of tables, and then click the Seminar Offerings table to select it.

- Click the Total Hours field to select it and then click the Paste button to paste it into the expression.

- Click the minus sign to add it to the expression.

- Click the Hours Spent field to select it and then click the Paste button to paste it into the expression (Figure 7–4).

Figure 7–4

Q&A Why are the fields preceded by a table name and an exclamation point?

This notation qualifies the field, that is, it indicates to which table the field belongs.

Q&A Could I type the expression instead of using the Expression Builder?

Yes. You could type it directly into the design grid. You also could right-click the column and click Zoom to allow you to type the expression in the Zoom dialog box. Finally, you could use the Expression Builder, but simply type the expression rather than clicking any buttons. Use whichever method you find most convenient.

3

- Click the OK button and then press the ENTER key to enter the expression.

- Click the field in the grid in which you entered the expression and then click the Property Sheet button on the Design tab to display the property sheet.

Q&A What if the wrong property sheet appears?

You either did not click in the right location or you have not yet completed entering the expression. The easiest way to ensure you have done both is to click any other column in the grid and then click the column with the expression.

- Click the Caption property box and type Hours Remaining as the caption (Figure 7–5).

Figure 7–5

4

- Close the property sheet and then view the results of the query (Figure 7–6). (Your results may be in a different order.)

5

- Verify that your query results match those in the figure. If not, return to Design view and make the necessary corrections.

- Click the Save button, type `Seminar Offerings and Seminars` as the name of the query, and then click the OK button to save the query.

- Close the query.

Figure 7–6

Plan Ahead

Determine the fields that belong on the report.

1. **Examine the requirements for the report in general to determine the tables.** Do the requirements only relate to data in a single table, or does the data come from multiple tables? How are the tables related? Is the data in a query or could a query be created that contains some or all of the fields necessary for the report?

2. **Examine the specific requirements for the report to determine the fields necessary.** Look for all the data items that are specified for the report. Each should correspond to a field in a table or be able to be computed from a field in a table. This information gives you the list of fields.

3. **Determine the order of the fields.** Examine the requirements to determine the order in which the fields should appear. Be logical and consistent in your ordering. For example, in an address, the city should come before the state and the state should come before the postal code unless there is some compelling reason for another order.

Plan Ahead

Determine the organization of the report.

1. **Determine sort order.** Is there a special order in which the records should appear?

2. **Determine grouping.** Should the records be grouped in some fashion? If so, what should appear before the records in a group? If, for example, clients are grouped by recruiter number, the number of the recruiter should probably appear before the group. Should the recruiter name also appear? What should appear after the group? For example, are there some fields for which subtotals should be calculated? If so, the subtotals would come after the group.

(continued)

<table>
<tr><td>**Plan
Ahead**</td><td>*(continued)*

3. **Determine whether to include a subreport.** Rather than grouping, you may choose to include a subreport as in the Recruiter Master List. The data concerning seminar offerings for the client could have been presented by grouping the seminar offerings data by client number. The headings currently in the subreport would have appeared in the group header. Instead, it is presented in a subreport. Subreports, which are reports in their own right, offer more flexibility in formatting than group headers and footers. More importantly in the Recruiter Master List, some clients do not have any seminar offerings. If this information were presented using grouping, the group header still will appear for these clients. With a subreport, clients who have no seminar offerings do not appear.</td></tr>
</table>

To Create an Initial Report in Design View

Creating the report shown in Figure 7–1a on page AC 459 from scratch involves creating the initial report in Design view, adding the subreport, modifying the subreport separately from the main report, and then making the final modifications to the main report.

When you want to create a report from scratch, you use Report Design rather than Report Wizard. The Report Wizard is suitable for simple, customized reports. With Report Design, you can make advanced design changes, such as adding subreports. The following steps create the initial version of the Recruiter Master List and select the **record source** for the report, that is the table or query that will furnish the data for the report. The steps then specify sorting and grouping for the report.

- Click Create on the Ribbon to display the Create tab.

- Click the Report Design button on the Create tab to create a report in Design view.

- Ensure the selector for the entire report, the box in the upper-left corner of the report, is selected.

- Click the Property Sheet button on the Design tab to display a property sheet.

- With the All tab selected, click the Record Source property box arrow to display the list of available tables and queries (Figure 7–7).

Figure 7–7

2

- Click the Recruiters and Clients query to select the query as the record source for the report.

Q&A

I only see portions of names and some are similar. How can I be sure I selected the correct query?

Click the Record Source property in the property sheet to produce an insertion point and then repeatedly press the RIGHT ARROW key to move through the letters in the name. You also can expand the property sheet by pointing to the right or left edge of the sheet and dragging.

- Close the property sheet by clicking the Property Sheet button on the Design tab.

- Click the Group & Sort button to display the Group, Sort, and Total pane (Figure 7–8).

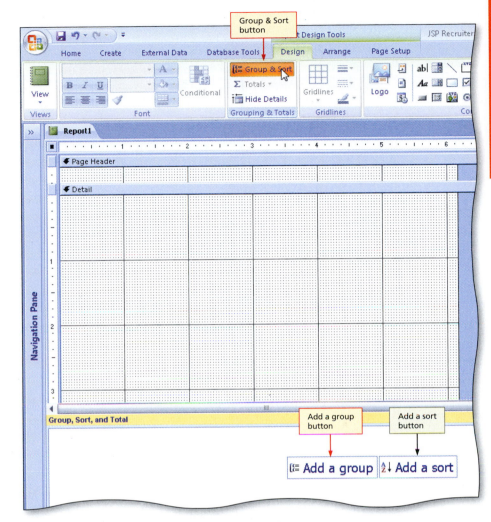

Figure 7–8

3

- Click the 'Add a group' button to display the list of available fields for grouping (Figure 7–9).

Figure 7–9

4

- Click the Recruiter Number field to group by Recruiter Number (Figure 7–10).

Figure 7–10

5

- Click the 'Add a sort' button to display the list of available fields for sorting (Figure 7–11).

6

- Click the Client Number field to sort by Client Number.

Figure 7–11

To Save the Report

Before proceeding with the next steps in the modification of the report, it is a good idea to save your work. The following steps save the report as Recruiter Master List.

1 Click the Save button.

2 Type `Recruiter Master List` as the report name.

3 Click the OK button.

Understanding Report Sections

As you create the report in Design view, you will place controls into sections on the form. There are three types of controls: bound controls, unbound controls, and calculated controls. **Bound controls** are used to display data that comes from fields in the database, such as the client number and name. **Unbound controls** are not associated with data from the database and are used to display such things as the report's title. Finally, **calculated controls** are used to display data that is calculated from other data, such as a total.

When you place a control, you will need to decide in which section to place the control. To do so, you must understand the purpose of each of the sections. The contents of the **Report Header section** print once at the beginning of the report. This section often contains a title. The contents of the **Report Footer section** print once at the end of the report. This section might contain grand totals of some of the items on the report. The contents of the **Page Header section** print once at the top of each page and often contain the column headings. The contents of the **Page Footer section** print once at the bottom of each page and may contain a date and a page number. The contents of the **Detail section** print once for each record in the table or query.

When the data in a report is grouped, there are two additional possible sections. The contents of the **Group Header section** are printed before the records in a particular group, and the contents of the **Group Footer section** are printed after the group. In the Discount Report (Figure 7–1b on page AC 459), for example, which is grouped by Recruiter Number, the Group Header section contains the recruiter number and name and the Group Footer section contains subtotals of Amount Paid and Current Due.

To Add Fields to the Report

When you have determined the fields that are necessary for the report, you need to add them. You can add the fields to the report by dragging them from the field list to the appropriate position on the report. The following steps add the fields to the report.

1

- Click the Add Existing Fields button on the Design tab to add a field list.

- Drag the Recruiter Number field to the approximate position shown in Figure 7–12.

Q&A

My field list does not look like the one in the figure. It has several tables listed and at the bottom it has Show only fields in the current record source. Yours has Show all tables. What should I do?

Click the 'Show only fields in the current record source' link. Your field list then should match the one in the figure.

Figure 7–12

- Release the left mouse button to place the field (Figure 7–13).

Figure 7–13

3

- Place the remaining fields in the positions shown in Figure 7–14.

- Click Arrange on the Ribbon to display the Arrange tab.

- Adjust the positions of the labels to those shown in the figure. If any field is not in the correct position, drag it to its correct location. To move the control or the attached label separately, drag the large handle in the upper-left corner of the control or label.

🔎 **Experiment**

- Select more than one control and then experiment with buttons on the Arrange tab to see their effect. After trying each one, click the Undo button on the Quick Access Toolbar to undo the change.

Figure 7–14

4

- Click Design on the Ribbon to display the Design tab.

- Remove the field list by clicking the Add Existing Fields button.

- Remove the Group, Sort, and Total pane by clicking the Group & Sort button on the Design tab.

Aligning Controls Using the Arrange Tab

When working on a report in Design view, you can make changes to the alignment of the controls in your report by using the Arrange tab, which is shown in Figure 7–14. Table 7–1 shows the groups that contain buttons relevant to aligning controls along with a description of the use of the buttons in the group.

Table 7–1 Arrange Tab	
Group	**Description**
Control Alignment	Click To Grid button to align upper-left corner of selected object to closest grid location. With multiple controls selected, click Left to align left edge of selected controls with left edge of leftmost control. Click Right to align right edge of selected controls with right edge of rightmost control. Click Top to align top edge of selected controls with top edge of topmost control. Click Bottom to align bottom edge of selected controls with bottom edge of bottommost control.
Position	Bring to Front or Send to Back is only relevant when two controls overlap. If so, Bring to Front will bring the selected control in front of other overlapping controls and Send to Back will place it behind other controls. The other controls in the group affect the spacing between controls. The buttons in the first row are Make Horizontal Spacing Equal and Make Vertical Spacing Equal. Both of these require at least three controls to be selected. Clicking the button will equalize the horizontal or vertical spacing between the controls. The buttons in the second row are Increase Horizontal Spacing and Increase Vertical Spacing. Clicking these buttons will increase the horizontal or vertical spacing between selected controls by one grid unit. The buttons in the third row are Decrease Horizontal Spacing and Decrease Vertical Spacing. Clicking these buttons will decrease the horizontal or vertical spacing between selected controls by one grid unit.
Size	The To Fit button sizes a control to best fit the data within it and the To Grid button sizes a control to the closest gridlines. The remaining controls require multiple controls be selected. To Tallest sizes the height of the selected controls to the height of the tallest control. To Widest sizes the width of the selected controls to the width of the widest control. To Shortest sizes the height of the selected controls to the height of the shortest control. To Narrowest sizes the width of the selected controls to the width of the narrowest control.
Show/Hide	The buttons in this group show or hide some component of a report. The first button in the first row shows or hides the grid. The second shows or hides the Report Header and Report Footer. The first button in the second row shows or hides the ruler. The second shows or hides the Page Header and Page Footer.

To Add Text Boxes

You can place a text box on a report or form by using the Text Box tool in the Controls group on the Design tab. The text box consists of a control that is initially unbound and an attached label. When you enter an expression in the text box, it becomes a calculated control. If the expression is just a single field (for example, =[Amount Paid]), it would be a bound control. Expressions also can be arithmetic operations, for example, calculating the sum of amount paid and current due. Many times, you need to **concatenate**, or combine, two or more text data items into a single expression; the process is called **concatenation**. To concatenate strings, you use the **ampersand (&)** operator. The process of converting an unbound control to a bound control is called **binding**.

The following steps add text boxes and create calculated controls.

1

- Click the Text Box tool on the Design tab and move the pointer to the approximate position shown in Figure 7–15.

Figure 7–15

2

- Click the position shown in Figure 7–15 to place a text box on the report (Figure 7–16).

Figure 7–16

3

- Click in the text box to produce an insertion point (Figure 7–17).

I inadvertently clicked somewhere else so the text box was no longer selected. When I clicked the text box a second time it was selected, but there was no insertion point. What should I do?

Simply click another time.

Figure 7–17

4

- Type =[First Name] &' '&[Last Name] as the entry in the text box.

What is the result of the expression I just entered?

The expression will display the first name of the recruiter followed by a space and then the last name of the recruiter. Any extra spaces at the end of the first name will be removed.

Could I use the Expression Builder instead of typing the expression?

Yes. Click the Property Sheet button and then click the Build button, which contains three dots, next to the Control Source property.

Do I need to use single quotes (')?

You also could use double quotes (").

- Click in the attached label to produce an insertion point (Figure 7–18).

Figure 7–18

5

- Use the BACKSPACE or DELETE key to erase the current entry in the label except for the colon and then type `Recruiter Name` prior to the colon as the new entry (Figure 7–19).

- Click outside the label to deselect it and then drag the label to the position shown in the figure by dragging the Move handle in the upper-left corner of the label.

Q&A

I inadvertently erased the colon. What should I do?

Just type a colon after the Recruiter Name.

Figure 7–19

6

- Use the techniques in Steps 1 to 5 to place a text box in the position indicated in Figure 7–20. Type `=[Amount Paid]+[Current Due]` as the expression in the text box, drag the label to the position shown in the figure, erase the contents of the label other than the colon and type `Total Amount` in the label.

Q&A

My label is not in the correct position. What should I do?

Click outside the label to deselect it, click the label, and then drag it to the desired position.

Figure 7–20

To View the Report

As you are working on a report in Design view, it is useful to periodically view the report to gauge how it will look containing data. One way to do so is to use Print Preview. The following steps view the report in Print Preview.

1

- Click the View button arrow to produce the View button menu.

- Click Print Preview on the View button menu to view the report in Print Preview (Figure 7–21).

What would happen if I clicked the View button instead of the View button arrow?

The icon on the View button is the icon for Report View, so you would view the results in Report view. This is another useful way to view a report, but compared to Print Preview, Report View does not give as accurate a picture of how the final printed report will look.

The total amount does not appear as currency and the Specialties Needed field does not display all the values. How can I fix these issues?

You will see how to fix these issues in the next sections.

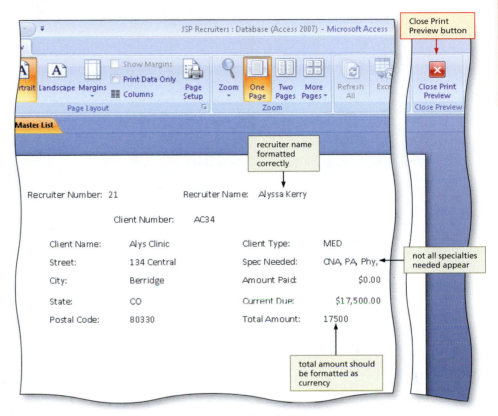

Figure 7–21

2

- Click the Close Print Preview button on the Print Preview tab to return to Design view.

To Format a Control

When you add a calculated control, you often need to format the control. You can use a control's property sheet and change the value in the appropriate property. If a property does not appear in the property sheet, you have two choices. You can click the tab on which the property is located. For example, if it is a control related to data, you would click the Data tab to show only data-related properties. Many people, however, prefer to click the All tab, which shows all properties, and then simply scroll through the properties, if necessary, until locating the appropriate property. The following steps change the format of the Total Amount by changing the value of the Format property and the Decimal Places property.

- Click the control containing the expression for Total Amount to select it and then click the Property Sheet button on the Design tab to display the property sheet.

- If necessary, click the All tab (Figure 7–22).

 Experiment

- Click the other tabs to see the types of properties on each tab. When finished, once again click the All tab.

- Click the Format property box, click the arrow that appears, and then click Currency to select Currency as the format.

- Click the Decimal Places property box, click the arrow that appears, and then click 2 to select 2 as the number of decimal places.

- Remove the property sheet by clicking the Property Sheet button.

Figure 7–22

To Group Controls

If there is a collection of controls that you frequently will want to modify in the same way, you can simplify the process of selecting all the controls by grouping them. Once they are grouped, selecting any control in the group automatically selects all of the controls in the group. You then can make the desired change and it will affect all the controls.

The following step groups the controls within the Detail section.

1

- Click the Client Number control to select it.

Q&A

Do I click the white space or the label?

The white space.

- While holding the SHIFT key down, click all the other controls in the Detail section to select them.

Q&A

Does it matter in which order I select the other controls?

No. It is only important that you ultimately select all the controls.

- Release the SHIFT key.

- Click Arrange on the Ribbon to display the Arrange tab.

- Click the Group button on the Arrange tab to group the controls (Figure 7–23).

Q&A

What if I make a mistake and group the wrong collection of controls?

Click the Ungroup button to ungroup the controls, select the collection you want, and then click the Group button.

Figure 7–23

To UNGROUP CONTROLS

If you no longer need to simultaneously modify all the controls you have placed in a group, you can ungroup the controls. To do so, you would use the following steps.

1. Click any of the controls in a group to select the entire group.

2. Click Arrange on the Ribbon to display the Arrange tab.

3. Click the Ungroup button on the Arrange tab to ungroup the controls.

To Update Grouped Controls

To update grouped controls, click any control in the group to select the entire group. Any change you then make affects all controls in the group. The following steps bold the controls in the group, resize them, and then change the border style.

- If necessary, click any one of the grouped controls to select the group.

- Click Design on the Ribbon to display the Design tab.

- Click the Bold button on the Design tab to bold all the controls in the group (Figure 7–24).

Figure 7–24

- Drag the right sizing handle of the Specialties Needed field to the approximate position shown in Figure 7–25 to resize all the controls in the group.

Q&A

What if I only want to change one control in the group?

Double-click the control to select just the one control and not the entire group. You then can make any change you wish to that one control.

Figure 7–25

3

- Click the Property Sheet button on the Design tab to display the property sheet for the grouped controls.

- With the All tab selected, click the Border Style property box to display an arrow and then click the arrow to display the list of available border styles (Figure 7–26).

4

- Click Solid to change the border styles for all the controls in the group to Solid.

 Experiment

- Try the other border styles to see their effect. When finished, once again select Solid as the border style.

- Close the property sheet.

Figure 7–26

To Update Multiple Controls that Are Not Grouped

To update multiple controls that are not grouped together, you must select all the controls. To do so, click one of the controls and then hold the SHIFT key down while selecting the others. The following steps italicize all the labels in the Detail section and then bold all the controls and labels in the Recruiter Number Header section.

- Click the label for the Client Number control to select it.

- While holding the SHIFT key down, click the labels for all the other controls in the Detail section to select them.

- Release the SHIFT key.

- Click the Italic button to italicize the labels (Figure 7–27).

Figure 7–27

- Click in the vertical ruler to the left of the Recruiter Number Header section to select all the controls in the section.

Q&A

What exactly is selected when I click in the vertical ruler?

If you picture a horizontal line through the point you clicked, any control that intersects that horizontal line would be selected.

- Click the Bold button on the Design tab to bold all the selected controls (Figure 7–28).

Figure 7–28

3

- Click outside the selected controls to deselect them. Click the control containing the expression for the recruiter's name to select it.

Q&A

Why do I have to deselect the controls and then select one of them a second time?

If you do not do so, any action you take would apply to all the selected controls rather than just the one you want.

- Drag the right sizing handle of the selected control to the approximate position shown in Figure 7–29.

Figure 7–29

Undoing and Saving

Remember that if you make a mistake, you often can correct it by clicking the Undo button on the Quick Access Toolbar. Clicking the Undo button will reverse your most recent change. You also can click the Undo button more than once to reverse multiple changes.

You should save your work frequently. That way, if you have problems that the Undo button will not fix, you can close the report without saving it and open it again. The report will be in exactly the state it was in at the time you saved it.

To Add a Subreport

To add a subreport to a report, you use the Subform/Subreport tool on the Design tab. Provided the Use Control Wizards button is selected, a wizard will guide you through the process of adding the subreport. The following steps add a subreport.

1

- Click the Use Control Wizards button, click the Subform/Subreport tool, and then move the pointer, which has changed to a plus sign with a subreport, to the approximate position shown in Figure 7–30.

Figure 7–30

2

- Click the position shown in Figure 7–30 to place the subreport and display the SubReport Wizard dialog box. Be sure the 'Use existing Tables and Queries' option button is selected (Figure 7–31).

Figure 7–31

3

- Click the Next button.

- Click the Tables/Queries box arrow.

- Scroll down until Query: Seminar Offerings and Seminars is visible, click Query: Seminar Offerings and Seminars, and then click the Add All Fields button to select all the fields in the query (Figure 7–32).

Q&A

Why did I select Client Number for the subreport when I already have the field on the main report?

Client Number is the field that links the subreport to the main report.

Figure 7–32

4

- Click the Next button and then ensure the 'Choose from a list' option button is selected (Figure 7–33).

Q&A

What is the purpose of this dialog box?

You use this dialog box to indicate the fields that link the main report (referred to as "report") to the subreport (referred to as "subreport"). If the fields have the same name, as they often will, you can simply select Choose from a list and then accept the selection Access already has made.

Figure 7–33

5

- Click the Next button, type `Seminar Offerings by Client` as the name of the subreport, and then click the Finish button to add the subreport (Figure 7–34).

6

- Click outside the subreport to deselect the subreport.

- Click the Save button on the Quick Access Toolbar to save your changes.

- Close the Recruiter Master List report.

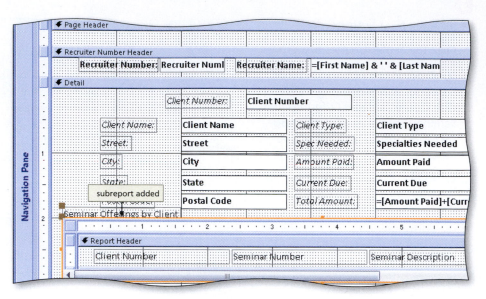

Figure 7–34

To Open the Subreport in Design View

The subreport appears as a separate report in the Navigation Pane. It can be modified just like any other report. The following steps open the subreport in Design view.

1

- Show the Navigation Pane, scroll down so that the Seminar Offerings by Client report appears, and then right-click the Seminar Offerings by Client report to produce a shortcut menu (Figure 7–35).

Figure 7–35

2

- Click Design View on the shortcut menu to open the subreport in Design view.

- Hide the Navigation Pane.

- Click the Client Number control in the Detail section to select the control (Figure 7–36).

Q&A

My screen does not look the same as yours. My headings have a blue background. How can I remove the background?

Click the ruler to the left of the Report Header section to select all the controls in the section. Click the Fill/Back Color arrow and then click Transparent.

Figure 7–36

Print Layout Issues

The green triangular symbol in the upper-left corner of the report is an error indicator. Pointing to it displays an Error Checking Options button. Clicking the Error Checking Options button produces the Error Checking Options menu, as shown in Figure 7–37.

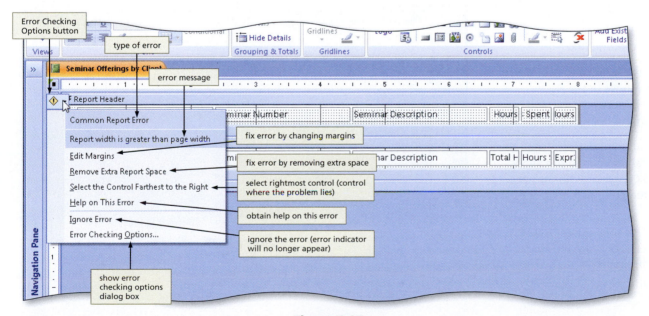

Figure 7–37

The first line in the menu is simply a statement of the type of error that occurred, and the second is a description of the specific error, in this case, the fact that the report width is greater than the page width, a situation that could lead to data not appearing where you expect it to as well as the printing of some blank pages.

BTW

Subreports
A main report can contain more than one subreport. If the main report is based on a table or query, each subreport must contain information related to the information in the main report. If the main report is not based on a table or query, it simply serves as a container for the subreports, which then have no restrictions on the information they contain.

The next three lines provide alternatives for addressing the error. You could change the margins to allow more space for the report. You could remove some extra space. You could select the control farthest to the right and move it. The next line gives more detailed help on the error. The Ignore Error command instructs Access to not consider this an error. The error indicator then would disappear. The final line displays the Error Checking Options dialog box where you can make other changes.

Later in this chapter, you will fix the problem by changing the width of the report, so you do not need to take any action at this time.

To Modify the Controls in the Subreport

Because the client number appears in the main report, it does not need to be duplicated in the subreport. Also, the column headers in the subreport should extend over two lines, as shown in Figure 7–1a on page AC 459. The following step modifies the subreport by deleting the Client Number control and revising the column headings.

1

- With the Client Number control selected, press the DELETE key to delete the control.

- Change the labels in the Report Header section to match those shown in Figure 7–38. To extend a heading over two lines, click prior to the second word to produce an insertion point and then press SHIFT+ENTER to move the second word to a second line.

- Change the sizes of the controls to match those in the figure by selecting the controls and dragging the sizing handles.

- Use the alignment buttons on the Design tab to change the alignment to Center or Right as necessary to match the labels in the figure.

Q&A Why does Expr1 appear in the Detail section under the Hours Remaining label?

Expr1 indicates that Hours Remaining is a calculated control.

Figure 7–38

Experiment

- There is currently a space between the two names in the labels. To delete the space, click immediately after the first word to produce an insertion point and then press the DELETE key. Try the various alignments (left, right, and center) before removing the space. Remove the space and try the various alignments again to see if the removal of the space makes any difference. When finished, make sure your labels look like the one in the figure.

To Change the Can Grow Property

Some of the seminar descriptions are too long to fit in the available space. This problem can be addressed in several ways.

1. Move the controls to allow more space in between controls. Then, drag the appropriate handles on the controls that need to be expanded to enlarge them.

2. Use the Font Size property to select a smaller font size. This will allow more data to fit in the same space.

3. Use the Can Grow property. By changing the value of this property from No to Yes, the data can be spread over two lines, thus allowing all the data to print. Access will split data at natural break points, such as commas, spaces, and hyphens.

The third approach is the easiest to use and also produces a very readable report. The following step changes the Can Grow property for the Seminar Description field.

- Click the Seminar Description control to select it.

- Click the Property Sheet button on the Design tab to display the property sheet.

- With the All tab selected, scroll down until the Can Grow property appears, click the Can Grow property box arrow to display the list of possible values for the Can Grow property (Figure 7–39).

- Click Yes in the list.

- Close the property sheet.

Q&A

What is the effect of the Can Shrink property?

If the Can Shrink property is set to Yes, Access will remove blank lines that occur when the field is empty.

Figure 7–39

To Change the Appearance of the Controls in the Subreport

The following steps change the appearance of the controls in the subreport.

1
- Drag the right boundary of the subreport to the approximate position shown in Figure 7–40.

2
- Click the ruler to the left of the controls in the Detail section to select the controls, and then click the Bold button on the Design tab to bold the controls.

- Click the ruler to the left of the labels in the Report Header section to select the labels, and then click the Italic button on the Design tab to italicize the controls.

- Click the Save button on the Quick Access Toolbar to save the changes.

- Close the Seminar Offerings by Client subreport.

Figure 7–40

To Resize the Subreport and the Report

The following steps resize the subreport control in the main report and then resize the main report.

1
- Show the Navigation Pane.

- Open the Recruiter Master List in Design view.

- Click the subreport and then drag the right sizing handle to change the size to the approximate size shown in Figure 7–41, and then drag the subreport to the approximate position shown in the figure.

- Drag the right boundary of the report to the approximate position shown in the figure.

Figure 7–41

2

- Scroll down so that the lower boundary of the Detail section appears and then drag the lower boundary of the section to the approximate position shown in Figure 7–42.

Q&A

I scrolled down to see the lower boundary of the Detail section and the controls are no longer on the screen. What is the easiest way to drag the boundary when the position to which I want to drag it is not visible?

You don't need to see the location to drag to it. As you get close to the top of the visible portion of the screen, Access automatically will scroll. You might find it easier, however to drag it near the top of the visible portion of the report, use the scroll bar to scroll up, and then drag some more. You might have to scroll a couple of times.

Figure 7–42

To Modify Section Properties

The following step first deletes the label for the subreport and then makes two modifications to the Recruiter Number Header section. The first modification, which causes the contents of the group header section to appear at the top of each page, changes the Repeat Section property to Yes. Without this change, the recruiter number and name only would appear at the beginning of the group of clients of that recruiter. If the list of clients occupies more than one page, it would not be apparent on subsequent pages which recruiter is associated with those clients. The second modification changes the Force New Page property to Before Section, causing each section to begin at the top of a page.

- Click the label for the subreport (the label that reads Seminar Offerings by Client), and then press the DELETE key to delete the label.

- Click the Recruiter Number Header bar to select the header and then click the Property Sheet button on the Design tab to display the property sheet.

- With the All tab selected, click the Repeat Section property box, click the arrow that appears, and then click Yes to cause the contents of the group header to appear at the top of each page.

- Click the Force New Page property box, click the arrow that appears, and then click Before Section to cause a new group to begin at the top of the next page (Figure 7–43).

- Close the property sheet.

Figure 7–43

To Add a Title, Page Number, and Date

You can add a title, a page number, and a date to a report using the Title button, the Insert Page Number button, and the Date & Time button respectively. The buttons are found on the Design tab. The following steps add a title, page number, and date to the Recruiter Master List report.

- Click the Title button on the Design tab to add a title and then drag the title to the middle of the Report Header section.

Q&A

The title is the same as the name of the report object. Can I change the report title without changing the name of the report object in the database?

Yes. The report title is a label and you can change it using any of the techniques that we used for changing column headings and other labels.

- Click the Insert Page Number button on the Design tab to display the Page Numbers dialog box.

Figure 7–44

- Be sure Page N and Top of Page [Header] option buttons are selected and then, if necessary, click the Alignment arrow and select Left (Figure 7–44).

2

- Click the OK button to add the page number.

- Click the Date & Time button on the Design tab to display the Date and Time dialog box.

- Click the option button for the third date format and click the Include Time check box to remove the check mark (Figure 7–45).

Figure 7–45

3

- Click the OK button to add the date to the Report Header.

- Drag the Date control to the position shown in Figure 7–46.

- Drag the boundary of the report to the position shown in the figure.

Figure 7–46

To Save and Close the Report

The following steps save the final report and then close the report.

1 Click the Save button on the Quick Access Toolbar to save the report.

2 Close the report by clicking the Close 'Recruiter Master List' button.

To Print the Report

The following steps print the Recruiter Master List report.

1 Show the Navigation Pane, ensure the Recruiter Master List report is selected, and then click the Office Button to display the Microsoft Office Button menu.

2 Point to Print on the Office Button menu and then click Quick Print on the Print submenu to print the report.

To Create a Second Report

JSP Recruiters also would like a report that groups clients by recruiter. The report should include subtotals and grand totals. Finally, it should show the discount amount for each client. The discount amount is based on the current due amount. Clients who owe more than $20,000 will receive a 4 percent discount and clients who owe $20,000 or less will receive a 2 percent discount. The following steps create the Discount Report, select the record source, and specify grouping and sorting options.

1 Hide the Navigation Pane.

2 Click Create on the Ribbon to display the Create tab and then click the Report Design button on the Ribbon to create a report in Design view.

3 Ensure the selector for the entire report, which is the box in the upper-left corner of the report, is selected and then click the Property Sheet button on the Design tab to display a property sheet.

4 With the All tab selected, click the Record Source property box, click the arrow that appears, and then click the Recruiters and Clients query to select the query as the record source for the report.

5 Close the property sheet by clicking the Property Sheet button on the Design tab.

6 Click the Group & Sort button to display the Group, Sort, and Total pane.

7 Click the 'Add a group' button to display the list of available fields for grouping and then click the Recruiter Number field to group by Recruiter Number.

8 Click the 'Add a sort' button to display the list of available fields for sorting, and then click the Client Number field to sort by Client Number.

9 Remove the Group, Sort, and Total pane by clicking the Group & Sort button on the Design tab.

To Add a Field to the Report

As with the previous report, you can add a field to the report by dragging the field from the field list. You can drag an attached label separately from the control to which it is attached by dragging the Move handle in its upper-left corner. This technique does not work, however, if you want to drag the attached label to a different section from the control's section. If you want the label to be in a different section, you must select the label, cut the label, select the section to which you want to move the label, and then paste the label. You then can move the label to the desired location.

The following steps add the Recruiter Number field to the Recruiter Number Header section and then move the label to the Page Header Section.

1

- Click the Add Existing Fields button on the Design tab to add a field list.

- If necessary, click the 'Show only fields in the current record source' link at the bottom of the field list to display only those fields in the Recruiters and Clients query (Figure 7–47).

Q&A

Why does the text on the button in Figure 7–47 display Show all tables?

The button text changes based on what appears in the Field List pane. If only the fields from the current record source appear, then the button text is Show all tables. If you click the button, all tables in the database will appear in the Field List pane and the button text will display 'Show only fields in the current record source'.

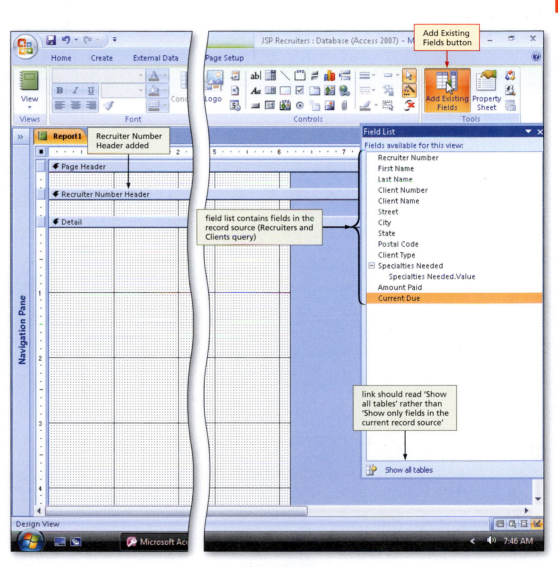

Figure 7–47

2

- Drag the Recruiter Number field to the approximate position shown in Figure 7–48.

Figure 7–48

3

- Click the label for the Recruiter Number control to select it (Figure 7–49).

Figure 7–49

4

- Click Home on the Ribbon to display the Home tab.

- Click the Cut button on the Home tab to cut the label.

- Click the Page Header bar to select the page header (Figure 7–50).

Q&A

Do I have to click the bar or could I click somewhere else within the section?

You also could click within the section. Clicking the bar is usually safer, however. If you click in a section intending to select the section, but click within one of the controls in the section, you will select the control rather than the section. Clicking the bar always selects the section.

Figure 7–50

5

- Click the Paste button on the Home tab to paste the label in the Page Header section (Figure 7–51).

Q&A When would I want to click the Paste button arrow rather than just the button?

Clicking the arrow displays the Paste button menu, which includes the Paste command and two additional commands. Paste Special allows you to paste data into different formats. Paste Append, which is available if you have cut or copied a record, allows you to paste the record to a table with a similar structure. If you want the simple Paste command, you can just click the button.

Figure 7–51

6

- Click in the label in front of the word, Number, to produce an insertion point.

- Press SHIFT+ENTER to move the word, Number, to a second line.

- Erase the colon following the word, Number.

To Add the Remaining Fields

The following steps add the remaining fields by dragging them into the Detail section. They next save the report, move the labels into the Page Header section, and move the controls containing the fields to the appropriate locations.

1

- Resize and move the Recruiter Number control to the approximate size and position shown in Figure 7–52.

- Resize the Recruiter Number label to the size shown in the figure.

- Drag the First Name, Last Name, Client Number, Client Name, Amount Paid, and Current Due fields into the Detail section, as shown in the figure.

Q&A Why drag them to the positions shown in the figure? That is not where they go. Could I drag them all at once?

Dragging them gets them onto the report, where you now can move

Figure 7–52

the controls and labels individually to the desired locations. You can drag multiple fields by selecting the first field, holding down the SHIFT key and then selecting other adjacent fields. To select fields that are not adjacent to each other use the CTRL key. How you choose to select fields and drag them onto the report is a matter of personal preference.

2

- Close the field list.

- Click the Save button on the Quick Access toolbar, type `Discount Report` as the report name, and click the OK button to save the report.

Q&A

Why save it at this point?

You do not have to save it at this point. Because you are about to move several labels between sections, however, saving it here gives you a convenient point from which to restart if you have problems.

- One at a time, cut each of the labels, paste the label into the Page Header section, resize, reformat, delete the colon, and move the labels to the approximate positions shown in Figure 7–53.

Q&A

When I paste the label, it always places it at the left edge, superimposing the Recruiter Number control. Can I change where Access places it?

Unfortunately, when you paste to a different section, Access places the control at the left edge. You will need to drag each control to its proper location after pasting it into the Page Header section.

Figure 7–53

- One at a time, resize and move the First Name and Last Name controls to the approximate positions in the Recruiter Number Header section shown in the figure.

- One at a time, resize and move the Client Number, Client Name, Amount Paid, and Current Due controls to the approximate positions in the Detail section shown in the figure.

- Select both the Amount Paid and Current Due labels and click Home on the Ribbon to display the Home tab.

- Click the Align Text Right button on the Design tab to align the headings to the right, as shown in the figure.

To Resize the Detail Section

The following step resizes the detail section of the Discount Report to remove most of the extra space below the controls in the section.

1 Scroll down so that the lower boundary of the Detail section appears and then drag the lower boundary of the section to a position just slightly below the controls in the section.

Q&A I scrolled down to see the lower boundary of the Detail section and the controls are no longer on the screen. What is the easiest way to drag the boundary when the position to which I want to drag it is not visible?

You don't need to see the location to drag to it. As you get close to the top of the visible portion of the screen, Access automatically will scroll. You might find it easier, however to drag it near the top of the visible portion of the report, use the scroll bar to scroll up, and then drag some more. You might have to scroll a couple of times.

Determine any calculations required for the report.

1. **Determine whether to include calculations in the group and report footers.** Should the report contain subtotals? Should the report contain grand totals? Are there other statistics that should be calculated (for example, averages)?

2. **Determine whether any special calculations are required.** Are there any special calculations? What are they? What fields are involved and how are they to be combined? Are any of the calculations conditional, that is, does the calculation depend on whether a certain criterion is true or false?

Plan Ahead

Totals and Subtotals

To add totals or other statistics to a footer, add a text box. You can use any of the aggregate functions: COUNT, SUM, AVG (average), MAX (largest value), MIN (smallest value), STDEV (standard deviation), VAR (variance), FIRST, and LAST. To use a function, type an equal (=) sign, followed by the function name. You then include a set of parentheses containing the item for which you want to perform the calculation. If the item name contains spaces, such as Amount Paid, you must enclose it in square brackets. For example, to calculate the sum of the amount paid values, the expression would be =SUM([Amount Paid]). Calculated controls that contain aggregate functions also are called aggregate fields.

Access will perform the calculation for the appropriate collection of records. If you enter this expression in the Recruiter Number Footer section, Access only will calculate the total for clients with the given recruiter; that is, it will calculate the appropriate subtotal. If you enter the expression in the Report Footer section, Access will calculate the total for all clients.

To Add Totals and Subtotals

An analysis of requirements at JSP indicated that the Discount Report should contain subtotals and grand totals of amounts paid and current due. The following steps first display the Recruiter Number Footer section and then add the total of amount paid and current due to both the Recruiter Number Footer section and the Report Footer section. The steps label the totals in the Recruiter Number Footer section as subtotals and the totals in the Report Footer section as grand totals. The steps also change the format of the new controls to currency and the number of decimal places to 2.

- Click the Group & Sort button on the Design tab to display the Group, Sort, and Total pane (Figure 7–54).

Figure 7–54

- Click Group on Recruiter Number and then click the More Options arrow to display additional options.

- Click the 'without a footer section' arrow to display the available options (Figure 7–55).

Figure 7–55

❸

- Click 'with a footer section' to add a footer.

- Close the Group, Sort, and Total pane by clicking the Group & Sort button on the Design tab.

- Click the Text Box tool on the Design tab, and then point to the position shown in Figure 7–56.

Figure 7–56

4

- Click the position shown in Figure 7–56 on the previous page to place a text box (Figure 7–57).

Figure 7–57

5

- Type =Sum([Current Due]) in the control, and then press the ENTER key.

- Click the label to select it.

- Click the label a second time to produce an insertion point.

- Use the DELETE or BACKSPACE key to delete the Text8 (your number might be different). Do not delete the colon.

- Type Subtotals as the label.

- Click outside the label to deselect it.

- Resize and align the Current Due controls in the Detail section and the Recruiter Number footer section as shown in Figure 7–58.

Figure 7–58

6

- Click the Text Box tool on the Design tab, and then click in the Recruiter Number Footer just to the left of the control for the sum of Current Due to place another text box.

- Click the text box to produce an insertion point, type =Sum ([Amount Paid]) in the control, and then press the ENTER key to enter the expression (Figure 7–59).

Q&A

Could I add the controls in the other order?

Yes. The only problem is that the label of the second control overlaps the first control. Adding the controls in the order shown in the steps cuts down on the overlap. It is not a major difference, however.

Figure 7–59

7

- Click the label to select it, and then press the DELETE key to delete the label.

Q&A

I inadvertently deleted the other control rather than the label. What should I do?

The first thing to try is to click the Undo button on the Quick Access Toolbar to reverse your deletion. You then can delete the correct control. If that does not work for you, you simply can delete the remaining control or controls in the section and start these steps over.

- Click the control for the sum of Amount Paid to select it and then hold the SHIFT key down and click the control for the sum of Current Due to select both controls.

- Click the Property Sheet button on the Design tab to display the property sheet.

Figure 7–60

- Change the format to Currency and the number of decimal places to 2 (Figure 7–60).

- Close the property sheet.

8

- Click Arrange on the Ribbon to display the Arrange tab.

- Click the Report Header/Footer button to display the Report Footer section (Figure 7–61).

Figure 7–61

- Click the ruler in the Recruiter Number Footer to the left of the controls in the section to select the controls.

- Click Home on the Ribbon to display the Home tab.

- Click the Copy button on the Home tab to copy the selected controls to the clipboard (Figure 7–62).

Figure 7–62

- Click the Report Footer bar to select the footer and then click the Paste button on the Home tab to paste a copy of the controls into the report footer.

- Move the controls to the positions shown in Figure 7–63.

- Click the label in the Report Footer section to select the label and then click a second time to produce an insertion point.

- Use the BACKSPACE or DELETE key to erase the current contents other than the colon and then type Grand totals in front of the colon to change the label (Figure 7–63).

Q&A Could I enter the controls just as I did earlier rather than copying and pasting?

Yes. Copying and pasting is a little simpler, but it is a matter of personal preference.

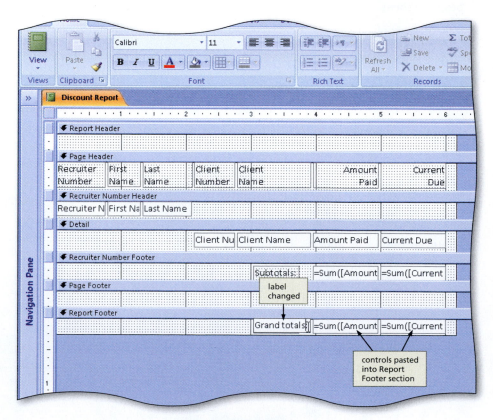

Figure 7–63

To View the Report

The following steps view the report in Print Preview.

1 Click the View button arrow on the Home tab to display the View button menu.

2 Click Print Preview on the View button menu to view the report in Print Preview (Figure 7–64).

Figure 7–64

To Assign a Conditional Value

The JSP requirements for this report also involved a conditional value related to the amount of a client's discount. To assign a conditional value, you will use the **IIF function**. The IIF function consists of the letters IIF followed by three items, called **arguments**, in parentheses. The first argument is a criterion; the second and third arguments are expressions. If the criterion is true, the function assigns the value of the expression in the second argument. If the criterion is false, the function assigns the value of the expression in the third argument. The IIF function you will use is IIF([Amount Paid]>20000, .04*[Current Due], .02*[Current Due]). If the amount paid is greater than $20,000, the value assigned would be .04*[Current Due]; that is, 4 percent of the current due amount. If the amount paid is not greater than $20,000, the value assigned would be .02*[Current Due]; that is, 2 percent of the current due amount.

The following steps add a text box and then use the Expression Builder to enter the appropriate IIF function in the text box. The steps then change the format of the text box. The steps modify and move the label for the text box. The steps add a title, page number, and date, and then change the size of the report.

1

- Click the Close Print Preview button arrow on the Print Preview tab to return to Design view.

- If necessary, click Design on the Ribbon to display the Design tab.

- Click the Text Box tool on the Design tab and point to the approximate position shown in Figure 7–65.

Figure 7–65

2

- Click the position shown in Figure 7–65 to place a text box.

- Click the attached label to select it and then press the DELETE key to delete the attached label.

- Click the text box to select it and then click the Property Sheet button on the Design tab to display a property sheet.

- Click the Control Source property to select it (Figure 7–66).

 Q&A

Why did I choose Control Source not Record Source?

You use Record Source to select the source of the records in a report, usually a table or a query. You use the Control Source property to specify the source of data for the control. This allows you to bind an expression or field to a control.

Figure 7–66

3

- Click the Build button to display the Expression Builder dialog box.

- Double-click Functions in the first column to display the function subfolders.

- Click Built-In Functions in the first column to display the various function categories in the second column.

- Scroll down in the second column so that Program Flow appears, and then click Program Flow to display the available program flow functions in the third column.

- Click IIF in the third column to select the IIF function and then click the Paste button (Figure 7–67).

Figure 7–67

Q&A Do I have to select Program Flow? Couldn't I just scroll down to IIF?

You do not have to select Program Flow. You indeed could scroll down to IIF. You will have to scroll through a large number of functions in order to get to IIF, however.

4

- Click the <expr> argument to select it and type [Amount Paid]>20000 as the expression.

- Click the <truepart> argument and type .04*[Current Due] as the true part.

- Click the <falsepart> argument and type .02*[Current Due] as the false part (Figure 7–68).

Q&A Are there other ways I could enter the expression?

Yes. You could just type the whole expression. On the other hand, you could select the function just as in these steps and when entering each argument you could select the fields from the list of fields and click the desired operators.

Figure 7–68

5

- Click the OK button in the Expression Builder dialog box to specify the expression as the control source for the text box.

- Change the format to Currency.

- Change the number of decimal places to 2.

- Close the property sheet by clicking the Property Sheet button.

- Click the Label (Form Control) tool on the Design tab and point to the approximate position shown in Figure 7–69.

Figure 7–69

6

- Press and hold the left mouse button, drag the pointer to the approximate position for the lower-right corner of the label shown in Figure 7–70, and then release the left mouse button to place the label.

Q&A

I made the label the wrong size. What should I do?

With the label selected, drag the sizing handles to resize the label as needed. Drag the control in a position away from the sizing handles if you need to move the label.

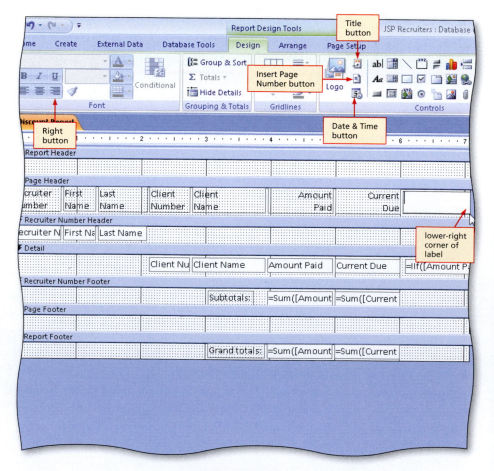

Figure 7–70

7

- Type Discount to enter the name of the label.

- Click outside the label to deselect the label and then click the label to select it once more.

- Click the Align Text Right button on the Design tab to right-align the text within the label.

- Move or resize the label as necessary so that it aligns with the new text box and with the other controls in the Page Header section.

Figure 7–71

- Using the techniques on Pages AC 490 and AC 491, add a title, page number, and date at the positions shown in Figure 7–71.

- Resize the Report Header section to the approximate size shown in the figure by dragging its lower edge.

- If necessary, drag the right boundary of the report to the position shown in the figure.

- Click Page Setup on the Ribbon to display the Page Setup tab as shown in the figure.

Obtaining Help on Functions

There are many functions available in Access for a variety of purposes. To see the list of functions, use the Expression Builder. Double-click Functions in the first column and then click Built-In Functions. You then can scroll through the entire list of functions in the third column. Alternatively, you can click a function category in the second column, in which case the third column only will contain the functions in that category. To obtain detailed help on a function, highlight the function in the third column and click the Help button. The Help presented will show the syntax of the function, that is, the specific rule for how you must type the function and any arguments. It will give you general comments on the function as well as examples illustrating the use of the function.

BTW

Changing the Date Format
To change the format used to display the date, right-click the date control and then click Properties on the short-cut menu. You then can select a format for the date and/or the time by changing the value for the Format property.

To Change the Report Margins

If you look at the horizontal ruler in Figure 7–71 on the previous page, you will notice that the report width is slightly over seven inches. Because the report probably will print on standard 8 ½ × 11 paper, it is a good idea to reduce the margins. This will allow the report to fit better onto the paper. There are two ways to change the margins. You can click the Margins button on the Page Setup tab and then select from some predefined options: Normal (right and left margins of .35"), Wide (right and left margins of .75"), and Narrow (right and left margins of .25"). If you want more control, you can click the Page Setup button to display the Page Setup dialog box. You then can specify your own margins, change the orientation, and also specify multiple columns if you want a multi-column report.

The following steps use the Margins button to select Narrow margins.

1 Click the Margins button on the Page Setup tab.

2 If necessary, click Narrow to specify the Narrow margin option.

Fine-Tuning a Report

When you have finished a report, you should review it to make sure the layout is precisely what you want. You may find that not all the data in a particular column appears as you intended. For example, in Figure 7–64 on page AC 503, the final n in the name Camden does not appear. To correct such a problem you could increase the size of the control by selecting the control and dragging the appropriate sizing handle. You may realize you need an additional control, which you could add by using the appropriate tool in the Controls group or by dragging a field from the field list.

In both cases, you have a potential problem. You may not have the room to increase the size or to add an additional control. If the control is part of a control layout as you had when you modified earlier reports in Layout view, you can resize controls or add new fields, and the remaining fields automatically adjust for the change. In Design view with individual controls, you must make any necessary adjustments yourself.

TO MAKE ROOM FOR RESIZING OR ADDITIONAL CONTROLS

To make room for resizing a control or for adding additional controls, you would use the following steps.
1. Select all controls to the right of the control you wish to resize or the position where you wish to add another control.
2. Drag any of the selected controls to the right to make room for the change.

To Save and Close the Report

The following steps save the final report and then close the report.

1 Click the Save button on the Quick Access Toolbar to save the report.

2 Close the report by clicking the Close 'Discount Report' button.

To Print the Report

The following steps print the Discount Report.

1 Show the Navigation Pane, ensure that Discount Report is selected, and then click the Office Button to display the Microsoft Office Button menu.

2 Point to Print on the Office Button menu and then click Quick Print on the Print submenu to print the report.

Mailing Labels

Organizations need to send invoices and other correspondence to clients on a regular basis. Using preprinted mailing labels eliminates much of the manual labor involved in preparing materials to be sent through the mail system. To print mailing labels, you create a special type of report. When this report prints, the data will appear on the mailing labels aligned correctly and in the order you specify.

To Create Labels

In Access, labels are a special type of report. Therefore, you create labels just as you create reports. The Label Wizard assists you in the process. Using the wizard, you can specify the type and dimensions of the label, the font used for the label, and the content of the label. The following steps create the labels.

1

• Show the Navigation Pane and select the Client table.

• Click Create on the Ribbon to display the Create tab.

• Click the Labels button on the Ribbon to display the Label Wizard dialog box.

• Ensure that English is selected as the Unit of Measure and that Avery is selected in the "Filter by manufacturer" box.

• Click C2163 in the Product number list (Figure 7–72).

Figure 7–72

2

- Click the Next button (Figure 7–73).

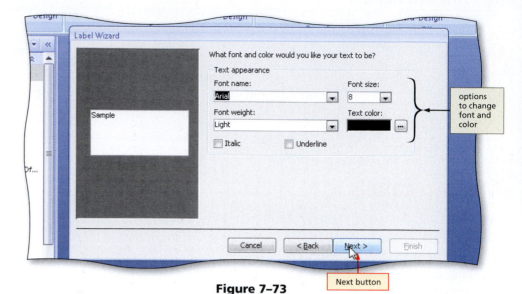

Figure 7–73

3

- Click the Next button to accept the default font and color settings.

- Click the Client Name field and then click the Add Field button (Figure 7–74).

Figure 7–74

4

- Click the second line in the label, and then add the Street field.

- Click the third line of the label.

- Add the City field, type , (a comma), press the SPACEBAR, add the State field, press the SPACEBAR, and then add the Postal Code field (Figure 7–75).

Figure 7–75

5

- Because the label now is complete, click the Next button.

- Select the Postal Code field as the field to sort by, and then click the Add Field button (Figure 7–76).

Why am I sorting by postal code?

When you need to do a bulk mailing, that is, mail a large number of items using a special mail rate, mail organizations require that the mail be sorted in postal code order.

Figure 7–76

6

- Click the Next button.

- Ensure the name for the report (that is, the labels) is Labels Client (Figure 7–77).

Figure 7–77

- Click the Finish button to complete the labels (Figure 7–78).

8
- Close the Labels Client report.

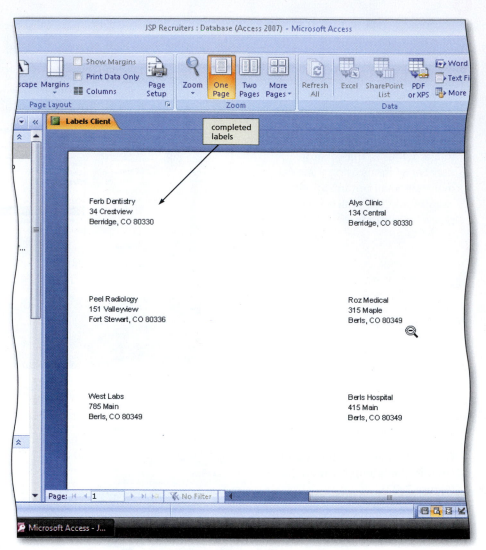

Figure 7–78

To Print Labels

Certification
The Microsoft Certified Application Specialist (MCAS) program provides an opportunity for you to obtain a valuable industry credential — proof that you have the Access 2007 skills required by employers. For more information, see Appendix G or visit the Access 2007 Certification Web page (scsite.com/ac2007/cert).

You print labels just as you print a report. The only difference is that you would want to load the labels in the printer before printing. The following steps print the labels.

1 Show the Navigation Pane and ensure the Labels Client report is selected and then click the Office Button to display the Microsoft Office menu.

2 Point to Print on the Office Button menu and then click Quick Print on the Print submenu to print the report.

Q&A I want to load the correct number of labels. How do I know how many pages of labels will print?

If you are unsure how many pages of labels will print, open the labels in Print Preview first. Use the Navigation buttons in the status bar of the Print Preview window to determine how many pages of labels will print.

To Quit Access

You saved all your changes and are ready to quit Access. The following step quits Access.

 Click the Close button on the right side of the Access title bar to quit Access.

BTW

Quick Reference
For a table that lists how to complete the tasks covered in this book using the mouse, Ribbon, shortcut menu, and keyboard, see the Quick Reference Summary at the back of this book, or visit the Access 2007 Quick Reference Web page (scsite.com/ac2007/qr).

Chapter Summary

In this chapter you have learned to change captions; create queries for a report; create reports in Design view; add fields and text boxes to a report; format controls; group and ungroup controls; update multiple controls; add and modify a subreport; modify section properties; add a title, page number, and date; add totals and subtotals; use a function in a text box; and create and print mailing labels. The following list includes all the new Access skills you have learned in this chapter.

1. Change a Caption (AC 462)
2. Create a Query for the Report (AC 462)
3. Create an Additional Query for the Report (AC 463)
4. Create an Initial Report in Design View (AC 466)
5. Add Fields to the Report (AC 469)
6. Add Text Boxes (AC 471)
7. View the Report (AC 475)
8. Format a Control (AC 475)
9. Group Controls (AC 476)
10. Ungroup Controls (AC 477)
11. Update Grouped Controls (AC 478)
12. Update Multiple Controls that are not Grouped (AC 480)
13. Add a Subreport (AC 482)
14. Open the Subreport in Design View (AC 484)
15. Modify the Controls in the Subreport (AC 486)
16. Change the Can Grow Property (AC 487)
17. Change the Appearance of the Controls in the Subreport (AC 488)
18. Resize the Subreport and the Report (AC 488)
19. Modify Section Properties (AC 489)
20. Add a Title, Page Number, and Date (AC 490)
21. Create a Second Report (AC 492)
22. Add a Field to the Report (AC 493)
23. Add the Remaining Fields (AC 495)
24. Resize the Detail Section (AC 497)
25. Add Totals and Subtotals (AC 498)
26. Assign a Conditional Value (AC 503)
27. Change the Report Margins (AC 508)
28. Make Room for Resizing or Additional Controls (AC 508)
29. Create Labels (AC 509)
30. Print Labels (AC 512)

 If you have a SAM user profile, you may have access to hands-on instruction, practice, and assessment. Log in to your SAM account (http://sam2007.course.com) to launch any assigned training activities or exams that relate to the skills covered in this chapter.

Learn It Online

Test your knowledge of chapter content and key terms.

Instructions: To complete the Learn It Online exercises, start your browser, click the Address bar, and then enter the Web address scsite.com/ac2007/learn. When the Access 2007 Learn It Online page is displayed, click the link for the exercise you want to complete and then read the instructions.

Chapter Reinforcement TF, MC, and SA
A series of true/false, multiple choice, and short answer questions that test your knowledge of the chapter content.

Flash Cards
An interactive learning environment where you identify chapter key terms associated with displayed definitions.

Practice Test
A series of multiple choice questions that test your knowledge of chapter content and key terms.

Who Wants To Be a Computer Genius?
An interactive game that challenges your knowledge of chapter content in the style of a television quiz show.

Wheel of Terms
An interactive game that challenges your knowledge of chapter key terms in the style of the television show *Wheel of Fortune*.

Crossword Puzzle Challenge
A crossword puzzle that challenges your knowledge of key terms presented in the chapter.

Apply Your Knowledge

Reinforce the skills and apply the concepts you learned in this chapter.

Creating a Report with a Subreport
Instructions: Start Access. If you are using the Microsoft Office Access 2007 Comprehensive text, open The Bike Delivers database that you used in Chapter 6. Otherwise, see your instructor for information on accessing the files required in this book.

Perform the following tasks:
1. Create a query that joins the Courier and Customer tables. Include the Courier Number, First Name, and Last Name fields from the Courier table. Include all fields except the courier number from the Customer table. Save the query as Couriers and Customers.

2. Create a query that joins the Weekly Services and Services Offered tables. Include the Customer Number, Service Code, Service Description, Service Date, Service Time, and Service Fee. Save the query as Weekly Services and Descriptions.

3. Create the report shown in Figure 7–79. The report uses the two queries that you created in steps 1 and 2. Use the name, Courier Master List, for the report. The report is in the same style as the Recruiter Master List shown in Figure 7–1a on page AC 459.

4. Submit the revised database in the format specified by your instructor.

Courier Master List

Page 1   4/25/2008

Courier Number 102   **Courier Name:**   Chou Dang

Customer Number: AS36

Customer Name: Asterman Ind.   *Telephone Number:*   555-2050
Street: 200 Bard   *Balance:* $185.00

Service Code	Service Description	Service Date	Service Time	Service Fee
01	Medical Supplies Delivery	4/7/2008	9:30 AM	$10.00
01	Medical Supplies Delivery	4/7/2008	1:15 PM	$10.00

Customer Number: CJ16

Customer Name: CJ Gallery   *Telephone Number:*   555-1304
Street: 277 Fordham   *Balance:* $195.00

Service Code	Service Description	Service Date	Service Time	Service Fee
02	Post Office Pick-up or Delivery	4/9/2008	3:30 PM	$7.00
04	Document Delivery	4/9/2008	11:00 AM	$6.50

Customer Number: ME71

Customer Name: Mentor Group   *Telephone Number:*   555-4110
Street: 543 Fleming   *Balance:* $138.00

Service Code	Service Description	Service Date	Service Time	Service Fee
04	Document Delivery	4/11/2008	10:00 AM	$6.50

Figure 7–79

Extend Your Knowledge

Extend the skills you learned in this chapter and experiment with new skills. You may need to use Help to complete the assignment.

Modifying Reports

Instructions: Copy the JSP Recruiters database and rename the database to your last name. For example, if your last name is Smith, then name the database Smith Recruiters. Start Access and open the database that you copied and renamed.

Perform the following tasks:
1. Open the Recruiter Master List in Design view. Add your name to the report footer. Your name should appear at the left.
2. Change the report title from Recruiter Master List to Recruiter/Seminar Master List. Change the font color to red and underline the title.
3. Open the Discount Report in Design view. Calculate the average, maximum, and minimum aggregate statistics for both the amount paid and current due columns. These statistics should be displayed in the report footer. Include an appropriate label for the statistics.
4. Submit the revised database in the format specified by your instructor.

Make It Right

Analyze a database and correct all errors and/or improve the design.

Correcting Form Design Errors

Instructions: Start Access. Open the InPerson Fitness database. See the inside back cover of this book for instructions on downloading the Data Files for Students, or contact your instructor for more information about accessing the required files.

The InPerson Fitness database contains data about an organization that does personal fitness training in an individual's home. The owner of the company has created the report shown in Figure 7–80, but there are a few problems. She really wanted to concatenate the first and last name of the trainer. The title of the report should appear in the report header, not in the page header. She wants to know the total amount for each client. Finally, she would like to add page numbers and a date to the report.

Figure 7–80

Correct these errors and submit the revised database in the format specified by your instructor.

In the Lab

Design, create, modify, and/or use a database following the guidelines, concepts, and skills presented in this chapter. Labs are listed in order of increasing difficulty.

Lab 1: Creating Reports and Mailing Labels for the JMS TechWizards Database

Problem: JMS TechWizards needs a report that displays technician information as well as information about client accounts. The company would like to show its appreciation to current clients by discounting the amount clients currently owe. JMS also needs mailing labels for its clients.

Instructions: If you are using the Microsoft Office Access 2007 Comprehensive text, open the JMS TechWizards database that you used in Chapter 6. Otherwise, see the inside back cover of this book for instructions on downloading the Data Files for Students, or contact your instructor for more information about accessing the required files.

Figure 7–81

Perform the following tasks:

1. Create a query that includes the technician number, first name and last name from the Technician table and all the fields from the Client table except technician number. Name the query, Technicians and Clients.

2. Create a query that joins the Category and the Work Orders tables. Include the client number, category number, category description, total hours, and hours spent. Create a calculated field that subtracts hours spent from total hours. Use Hours Remaining as the caption for the field. Name the query, Categories and Work Orders.

3. Create the report shown in Figure 7–81. The report uses the Technicians and Clients query as the basis for the main report and the Categories and Work Orders query as the basis for the subreport. Use the name, Technician Master List, for the report. The report is similar in style to the Recruiter Master List shown in Figure 7–1a on page AC 459.

4. Create mailing labels for the Technician table. Use Avery labels C2163 and format the label with first and last name on the first line, street on the second line, and city, state, and postal code on the third line. There is a comma and a space after city and a space between state and postal code. Sort the labels by postal code.

5. Submit the revised database in the format specified by your instructor.

In the Lab

Lab 2: Creating Reports for the Hockey Fan Zone Database

Problem: The management of the Hockey Fan Zone store needs a report that displays supplier information as well information about items and the order status of items. The company also is considering an in-store sale and would like a report that shows the regular selling price as well as the sale price of all items.

Instructions: If you are using the Microsoft Office Access 2007 Comprehensive text, open the Hockey Fan Zone database that you used in Chapter 6. Otherwise, see the inside back cover of this book for instructions on downloading the Data Files for Students, or contact your instructor for more information about accessing the required files.

Perform the following tasks:

1. Create the report shown in Figure 7–82. The report uses the Supplier-Item Query that previously was created as the basis for the main report and the Reorder table as the basis for the subreport. Use the name, Supplier Master Report, for the report. The report is the same style as that demonstrated in the project. Use conditional formatting to display the on hand value in red for all items with fewer than 10 items on hand.

2. Open the Supplier-Item Query in Design view and add the Selling Price field to the query. Save the query.

3. Create the report shown in Figure 7–83. The report uses the Supplier-Item Query and calculates the sale amount for each item. Items with a selling price greater than $15.00 have a 10 percent discount and 5 percent otherwise. Note that the report shows the sale price, not the discount. The report is similar to the Discount Report shown in Figure 7–1b on page AC 459. However, there are no group subtotals or report totals. Use the name, Item Discount Report.

4. Submit the revised database in the format specified by your instructor.

Figure 7–82

Figure 7–83

In the Lab

Lab 3: Creating Reports for the Ada Beauty Supply Database

Problem: Ada Beauty Supply needs a report that displays sales rep information as well as information about customers and any open orders that the customer has. The company also needs mailing labels for its sales reps.

Instructions: If you are using the Microsoft Office Access 2007 Comprehensive text, open the Ada Beauty Supply database that you used in Chapter 6. Otherwise, see the inside back cover of this book for instructions on downloading the Data Files for Students, or contact your instructor for more information about accessing the required files. Submit the revised database in the format specified by your instructor.

Figure 7–84

Instructions Part 1:   In the Customer table, change the caption for the Services Offered field to Services. Create a query that includes the sales rep number, first name, and last name from the Sales Rep table and all fields from the Customer table except the sales rep number. Use the name, Reps and Customers, for the query.

Instructions Part 2:   Create the report shown in Figure 7–84. The report is similar in style to the Recruiter Master List shown in Figure 7–1a on page AC 459.

Instructions Part 3:   Create mailing labels for the Sales Rep table. Use Avery labels C2163 and format the label with first and last name on the first line, street on the second line, and city, state, and postal code on the third line. There is a comma and a space after city and a space between state and postal code. Use a font size of 10 and a font weight of semi-bold. Sort the labels by postal code.

Cases and Places

Apply your creative thinking and problem solving skills to design and implement a solution.

• EASIER   •• MORE DIFFICULT

• 1: Creating Reports for the Second Hand Goods Database

If you are using the Microsoft Office Access 2007 Comprehensive text, open the Second Hand Goods database that you used in Chapter 6. Otherwise, see the inside back cover of this book for instructions on downloading the Data Files for Students, or contact your instructor for more information about accessing the required files. Create a report that is similar in style to the Discount Report shown in Figure 7–1b on page AC 459. Group the report by seller code and include the seller's first name and last name. The detail section should include the item number, description, date posted, and price. Create a calculated control, Sale Price, that displays the sale price (not the discount) for all items. Items that have a price of $10.00 or more will have a 5 percent discount. Items that have a price of less than $10.00 will have a 3 percent discount. Name the report Item Sale Report. Select your own fonts for the report. Filter the report to find all items that have a price less than $10. Print the filtered report and

Continued >

Cases and Places *continued*

then remove the filter. Submit the revised database and the printed filtered report in the format specified by your instructor.

• 2: Creating Reports and Mailing Labels for the BeachCondo Rentals Database

If you are using the Microsoft Office Access 2007 Comprehensive text, open the BeachCondo Rentals database that you used in Chapter 6. Otherwise, see the inside back cover of this book for instructions on downloading the Data Files for Students, or contact your instructor for more information about accessing the required files. Create a report that is similar in style to the Recruiter Master List shown in Figure 7–1a on page AC 459. You will need two queries for the report. The first query should include the owner code, owner first and last name, unit number, and weekly rate. The second query should include the renter number, renter first and last name, unit number, start date, and length. Group the report by owner and display the unit number and weekly rate in the detail section. Include a subreport with information about the current rentals using the second query. Create mailing labels for the Owner table. Submit the revised database in the format specified by your instructor.

•• 3: Creating Reports for the Restaurant Database

If you are using the Microsoft Office Access 2007 Comprehensive text, open the restaurant database that you used in Chapter 6. Otherwise, see the inside back cover of this book for instructions on downloading the Data Files for Students, or contact your instructor for more information about accessing the required files. Using the Plan Ahead guidelines presented in this chapter, determine what additional reports you need for your database. For example, you want to prepare listings of restaurants for conference attendees. These listings are really reports. How should the reports be organized? What data should appear in the reports? Are subreports needed? Do you want to create listings grouped by food type, by distance from the university, or by cost?

•• 4: Creating Reports for Your Contacts Database

Make It Personal

If you are using the Microsoft Office Access 2007 Comprehensive text, open the Contacts database that you used in Chapter 6. Otherwise, see the inside back cover of this book for instructions on downloading the Data Files for Students, or contact your instructor for more information about accessing the required files. Using the Plan Ahead guidelines presented in this chapter, determine what additional reports you need for your database. Do these reports require subreports? For example, if you have contacted several individuals at the same company, you may want to display the names of the individuals in a subreport. Concatenate the first and last names of the individuals to give the report a professional appearance.

•• 5: Understanding Reports

Working Together

Copy the JSP Recruiters database and rename the database to your team name. For example if your team is FabFour, then name the database FabFour Recruiters. As a team, design an appropriate company letterhead for the Recruiter Master List and the Discount Report. Try different fonts and incorporate a picture or clip art. Modify the report header sections in both reports to accommodate the letterhead. Add a label to the page footer section that includes the names of the team members.

8 | Advanced Form Techniques

Objectives

You will have mastered the material in this project when you can:

- Create a form in Design view
- Add a calculated field
- Add combo boxes that include selection lists and search boxes
- Format and resize controls
- Add command buttons to a form
- Modify buttons and combo boxes
- Add an option group and create a macro for the option group

- Use tab controls to create a multipage form
- Add and modify a subform
- Insert charts
- Modify a chart type
- Format a chart

8 | Advanced Form Techniques

Introduction

This chapter creates two new forms. The first form contains two combo boxes, one for selecting data from a related table and one for finding a record on the form. It also contains command buttons to accomplish various tasks as well as an **option group**, a rectangle containing a collection of option buttons. For the command buttons and the option group to function correctly, you will create macros. In addition to the actions, the macro for the option group also contains conditions.

You also will create a **multipage form**, a form that contains more than one page of information. The form contains a tab control that allows you access two different pages. Clicking the first tab displays a page containing a subform. Clicking the second tab displays a page containing two charts.

Project — Advanced Form Techniques

JSP Recruiters wants two additional forms to use with its Client and Recruiters tables. The first form, Client View and Update Form (Figure 8–1a), contains the fields in the Client table as well as the Total Amount, which is the sum of the amount paid and the current due. Because users should not update the total amount, it appears dim on the form. Users cannot tab to it, nor will clicking it have any effect. The form has several command buttons: Next Record, Previous Record, Add Record, Delete Record, and Close Form. Clicking any of these buttons causes the action indicated on the button to take place.

In the lower-right corner of the form is an option group called Form Options. Users can click one of the options to indicate the portion of the form they wish to be able to update. If they click the Change Address Data option button, for example, they would be able to update the client number, the client name, the street, the city, the state, and the postal code, but no other data related to the client. All other fields would be dim, just like Total Amount. This restriction prevents users from inadvertently changing something they should not change.

The form also contains a combo box for the Recruiter Number field that assists users in selecting the correct recruiter (Figure 8–1b).

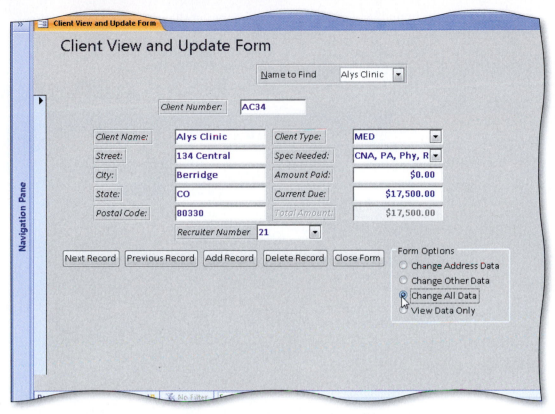

Figure 8–1a Form with Total Amount dimmed

Figure 8–1b Using combo box control for Recruiter Number

To assist users in finding a client when they know the client's name, the form also includes a combo box they can use for this purpose (Figure 8–1c). After clicking the arrow, the user simply can click the client they wish to find and Access will locate the client (Figure 8–1d) and display that client's data in the form.

Figure 8–1c Using combo box to search for Client Name

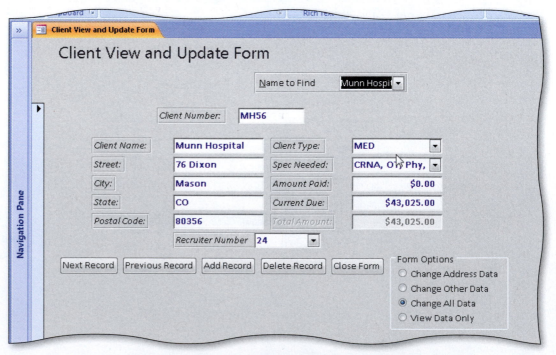

Figure 8–1d Client data found using combo box

For the second new form, JSP Recruiters needs a multipage form that lists the number and name of recruiters. Selecting the first tab, the one labeled Datasheet, displays a subform listing information about the seminar offerings for clients of the recruiter (Figure 8–2a).

Figure 8–2a

Selecting the other tab, the one labeled Charts, displays two charts that illustrate the total hours spent and hours remaining by the recruiter for the various seminars (Figure 8–2b). In both charts, the slices of the pie represent the various seminars. They are color-coded and the legend at the bottom indicates the meaning of the various colors. The size of the pie gives a visual representation of the portion of the hours spent or hours remaining by the recruiter for that particular seminar. The chart also includes specific percentages. If you look at the bottom (light blue) slice in the Hours Spent by Seminar Offering, for example, you see that the color indicates it represents seminar S06. It represents 34 percent of the total. Thus, for all the hours already spent on the various seminar offerings by recruiter 24, 34 percent have been spent on seminar S06.

Figure 8–2b

Overview

As you read through this chapter, you will learn how to create the forms by performing these general tasks:

- Create a form with a calculated field, a combo box for finding records in a related table, and a combo box for finding a record.
- Add command buttons and an option group to the form.
- Create macros for the option group and for one of the buttons.
- Create a form with a tab control.
- Add a subform to one of the tabbed pages.
- Add charts to the other tabbed page.

Plan Ahead

> **Form Design Guidelines**
>
> 1. **Determine the intended audience and the purpose of the form.** Who will use the form? How will they use it? What data do they need? What level of detail do they need?
>
> 2. **Determine the source of data for the form.** Is all the data found in a single table, or does it come from multiple related tables? Which table or tables contain the data?
>
> 3. **Determine the fields that belong on the form.** What data items are needed by the user of the form?
>
> 4. **Determine any calculations required for the form.** Should the form contain any special calculations? For example, the Client View and Update Form contains a Total Amount field that is calculated by adding the contents of the Amount Paid field and the Current Due field.
>
> 5. **Determine the organization of the form along with any additional items that should be on the form.** In what order should the fields appear? How should they be arranged? Should the form contain a subform? Should the form contain a chart? Should the form contain command buttons to assist the user in performing various functions? Should the form contain a combo box to assist the user in searching for a record?
>
> 6. **Determine the format and style of the form.** What should be in the form heading? Do you want a title, for example? Do you want a logo? What should be in the body of the form? What should the style be? In other words, what visual characteristics should the various portions of the form have?
>
> When necessary, more specific details concerning the above decisions and/or actions are presented at appropriate points in the chapter. The chapter also will identify the use of these guidelines in the design of the forms such as the ones shown in Figure 8–1 on pages AC 523 and AC 524.

Starting Access

If you are using a computer to step through the project in this chapter and you want your screen to match the figures in this book, you should change your screen's resolution to 1024 × 768. For information about how to change a computer's resolution, read Appendix E.

To Start Access

The following steps, which assume Windows Vista is running, start Access.

Note: If you are using Windows XP, see Appendix F for alternate steps.

 Click the Start button on the Windows Vista taskbar to display the Start menu.

2 Click All Programs at the bottom of the left pane on the Start menu to display the All Programs list and then click Microsoft Office on the All Programs list to display the Microsoft Office list.

3 Click Microsoft Office Access 2007 on the Microsoft Office list to start Access and display the Getting Started with Microsoft Office Access window.

4 If the Access window is not maximized, click the Maximize button on its title bar to maximize the window.

To Open a Database

In Chapter 1, you created your database on a USB flash drive using the file name, JSP Recruiters. There are two ways to open the file containing your database. If the file you created appears in the Recent Documents list, you could click it to open the file. If not, you can use the More button to open the file. The following steps use the More button to open the JSP Recruiters database from the USB flash drive.

Note: If you are using Windows XP, see Appendix F for alternate steps.

1 With your USB flash drive connected to one of the computer's USB ports, click the More button to display the Open dialog box.

2 If the Folders list is displayed below the Folders button, click the Folders button to remove the Folders list.

3 If necessary, click Computers in the Favorite Links section and then double-click UDISK 2.0 (E:) to select the USB flash drive, Drive E in this case, as the new open location. (Your drive letter might be different.)

4 Click JSP Recruiters to select the file name.

5 Click the Open button to open the database.

6 If a Security Warning appears, click the Options button to display the Microsoft Office Security Options dialog box.

7 With the option button to enable the content selected, click the OK button to enable the content.

Determine the fields that belong on the form.

1. **Examine the requirements for the form in general to determine the tables.** Do the requirements only relate to data in a single table, or does the data come from multiple tables? How are the tables related?

2. **Examine the specific requirements for the form to determine the fields necessary.** Look for all the data items that are specified for the form. Each should correspond to a field in a table or be able to be computed from a field in a table. This information gives you the list of fields.

3. **Determine whether there are any special calculations required.** Are there any special calculations? What are they? What fields are involved and how are they to be combined?

Plan Ahead

Plan Ahead

Determine the organization of the form.

1. **Determine the order of the fields.** Examine the requirements to determine the order in which the fields should appear. Be logical and consistent in your ordering. For example, in an address, the city should come before the state and the state should come before the postal code, unless there is some compelling reason for another order.

2. **Determine whether to include a subform.** If the fields for the form come from exactly two tables and there is a one-to-many relationship between the two tables and if the form is based on the "one" table, you often will place the data for the "many" table in a subform. If there are multiple tables involved, you may be able to create a query on which you can base the subform.

3. **Determine whether to include a chart.** Do you want to represent data in a visual manner? If so, you can include a chart. If you do decide to use a chart, which type of chart would best represent the data? If you want to represent total amounts, for example, a bar chart may be appropriate. If, instead, you want to represent portions of the whole, a pie chart may be better.

Plan Ahead

Determine any additional items that should be on the form.

1. **Determine whether the form should include any combo boxes.** A combo box is a combination of a text box, where users can type data, and a list box, where users can click an arrow to display a list. Would a combo box improve the functionality of the form? Is there a place where it would be convenient for users to enter data by selecting the data from a list, either a list of predefined items or a list of values from a related table? If users need to search for records, you may wish to include a combo box to assist in the process.

2. **Determine whether the form should include any command buttons.** Can you make certain actions more convenient for users by including command buttons? Buttons can carry out record navigation actions (for example, go to the next record), record operation actions (for example, add a record), form operation actions (for example, close a form), report operation actions (for example, print a report), an application action (for example, quit application), and some miscellaneous actions (for example, run a macro).

3. **Determine whether the form should contain any option groups.** If users are to select from a list of predefined choices, you can consider adding an option group. If, for example, there are different ways users might choose to interact with the form, you could include an option group. In the Client View and Update Form, for example, there is an option group in which users can select the portion of the form they will be able to update.

4. **Determine whether the form should contain a tab control.** If the form contains more information than conveniently will fit on the screen at a time, consider adding a tab control. With a tab control, you can organize the information within a collection of tabbed pages. To access any of the tabbed pages, users need only click the corresponding tab.

Creating a Form with Combo Boxes, Command Buttons, and Option Groups

After planning a form, you may decide that you need to use features such as combo boxes, command buttons, and option groups. You can include such items while modifying the form in Design view. Selecting the Use Control Wizards button on the Design tab activates a wizard that will assist you in the process.

To Create a Form in Design View

You can create a form using several different form tools, such as the Form Wizard and the Split Form. Creating a form in Design view gives you the most flexibility in laying out the form. You will be presented with a blank design on which to place objects. The following steps create a form in Design view.

- Click Create on the Ribbon to display the Create tab.

- Click Form Design on the Create tab to create a new form in Design view.

- Hide the Navigation Pane.

- Click the Property Sheet button on the Design tab to display a property sheet.

- With the All tab selected, click the Record Source property, click the arrow, and then click the Client table to select the Client table as the record source.

- Click the Save button on the Quick Access Toolbar, then type `Client Master Form` as the form name (Figure 8–3).

Figure 8–3

- Click the OK button to save the form.

- Click the Caption property in the property sheet, and then type `Client View and Update Form` as the new caption.

- Close the property sheet by clicking the Property Sheet button on the Design tab.

- Click the Add Existing Fields button to display the Field List (Figure 8–4).

Why doesn't the name on the tab change to the new caption, Client View and Update Form?

The name on the tab will change to the new caption in Form view. In Design view, you still see the name of the form.

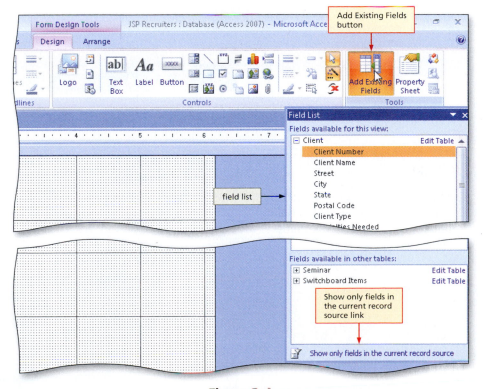

Figure 8–4

To Add Fields to the Form Design

After deciding the fields to add to the Client View and Update Form, you can place them on the form by dragging the fields from the field list to the desired position. The following steps place all the fields except the Recruiter Number field on the form.

- If necessary, click the 'Show only fields in the current record source' link at the bottom of the field list to show only the fields in the Client table.

- Drag the Client Number field from the field list to the approximate position shown in Figure 8–5.

Figure 8–5

- Click the Client Name field in the field list.

- While holding the SHIFT key down, click the Postal Code field in the field list to select multiple fields (Figure 8–6).

Figure 8–6

3

- Drag the selected fields to the approximate position shown in Figure 8–7.

- Select the Client Type through Current Due fields and then drag the selected fields to the approximate position shown in the figure.

- If controls for any of the fields are not aligned properly, align them by dragging them to the desired location or by using the alignment buttons on the Arrange tab.

- Close the field list.

Figure 8–7

To Add a Calculated Field to the Form

If you have determined that a calculated field is appropriate for a form, you can create one by using the Text Box tool in the Controls group on the Design tab. Place the text box on the form, and then indicate the contents of the field.

The following steps add the Total Amount field to the form. The total amount is calculated by adding the contents of the Amount Paid field and the contents of the Current Due field.

1

- Click the Text Box tool in the Controls group on the Design tab, and then move the mouse pointer, which has changed shape to a small plus symbol accompanied by a text box, to the position shown in Figure 8–8.

Figure 8–8

2

- Click the position shown in Figure 8–8 on the previous page to place a text box.

- Click inside the text box and type =[Amount Paid]+[Current Due] as the expression in the text box.

- Click the attached label (the box that contains the word, Text) twice, once to select it and a second time to produce an insertion point.

- Use the DELETE key or the BACKSPACE key to delete the current entry.

- Type Total Amount: as the new entry (Figure 8–9).

Could I use the expression builder instead to create the calculation?

Yes. Click the field, click the Property Sheet button on the Design tab, and then click the Build button (the three dots). You then can use the expression builder to create the expression. Use whichever method you find most convenient.

3

- Ensure that the newly added text box aligns properly with the other controls as shown in Figure 8–9.

Figure 8–9

To Change the Format of a Field

Access automatically formats fields from the database appropriately because it knows their data types. Usually, you will find the formats assigned by Access to be acceptable. For calculated fields, such as Total Amount, however, Access just assigns a general number format. The value will not appear automatically with two decimal places and a dollar sign.

To change to another format, such as Currency, which displays the number with a dollar sign and two decimal places, use the field's property sheet to change the Format property. The following steps change the format for the Total Amount field to Currency.

- Click the control for the Total Amount field (the box containing the expression), and then click the Property Sheet button to display the property sheet.

- With the All tab selected, click the Format property, click the Format property box arrow to produce a list of available formats, and then select Currency.

- Click the Decimal Places property, click the Decimal Places property box arrow, and then select 2 (Figure 8–10).

2

- Close the property sheet by clicking the Property Sheet button on the Design tab.

Figure 8–10

Combo Boxes

When entering a recruiter number, the value must match the number of a recruiter currently in the Recruiter table. To assist the users in entering this data, the form will contain a combo box. A **combo box** combines the properties of a **text box**, a box into which you can type an entry, and a **list box**, a box you can use to display a list. With a combo box, the user either can enter the data or click the combo box arrow to display a list of possible values and then select an item from the list.

To Add a Combo Box that Selects Values from a Related Table

If you have determined that a combo box that selects values from a related table would be useful on your form, you can add the combo box to a form using the Combo Box tool in the Controls group on the Design tab. If the Use Control Wizards button in the Controls group on the Design tab is selected, you can use a wizard to guide you through the process of creating the combo box. The following steps place a combo box that selects values from a related table for the Recruiter Number field on the form.

1

- With the Use Control Wizards button in the Controls group on the Design tab selected, click the Combo Box (Form Control) tool in the Controls group, and then move the mouse pointer, whose shape has changed to a small plus symbol accompanied by a combo box, to the position shown in Figure 8–11.

Figure 8–11

2

- Click the position shown in Figure 8–11 to place a combo box.

- If necessary, in the Combo Box Wizard dialog box, click the 'I want the combo box to look up the values in a table or query.' option button (Figure 8–12).

Q&A

What is the purpose of the other options?

Use the second option if you want to type a list from which the user will choose. Use the third option if you want to use the combo box to search for a record.

Figure 8–12

• Click the Next button and then, with the Tables option button selected, click Table: Recruiter to specify that the combo box values will come from the Recruiter table (Figure 8–13).

Figure 8–13

4

• Click the Next button to display the next Combo Box Wizard screen.

• Click the Add Field button to add the Recruiter Number as a field in the combo box.

• Click the First Name field and then click the Add Field button.

• Click the Last Name field and then click the Add Field button (Figure 8–14).

Figure 8–14

• Click the Next button to display the next Combo Box Wizard screen.

• Click the arrow in the first text box, and then select the Recruiter Number field (Figure 8–15).

Figure 8–15

6

- Click the Next button to display the next Combo Box Wizard screen (Figure 8–16).

Q&A

What is the key column? Do I want to hide it?

The key column would be the Recruiter Number, the column that identifies both a first name and a last name. Because the purpose of this combo box is to update recruiter numbers, you certainly do not want them hidden.

Figure 8–16

7

- Click the 'Hide key column (recommended)' check box to remove the check mark so that the Recruiter Number field will appear along with the First Name and Last Name fields.

- Click the Next button to display the next Combo Box Wizard screen (Figure 8–17).

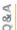

Q&A

Do I need to make any changes here?

No. The Recruiter Number field, which is the field you want to store, already is selected.

Figure 8–17

- Click the Next button to display the next Combo Box Wizard screen.

- Click the 'Store that value in this field:' option button.

- Because you want to store the value in the Recruiter Number field, click the 'Store that value in this field:' box arrow, and then click Recruiter Number (Figure 8–18).

- Click the Next button to display the next Combo Box Wizard screen.

- Be sure `Recruiter Number` is entered as the label for the combo box, and then click the Finish button to place the combo box.

Q&A | Could I change the label to something else?
| Yes. If you think something else would be better, you could change it.

- Save your changes to the form.

Figure 8–18

To Change the Background Color

You can use the Fill/Back Color button on the Design tab to change the background color of a form. The following steps change the background color of the form to Light Gray 2.

- Click anywhere in the Detail section but outside all the controls to select the section.

- Click the Fill/Back Color button arrow on the Design tab to display a color palette (Figure 8–19).

- Click the Light Gray 2 color, the first color in the third row under Standard Colors, to change the background color.

 Experiment

- Try other colors to see their effect. When finished, once again select the Light Gray 2 color.

Figure 8–19

To Format a Control

You can use buttons on the Design tab to format a control in a variety of ways. You have even more control over the types of changes you can make, however, if you use the property sheet. The following steps make a variety of changes to the format of the Client Number control.

- Click the Client Number control (the white space, not the label) to select it.

- Click the Property Sheet button on the Design tab to display the property sheet.

- Click the Format tab.

- Change the Font Weight to Semi-bold.

- Change the Special Effect to Sunken.

- Close the Property Sheet by clicking the Property Sheet button.

- Click the Font color arrow on the Design tab to display a color palette (Figure 8–20).

Figure 8–20

- Click the Dark Blue color (the second color from the right in the bottom row) to select it as the font color.

- Click the label for the Client Number field to select it.

- Click the Italic button on the Design tab to italicize the label.

- Click the Property Sheet button on the Design tab to display a property sheet.

- Change the Special Effect to Etched (Figure 8–21).

- Close the property sheet.

Figure 8–21

To Use the Format Painter

Once you have formatted a control and its label the way you want, you can format other controls in exactly the same way by using the format painter. To do so, click the control whose format you want to copy, click the Format Painter button on the Design tab and then click the other control. If you want to copy the format to more than one other control, double-click the Format Painter button instead of simply clicking the button, then click each of the controls that you want to change. The following steps copy the formatting of the Client Number control and label to the other controls.

- With the Client Number control selected, double-click the Format Painter button on the Design tab.
- Point to the Client Name control (Figure 8–22).

- Click the Client Name control to assign it the same formatting as the Client Number control.
- Click all the other controls on the form to assign them the same formatting.
- Click the Format Painter button to prevent further format copying.

Q&A Should I always click the Format Painter button when I have finished copying the formatting?

If you double-clicked the Format Painter button to enable you to copy the formatting to multiple controls, you need to click the Format Painter button again to turn off the copying. If you simply clicked the Format Painter button to enable you to copy the formatting to a single control, you do not need to click the button again. As soon as you copy the formatting to the single control, the copying will be turned off.

Q&A Does the order in which I click the other controls matter?

No. The only thing that is important is that you ultimately click all the controls whose formatting you want to assign.

Figure 8–22

To Resize Multiple Controls

You can resize multiple controls at the same time by selecting all the controls to be resized before dragging a sizing handle. The following step resizes multiple controls.

- Click the Client Name control to select it.

- While holding the SHIFT key down, click the Street, City, State, Postal Code, Client Type, Specialties Needed, Amount Paid, Current Due, and Total Amount controls to select them.

- Drag the right sizing handle of any of the selected controls to resize the controls to the approximate size shown in Figure 8–23.

Figure 8–23

To Add a Title and Expand the Form Header Section

The form you are creating has a title, Client Master Form. The following step adds the title to the form.

- Click the Title button on the Design tab to add a Form Header section and to add a control for the title to the Form Header section (Figure 8–24).

Q&A Why is the title Client View and Update Form rather than Client Master Form?

If you have changed the caption, the title will use the new value of the Caption property.

Q&A Could I add the Form Header section before adding the title? If I do, what happens when I add the title?

Access will place the title in the Form Header section that you already added.

Figure 8–24

2

• Drag the lower boundary of the Form Header section down to the approximate position shown in Figure 8–25.

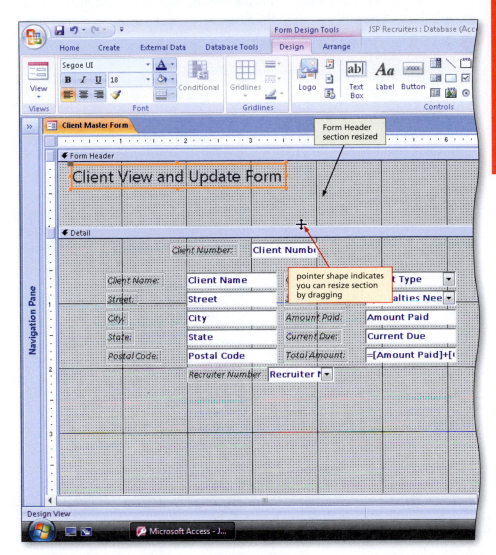

Figure 8–25

To Add Command Buttons to a Form

You may find that you can improve the functionality of your form by adding command buttons. To add command buttons, you use the Use Control Wizards button and Button (Form Control) tool in the Controls group on the Design tab. When using the series of Command Button Wizard dialog boxes, you provide the action that should be taken when the button is clicked. Several categories of actions are available.

In the Record Navigation category, you will select the Go To Next Record action for one of the buttons. From the same category, you will select the Go To Previous Record action for another. Other buttons will use the Add New Record and the Delete Record actions from the Record Operations category. The Close Form button will use the Close Form action from the Form Operations category.

The following steps add command buttons to move to the next record, move to the previous record, add a record, delete a record, and close the form.

1

- Make sure the Use Control Wizards button is selected.

- Click the Button (Form Control) tool and move the mouse pointer to the approximate position shown in Figure 8–26.

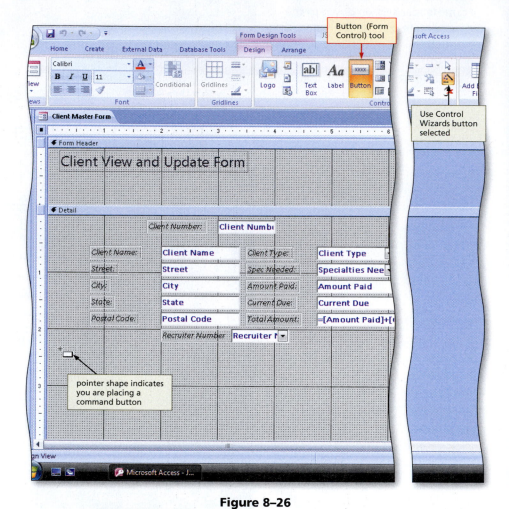

Figure 8–26

2

- Click the position shown in Figure 8–26 to display the Command Button Wizard dialog box.

- With Record Navigation selected in the Categories box, click Go To Next Record in the Actions box (Figure 8–27).

Figure 8–27

3

- Click the Next button to display the next Command Button Wizard screen (Figure 8–28).

Q&A

What is the purpose of these option buttons?

Choose the first option button to place text on the button. You then can specify the text to be included or accept the default choice. Choose the second option button to place a picture on the button. You then can select a picture.

Figure 8–28

4

- Click the Text option button.

- Because Next Record is the desired text and does not need to be changed, click the Next button.

- Type `Next Record` as the name of the button (Figure 8–29).

Figure 8–29

5

- Click the Finish button to finish specifying the button.

- Use the techniques in Steps 1 through 4 to place the Previous Record button directly to the right of the Next Record button. The action is Go To Previous Record in the Record Navigation category. Choose the Text option button and Previous Record on the button, and then type `Previous Record` as the name of the button.

- Use the techniques in Steps 1 through 4 to place a button directly to the right of the Previous Record button. The action is Add New Record in the Record Operations category. Choose the Text option button and Add Record on the button, and then type `Add Record` as the name of the button.

- Use the techniques in Steps 1 through 4 to place the Delete Record and Close Form buttons in the positions shown in Figure 8–30. For the Delete Record button, the category is Record Operations and the action is Delete Record. For the Close Form button, the category is Form Operations and the action is Close Form.

Q&A

My buttons are not aligned like yours are. What should I do?

If your buttons are not aligned properly, you can drag them to the correct positions. You also can use the Arrange tab.

Figure 8–30

To Add a Combo Box that Is Used to Find a Record

Although you can use the Ribbon to locate records on a form, it may be more convenient to use a combo box. You could type the client's name directly into the box. Alternatively, you can click the Name to Find box arrow, and Access displays a list of client names. To select a name from the list, simply click the name.

To create a combo box, use the Combo Box tool in the Controls group on the Design tab. The Combo Box Wizard then will guide you through the steps of adding the combo box. The following steps show how to place a combo box for names on the form.

1

- With the Use Control Wizards button selected, click the Combo Box (Form Control) tool and then move the mouse pointer, whose shape has changed to a small plus sign with a combo box, to the position shown in Figure 8–31.

Figure 8–31

2

- Click the position shown in Figure 8–31 to display the Combo Box Wizard.

- Click the 'Find a record on my form based on the value I selected in my combo box.' option button.

- Click the Next button, click the Client Name field, and then click the Add Field button to select the Client Name field for the combo box (Figure 8–32).

Figure 8–32

3

- Click the Next button.

- Drag the right boundary of the column heading to the approximate size shown in Figure 8–33.

Q&A Can I also resize the column to best fit the data by double-clicking the right boundary of the column heading?

Yes.

Figure 8–33

4

- Click the Next button, and then type &Name to Find as the label for the combo box.

Q&A What is the purpose of the ampersand in front of the letter, N?

The ampersand (&) in front of the letter N indicates that users can select the combo box by pressing ALT+N.

- Click the Finish button. Position the control and label in the approximate position shown in Figure 8–34.

Q&A Why is the letter, N, underlined?

The underlined N in Name indicates that you can press ALT+N to select the combo box. It is underlined because you preceded the letter N with the ampersand.

Figure 8–34

To Place a Rectangle

To emphasize the special nature of the combo box, you can place a rectangle around it as a visual cue. The following steps use the Rectangle tool to place a rectangle.

- Click the Rectangle tool in the Controls group on the Design tab, point to the upper-left corner of the rectangle in Figure 8–35, press the left mouse button, drag the pointer to the lower-right corner of the rectangle, and then release the left mouse button to place the rectangle.

- Click the Property Sheet button on the Design tab to display the property sheet for the rectangle.

- Change the value of the Special Effect property to Etched.

- Make sure the value of the Back Style property is Transparent, so the combo box will appear within the rectangle.

Q&A

What if the value is not Transparent?

If the value is not Transparent, the rectangle would cover the combo box completely and the combo box would not be visible.

- Close the property sheet.

- Save and then close the form.

Figure 8–35

BTW

Font versus Foreground Color
The font color also is called the foreground color. When you change the font color using the Ribbon, you click the Font Color button. If you use the property sheet to change the color, you click the Fore Color property, click the Build button, and then click the desired color.

To Open a Form

Once you have created the form, you can use it at any time by opening it. The following step opens the Client Master Form.

- Show the Navigation Pane. Right-click the Client Master Form to display the shortcut menu.

- Click Open on the shortcut menu to open the form (Figure 8–36).

- Hide the Navigation Pane.

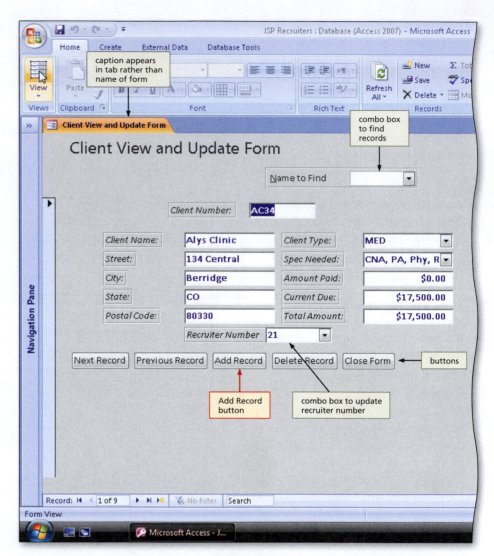

Figure 8–36

Using the Buttons

To move around on the form, you can use the buttons to perform the actions you specify. To move to the next record, click the Next Record button. Click the Previous Record button to move to the previous record. Clicking the Delete Record button will delete the record currently on the screen. You will get a message requesting that you verify the deletion before the record actually is deleted. Clicking the Close Form button will remove the form from the screen.

To Use the Add Record Button

Clicking the Add Record button will clear the contents of the form so you can add a new record. The following step uses the Add Record button.

- Click the Add Record button (Figure 8–37).

Q&A There is no insertion point in the Client Number field. How would I begin entering a new record?

To begin entering a record, you would have to click the Client Number field before you can start typing.

Q&A Why does MED appear in the Client Type field?

The value MED is the default value assigned to the Client Type field.

Experiment

- Try each of the other buttons to see their effect. Do not delete any records. After clicking the Close Form button, open the form once again.

Figure 8–37

To Use the Combo Box

Using the combo box, you can search for a client in two ways. First, you can click the combo box arrow to display a list of client names, and then select the name from the list by clicking it. Alternatively, you can begin typing the name. As you type, Access will display automatically the name that begins with the letters you have typed. Once the correct name is displayed, select the name by pressing the TAB key. Regardless of the method you use, the data for the selected client appears on the form once the selection is made.

The following steps first locate the client whose name is Munn Hospital, and then use the Next Record button to move to the next client.

- Click the Name to Find box arrow to display a list of client names (Figure 8–38).

Q&A The list is not in alphabetical order, because Ferb Dentistry is before Family Health. Wouldn't it be easier to use if the list was in alphabetical order?

Yes. You will change the combo box later so that the names appear in alphabetical order.

Figure 8–38

2

- Click Munn Hospital to display the data for Munn Hospital in the form (Figure 8–39).

Figure 8–39

3

- Click the Next Record button to display the next record (Figure 8–40).

Q&A Why does the combo box still contain Munn Hospital, rather than Peel Radiology?

This is a problem with the combo box. You will address this issue later.

Figure 8–40

Issues with the Add Record Button

Although clicking the Add Record button does erase the contents of the form in preparation for adding a new record, there is a problem with it. After clicking the Add Record button there should be an insertion point in the control for the first field, the Client Number field, but there is not. To display an insertion point automatically when you click the Add Record button, you need to change the focus. A control is said to have the **focus** when it becomes active; that is, when it becomes able to receive user input through mouse or keyboard actions. At any point in time, only one item on the form has the focus. In addition to adding a new record, clicking the Add Record button needs to update the focus to the Client Number field.

Issues with the Combo Box

The combo box has the following issues. First, if you examine the list of names in Figure 8–38 on page AC 549, you will see that they are not in alphabetical order (Ferb Dentistry comes before Family Health). Second, when you move to a record without using the combo box, the name in the combo box does not change to reflect the name of the client currently on the screen. Third, one way to change the focus from one field to another is to press the TAB key. As you repeatedly press the TAB key, the focus should move through all the fields on the form. It should not move to the combo box, however, because that does not represent a field to be updated.

BTW

Focus
A visual way exists to determine which object on the screen has the focus. If a field has the focus, an insertion point will appear in the field. If a button has the focus, a small rectangle will appear inside the button.

BTW

VBA
Visual Basic for Applications (VBA) is a programming language that can be used with Access. As with other programming languages, programs in VBA consist of code; that is, a collection of statements, also called commands, which are instructions that will cause actions to take place when the program executes. VBA is included with all of the Microsoft Office applications.

To Modify the Add Record Button

To correct the problem with the Add Record button not displaying an insertion point, you will update a macro that is associated with the clicking of the button. You need to add an action to the macro that will move the focus to the control for the Client Number field. The appropriate action is GoToControl and the argument is the name of the control.

When creating macros, it is desirable for control names not to contain spaces. If you are programming in VBA (Visual Basic for Applications), it is a requirement. There are a variety of approaches you can use for changing the names so that they don't contain spaces. The one you will use is to insert an underscore (_) in place of the space. For example, you will change Client Number to Client_Number.

The following steps first change the name of the controls to remove spaces. They then modify the macro that is associated with the clicking of the Add Record button by adding an action that will change the focus to the control for the Client Number field.

1

- Click the View button arrow and then click Design View to return to Design view.

- Click the control for the Client Number field (the white space, not the label), and then click the Property Sheet button to display the property sheet.

- If necessary, click the All tab. Ensure the Name property is selected, click immediately following the word Client, press the DELETE key to delete the space, and then type an underscore (_) to change the name to Client_Number (Figure 8–41).

Figure 8–41

Q&A

Could I just erase the old name and type Client_Number?

Yes. Use whichever method you find most convenient.

2

- Click the control for the Client Name field to display its property sheet and then change the name to Client_Name.

- Using the same technique, change the name for the controls for the Postal Code, Client Type, Specialties Needed, Amount Paid, Current Due, and Recruiter Number fields by replacing the space with an underscore (_).

- Close the property sheet and then right-click the Add Record button to display a shortcut menu (Figure 8–42).

Figure 8–42

3

- Click Build Event on the shortcut menu to display the macro associated with the On Click event (Figure 8–43).

Q&A

What is the purpose of the three actions currently in the macro?

The first command indicates that if there is an error, Access should proceed to the next action in the macro rather than immediately stopping the macro. The second action causes Access to go to the record indicated by the values in the arguments. The value New indicates that it is to go to a new record. Because the final action has a condition, it only will be executed if the condition is true, that is, the error code contains a value other than 0. In that case, the MsgBox action will display a description of the error.

Figure 8–43

4

- Click the row selector for the third row, the row that contains a criterion, and then press the INSERT key to insert a new row.

- Click the Action column on the newly inserted row, click the arrow, and select the GoToControl action to indicate that the focus will move to another control.

- Type `Client_Number` as the Control Name argument (Figure 8–44).

What is the effect of the GoToControl action?

When Access executes this action, the focus will move to the control indicated in the Control Name argument, in this case, the Client_Number control.

5

- Click the Save button on the Quick Access Toolbar to save your changes.

- Click the Close button on the Design tab to close the macro and return to the form design.

Figure 8–44

Events

Events are actions that have happened or are happening at the present time. An event can be caused by a user action. For example, one of the events associated with a button on a form is clicking the button. The corresponding event property is On Click. If you associate VBA code with the On Click event property, that code will execute whenever you click the button. Using properties associated with events, you can tell Access to run a macro, call a Visual Basic function, or run an event procedure in response to an event.

To Modify the Combo Box

You need to take special action to correct the issues with the combo box. To ensure the data is sorted in the correct order, you need to modify the query that Access has created for the combo box so the data is sorted by client name. You also need to modify the VBA (Visual Basic for Applications) code associated with what is termed the On Current event property of the entire form. The modification to the On Current event property will ensure that the combo box is kept current with the rest of the form; that is, it contains the name of the client whose number currently appears in the Client Number field. The following steps modify the query and then the code associated with the On Current event property appropriately. The final step changes the Tab Stop property for the combo box from Yes to No.

● Click the Name to Find combo box (the white space, not the label), and then click the Property Sheet button.

● Change the name to Name_to_Find.

● Scroll down in the property sheet so that the Row Source property appears, click the Row Source property, and then click the Build button (the three dots) to display the Query Builder.

● Click the Sort row in the Client Name field, click the box arrow that appears, and then click Ascending to change the order (Figure 8–45).

Figure 8–45

2

- Click the Save button to save your changes.

- Close the Query Builder window by clicking the Close button on the Design tab.

- Close the property sheet.

- Click the form selector (the box in the upper-left corner of the form) to select the form.

- Click the Property Sheet button on the Design tab, scroll down until the On Current property appears, and then click the On Current property.

- Click the Build button (the three dots) to display the Choose Builder dialog box (Figure 8–46).

Figure 8–46

3

- Click Code Builder in the Choose Builder dialog box, and then click the OK button to display the VBA code generated for the form (Figure 8–47).

Figure 8–47

4

- Press the TAB key and then type `Name_to_Find = Client_Number ' Update the combo box` as shown in Figure 8–48.

Q&A

How would I construct a command like this in my own form?

Begin with the name you assigned to the combo box followed by an equal sign and then the name of the control containing the primary key of the table. The portion of the statement following the apostrophe is a comment, describing the purpose of the command. You simply could type the same thing that you see in this command.

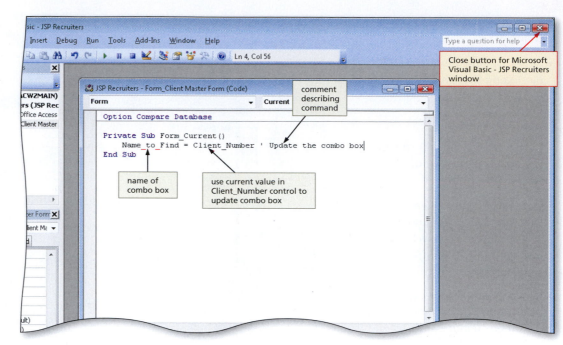

Figure 8–48

5

- Click the Close button for the Microsoft Visual Basic - JSP Recruiters - window, and then close the Form property sheet.

- Click the Name to Find combo box and then click the Property Sheet button.

- Scroll down until the Tab Stop property appears, click the Tab Stop property, and then click the Tab Stop property box arrow.

- Click No, and then close the property sheet.

- Save your changes.

To Change the Enabled Property

In the form in Figure 8–1 on pages AC 523 and AC 524 , the Total Amount field is dimmed, indicating that you cannot change the value in the field. To dim the field, you need to change the field's Enabled property from Yes to No. The following steps change the Enabled property.

1 Click the Total Amount field (the white space, not the label), click the Property Sheet button to display the property sheet, and then scroll down until the Enabled Property appears.

2 Click the Enabled property, click the Enabled property arrow, and then click No to change the value from Yes to No.

3 Close the property sheet and then save your changes.

Using the Modified Form

The problems with the Add Record button and the combo box now are corrected and the Total Amount field is dimmed. When you click the Add Record button, an insertion point appears in the Client Number field (Figure 8–49a). When you click the Name to Find box arrow, the list of names is in alphabetical order (Figure 8–49b). After using the Name to Find box to find a client (Figure 8–49c on page AC 558) and clicking the Next button, the Name to Find box is updated with the correct client name (Figure 8–49d on page AC 558).

Figure 8–49a Using the Add Record button

Figure 8–49b Using the Name to Find box

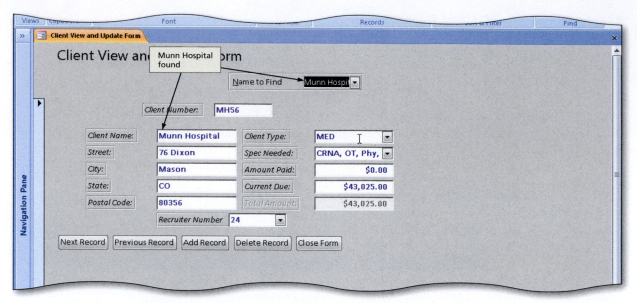

Figure 8–49c Results of using the Name to Find box

Figure 8–49d Using the Next Record button

To Add an Option Group

You may decide to allow users to make a selection from some predefined options by including an option group. An **option group** is a rectangle containing a collection of option buttons. To select an option, you simply click the corresponding option button. The form you are creating contains an option group called Form Options. In this group, you select an option button to indicate the portion of the form that should be enabled for update.

The following steps use the Option Group tool to create the Form Options option group.

1

- With the Use Control Wizards button selected, click the Option Group tool in the Controls group on the Design tab and then move the pointer to the approximate position shown in Figure 8–50.

Figure 8–50

2

- Click the position shown in Figure 8–50 to place an option group and start the Option Group Wizard.

- Type `Change Address Data` in the first row of label names and press the DOWN ARROW key.

- Type `Change Other Data` in the second row of label names and press the DOWN ARROW key.

- Type `Change All Data` in the third row of label names and press the DOWN ARROW key.

- Type `View Data Only` in the fourth row of label names (Figure 8–51).

Figure 8–51

● Click the Next button to move to the next Option Group Wizard screen.

● With the 'Yes, the default choice is' option button selected, click the arrow and select View Data Only as the default choice (Figure 8–52).

Q&A What is the effect of specifying one of the options as the default choice?

The default choice is the one that initially will be selected when you open the form.

Figure 8–52

● Click the Next button to move to the next Option Group Wizard screen and then verify that the values assigned to the labels match those shown in Figure 8–53.

Q&A How do I use the values that I have assigned?

You can use them in macros or VBA. You will use them in a macro later in this chapter.

Figure 8–53

● Click the Next button to move to the next Option Group Wizard screen and then ensure that the 'Save the value for later use.' option button is selected.

Q&A What is the alternative?

You could store the value in a field.

● Click the Next button to move to the next Option Group Wizard screen and then ensure that the 'Option buttons' option button and the Etched option button are selected.

Q&A What are the alternatives?

Rather than option buttons, you could choose Check boxes or Toggle buttons. Rather than Etched, you could select Flat, Raised, Shadowed, or Sunken.

● Click the Next button to move to the next Option Group Wizard screen, type `Form Options` as the caption, and then click the Finish button.

To Create a Macro for the Option Group

In order to take appropriate action when the user clicks an option button in the option group, you will create a macro. The macro will set the Enabled property of the controls on the form to the appropriate value. Those controls that should be enabled, that is, those controls the user should be able to update will have the Enabled value set to 1; the rest will have the value set to 0.

Because the specific actions to be taken depend on the option button the user selects, the macro will contain conditions. There will be four conditions: one to test if the user selected option 1, one to test if the user selected option 2, one for option 3, and one for option 4. The expression that contains this number is [Forms]![Client Master Form]![Form_Options]. Because this expression is fairly lengthy, the macro will begin by setting a temporary variable, Optno (short for option number), to this expression. This simply means that Optno is a named location in computer memory. This location can contain a value, in this case the option number on the form. In each of the conditions, you then can use Optno rather than the full expression.

The following steps begin creating the macro and add an action to set the temporary variable to the desired value.

1

- With the option group selected, click the Property Sheet button on the Design tab to display a property sheet.

- Change the name to Form_Options.

- Click the After Update property.

- Click the Build button to display the Choose Builder dialog box (Figure 8–54).

Figure 8–54

2

- With Macro Builder selected in the Choose Builder dialog box, click the OK button to create a macro.

- Click the Conditions button, if necessary, to display the Condition column.

- Select SetTempVar as the action on the first row.

- Enter `Optno` as the value for the Name argument.

- Enter `[Forms]![Client Master Form]![Form_Options]` as the value for the Expression argument (Figure 8–55).

Q&A What does this expression mean?

The first part indicates that the value is found in a control on a form. The second part indicates that it is the Client Master Form. The final part indicates that it is the control called Form_Options on the Client Master Form. The end result is that the temporary variable Optno will be set to the value of the Form_Options control.

Figure 8–55

BTW

Variables
Variables are named locations in computer memory. You can place a value in a variable, change the value in a variable, and use the value in a variety of ways, such as computations and comparisons.

Macro for Options Group

The macro contains four conditions. The first is [TempVars]![Optno]=1, which simply means the value in the temporary variable Optno is equal to 1. In other words, the user selected the first option button. The actions associated with this condition are all SetProperty. The arguments will be the name of the control (for example, Client_Number), the property to be set (Enabled), and the value (1 for enabled, 0 for not enabled). For option 1, the Client_Number, Client_Name, Street, City, State, and Postal_Code should all have the value of the Enabled property set to 1; the remaining controls should have the value set to 0. If more than one action is associated with the same condition, the condition column for all actions other than the first should contain three periods (...).

The conditions and actions for options 2, 3, and 4 are similar. The only difference is which controls have their enabled property set to 1. For option 2, the Client_Number, Client_Name, Client_Type, Specialties_Needed, Amount_Paid, Current_Due, and Recruiter_Number should all have the value of the Enabled property set to 1; the remaining controls should have the value set to 0. For option 3, all controls should have their Enabled property set to 1 and for option 4, all controls should have their Enabled property set to 0. Because the temporary variable, Optno, is not needed once the actions in this macro have been performed, the final action removes this temporary variable.

Table 8–1 shows the macro for the option group.

Condition	Action	Arguments
	SetTempVar	Name: Optno Expression: [Forms]![Client Master Form]![Form_Options]
[TempVars]![Optno]=1	SetProperty	Control Name: Client_Number Property: Enabled Value: 1
…	SetProperty	Control Name: Client_Name Property: Enabled Value: 1
…	SetProperty	Control Name: Street Property: Enabled Value: 1
…	SetProperty	Control Name: City Property: Enabled Value: 1
…	SetProperty	Control Name: State Property: Enabled Value: 1
…	SetProperty	Control Name: Postal_Code Property: Enabled Value: 1
…	SetProperty	Control Name: Client_Type Property: Enabled Value: 0
…	SetProperty	Control Name: Specialties_Needed Property: Enabled Value: 0
…	SetProperty	Control Name: Amount_Paid Property: Enabled Value: 0
…	SetProperty	Control Name: Current_Due Property: Enabled Value: 0
…	SetProperty	Control Name: Recruiter_Number Property: Enabled Value: 0
[TempVars]![Optno]=2	SetProperty	Control Name: Client_Number Property: Enabled Value: 1
…	SetProperty	Control Name: Client_Name Property: Enabled Value: 1
…	SetProperty	Control Name: Street Property: Enabled Value: 0
…	SetProperty	Control Name: City Property: Enabled Value: 0
…	SetProperty	Control Name: State Property: Enabled Value: 0
…	SetProperty	Control Name: Postal_Code Property: Enabled Value: 0

Table 8–1 Macro for After Update Property of the Option Group

Table 8–1 Macro for After Update Property of the Option Group (*continued*)		
Condition	**Action**	**Arguments**
...	SetProperty	Control Name: Client_Type Property: Enabled Value: 1
...	SetProperty	Control Name: Specialties_Needed Property: Enabled Value: 1
...	SetProperty	Control Name: Amount_Paid Property: Enabled Value: 1
...	SetProperty	Control Name: Current_Due Property: Enabled Value: 1
...	SetProperty	Control Name: Recruiter_Number Property: Enabled Value: 1
[TempVars]![Optno]=3	SetProperty	Control Name: Client_Number Property: Enabled Value: 1
...	SetProperty	Control Name: Client_Name Property: Enabled Value: 1
...	SetProperty	Control Name: Street Property: Enabled Value: 1
...	SetProperty	Control Name: City Property: Enabled Value: 1
...	SetProperty	Control Name: State Property: Enabled Value: 1
...	SetProperty	Control Name: Postal_Code Property: Enabled Value: 1
...	SetProperty	Control Name: Client_Type Property: Enabled Value: 1
...	SetProperty	Control Name: Specialties_Needed Property: Enabled Value: 1
...	SetProperty	Control Name: Amount_Paid Property: Enabled Value: 1
...	SetProperty	Control Name: Current_Due Property: Enabled Value: 1
...	SetProperty	Control Name: Recruiter_Number Property: Enabled Value: 1
[TempVars]![Optno]=4	SetProperty	Control Name: Client_Number Property: Enabled Value: 0
...	SetProperty	Control Name: Client_Name Property: Enabled Value: 0

Condition	Action	Arguments
...	SetProperty	Control Name: Street Property: Enabled Value: 0
...	SetProperty	Control Name: City Property: Enabled Value: 0
...	SetProperty	Control Name: State Property: Enabled Value: 0
...	SetProperty	Control Name: Postal_Code Property: Enabled Value: 0
...	SetProperty	Control Name: Client_Type Property: Enabled Value: 0
...	SetProperty	Control Name: Specialties_Needed Property: Enabled Value: 0
...	SetProperty	Control Name: Amount_Paid Property: Enabled Value: 0
...	SetProperty	Control Name: Current_Due Property: Enabled Value: 0
...	SetProperty	Control Name: Recruiter_Number Property: Enabled Value: 0
	RemoveTempVar	Name: Optno

Table 8–1 Macro for After Update Property of the Option Group (*continued*)

To Add Actions to the Macro

The following steps add the remaining conditions and actions to the macro.

1

• Add the condition and actions associated with option number 1 and specify the arguments for the actions (Figure 8–56).

Figure 8–56

2

- Add the conditions and actions associated with options 2, 3, and 4 and specify the arguments for the actions.

Q&A

Do I have to type all these actions? They seem to be very similar to the ones associated with option 1.

You can copy and paste the actions for option 1. (Click the row selector for the row with the condition and then click the final action in the list while holding the SHIFT key down to select the actions. Click the Home tab, click the Copy button, click the row selector for the first empty row, and then click the Paste button.) You then can change the number in the condition to the appropriate option number and then make the appropriate changes to the Enabled argument on the new rows.

- Add the RemoveTempVar action and argument as shown in Figure 8–57.

Q&A

Do I need to remove the temporary variable?

Technically, no. In fact, if you plan to use this temporary variable in another macro and wanted it to retain the value you assigned in this macro, you definitely would not remove it. If you don't plan to use it elsewhere, it is a good idea to remove it, however.

3

- Click the Save button to save the macro.

- Click the Close button on the Design tab to close the macro and return to the form.

Figure 8–57

To Create a Macro for the On Load Property of the Form

There are occasions where there is some special action to be taken when a form first loads into memory. For example, when this form loads, you want to ensure that the correct fields are enabled. In particular, because the View Data Only option is the one that initially is selected, the enabled property for all controls initially should be set to 0. Such an action would be included in a macro that is to be executed when the Form Load event occurs. The macro should set the enabled property for all controls to 0. The following steps create the required macro.

1

- Click the form selector (the box in the upper-left corner of the form) to select the form.

- If necessary, click the Property Sheet button on the Design tab, scroll down until the On Load property appears, and then click the On Load property.

- Click the Build button (the three dots) to display the Choose Builder dialog box.

- With Macro Builder selected in the Choose Builder dialog box, click the OK button to create a macro.

- Click the Conditions button, if necessary, to remove the Condition column.

- Enter the actions and arguments shown in Figure 8–58.

2

- Save the changes to the macro.

- Click the Close button on the Design tab to close the macro and return to the form.

- Close the property sheet.

- Save and then close the form.

Figure 8–58

Using the Option Group

When you first open the form, the View Data Only option button will be selected (Figure 8–59a on the following page) and none of the controls will be enabled; they all will be dimmed. If you click the Change Address Data option button (Figure 8–59b on the following page), the Client Number, Client Name, Street, City, State, and Postal Code controls will be enabled. The rest will be dimmed. If you click the Change Other Data option button (Figure 8–59c on page AC 569), the Client Number, Client Name, Client Type, Specialties Needed, Amount Paid, Current Due, and Recruiter Number controls will be enabled. Finally, if you click the Change All Data option button (Figure 8–59d on page AC 569), all controls are enabled except the Total Amount control, which cannot be updated.

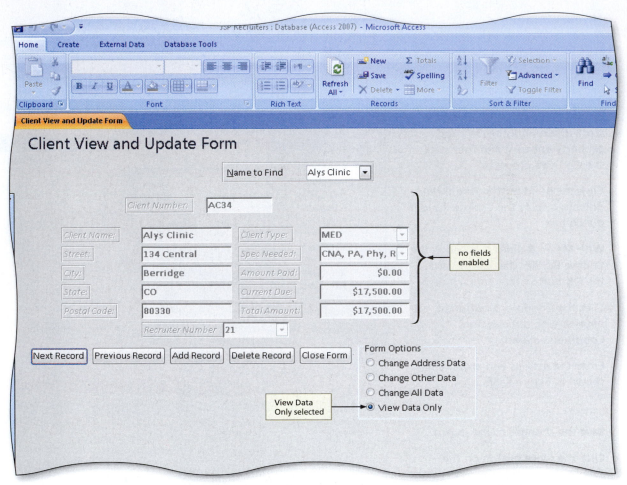

Figure 8–59a Open form with View Data Only option button default

Figure 8–59b Controls enabled for changing client address data

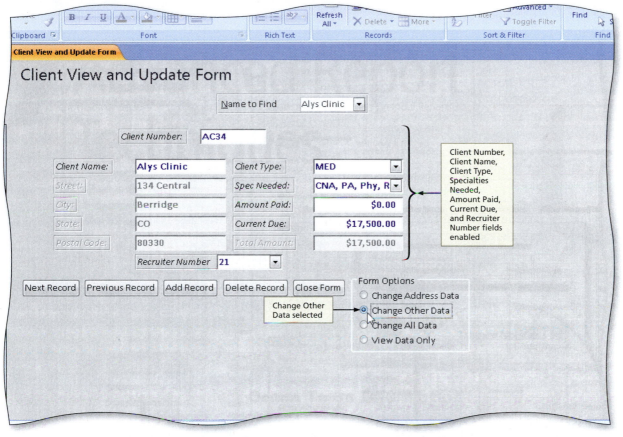

Figure 8–59c Controls enabled for changing other client data

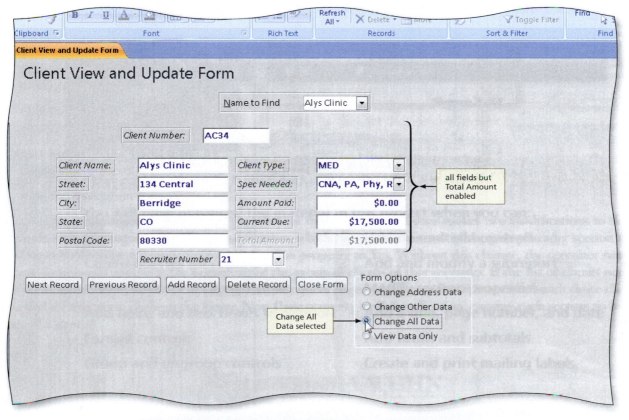

Figure 8–59d All controls enabled except Total Amount

Creating a Multipage Form

If you have determined that you have more data than will fit conveniently on one screen, you can create a **multipage form**, a form that includes more than a single page. There are two ways to create a multipage form. You can insert a page break at the desired location. An alternative that produces a nice-looking and easy-to-use multipage form is to insert a tab control. Once you have done so, users can change from one page to another by clicking the desired tab.

To Create a Form

The following steps create a form in Design view. The form will include two tabs, one that displays a datasheet and another that displays two charts.

 1

- If necessary, hide the Navigation Pane.

- Click Create on the Ribbon to display the Create tab.

- Click Form Design on the Create tab to create a new form in Design view.

- Click the Property Sheet button on the Design tab to display a property sheet.

- With the All tab selected, click the Record Source property, click the arrow that appears, and then click the Recruiter table to select the Recruiter table as the row source.

- Close the property sheet.

- Click the Add Existing Fields button to display a field list, drag the Recruiter Number, First Name, and Last Name fields to the approximate positions shown in Figure 8–60.

- Move the attached labels for the First Name and Last Name fields to the positions shown in the figure by dragging their move handles.

- Close the field list by clicking the Add Existing Fields button a second time.

Figure 8–60

To Use Tab Controls to Create a Multipage Form

To use tabs on a form, you need to insert a tab control. The following steps insert a tab control with two tabs — Datasheet and Charts. Users will be able to click the Datasheet tab in the completed form to view seminar offerings in Datasheet view. Clicking the Charts tab will display two charts representing the same seminar data.

- Click the Tab Control tool and move the mouse pointer to the approximate location shown in Figure 8–61.

Figure 8–61

- Click the position shown in Figure 8–61 to place a tab control on the form.

- Click the leftmost tab and then click the Property Sheet button on the Design tab to display a property sheet.

- Change the value for the Name property to `Datasheet` (Figure 8–62).

- Click the second tab without closing the property sheet.

- Change the value for the Name property to `Charts`.

- Close the property sheet.

- Save the form using the name, Recruiter Seminar Data.

Figure 8–62

To Add a Subform

To add a subform to a form, you use the Subform/Subreport tool in the Controls group on the Design tab. If the Use Control Wizards button is selected, a wizard will guide you through the process of adding the subform. The following steps place a subform on the Datasheet tab.

- Resize the tab control to the approximate size shown in Figure 8–63 by dragging the appropriate sizing handles.

Figure 8–63

- Click the Datasheet tab.

- With the Use Control Wizards button selected, click the Subform/Subreport tool in the Controls group on the Design tab, and then move the mouse pointer to the approximate position shown in Figure 8–64.

Figure 8–64

3

- Click the position shown in Figure 8–64 to open the SubForm Wizard.

- Be sure the 'Use existing Tables and Queries' option button is selected.

- Click the Next button to display the next SubForm Wizard screen.

- Click the Tables/Queries box arrow and then click the Recruiters and Seminar Offerings query.

- Click the Add All Fields button (Figure 8–65).

Figure 8–65

4

- Click the Next button.

- Be sure the 'Choose from a list' option button is selected.

- Click the Next button.

- Type `Seminar Offerings for Recruiter` as the name of the subform and then click the Finish button to complete the creation of the subform (Figure 8–66).

5

- Save and then close the Recruiter Seminar Data form.

Figure 8–66

To Modify a Subform

The next task is to modify the subform. The Recruiter Number field needed to be in the subform because it is used to link the data in the subform to the data in the main form. It is not supposed to appear in the form, however. In addition, the remaining columns need to be resized to appropriate sizes. The following steps illustrate how to first remove the Recruiter Number field and then convert to Datasheet view to resize the remaining columns.

1

- Show the Navigation Pane, right-click the Seminar Offerings for Recruiter form, and then click Design View on the shortcut menu.

- Click the Recruiter Number control, and then press the DELETE key to delete the control.

- Click the View button to view the subform in Datasheet view.

- Resize each column to best fit the data by double-clicking the right boundary of the column's field selector (Figure 8–67).

2

- Save the subform and then close it.

Figure 8–67

To Change the Background Color

The following steps change the background color of the form to Light Gray 2.

1

- If necessary, show the Navigation Pane, right-click Recruiter Seminar Data, and then click Design View on the shortcut menu.

- Hide the Navigation Pane.

- Click anywhere in the Detail section but outside all the controls to select the section.

- Click the Fill/Back Color button arrow on the Design tab to display a color palette (Figure 8–68).

2

- Click the Light Gray 2 color, the first color in the third row under Standard Colors, to change the background color.

Figure 8–68

To Resize the Subform

The following step resizes the subform to the size shown in Figure 8–2a on page AC 525.

- Resize the subform to the size shown in Figure 8–69 by dragging the right sizing handle.

Figure 8–69

To Insert Charts

You may decide that you want to represent data visually in a table or query. If so, you can create a chart. To insert a chart, use the Insert Chart tool on the Design tab. The Chart Wizard then will ask you to indicate the fields to be included on the chart and the type of chart you wish to insert. The following steps insert a chart.

- Click the Charts tab and then click the Insert Chart tool in the Controls group on the Design tab.

- Move the pointer to the approximate position shown in Figure 8–70.

Figure 8–70

- Click the position shown in Figure 8–70 on the previous page to display the Chart Wizard dialog box.

- Click the Queries option button in the Chart Wizard dialog box, click the Recruiters and Seminar Offerings query, and then click the Next button.

- Select the Seminar Number and Hours Spent fields by clicking them and then clicking the Add Field button (Figure 8–71).

Figure 8–71

- Click the Next button.

- Click the Pie chart, the chart in the lower-left corner (Figure 8–72).

Experiment

- Click the other chart types and read the description of each chart type in the lower-right corner of the Chart Wizard dialog box. When finished, click the Pie chart in the lower-left corner.

Figure 8–72

4

 • Click the Next button (Figure 8–73). (Your chart may not appear.)

Q&A What do the chart fields mean?

The field under the chart represents the data that will be summarized by slices of the pie. The other field is used to indicate the series. In this example, the field for the series is the seminar number and the sizes of the slices of the pie will represent the sum of the number of hours spent. You can change these by dragging the fields to the desired locations.

Q&A These fields make sense for a pie chart. What if I selected a different chart type?

The items on this screen will be relevant to the particular chart type you select. Just as with the pie chart, the correct fields often will be selected automatically. If not, you can drag the fields to the correct locations.

Figure 8–73

5

• Click the Next button (Figure 8–74).

Q&A The Recruiter Number field does not appear in my chart. Can I still use it to link the form and the chart?

Yes. Even though the Recruiter Number does not appear, it still is included in the query on which the chart is based. In fact, it is essential that it is included so that you can link the document (that is, the form) and the chart. Linking the document and the chart ensures that the chart will reflect accurately the data for the correct recruiter, that is, the recruiter who currently appears in the form.

Figure 8–74

6

• Click the Next button, type `Hours Spent by Seminar Offering` as the title, and then click the Finish button (Figure 8–75).

 Q&A

The data does not look right. What's wrong and what do I need to do to fix it?

The data in the chart is fictitious. The data simply represents the general way the chart will look. When you view the actual form, the data represented in the chart should be correct.

Figure 8–75

7

• Use the techniques shown in Steps 1 through 6 to add a second chart at the position shown in Figure 8–76. In this chart, select Hours Remaining instead of Hours Spent and type `Hours Remaining by Seminar Offering` as the title of the chart instead of Hours Spent by Seminar Offering.

 8

• Save your changes.

• Close the form.

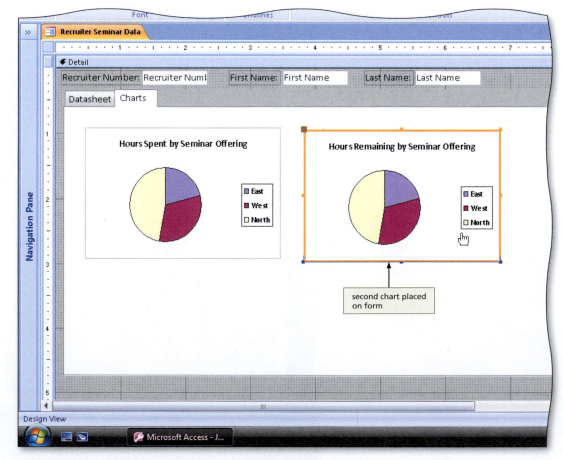

Figure 8–76

To Use the Form

You use this form just like the other forms you have created and used. To move from one tabbed page to another, simply click the desired tab. The corresponding page then will appear. The following steps use the form to view the seminar data.

 1
- Show the Navigation Pane, open the Recruiter Seminar Data form in Form view, and hide the Navigation Pane.

- With the Datasheet tab selected, click the Next Record button at the bottom of the form to move to the second record in the Recruiter table (Figure 8–77).

Q&A What is the purpose of the navigation buttons in the subform?

These navigation buttons allow you to move within the records in the subform, that is, within the seminar offerings for the recruiter whose number and name appear at the top of the form.

Figure 8–77

2
- Click the Charts tab to display the charts (Figure 8–78).

Q&A My chart does not appear when I move to another record. What's wrong and what do I need to do to fix it?

Nothing is wrong. You may need to refresh the data. To do so, click the Datasheet tab and then click the Charts tab.

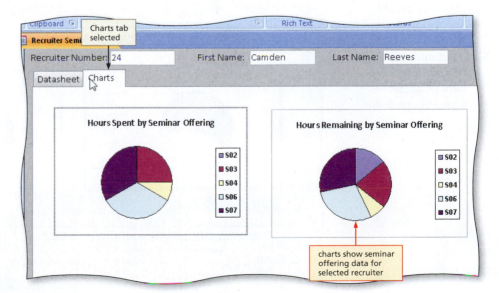

Figure 8–78

To Modify a Chart Type

When you first create a chart you specify the chart type. You later can change the type by editing the chart and selecting the Chart Type command. The following steps change the chart type.

• Right-click the Hours Spent by Seminar Offering chart to display a shortcut menu.

Q&A

Does it matter where I right-click?

You should right-click within the rectangle but outside any of the items within the rectangle, in other words, in the white space.

Q&A

My shortcut menu is very different. What should I do?

Click the View button arrow and then click Form View to ensure that you are viewing the form in Form view and then try again.

Figure 8–79

• Point to Chart Object on the shortcut menu to display the Chart Object submenu (Figure 8–79).

• Click Edit on the Chart Object sub-menu to edit the chart and display the underlying chart data in datasheet view (Figure 8–80).

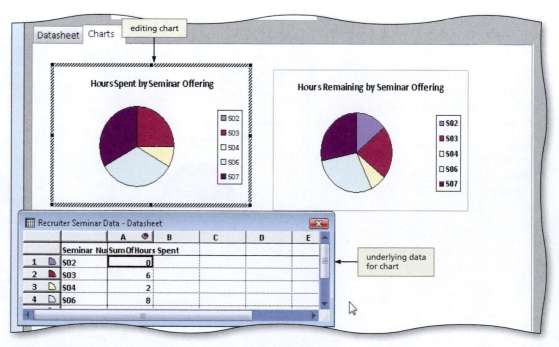

Figure 8–80

3

- Right-click the chart to display the shortcut menu for editing the chart (Figure 8–81).

Q&A Does it matter where I right-click?

You should right-click within the rectangle but outside any of the items within the rectangle, in other words, in the white space.

Q&A What types of changes can I make if I select Format Chart Area?

You can change such things as border style, color, fill effects, and fonts.

Q&A How do I make other changes?

By clicking Chart Options on the shortcut menu, you can change titles, legends, and labels. For 3-D charts, by clicking 3-D View on the shortcut menu, you can change the elevation and rotation of the chart. You also can format specific items on the chart, as you will see in the next section.

Figure 8–81

4

- Click the Chart Type command on the shortcut menu to display the Chart Type dialog box (Figure 8–82).

Q&A What is the relationship between the Chart type and the Chart sub-type?

You can think of Chart types as categories of charts. There are column charts, bar charts, line charts, and so on. Once you have selected a category, the chart sub-types are those charts in that category. If you have selected the Pie chart category, for example, the charts within the category are the ones shown in the list of chart sub-types in Figure 8–82.

Figure 8–82

5

- Click the chart sub-type in the middle of the first row of chart sub-types to select it as the chart sub-type.

Experiment

- Click each of the chart types and examine the chart sub-types associated with that chart type. When finished, select Pie as the chart type and the sub-type in the middle of the first row as the chart sub-type.

- Click the OK button to change the chart sub-type.

- Click outside the chart and the datasheet to deselect the chart.

- Make the same change to the other chart (Figure 8–83).

Figure 8–83

To Format a Chart

You can change the border style, color, fill effects, and fonts by using the Format Chart Area command. You can change titles, legends, and labels by using the Chart Options command. You also can format specific portions of a chart by right-clicking the portion you wish to format and then clicking the appropriate command on the shortcut menu. The following steps use this technique to move the legend so that it is at the bottom of the chart and then include percentages in the chart.

- Right-click the Hours Spent by Seminar Offering chart to display a shortcut menu, point to Chart Object on the shortcut menu to display the Chart Object submenu, and then click Edit on the Chart Object submenu.

- Right-click the legend to display a shortcut menu, and then click Format Legend on the shortcut menu to display the Format Legend dialog box.

- Click the Placement tab (Figure 8–84).

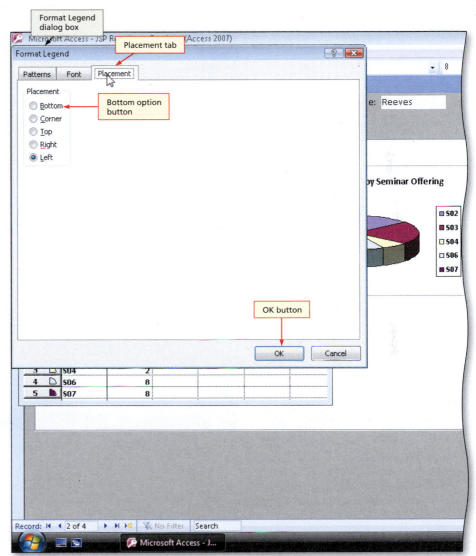

Figure 8–84

2

- Click the Bottom option button to specify that the legend should appear at the bottom of the chart.

What other types of changes can I make in this dialog box?

Click the patterns tab to change such things as border style, color, and fill effects. Click the Font tab to change the font and/or font characteristics.

- Click the OK button to place the legend at the location you selected.

- Right-click the pie chart to display a shortcut menu, and then click Format Data Series on the shortcut menu to display the Format Data Series dialog box.

- Click the Data Labels tab.

- Click the Percentage check box to specify that percentages are to be included (Figure 8–85).

I see a Patterns tab just as with the legend, but how would I use the Options tab? Also, does the fact these are check boxes rather than option buttons mean that I can select more than one?

Use the Options tab to indicate whether the color is to vary by slice and also to specify the angle of the first slice in the pie. Because these are check boxes, you can select as many as you wish. Selecting too many can clutter the chart, however.

These options make sense for a pie chart, but what about other chart types?

The options that you see will vary from one chart type to another. They will be relevant for the selected chart type.

Figure 8–85

3

- Click the OK button to include percentages on the chart (Figure 8–86).

4

- Click outside the chart and the datasheet to deselect the chart.
- Make the same changes to the other chart.
- Save and then close the form.

Figure 8–86

Using Other Tools in the Controls Group

You have used several tools within the Controls group on the Design tab. There are additional tools available (Figure 8–87) to customize a form's controls.

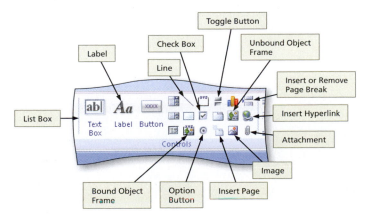

Figure 8–87

BTW

Quick Reference
For a table that lists how to complete the tasks covered in this book using the mouse, Ribbon, short-cut menu, and keyboard, see the Quick Reference Summary at the back of this book, or visit the Access 2007 Quick Reference Web page (scsite.com/ac2007/qr).

A list of the additional tools and a description of their respective uses appears in Table 8–2.

Table 8–2 Additional Tools in the Controls Group	
Tool	**Description**
Label	Create a label, a box containing text that cannot be edited and is independent of other controls, such as a title.
List Box	Create a list box, a box that allows the user to select from a list of options.
Line	Draw a line on a form or report.
Bound Object Frame	Insert an OLE object (for example, a graph, picture, sound file, or video) that is contained in a field in a table within the database.
Check Box	Insert a check box. With a check box, a user can make multiple Yes/No selections.
Option Button	Insert an option button. With an option button, a user can make a single Yes/No selection from among a collection of at least two choices.
Toggle Button	Add a toggle button. With a toggle button, a user can make a Yes/No selection by clicking the button. The button either appears to be pressed (for Yes) or not pressed (for No).
Insert Page	Insert an additional page into a tab control.
Unbound Object Frame	Insert an OLE object (for example, a graph, picture, sound file, or video) that is not contained in a field in a table within the database.
Image	Insert a frame into which you can insert a graphic. The graphic will be the same for all records.
Insert or Remove Page Break	Insert or remove a physical page break (typically in a report).
Insert Hyperlink	Insert a hyperlink to an existing file, Web page, database object, or e-mail address.
Attachment	Insert an Attachment field.

To Quit Access

BTW

Certification
The Microsoft Certified Application Specialist (MCAS) program provides an opportunity for you to obtain a valuable industry credential — proof that you have the Access 2007 skills required by employers. For more information, see Appendix G or visit the Access 2007 Certification Web page (scsite.com/ac2007/cert).

You saved all your changes and are ready to quit Access. The following step quits Access.

 Click the Close button on the right side of the Access title bar to quit Access.

Chapter Summary

In this chapter you have learned to add a calculated field to a form; add a combo box that selects from a related table as well as a combo box that is used to find records on a form; format controls and use the format painter; add command buttons to a form; modify a button and a combo box; add and modify an option group; create macros with conditions as well as modify properties using a macro; use a tab control to create a multipage form; add and modify a subform; insert charts; change chart types; and format charts. The following list includes all the new Access skills you have learned in this chapter.

1. Create a Form in Design View (AC 529)
2. Add Fields to the Form Design (AC 530)
3. Add a Calculated Field to the Form (AC 531)
4. Change the Format of a Field (AC 532)
5. Add a Combo Box that Selects Values from a Related Table (AC 534)
6. Change the Background Color (AC 537)
7. Format a Control (AC 538)
8. Use the Format Painter (AC 539)
9. Resize Multiple Controls (AC 540)
10. Add a Title and Expand the Form Header Section (AC 540)
11. Add Command Buttons to a Form (AC 541)
12. Add a Combo Box that is Used to Find a Record (AC 544)
13. Place a Rectangle (AC 547)
14. Open a Form (AC 548)
15. Use the Add Record Button (AC 549)
16. Use the Combo Box (AC 549)

17. Modify the Add Record Button (AC 551)
18. Modify the Combo Box (AC 554)
19. Change the Enabled Property (AC 556)
20. Add an Option Group (AC 558)
21. Create a Macro for the Option Group (AC 561)
22. Add Actions to the Macro (AC 565)
23. Create a Macro for the On Load Property of the Form (AC 566)
24. Use Tab Controls to Create a Multipage Form (AC 571)
25. Add a Subform (AC 572)
26. Modify a Subform (AC 574)
27. Change the Background Color (AC 574)
28. Resize the Subform (AC 575)
29. Insert Charts (AC 575)
30. Use the Form (AC 579)
31. Modify a Chart Type (AC 580)
32. Format a Chart (AC 583)

 If you have a SAM user profile, you may have access to hands-on instruction, practice, and assessment. Log in to your SAM account (http://sam2007.course.com) to launch any assigned training activities or exams that relate to the skills covered in this chapter.

STUDENT ASSIGNMENTS

Learn It Online

Test your knowledge of chapter content and key terms.

Instructions: To complete the Learn It Online exercises, start your browser, click the Address bar, and then enter the Web address scsite.com/ac2007/learn. When the Access 2007 Learn It Online page is displayed, click the link for the exercise you want to complete and then read the instructions.

Chapter Reinforcement TF, MC, and SA
A series of true/false, multiple choice, and short answer questions that test your knowledge of the chapter content.

Flash Cards
An interactive learning environment where you identify chapter key terms associated with displayed definitions.

Practice Test
A series of multiple choice questions that test your knowledge of chapter content and key terms.

Who Wants To Be a Computer Genius?
An interactive game that challenges your knowledge of chapter content in the style of a television quiz show.

Wheel of Terms
An interactive game that challenges your knowledge of chapter key terms in the style of the television show *Wheel of Fortune*.

Crossword Puzzle Challenge
A crossword puzzle that challenges your knowledge of key terms presented in the chapter.

Apply Your Knowledge

Reinforce the skills and apply the concepts you learned in this chapter.

Creating a Multipage Form for The Bike Delivers Database
Instructions: Start Access. If you are using the Microsoft Office Access 2007 Comprehensive text, open The Bike Delivers database that you used in Chapter 7. Otherwise, see your instructor for information on accessing the files required in this book.

Perform the following tasks:
1. Open the Couriers and Services query in Design view. Sort the query in ascending order by Courier Number, Customer Number, and Service Code. Save the changes to the query.
2. Create the Courier Service Data form shown in Figure 8–88. The Datasheet tab displays a subform listing information about services for clients of the courier (Figure 8–88a). Data for the subform is based on the Couriers and Services query. Data for the Charts tab also is based on the Couriers and Services query (Figure 8–88b).

(a)

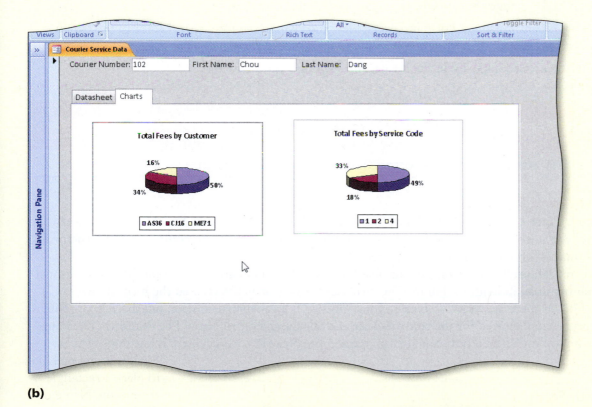

(b)

Figure 8–88

3. Submit the revised database in the format specified by your instructor.

Extend Your Knowledge

Extend the skills you learned in this chapter and experiment with new skills. You may need to use Help to complete the assignment.

Modifying Forms

Instructions: Copy the JSP Recruiters database and rename the database to Chapter 8_last name Recruiters. For example, if your last name is Smith, then name the database Chapter 8_Smith Recruiters. Start Access and open the database that you copied and renamed.

Perform the following tasks:

1. Open the Recruiter Seminar Data Form in Design view. Add a title to the form and insert the current date in the form header.
2. Add a third tab control to the form. Name the tab control, Clients.
3. Add a subform to the Clients tab control. The Client table is the basis of the subform. Display the Client Number, Client Name, Client Type, Amount Paid, and Current Due in a datasheet on the subform.
4. Open the Client Master Form in Design view. Change the font color for the command button text to Dark Red. Change the label for the option group to Dark Red.
5. Open the Client Financial Form in Design view and change the foreground color of the Client Number field to red.
6. Submit the revised database in the format specified by your instructor.

Make It Right

Analyze a database and correct all errors and/or improve the design.

Correcting Form Design Errors

Instructions: Start Access. Open the YourHouse Fitness Company database. See the inside back cover of this book for instructions on downloading the Data Files for Students, or contact your instructor for more information about accessing the required files.

The YourHouse Fitness Company database contains data about an organization that does personal fitness training in an individual's home. The owner of the company has created the form shown in Figure 8–89, but there are a few problems. Total Amount is a calculated control, but there is a problem with the expression entered for the control. Also, the calculated control should be dimmed. The name in the Name to Find combo box should change when the Next Record navigation button is clicked. Finally, she would like to place a rectangle around the Name to Find combo box and apply the raised special effect.

Correct these errors and submit the revised database in the format specified by your instructor.

Figure 8–89

In the Lab

Design, create, modify, and/or use a database following the guidelines, concepts, and skills presented in this chapter. Labs are listed in order of increasing difficulty.

Lab 1: Applying Advanced Form Techniques to the JMS TechWizards Database

Problem: JMS TechWizards needs a form for the Client table that will allow users to update data in the table. JMS also needs a form to display work order data for technicians.

Instructions: If you are using the Microsoft Office Access 2007 Comprehensive text, open the JMS TechWizards database that you used in Chapter 7. Otherwise, see the inside back cover of this book for instructions on downloading the Data Files for Students, or contact your instructor for more information about accessing the required files.

Perform the following tasks:

1. Open the Technicians and Work Orders query and sort the query by Technician Number, Client Number, and Category Number. Save the changes to the query.

2. Create the Client Master Form shown in Figure 8–90. Total Amount is a calculated control and is the sum of the Billed and Paid amounts. Users should not be able to update the Total Amount control. The form includes command buttons, a combo box for the Technician Number field, and a combo box to search for clients by name. Be sure to sort the client names in ascending order, place a rectangle around the combo box, and update the combo box. The user should not be able to tab to the combo box. When the Add Record button is clicked, the insertion point should be in the Client Number field. The form is similar in style to the form shown in Figure 8–1a on page AC 523.

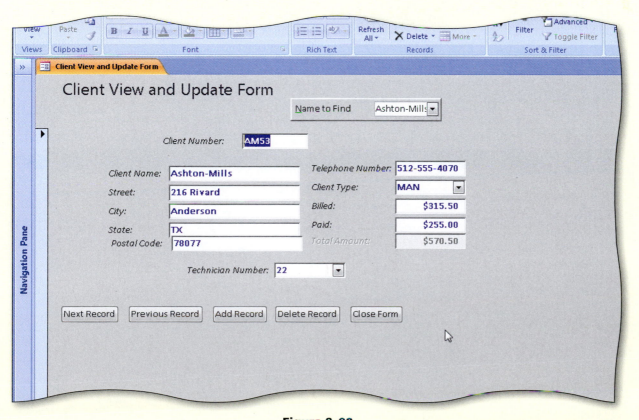

Figure 8–90

Continued >

In the Lab *continued*

3. Create the form shown in Figure 8–91. The subform that appears in the Datasheet tab uses the Technicians and Work Orders query (Figure 8–91a). The charts that appear in the Charts tab use the same query and the exploded pie subchart (Figure 8–91b).

Figure 8–91a

Figure 8–91b

4. Submit the revised database in the format specified by your instructor.

In the Lab

Lab 2: Applying Advanced Form Techniques to the Hockey Fan Zone Database

Problem: The management of the Hockey Fan Zone store needs a form that displays item information. The form should display the total cost of items on hand. It also should include command buttons to perform common operations, a combo box to search for items by description, and an option group that allows different views of the Item table. The company also needs a form that displays supplier information as well as items on order and all items associated with a supplier.

Instructions: If you are using the Microsoft Office Access 2007 Comprehensive text, open the Hockey Fan Zone database that you used in Chapter 7. Otherwise, see the inside back cover of this book for instructions on downloading the Data Files for Students, or contact your instructor for more information about accessing the required files.

Continued >

In the Lab *continued*

Perform the following tasks:

1. Create the Item View and Update Form shown in Figure 8–92. Total Cost is a calculated control and is the result of multiplying On Hand by Cost. Users should not be able to update the Total Cost control. The form includes command buttons, a combo box for the Supplier Code field, and a combo box to search for items by description. Be sure to sort the descriptions in ascending order, place a rectangle around the combo box, and update the combo box. The user should not be able to tab to the combo box. When the Add Record button is clicked, the insertion point should be in the Item Number field. If the user clicks the Change Item Description Data option, they should be able to change only the item number, description, and item type. If the user clicks the Change Other Data option, they should be able to change all data except description and item type. When the form first opens, the View Data Only option should apply. The form is similar in style to that shown in Figure 8–1a on page AC 523.

Figure 8–92

2. Open the Supplier and Number of Items query in Design view and add the Description and Date Ordered fields to the query. Sort the query by Item Number and Date Ordered. Save the query.

3. Create the Supplier Master Data form shown in Figure 8–93. The On Order tab (Figure 8–93a) uses the Supplier and Number of Items query for the subform. The Items tab uses the Item table for the subform. Note that the labels for Supplier Code and Supplier Name have been changed and that there is a title on the form. The form's title is bold. Use red as the font for the labels and dark blue as the font for the text boxes. You can use the Format Painter to copy formatting for text boxes and labels.

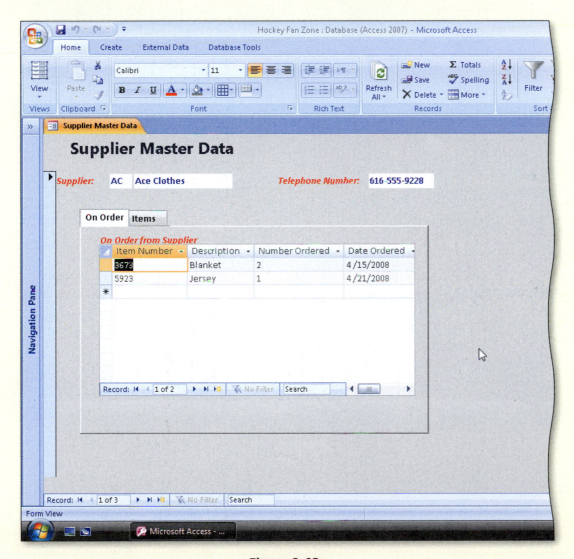

Figure 8–93a

Continued >

In the Lab *continued*

Figure 8–93b

4. Submit the revised database in the format specified by your instructor.

In the Lab

Lab 3: Applying Advanced Form Techniques to the Ada Beauty Supply Database

Problem: Ada Beauty Supply needs a form that displays customer information. The form should display a calculated control that sums the Balance and Amount Paid fields. It also should include a combo box to search for customers by name and an option group that allows different views of the Customer table. The company also needs a form that displays sales rep information as well as open orders for customers.

Instructions: If you are using the Microsoft Office Access 2007 Comprehensive text, open the Ada Beauty Supply database that you used in Chapter 7. Otherwise, see the inside back cover of this book for instructions on downloading the Data Files for Students, or contact your instructor for more information about accessing the required files. Submit the revised database in the format specified by your instructor.

Instructions Part 1: Create the Customer View and Update Form shown in Figure 8–94.

Instructions Part 2: Create a query that joins the Sales Rep, Customer, and Open Orders tables. Include the sales rep number, customer number, customer name, order number, and amount in the query. Sort the query by sales rep number, customer number, and order numbers. Save the query as Sales Reps and Orders.

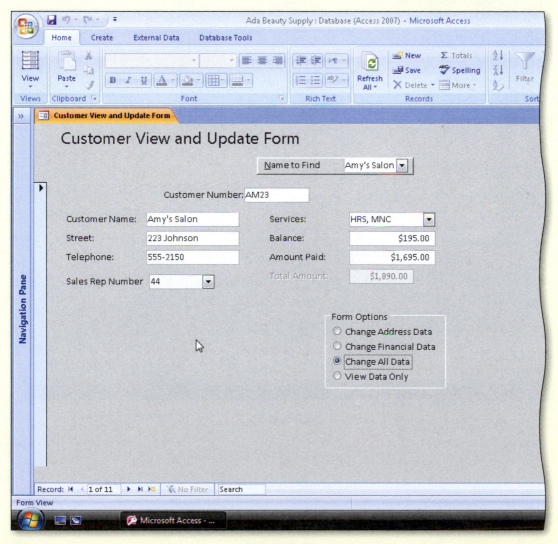

Figure 8–94

Continued >

In the Lab *continued*

Instructions Part 3: Create the Sales Rep Data form shown in Figure 8–95. This form uses the query you created in Part 2. The Chart tab has only one chart that displays the customer number and the total amount of open orders for the customer. The chart uses a 3D column chart style.

Figure 8–95

Cases and Places

Apply your creative thinking and problem-solving skills to design and implement a solution.

● Easier   ●● More Difficult

● 1: Applying Advanced Form Techniques to the Second Hand Goods Database

If you are using the Microsoft Office Access 2007 Comprehensive text, open the Second Hand Goods database that you used in Chapter 7. Otherwise, see the inside back cover of this book for instructions on downloading the Data Files for Students, or contact your instructor for more information about accessing the required files. Modify the Item Update Form that you created previously to include command buttons to move to the next record, move to the previous record, add a record, and delete a record. Delete the seller data that appears on the form and re-add this information as a combo box. When users add a record, the insertion point should be in the item number field. Sort the records in order by Description. Print the form for the record that now appears as the first record. Apply a filter to the form to find only those items that are in Excellent condition. Write the item numbers of the filtered records on the form that you printed. Submit the printed form and the revised database in the format specified by your instructor.

● 2: Applying Advanced Form Techniques to the BeachCondo Rentals Database

If you are using the Microsoft Office Access 2007 Comprehensive text, open the BeachCondo Rentals database that you used in Chapter 7. Otherwise, see the inside back cover of this book for instructions on downloading the Data Files for Students, or contact your instructor for more information about accessing the required files. Modify the Owner Master Form that you created previously to include command buttons to move to the next record, move to the previous record, find a record, and close the form. Use pictures instead of text on the command buttons. Submit the revised database in the format specified by your instructor.

●● 3: Applying Advanced Form Techniques to the Restaurant Database

If you are using the Microsoft Office Access 2007 Comprehensive text, open the restaurant database that you used in Chapter 7. Otherwise, see the inside back cover of this book for instructions on downloading the Data Files for Students, or contact your instructor for more information about accessing the required files. Using the Plan Ahead guidelines presented in this chapter, determine what additional forms you need for your database. Also, determine if you need to make any changes to existing forms. For example, if attendees are using your forms, you want to make them as easy to use as possible. Combo boxes and command buttons may be useful. Should attendees be allowed to change any data? If not, perhaps, you should set certain fields to view only. What data should appear on the forms? Are multipage forms needed? Modify the database as appropriate and submit the revised database in the format specified by your instructor.

Continued >

Cases and Places *continued*

•• 4: Applying Advanced Form Techniques to Your Contacts Database

Make It Personal

If you are using the Microsoft Office Access 2007 Comprehensive text, open the contacts database that you used in Chapter 7. Otherwise, see the inside back cover of this book for instructions on downloading the Data Files for Students, or contact your instructor for more information about accessing the required files. Review the current forms you have in your Contacts database. Could any forms be enhanced by the addition of command buttons? Would a combo box to search for contacts be beneficial? Do you need a multipage form? Modify the forms as necessary. Submit the revised database in the format specified by your instructor.

•• 5: Understanding Forms

Working Together

As a team, choose one of the In the Lab databases. Then, copy and rename the database. Research the purpose of the tools listed in Table 8–2 on page AC 586. Modify the Client Master Form by adding lines and adding a picture. Modify the Recruiter Seminar Data form by adding command buttons. Place pictures instead of text on the command buttons. Submit the revised database in the format specified by your instructor.

9 | Administering a Database System

Objectives

You will have mastered the material in this project when you can:

- Convert a database to and from earlier versions of Access

- Use the Table Analyzer, Performance Analyzer, and Documenter

- Create custom categories and groups in the Navigation Pane

- Use table and database properties

- Use field properties to create a custom input mask and to allow zero length

- Create indexes

- Enable and use automatic error checking

- Create and use smart tags

- Select a startup form

- Encrypt a database and set a password

- Understand and use digital certificates

- Understand the purpose and use of options within the Trust Center

- Lock a database

- Split a database

9 | Administering a Database System

Introduction

Administering a database system is an important activity that has many facets. These activities go far beyond the simple updating of a database. They include activities to improve the usability, accessibility, security, and efficiency of the database.

Project — Administering a Database System

Security
Security is the prevention of unauthorized access to a database. Within an organization, the database administrator determines the types of access individual users can have to the database. Various government rules and regulations, such as Sarbannes-Oxley (SOX) and the Health Insurance Portability and Accountability Act (HIPAA) require database administrators to have strict security procedures in place to protect data from unauthorized access.

JSP Recruiters realizes the importance of database administration, that is, the importance of administering its database system properly. Management realizes that doing so encompasses a wide variety of activities (Figure 9–1). Database administration can include conversion of an Access 2007 database to an earlier version. Database administration usually includes such activities as analyzing tables for potential problems, analyzing performance to see if changes are warranted to make the system perform more efficiently, and documenting the various objects in the database. It can include creating custom categories and groups in the Navigation Pane as well as changing table and database properties. It also can include the use of field properties in such tasks as creating a custom input mask and allowing zero length strings. It can include the creation of indexes to speed up retrieval. The inclusion of automatic error checking and smart tags in tables, queries, forms, and reports is part of the administration of a database system. Securing the database through the use of passwords and encryption also are database administration tasks, as is the selection of a startup form. Understanding the purpose of digital certificates and the trust center is critical to the database administration function. Another important area of database administration is the protection of the database. This protection includes locking the database through the creation of an ACCDE file to prevent unauthorized changes from being made to the VBA source code or to the design of forms and reports. Splitting the database into a front-end and a back-end database is another way to protect the functionality and efficiency of a database.

- Convert a database to an earlier version of Access
- Use the Table Analyzer
- Use the Performance Analyzer
- Use the Documenter
- Enable error checking
- Create a custom input mask
- Specify and use smart tags
- Import and link SharePoint Services lists
- Set startup options
- Set a password
- Encode a database
- Create and use a replica
- Set macro security level
- Synchronize a Design Master and a replica
- Split a database
- Create an MDE file
- Specify user-level security

SONY

Use the Table Analyzer

Use the Performance Analyzer

Use the Documenter

Create custom categories and groups in the Navigation Pane

Create custom properties

Create indexes

Enable error checking

Specify and use smart tags

Encrypt a database and set a password

Figure 9–1

Overview

As you read this chapter, you will learn how to administer a database by performing these general tasks:

- Learn how to convert databases to and from earlier versions of Access as well as how to use tools for analyzing and documenting Access databases.
- Create custom categories and groups in the Navigation Pane.
- Use table, database, and field properties.
- Create indexes.
- Learn how to use automatic error checking.
- Use smart tags.
- Understand digital certificates and the Trust Center.
- Lock a database.
- Split a database.

Plan Ahead

> **Database Administration Guidelines**
>
> 1. **Determine whether a database needs to be converted to or from an earlier version.** Do users of a previous version of Access need to be able to use the database? If so, you will need to be sure the database does not contain any features that would prevent it from being converted. Is there a database that was created in an earlier version of Access that you would like to use in Access 2007?
>
> 2. **Determine when to analyze and/or document the database.** Once you create a database you should use the table and performance analyzers to determine if any changes to the structure are warranted. You also should document the database. You should perform these tasks whenever you change the structure.
>
> 3. **Determine the most useful way to customize the Navigation Pane.** Would it be helpful to have custom categories and groups? What items should be in the groups? Would it be helpful to restrict the items that appear to only those whose names contain certain characters?
>
> 4. **Determine any table-wide validation rules.** Are there any validation rules that involve more than a single field? For example, a validation rule that states that the hours spent cannot exceed the total hours would involve both the Hours Spent and the Total Hours fields.
>
> 5. **Determine any custom database properties.** Are there properties that would be helpful in documenting the database that are not included in the list of database properties you can use? If so, you can add custom properties.
>
> 6. **Determine indexes.** Examine retrieval and sorting requirements to determine possible indexes. Indexes can make both retrieval and sorting more efficient.
>
> 7. **Determine whether a startup form is appropriate.** Is there a form that should be displayed automatically whenever a user opens the database? If the database includes a switchboard, the switchboard is usually a good candidate for such a form.
>
> 8. **Determine whether the database should be encrypted.** Encrypting a database is an excellent security feature. If there are any potential security issues, you should strongly consider encryption. As part of the process, you also will set a password.
>
> 9. **Determine whether the database should be locked.** Should users be able to change the design of forms, reports, and/or VBA code? If not, you should lock the database to prevent such changes.
>
> *(continued)*

(continued)

**Plan
Ahead**

10. **Determine whether the database should be split.** Would it be preferable to have the database split into a back-end database, which contains only the table data, and a front-end database, which contains other objects, such as queries, forms, and reports? If so, you should split the database.

   When necessary, more specific details concerning the above decisions and/or actions are presented at appropriate points in the chapter. The chapter also will identify the use of these guidelines in the administration of a database.

Starting Access

If you are using a computer to step through the project in this chapter and you want your screen to match the figures in this book, you should change your screen's resolution to 1024 × 768. For information about how to change a computer's resolution, read Appendix E.

To Start Access

The following steps, which assume Windows Vista is running, start Access.

Note: If you are using Windows XP, see Appendix F for alternate steps.

1 Click the Start button on the Windows Vista taskbar to display the Start menu.

2 Click All Programs at the bottom of the left pane on the Start menu to display the All Programs list, and then click Microsoft Office on the All Programs list to display the Microsoft Office list.

3 Click Microsoft Office Access 2007 on the Microsoft Office list to start Access and display the Getting Started with Microsoft Office Access window.

4 If the Access window is not maximized, click the Maximize button on its title bar to maximize the window.

To Open a Database

In Chapter 1, you created your database on a USB flash drive using the file name, JSP Recruiters. There are two ways to open the file containing your database. If the file you created appears in the Recent Documents list, you could click it to open the file. If not, you can use the More button to open the file. The following steps use the More button to open the JSP Recruiters database from the USB flash drive.

Note: If you are using Windows XP, see Appendix F for alternate steps.

1 With your USB flash drive connected to one of the computer's USB ports, click the More button to display the Open dialog box.

2 If the Folders list is displayed below the Folders button, click the Folders button to remove the Folders list.

3 If necessary, click Computers in the Favorite Links section and then double-click UDISK 2.0 (E:) to select the USB flash drive, Drive E in this case, as the new open location. (Your drive letter might be different.)

4 Click JSP Recruiters to select the file name.

5 Click the Open button to open the database.

6 If a Security Warning appears, click the Options button to display the Microsoft Office Security Options dialog box.

7 With the option button to enable the content selected, click the OK button to enable the content.

Converting Databases

There are occasions when you may need to convert from one version of Access to another. For example, an employee in a different location may have an earlier version of Access. Perhaps, you have a database created in an earlier version of Access that you want to use in Access 2007. You can convert from an Access 2007 database to earlier versions. You also can convert from earlier versions to Access 2007.

TO CONVERT AN ACCESS 2007 DATABASE TO AN EARLIER VERSION

To convert an Access 2007 database to an earlier version, the database cannot contain any features that are specific to Access 2007. These include attachments, multivalued fields, offline data, or links to external files not supported in earlier versions of Access. If the database does contain any of these features, Access will not allow you to convert to an earlier version. Provided the database does not contain such features, you can convert the database by pointing to the Save As command on the Microsoft Office Button menu (Figure 9–2). You then can choose the appropriate format.

Figure 9–2

Specifically, to convert an Access 2007 database to an earlier version, you would use the following steps.

1. With the database to be converted open, click the Microsoft Office Button to display the Microsoft Office Button menu.

2. Point to the Save As arrow to display the Save As submenu.

3. Click the desired format.

4. Type the name you want for the converted database, select a location, and click the Save button.

To Convert an Access 2000 or Access 2002-2003 Database to Access 2007

To convert an Access 2000 or Access 2002-2003 database to an Access 2007 database, you open the database. Initially, the database is open in compatibility mode, where new features that cannot easily be displayed or converted are disabled. In this mode, the database remains in its original format. If you want to convert it, you use the Convert command on the Microsoft Office Button menu. Once the database is converted, the disabled features will be enabled. You will no longer be able to share the database with users of Access 2000 or Access 2002-2003, however.

Specifically, to convert an Access 2000 or 2002-2003 database to Access 2007, you would use the following steps.

1. With the database to be converted open, click the Microsoft Office Button to display the Microsoft Office Button menu.

2. Click Convert on the Microsoft Office Button menu.

3. Type the name you want for the converted database, select a location, and click the Save button.

BTW

Opening Earlier Versions of Access
You can open a database having an Access 2000 or Access 2002-2003 file format directly, without converting the database to Access 2007. When you open a database that has an Access 2000 or Access 2002-2003 file format, the file format appears in parentheses following the database file name in the title bar.

Microsoft Access Tools

Microsoft Access has a variety of tools that are useful in analyzing databases. These include tools to analyze table structures, to analyze performance, and to create detailed documentation.

To Use the Table Analyzer

Access contains three tools that allow you to analyze the design and performance of your database. The Table Analyzer can analyze tables while looking for potential redundancy. The Performance Analyzer can analyze performance and check for ways to make queries, reports, or forms more efficient. Then, the tool will make suggestions for possible changes. The Database Documenter produces detailed documentation describing the structure and content of the various tables, queries, forms, reports, and other objects in the database.

The Table Analyzer examines tables for **redundancy**, which is duplicated data. If redundancy is found, the Table Analyzer will suggest ways to split the table to eliminate the redundancy. The following steps illustrate how to use the Table Analyzer.

- If necessary, hide the Navigation Pane.

- Click Database Tools on the Ribbon to display the Database Tools tab (Figure 9–3).

Figure 9–3

- Click the Analyze Table button on the Database Tools tab to display the Table Analyzer Wizard dialog box (Figure 9–4).

Figure 9–4

3

• Click the Next button to display the next Table Analyzer Wizard screen (Figure 9–5).

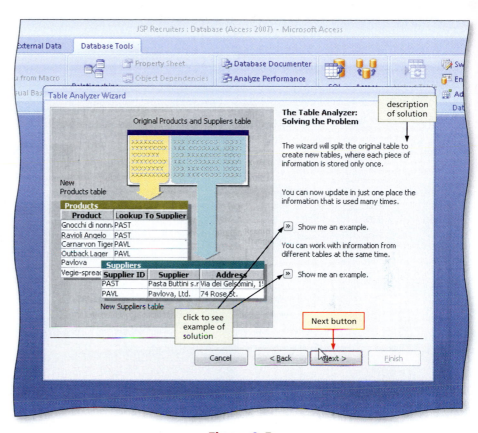

Figure 9–5

4

• Click the Next button to display the next Table Analyzer Wizard screen.

• Make sure the Client table is selected (Figure 9–6).

Figure 9–6

5

- Click the Next button.

- Be sure the 'Yes, let the wizard decide.' option button is selected (Figure 9–7).

Figure 9–7

6

- Click the Next button to run the analysis (Figure 9–8).

Q&A I can't see all the fields in the field lists on the right. What can I do?

You either can resize the field lists or use the scroll bar to see the other fields.

Q&A I don't really want to put the state in a different table, even though I realize that states are duplicated. Do I have to follow this advice?

Certainly not. This is only a suggestion.

7

- Because the type of duplication identified by the analyzer does not pose a problem, click the Cancel button.

Figure 9–8

To Use the Performance Analyzer

The Performance Analyzer will examine the tables, queries, reports, forms, and other objects in your system, looking for changes that would improve the efficiency of database operations. This could include changes to the way data is stored, as well as changes to the indexes created for the system (you will learn about indexes later in this chapter). Once it has finished, it will make recommendations concerning possible changes. The following steps use the Performance Analyzer.

- Click the Analyze Performance button on the Database Tools tab to display the Performance Analyzer dialog box.

- If necessary, click the Tables tab (Figure 9–9).

Figure 9–9

- Click the Select All button to select all tables.

- Click the OK button to display the results (Figure 9–10).

Q&A

What do the results mean?

Access has no changes to suggest. If it did, you could decide whether to follow the suggestions.

- Click the OK button to finish working with the Performance Analyzer.

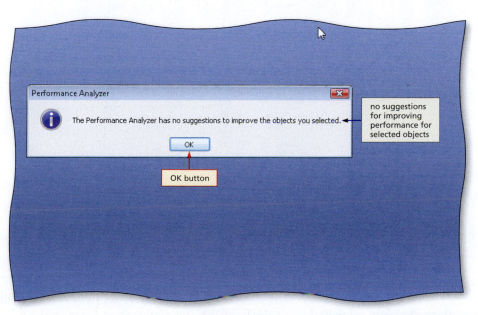

Figure 9–10

To Use the Documenter

The Documenter allows you to produce detailed documentation of the various tables, queries, forms, reports, and other objects in your database. Figure 9–11 shows a portion of the documentation of the Client table. The complete documentation is much lengthier than the one shown in the figure. In the actual documentation, all fields would display as much information as the Client Number field. In the sample documentation shown in the figure, only those items of interest are shown for the other fields.

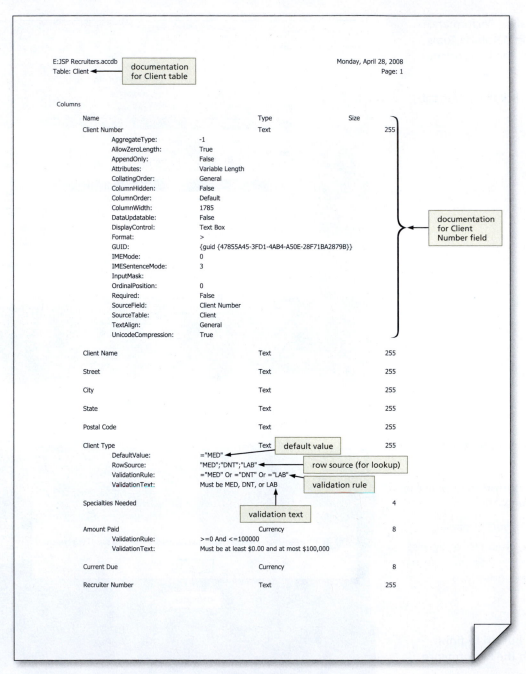

Figure 9–11

Notice that the documentation of the Client Type field contains the default value and the row source associated with the Lookup information for the field. The documentation for both the Client Type and Amount Paid fields contains validation rules and validation text.

The following steps use the Documenter to produce documentation for the Client table.

1

- Click the Database Documenter button on the Database Tools tab to display the Documenter dialog box.

- If necessary, click the Tables tab and then click the Client check box (Figure 9–12).

Figure 9–12

2

- Click the OK button to produce a preview of the documentation (Figure 9–13).

Q&A

What can I do with this documentation?

You could print it by clicking the Print button. You could create a PDF or XPS file containing the documentation by clicking the PDF or XPS button and following the directions. You could create a file that is accessible from Word by clicking the Word button and following the directions. You may need to use this documentation later if you make changes to the database.

- Click the Close Print Preview button to close the preview of the documentation.

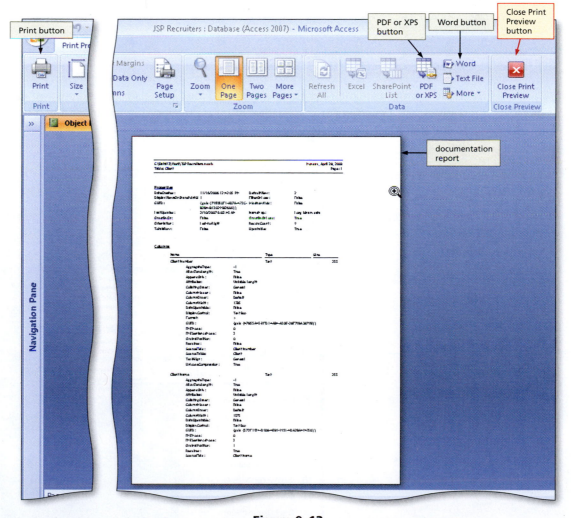

Figure 9–13

Experiment

- Try other options within the Documenter to see the effect of your choice on the documentation produced. Each time, close the preview of the documentation.

BTW

Database Documenter
The Options button in the Documenter dialog box allows you to further specify what to include for each table and for each field in a table.

Navigation Pane

You already have seen how to customize the Navigation Pane by selecting the category and the filter. You also can create custom categories and groups that you can use to categorize the items in the database in ways that are most useful to you. In addition, you can use the Search Bar to restrict the items that appear in the Navigation Pane to only those that have the collection of characters you specify in their names.

Plan Ahead

Determine the most useful way to customize the Navigation Pane.
Determine the customization of the Navigation Pane that would be most helpful to your users. The types of issues to consider are the following:

1. Is there a new category that would be useful?

2. If so, are there new groups that would be useful to include in the new category?

3. If you have created a new category and a new group, which items should be included in one of the new groups and which should be left uncategorized?

To Create Custom Categories and Groups

You can create custom categories in the Navigation Pane. You also can add custom groups to the categories. The following steps create a custom category called Financial Items. They then add two custom groups, Detailed and Summary, to the Financial Items category.

- Show the Navigation Pane.

- Right-click the Navigation Pane title bar to display a shortcut menu (Figure 9–14).

Figure 9–14

2

- Click the Navigation Options command on the shortcut menu to display the Navigation Options dialog box (Figure 9–15).

Q&A What else could I do with the shortcut menu?

You could select a category, select sort order, or select how to view the items within the Navigation Pane.

Figure 9–15

3

- Click the Add Item button to add a new category (Figure 9–16).

Q&A Could I use the Custom category?

Yes. It is a good idea to reserve that category by creating your own new category, however.

Q&A If I made a mistake in creating a new category, how can I fix it?

Select the category that is incorrect. If the name is wrong, click the Rename Item button and change the name appropriately. If you do not want the category, click the Delete Item button to delete the category and then click the OK button.

Figure 9–16

4

- Type Financial
  Items as the name
  of the category.

- Click the Add Group
  button to add a
  group, and then type
  Detailed as the
  name of the group.

- Click the Add Group
  button to add a
  group, and then
  type Summary as the
  name of the group
  (Figure 9–17).

Q&A

I added the groups
in the wrong order.
How can I change
the order?

Select the group
that is in the wrong
position. Click the UP
or DOWN arrows to
move the group to
the correct location.

5

- Click the OK button
  to create the new
  category and groups.

Figure 9–17

To Add Items to Groups

Once you have created new groups, you can add existing items to the new groups. The following steps add items to the Summary and Detailed groups in the Financial Items category.

1

- Click the Navigation Pane arrow to produce the Navigation Pane menu (Figure 9–18).

Q&A Do I have to click the arrow?

No. If you prefer, you can click anywhere in the title bar for the Navigation Pane. Clicking arrows is a good habit, however, because there are many situations where you must click the arrow.

Figure 9–18

2

- Click the Financial Items category to display the groups within the category.

- Right-click Client-Recruiter Crosstab to display the shortcut menu.

- Point to the 'Add to group' command on the shortcut menu to display the list of available groups (Figure 9–19).

Q&A I didn't create an Unassigned Objects group. Where did it come from?

Access creates the Unassigned Objects group automatically. Until you add an object to one of the groups you created, it will be in the Unassigned Objects group.

Q&A What is the purpose of the New Group on the submenu?

You can create a new group using this submenu. This is an alternative to using the Navigation Options dialog box. Use whichever approach you find most convenient.

Figure 9–19

3

- Click Summary to add the Client-Recruiter Crosstab to the Summary group.

- Using the same technique, add the items shown in Figure 9–20 to the Detailed and Summary groups.

Q&A

Why do all the items in the Detailed and Summary groups have the link symbol in front of them?

You actually don't add an object to your group. Rather, you create a link to the object. In practice, you don't have to worry about this. The process for opening an object in one of your custom groups remains the same.

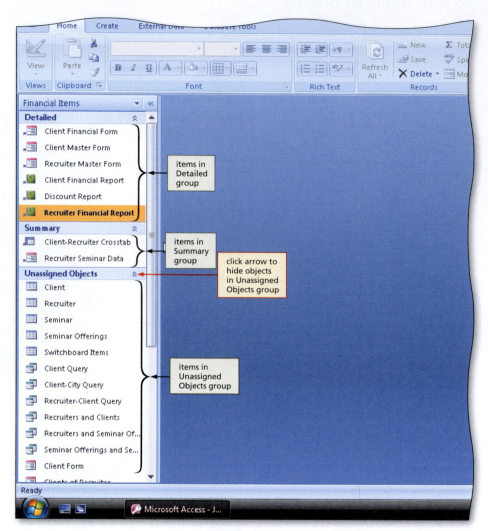

Figure 9–20

4

- Click the arrow in the Unassigned Objects bar to hide the unassigned objects (Figure 9–21).

Q&A

Do I have to click the arrow?

No. Just as with the Navigation Pane, you can click anywhere in the Unassigned Objects bar.

Figure 9–21

To Use the Search Bar

You can reduce the number of items that appear in the Navigation Pane by hiding some of the groups. An alternative method for reducing the number of items that appear is to display only those names that contain a certain collection of characters. To do so, you use the Search Bar. The following steps use the Search Bar to display only those items whose names contain the letters, Sem.

- Return the Navigation Pane to its default state by selecting Tables and Related Views as the category and All Tables as the filter.

- Right-click the Navigation Pane title bar to display a shortcut menu.

- Click Search Bar on the shortcut menu to display the Search Bar.

- Type Sem in the Search Bar to display only items containing Sem (Figure 9–22).

Experiment

- Try other combinations of letters in the search bar to see their effect.

2

- Right-click the Navigation Pane title bar to display a shortcut menu.

- Click Search Bar on the shortcut menu to remove the Search Bar.

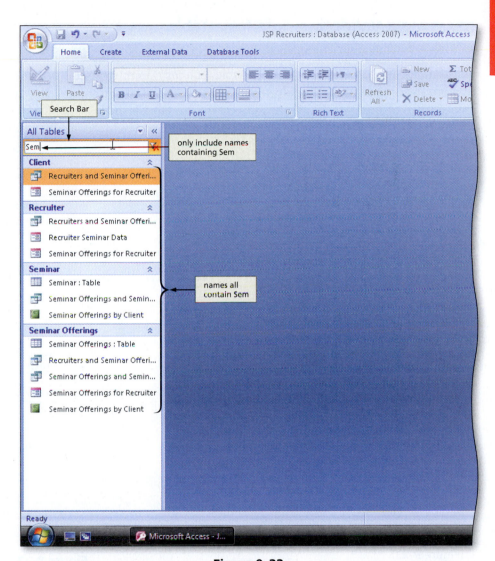

Figure 9–22

Table and Database Properties

You can assign properties to tables. For example, you could assign a validation rule and validation text to an entire table. You also can assign properties to the database, typically for documentation purposes.

To Create a Validation Rule for a Table

Many validation rules apply to individual fields within a table. Some, however, apply to more than one field. For example, in the Seminar Offerings table, you may want to require that the hours spent must be less than or equal to the total hours. This rule involves two fields, Hours Spent and Total Hours. To create a validation rule that involves two or more fields, you need to create the rule for the table using the table's Validation Rule property. The following steps create the appropriate validation rule for the Seminar Offerings table.

 1

- Open the Seminar Offerings table in Design view and hide the Navigation Pane.

- Click the Property Sheet button on the Design tab to display the table's property sheet.

- Click the Validation Rule property and type [Hours Spent]<=[Total Hours] as the validation rule.

- Click the Validation Text property and type Hours spent cannot exceed total hours as the validation text (Figure 9–23).

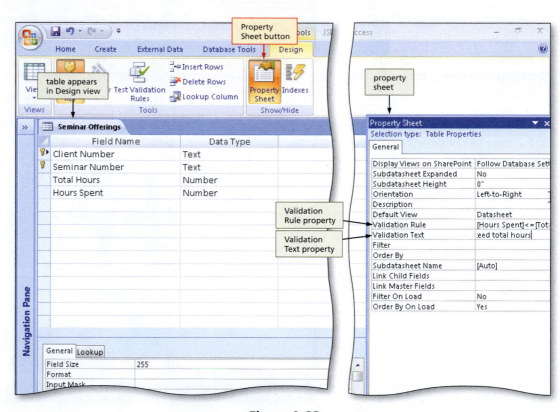

Figure 9–23

Q&A
Could I use the expression builder to create the validation rule?

Yes. Use whichever method you find the most convenient.

 2

- Close the property sheet.

- Click the Save button on the Quick Access Toolbar to save the validation rule and the validation text.

- When asked if you want to test existing data, click the No button.

- Close the Seminar Offerings table.

Effect of the Validation Rule

With this validation rule in place, an attempt to add or change a record on which the hours spent was greater than the total hours would produce the error message shown in Figure 9–24.

Figure 9–24

To Create Custom Properties

Custom properties are a collection of properties that you can choose from to supplement the general database property categories included in the property sheet. You can use custom properties to further document your database. If you have needs that go beyond the custom properties, you can create your own original or unique properties. The following steps **populate** the Status custom property, that is, they set a value for the property. In this case, they set the Status property to "Live Version," indicating this is the live version of the database. If the database were still in a test environment, the property would be set to "Test Version." The steps also create and populate a new property called Production that represents the date the database was placed into production.

1
- Click the Microsoft Office Button to display the Microsoft Office Button menu.

- Point to the Manage arrow to display a submenu (Figure 9–25).

Figure 9–25

2

- Click Database Properties to display the JSP Recruiters.accdb Properties dialog box.

- Click the Custom tab.

- Scroll down in the Name list so that Status appears, and then click Status.

- Ensure that the Type is Text.

Q&A What if it is not?

Click the Type arrow and then click Text.

- Click the Value box and type `Live Version` as the value (Figure 9–26).

Figure 9–26

3

- Click the Add button to add the property.

- Type Production in the Name box.

- Select Date as the Type.

- Type `04/03/2008` as the value (Figure 9–27) to indicate that the database went into production on April 3, 2008.

Figure 9–27

4
- Click the Add button to add the property (Figure 9–28).

What if I add a property that I decide I don't want?

You can delete it. To do so, click the property you no longer want and then click the Delete button.

5
- Click the OK button to close the JSP Recruiters.accdb Properties dialog box.

How do I view these properties in the future?

The same way you created them. Click the Microsoft Office Button, point to Manage, and then click Database Properties. Click the desired tab to see the properties you want.

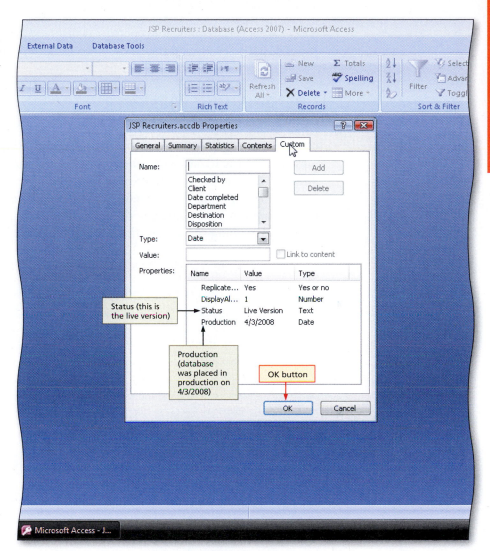

Figure 9–28

Special Field Properties

There are a variety of field properties available. Two special field properties, the Custom Input Mask property and the Allow Zero Length property, are described in this section.

Custom Input Masks

A way to prevent users from entering data that does not have a certain format is to use an input mask. You already may have used the Input Mask Wizard to create an input mask. Using the wizard, you can select the input mask that meets your needs from a list. This often is the best way to create the input mask.

If the input mask you need to create is not similar to any in the list, you can create a custom input mask by entering the appropriate characters as the value for the Input Mask property. In doing so, you use the symbols from Table 9–1.

Table 9–1 Input Mask Symbols		
Symbol	**Type Of Data Accepted**	**Data Entry Optional**
0	Digits (0 through 9) without plus (+) or minus (-) sign. Positions left blank appear as zeros.	No
9	Digits (0 through 9) without plus (+) or minus (-) sign. Positions left blank appear as spaces.	Yes
#	Digits (0 through 9) with plus (+) or minus (-) sign. Positions left blank appear as spaces.	Yes
L	Letters (A through Z).	No
?	Letters (A through Z).	Yes
A	Letters (A through Z) or digits (0 through 9).	No
a	Letters (A through Z) or digits (0 through 9).	Yes
&	Any character or a space.	No
C	Any character or a space.	Yes
<	Converts any letter entered to lowercase.	Does not apply
>	Converts any letter entered to uppercase.	Does not apply
!	Characters typed in the input mask fill it from left to right.	Does not apply
\	Character following the slash is treated as a literal in the input mask.	Does not apply

For example, to indicate that client numbers must consist of two letters followed by two numbers, you would enter LL99. The Ls in the first two positions indicate that the first two positions must be letters. Using L instead of a question mark indicates that the users must enter these letters; that is, they are not optional. With the question mark, they could leave these positions blank. The 9s in the last two positions indicate that the users must enter digits (0 through 9). Using 9 instead of 0 indicates that they could leave these positions blank; that is, they are optional. Finally, to ensure that any letters entered are converted to uppercase, you would use the > symbol at the beginning of the input mask. The complete mask would be >LL99.

To Create a Custom Input Mask

The following step creates a custom input mask for the Client Number field.

- Open the Client table in Design view and hide the Navigation Pane.

- With the Client Number field selected, click the Input Mask property, and then type >LL99 as the value (Figure 9–29).

Q&A What is the difference between the Format property and the Input Mask property?

The Format property ensures that data is displayed consistently, for example, always in uppercase. The Input Mask property controls how data is entered.

Q&A What is the effect of this input mask?

From this point on, anyone entering a client number will be restricted to letters in the first two positions and numeric digits in the last two. Further, any letters entered in the first two positions will be converted to uppercase.

Q&A In Figure 9–29, the Client Number field has both a custom input mask and a format. Is this a problem?

Technically, you do not need both. When the same field has both an input mask and a format, the format takes precedence. Because the format specified for the Client Number field is the same as the input mask (uppercase), it will not affect the data.

Figure 9–29

To Allow Zero Length

You can use zero-length strings to distinguish data that does not exist from data that is unknown. For example, in the Recruiter table, you may want to set the Required property for the Comment field to Yes, so that users cannot forget to enter a comment. If you do forget to enter a comment, Access will display an error message and not let you add the record. If, on the other hand, you find a certain recruiter for whom no comment is appropriate, you can enter a zero-length string ("") and Access will accept the record without giving you an error message. A **zero-length string** is a string whose length is zero. To enter a zero-length string you type two quotation marks with no spaces in between (""). If you enter a zero-length string into a Text or Memo field whose Required property is set to Yes, Access will not report an error, because entering a zero-length string is not the same as leaving the field blank.

If you want to ensure that data is entered in the field and that a zero-length string is not appropriate, you can set the Required property to Yes and the Allow Zero Length property to No. The following steps set the Allow Zero Length property for the Client Name field to No. (The Required property already has been set to Yes.)

1

- Click the row selector for the Client Name field to select the field.

- Click the Allow Zero Length property and then click the arrow that appears to display a menu.

- Click No in the menu to change the value of the Allow Zero Length property from Yes to No (Figure 9–30).

Q&A Could I just type the word, No?

Yes. In fact, you could type the letter N and Access would complete the word No. Use whichever technique you prefer.

2

- Save your changes and click the No button when asked if you want to test existing data.

- Close the table.

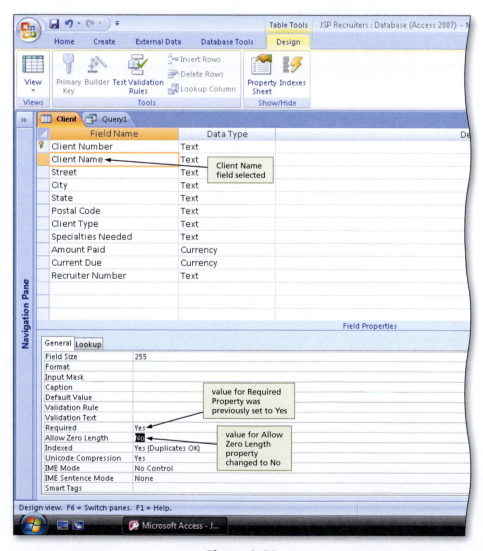

Figure 9–30

Effect of Allowing Zero Length

If the value for the Allow Zero Length property is set to No, an attempt to enter a zero length string ("") will result in an error message (Figure 9–31).

Figure 9–31

Creating and Using Indexes

You already are familiar with the concept of an index. The index in the back of a book contains important words or phrases together with a list of pages on which the given words or phrases can be found. An **index** for a table is similar. An index is created based on a field or combination of fields. An index on the Client Name field, for example, would enable Access to rapidly locate a record that contains a particular client name. In this case, the items of interest are client names instead of keywords or phrases, as is the case in the back of this book. The field or fields on which the index is built is called the **index key**. Thus, in the index on client names, the Client Name field is the index key.

Each name occurs in the index along with the number of the record on which the corresponding client is located. Further, the names appear in the index in alphabetical order, so Access could use this index to rapidly produce a list of clients alphabetized by client name.

Indexes make the process of retrieving records very fast and efficient. (With relatively small tables, the increased efficiency associated with indexes will not be as apparent as in larger tables. In practice, it is common to encounter tables with thousands, tens of thousands,

Define and Modify Multi-Field Primary Keys

When you define a multi-field primary key (a primary key that includes more than one field), you should examine carefully the length and data type of the fields that participate in the primary key. For example, in the Seminar Offerings table, both the Client Number and the Seminar Number participate in the primary key. Both fields have a data type of Text and a length of 255. You should be certain that this data type and length match the Client Number field in the Client table and the Seminar Number field in the Seminar table. If either field that participates in the primary key does not match, then you can modify the data type and/or length in Design view.

or even hundreds of thousands of records. In such cases, the increase in efficiency provided by indexes is dramatic. In fact, without indexes, many operations in such databases simply would not be practical. They would take too long to complete.)

Another benefit of indexes is that they provide an efficient way to order records. That is, if the records are to appear in a certain order, Access can use an index instead of physically having to rearrange the records in the database. Physically rearranging the records in a different order can be a very time-consuming process.

To gain the benefits of an index, you first must create one. Access automatically creates an index on the primary key as well as on some other special fields. If, as is the case with both the Client and Recruiter tables, a table contains a field called Postal Code, for example, Access will create an index for it automatically. You must create any other indexes you determine would be useful, indicating the field or fields on which the index is to be built.

Although the index key usually will be a single field, it can be a combination of fields. For example, you might want to sort records by amount paid within client type. In other words, the records are ordered by a combination of fields: Client Type and Amount Paid. An index can be used for this purpose by using a combination of fields for the index key. In this case, you must assign a name to the index. It is a good idea to assign a name that represents the combination of fields. For example, an index whose key is the combination of the Client Type and Amount Paid fields might be called TypePaid.

How Access Uses Indexes

Access creates an index whenever you request that it do so. It takes care of all the work in setting up and maintaining the index. In addition, Access will use the index automatically.

If you request that data be sorted in a particular order and Access determines that an index is available that it can use to make the process efficient, it will do so. If no index is available, it still will sort the data in the order you requested; it will just take longer than with the index.

Similarly, if you request that Access locate a particular record that has a certain value in a particular field, Access will use an index if an appropriate one exists. If not, it will have to examine each record until it finds the one you want.

In both cases, the added efficiency provided by an index will not be readily apparent in tables that have only a few records. As you add more records to your tables, however, the difference can be dramatic. Even with only 50 to 100 records, you will notice a difference. You can imagine how dramatic the difference would be in a table with 50,000 records.

Plan Ahead

> **Determine indexes.**
> An index improves efficiency for sorting and finding records. On the other hand, indexes occupy space on your disk. They also require Access to do extra work. Access must keep up-to-date all the indexes that have been created. Thus, both advantages and disadvantages exist to using indexes. Consequently, the decision as to which indexes to create is an important one. The following guidelines should help you in this process.
>
> Create an index on a field (or combination of fields) if one or more of the following conditions are present:
>
> 1. The field is the primary key of the table (Access creates this index automatically).
>
> 2. The field is the foreign key in a relationship you have created.
>
> 3. You frequently will need your data to be sorted on the field.
>
> 4. You frequently will need to locate a record based on a value in this field.
>
> *(continued)*

(continued)

Because Access handles 1 automatically, you only need to concern yourself about 2, 3, and 4. If you think you will need to see client data arranged in order of current due amounts, for example, you should create an index on the Current Due field. If you think you will need to see the data arranged by amount paid within client type, you should create an index on the combination of the Client Type field and the Amount Paid field. Similarly, if you think you will need to find a client given the client's name, you should create an index on the Client Name field.

**Plan
Ahead**

To Create a Single-Field Index

A **single-field index** is an index whose key is a single field. If you need to frequently locate clients by name, you would create a single-field index. The index key would be the Client Name field. In creating an index, you need to indicate whether to allow duplicates in the index key; that is, two records that have the same value. For example, in the index for the Client Name field, if duplicates are not allowed, Access would not allow the addition of a client whose name is the same as the name of a client already in the database. In the index for the Client Name field, duplicates will be allowed. The following steps create a single-field index.

1

- Open the Client table in Design view and hide the Navigation Pane.

- Select the Client Name field.

- Click the Indexed property box in the Field Properties pane to select the property.

- Click the down arrow that appears to display the Indexed list (Figure 9–32).

2

- If necessary, click the Yes (Duplicates OK) value in the list to specify that duplicates are to be allowed.

Figure 9–32

To Create a Multiple-Field Index

Creating **multiple-field indexes**, that is, indexes whose key is a combination of fields, involves a different process from creating single-field indexes. To create multiple-field indexes, you will use the Indexes button, enter a name for the index, and then enter the combination of fields that make up the index key. Assuming there is a need to sort records on the combination of Client Type and Amount Paid, you would create a multiple-field index whose key is the combination of the Client Type field and the Amount Paid field. The following steps create this multiple-field index and assign it the name TypePaid.

- Click the Indexes button on the Design tab to display the Indexes: Client dialog box (Figure 9–33).

Figure 9–33

2

- Click the blank row (the row following Client Name) in the Index Name column in the Indexes: Client dialog box to select the position to enter the name of the new index.

- Type `TypePaid` as the index name, and then press the TAB key.

- Click the down arrow in the Field Name column to produce a list of fields in the Client table and then select Client Type to enter the first of the two fields for the index.

- Press the TAB key three times to move to the Field Name column on the following row.

Figure 9–34

- Select the Amount Paid field in the same manner as the Client Type field (Figure 9–34).

3

- Close the Indexes: Client dialog box by clicking its Close button.

- Click the Save button to save your changes.

- Close the Client table.

Automatic Error Checking

Access automatically can check for several types of errors in forms and reports. When Access detects an error, it warns you about the existence of the error and provides you with options for correcting it. The types of errors that Access can detect and correct are shown in Table 9–2.

Table 9–2 Types of Errors

Data Type	Description
Unassociated label and control	A label and control are selected that are not associated with each other.
New unassociated labels	A newly added label is not associated with any other control.
Keyboard shortcut errors	A shortcut key is invalid. This can happen because an unassociated label has a shortcut key, there are duplicate shortcut keys assigned, or a blank space is assigned as a shortcut key.
Invalid control properties	A control property is invalid. For example, the property can contain invalid characters.
Common report errors	The report has invalid sorting or grouping specifications or the report is wider than the page size.

To Enable Error Checking

For automatic error checking to take place, it must be enabled. The following steps ensure that error checking is enabled.

- Click the Microsoft Office Button and then click Access Options to display the Access Options dialog box.

- Click Object Designers to display the options for creating and modifying objects.

- Scroll down so that the Error Checking section appears.

- Be sure the Enable error checking box is checked (Figure 9–35).

Q&A

What is the purpose of the other check boxes in the section?

All the other check boxes are checked, indicating that Access will perform all the various types of automatic error checking that are possible. If there were a particular type of error checking that you would prefer to skip, you would remove its check mark before clicking the OK button.

2

- Click the OK button to close the Access Options dialog box.

Figure 9–35

Error Indication

If an error occurs, a small triangle called an **error indicator** appears in the appropriate field or control. In Figure 9–36, the label for Recruiter Number in the Client View and Update Form is changed to include an ampersand (&) before the letter N. This will make the letter N a keyboard shortcut for this control, which is a problem because the letter N already is a shortcut for Name to Find.

Figure 9–36

Once the change is complete, an error indicator appears in both controls in which the letter N is the keyboard shortcut, as shown in Figure 9–37.

Figure 9–37

Selecting a control containing an error indicator displays an Error Checking Options button. In Figure 9–38, the Error Checking Options button appears next to the Recruiter Number label, which currently is selected.

Figure 9–38

Clicking the Error Checking Options button produces the Error Checking Options menu, as shown in Figure 9–39. The first line in the menu is simply a statement of the type of error that occurred, and the second is a description of the specific error. The Change Caption command gives a submenu of the captions that can be changed. The Edit Caption Property command allows you to change the caption directly and is the simplest way to correct this error. The Help on This Error command gives help on the specific error that occurred. You can choose to ignore the error by using the Ignore Error command. The final command, Error Checking Options, allows you to change the same error checking options shown in Figure 9–35 on page AC 632.

Figure 9–39

The simplest way to fix the keyboard shortcut error is to edit the caption property. Clicking the Edit Caption Property command produces a property sheet with the Caption property highlighted (Figure 9–40). You then can change the Caption property to make another letter the shortcut key. For example, you could make the letter R the shortcut key by typing `&Recruiter Number` as the entry.

Figure 9–40

Smart Tags

In Access, a **smart tag** is a button that appears in a table, query, form, or report that assists users in accomplishing various tasks, including connecting to the Web. Smart tags are available in other Office applications as well. You can assign smart tags to fields in tables and queries. You also can assign smart tags to controls in forms and reports. For example, adding a smart tag to a name field provides quick access to commands related to names, such as sending mail or scheduling a meeting.

To Add a Smart Tag to a Field in a Table

You use the Smart Tag property for a field to add a smart tag to the field. The following steps add a smart tag to the Last Name field in the Recruiter table.

- Open the Recruiter table in Design view and hide the Navigation Pane.

- Click the row selector for the Last Name field.

- Click the Smart Tags text box to select it (Figure 9–41).

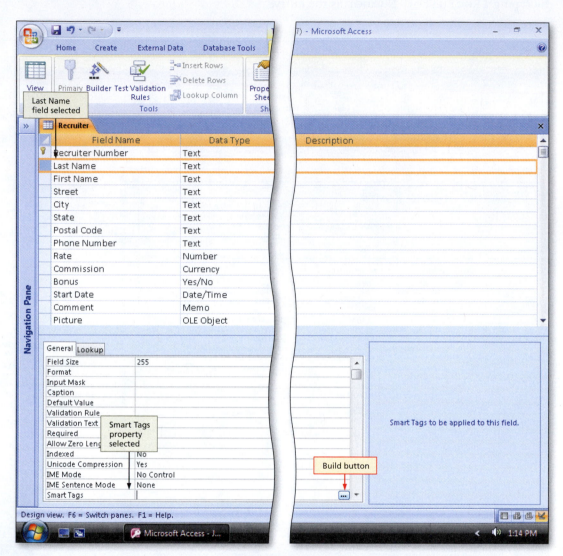

Figure 9–41

BTW

Smart Tags
Other available smart tags are: Date, Telephone Number, and Financial Symbol. The actions associated with the Date smart tag allow you to schedule a meeting and show your calendar. The Telephone Number smart tag adds the phone number to your contacts. The Financial Symbol smart tag accesses data from MSN Money Central.

2

- Click the Build button.

- Click the check box for the Person Name smart tag (Figure 9–42).

Figure 9–42

3

- Click the OK button to add the smart tag (Figure 9–43).

Q&A

Do I have to type that long expression in the Smart Tags box?

No. Access creates it for you automatically.

4

- Save your changes.

- Close the table.

Figure 9–43

Showing Smart Tags

In addition to assigning smart tags, you need to take special action to be sure that the smart tags appear. There actually are two options you have to address. One option concerns smart tags appearing in forms and reports. The other concerns smart tags appearing in tables and queries.

TO SHOW SMART TAGS IN FORMS AND REPORTS

1. Click the Microsoft Office Button.

2. Click Access Options.

3. Click Advanced.

4. If necessary, scroll to the Display section.

5. Be sure the Show Smart Tags on Forms and Reports check box is checked.

6. Click the OK button.

TO SHOW SMART TAGS IN TABLES AND QUERIES

1. Click the Microsoft Office Button.

2. Click Access Options.

3. Click Advanced.

4. If necessary, scroll to the Display section.

5. Be sure the Show Smart Tags on Datasheets check box is checked.

6. Click the OK button.

Hiding Smart Tags

Just as you need to take special action to be sure that smart tags appear, you also need to take special action to hide the smart tags, that is, to be sure that the smart tags do not appear. Again there are two options you have to address. One concerns forms and reports. The other concerns tables and queries.

TO HIDE SMART TAGS IN FORMS AND REPORTS

1. Click the Microsoft Office Button.

2. Click Access Options.

3. Click Advanced.

4. If necessary, scroll to the Display section.

5. Be sure the Show Smart Tags on Forms and Reports check box is not checked.

6. Click the OK button.

TO HIDE SMART TAGS IN TABLES AND QUERIES

1. Click the Microsoft Office Button.

2. Click Access Options.

3. Click Advanced.

4. If necessary, scroll to the Display section.

5. Be sure the Show Smart Tags on Datasheets check box is not checked.

6. Click the OK button.

Using the Smart Tag in the Table

After you have created a smart tag for a field in a table, it will appear in the field whenever you view the table. In Figure 9–44, for example, the small triangles indicate smart tags.

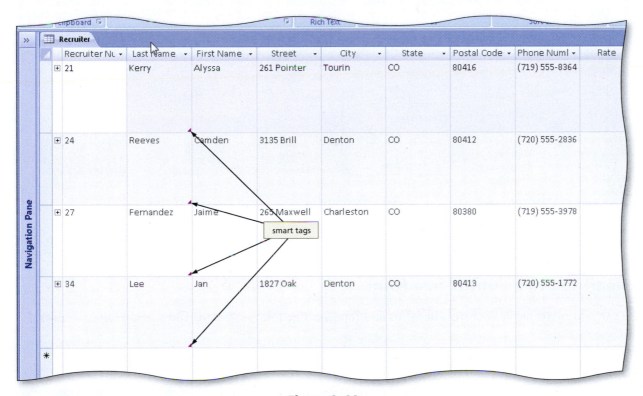

Figure 9–44

When you click a field containing a smart tag, the Smart Tag Actions button appears. In Figure 9–45, the Smart Tag Actions button for the last name Kerry appears next to the field.

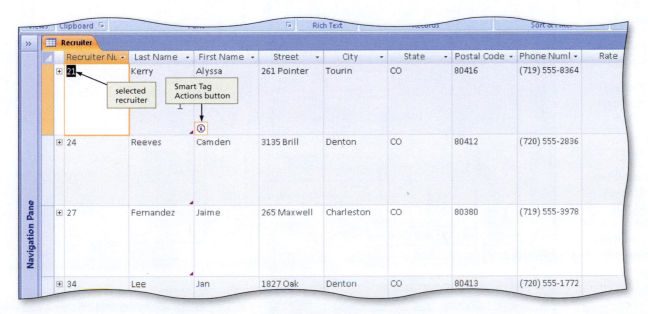

Figure 9–45

Clicking the Smart Tag Actions button produces a menu of possible actions (Figure 9–46). You can click an action on this menu to take the corresponding action.

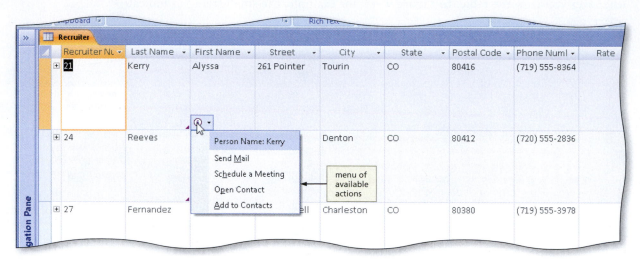

Figure 9–46

To Add a Smart Tag to a Control in a Form

You also can add smart tags to controls in forms and reports. The following steps add a smart tag to a control in a form.

- Open the Recruiter Master Form in Design view and hide the Navigation Pane.

- If a field list appears, close the field list by clicking the Add Existing Fields button on the Design tab.

- Click the Last Name control to select it.

- Click the Property Sheet button on the Design tab to display a property sheet.

- Be sure the All tab is selected. Scroll down until the Smart Tags property appears, and then click the Smart Tags property (Figure 9–47).

Figure 9–47

2

- Click the Build button to display the Smart Tags dialog box.

- Click the check box for the Person Name smart tag (Figure 9–48).

3

- Click the OK button to add the smart tag to the control.

- Close the property sheet.

- Save your changes.

- Close the form.

Figure 9–48

Using the Smart Tag in the Form

Once you have created a smart tag for a control in a form, it will appear whenever you view the form, as shown in Figure 9–49.

Figure 9–49

When you click a field containing a smart tag, the Smart Tag Actions button will appear. In Figure 9–50, the Smart Tag Actions button for the Last Name control appears next to the control.

Figure 9–50

Clicking the Smart Tag Actions button produces a menu of possible actions (Figure 9–51). You can click an action on this menu to take the corresponding action.

Figure 9–51

Additional Smart Tags

To use other smart tags created by Microsoft or by other companies, click the More Smart Tags button (shown in Figure 9–48 on page AC 641), and then search the Web for the desired smart tag.

Database Options

You can configure the way users will interact with the database by changing database options. Database options are settings that affect how the database appears or functions. For example, you can select a form to display automatically when the database is opened. You also can hide the Navigation Pane. You already have been hiding the Navigation Pane by clicking the Shutter Bar Open/Close Button. Technically, that action closes the Navigation

Pane but leaves the shutter bar on the screen. You then can show the Navigation Pane by clicking the button a second time. You also can completely hide the Navigation Pane, which removes the shutter bar. To make either of these changes, you will click Current Database in the Access Options dialog box and then select the appropriate options.

To Select a Startup Form

If the database includes a switchboard, it is common to select the switchboard as the startup form — that is, the form that appears when a user opens the database. The following steps ensure that the switchboard appears automatically when the JSP Recruiters database is opened.

- Click the Microsoft Office Button and then click Access Options to display the Access Options dialog box.

- Click Current Database to select the options for the current database.

- Click the Display Form box arrow to display the list of available forms (Figure 9–52).

- Click Switchboard and then click the OK button to select the switchboard as the form that will automatically be displayed whenever the database is opened.

- Click the OK button when Access displays a message indicating that you must close and reopen the database for the change to take effect.

Figure 9–52

Opening a Database with a Startup Form

Whenever you open a database with a startup form, Access automatically displays the startup form. If you have selected the switchboard as the startup form, as in the previous set of steps, the switchboard would be displayed without requiring any special action on the user's part (Figure 9–53).

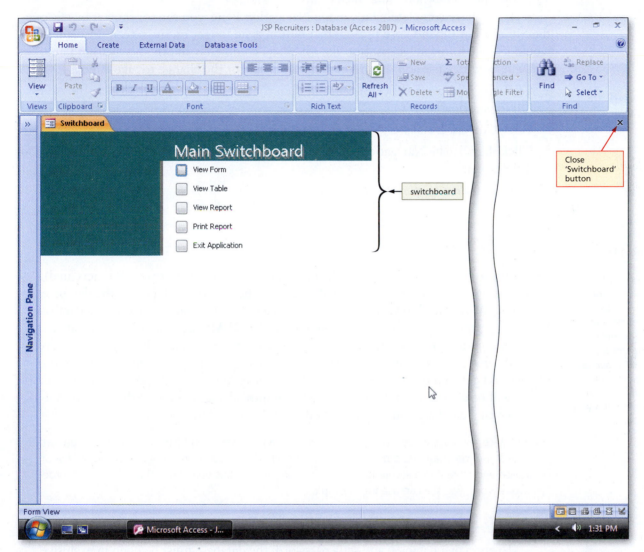

Figure 9–53

You then could use the switchboard by clicking the various buttons in the switchboard. If you click Exit Application, the database will be closed. If you want to exit the switchboard but leave the database open, click the Close 'Switchboard' button.

To Completely Hide the Navigation Pane

Normally, simply hiding the Navigation Pane by closing it is desirable. The shutter bar remains on the screen so you easily can open the Navigation Pane whenever you need it. If you want to completely hide the Navigation Pane, that is, remove the shutter bar from the screen, you would use the following steps. Notice that it is necessary to close and then reopen the database for this change to take effect.

1. Click the Microsoft Office Button and then click Access Options to display the Access Options dialog box.

2. Click Current Database to select the options for the current database.

3. Click the Display Navigation Pane check box (see Figure 9–52 on page AC 644) to remove the check mark.

4. Close and then reopen the database.

To Show the Navigation Pane when it has been Hidden

If you have completely hidden the Navigation Pane, you cannot show it by clicking the Shutter Bar Open/Close Button; that button is no longer on the screen. Instead, you would use the following steps. Just like when you completely hid the Navigation Pane, you will need to close and then reopen the database for the change to take effect.

1. Click the Microsoft Office Button and then click Access Options to display the Access Options dialog box.

2. Click Current Database to select the options for the current database.

3. Click the Display Navigation Pane check box (see Figure 9–52 on page AC 644) to add a check mark.

4. Close and then reopen the database.

BTW

Passwords
Passwords should be eight or more characters in length. The longer the length of the password and the more random the characters, the more difficult it is for someone to determine. Use a combination of uppercase and lowercase letters as well as numbers and special symbols when you create a password.

Encrypting a Database

Encrypting refers to the storing of the data in the database in an encoded (encrypted) format. Any time a user stores or modifies data in the encrypted database, the database management system (DBMS) will encode the data before actually updating the database. Before a legitimate user retrieves the data using the DBMS, the data will be decoded. The whole encrypting process is transparent to a legitimate user; that is, he or she is not even aware it is happening. If an unauthorized user attempts to bypass all the controls of the DBMS and get to the database through a utility program or a word processor, however, he or she will be able to see only the encoded, and unreadable, version of the data. In Access, you encrypt a database and set a password as part of the same operation.

Note: Once you have encrypted a database and set a password, you MUST remember the password to access your database. As a precaution, it is a good idea for you to make a backup copy of your database and store it in a secure location before performing this operation. That way, if you forget your password, you still can use the backup copy.

To Open a Database in Exclusive Mode

To encrypt a database and set a password, the database must be open in exclusive mode, that is, no other user can access the database in any way. The following steps open the Camashaly database in exclusive mode in preparation for setting a password.

1 Close the open database by clicking the Microsoft Office Button and then clicking Close Database on the Microsoft Office Button menu.

2 With your USB flash drive connected to one of the computer's USB ports, click the More button to display the Open dialog box.

3 If the Folders list is displayed below the Folders button, click the Folders button to remove the Folders list.

4 If necessary, click Computer in the Favorite Links section and then double-click UDISK 2.0 (E:) to select the USB flash drive, Drive E in this case, as the new open location. (Your drive letter might be different.)

5 Click Camashaly to select the file name.

6 Click the Open button arrow to display the Open button menu (Figure 9–54).

7 Click Open Exclusive to open the database in exclusive mode.

◄ | What is the purpose of the other modes?

Q&A | The mode you use affects how you and other users interact with the database. The first option, Open, opens the database in a mode that allows it to be shared by other users. The second, Open Read-Only, allows you to read the data in the database, but not update the database. Other users can both read and update. The fourth, Open Exclusive Read-Only allows you to read but not update. Other users also can read the data, but they cannot perform updates.

8 If a Security Warning appears, click the Options button to display the Microsoft Office Security Options dialog box.

9 With the option button to enable the content selected, click the OK button to enable the content.

Figure 9–54

To Encrypt a Database with a Password

With the database open in exclusive mode, the following steps encrypt the database with a password. Be sure to remember the password that you type. You will use it again in the next sections.

- Click Database Tools on the Ribbon to display the Database Tools tab.

- Click the Encrypt with Password button on the Database Tools tab to display the Set Database Password dialog box.

- Type a password in the Password text box in the Set Database Password dialog box.

- Press the TAB key and then type your password again in the Verify text box (Figure 9–55).

Q&A Are passwords case sensitive?

Yes.

Q&A What if I forget my password?

You will not be able to open your database. You would have to use the backup copy you made of your database.

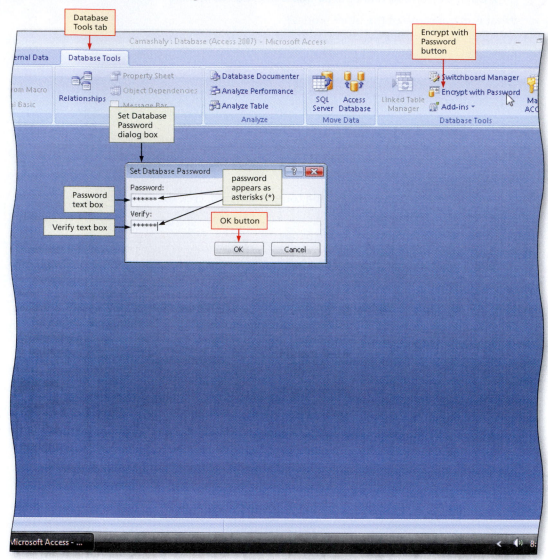

Figure 9–55

- Click the OK button to encrypt the database and set the password.

- Close the database.

Opening a Database with a Password

When you open a database that has a password, you will be prompted to enter your password in the Password Required dialog box. Once you have done so, click the OK button. Assuming yo u have entered your password correctly, Access then will open the database.

To Decrypt the Database and Remove the Password

If you no longer feel the encryption and the password are necessary, you can decrypt the database and remove the password. The following steps accomplish this task.

- Open the Camashaly database in exclusive mode (see the steps on page AC 647), entering your password when requested. If necessary, enable the content.

- Click Database Tools on the Ribbon to display the Database Tools tab.

- Click the Decrypt Database button on the Ribbon to display the Unset Database Password dialog box (Figure 9–56).

Q&A Why does clicking the Decrypt Database button display a dialog box that is called Unset Database Password?

The use of passwords and encryption are part of the same process, as the button you clicked earlier, Encrypt with Password, indicates. The same is true for decryption, even though the word, Password, does not appear on the button.

Figure 9–56

- Type the password in the Password dialog box.

- Click the OK button to remove the password and decrypt the database.

- Close the Camashaly database.

Q&A What is the effect of this change?

Users no longer will need to enter a password when they open the database.

Digital Certificates

When you have created your database, you can convey to others that your database can be trusted by adding a **digital signature**, a stamp of authentication, which is contained within a **digital certificate**. To do so, you package and sign your database. You then can send the resulting package to others. The signature confirms that no one has tampered with the database. If the users trust the author, they then can enable the content of the database with confidence.

Note: Do not complete the following section (pages AC 650 through 653) unless your instructor tells you to do so. Even if you are not completing the section, however, you should read it to make sure you understand the process. The steps create a database called JSP Recruiters New, which is used later in the chapter. If you do not complete the steps, you should use the Back Up Database command on the Manage submenu of the Microsoft Office Button menu to create the JSP Recruiters New database.

To Create a Self-Signed Certificate

To use a verified, authenticated digital certificate, you must obtain one from a trusted Microsoft partner certification authority (CA). If you don't have such a certificate you can create your own digital certificate, known as a **self-signed certificate**. In the process, you are creating a certificate that can be used for personal macros only on the machine on which they were created. The following steps create a self-signed certificate.

- Open the JSP Recruiters database and close the switchboard. If necessary, enable the content.

- Click the Start button on the Windows Vista taskbar to display the Start menu.

- Click All Programs at the bottom of the left pane on the Start menu to display the All Programs list and then click Microsoft Office on the All Programs list to display the Microsoft Office list.

- Click Microsoft Office Tools on the Microsoft Office list to display the Microsoft Office Tools list.

- Click Digital Certificate for VBA Projects to display the Create Digital Certificate dialog box.

- Type your name in the 'Your certificate's name' text box (Figure 9–57).

Figure 9–57

- Click the OK button to create the certificate (Figure 9–58).

- Click the OK button in the SelfCert Success message box to close the message box.

Q&A Do I have to do this from within Access?

No. The digital certificate steps occur in a separate program.

Figure 9–58

To Package and Sign a Database

You can package, digitally sign, and distribute an Access database with a single operation. Access will save the result in the Access Deployment file format (.accdc). Other users then can extract the database from the package and use it. The following steps package and sign the JSP Recruiters database, using the self-signed certificate you created earlier.

- Click the Microsoft Office Button to display the Microsoft Office Button menu.

- Point to the Publish arrow to display the Publish submenu (Figure 9–59).

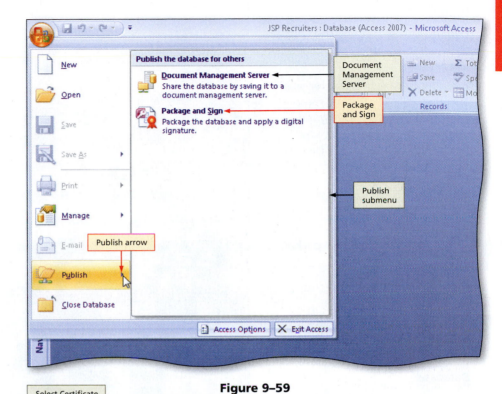

Figure 9–59

2

- Click Package and Sign to display the Select Certificate dialog box (Figure 9–60).

Q&A What can I do with this dialog box?
You can select a certificate or view details of the selected certificate.

Figure 9–60

● With the desired certificate selected, click the OK button.

● Select the location where you will save the certificate, and enter a name for the signed package (Figure 9–61).

Q&A

Did I need to select Microsoft Office Access Signed Package as the Save as type?

No. Access should do this for you automatically. If for some reason Microsoft Office Access Signed Package was not selected, you could select it yourself by clicking the arrow and then clicking the signed package in the list.

4

● Click the Create button to package and sign the database.

● If the switchboard opens, close it by clicking its Close button.

● Close the existing database by clicking the Microsoft Office button and then clicking Close Database.

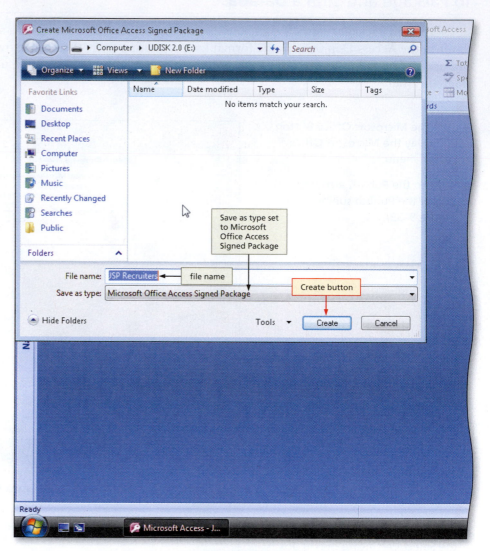

Figure 9–61

BTW

Packaging
Packaging places the database in an Access Deployment (.accdc) file, signs the package, and then places the code-signed package at a location on the user's computer that you determine. Users then can extract the database from the package and work directly in the database (not in the package file).

To Open a Signed Package

The following steps open the signed package you just created and then extract the JSP Recruiters database from the package, giving it the name, JSP Recruiters New.

- From the Getting Started with Microsoft Office Access screen, click the More button to display the Open dialog box.

- Select the location for the package and then change the file type by clicking the 'Files of type' box arrow and selecting Microsoft Office Access Signed Packages.

- Ensure the package you wish to open is selected (Figure 9–62).

Figure 9–62

- Click the Open button to open the package and, if there is a security concern detected, to display the Microsoft Office Access Security Notice dialog box (Figure 9–63).

- Click the Open button to display the Extract Database To dialog box.

- Select your USB drive as the location and change the database name to JSP Recruiters New.

- Click the OK button to extract the database.

- Because you will not be using this database, close the database and reopen the JSP Recruiters database.

Figure 9–63

The Trust Center

The Trust Center is a place within Access where you can set security options and also find the latest information on technology related to privacy, safety, and security. To use the Trust Center, you click the Microsoft Office Button and then click Access Options to display the Access Options dialog box. You then click Trust Center to display the Trust Center content (Figure 9–64). You then would click the Trust Center Settings button to display the Trust Center dialog box in which you can make changes in the following categories.

Figure 9–64

Trusted Publishers

Clicking Trusted Publishers in the Trust Center dialog box shows the list of trusted publishers (Figure 9–65). Currently there are none. To view details about a trusted publisher, click the publisher and then click the View button. To remove a trusted publisher from the list, click the publisher and then click the Remove button.

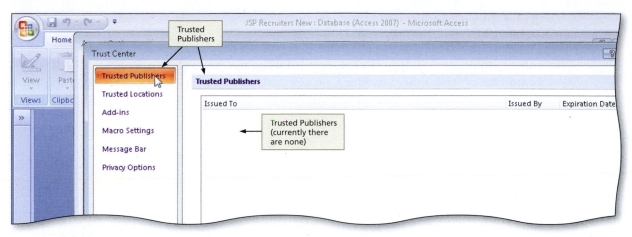

Figure 9–65

Trusted Locations

Clicking Trusted Locations shows the list of trusted locations (Figure 9–66). To add a new location, click the 'Add new location' button. To remove or modify an existing location, click the location and then click the Remove or Modify button.

Figure 9–66

Add-Ins

Add-ins are additional programs that you can install and use within Access. Some come with Access and typically are installed using the Access Setup program. Others can be purchased from other vendors. Clicking Add-ins gives you the opportunity to specify restrictions concerning Add-ins (Figure 9–67).

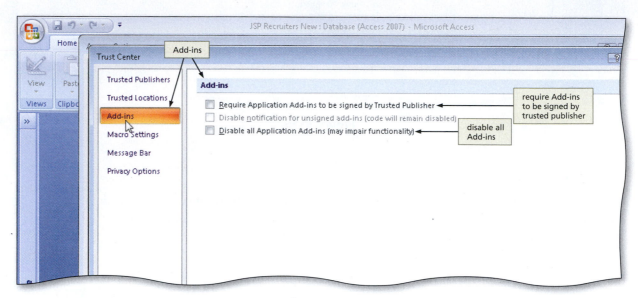

Figure 9–67

Macro Settings

Macros written by others have the potential to harm your computer, for example by spreading a virus. The Trust Center uses special criteria, including valid digital signatures, reputable certificates, and trusted publishers, to ensure a macro is safe. If the Trust Center discovers a macro that potentially is unsafe, it will take appropriate action. The action the Trust Center takes depends on the Macro setting you have selected. Clicking Macro Settings enables you to select or change this setting (Figure 9–68).

Figure 9–68

Message Bar

Clicking Message Bar lets you choose whether the message bar should appear when content has been blocked (Figure 9–69).

Figure 9–69

Privacy Options

Clicking Privacy Options lets you set security settings to protect your personal privacy (Figure 9–70).

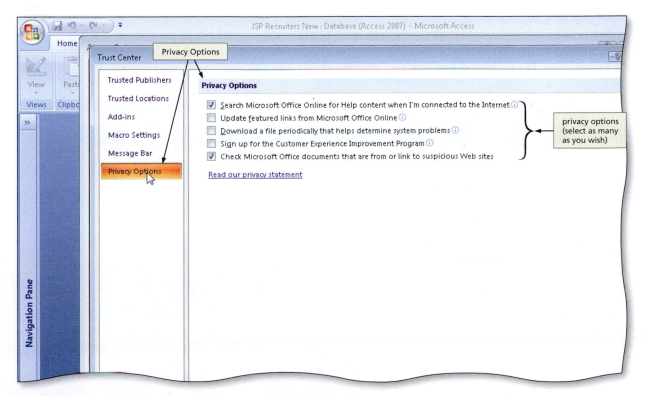

Figure 9–70

Managing Add-Ins

You can manage add-ins by clicking the Microsoft Office Button, clicking Access Options, and then clicking Add-ins (Figure 9–71). You can view details concerning existing add-ins. You also can manage existing add-ins or add new ones by selecting the add-in category in the Manage box and then clicking the Go button to start the Add-in Manager.

Figure 9–71

You also can start the Add-in Manager by clicking Database Tools on the Ribbon to display the Database Tools tab and then clicking the Add-ins button (Figure 9–72).

Figure 9–72

Locking a Database

By **locking** a database, you can prevent users from viewing or modifying VBA code in your database or from making changes to the design of forms or reports. When you lock the database, Access changes the file name extension from .accdb to .accde.

TO CREATE A LOCKED DATABASE (ACCDE FILE)

To lock a database, you would use the following steps.

1. With the database to be locked open, click Database Tools on the Ribbon to display the Database Tools tab.

2. Click the Make ACCDE button on the Database Tools tab to display the Save As dialog box.

3. In the Save As dialog box, indicate a location and name for the ACCDE file.

4. Click the Save button in the Save As dialog box to create the file.

Using the Locked Database

You use an ACCDE file just as you use the databases with which you now are familiar with two exceptions. First, you must select ACCDE files in the Files of type box when opening the file. Second, you will not be able to modify any source code or change the design of any forms or reports. If you right-clicked the Client Master Form, for example, you would find that the Design View command on the shortcut menu is dimmed, as are many other commands (Figure 9–73).

Figure 9–73

It is very important that you save your original database in case you ever need to make changes to VBA code or to the design of a form or report. You cannot use the ACCDE file to make such changes.

Record Locking

You can indicate how records are to be locked when multiple users are using a database at the same time. To do so, click the Microsoft Office Button, click Access Options, and then click Advanced. Scroll down so that the Advanced section appears on the screen (Figure 9–74).

Figure 9–74

If you wanted the default open mode to be exclusive rather than shared, you could click the Exclusive option button. You can select the approach you want for record locking by clicking the appropriate record locking option button. The possible approaches to record locking are shown in Table 9–3.

Table 9–3 Record Locking Approaches	
Locking Type	**Description**
No locks	When you edit a record, Access will not lock the record. Thus, other users also could edit the same record at the same time. When you have finished your changes and attempt to save the record, Access will give you the option of overwriting the other user's changes (not recommended), copying your changes to the clipboard for pasting into a new record, or canceling your changes.
All records	All records will be locked as long as you have the database open. Other users are prevented from editing or locking the records during this time.
Edited record	When you edit a record, Access will lock the record for your use. When other users attempt to edit the same record, they will not be able to do so. Instead, they will see the locked record indicator.

Splitting a Database

You can **split** a database into two databases, one called the **back-end database** that contains only the table data, and another database called the **front-end database** that contains the other objects. While there only would be a single copy of the back-end database, each user could have his or her own copy of the front-end database. Each user would create the desired custom reports, forms, and other objects in his or her own front-end database, thereby not interfering with any other user.

BTW

Quick Reference
For a table that lists how to complete the tasks covered in this book using the mouse, Ribbon, shortcut menu, and keyboard, see the Quick Reference Summary at the back of this book, or visit the Access 2007 Quick Reference Web page (scsite.com/ac2007/qr).

<table>
<tr><td>**Plan Ahead**</td><td>**Determine whether the database should be split.**
Should the database be split into a front-end and a back-end? Issues to consider are the following:</td></tr>
</table>

> **Determine whether the database should be split.**
> Should the database be split into a front-end and a back-end? Issues to consider are the following:
>
> 1. In many cases, when multiple users share a database, individual users would like to develop their own custom forms, reports, queries, or other objects. If this is the case and each user develops such custom objects, the database can become cluttered and confusing. Many reports, for example, could be developed by different users for different purposes. Further, unless some special action is taken, there is nothing to protect one user's object (for example, a report or form) from being modified by another user. Splitting the database solves this problem.
>
> 2. Is there a size issue with the database? Splitting the database into a front-end and a back-end produces smaller databases.

To Split the Database

When splitting a database, the database to be split must be open. In the process, you will identify a name and location for the back-end database that will be created by the splitter. The following steps show how to split the JSP Recruiters New database (the one you extracted earlier).

1

- Open the JSP Recruiters New database. If necessary, enable the content and close the Switchboard.

- Click Database Tools on the Ribbon to display the Database Tools tab.

- Click the Access Database button on the Database Tools tab to display the Database Splitter dialog box (Figure 9–75).

The instructions say that I should make a backup copy of my database before splitting it. Should I do that now?

It definitely is a good idea to make a backup copy. Here, because you are using the JSP Recruiters New database rather than the main JSP Recruiters database, it is not necessary. Your JSP Recruiters database still will be intact.

Figure 9–75

2

• Click the Split Database button to display the Create Back-end Database dialog box (Figure 9–76).

Figure 9–76

3

• Be sure the file name in the Create Back-end Database dialog box that appears is JSP Recruiters New_acc.mdb.

• Select a location for the back-end database, for example, drive E:, and then click the Split button (Figure 9–77).

4

• Click the OK button.

Figure 9–77

The Front-End and Back-End Databases

The database now has been split into separate front-end and back-end databases. The front-end database is the one that you will use. This database contains all the queries, reports, forms, and so on, from the original database. The front-end database only contains links to the tables, however, instead of the tables themselves (Figure 9–78). The back-end database contains the actual tables, but does not contain any other objects.

Figure 9–78

To Quit Access

You are ready to quit Access. The following step quits Access.

1 Click the Close button on the right side of the Access title bar to quit Access.

Chapter Summary

In this chapter you have learned to convert Access databases to and from earlier versions; use Microsoft Access tools to analyze and document an Access database; add custom categories and groups to the Navigation Pane; use table and database properties; use field properties to create a custom input mask and to allow zero-length strings; create indexes; use automatic error checking; use smart tags; select a startup form; encrypt a database and set a password; use digital certificates; use the Trust Center; lock a database; and split a database. The following list includes all the new Access skills you have learned in this chapter.

1. Convert an Access 2007 Database to an Earlier Version (AC 606)
2. Convert an Access 2000 or Access 2002-2003 Database to Access 2007 (AC 607)
3. Use the Table Analyzer (AC 608)
4. Use the Performance Analyzer (AC 611)
5. Use the Documenter (AC 612)
6. Create Custom Categories and Groups (AC 614)
7. Add Items to Groups (AC 617)
8. Use the Search Bar (AC 619)
9. Create a Validation Rule for a Table (AC 620)
10. Create Custom Properties (AC 621)
11. Create a Custom Input Mask (AC 625)
12. Allow Zero Length (AC 626)
13. Create a Single-Field Index (AC 629)
14. Create a Multiple-Field Index (AC 630)
15. Enable Error Checking (AC 632)
16. Add a Smart Tag to a Field in a Table (AC 636)
17. Show Smart Tags in Forms and Reports (AC 638)
18. Show Smart Tags in Tables and Queries (AC 638)
19. Hide Smart Tags in Forms and Reports (AC 638)
20. Hide Smart Tags in Tables and Queries (AC 638)
21. Add a Smart Tag to a Control in a Form (AC 640)
22. Select a Startup Form (AC 644)
23. Completely Hide the Navigation Pane (AC 645)
24. Show the Navigation Pane when it has been Hidden (AC 646)
25. Open a Database in Exclusive Mode (AC 646)
26. Encrypt a Database with a Password (AC 648)
27. Decrypt the Database and Remove the Password (AC 649)
28. Create a Self-Signed Certificate (AC 650)
29. Package and Sign a Database (AC 651)
30. Open a Signed Package (AC 653)
31. Create a Locked Database (ACCDE File) (AC 659)
32. Split the Database (AC 662)

Learn It Online

Test your knowledge of chapter content and key terms.

Instructions: To complete the Learn It Online exercises, start your browser, click the Address bar, and then enter the Web address scsite.com/ac2007/learn. When the Access 2007 Learn It Online page is displayed, click the link for the exercise you want to complete and then read the instructions.

Chapter Reinforcement TF, MC, and SA
A series of true/false, multiple choice, and short answer questions that test your knowledge of the chapter content.

Flash Cards
An interactive learning environment where you identify chapter key terms associated with displayed definitions.

Practice Test
A series of multiple choice questions that test your knowledge of chapter content and key terms.

Who Wants To Be a Computer Genius?
An interactive game that challenges your knowledge of chapter content in the style of a television quiz show.

Wheel of Terms
An interactive game that challenges your knowledge of chapter key terms in the style of the television show *Wheel of Fortune*.

Crossword Puzzle Challenge
A crossword puzzle that challenges your knowledge of key terms presented in the chapter.

Apply Your Knowledge

Reinforce the skills and apply the concepts you learned in this chapter.

Administering The Bike Delivers Database
Instructions: Start Access. If you are using the Microsoft Office Access 2007 Comprehensive text, open The Bike Delivers database that you used in Chapter 8. Otherwise, see your instructor for information on accessing the files required in this book.

Perform the following tasks:
1. Open the Customer table in Design view and create an index that allows duplicates on the Customer Name field.
2. Create a custom input mask for the Customer Number field. The first two characters of the customer number must be uppercase letters and the last two characters must be digits. No position may be blank.
3. Create a smart tag for the Customer Name field.
4. Save the changes to the Customer table.
5. Populate the Status property for the database with the value, End of Chapter Exercise.
6. Create a custom property with the name Semester. Use Date as the Type and enter the current date as the value.
7. Submit the revised database in the format specified by your instructor.

Extend Your Knowledge

Extend the skills you learned in this chapter and experiment with new skills. You may need to use Help to complete the assignment.

Changing Access Options and Table Properties

Instructions: Copy the JSP Recruiters database and rename the database to Chapter 9_last name Recruiters. For example, if your last name is Smith, then name the database Chapter 9_Smith Recruiters. Start Access and open the database that you copied and renamed.

Perform the following tasks:

1. The switchboard no longer should appear when the database is opened. Change the Access options to ensure that the switchboard does not appear automatically.

2. Change the Navigation options so that the Search Bar always should appear in the Navigation Pane.

3. Open the Seminar table in Design view and create a validation rule that specifies that the value in the Hours field must be greater than or equal to the value in the Increments field.

4. Currently, when you open the Seminar table in Datasheet view, the table is in order by Seminar Number. Change the property for the table so the table is in order by Seminar Description.

5. Change the length of the Seminar Number field in the Seminar table and in the Seminar Offerings table to 20. You will need to delete the relationship between the tables before you can change the length. Re-create the relationship between the Seminar and Seminar Offerings table.

6. In the Integration Feature, you saved the export steps to export the Recruiter-Client Query. Run those saved export steps. Overwrite the existing Excel file.

7. Submit the revised database in the format specified by your instructor.

Make It Right

Analyze a database and correct all errors and/or improve the design.

Correcting Table Design Errors

Instructions: Start Access. Open the Pets and More database. See the inside back cover of this book for instructions on downloading the Data Files for Students, or contact your instructor for more information about accessing the required files.

 The Pets and More database contains data about a company that provides a variety of services to pet owners. The owner added the index shown in Figure 9–79 on the next page to the Customer table. The index is to sort records first by City and then by Last Name, but she gets an error message when she tries to save the table change. Create the index correctly.

Continued >

Make It Right *continued*

She also created an input mask for the Customer Number field. The input mask she created is shown in Figure 9–79, however she found that it does not work correctly. It allows a user to input a customer number that does not include letters. The customer number must be two letters followed by two numbers.

Figure 9–79

Correct these errors and submit the revised database in the format specified by your instructor.

In the Lab

Design, create, modify, and/or use a database following the guidelines, concepts, and skills presented in this chapter. Labs are listed in order of increasing difficulty.

Lab 1: Administering the JMS TechWizards Database

Problem: JMS TechWizards has determined a number of database administration tasks that need to be done. These include creating indexes, setting start up options, creating input masks, creating smart tags, and converting to an earlier version of Access.

Instructions: If you are using the Microsoft Office Access 2007 Comprehensive text, open the JMS TechWizards database that you used in Chapter 8. Otherwise, see the inside back cover of this book for instructions on downloading the Data Files for Students, or contact your instructor for more information about accessing the required files.

Perform the following tasks:
1. Technician Number is a field in both the Client and Technician tables. Create an input mask for the Technician Number field in both tables.
2. Create an index on the Last Name and First Name fields in the Technician table. Name the index, FullName.
3. Open the Client Master Form and create a smart tag for the Client Name field.
4. Select the switchboard as the startup form.
5. Convert the database to an Access 2002-2003 database.
6. Submit the revised database in the format specified by your instructor.

In the Lab

Lab 2: Administering the Hockey Fan Zone Database

Problem: The management of the Hockey Fan Zone store has determined a number of database administration tasks that need to be done. These include creating indexes, setting startup options, creating input masks, creating smart tags, and using table properties.

Instructions: If you are using the Microsoft Office Access 2007 Comprehensive text, open the Hockey Fan Zone database that you used in Chapter 8. Otherwise, see the inside back cover of this book for instructions on downloading the Data Files for Students, or contact your instructor for more information about accessing the required files.

Perform the following tasks:
1. Open the Item table in Design view and create an index on the combination of Item Type and Description. Name the index, TypeDescription.
2. Create a custom input mask for the Item Number field. The values in the field must be four digits in length.
3. Ensure that the cost of an item is less than the selling price of an item.
4. Ensure that the switchboard appears when the database is opened.
5. Open the Supplier table in Design view and create a smart tag for the Supplier Name field.
6. Populate the Status database property with the value, Current Version.
7. Submit the revised database in the format specified by your instructor.

In the Lab

Lab 3: Administering the Ada Beauty Supply Database

Problem: Ada Beauty Supply has determined a number of database administration tasks that need to be done. These include creating indexes, setting startup options, creating input masks, allowing zero-length fields, creating smart tags, and populating database properties.

Instructions: If you are using the Microsoft Office Access 2007 Comprehensive text, open the Ada Beauty Supply database that you used in Chapter 8. Otherwise, see the inside back cover of this book for instructions on downloading the Data Files for Students, or contact your instructor for more information about accessing the required files. Submit the revised database in the format specified by your instructor.

Continued >

In the Lab *continued*

Instructions Part 1: The management of Ada Beauty Supply is concerned that as the database grows, it will take longer to retrieve information on customer names. An index would speed up the retrieval process. The management also feels that an index on the last name and first name of the sales rep would improve efficiency.

Instructions Part 2: The management wants to ensure that the customer number field always contains two uppercase letters followed by two numeric digits. Also, errors are occurring because individuals are entering text instead of numbers in the Postal Code field in the Sales Rep table. In addition, empty strings should not be allowed in the Customer Name field.

Instructions Part 3: Management would like an easy way to select a customer name and send them an e-mail. Management wants to be able to do this from within the Customer table and the Customer Master Form. Management also wants the switchboard to appear when the database is opened.

Instructions Part 4: Management needs to contact all customers with an amount paid greater than $1,000.00. Apply a filter to the Sales Rep-Customer query and print the filtered query results.

Cases and Places

Apply your creative thinking and problem solving skills to design and implement a solution.

● EASIER   ●● MORE DIFFICULT

●1 Administering the Second Hand Goods Database

If you are using the Microsoft Office Access 2007 Comprehensive text, open the Second Hand Goods database that you used in Chapter 8. Otherwise, see the inside back cover of this book for instructions on downloading the Data Files for Students, or contact your instructor for more information about accessing the required files. Perform the following database administration tasks:

a. Copy the Second Hand Goods database and rename it as Second Hand Furniture.

b. Split the Second Hand Furniture database into a front-end and a back-end database.

c. Open the front-end database and open the switchboard form in Design view.

d. Add a label to the upper-left corner of the form and type your name in the label. Change the font color to white and the font size to 12.

e. Submit the revised databases in the format specified by your instructor.

●2 Administering the BeachCondo Rentals Database

If you are using the Microsoft Office Access 2007 Comprehensive text, open the BeachCondo Rentals database that you used in Chapter 8. Otherwise, see the inside back cover of this book for instructions on downloading the Data Files for Students, or contact your instructor for more information about accessing the required files. Perform the following database administration tasks:

a. Use the Database Documenter to produce detailed documentation on the Current Rentals table. Export the documentation to a Word RTF file. Change the name of the file to LastName_ Documentation.rtf where LastName is your last name.

b. Use the Table Analyzer to analyze the table structure of each table in the database. Open the RTF file that you created in the previous step and report the results of the analysis at the end of the file.

c. Use the Performance Analyzer to analyze all the tables and queries in the database. Report the results of the analysis in your RTF file.

d. Customize the Navigation Pane by adding a custom category called Rentals. Then add two custom groups, Potential and Current, to the Rentals category.

e. Add the Available Rentals report and the Condos by Bedroom report to the Potential group. Add the Current Rentals table and the report that you created in Chapter 7 to the Current category.

f. Print the relationships for the database.

g. Submit the RTF file and the revised database in the format specified by your instructor.

●●3 Administering the Restaurant Database

If you are using the Microsoft Office Access 2007 Comprehensive text, open the restaurant database that you used in Chapter 8. Otherwise, see the inside back cover of this book for instructions on downloading the Data Files for Students, or contact your instructor for more information about accessing the required files. Using the Plan Ahead guidelines presented in this chapter, determine what administrative tasks you need to perform on your database. Do you need to customize the Navigation Pane? Do you need to add any indexes, input masks, or smart tags? Are any custom properties needed? Because you probably will have different people using the database, you may want to split the database. Is error checking enabled? Perform the necessary database administration tasks and submit the revised database to your instructor.

Continued >

Cases and Places *continued*

••4 Creating a Digital Certificate for Your Contacts Database

Make It Personal

If you are using the Microsoft Office Access 2007 Comprehensive text, open the contacts database that you used in Chapter 8. Otherwise, see the inside back cover of this book for instructions on downloading the Data Files for Students, or contact your instructor for more information about accessing the required files. If you have your instructor's permission and the ability to create digital certificates, create a digital certificate for your contacts database. Submit the revised database in the format specified by your instructor.

••5 Understand Database Administration Tasks

Working Together

Copy the Hockey Fan Zone database and rename the database to your team name. For each of the database administration tasks listed below, perform the task and record the outcome. Write a short paper that explains what happened when you did these tasks.

    a. Create an earlier version of the database

    b. Encrypt the database and set a password

    c. Create a locked database

    d. Change the macro settings

    e. Change privacy options

    f. Export the AC_History.xlsx file attachment and then detach (remove) the attachment.

Web Feature
Sharing Access Data

Objectives

You will have mastered the material in this feature when you can:

- Create a SharePoint Services list by exporting an Access table

- Open a SharePoint Services list from within SharePoint

- Import or link a SharePoint Services list to an Access table

- Move a database to SharePoint and share the database

- Insert a hyperlink to a file or Web page

- Export to HTML

SharePoint Services
Windows SharePoint offers users the ability to store data on the Web so that access to that data can be shared across a network. It is essentially a storage location that can be accessed collaboratively. No special software is required on the client side. SharePoint Services technology is particularly useful for sharing information across an intranet.

Web Feature Introduction

Access users often need to work with their data from a remote location or share database information with colleagues working in another location. You can use the Web for this type of access in one of two ways, either with Windows SharePoint Services or by saving Access objects as HTML files. Using the current version of Windows SharePoint Services 3.0, you can create lists that are like Access tables. Other users with appropriate privileges can access the site and share the lists. Windows SharePoint offers users the ability to store data on the Web so that access to that data can be shared across a network. The other method, saving Access objects as HTML files, lets users view them over the Web in a browser, such as Internet Explorer.

Project — Sharing Access Data

Like other applications, Access allows you to share data with others using SharePoint Services. You can import, export, and link data to a SharePoint Services Web site. The data will reside on the Web site in the form of lists.

A SharePoint Services list is similar to a table in a database. The list is a grid with column headings, which are similar to field names, and data in the columns that match the column headings. Figure 1a shows a list with information about computer items. The first column heading is Item Id, and the items in the column are item ids. The second column heading is Description, and the items in the column are descriptions of products. The data in the list can be imported or linked to a table in an Access database. Figure 1b shows the results of importing the data into a table. Notice that Access has added an additional field, the ID field, which is an AutoNumber field that serves as the primary key.

Figure 1

You also can make objects in the database available for viewing by others by exporting the object as an HTML file. Figure 2 shows an HTML version of the Discount Report for JSP Recruiters viewed in a browser. The figure also contains a hyperlink to the JSP Recruiter's Home Page. To display that home page while viewing this data, simply click the link. Unlike the data in SharePoint lists, the HTML versions of objects in the database are static. That is, they do not change when the data in the database changes. If you were to change client data tomorrow and wanted the HTML version to contain the new data, you would need to export the file again, creating an updated version.

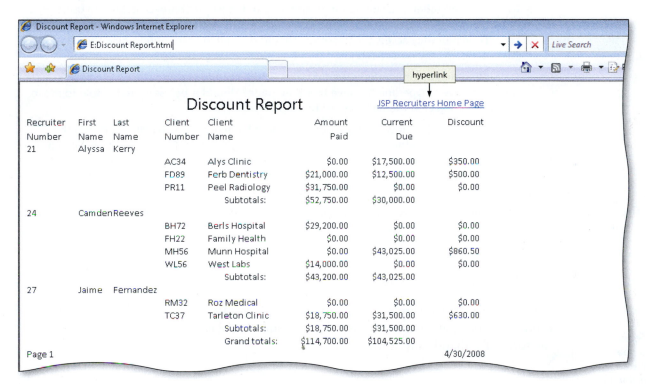

Figure 2

Overview

As you read through this feature, you will learn how to perform the following tasks.

- Create a SharePoint list by exporting an Access table.
- Open and use a SharePoint list.
- Import or link a SharePoint list to an Access database.
- Move a database to SharePoint.
- Use a shared database.
- Add a hyperlink to an Access object.
- Export Access data to HTML.

Plan Ahead

> **Guidelines for Sharing Data**
>
> 1. **Determine tables to be shared.** Which tables contain data that should be shared with others over the Internet?
>
> 2. **Determine whether users should import or link SharePoint lists to their Access tables.** If they link the data, any changes they make either in SharePoint or Access will be available to others. If they import the data, the changes only will affect the database on which they are working. For each list and each user, you need to determine whether changes should be immediately available to others.
>
> 3. **Determine whether you should move an entire database to SharePoint.** Should users have access to all the tables in the database? Should they have access to the forms or reports? When they access the database, should they be able to merely view the data (that is, Read-Only mode) or should they be able to change data (that is, Edit mode)?
>
> 4. **Determine whether hyperlinks would be useful in any forms or reports.** Would it be useful to have a hyperlink to move to a Web page? Would it be useful to be able to move to another object in the database or to send e-mail?
>
> 5. **Determine whether any database objects should be exported as HTML.** Exporting the objects as HTML enables them to be viewed over the Internet. They also can be viewed using a Web browser on the local computer. It is important to remember that data that has been exported as HTML does not change when the underlying data in the database changes.
>
> When necessary, more specific details concerning the above decisions and/or actions are presented at appropriate positions within the feature.

SharePoint Services

Access allows you to share data with others using SharePoint Services. You can import, export, and link data to a SharePoint Services site. The data will reside on the Web site in the form of a SharePoint Services list.

Creating a SharePoint Services List

You can create a SharePoint Services list directly on a SharePoint Services site. You also can create one by exporting an Access table or an Excel worksheet. The process for creating one from an Access table is similar to exporting a table to any other format. The only difference is that you would use the SharePoint List button in the Export group on the External Data tab, rather than the Excel, Word, or any of the other buttons (Figure 3).

Figure 3

You then would need to identify the site, give a name for the list to be created, and include an optional description of the list (Figure 4).

Figure 4

To Create a SharePoint Services List by Exporting an Access Table

To create a SharePoint Services List by exporting an Access table, you would use the following steps.

1. With the table selected within Access, click External Data on the Ribbon to display the External Data tab.
2. Click the SharePoint List button in the Export group on the External Data tab to display the Export - SharePoint Site dialog box.
3. Specify the SharePoint site, specify the name for the list, and, optionally, enter a description of the list.
4. Click the OK button and then enter your user name and password when prompted.
5. Decide whether you want to save the export steps.

Opening a SharePoint Services List

You can use a list directly from the SharePoint site. You can open the list by selecting from the available lists (Figure 5).

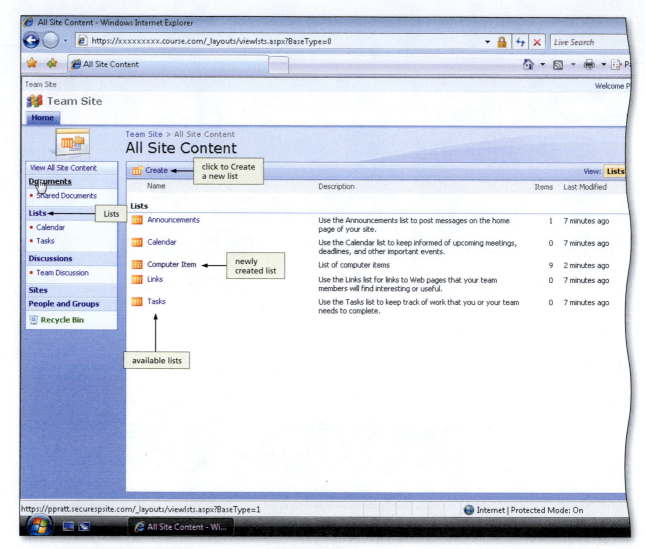

Figure 5

TO OPEN A SHAREPOINT SERVICES LIST FROM WITHIN SHAREPOINT

To open a list from within SharePoint, you would use the following steps.

1. Enter the SharePoint site, giving your username and password when prompted.

2. Click the Lists link.

3. Click the desired list.

Using a SharePoint Services List

When the list is open, you can view it in Datasheet view, which is very similar to Datasheet view within Access (Figure 6).

Figure 6

You can filter or sort on a field by clicking the arrow in the column heading for the field (Figure 7). You can click either Sort Ascending or Sort Descending to change the sort order. By clicking a value, only those rows containing that value will appear. By once again clicking Show All you can redisplay all records. If you need more complex filtering, you can click Custom Filter and then specify individual conditions. You also can connect the individual conditions with "and" or "or."

Figure 7

The New tab allows you to add a new row (record) in Form view (Figure 8). You also could add a new row by typing in the blank row at the end of the datasheet.

Figure 8

By clicking the Actions arrow, you can display a menu with several useful commands (Figure 9).

Figure 9

The Task Pane command in the Actions list lets you display a task pane with still additional commands. By clicking the Totals command in the Actions list, you can display totals for numeric fields (Figure 10). Clicking the Settings arrow produces a list of commands that allow you to create a new column, create a view (similar to an Access query), or manage settings for the list.

Figure 10

Importing a SharePoint Services List

There are two ways to import a SharePoint Services list to an Access table. You can use the SharePoint Lists button in the Import group on the External Data tab. You also can use the SharePoint Lists button on the Create tab (Figure 11). Clicking Existing SharePoint List on the SharePoint Lists button menu produces the same effect as clicking the SharePoint Lists button in the Import Group. The SharePoint Lists button gives you additional options, because it lists the various SharePoint List templates.

Figure 11

Regardless of which approach you take, Access will display the Get External Data - SharePoint Site dialog box (Figure 12). In this dialog box, you will give the address for the site from which to import, and then select the option button to import the source data into a new table. You also will be prompted to give your user name and password.

Figure 12

Versioning
You can set Microsoft Windows SharePoint Services 3.0 lists so that you can track versions of the items they contain. When version tracking is enabled for the list, each time the data in a row changes, Windows SharePoint Services creates a new version of that row. You do not see the versions in the list itself, but you can access them while viewing the list.

Assuming your user name and password are valid, you will see the available lists from which you can select (Figure 13). You check the list or lists you want to import.

Figure 13

The imported table is shown in Figure 14. The name of the table is Computer Item. Access also has added automatically the ID field, which is an AutoNumber field that functions as the primary key.

Figure 14

TO IMPORT A SHAREPOINT SERVICES LIST

To import a SharePoint Services List to an Access table, you would use the following steps.

1. With the database to which you wish to import the list open, click Create on the Ribbon to display the Create tab.
2. Click the SharePoint Lists button on the Create tab to display the available SharePoint List templates.
3. Click Existing SharePoint List to display the Get External Data - SharePoint Site dialog box. (Rather than clicking SharePoint Lists on the Create tab, you could have clicked SharePoint List in the Import Group on the External Data tab. In that approach, you would not see the available SharePoint List templates.)
4. Enter the site address for the SharePoint site.
5. Click the 'Import the source data into a new table in the current database' option button.
6. Click the Next button, enter your user name and password when prompted, and then click the check box for the list you want to import (you can click more than one).
7. Click the OK button to import the list.
8. Decide whether you want to save the import steps.

Linking a SharePoint Services List

You also can link a SharePoint Services list to a table in an Access database. The linked table appears in the Navigation Pane preceded by the symbol that indicates it is linked (Figure 15).

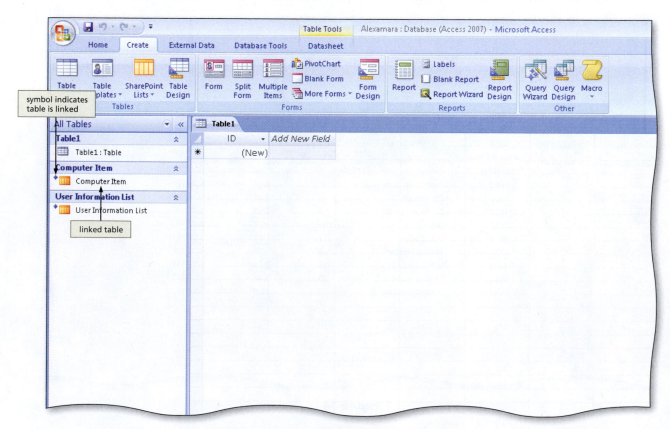

Figure 15

To Link a SharePoint Services List

To link a SharePoint Services list to an Access table, you would use the following steps.

1. With the database to which you wish to link the list open, click Create on the Ribbon to display the Create tab.

2. Click the SharePoint Lists button on the Create tab to display the available SharePoint List templates.

3. Click Existing SharePoint List to display the Get External Data - SharePoint Site dialog box.

4. Enter the site address for the SharePoint site.

5. Be sure the 'Link to the data source by creating a linked table' option button is selected.

6. Click the Next button, enter your user name and password when prompted, and then click the check box for the list you want to link.

7. Click the OK button to import the list.

8. Decide whether you want to save the import steps.

Using a Linked Table

Because this is a linked table, any change in either the linked table or the list is automatically reflected in the other. In Figure 16, for example, the Units on Hand quantity for Desktop Holder is changed from 4 to 6 in the linked table in Access. Notice that Access automatically has added an Attachments field.

Figure 16

The corresponding SharePoint Services list is shown in Figure 17. The change to the units on hand is reflected in the list. If you already had the SharePoint Services list open when you made the change to the linked table, the change may not immediately be reflected on your screen. You would have needed to click the Action arrow and then click the Refresh Data command.

Figure 17

TO MOVE A DATABASE TO SHAREPOINT

You can move an entire database to SharePoint. This makes your database available to a wide variety of users. To do so, you click the Move to SharePoint button to start the Move to SharePoint Site Wizard (Figure 18).

Figure 18

The Wizard will perform the following tasks for you.

1. Create a backup copy of your database so that you can go back to the non-SharePoint version if you need to do so.

2. Create a SharePoint list for every table in the database.

3. Remove the tables from the database and replace them with linked tables, ensuring that all the data is managed by SharePoint.

4. Optionally upload a copy of the database to the SharePoint site so that other users can access your queries, forms, and reports.

To move a database to a SharePoint site, you would use the following steps.

1. With the database to be moved open, click the Move to SharePoint button in the SharePoint Lists group on the External Data tab to start the Move to SharePoint Site Wizard.

2. Enter the address of the SharePoint site, giving your user name and password when requested.

3. If you want to give other users the ability to use your forms and reports, be sure the 'Save a copy of my database to the SharePoint site and create shortcuts to my Access forms and reports' check box is selected.

4. Click the Browse button, select a location for the shared database (for example, the shared document library), and then click the OK button.

5. Click the Next button.

6. If you want to see details concerning issues encountered while moving your data, click the Show Details button.

7. Click the Finish button to complete the movement of the database. If any problems occurred during the movement, a table called Move to SharePoint Site Issues will be created in the database; this table contains details concerning these issues.

TO OPEN A SHARED DATABASE

You can open a shared database (one that has been moved to SharePoint) from within SharePoint (Figure 19). In the process, you can determine whether to open the database in Read-Only mode, where you cannot make any changes, or Edit mode, where you can change the data.

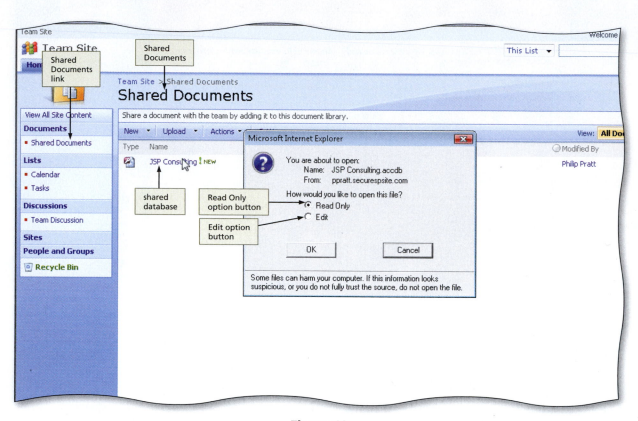

Figure 19

BTW

Working Offline
You can use Microsoft Office Access 2007 to work offline with data that is linked to a list on a Microsoft Windows SharePoint Services 3.0 site. To work offline, open the database that is linked to SharePoint lists, click the External Data tab, and then click Work Offline. To reconnect to the SharePoint server, click Work Online on the External Data tab. To synchronize your data, that is, update the database and lists, click Synchronize on the External Data tab.

To open a shared database, you would use the following steps.

1. Enter the SharePoint Site, giving your user name and password when requested.
2. Select the location of the shared database (for example, Shared Documents).
3. Click the name of the database you wish to open.
4. Select whether you want to open the database in Read-Only mode or in Edit mode.
5. Click the OK button.
6. If you wish to save a local copy, select a location for the local copy.

Update Shared Data

If you open the database in Edit mode, you can make changes to the data and your changes will be sent to the SharePoint server, where they will be available to others. There is a potential problem, however. Another user may be attempting to edit the same record that you are editing. If the other user completes his or her update before you complete yours, you will receive the message shown in Figure 20. You then can choose how you wish to handle the issue.

Figure 20

If you click the Save Record button, your changes will be saved. This can be dangerous because the other user's update typically will be lost in the process. If you click the Copy to Clipboard button, the contents of your change will be copied to the clipboard. You then could examine the record to see the effect of the other user's changes. If your changes still are appropriate, you then could paste your changes into the database. Finally, if you click Drop Changes, your changes are abandoned.

Hyperlinks and HTML

In a Web page, a **hyperlink** is an element that you can activate, typically with a click of the mouse, to open another Web document. You can add hyperlinks to forms and reports in an Access database to perform a similar function. The link could be to a Web page, as shown in Figure 21. It also could be to another object in the database or to an e-mail address.

Figure 21

Web pages typically are created using HTML (Hypertext Markup Language). You can create an HTML document from an Access table, query, or report. Such an HTML document can be displayed in a Web browser (Figure 22).

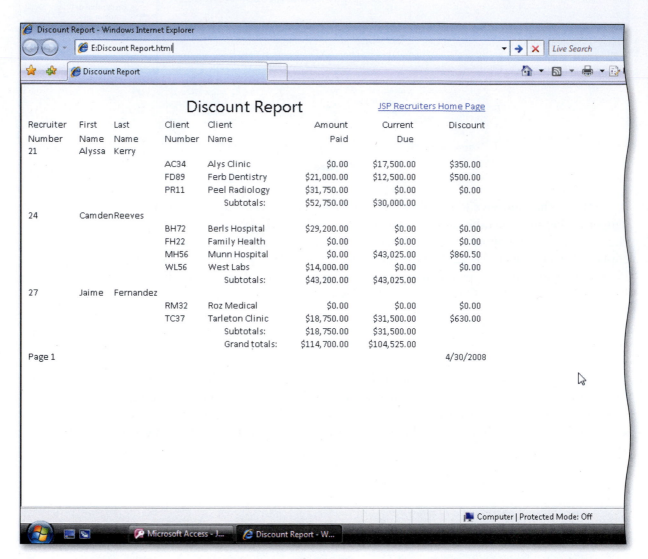

Figure 22

Adding Hyperlinks

To add a hyperlink to a form or report, you use the Insert Hyperlink tool in the Controls group on the Design tab (Figure 23). If the link is to an existing file or Web page, you make sure Existing File or Web Page is selected in the Link to pane, enter the text to display as the link name, and add the address.

Figure 23

By clicking Object in This Database instead of Existing File or Web Page, you can link to the report, form, or other object. In the process of creating the link, you will identify the specific object to which you wish to link. You can insert a hyperlink with an e-mail address by clicking E-mail Address and then giving the address and, optionally, a subject.

Once you have added the hyperlink, you can drag it to the desired location on the form or report (Figure 24).

Figure 24

BTW

Certification
The Microsoft Certified Application Specialist (MCAS) program provides an opportunity for you to obtain a valuable industry credential — proof that you have the Access 2007 skills required by employers. For more information, see Appendix G or visit the Access 2007 Certification Web page (scsite.com/ac2007/cert).

TO INSERT A HYPERLINK TO A FILE OR WEB PAGE
To insert a hyperlink to a file or Web page, you would use the following steps.

1. With the object to contain the hyperlink open in Design view, click the Insert Hyperlink tool in the Controls group on the Design tab.

2. Type the text to display for the hyperlink.

3. With Existing File or Web Page selected, select the file or type the address.

4. Click the OK button to add the hyperlink.

5. Drag the hyperlink to the desired location.

Exporting to HTML

You can create an HTML version of a table, query, form, or report. This version would be suitable for posting on the Web or for viewing using a Web browser, but cannot be edited by another user. To create an HTML version, you would use the HTML Document command on the More button menu in the Export group on the External Data tab (Figure 25).

Figure 25

After you have clicked the HTML Document command, you would use the Export - HTML Document dialog box to enter a file name and select a location for the file (Figure 26).

Figure 26

To Export to HTML

To export an object to HTML, you would use the following steps.

1. With the table, query, form, or report to be exported selected in the Navigation Pane, click the More button in the Export group on the External Data tab to display the More menu.
2. Click HTML Document on the More menu.
3. Enter the file name and location for the HTML file to be created and then click the OK button.
4. In the HTML Output Options dialog box, click the OK button.

Feature Summary

In this feature you have learned to share Access data by using SharePoint; create a SharePoint list by exporting an Access table; open and use a SharePoint list; import or link a SharePoint list to an Access database; move a database to SharePoint; use a shared database; add a hyperlink to an Access object; and export Access data to HTML. The following list includes all the new Access skills you have learned in this feature.

1. Create a SharePoint Services List by Exporting an Access Table (AC 677)
2. Open a SharePoint Services List from within SharePoint (AC 678)
3. Import a SharePoint Services List (AC 684)
4. Link a SharePoint Services List (AC 685)
5. Move a Database to SharePoint (AC 686)
6. Open a Shared Database (AC 688)
7. Insert a Hyperlink to a File or Web Page (AC 692)
8. Export to HTML (AC 693)

STUDENT ASSIGNMENTS

In the Lab

Design, create, modify, and/or use a database following the guidelines, concepts, and skills presented in this feature. Labs are listed in order of increasing difficulty.

Lab 1: Inserting Hyperlinks into and Exporting HTML Files from the JMS TechWizards Database

Problem: The management of JMS TechWizards would like to learn to export a report and a query to HTML. They also would like to insert a hyperlink to a Web page.

Instructions: Start Access. If you are using the Microsoft Office Access 2007 Comprehensive text, open the JMS TechWizards database that you used in Chapter 9. Otherwise, see the inside back cover of this book for instructions on downloading the Data Files for Students, or contact your instructor for more information about accessing the required files.

Perform the following tasks:

1. Open the Client Master Form in Design view and insert a hyperlink as shown in Figure 27. Use the scsite.com Web page as the address.

2. Export the City-Technician crosstab as an HTML file.

3. Export the Billing Summary Report as an HTML file.

4. Submit the HTML files and the revised database in the format specified by your instructor.

Figure 27

In the Lab

Lab 2: Sharing Data in the Hockey Fan Zone Database

Problem: The management of Hockey Fan Zone would like to learn more about how they might use Windows SharePoint Services to share data.

Instructions: If you are using the Microsoft Office Access 2007 Comprehensive text, use the Hockey Fan Zone database that you used in Chapter 9. Otherwise, see the inside back cover of this book for instructions on downloading the Data Files for Students, or contact your instructor for more information about accessing the required files.

Perform the following tasks:

1. Open Microsoft Office Word, create a new document, and then type your name at the top. List the steps to do the following.

   a. Create a SharePoint Services list by exporting the Supplier table.

   b. Open the Supplier table in SharePoint Services and sort the suppliers in descending order by Last Order Date.

   c. Link the Item table from a SharePoint Services list to a database named FanShare.

   d. Change the cost of ball caps to $10.00.

   e. Import the Supplier table from a SharePoint Services list to a database named FanShare.

2. Submit the Word document in the format specified by your instructor.

3. If you have access to a SharePoint Server, perform the tasks in step 1 and submit the database in the format specified by your instructor.

Appendix A

Project Planning Guidelines

Using Project Planning Guidelines

The process of communicating specific information to others is a learned, rational skill. Computers and software, especially Microsoft Office 2007, can help you develop ideas and present detailed information to a particular audience.

Using Microsoft Office 2007, you can create projects such as Word documents, Excel spreadsheets, Access databases, and PowerPoint presentations. Computer hardware and productivity software such as Microsoft Office 2007 minimizes much of the laborious work of drafting and revising projects. Some communicators handwrite ideas in notebooks, others compose directly on the computer, and others have developed unique strategies that work for their own particular thinking and writing styles.

No matter what method you use to plan a project, follow specific guidelines to arrive at a final product that presents information correctly and effectively (Figure A–1). Use some aspects of these guidelines every time you undertake a project, and others as needed in specific instances. For example, in determining content for a project, you may decide that a bar chart communicates trends more effectively than a paragraph of text. If so, you would create this graphical element and insert it in an Excel spreadsheet, a Word document, or a PowerPoint slide.

Determine the Project's Purpose

Begin by clearly defining why you are undertaking this assignment. For example, you may want to track monetary donations collected for your club's fundraising drive. Alternatively, you may be urging students to vote for a particular candidate in the next election. Once you clearly understand the purpose of your task, begin to draft ideas of how best to communicate this information.

Analyze your Audience

Learn about the people who will read, analyze, or view your work. Where are they employed? What are their educational backgrounds? What are their expectations? What questions do they have?

PROJECT PLANNING GUIDELINES

1. DETERMINE THE PROJECT'S PURPOSE
Why are you undertaking the project?

2. ANALYZE YOUR AUDIENCE
Who are the people who will use your work?

3. GATHER POSSIBLE CONTENT
What information exists, and in what forms?

4. DETERMINE WHAT CONTENT TO PRESENT TO YOUR AUDIENCE
What information will best communicate the project's purpose to your audience?

Figure A–1

Design experts suggest drawing a mental picture of these people or finding photographs of people who fit this profile so that you can develop a project with the audience in mind.

By knowing your audience members, you can tailor a project to meet their interests and needs. You will not present them with information they already possess, and you will not omit the information they need to know.

Example: Your assignment is to raise the profile of your college's nursing program in the community. How much do they know about your college and the nursing curriculum? What are the admission requirements? How many of the applicants admitted complete the program? What percent pass the state Boards?

Gather Possible Content

Rarely are you in a position to develop all the material for a project. Typically, you would begin by gathering existing information that may reside in spreadsheets or databases. Web sites, pamphlets, magazine and newspaper articles, and books could provide insights of how others have approached your topic. Personal interviews often provide perspectives not available by any other means. Consider video and audio clips as potential sources for material that might complement or support the factual data you uncover.

Determine What Content to Present to your Audience

Experienced designers recommend writing three or four major ideas you want an audience member to remember after reading or viewing your project. It also is helpful to envision your project's endpoint, the key fact you wish to emphasize. All project elements should lead to this ending point.

As you make content decisions, you also need to think about other factors. Presentation of the project content is an important consideration. For example, will your brochure be printed on thick, colored paper or transparencies? Will your PowerPoint presentation be viewed in a classroom with excellent lighting and a bright projector, or will it be viewed on a notebook computer monitor? Determine relevant time factors, such as the length of time to develop the project, how long readers will spend reviewing your project, or the amount of time allocated for your speaking engagement. Your project will need to accommodate all of these constraints.

Decide whether a graph, photograph, or artistic element can express or emphasize a particular concept. The right hemisphere of the brain processes images by attaching an emotion to them, so audience members are more apt to recall these graphics long term rather than just reading text.

As you select content, be mindful of the order in which you plan to present information. Readers and audience members generally remember the first and last pieces of information they see and hear, so you should put the most important information at the top or bottom of the page.

Summary

When creating a project, it is beneficial to follow some basic guidelines from the outset. By taking some time at the beginning of the process to determine the project's purpose, analyze the audience, gather possible content, and determine what content to present to the audience, you can produce a project that is informative, relevant, and effective.

Appendix B

Introduction to Microsoft Office 2007

What Is Microsoft Office 2007?

Microsoft Office 2007 is a collection of the more popular Microsoft application software. It is available in Basic, Home and Student, Standard, Small Business, Professional, Ultimate, Professional Plus, and Enterprise editions. Each edition consists of a group of programs, collectively called a suite. Table B–1 lists the suites and their components. **Microsoft Office Professional Edition 2007** includes these six programs: Microsoft Office Word 2007, Microsoft Office Excel 2007, Microsoft Office Access 2007, Microsoft Office PowerPoint 2007, Microsoft Office Publisher 2007, and Microsoft Office Outlook 2007. The programs in the Office suite allow you to work efficiently, communicate effectively, and improve the appearance of the projects you create.

Table B–1

	Microsoft Office Basic 2007	Microsoft Office Home & Student 2007	Microsoft Office Standard 2007	Microsoft Office Small Business 2007	Microsoft Office Professional 2007	Microsoft Office Ultimate 2007	Microsoft Office Professional Plus 2007	Microsoft Office Enterprise 2007
Microsoft Office Word 2007	✓	✓	✓	✓	✓	✓	✓	✓
Microsoft Office Excel 2007	✓	✓	✓	✓	✓	✓	✓	✓
Microsoft Office Access 2007					✓	✓	✓	✓
Microsoft Office PowerPoint 2007		✓	✓	✓	✓	✓	✓	✓
Microsoft Office Publisher 2007				✓	✓	✓	✓	✓
Microsoft Office Outlook 2007	✓		✓				✓	✓
Microsoft Office OneNote 2007		✓				✓		
Microsoft Office Outlook 2007 with Business Contact Manager				✓	✓	✓		
Microsoft Office InfoPath 2007						✓	✓	✓
Integrated Enterprise Content Management						✓	✓	✓
Electronic Forms						✓	✓	✓
Advanced Information Rights Management and Policy Capabilities						✓	✓	✓
Microsoft Office Communicator 2007							✓	✓
Microsoft Office Groove 2007						✓		✓

Microsoft has bundled additional programs in some versions of Office 2007, in addition to the main group of Office programs. Table B–1 on the previous page lists the components of the various Office suites.

In addition to the Office 2007 programs noted previously, Office 2007 suites can contain other programs. Microsoft Office OneNote 2007 is a digital notebook program that allows you to gather and share various types of media, such as text, graphics, video, audio, and digital handwriting. Microsoft Office InfoPath 2007 is a program that allows you to create and use electronic forms to gather information. Microsoft Office Groove 2007 provides collaborative workspaces in real time. Additional services that are oriented toward the enterprise solution also are available.

Office 2007 and the Internet, World Wide Web, and Intranets

Office 2007 allows you to take advantage of the Internet, the World Wide Web, and intranets. The Microsoft Windows operating system includes a **browser**, which is a program that allows you to locate and view a Web page. The Windows browser is called Internet Explorer.

One method of viewing a Web page is to use the browser to enter the Web address for the Web page. Another method of viewing a Web page is clicking a hyperlink. A **hyperlink** is colored or underlined text or a graphic that, when clicked, connects to another Web page. Hyperlinks placed in Office 2007 documents allow for direct access to a Web site of interest.

An **intranet** is a private network, such as a network used within a company or organization for internal communication. Like the Internet, hyperlinks are used within an intranet to access documents, pages, and other destinations on the intranet. Unlike the Internet, the materials on the network are available only for those who are part of the private network.

Online Collaboration Using Office

Organizations that, in the past, were able to make important information available only to a select few, now can make their information accessible to a wider range of individuals who use programs such as Office 2007 and Internet Explorer. Office 2007 allows colleagues to use the Internet or an intranet as a central location to view documents, manage files, and work together.

Each of the Office 2007 programs makes publishing documents on a Web server as simple as saving a file on a hard disk. Once placed on the Web server, users can view and edit the documents and conduct Web discussions and live online meetings.

Using Microsoft Office 2007

The various Microsoft Office 2007 programs each specialize in a particular task. This section describes the general functions of the more widely used Office 2007 programs, along with how they are used to access the Internet or an intranet.

Microsoft Office Word 2007

Microsoft Office Word 2007 is a full-featured word processing program that allows you to create many types of personal and business documents, including flyers, letters, resumes, business documents, and academic reports.

Word's AutoCorrect, spelling, and grammar features help you proofread documents for errors in spelling and grammar by identifying the errors and offering suggestions for corrections as you type. The live word count feature provides you with a constantly updating word count as you enter and edit text. To assist with creating specific documents, such as a business letter or resume, Word provides templates, which provide a formatted document before you type the text of the document. Quick Styles provide a live preview of styles from the Style gallery, allowing you to preview styles in the document before actually applying them.

Word automates many often-used tasks and provides you with powerful desktop publishing tools to use as you create professional looking brochures, advertisements, and newsletters. SmartArt allows you to insert interpretive graphics based on document content.

Word makes it easier for you to share documents for collaboration. The Send feature opens an e-mail window with the active document attached. The Compare Documents feature allows you easily to identify changes when comparing different document versions.

Word 2007 and the Internet Word makes it possible to design and publish Web pages on the Internet or an intranet, insert a hyperlink to a Web page in a word processing document, as well as access and search the content of other Web pages.

Microsoft Office Excel 2007

Microsoft Office Excel 2007 is a spreadsheet program that allows you to organize data, complete calculations, graph data, develop professional looking reports, publish organized data to the Web, and access real-time data from Web sites.

In addition to its mathematical functionality, Excel 2007 provides tools for visually comparing data. For instance, when comparing a group of values in cells, you can set cell backgrounds with bars proportional to the value of the data in the cell. You can also set cell backgrounds with full-color backgrounds, or use a color scale to facilitate interpretation of data values.

Excel 2007 provides strong formatting support for tables with the new Style Preview gallery.

Excel 2007 and the Internet Using Excel 2007, you can create hyperlinks within a worksheet to access other Office documents on the network or on the Internet. Worksheets saved as static, or unchanging Web pages can be viewed using a browser. The person viewing static Web pages cannot change them.

In addition, you can create and run queries that retrieve information from a Web page and insert the information directly into a worksheet.

Microsoft Office Access 2007

Microsoft Office Access 2007 is a comprehensive database management system (DBMS). A **database** is a collection of data organized in a manner that allows access, retrieval, and use of that data. Access 2007 allows you to create a database; add, change, and delete data in the database; sort data in the database; retrieve data from the database; and create forms and reports using the data in the database.

Access 2007 and the Internet Access 2007 lets you generate reports, which are summaries that show only certain data from the database, based on user requirements.

Microsoft Office PowerPoint 2007

Microsoft Office PowerPoint 2007 is a complete presentation graphics program that allows you to produce professional looking presentations. With PowerPoint 2007, you can create informal presentations using overhead transparencies, electronic presentations using a projection device attached to a personal computer, formal presentations using 35mm slides or a CD, or you can run virtual presentations on the Internet.

PowerPoint 2007 and the Internet   PowerPoint 2007 allows you to publish presentations on the Internet or other networks.

Microsoft Office Publisher 2007

Microsoft Office Publisher 2007 is a desktop publishing program (DTP) that allows you to design and produce professional quality documents (newsletters, flyers, brochures, business cards, Web sites, and so on) that combine text, graphics, and photographs. Desktop publishing software provides a variety of tools, including design templates, graphic manipulation tools, color schemes or libraries, and various page wizards and templates. For large jobs, businesses use desktop publishing software to design publications that are **camera ready**, which means the files are suitable for production by outside commercial printers. Publisher 2007 also allows you to locate commercial printers, service bureaus, and copy shops willing to accept customer files created in Publisher.

Publisher 2007 allows you to design a unique image, or logo, using one of more than 45 master design sets. This, in turn, permits you to use the same design for all your printed documents (letters, business cards, brochures, and advertisements) and Web pages. Publisher includes 70 coordinated color schemes; 30 font schemes; more than 10,000 high-quality clip art images; 1,500 photographs; 1,000 Web-art graphics; 340 animated graphics; and hundreds of unique Design Gallery elements (quotations, sidebars, and so on). If you wish, you also can download additional images from the Microsoft Office Online Web page on the Microsoft Web site.

Publisher 2007 and the Internet   Publisher 2007 allows you easily to create a multipage Web site with custom color schemes, photographic images, animated images, and sounds.

Microsoft Office Outlook 2007

Microsoft Office Outlook 2007 is a powerful communications and scheduling program that helps you communicate with others, keep track of your contacts, and organize your schedule. Outlook 2007 allows you to view a To-Do bar containing tasks and appointments from your Outlook calendar. Outlook 2007 allows you to send and receive electronic mail (e-mail) and permits you to engage in real-time communication with family, friends, or coworkers using instant messaging. Outlook 2007 also provides you with the means to organize your contacts, and you can track e-mail messages, meetings, and notes with a particular contact. Outlook's Calendar, Contacts, Tasks, and Notes components aid in this organization. Contact information is available from the Outlook Calendar, Mail, Contacts, and Task components by accessing the Find a Contact feature. **Personal information management (PIM)** programs such as Outlook provide a way for individuals and workgroups to organize, find, view, and share information easily.

Microsoft Office 2007 Help

At any time while you are using one of the Office programs, you can interact with **Microsoft Office 2007 Help** for that program and display information about any topic associated with the program. Several categories of help are available. In all programs, you can access Help by pressing the F1 key on the keyboard. In Publisher 2007 and Outlook 2007, the Help window can be opened by clicking the Help menu and then selecting Microsoft Office Publisher or Outlook Help command, or by entering search text in the 'Type a question for help' text box in the upper-right corner of the program window. In the other Office programs, clicking the Microsoft Office Help button near the upper-right corner of the program window opens the program Help window.

The Help window in all programs provides several methods for accessing help about a particular topic, and has tools for navigating around Help. Appendix C contains detailed instructions for using Help.

Collaboration and SharePoint

While not part of the Microsoft Office 2007 suites, SharePoint is a Microsoft tool that allows Office 2007 users to share data using collaborative tools that are integrated into the main Office programs. SharePoint consists of Windows SharePoint Services, Office SharePoint Server 2007, and, optionally, Office SharePoint Designer 2007.

Windows SharePoint Services provides the platform for collaboration programs and services. Office SharePoint Server 2007 is built on top of Windows SharePoint Services. The result of these two products is the ability to create SharePoint sites. A SharePoint site is a Web site that provides users with a virtual place for collaborating and communicating with their colleagues while working together on projects, documents, ideas, and information. Each member of a group with access to the SharePoint site has the ability to contribute to the material stored there. The basic building blocks of SharePoint sites are lists and libraries. Lists contain collections of information, such as calendar items, discussion points, contacts, and links. Lists can be edited to add or delete information. Libraries are similar to lists, but include both files and information about files. Types of libraries include document, picture, and forms libraries.

The most basic type of SharePoint site is called a Workspace, which is used primarily for collaboration. Different types of Workspaces can be created using SharePoint to suit different needs. SharePoint provides templates, or outlines of these Workspaces, that can be filled in to create the Workspace. Each of the different types of Workspace templates contain a different collection of lists and libraries, reflecting the purpose of the Workspace. You can create a Document Workspace to facilitate collaboration on documents. A Document Workspace contains a document library for documents and supporting files, a Links list that allows you to maintain relevant resource links for the document, a Tasks list for listing and assigning To-Do items to team members, and other links as needed. Meeting Workspaces allow users to plan and organize a meeting, with components such as Attendees, Agenda, and a Document Library. Social Meeting Workspaces provide a place to plan social events, with lists and libraries such as Attendees, Directions, Image/Logo, Things To Bring, Discussions, and Picture Library. A Decision Meeting Workspace is a Meeting Workspace with a focus on review and decision-making, with lists and libraries such as Objectives, Attendees, Agenda, Document Library, Tasks, and Decisions.

Users also can create a SharePoint site called a WebParts page, which is built from modules called WebParts. WebParts are modular units of information that contain a title bar and content that reflects the type of WebPart. For instance, an image WebPart would contain a title bar and an image. WebParts allow you quickly to create and modify a SharePoint site, and allow for the creation of a unique site that can allow users to access and make changes to information stored on the site.

Large SharePoint sites that include multiple pages can be created using templates as well. Groups needing more refined and targeted sharing options than those available with SharePoint Server 2007 and Windows SharePoint Services can add SharePoint Designer 2007 to create a site that meets their specific needs.

Depending on which components have been selected for inclusion on the site, users can view a team calendar, view links, read announcements, and view and edit group documents and projects. SharePoint sites can be set up so that documents are checked in and out, much like a library, to prevent multiple users from making changes simultaneously. Once a SharePoint site is set up, Office programs are used to perform maintenance of the site. For example, changes in the team calendar are updated using Outlook 2007, and changes that users make in Outlook 2007 are reflected on the SharePoint site. Office 2007 programs include a Publish feature that allows users easily to save file updates to a SharePoint site. Team members can be notified about changes made to material on the site either by e-mail or by a news feed, meaning that users do not have to go to the site to check to see if anything has been updated since they last viewed or worked on it. The search feature in SharePoint allows users quickly to find information on a large site.

Appendix C
Microsoft Office Access 2007 Help

Using Microsoft Office 2007 Access Help

This appendix shows how to use Microsoft Office Access Help. At any time while you are using one of the Microsoft Office 2007 programs, you can use Office Help to display information about all topics associated with the program. This appendix uses Microsoft Office Access 2007 to illustrate the use of Office Help. Help in other Office 2007 programs responds in a similar fashion.

In Office 2007, Help is presented in a window that has Web browser-style navigation buttons. Each Office 2007 program has its own Help home page, which is the starting Help page that is displayed in the Help window. If your computer is connected to the Internet, the contents of the Help page reflect both the local help files installed on the computer and material from Microsoft's Web site. As shown in Figure C–1, two methods for accessing Access's Help are available:

1. Microsoft Office Access Help button near the upper-right corner of the Access window

2. Function key F1 on the keyboard

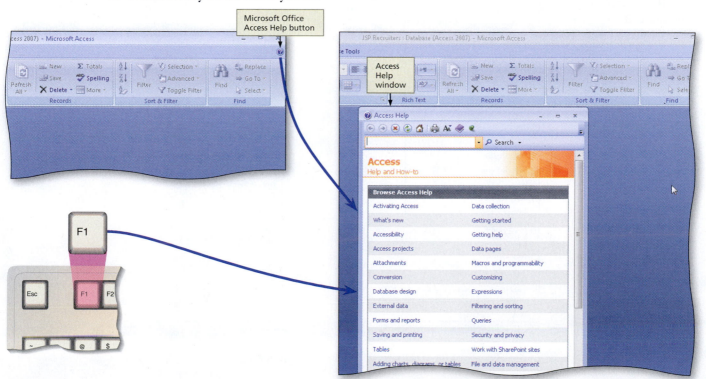

Figure C–1

To Open the Access Help Window

The following steps open the Access Help window and maximize the window.

1

- Start Microsoft Access, if necessary. Click the Microsoft Office Access Help button near the upper-right corner of the Access window to open the Access Help window (Figure C–2).

Figure C–2

2

- Click the Maximize button on the Help title bar to maximize the Help window (Figure C–3).

Figure C–3

The Access Help Window

The Access Help window provides several methods for accessing help about a particular topic, and also has tools for navigating around Help. Methods for accessing Help include searching the help content installed with Access, or searching the online Office content maintained by Microsoft.

Figure C–3 shows the main Access Help window. To navigate Help, the Access Help window includes search features that allow you to search on a word or phrase about which you want help; the Connection Status button, which allows you to control where Access Help searches for content; toolbar buttons; and links to major Help categories.

Search Features

You can perform Help searches on words or phrases to find information about any Access feature using the 'Type words to search for' text box and the Search button (Figure C–4a). Click the 'Type words to search for' text box and then click the Search button or press the ENTER key to initiate a search of Access Help.

Figure C–4

Access Help offers the user the option of searching the online Help Web pages maintained by Microsoft or the offline Help files placed on your computer when you install Access. You can specify whether Access Help should search online or offline from two places: the Connection Status button on the status bar of the Access Help window, or the Search button arrow on the toolbar. The Connection Status button indicates whether Help currently is set up to work with online or offline information sources. Clicking the Connection Status button provides a menu with commands for selecting online or offline searches (Figure C–4b). The Connection Status menu allows the user to select whether help searches will return content only from the computer (offline), or content from the computer and from Office Online (online).

Clicking the Search button arrow also provides a menu with commands for an online or offline search (Figure C–4a). These commands determine the source of information that Help searches for during the current Help session only. For example, assume that your preferred search is an offline search because you often do not have Internet access. You would set Connection Status to 'Show content only from this computer'. When you have Internet access, you can select an online search from the Search menu to search Office Online for information for your current search session only. Your search will use the Office Online resources until you quit Help. The next time you start Help, the Connection Status once again will be offline. In addition to setting the source of information that Help searches for during the current Help session, you can use the Search menu to further target the current search to one of four subcategories of online Help: Access Help, Access Templates, Access Training, and Developer Reference. The local search further can target one subcategory, Developer Reference.

In addition to searching for a word or string of text, you can use the links provided on the Browse Access Help area (Figure C–3 on page APP 10) to search for help on a topic. These links direct you to major help categories. From each major category, subcategories are available to further refine your search.

Finally, you can use the Table of Contents for Access Help to search for a topic the same way you would in a hard copy book. The Table of Contents is accessed through a toolbar button.

Toolbar Buttons

You can use toolbar buttons to navigate through the results of your search. The toolbar buttons are located on the toolbar near the top of the Help Window (Figure C–5). The toolbar buttons contain navigation buttons as well as buttons that perform other useful and common tasks in Access Help, such as printing.

Figure C–5

The Access Help navigation buttons are the Back, Forward, Stop, Refresh, and Home buttons. These five buttons behave like the navigation buttons in a Web browser window. You can use the Back button to go back one window, the Forward button to go forward one window, the Stop button to stop loading the current page, and the Home button to redisplay the Help home page in the Help window. Use the Refresh button to reload the information requested into the Help window from its original source. When getting Help information online, this button provides the most current information from the Microsoft Help Web site.

The buttons located to the right of the navigation buttons — Print, Change Font Size, Show Table of Contents, and Not on Top — provide you with access to useful and common commands. The Print button prints the contents of the open Help window. The Change Font Size button customizes the Help window by increasing or decreasing the size of its text. The Show Table of Contents button opens a pane on the left side of the Help window that shows the Table of Contents for Access Help. You can use the Table of Contents for Access Help to navigate through the contents of Access Help much as you would use the Table of Contents in a book to search for a topic. The Not On Top button is an example of a toggle button, which is a button that can be switched back and forth between two states. It determines how the Access Help window behaves relative to other windows. When clicked, the Not On Top button changes to Keep On Top. In this state, it does not allow other windows from Access or other programs to cover the Access Help window when those windows are the active windows. When in the Not On Top state, the button allows other windows to be opened or moved on top of the Access Help window.

You can customize the size and placement of the Help window. Resize the window using the Maximize and Restore buttons, or by dragging the window to a desired size. Relocate the Help window by dragging the title bar to a new location on the screen.

Searching Access Help

Once the Access Help window is open, several methods exist for navigating Access Help. You can search for help by using any of the three following methods from the Help window:

1. Enter search text in the 'Type words to search for' text box
2. Click the links in the Help window
3. Use the Table of Contents

To Obtain Help Using the Type Words to Search for Text Box

Assume for the following example that you want to know more about simple reports. The following steps use the 'Type words to search for' text box to obtain useful information about simple reports by entering the words, simple report, as search text. The steps also navigate in the Access Help window.

1

- Type simple report in the 'Type words to search for' text box at the top of the Access Help window.

- Click the Search button arrow to display the Search menu.

- If it is not selected already, click All Access on the Search menu to select the command. If All Access is already selected, click the Search button arrow again to close the Search menu.

Q&A

Why select All Access on the Search menu?

Selecting All Access on the Search menu ensures that Access Help will search all possible sources for information on your search term. It will produce the most complete search results.

Figure C–6

2

● Click the Search button to display the search results (Figure C–7).

Why might my results differ?

If you do not have an Internet connection, your results will reflect only the content of the Help files on your computer. When searching for help online, results also can change as material is added, deleted, and updated on the online Help Web pages maintained by Microsoft.

Why were my search results not very helpful?

When initiating a search, keep in mind to check the spelling of the search text; and to keep your search very specific, with fewer than seven words, to return the most accurate results.

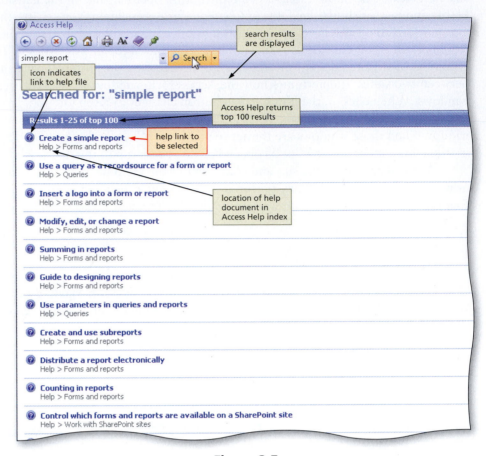

Figure C–7

3

● Click the 'Create a simple report' link to open the Help document associated with the link in the Help window (Figure C–8).

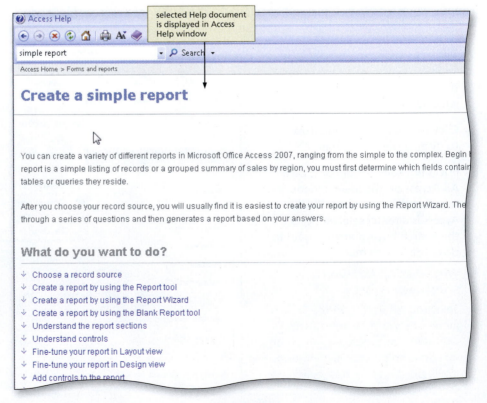

Figure C–8

4

- Click the Home button on the taskbar to clear the search results and redisplay the Access Help home page (Figure C–9).

Figure C–9

To Obtain Help Using the Help Links

If your topic of interest is listed in the Browse Access Help area, you can click the link to begin browsing Access Help categories instead of entering search text. You browse Access Help just like you would browse a Web site. If you know in which category to find your Help information, you may wish to use these links. The following steps find the simple report Help information using the category links from the Access Help home page.

1

- Click the 'Forms and reports' link to open the Forms and Reports page.

- Click the 'Create a simple report' link to open the Help document associated with the link (Figure C–10).

Q&A

What does the Show All link do?

In many Help documents, additional information about terms and features is available by clicking a link in the document to display additional information in the Help document. Clicking the Show All link opens all the links in the Help document that expand to additional text.

Figure C–10

To Obtain Help Using the Help Table of Contents

A third way to find Help in Word is through the Help Table of Contents. You can browse through the Table of Contents to display information about a particular topic or to familiarize yourself with Access. The following steps access the simple report Help information by browsing through the Table of Contents.

- Click the Home button on the toolbar.

- Click the Show Table of Contents button on the toolbar to open the Table of Contents pane on the left side of the Help window. If necessary, click the Maximize button on the Help title bar to maximize the window (Figure C–11).

Figure C–11

- Click the 'Forms and reports' link in the Table of Contents pane to view a list of Help subtopics.

- Click the 'Create a simple report' link in the Table of Contents pane to view the selected Help document in the right pane (Figure C–12).

Q&A

How do I remove the Table of Contents pane when I am finished with it?

The Show Table of Contents button acts as a toggle switch. When the Table of Contents pane is visible, the button changes to Hide Table of Contents. Clicking it hides the Table of Contents pane and changes the button to Show Table of Contents.

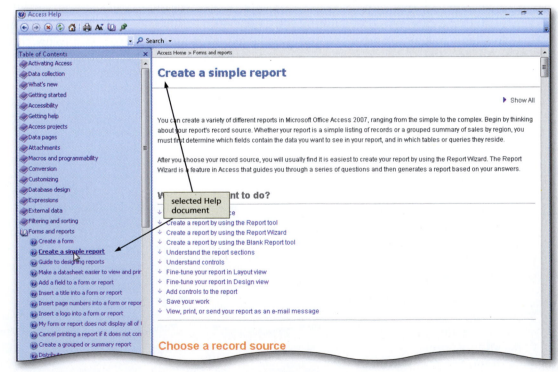

Figure C–12

Obtaining Help while Working in Access

Often you may need help while working on a database without already having the Help window open. For example, you may be unsure about how a particular command works, or you may be presented with a dialog box that you are not sure how to use. Rather than opening the Help window and initiating a search, Access Help provides you with the ability to search directly for help.

Figure C–13 shows one option for obtaining help while working in Access. If you want to learn more about a command, point to the command button and wait for the Enhanced ScreenTip to appear. If the Help icon appears in the Enhanced ScreenTip, press the F1 key while pointing to the command to open the Help window associated with that command.

Figure C–13

Figure C–14 shows a dialog box with a Get help button in it. Pressing the F1 key while the dialog box is displayed opens a Help window. The Help window contains help about that dialog box, if available. If no help file is available for that particular dialog box, then the main Help window opens.

Figure C–14

Use Help

1 Obtaining Help Using Search Text

Instructions: Perform the following tasks using Access Help.

1. Use the 'Type words to search for' text box to obtain help about the Navigation Pane. Use the Connection Status menu to search online help if you have an Internet connection.

2. Click Guide to the Navigation Pane in the list of links in the search results. Double-click the Microsoft Office Access Help window title bar to maximize it. Read and print the information. At the top of the printout, write down the number of links Access Help found.

3. Use the Search menu to search for help offline. Repeat the search from Step 1. At the top of the printout, write down the number of links that Access Help found searching offline. Submit the printouts as specified by your instructor.

4. Use the 'Type words to search for' text box to search for information online about keyboard shortcuts. Click the 'Keyboard Shortcuts for Access' link in the search results. If necessary, maximize the Microsoft Office 2007 Access Help window. Read and print the contents of the window. Close the Microsoft Office Access Help window. Submit the printouts as specified by your instructor.

5. For each of the following words and phrases, click one link in the search results, click the Show All link, and then print the page: multivalued field; Ribbon; wildcards; relationship; datasheet totals; and update. Submit the printouts as specified by your instructor.

2 Expanding on Access Help Basics

Instructions: Use Access Help to better understand its features and answer the questions listed below. Answer the questions on your own paper, or submit the printed Help information as specified by your instructor.

1. Use Help to find out how to customize the Help window. Change the font size to the smallest option and then print the contents of the Microsoft Office Access Help window. Change the font size back to its original setting. Close the window.

2. Press the F1 key. Search for information about tables, restricting the search results to Access Templates. Print the first page of the Search results.

3. Search for information about tables, restricting the search results to Access Help files. Print the first page of the Search results.

4. Use Access Help to find out what happened to the Office Assistant, a feature in the previous version of Access. Print out the Help document that contains the answer.

Appendix D

Publishing Office 2007 Web Pages to a Web Server

With the Office 2007 programs, you use the Save As command on the Office Button menu to save a Web page to a Web server using one of two techniques: Web folders or File Transfer Protocol. A **Web folder** is an Office shortcut to a Web server. **File Transfer Protocol** (**FTP**) is an Internet standard that allows computers to exchange files with other computers on the Internet.

You should contact your network system administrator or technical support staff at your Internet access provider to determine if their Web server supports Web folders, FTP, or both, and to obtain necessary permissions to access the Web server. If you decide to publish Web pages using a Web folder, you must have the Office Server Extensions (OSE) installed on your computer.

Using Web Folders to Publish Office 2007 Web Pages

When publishing to a Web folder, someone first must create the Web folder before you can save to it. If you are granted permission to create a Web folder, you must obtain the Web address of the Web server, a user name, and possibly a password that allows you to access the Web server. You also must decide on a name for the Web folder. Table D–1 explains how to create a Web folder.

Office 2007 adds the name of the Web folder to the list of current Web folders. You can save to this folder, open files in the folder, rename the folder, or perform any operations you would to a folder on your hard disk. You can use your Office 2007 program or Windows Explorer to access this folder. Table D–2 explains how to save to a Web folder.

Table D–1 Creating a Web Folder
1. Click the Office Button and then click Save As or Open.
2. When the Save As dialog box (or Open dialog box) appears, click the Tools button arrow, and then click Map Network Drive... When the Map Network Drive dialog box is displayed, click the 'Connect to a Web site that you can use to store your documents and pictures' link.
3. When the Add Network Location Wizard dialog box appears, click the Next button. If necessary, click Choose a custom network location. Click the Next button. Click the View examples link, type the Internet or network address, and then click the Next button. Click 'Log on anonymously' to deselect the check box, type your user name in the User name text box, and then click the Next button. Enter the name you want to call this network place and then click the Next button. Click to deselect the 'Open this network location when I click Finish' check box, and then click the Finish button.

Table D–2 Saving to a Web Folder
1. Click the Office Button, click Save As.
2. When the Save As dialog box is displayed, type the Web page file name in the File name text box. Do not press the ENTER key.
3. Click the Save as type box arrow and then click Web Page to select the Web Page format.
4. Click Computer in the Navigation pane.
5. Double-click the Web folder name in the Network Location list.
6. If the Enter Network Password dialog box appears, type the user name and password in the respective text boxes and then click the OK button.
7. Click the Save button in the Save As dialog box.

Using FTP to Publish Office 2007 Web Pages

When publishing a Web page using FTP, you first must add the FTP location to your computer before you can save to it. An FTP location, also called an **FTP site**, is a collection of files that reside on an FTP server. In this case, the FTP server is the Web server.

To add an FTP location, you must obtain the name of the FTP site, which usually is the address (URL) of the FTP server, and a user name and a password that allows you to access the FTP server. You save and open the Web pages on the FTP server using the name of the FTP site. Table D–3 explains how to add an FTP site.

Office 2007 adds the name of the FTP site to the FTP locations list in the Save As and Open dialog boxes. You can open and save files using this list. Table D–4 explains how to save to an FTP location.

Table D–3 Adding an FTP Location
1. Click the Office Button and then click Save As or Open.
2. When the Save As dialog box (or Open dialog box) appears, click the Tools button arrow, and then click Map Network Drive... When the Map Network Drive dialog box is displayed, click the 'Connect to a Web site that you can use to store your documents and pictures' link.
3. When the Add Network Location Wizard dialog box appears, click the Next button. If necessary, click Choose a custom network location. Click the Next button. Click the View examples link, type the Internet or network address, and then click the Next button. If you have a user name for the site, click to deselect 'Log on anonymously' and type your user name in the User name text box, and then click Next. If the site allows anonymous logon, click Next. Type a name for the location, click Next, click to deselect the 'Open this network location when I click Finish' check box, and click Finish. Click the OK button.
4. Close the Save As or the Open dialog box.

Table D–4 Saving to an FTP Location
1. Click the Office Button and then click Save As.
2. When the Save As dialog box appears, type the Web page file name in the File name text box. Do not press the ENTER key.
3. Click the Save as type box arrow and then click Web Page to select the Web Page format.
4. Click Computer in the Navigation pane.
5. Double-click the name of the FTP site in the Network Location list.
6. When the FTP Log On dialog box appears, enter your user name and password and then click the OK button.
7. Click the Save button in the Save As dialog box.

Appendix E

Customizing Microsoft Office Access 2007

This appendix explains how to change the screen resolution in Windows Vista to the resolution used in this book. It also describes how to customize the Word window by changing the Ribbon, Quick Access Toolbar, and the color scheme.

Changing Screen Resolution

Screen resolution indicates the number of pixels (dots) that the computer uses to display the letters, numbers, graphics, and background you see on the screen. When you increase the screen resolution, Windows displays more information on the screen, but the information decreases in size. The reverse also is true: as you decrease the screen resolution, Windows displays less information on the screen, but the information increases in size.

The screen resolution usually is stated as the product of two numbers, such as 1024×768 (pronounced "ten twenty-four by seven sixty-eight"). A 1024×768 screen resolution results in a display of 1,024 distinct pixels on each of 768 lines, or about 786,432 pixels. The figures in this book were created using a screen resolution of 1024×768.

The screen resolutions most commonly used today are 800×600 and 1024×768, although some Office specialists set their computers at a much higher screen resolution, such as 2048×1536.

To Change the Screen Resolution

The following steps change the screen resolution from 1280×1024 to 1024×768. Your computer already may be set to 1024×768 or some other resolution.

- If necessary, minimize all programs so that the Windows Vista desktop appears.

- Right-click the Windows Vista desktop to display the Windows Vista desktop shortcut menu (Figure E–1).

Figure E–1

● Click Personalize on the shortcut menu to open the Personalization window.

● Click Display Settings in the Personalization window to display the Display Settings dialog box (Figure E–2).

Figure E–2

● Drag the slider in the Resolution area so that the screen resolution changes to 1024 × 768 (Figure E–3).

Figure E–3

4

- Click the OK button to change the screen resolution from 1280 × 1024 to 1024 × 768 (Figure E–4).

Figure E–4

5

- Click the Yes button in the Display Settings dialog box to accept the new screen resolution (Figure E–5).

What if I do not want to change the screen resolution after seeing it applied after I click the OK button?

You either can click the No button in the inner Display Settings dialog box, or wait for the timer to run out, at which point Windows Vista will revert to the original screen resolution.

- Click the Close button to close the Personalization Window.

Figure E–5

Screen Resolution and the Appearance of the Ribbon in Office 2007 Programs

Changing the screen resolution affects how the Ribbon appears in Office 2007 programs. Figure E–6 shows the Access Ribbon at the screen resolutions of 800 × 600, 1024 × 768, and 1280 × 1024. All of the same commands are available regardless of screen resolution. Access, however, makes changes to the groups and the buttons within the groups to accommodate the various screen resolutions. The result is that certain commands may need to be accessed differently depending on the resolution chosen. A command that is visible on the Ribbon and available by clicking a button at one resolution may not be visible and may need to be accessed using its group button at a different resolution.

Figure E–6

Comparing the three Ribbons, notice changes in content and layout of the groups and galleries. In some cases, the content of a group is the same in each resolution, but the layout of the group differs. For example, the same buttons appear in the Font group in the three resolutions, but the layouts differ. The buttons are displayed in three rows at the 800 × 600 resolution, and in two rows in the 1024 × 768 and 1280 × 1024 resolutions. In other cases, the content and layout are the same across the resolution, but the level of detail differs with the resolution. In the Clipboard group, when the resolution increases to 1280 × 1024, the names of all the buttons in the group appear in addition to the buttons themselves. At the lower resolution, only the buttons appear.

Changing resolutions also can result in fewer commands being visible in a group. Comparing the Records group, notice that the group at the 800 × 600 resolution consists of a Records button, while at the higher resolutions, the group has three buttons visible. The commands that are available on the Ribbon at the higher resolutions must be accessed using the Editing button at the 800 × 600 resolution.

Customizing the Access Window

When working in Access, you may want to make your working area as large as possible. One option is to minimize the Ribbon. You also can modify the characteristics of the Quick Access Toolbar, customizing the toolbar's commands and location to better suit your needs.

To Minimize the Ribbon in Access

The following steps minimize the Ribbon.

1
- Start Access.

- Maximize the Access window, if necessary.

- Click the Customize Quick Access Toolbar button on the Quick Access Toolbar to display the Customize Quick Access Toolbar menu (Figure E–7).

Figure E–7

2
• Click Minimize the Ribbon on the Quick Access Toolbar menu to reduce the Ribbon display to just the tabs (Figure E–8).

Figure E–8

Other Ways

1. Double-click the active Ribbon tab
2. Press CTRL+F1

Customizing and Resetting the Quick Access Toolbar

The Quick Access Toolbar, located to the right of the Microsoft Office Button by default, provides easy access to some of the more frequently used commands in Access (Figure E–7). By default, the Quick Access Toolbar contains buttons for the Save, Undo, and Redo commands. Customize the Quick Access Toolbar by changing its location in the window and by adding additional buttons to reflect which commands you would like to be able to access easily.

To Change the Location of the Quick Access Toolbar

The following steps move the Quick Access Toolbar to below the Ribbon.

1
• Double-click the Home tab to redisplay the Ribbon.

• Click the Customize Quick Access Toolbar button on the Quick Access Toolbar to display the Customize Quick Access Toolbar menu (Figure E–9).

Figure E–9

● Click Show Below the Ribbon on the Quick Access Toolbar menu to move the Quick Access Toolbar below the Ribbon (Figure E–10).

Quick Access Toolbar moved below Ribbon

Figure E–10

To Add Commands to the Quick Access Toolbar Using the Customize Quick Access Toolbar Menu

Some of the more commonly added commands are available for selection from the Customize Quick Access Toolbar menu. The following steps add the Quick Print button to the Quick Access Toolbar.

● Click the Customize Quick Access Toolbar button to display the Customize Quick Access Toolbar menu (Figure E–11).

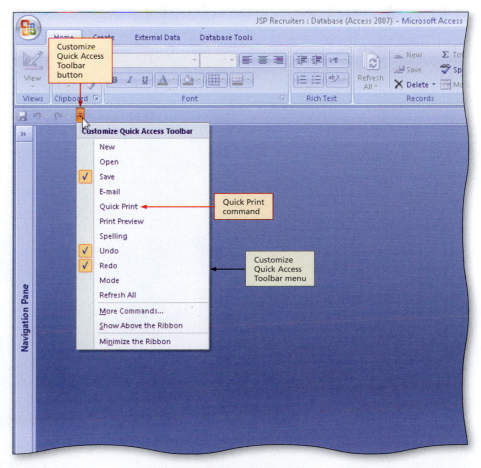

Customize Quick Access Toolbar button

Quick Print command

Customize Quick Access Toolbar menu

Figure E–11

• Click Quick Print on the Quick Access Toolbar menu to add the Quick Print button to the Quick Access Toolbar (Figure E–12).

Quick Print button added to Quick Access Toolbar

Figure E–12

To Add Commands to the Quick Access Toolbar Using the Shortcut Menu

Commands also can be added to the Quick Access Toolbar from the Ribbon. Adding an existing Ribbon command that you use often to the Quick Access Toolbar makes the command immediately available, regardless of which tab is active.

• Click the Create tab on the ribbon to make it the active tab.

• Right-click the Table button on the Create tab to display a shortcut menu (Figure E–13).

Table button

Create tab

Add to Quick Access Toolbar command

shortcut menu

Figure E–13

2

• Click Add to Quick Access Toolbar on the shortcut menu to add the Table button to the Quick Access Toolbar (Figure E–14).

Figure E–14

To Add Commands to the Quick Access Toolbar Using Access Options

Some commands do not appear on the Ribbon. They can be added to the Quick Access Toolbar using the Access Options dialog box.

1

• Click the Office Button to display the Office Button menu (Figure E–15).

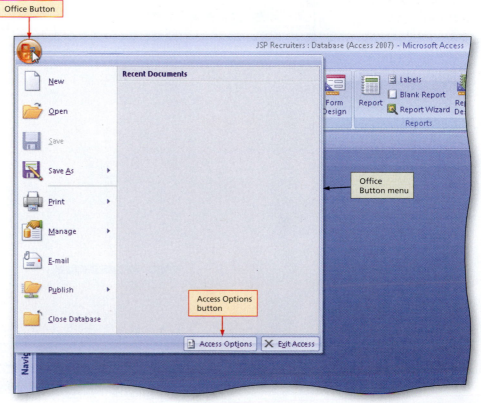

Figure E–15

2

- Click the Access
Options button on
the Office Button
menu to display
the Access Options
dialog box
(Figure E–16).

Figure E–16

3

- Click Customize in
the left pane.

- Click the 'Choose
commands from'
box arrow to display
the 'Choose
commands from' list.

- Click Commands Not
in the Ribbon in the
'Choose commands
from' list.

- Scroll to display the
Split command.

- Click Split to select it
(Figure E–17).

Figure E–17

4

● Click the Add button to add the Split button to the list of buttons on the Quick Access Toolbar (Figure E–18).

Figure E–18

5

● Click the OK button to add the Split button to the Quick Access Toolbar (Figure E–19).

Figure E–19

Other Ways

1. Click Customize Quick Access Toolbar button, click More Commands, select commands to add, click Add button, click OK button

To Remove a Command from the Quick Access Toolbar

1

- Right-click the Split button on the Quick Access Toolbar to display a shortcut menu (Figure E–20).

Figure E–20

2

- Click Remove from Quick Access Toolbar on the shortcut menu to remove the button from the Quick Access Toolbar (Figure E–21).

Figure E–21

Other Ways

1. Click Customize Quick Access Toolbar button, click More Commands, click the command you wish to remove in the Customize Quick Access Toolbar list, click Remove button, click OK button

2. If the command appears on the Customize Quick Access Toolbar menu, click the Customize Quick Access Toolbar button, click the command you wish to remove

To Reset the Quick Access Toolbar

1

- Click the Customize Quick Access Toolbar button on the Quick Access Toolbar.

- Click More Commands on the Quick Access Toolbar menu to display the Access Options Dialog box.

- Click the Show Quick Access Toolbar below the Ribbon check box to deselect it (Figure E–22).

Figure E–22

- Click the Reset button, click the Yes button in the dialog box that appears, and then click the OK button in the Word Options dialog box, to reset the Quick Access Toolbar to its original position to the right of the Office Button, with the original three buttons (Figure E–23).

Figure E–23

Changing from Tabbed Documents to Overlapping Windows

In Access 2007, tables, queries, forms, reports, and other objects are displayed as tabbed documents rather than overlapping windows as they were in previous versions. You can change to overlapping windows if you wish. The following steps change the display from tabbed documents to overlapping windows.

To Change from Tabbed Documents to Overlapping Windows

- Click the Office Button to display the Office Button menu.

- Click the Access Options button to display the Access Options dialog box.

- If necessary, click Current Database in the left pane. Click the Overlapping Windows option button to select overlapping windows (Figure E–24).

- Click the OK button to change to overlapping windows.

- When Access informs you that you must close and reopen the database for the change to take effect, click the OK button.

- Close and reopen the database.

- Open both the Client and Recruiter tables to see the effect of overlapping windows (Figure E–25).

Q&A

How do I switch back to the tabbed documents?

Follow the steps for changing to overlapping windows, but click the Tabbed Documents option button.

Figure E–24

Figure E–25

Appendix F

Steps for the Windows XP User

For the XP User of this Book

For most tasks, no differences exist between using Access under the Windows Vista operating system and using Access under the Windows XP operating system. With some tasks, however, you will see some differences, or need to complete the tasks using different steps. This appendix shows how to Start Access, Create a Database, and Open a Database while using Microsoft Office under Windows XP.

To Start Access

The following steps, which assume Windows is running, start Access based on a typical installation. You may need to ask your instructor how to start Access for your computer.

- Click the Start button on the Windows taskbar to display the Start menu.

- Point to All Programs on the Start menu to display the All Programs submenu.

- Point to Microsoft Office on the All Programs submenu to display the Microsoft Office submenu (Figure F–1).

Figure F–1

2

- Click Microsoft Office Access 2007 to start Access and display the Getting Started with Microsoft Office Access screen (Figure F–2).

- If the Access window is not maximized, click the Maximize button next to the Close button on its title bar to maximize the window.

Q&A

What is a maximized window?

A maximized window fills the entire screen. When you maximize a window, the Maximize button changes to a Restore Down button.

Figure F–2

Other Ways

1. Double-click Access icon on desktop, if one is present

2. Click Microsoft Office Access 2007 on Start menu

To Create a Database

The following steps create a database, using the file name JSP Recruiters, on a USB flash drive.

1

- With a USB flash drive connected to one of the computer's USB ports, click Blank Database to create a new blank database.

2

- Repeatedly press the DELETE key to delete the default name of Database1.

- Type `JSP Recruiters` in the File Name text box to replace the default file name of Database1 (your screen may show Database1.accdb). Do not press the ENTER key after typing the file name.

Q&A

What characters can I use in a file name?

A file name can have a maximum of 255 characters, including spaces. The only invalid characters are the backslash (\), slash (/), colon (:), asterisk (*), question mark (?), quotation mark ("), less than symbol (<), greater than symbol (>), and vertical bar (|).

3

- Click the 'Browse for a location to put your database' button to display the File New Database dialog box (Figure F–3).

Q&A

Do I have to save to a USB flash drive?

No. You can save to any device or folder. A **folder** is a specific location on a storage medium. You can save to the default folder or a different folder. You also can create your own folders, which is explained later in this book.

Figure F–3

4

- Click the Save in box arrow to display a list of available drives and folders.

Q&A

Why is my list of files, folders, and drives arranged and named differently from those shown in the figure?

Your computer's configuration determines how the list of files and folders is displayed and how drives are named. You can change the save location by clicking shortcuts on the My Places bar.

Q&A

How do I save the file if I am not using a USB flash drive?

Use the same process, but be certain to select your device in the Save in list.

5

- Click UDISK 2.0 (E:) in the Save in list to select the USB flash drive, Drive E in this case, as the new save location.

Q&A

What if my USB flash drive has a different name or letter?

It is very likely that your USB flash drive will have a different name and drive letter and be connected to a different port. Verify that the device in your Save in list is correct.

6

- Click the OK button to select the USB flash drive as the location for the database and to return to the Getting Started with Microsoft Office Access screen.

7

- Click the Create button to create the database on the USB flash drive with the file name, JSP Recruiters.

Q&A

How do I know that the JSP Recruiters database is created?

The name of the database appears in the title bar.

8

- If a Field List appears, click its Close button to remove the Field List from the screen (Figure F–4).

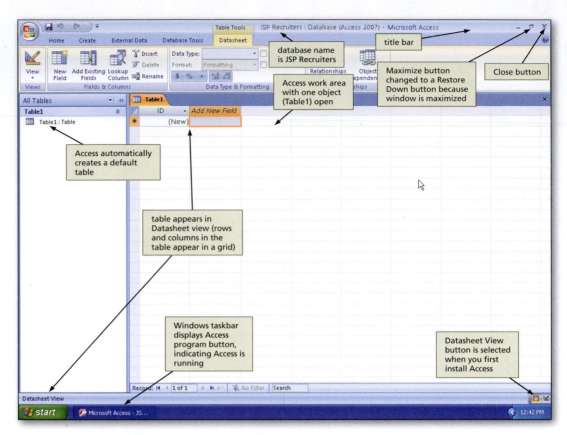

Figure F–4

Other Ways

1. Click Office Button, click Save, type file name, select drive or folder, click Save button

2. Press CTRL+S or press SHIFT+F12, type file name, select drive or folder, click Save button

To Open a Database

The following steps use the More button to open the JSP Recruiters database from the USB flash drive.

1
- With your USB flash drive connected to one of the computer's USB ports, click the More button, shown in Figure F–2 on page APP 36, to display the Open dialog box (Figure F-5).

Figure F–5

- If necessary, click the Look in box arrow and then click UDISK 2.0 (E:) to select the USB flash drive, Drive E in this case, in the Look in list as the new open location.

- Click JSP Recruiters to select the file name.

Q&A How do I open the file if I am not using a USB flash drive?

Use the same process, but be certain to select your device in the Look in list. You might need to open multiple folders.

2
- Click the Open button to open the database (Figure F–6).

3
- If a Security Warning appears, as shown in Figure F–6, click the Options button to display the Microsoft Office Security Options dialog box.

4
- Click the 'Enable this content' option button.

- Click the OK button to enable the content.

Figure F–6

Q&A When would I want to disable the content?

You would want to disable the content if you suspected that your database might contain harmful content or damaging macros. Because you are the one who created the database and no one else has used it, you should have no such suspicions.

Other Ways

1. Click Office Button, double-click file name in Recent Documents list

2. Press CTRL+O, select file name, press ENTER

Appendix G
Microsoft Business Certification Program

What Is the Microsoft Business Certification Program?

The Microsoft Business Certification Program enables candidates to show that they have something exceptional to offer – proved expertise in Microsoft Office 2007 programs. The two certification tracks allow candidates to choose how they want to exhibit their skills, either through validating skills within a specific Microsoft product or taking their knowledge to the next level and combining Microsoft programs to show that they can apply multiple skill sets to complete more complex office tasks. Recognized by businesses and schools around the world, more than 3 million certifications have been obtained in more than 100 different countries. The Microsoft Business Certification Program is the only Microsoft-approved certification program of its kind.

What Is the Microsoft Certified Application Specialist Certification?

The Microsoft Certified Application Specialist certification exams focus on validating specific skill sets within each of the Microsoft Office system programs. Candidates can choose which exam(s) they want to take according to which skills they want to validate. The available Application Specialist exams include:

- Using Windows Vista™
- Using Microsoft® Office Word 2007
- Using Microsoft® Office Excel® 2007
- Using Microsoft® Office PowerPoint® 2007
- Using Microsoft® Office Access™ 2007
- Using Microsoft® Office Outlook® 2007

> For more information and details on how Shelly Cashman Series textbooks map to Microsoft Certified Application Specialist certification, visit scsite.com/off2007/cert.

What Is the Microsoft Certified Application Professional Certification?

The Microsoft Certified Application Professional certification exams focus on a candidate's ability to use the 2007 Microsoft® Office system to accomplish industry-agnostic functions, for example Budget Analysis and Forecasting, or Content Management and Collaboration. The available Application Professional exams currently include:

- Organizational Support
- Creating and Managing Presentations
- Content Management and Collaboration
- Budget Analysis and Forecasting

Appendix H
Database Design

Introduction

This appendix presents a method for designing a database to satisfy a set of requirements. In designing a database, you must identify the tables in the database, the columns in the tables, the primary keys of the tables, and the relationships between the tables.

The appendix begins by examining some important concepts concerning relational databases and then presents the design method. To illustrate the process, the appendix presents the requirements for the JSP Recruiters database. The appendix then applies the design method to those requirements to produce the database design. The appendix concludes by examining normalization, a process that you can use to identify and fix potential problems in database designs.

Relational Databases

A **relational database** is a collection of tables similar to the tables for JSP Recruiters that appear in Figure H–1 on the next page. The Client table contains information about the clients to which JSP Recruiters provides recruiting services. JSP assigns each client to a specific recruiter. The Recruiter table contains information about the recruiters to whom these clients are assigned.

The Seminar table lists the specific seminars that the recruiters at JSP Recruiters offer to their clients. Each seminar has a number and a description. The table also includes the number of hours for which the seminar usually is offered and the increments, that is, the standard time blocks, in which the seminar usually is offered. The first row, for example, indicates that seminar S01 is Assessing Patient Satisfaction. The seminar typically is offered in 2-hour increments for a total of 8 hours.

The Seminar Offerings table contains a client number, a seminar number, the total number of hours for which the seminar is scheduled, and the number of hours the client already has spent in the seminar. The second record shows that client BH72 currently has scheduled seminar S03 (Medical Powers of Attorney). The seminar is scheduled for 12 hours, of which 6 hours already have been spent.

The formal term for a table is relation. A **relation** essentially is a two-dimensional table. If you study the tables shown in Figure H–1 on the next page, you might see that there are certain restrictions you can place on relations. Each column in a table should have a unique name, and entries in each column should match this column name. For example, in the Postal Code column, all entries in fact should *be* postal codes. In addition, each row should be unique. After all, if two rows in a table contain identical data, the second row does not provide any information that you do not already have. In addition, for maximum flexibility, the order in which columns and rows appear in a table should be immaterial. Finally, a table's design is less complex if you restrict each position in the table to a single entry; that is, you do not permit multiple entries (often called **repeating groups**) in the table. These restrictions lead to the following definition:

Client

Client Number	Client Name	Street	City	State	Postal Code	Amount Paid	Current Due	Recruiter Number
AC34	Alys Clinic	134 Central	Berridge	CO	80330	$0.00	$17,500.00	21
BH72	Berls Hospital	415 Main	Berls	CO	80349	$29,200.00	$0.00	24
FD89	Ferb Dentistry	34 Crestview	Berridge	CO	80330	$21,000.00	$12,500.00	21
FH22	Family Health	123 Second	Tarleton	CO	80409	$0.00	$0.00	24
MH56	Munn Hospital	76 Dixon	Mason	CO	80356	$0.00	$43,025.00	24
PR11	Peel Radiology	151 Valleyview	Fort Stewart	CO	80336	$31,750.00	$0.00	21
RM32	Roz Medical	315 Maple	Berls	CO	80349	$0.00	$0.00	27
TC37	Tarleton Clinic	451 Hull	Tarleton	CO	80409	$18,750.00	$31,500.00	27
WL56	West Labs	785 Main	Berls	CO	80349	$14,000.00	$0.00	24

Recruiter

Recruiter Number	Last Name	First Name	Street	City	State	Postal Code	Rate	Commission
21	Kerry	Alyssa	261 Pointer	Tourin	CO	80416	0.10	$17,600.00
24	Reeves	Camden	3135 Brill	Denton	CO	80412	0.10	$19,900.00
27	Fernandez	Jaime	265 Maxwell	Charleston	CO	80380	0.09	$9,450.00
34	Lee	Jan	1827 Oak	Denton	CO	80413	0.08	$0.00

Seminar

Seminar Number	Seminar Description	Hours	Increments
S01	Assessing Patient Satisfaction	8	2
S02	HIPAA Fundamentals	4	2
S03	Medical Powers of Attorney	12	4
S04	OSHA Fundamentals	4	2
S05	Using Basic Medical Terminology	16	4
S06	Working in Teams	16	4
S07	Coping with Crisis Situations	8	2
S08	Personal Hygiene in the Medical Environment	2	1

Seminar Offerings

Client Number	Seminar Number	Total Hours	Hours Spent
BH72	S02	4	0
BH72	S03	12	6
FH22	S04	4	2
FH22	S07	8	4
MH56	S06	16	8
MH56	S07	8	4
PR11	S05	16	4
TC37	S01	8	2
TC37	S07	10	2
TC37	S08	2	0

Figure H–1

A relation is a two-dimensional table in which:

1. The entries in the table are single-valued; that is, each location in the table contains a single entry.

2. Each column has a distinct name (technically called the attribute name).

3. All values in a column are values of the same attribute (that is, all entries must correspond to the column name).

4. The order of columns is immaterial. You can view the columns in any order you want.

5. Each row is distinct; that is, no two rows are identical.

6. The order of rows is immaterial. You can view the rows in any order you want.

A relational database is a collection of relations. Rows in a table (relation) often are called **records** or **tuples**. Columns in a table (relation) often are called **fields** or **attributes**.

To depict the structure of a relational database, you can use a commonly accepted shorthand representation: you write the name of the table and then, within parentheses, list all of the columns in the table. Each table should begin on a new line. If the entries in the table occupy more than one line, the entries that appear on the next line should be indented so it is clear that they do not constitute another table. Using this method, you would represent the JSP Recruiters database as follows:

Client (Client Number, Client Name, Street, City, State, Postal Code, Amount Paid, Current Due, Recruiter Number)

Recruiter (Recruiter Number, Last Name, First Name, Street, City, State, Postal Code, Rate, Commission)

Seminar (Seminar Number, Seminar Description, Hours, Increments)

Seminar Offerings (Client Number, Seminar Number, Total Hours, Hours Spent)

The JSP Recruiters database contains some duplicate column names. For example, the Recruiter Number column appears in *both* the Recruiter table *and* the Client table. Suppose a situation exists wherein the two columns might be confused. If you write Recruiter Number, how would the computer or another individual know which Recruiter Number column in which table you intended to use? When duplicate column names exist in a database, you need to indicate the column to which you are referring. One common approach to this problem is to write both the table name and the column name, separated by a period. Thus, you would write the Recruiter Number column in the Client table as Client.Recruiter Number and the Recruiter Number column in the Recruiter table as Recruiter.Recruiter Number. Technically, when you combine a column name with a table name, you say that you **qualify** the column names. It *always* is acceptable to qualify column names, even if there is no possibility of confusion. If confusion may arise, however, it is *essential* to qualify column names.

Functional Dependence

In the JSP Recruiters database (Figure H–1), a given client number in the database will correspond to a single client because client numbers are unique. Thus, you could look up a client number and find a single name that corresponds to it. No ambiguity exists. If you know a value for an attribute guarantees that you also know a single value for a second attribute, the second attribute is said to be **functionally dependent** on the first. Thus, Client Name is functionally dependent on Client Number because if you know a value for Client Number, you automatically know a single value for Client Name. In other words, Client Number determines Client Name. This often is indicated as Client Number → Client Name. The attribute following the arrow is functionally dependent on the attribute preceding the arrow.

If you were given a city and asked to find a single client's name, however, you could not do it. Given Berridge as the city, for example, you would find two client names (Alys Clinic and Ferb Dentistry). Formally, you would say the Client Name is *not* functionally dependent on City.

In the Recruiter table, Last Name is functionally dependent on Recruiter Number. If you are given a value for Recruiter Number, for example 24, you always will find a *single* last name, in this case Reeves, associated with it.

In the Client table, Client Name is not functionally dependent on Recruiter Number. Given Recruiter Number 21, for example, you would not be able to find a single client name, because 21 appears on more than one row in the table.

In the Seminar Offerings table, Hours Spent is not functionally dependent on Client Number. Client Number does not give enough information. For example, in the first row, Client Number is BH72 and Hours Spent is 0. In the second row, however, the Client Number also is BH72, but the Hours Spent is 6. Hours Spent also is not functionally dependent on Seminar Number, because Seminar Number does not give enough information. For example, in the fourth row, Seminar Number is S07 and Hours Spent is 4. In the ninth row, however, Seminar Number also is S07, but Hours Spent is 2.

Hours Spent actually is functionally dependent on the combination (formally called the **concatenation**) of Client Number and Seminar Number. Given a client number *and* a seminar number, you can determine a single value for Hours Spent. This would be written as Client Number, Seminar Number → Hours Spent.

Primary Key

The **primary key** of a table (relation) is the column or minimum collection of columns that uniquely identifies a given row in that table. In the Recruiter table, the recruiter's number uniquely identifies a given row. Any recruiter number appears on only one row of the table. Thus, Recruiter Number is the primary key. Similarly, Client Number is the primary key of the Client table and Seminar Number is the key of the Seminar table.

The primary key of the Seminar Offerings table consists of two columns, Client Number and Seminar Number. Total Hours and Hours Spent neither are dependent on just Client Number nor are they dependent on just Seminar Number. Rather, they are dependent on the combination of Client Number and Seminar Number. Thus, neither Client Number nor Seminar Number alone can be the primary key. Both columns are required.

The primary key provides an important way of distinguishing one row in a table from another. In the shorthand representation, you underline the column or collection of columns that comprise the primary key for each table in the database. Thus, the complete shorthand representation for the JSP Recruiters database is as follows:

Client (<u>Client Number</u>, Client Name, Street, City, State, Postal Code, Amount Paid, Current Due, Recruiter Number)

Recruiter (<u>Recruiter Number</u>, Last Name, First Name, Street, City, State, Postal Code, Rate, Commission)

Seminar (<u>Seminar Number</u>, Seminar Description, Hours, Increments)

Seminar Offerings (<u>Client Number</u>, <u>Seminar Number</u>, Total Hours, Hours Spent)

Occasionally (but not often) there might be more than one possibility for the primary key. For example, if the JSP Recruiters database included the recruiter's Social Security number in the Recruiter table, either the recruiter number or the Social Security number could serve as the primary key. In this case, both columns are referred to as candidate keys. Similarly to a primary key, a **candidate key** is a column or collection of columns on which all columns in the table are functionally dependent — the definition for primary key really defines candidate key as well. From all the candidate keys, the user chooses one to be the primary key.

Database Design

This section presents a specific database design method, given a set of requirements that the database must support. The section then presents a sample of such requirements and illustrates the design method by designing a database to satisfy these requirements.

Design Method

The following steps illustrate how to design a database for a set of requirements.

1. Read through the requirements and identify the entities (objects) involved. Assign names to the entities. If, for example, the design involves departments and employees, you could assign the names Department and Employee. If the design involves customers, orders, and parts, you could assign the names Customer, Order, and Part.

2. Identify a unique identifier for each entity. For example, if one of the entities is parts, you would determine what it takes to uniquely identify each individual part. In other words, what enables the organization to distinguish one part from another? For a part entity, it may be Part Number. For a customer entity, it may be Customer Number. If there is no such unique identifier, it probably is a good idea to add one. Perhaps the previous system was a manual one in which customers were not assigned numbers, in which case this would be a good time to add customer numbers to the system. If there is no natural candidate for a primary key, you can add an AutoNumber field (like the ID field that Access automatically adds when you create a new table).

3. Identify the attributes for all the entities. These attributes will become the columns in the tables. It is possible that more than one entity has the same attribute. At JSP Recruiters, for example, clients and recruiters both have the attributes of street address, city, state, and postal code. To clarify this in your planning, you can follow the name of the attribute with the corresponding entity in parentheses. Thus, Street (Client) would be the street address of a client, whereas Street (Recruiter) would be the street address of a recruiter.

4. Identify the functional dependencies that exist among the attributes.

5. Use the functional dependencies to identify the tables. You do this by placing each attribute with the attribute or minimum combination of attributes on which it is functionally dependent. The attribute or attributes on which all other attributes in the relation are dependent will be the primary key of a relation. The remaining attributes will be the other columns in the relation. Once you have determined all the columns in the relation, you can assign an appropriate name to the relation.

6. Identify any relationships between tables by looking for matching columns.

The following sections illustrate the design process by designing the database for JSP Recruiters. The next section gives the requirements that this database must support, and the last section creates a database design based on those requirements.

BTW

Physical Database Design
Database design includes both logical design and physical design. Logical database design includes determining the fields (attributes) for the various tables (relations). With physical database design, you need to determine the appropriate data type for each field. For example, should the Client Number field be a Text field or a Number field? What format would be best for each data type? To do so, use the guidelines given on pages AC 10 and 301.

BTW

Boolean Operators
The Boolean operators (AND, OR, and NOT) have a special restriction on the expressions involved. Each expression must be either true or false. When using the Boolean operator AND, for example, the expressions before and after the word AND are examined to determine whether they are true or false. If both are true, the result is true. Otherwise, the result is false. Typically, the expressions involve either a field and a value ([Amount Paid]>20000) or two fields ([Hours Spent]<[Total Hours]). There is one type of field that is appropriate for the Boolean operators without needing to be part of an expression — the Yes/No field. For example, there might be a Yes/No field in the Recruiter table called Bonus that is set to Yes (true) if the recruiter is eligible for a bonus and set to No (false) if the Recruiter is not. This field could be used in a Boolean expression by itself (Bonus AND [Commission]>15000). This expression would be true if Bonus is Yes and the value in the Commission field is greater than 15,000. It would be false otherwise. For details on determining when to use a Yes/No field, see the Plan Ahead on page AC 301.

Requirements for the JSP Recruiters Database

The JSP Recruiters database must support the following requirements:

1. For a client, JSP needs to maintain the client number, name, street address, city, state, postal code, amount paid, and the amount that currently is due. They also need the total amount, which is the sum of the amount already paid and the current due.

2. For a recruiter, store the recruiter number, last name, first name, street address, city, state, postal code, rate, and commission.

3. For a seminar, store the seminar number, seminar description, hours, and increments. In addition, for each offering of the seminar, store the number of the client for whom the seminar is offered, the total number of hours planned for the offering of the seminar, and the number of hours already spent. The total hours may be the same as the normal number of hours for the seminar, but it need not be. This gives JSP the flexibility of tailoring the offering of the seminar to the specific needs of the client.

4. Each client has a single recruiter to which the client is assigned. Each recruiter may be assigned many clients.

5. A client may be offered many seminars and a seminar may be offered to many clients.

Database Design Example

The following represents the application of the design method for the JSP Recruiters requirements.

1. There are three entities: clients, recruiters, and seminars. The names assigned to them are Client, Recruiter, and Seminar, respectively.

2. The unique identifier for clients is the client number. The unique identifier for recruiters is the recruiter number. The unique identifier for seminars is the seminar number. The names assigned to these identifiers are Client Number, Recruiter Number, and Seminar Number, respectively.

3. The attributes are:

>Client Number
>Client Name
>Street (Client)
>City (Client)
>State (Client)
>Postal Code (Client)
>Amount Paid
>Current Due
>Recruiter Number
>Last Name
>First Name
>Street (Recruiter)
>City (Recruiter)
>State (Recruiter)
>Postal Code (Recruiter)
>Rate
>Commission
>Seminar Number

Seminar Description

Hours

Increments

Total Hours

Hours Spent

Remember that parentheses after an attribute indicate the entity to which the attribute corresponds. Thus, Street (Client) represents the street address of a client in a way that distinguishes it from Street (Recruiter), which represents the street address of a recruiter.

Question: Why isn't Total Amount included?

Answer: Total Amount, which is Amount Paid plus Current Due, can be calculated from other columns. You can perform this calculation in queries, forms, and reports. Thus, there is no need to include it as a column in the Client table. Further, by including it, you introduce the possibility of errors in the database. For example, if Amount Paid is $5,000, Current Due is $2,000, and yet you set Total Amount equal to $8,000, you have an error. You also need to be sure to change Total Amount appropriately whenever you change either Amount Paid or Current Due. If Total Amount is not stored, but rather is calculated when needed, you avoid all these problems.

4. The functional dependencies among the attributes are:

Client Number → Client Name, Street (Client), City (Client), State (Client),
   Postal Code (Client), Amount Paid, Current Due, Recruiter Number

Recruiter Number → Last Name, First Name, Street (Recruiter), City (Recruiter),
   State (Recruiter), Postal Code (Recruiter), Rate, Commission

Seminar Number → Seminar Description, Hours, Increments

Client Number, Seminar Number → Total Hours, Hours Spent

Question: Why is Total Hours listed with Client Number and Seminar Number rather than just with Seminar Number?

Answer: If the Total Hours was required to be the same as the number of hours for the seminar, then it indeed would be listed with Seminar Number. (It would not vary from one client to another.) Because JSP wants the flexibility of tailoring the number of hours for which a particular seminar is offered to the specific needs of the client, Total Hours also is dependent on Client Number.

The client's name, street address, city, state, postal code, amount paid, and current due are dependent only on Client Number. Because a client has a single recruiter, the recruiter number is dependent on Client Number as well. The recruiter's last name, first name, street address, city, state, postal code, rate, and commission are dependent only on Recruiter Number. A seminar description, the number of hours for the seminar, and the increments in which the seminar is offered are dependent only on Seminar Number. The total hours for a particular seminar offering as well as the hours already spent are dependent on the combination of Client Number and Seminar Number.

5. The tables are:

Client (<u>Client Number</u>, Client Name, Street, City, State, Postal Code, Amount Paid, Current Due, Recruiter Number)

Recruiter (<u>Recruiter Number</u>, Last Name, First Name, Street, City, State, Postal Code, Rate, Commission)

Seminar (<u>Seminar Number</u>, Seminar Description, Hours, Increments)

Seminar Offerings (<u>Client Number</u>, <u>Seminar Number</u>, Total Hours, Hours Spent)

The primary keys are underlined.

6. The following are the relationships between the tables:

a. The Client and Recruiter tables are related using the Recruiter Number fields.

b. The Client and Seminar Offerings tables are related using the Client Number fields.

c. The Seminar and Seminar Offerings tables are related using the Seminar Number fields.

Question: Is there a relationship between the Client table and the Seminar table? If so, what type of relationship is it?

Answer: There actually is a many-to-many relationship between the Client table and the Seminar table. A client can schedule many seminars and a seminar can be offered to many clients. The typical way a many-to-many relationship between two tables is implemented is by creating a third table whose primary key is the combination of the primary keys of the individual tables. In this case, the Seminar Offerings table plays exactly that role.

Normalization

After you create your database design, you should analyze it to make sure the design is free of potential problems. To do so, you use a process called normalization. The **normalization** process enables you to identify the existence of potential problems. This process also supplies methods for correcting these problems.

The normalization process involves converting tables into various types of **normal forms**. A table in a particular normal form possesses a certain desirable set of properties. Several normal forms exist, the most common being first normal form (1NF), second normal form (2NF), and third normal form (3NF). The forms create a progression in which a table that is in 1NF is better than a table that is not in 1NF; a table that is in 2NF is better than one that is in 1NF; and so on. The goal of normalization is to take a table or collection of tables and produce a new collection of tables that represents the same information but is free of problems.

First Normal Form

A relation (table) that contains a **repeating group** (or multiple entries for a single row) is called an **unnormalized relation**. Removal of repeating groups is the starting point in the goal for tables that are as free of problems as possible. In fact, in most database management systems, tables cannot contain repeating groups. A table (relation) is in **first normal form (1NF)** if it does not contain repeating groups.

In designing a database, you may have created a table with a repeating group. For example, you might have created a Seminar Offerings table, in which the primary key is the Client Number and there is a repeating group consisting of Seminar Number, Total Hours, and Hours Spent. In the example, there is one row per client with Seminar Number, Total Hours, and Hours Spent repeated as many times as necessary (Figure H–2).

Seminar Offerings			
Client Number	**Seminar Number**	**Total Hours**	**Hours Spent**
BH72	S02	4	0
	S03	12	6
FH22	S04	4	2
	S07	8	4
MH56	S06	16	8
	S07	8	4
PR11	S05	16	4
TC37	S01	8	2
	S07	10	2
	S08	2	0

Figure H–2

In the shorthand notation, you represent a repeating group by enclosing the repeating group within parentheses. The Seminar Offerings table in Figure H–2 would be represented as:

Seminar Offerings (<u>Client Number</u>, (Seminar Number, Total Hours, Hours Spent))

Conversion to First Normal Form

To convert the table to 1NF, remove the repeating group symbol to give the following:

Seminar Offerings (<u>Client Number</u>, <u>Seminar Number</u>, Total Hours, Hours Spent)

The corresponding example of the new table is shown in Figure H–3.

Seminar Offerings			
Client Number	**Seminar Number**	**Total Hours**	**Hours Spent**
BH72	S02	4	0
BH72	S03	12	6
FH22	S04	4	2
FH22	S07	8	4
MH56	S06	16	8
MH56	S07	8	4
PR11	S05	16	4
TC37	S01	8	2
TC37	S07	10	2
TC37	S08	2	0

Figure H–3

Note that the first row of the unnormalized table (Figure H–2 on the previous page) indicates that client BH72 currently is being offered both seminar S02 and seminar S03. In the normalized table, this information is represented by *two* rows, the first and the second (Figure H–3 on the previous page). The primary key for the unnormalized Seminar Offerings table was the Client Number only. The primary key for the normalized table now is the combination of Client Number and Seminar Number.

In general, when converting a non-1NF table to 1NF, the primary key typically will include the original primary key concatenated with the key of the repeating group; that is, the column that distinguishes one occurrence of the repeating group from another within a given row in the table. In this case, Seminar Number is the key to the repeating group and thus becomes part of the primary key of the 1NF table.

Second Normal Form

Even though the following table is in 1NF, problems may exist that will cause you to want to restructure the table. You might have created the following Seminar Offerings table:

Seminar Offerings (<u>Client Number</u>, Client Name, <u>Seminar Number</u>, Seminar Description, Total Hours, Hours Spent)

with the functional dependencies:

Client Number → Client Name

Seminar Number → Seminar Description

Client Number, Seminar Number → Total Hours, Hours Spent

This notation indicates that Client Number alone determines Client Name, Seminar Number alone determines Seminar Description, but it requires *both* a Client Number *and* a Seminar Number to determine either Total Hours or Hours Spent. Consider the sample of this table shown in Figure H–4.

Seminar					
Client Number	**Client Name**	**Seminar Number**	**Seminar Description**	**Total Hours**	**Hours Spent**
BH72	Berls Hospital	S02	HIPAA Fundamentals	4	0
BH72	Berls Hospital	S03	Medical Powers of Attorney	12	6
FH22	Family Health	S04	OSHA Fundamentals	4	2
FH22	Family Health	S07	Coping with Crisis Situations	8	4
MH56	Munn Hospital	S06	Working in Teams	16	8
MH56	Munn Hospital	S07	Coping with Crisis Situations	8	4
PR11	Peel Radiology	S05	Using Basic Medical Terminology	16	4
TC37	Tarleton Clinic	S01	Assessing Patient Satisfaction	8	2
TC37	Tarleton Clinic	S07	Coping with Crisis Situations	10	2
TC37	Tarleton Clinic	S08	Personal Hygiene in the Medical Environment	2	0

Figure H–4

The name of a specific client, BH72 for example, occurs multiple times in the table. This redundancy causes several problems. It certainly is wasteful of space, but that is not nearly as serious as some of the other problems. These other problems are called **update anomalies** and they fall into four categories:

1. **Update.** A change to the name of client BH72 requires not one change to the table, but several — you must change each row in which BH72 appears. This certainly makes the update process much more cumbersome; it is more complicated logically and takes longer to update.

2. **Inconsistent data.** There is nothing about the design that would prohibit client BH72 from having two or more different names in the database. The first row, for example, might have Berls Hospital as the name, whereas the second row might have Berl Hospital.

3. **Additions.** There is a real problem when you try to add a new seminar and its description to the database. Because the primary key for the table consists of both Client Number and Seminar Number, you need values for both of these to add a new row. If you have a client to add but there are as yet no seminars scheduled for it, what do you use for a seminar number? The only solution would be to make up a dummy seminar number and then replace it with a real seminar number once the client requests a seminar. This is not an acceptable solution.

4. **Deletions.** In Figure H–4, if you delete client BH72 from the database, you also *lose* all the information about seminar S02. For example, you would no longer know that the description of seminar S02 is HIPAA Fundamentals.

These problems occur because there is a column, Client Name, that is dependent on only a portion of the primary key, Client Number, and *not* on the complete primary key. The problem with Seminar Description is that it is dependent on only the Seminar Number. This leads to the definition of second normal form. Second normal form represents an improvement over first normal form because it eliminates update anomalies in these situations. In order to understand second normal form, you need to understand the term nonkey column.

A column is a **nonkey column** (also called a **nonkey attribute**) if it is not a part of the primary key. A table (relation) is in **second normal form** (**2NF**) if it is in first normal form and no nonkey column is dependent on only a portion of the primary key.

Note that if the primary key of a table contains only a single column, the table automatically is in second normal form. In that case, there could not be any column dependent on only a portion of the primary key.

Conversion to Second Normal Form

To correct the problems, convert the table to a collection of tables in second normal form. Then name the new tables. The following is a method for performing this conversion.

First, take each subset of the set of columns that make up the primary key, and begin a new table with this subset as its primary key. For the Seminar Offerings table, this would give:

(<u>Client Number</u>)

(<u>Seminar Number</u>)

(<u>Client Number</u>, <u>Seminar Number</u>)

Next, place each of the other columns with the appropriate primary key; that is, place each one with the minimal collection of columns on which it depends. For the Seminar Offerings table, this would yield:

(<u>Client Number</u>, Client Name)

(<u>Seminar Number</u>, Seminar Description)

(<u>Client Number</u>, <u>Seminar Number</u>, Total Hours, Hours Spent)

Each of these new tables now can be given a name that is descriptive of the meaning of the table, such as Client, Seminar, and Seminar Offerings. Figure H–5 shows samples of the tables involved.

Client

Client Number	Client Name
BH72	Berls Hospital
FH22	Family Health
MH56	Munn Hospital
PR11	Peel Radiology
TC37	Tarleton Clinic

Seminar

Seminar Number	Seminar Description
S01	Assessing Patient Satisfaction
S02	HIPAA Fundamentals
S03	Medical Powers of Attorney
S04	OSHA Fundamentals
S05	Using Basic Medical Terminology
S06	Working in Teams
S07	Coping with Crisis Situations
S08	Personal Hygiene in the Medical Environment

Seminar Offerings

Client Number	Seminar Number	Total Hours	Hours Spent
BH72	S02	4	0
BH72	S03	12	6
FH22	S04	4	2
FH22	S07	8	4
MH56	S06	16	8
MH56	S07	8	4
PR11	S05	16	4
TC37	S01	8	2
TC37	S07	10	2
TC37	S08	2	0

Figure H–5

The new design eliminates the update anomalies. A client name occurs only once for each client, so you do not have the redundancy that you did in the earlier design. Changing the name of a client now is a simple process involving a single change. Because the name of a client occurs in a single place, it is not possible to have multiple names for the same client in the database at the same time.

To add a new client, you create a new row in the Client table and thus there is no need to have a seminar offering already scheduled for that client. Also, deleting client BH72 has nothing to do with the Seminar table and, consequently, does not cause seminar S02 to be deleted. Thus, you still have its description (HIPAA Fundamentals) in the database. Finally, you have not lost any information in the process. The data in the original design can be reconstructed from the data in the new design.

Third Normal Form

Problems still can exist with tables that are in 2NF as illustrated in the following Client table:

Client (<u>Client Number</u>, Client Name, Street, City, State, Postal Code, Amount Paid, Current Due, Recruiter Number, Last Name, First Name)

The functional dependencies in this table are:

Client Number → Client Name, Street, City, State, Postal Code, Amount Paid, Current Due, Recruiter Number

Recruiter Number → Last Name, First Name

Client Number determines all the other columns. In addition, Recruiter Number determines Last Name and First Name.

Because the primary key of the table is a single column, the table automatically is in second normal form. As the sample of the table shown in Figure H–6 demonstrates, however, this table has problems similar to those encountered earlier, even though it is in 2NF. In this case, it is the last name and first name of a recruiter that can occur many times in the table (see recruiter 21, Alyssa Kerry, for example).

BTW

3NF
The actual definition of third normal form is that no nonkey column is functionally dependent on any other nonkey column. The relation in Figure H-6 also violates this definition because the nonkey column Last Name is functionally dependent on the nonkey column Recruiter Number.

Client							
Client Number	**Client Name**	**...**	**Amount Paid**	**Current Due**	**Recruiter Number**	**Last Name**	**First Name**
AC34	Alys Clinic	...	$0.00	$17,500.00	21	Kerry	Alyssa
BH72	Berls Hospital	...	$29,200.00	$0.00	24	Reeves	Camden
FD89	Ferb Dentistry	...	$21,000.00	$12,500.00	21	Kerry	Alyssa
FH22	Family Health	...	$0.00	$0.00	24	Reeves	Camden
MH56	Munn Hospital	...	$0.00	$43,025.00	24	Reeves	Camden
PR11	Peel Radiology	...	$31,750.00	$0.00	21	Kerry	Alyssa
RM32	Roz Medical	...	$0.00	$0.00	27	Fernandez	Jaime
TC37	Tarleton Clinic	...	$18,750.00	$31,500.00	27	Fernandez	Jaime
WL56	West Labs	...	$14,000.00	$0.00	24	Reeves	Camden

Figure H–6

This redundancy results in the same set of problems described previously with the Seminar Offerings table. In addition to the problem of wasted space, you have similar update anomalies, as follows:

1. **Updates.** A change to the name of a recruiter requires not one change to the table, but several. Again the update process becomes very cumbersome.

2. **Inconsistent data.** There is nothing about the design that would prohibit a recruiter from having two different names in the database. On the first row, for example, the name for recruiter 21 might read Alyssa Kerry; whereas on the third row (another row on which the recruiter number is 21), the name might be Stacy Webb.

3. **Additions.** In order to add recruiter 39, whose name is Tati Angelo, to the database, she must have at least one client. If she has not yet been assigned any clients, either you cannot record the fact that her name is Tati Angelo or you have to create a fictitious client for her to represent. Again, this is not a desirable solution to the problem.

4. **Deletions.** If you were to delete all the clients of recruiter 24 from the database, then you also would lose all information concerning recruiter 24.

These update anomalies are due to the fact that Recruiter Number determines Last Name and First Name, but Recruiter Number is not the primary key. As a result, the same Recruiter Number and consequently the same Last Name and First Name can appear on many different rows.

You have seen that 2NF is an improvement over 1NF, but to eliminate 2NF problems, you need an even better strategy for creating tables in the database. Third normal form provides that strategy. Before looking at third normal form, however, you need to become familiar with the special name that is given to any column that determines another column (like Recruiter Number in the Client table).

Any column (or collection of columns) that determines another column is called a **determinant**. Certainly the primary key in a table is a determinant. In fact, by definition, any candidate key is a determinant. (Remember that a candidate key is a column or collection of columns that could function as the primary key.) In this case, Recruiter Number is a determinant, but it certainly is not a candidate key, and that is the problem.

A table is in **third normal form** (**3NF**) if it is in second normal form and if the only determinants it contains are candidate keys. This definition is not the original definition of third normal form. This more recent definition, which is preferable to the original, also is referred to as **Boyce-Codd normal form** (**BCNF**). However, in this text, it simply is referred to as third normal form.

Conversion to Third Normal Form

You now have identified the problem with the Client table: it is not in 3NF. You now need a scheme to correct the deficiency in the Client table and in all tables having similar deficiencies. Such a method follows.

First, for each determinant that is not a candidate key, remove from the table the columns that depend on this determinant, but do not remove the determinant. Next, create a new table containing all the columns from the original table that depend on this determinant. Finally, make the determinant the primary key of this new table.

In the Client table, for example, Last Name and First Name are removed because they depend on the determinant Recruiter Number, which is not a candidate key. A new table is formed, consisting of Recruiter Number as the primary key, Last Name and First Name. Specifically:

Client (<u>Client Number</u>, Client Name, Street, City, State, Postal Code,
    Amount Paid, Current Due, Recruiter Number, Last Name, First Name)

is replaced by:

Client (<u>Client Number</u>, Client Name, Street, City, State, Postal Code,
    Amount Paid, Current Due, Recruiter Number)

and

Recruiter (<u>Recruiter Number</u>, Last Name, First Name)

Figure H–7 shows samples of the tables involved.

Client

Client Number	Client Name	...	Amount Paid	Current Due	Recruiter Number
AC34	Alys Clinic	...	$0.00	$17,500.00	21
BH72	Berls Hospital	...	$29,200.00	$0.00	24
FD89	Ferb Dentistry	...	$21,000.00	$12,500.00	21
FH22	Family Health	...	$0.00	$0.00	24
MH56	Munn Hospital	...	$0.00	$43,025.00	24
PR11	Peel Radiology	...	$31,750.00	$0.00	21
RM32	Roz Medical	...	$0.00	$0.00	27
TC37	Tarleton Clinic	...	$18,750.00	$31,500.00	27
WL56	West Labs	...	$14,000.00	$0.00	24

Recruiter

Recruiter Number	Last Name	First Name
21	Kerry	Alyssa
24	Reeves	Camden
27	Fernandez	Jaime

Figure H–7

This design corrects the previously identified problems. A recruiter's name appears only once, thus avoiding redundancy and making the process of changing a recruiter's name a very simple one. It is not possible with this design for the same recruiter to have two different names in the database. To add a new recruiter to the database, you add a row in the Recruiter table so it is not necessary to have a pre-existing client for the recruiter. Finally, deleting all the clients of a given recruiter will not remove the recruiter's record from the Recruiter table, so you retain the recruiter's name; all the data in the original table can be reconstructed from the data in the new collection of tables. All previously mentioned problems indeed have been solved.

In the Lab

Design, create, modify, and/or use a database following the guidelines, concepts, and skills presented in this appendix.

Lab 1: Designing a Database

Instructions: Answer the following questions in the format specified by your instructor.

1. List three relational table characteristics that are violated in the table shown in Figure H–8.

Orders			
Date	Part Number	Number Ordered	Date
11/01/2008	AX12	11	11/12/2008
11/01/2008	BT04	1	11/09/2008
	BZ66	1	Friday
11/03/2008	CB03	4	11/13/2008
11/03/2008	CX11	2	11/12/2008
11/04/2008	AZ52	2	11/12/2008
	BA74	4	$182.91
11/04/2008	BT04	1	11/15/2008
11/03/2008	CX11	2	11/12/2008
11/04/2008	CZ81	2	11/13/2008

Figure H–8

2. The following table is a student's first attempt to create a database design:

   Student (<u>StudentID</u>, Student Name, Credit Hours, AdvisorID, Advisor Name, (CourseID, Course Name, Grade))

   a. Identify the functional dependencies.

   b. Convert this table to an equivalent collection of tables in 3NF.

3. The following table concerns invoice information. For a given invoice (identified by invoice number), there will be a single customer. The customer's number, name, and address appear on the invoice as well as the invoice date. Also, there may be several different items appearing on the invoice. For every item that appears, the item number, description, price, and number shipped will be displayed. Convert this table into an equivalent collection of tables in 3NF.

   Invoice (<u>Invoice Number</u>, Customer Number, Customer Name,

   Street Address, City, State, Postal Code, Country, Invoice Date, (Item Number,

   Item Description, Price, Number Shipped))

4. Consider the following set of requirements for Sun City Limo:

   For each driver, the company keeps track of the driver's name, driver's license number, home telephone number, and cell telephone number.

   For each limo, the company keeps track of a unique limousine ID number, limousine color, and number of passengers the limo can hold.

   One driver can be assigned to more than one limo.

   Based on these requirements, create a set of 3NF relations.

Index

Quick Reference Summary

In the Microsoft Office Access 2007 program, you can accomplish a task in a number of ways. The following table provides a quick reference to each task presented in this textbook. The first column identifies the task. The second column indicates the page number on which the task is discussed in the book. The subsequent four columns list the different ways the task in column one can be carried out.

Microsoft Office Access 2007 Quick Reference Summary

Task	Page Number	Mouse	Ribbon	Shortcut Menu	Keyboard Shortcut
Add Additional Field Control	AC 316	Drag field name from field list to form			
Add Calculated field to form	AC 531		Text Box tool on Design tab		
Add Chart to Form	AC 575		Insert Chart tool on Design tab		
Add Combo Box	AC 534		Use Controls Wizard on Design tab | Combo Box (Form Control) tool		
Add Date and Time to Report	AC 490		Date & Time button on Design tab		
Add Date and Time to Form	AC 274		Date and Time button on Format tab		
Add Fields to Form	AC 279, 530		Add Existing Fields button on Format or Design tab | select field in field list | drag field to form		
Add Fields to Report	AC 265, 469		Add Existing Fields button on Format or Design tab | drag new field to report		
Add Fields to Table	AC 302			Right-click table in Navigation Pane | click Design View | click first open field	
Add Form Command Buttons	AC 541		Use Control Wizards button on Design tab | Button (Form Control) tool		

Microsoft Office Access 2007 Quick Reference Summary *(continued)*

Task	Page Number	Mouse	Ribbon	Shortcut Menu	Keyboard Shortcut
Add Form Option Group	AC 558		Use Control Wizards button on Design tab | Option group tool		
Add Form Rectangle	AC 547		Rectangle tool on Design tab		
Add Form Title	AC 323		Title button on Design tab		
Add Macro Actions	AC 368	In macro action column click box arrow | select action			
Add New Field	AC 24	Right-click Add New Field in Datasheet	Insert Rows button on Design Tab	Design View | INSERT	
Add Page Number to Report	AC 490		Insert Page Number button on Design tab		
Add Record	AC 30, 38	New (blank) record button	New button on Home tab	Open | Click in field	CTRL+PLUS SIGN (+)
Add Smart Tag to Field	AC 636		Open table in Design view | select field | select Smart Tags text box | click Build button | select desired smart tag(s)		
Add Smart Tag to Form Control	AC 640		Open form in Design view | select control | click Property Sheet button on Design tab | click All tab | click Smart Tags property | click Build button | select desired smart tag(s)		
Add Subform	AC 324, 572		Subform/Subreport tool on Design tab | Control Wizards tool | click form		
Add Subreport	AC 482		Subform/Subreport tool on Design tab | click report		
Add Text Box to Report or Form	471		Text Box tool on Design tab | click report or form | enter text box text		
Add Title to Report	AC 490		Title button on Design tab		
Add Total and Subtotals to Report	AC 498		Group & Sort button on Design tab		
Align Controls	AC 319		Select controls | click desired alignment button on Arrange tab		

Microsoft Office Access 2007 Quick Reference Summary *(continued)*

Task	Page Number	Mouse	Ribbon	Shortcut Menu	Keyboard Shortcut
Allow Zero-Length Strings	AC 626		Open table in Design view | select field | click Allow Zero Length property | change Allow Zero Length property to Yes		
Assign Conditional Value	AC 503		Text Box tool on the Design tab | place text box on form | delete text box label | select text box | click Property Sheet button | click Control Source property | click Build button | assign conditions using Expression Builder dialog box		
AutoFormat Report or Form	AC 284		More button in AutoFormat group on Format tab		
Calculate Statistics	AC 118		Totals button on Design tab		
Change Control's Color	AC 275		Select control | click Font Color arrow on Format tab | click desired color		
Change Back Color on Form	AC 322			Right-click form | point to Fill/Back Color arrow | click desired color	
Change Can Grow Property	AC 487		Select control | Property Sheet button on Design tab | All tab | change Can Grow property to Yes		
Change Caption	462	Select row | Caption property			
Change Chart Orientation	AC 407		Switch Row/Column button on Design tab		
Change Chart Type	AC 405		Change Chart Type button on Design tab | Type tab | select desired chart		
Change Colors and Font	AC 180		Alternate Fill/Back Color button arrow or Font Color button arrow or Font box arrow on Home tab		
Change Column Size	AC 309	Drag column boundary			
Change Database Properties	AC 60	Office button | Manage | Database Properties			

Microsoft Office Access 2007 Quick Reference Summary *(continued)*

Task	Page Number	Mouse	Ribbon	Shortcut Menu	Keyboard Shortcut
Change Field Format	AC 532		Select field | Property Sheet button on Design tab |		
Change Form Background Color	AC 537		Click form | Fill/Back Color button arrow on Design tab		
Change Form Label Color	AC 330		View button on Design tab | select label | click Font Color arrow | select color		
Change Form Tab Order	AC 336		Tab Order button on Arrange tab | Tab Order dialog box		
Change Form Title Format	AC 333		Design View on View Button menu on Design tab | select control | Property Sheet button		
Change Gridlines	AC 179		Gridlines button on Home tab		
Change PivotTable Properties	AC 398		Property Sheet button on Design tab		
Change Primary Key	AC 28	Delete field | Primary Key button	Design View button on Design tab | select field | Primary Key button		
Change Report Margins	AC 508		Page Setup button on Design tab | Margins		
Change Row Size	AC 309	Drag record selector boundary		Right-click field or record selector | click Column Width or Row Height	
Change Size Mode	AC 330		Click control | Property Sheet button on Design tab | Size Mode		
Chart Axis Title	AC 408		Select axis title | Property Sheet button on Design tab | Format tab | Caption box | replace caption		
Chart Title	AC 409		Select chart | Property Sheet button on Design tab | General tab | Add title button | close property sheet | click title | Property Sheet button on design tab | Format tab | replace title (caption)		
Clear Form Filter	AC 282				
Clear Query	AC 98				Select all entries | DELETE

Microsoft Office Access 2007 Quick Reference Summary *(continued)*

Task	Page Number	Mouse	Ribbon	Shortcut Menu	Keyboard Shortcut
Clear Report Filter	AC 254			Right-click field | clear selected filter	
Close Object	AC 35	Close button for object		Right-click item | Close	
Close Switchboard	AC 388	Close button			
Completely Hide Navigation Pane	AC 645	Microsoft Office Button | click Access Options | click Current Database | clear Display Navigation Pane check box			
Composite Primary Key	AC 391	Click row selector for first field | press and hold SHIFT | click row selector for second field | Primary key button			
Conditionally Format Controls	AC 250		Select field | Conditional button on Format tab		
Convert Database from an Earlier Version of Access	AC 607	Open database to convert | Microsoft Office button | Convert			
Convert Database to an Earlier Version of Access	AC 606-607	Open database to convert | Microsoft Office button | Save As			
Create Calculated Field	AC 113			Zoom	SHIFT+F2
Create Crosstab Query	AC 123		Query Wizard button on Create tab | Crosstab Query Wizard		
Create Custom Categories for Navigation Pane	AC 614	Show Navigation Pane | right-click Navigation Pane | Navigation Options | Add Item button or Add Group button | OK button			
Create Custom Input Mask	AC 625		Open table in Design view | select field for mask | click Input Mask property | enter mask		
Create Custom Properties	AC 621	Microsoft Office button | point to Manage arrow | click Database Properties | click Custom tab | revise properties as needed			
Create Database	AC 14	Blank Database button or Office Button | Save			CTRL+S or SHIFT+F12 or ALT+I
Create Form	AC 142		Form button on Create tab		
Create Form in Design View	AC 315, 529		Form Design button on Create tab		

Microsoft Office Access 2007 Quick Reference Summary *(continued)*

Task	Page Number	Mouse	Ribbon	Shortcut Menu	Keyboard Shortcut
Create Form with Datasheet	AC 343		Select "one" table in Navigation Pane | Form button on Create tab		
Create Form with Datasheet in Layout View	AC 345		Blank Form button on Create tab | Show All Tables | plus sign for "one" table | drag fields to form | plus sign for "many" table | drag first field to form | select datasheet | drag remaining fields		
Create Form with Form Wizard	AC 269		More Forms button on Create tab | Form Wizard		
Create Initial Report in Design View	466		Report Design button on Create tab | select entire report | Property sheet button | select record source		
Create Labels	AC 509		Labels button on Create tab		
Create Macro	AC 366		Macro button arrow on Create tab | Macro		
Create Multipage Form Using Tabs	AC 571		Design tab | create new form | Tab control tool		
Create Multiple-Field Index	AC 630		Indexes button on Design tab		
Create Multi-Table Report	AC 257		Report Wizard button on Create tab | add fields for first table | click Tables/Queries arrow | select second table | add fields for second table		
Create PivotChart	AC 404	Open query | View button arrow | PivotChart View		PivotChart view on status bar	
Create PivotChart Legend	AC 404		Legend button on Design tab		
Create PivotTable	AC 396	Open query | View button arrow | PivotTable View | add fields to drop zones		PivotTable view on status bar	
Create Query	AC 78		Query Design button on Create tab		
Create Report	AC 51		Report Wizard button on Create tab		
Create Report using Report Wizard	AC 239		Report Wizard button on Create tab		

Microsoft Office Access 2007 Quick Reference Summary *(continued)*

Task	Page Number	Mouse	Ribbon	Shortcut Menu	Keyboard Shortcut
Create Self-Signed Certificate	AC 650	Start button on Windows Vista taskbar | All Programs | Microsoft Office | Microsoft Office tools | click Digital Certificate for VBA Projects | type your name | OK button | OK button			
Create Space on Report by Moving Controls	AC 508	Select controls | drag controls to new location			
Create SQL Query	AC 430		Query Design button on Create tab | close Show Table dialog box | View button arrow | SQL View		
Create Switchboard	AC 380		Switchboard Manager button on Database Tools tab		
Create Table	AC 23	Office Button | Save button	Table button on Create tab		CTRL+S or SHIFT+F12
Create Validation Rules for Tables	AC 620		Open table in Design view | Property Sheet button on Design tab | Validation Rule property | type rule		
Customize Navigation Pane	AC 126	Navigation Pane arrow | Object Type			
Decrypt Database and Remove Password	AC 649		Close database | More button | Computer | click file name | click Open button arrow | Open Exclusive | OK button | Decrypt Database button on Database Tools tab | type password | click OK button		
Define Fields in a Table	AC 24		Right-click Add New Field on Datasheet tab | Rename Column	Right-click Add New Field | Rename Column	
Delete Record	AC 148	Click Record Selector | DELETE	DELETE button		
Enable Error Checking	AC 632	Microsoft Office Button | click Access Options | click Object Designers | check Enable error checking check box			

Microsoft Office Access 2007 Quick Reference Summary *(continued)*

Task	Page Number	Mouse	Ribbon	Shortcut Menu	Keyboard Shortcut
Encrypt Database with Password	AC 648		Encrypt with Password button on Database Tools tab | type password | verify password | click OK button		
Enter Data in Attachment Field	AC 312			Right-click field | click Manage Attachments | click Add | navigate to file to add	
Enter Data in Date Field	AC 308	Type date in date field			Calendar button | select date
Enter Data in Hyperlink Field	AC 314			Right-click field | click Hyperlink | click Edit Hyperlink | enter desired Web address	
Enter Data in Memo Field	AC 308	Type data in memo field			
Enter Data in OLE Field	AC 310			Right-click field | click Insert Object	
Enter Data in Yes/No Field	AC 307	Click field's check box to indicate Yes			
Exclude Field from Query Results	AC 112	Show check box			
Export Query	AC 221		Select query | desired application button in Export group on External Data tab		
Field Size	AC 46		Design View button on Design tab | select field | Field Size box		
Filter by Selection	AC 149		Selection button on Home tab | select criterion		
Filter Records in Report	AC 252			Right-click field | click selected filter	
Form Filter and Sort	AC 280		Advanced button on Home tab | Advanced Filter/Sort | select fields on which to sort | enter sort criteria | Toggle Filter button		
Format Calculated Field	AC 116		Property Sheet button on Design tab		
Format Chart	AC 583	Right-click chart | point to Chart Object | click Edit			
Format Control	475, 538		Select control | Property Sheet button on Design tab | Format property box | select desired format		

Microsoft Office Access 2007 Quick Reference Summary *(continued)*

Task	Page Number	Mouse	Ribbon	Shortcut Menu	Keyboard Shortcut
Format Field	AC 168	Select field | Format property box			
Gridlines in Form	AC 273		Gridlines button on Format tab		
Group Controls	476		Select controls | Group button on Arrange tab		
Group in Query	AC 121	Total row or include multiple fields in query			
Group in Report	AC 244		Group & Sort button on Format tab | Add a group button		
Hide Smart Tags	AC 638	Microsoft Office Button | click Access Options | click Advanced | clear Show Smart Tags on Forms and Reports or Show Smart Tags on Datasheet check box			
Import Data	AC 212		Desired application in Import group on External Data tab		
Include All Fields in Query	AC 85	Double-click asterisk in field list	Query Design button on Create tab | Add All Fields button		
Include Field in Query	AC 85		Query Design button on Create tab | select field | Add Field button		
Input Mask	AC 304	In Design View | Input Mask property box | Build button			
Join Tables	AC 105		Query Design button on Create tab | bring field lists for tables into upper pane		
Link Tables	AC 217		Access button on External Data tab | select database | OK button		
Lock Database	AC 659		Make ACCDE button on Database Tools tab | select location and name for ACCDE file | Save button		
Lookup Field	AC 172	Data Type column for field | Lookup Wizard			
Macro Group	AC 377		Macro button arrow on Design tab | Macro | Macro Names button | enter macro names		
Modify Chart Type	AC 587			Right-click chart | Chart object | Edit | right-click chart	

Microsoft Office Access 2007 Quick Reference Summary *(continued)*

Task	Page Number	Mouse	Ribbon	Shortcut Menu	Keyboard Shortcut
Modify Controls in Subreport	AC 486	Click controls in report | resize using sizing handles or delete using DELETE key			
Modify Macro	AC 373			Right-click macro | Design view | insert new row | select new action	
Modify Section Properties	AC 489	Select section header | Property Sheet button on Design tab			
Modify Switchboard Page	AC 383, 385		Switchboard Manager button on Database Tools tab | Edit | New | select item to add to switchboard		
Move Controls in Stacked or Tabular Control Layout	AC 277	Select controls | drag to new location			
Move Field List	AC 320	Drag field list title bar			
Move Form Control	AC 276	Point to control | drag to desired location			
Move to First Record	AC 39	First Record button			
Move to Last Record	AC 39	Last Record button			
Move to Next Record	AC 39	Next Record button			
Move to Previous Record	AC 39	Previous Record button			
New Item	various	Office button | Open			
Object Dependencies	AC 339		Select object in Navigation Pane | Object Dependencies button on the Database Tools tab | Objects that depend on me button		
Omit Duplicates	AC 100	Open Property Sheet, set Unique Values to Yes	Property Sheet button on Design tab | Unique Values	Properties | Unique Values	
Open Database	AC 37	More button | Open button or Office button | double-click file name			CTRL+O
Open Database in Exclusive Mode	AC 646	Close database | More button | Computer | click file name | click Open button arrow | Open Exclusive | OK button			

Microsoft Office Access 2007 Quick Reference Summary *(continued)*

Task	Page Number	Mouse	Ribbon	Shortcut Menu	Keyboard Shortcut
Open Signed Package	AC 653	Close database | More button | select package location | click Files of Type box arrow | click Microsoft Office Access Signed Packages | select package | click Open button | select location | click OK button			
Open Subreport in Design View	484	Right-click report in Navigation Pane | click Design View			
Open Switchboard	AC 387			Right-click switchboard in Navigation Pane | Open	
Open Table	AC 26	Open button		Open	
Package and Sign Database	AC 651	Microsoft Office Button | Publish arrow | click Package and Sign | select desired certificate | name package | click Create button | close database			
Preview Table	AC 41	Office button | Print | Print Preview			ALT+F, W, V
Print Form	AC 282	Office button | Print | Quick Print			
Print Labels	AC 512	Select labels report in Navigation Pane | Office Button menu | Print | Quick Print			
Print Report	AC 256	Office button | Print | Quick Print			
Print Object	AC 41, 56	Office button | Print | Quick Print or Print			CTRL+P
Quit Access	AC 36	Close button			
Referential Integrity	AC 186		Relationships button on Database Tools tab		
Remove Chart Drop Zones	AC 409		Drop Zones button on Design tab		
Remove Form Tab Stops	AC 335		Select controls | Property Sheet button on Design tab | select All tab | change Tab Stop property to No		
Resize Column	AC 175	In Datasheet view, double-click right boundary of the field selector		Right-click field name | Column Width	
Resize Column Headings	AC 263	Select column header | drag upper or lower boundary			

Microsoft Office Access 2007 Quick Reference Summary *(continued)*

Task	Page Number	Mouse	Ribbon	Shortcut Menu	Keyboard Shortcut
Resize Column in Report	AC 249	Select column | drag right column boundary			
Resize Detail Section	AC 497	Drag section boundary			
Resize Multiple Controls	AC 540	Select controls to resize | use resizing handle to resize any control			
Resize Subform	AC 575	Drag form borders			
Resize Subreport and Report	AC 488	Open report in Design view | resize with sizing handles | drag subreport			
Run Macro	AC 372			Select macro in Navigation Pane | right-click macro | click Run	
Save Form	AC 58	Office button | Save			CTRL+S
Save Query	AC 91	Save button or Office button | Save			CTRL+S
Save Report	AC 254	Save button			
Save Table	AC 27	Save button	Office button | Save	Save	CTRL+S
Search for Access Help	AC 62	Microsoft Office Access Help button			F1
Search for Record	AC 145		Find button on Home tab		CTRL+F
Search Memo Field in Query	AC 340	In Datasheet view, include wildcards in criterion			
Select Fields for Report	AC 51		Report Wizard button on Create tab | Add Field button		
Select Startup Form	AC 644	Microsoft Office Button | click Access Options | click Current Database | click Display Form | select form to display			
Show Navigation Pane that has been Completely Hidden	AC 646	Microsoft Office Button | click Access Options | click Current Database | check Display Navigation Pane check box			
Show Smart Tags	AC 638	Microsoft Office Button | click Access Options | click Advanced | check Show Smart Tags on Forms and Reports check box Or Show Smart Tags on Datasheet check box			
Simple Query Wizard	AC 78		Query Wizard button on Create tab		

Microsoft Office Access 2007 Quick Reference Summary *(continued)*

Task	Page Number	Mouse	Ribbon	Shortcut Menu	Keyboard Shortcut
Single-Field Index	AC 629		Open table in Design view	select field for index	Indexed property box	select Yes (Duplicates OK) or Yes (No Duplicates)		
Single-Step Macro	AC 371		Single Step button on Design tab	Run button in Design view		
Sort Data in Query	AC 98		Select field in Design grid	Ascending		
Sort in Report	AC 244		Group & Sort button on Format tab	Add a sort button		
Sort on Multiple Keys	AC 101	Assign two sort keys			
Special Effects for Form Labels	AC 330		Select label	Property Sheet button on Design tab	Special Effect property box arrow		
Split Database	AC 662		Access Database button on Database tools tab	click Split Database button	select file location	click Split button	click OK button		
Split Form	AC 57		Split Form button on Create tab		
Start Access	AC 12	Start button	All Programs	Microsoft Office	Microsoft Office Access 2007			
Subtotals in Reports	AC 268		For each subtotal, select field to sum	Totals button on Format tab	Sum		
Summary Report	AC 256		Group report on desired field	include calculations	Hide Details button on Format tab		
Switch Between Form and Datasheet Views	AC 57	Form View or Datasheet View button	.		
Totals in Report	AC 248		Select field	Totals button on Format tab	Sum		
Ungroup Controls	476		Select any control in group	Ungroup button on Arrange tab		
Update Grouped Controls	478		Select any control in group	Design tab	use buttons in Font group or options in property sheet		

Microsoft Office Access 2007 Quick Reference Summary *(continued)*

Task	Page Number	Mouse	Ribbon	Shortcut Menu	Keyboard Shortcut
Update Query	AC 162		Update button on Design tab | select field, Update To row, enter new value	Query Type | Update Query	
Use Advanced Filter/Sort	AC 155		Advanced button on Home tab | Advanced/Filter Sort		
Use AND Criterion	AC 95				Place criteria on same line
Use Criterion	AC 81	Right-click query | Design View | Criteria row			
Use Date Field in Query	AC 340	In Datasheet view, type date with slashes as criterion			
Use Documenter	AC 612		Database Documenter button on Database Tools tab		
Use Form	AC 337			Right-click form in Navigation Pane | Open | click navigation buttons	
Use Format Painter	AC 539		Select control whose format to copy | double-click Format Painter on Design tab | click control to format		
Use Navigation Pane Search Bar	AC 619	Right-click Navigation Pane | click Search Bar | enter search term			
Use OR Criterion	AC 96				Place criteria on separate lines
Use Performance Analyzer	AC 611		Analyze Performance button on Database Tools tab		
Use PivotChart	AC 411		Open query in PivotChart view | Drop Zones button on Design tab | click arrows and check boxes to experiment		
Use PivotTable	AC 400	View button arrow | PivotTable View | click plus or minus signs			
Use Table Analyzer	AC 608		Analyze Table button on Database Tools tab		
Use Yes/No Field in Query	AC 340	In Datasheet view, type Yes or No as criterion			
View Report in Print Preview	475		View button on Design tab | Print Preview		